ENDANGERED AND THREATENED SPECIES PROGRAMS IN PENNSYLVANIA AND OTHER STATES: Causes, Issues and Management

The Pennsylvania Academy of Science Publications

Books and Proceedings

Book Editor: Shyamal K. Majumdar
Professor of Biology
Lafayette College
Easton, Pennsylvania 18042

1. *Energy, Environment, and the Economy,* 1981. ISBN: 0-9606670-0-8. Editor: Shyamal K. Majumdar.

2. *Pennsylvania Coal: Resources, Technology and Utilization,* 1983. ISBN: 0-9606670-1-6. Editors: Shyamal K. Majumdar and E. Willard Miller.

3. *Hazardous and Toxic Wastes: Technology, Management and Health Effects,* 1984. ISBN: 0-9606670-2-4. Editors: Shyamal K. Majumdar and E. Willard Miller.

4. *Solid and Liquid Wastes: Management, Methods and Socioeconomic Considerations,* 1984. ISBN: 0-9606670-3-2. Editors: Shyamal K. Majumdar and E. Willard Miller.

5. *Management of Radioactive Materials and Wastes: Issues and Progress,* 1985. ISBN: 0-9606670-4-0. Editors: Shyamal K. Majumdar and E. Willard Miller.

6. *Endangered and Threatened Species Programs in Pennsylvania and Other States: Causes, Issues and Management,* 1986. ISBN: 0-9606670-5-9. Editors: Shyamal K. Majumdar, Fred J. Brenner, and Ann F. Rhoads.

7. *Proceedings* of the Pennsylvania Academy of Science. Two issues per year; current volume (1986) is 60. ISSN: 0096-9222. Editor: Daniel Klem, Jr.

ENDANGERED AND THREATENED SPECIES PROGRAMS IN PENNSYLVANIA AND OTHER STATES: Causes, Issues and Management

EDITED BY
SHYAMAL K. MAJUMDAR, Ph.D.
Professor of Biology
Lafayette College
Easton, Pennsylvania 18042

FRED J. BRENNER, Ph.D.
Professor of Biology
Grove City College
Grove City, Pennsylvania 16127

ANN F. RHOADS, Ph.D.
Director of Botany
Morris Arboretum
University of Pennsylvania
Philadelphia, Pennsylvania 19118

Founded on April 18, 1924

**A Publication of
The Pennsylvania Academy of Science**

Library of Congress Cataloging in Publication Data

Endangered and Threatened Species Programs in Pennsylvania and Other States: Causes, Issues and Management.

Bibliography
Index

Library of Congress Catalog Card No.: 86-61186

ISBN 0-9606670-5-9
 Copyright © 1986 By The Pennsylvania Academy of Science

All rights reserved. No part of this book may be reproduced in any form without written consent from the publisher, The Pennsylvania Academy of Science. For information write to The Pennsylvania Academy of Science, Attention: Dr. S.K. Majumdar, Editor, Department of Biology, Lafayette College, Easton, Pennsylvania 18042.

Printed in the United States of America by

Typehouse of Easton
Phillipsburg, New Jersey 08865

COMMONWEALTH OF PENNSYLVANIA
DEPARTMENT OF ENVIRONMENTAL RESOURCES
HARRISBURG, PA. 17120

THE SECRETARY

Nicholas DeBenedictis
Secretary, Department of Environmental Resources

FOREWORD

The quality of life in Pennsylvania has continued to improve, in large part due to partnerships established among government, the academic community, business and the general public. The Pennsylvania Academy of Science has made important contributions to this effort by gathering information from a wide variety of sources and focusing it on specific issues facing our state. I am confident that this new book on Endangered and Threatened Species will be as beneficial as the Academy's previous volumes.

The Pennsylvania Department of Environmental Resources is proud to play a major role in the protection of the habitats of endangered and threatened species in Pennsylvania. DER manages the Commonwealth's 113 state parks, and is the steward for nearly two million acres of state forest land—approximately 7 percent of all the land in the Commonwealth.

In April 1985, the Commonwealth Forest Resource Plan was completed following a statewide series of public meetings. The Pennsylvania Natural Diversity Inventory includes information from across the state on rare plant sitings, endangered plant populations, unique habitats, and other historical plant information to help manage and protect the state's natural diversity. DER is a member of the Wild Resources Conservation Board, described in more detail within this book.

Perhaps even more important than DER's direct role in programs to protect endangered and threatened species are the advancements Pennsylvania has made in providing a safe environment for all its habitants, be they human, animal, or plant life.

Over the past five years, water quality has improved in 173.5 miles of streams in Pennsylvania. Pennsylvania has been one of the leading states in obligating sewage facilities constructions grants. Abandoned mine land reclamation has been increased dramatically, utilizing both state and federal funds. Major environmental legislation, including Oil and Gas Protection, Radiation Protection, and Safe Drinking Water Acts, has been passed in recent years.

The legislature is currently considering legislation to help the Commonwealth better dispose of municipal solid waste in a responsible manner. In 1986, Pennsylvania assumed responsibility for the regulation of hazardous wastes within its borders. In 1985, Pennsylvania became a full partner in the effort to clean up the Chesapeake Bay. Knowledge gained from this unique multi-state effort to protect a sensitive habitat may be transferred to other future efforts.

The Pennsylvania Academy of Science is to be commended for its efforts in the study of environmental issues. Development of new techniques to protect our environment is dependent on new ideas, such as those included in these volumes.

Sincerely,

Nicholas DeBenedictis
Secretary
Pennsylvania Department
of Environmental Resources

PREFACE

Loss of genetic diversity due to the extinction of species of living organisms is a worldwide problem of major proportions. Considering the long range implications, it is second only to the threat of nuclear war.

Extinction is occurring today at a rate unequalled since the end of the Cretaceous Era, 65 million years ago, when the dinosaurs and many other kinds of plants and animals disappeared. Current estimates are that 15 to 25 percent of existing species are in danger of extinction due to human activity, a rate which will result in the loss of 40,000 species of plants alone within our lifetimes.

While the majority of these losses are occurring in the tropics due to the widespread destruction of tropical rain forests, species of the temperate zone are also threatened. Current data indicate that 62 species of vascular plants have been extirpated in Pennsylvania, one of these is extinct throughout its range. Loss of habitat due to ever increasing demand for land for housing and commercial development is easily documented. Less obvious is the full effect of various forms of pollution on plant and animal populations. The impact of acid deposition on aquatic and terrestrial ecosystems is the subject of current research. In addition, the subtle effects of other air pollutants, especially ozone, need further clarification.

The elimination of any species, exotic or native, represents a loss of genetic diversity for the ecosystem. Once a species is extirpated from an area its gene pool is lost forever and when individuals are re-introduced we have replaced the population with a genetically different population which may be similar but not identical to the original population. By allowing extinction to occur at the present rate we are denying future generations important options. Extinction is irreversible, once a species is gone it cannot be recovered. We must assume responsibility for protecting the biological diversity of the world, and what better place to start than in our own backyard?

The book is divided into four parts containing 37 chapters. The papers deal not only with the ecological problems and restoration of specific species but habitat and ecosystem management as well. In addition, the book offers information on the status of on-going programs as well as providing a basis for future research. Part one considers general concepts on endangered and threatened species programs. Part two covers factors that cause species to become threatened or endangered. Natural features and specific programs are discussed by 13 experts and their associates from eight states in part three. Part four considers atmospheric stressors and their contributions to changes in species composition.

This book will contribute to our understanding of the status of rare and endangered species in Pennsylvania and surrounding states, the pressures which threaten their continued existence, the programs in effect to protect them and help identify areas in need of further research. Increased awareness and understanding of the problem are essential to stimulating greater interest in both the scientific community and the general public.

We express our deep appreciation for the excellent cooperation and dedication of the contributors. For a task of this magnitude many individuals in addition to the authors made contributions, and we are most pleased to acknowledge them. Gratitude is extended to Dr. Robert S. Chase, Head, Department of Biology, Lafayette College for providing facilities for editorial work to Dr. S.K. Majumdar. Thanks are due to Caryn Golden of Lafayette College, and Mary Ellen Pearson and the Secretarial Staff of the Grove City College for competent secretarial assistance.

> Shyamal K. Majumdar, Ph.D.,
> Fred J. Brenner, Ph.D.,
> Ann F. Rhoads, Ph.D.,
> Editors
> May, 1986

Endangered and Threatened Species Programs in Pennsylvania and Other States: Causes, Issues and Management

Table of Contents

Foreword:
  Nicholas DeBenedictis, Secretary, Pennsylvania Department of
  Environmental Resources V
Preface VII
Contributors XII
Symposia and Acknowledgments XVII
Introduction:
  George C. Shoffstall, Jr., Immediate Past President of the
  Pennsylvania Academy of Science and President, National
  Association of Academies of Science XVIII

Part One: General Concepts and Programs

Chapter 1: FOUNDING POPULATIONS IN CONSERVATION: PROBLEMS AND CHARACTERISTICS OF SMALL POPULATIONS
Christine Schonewald-Cox 1

Chapter 2: INTERACTION OF FEDERAL AND STATE AGENCIES IN THE ENDANGERED SPECIES PROGRAMS
Jack Edmundson 17

Chapter 3: MANAGEMENT OF UNDERCOVER OPERATIONS IN ENDANGERED SPECIES AND OTHER WILDLIFE LAW ENFORCEMENT
Clark R. Bavin 21

Chapter 4: THE ROLE OF PENNSYLVANIA'S WILD RESOURCE CONSERVATION FUND IN ENDANGERED SPECIES MANAGEMENT
Frank H. Felbaum 33

Chapter 5: HABITAT PRESERVATION AND DEVELOPMENT FOR RARE AND ENDANGERED SPECIES MANAGEMENT
Fred J. Brenner 37

Chapter 6: ENDANGERED HABITATS AND HOW THEY AFFECT RARE AND ENDANGERED PLANT SPECIES
G.C. Boone 53

Chapter 7: COMPUTER-GENERATED MAPPING OF RARE/ENDANGERED SPECIES
Jay F. Watson 67

Chapter 8: THE FEDERAL ENDANGERED SPECIES PROGRAM: HOW DO SPECIES GET LISTED AND THEN WHAT?
Judy Jacobs 75

Part Two: Unifying Concepts that Cause Species to Become Threatened or Endangered

Chapter 9: ENDANGERED PLANTS IN PENNSYLVANIA: PRESENT STATUS AND FUTURE PROTECTION
Paul Wiegman 86

Chapter 10: RARE PLANTS OF EASTERN PENNSYLVANIA
Ann F. Rhoads 103

Chapter 11: AN OVERVIEW OF THE VASCULAR PLANT GEOGRAPHY OF PENNSYLVANIA
Carl S. Keener and Marilyn M. Park 111

Chapter 12: AMERICAN CHESTNUT (*CASTANEA DENTATA*)— REPLACEMENT SPECIES AND CURRENT STATUS
Franklin C. Cech 145

Chapter 13: RARE PLANTS OF THE DELAWARE ESTUARY IN PENNSYLVANIA
A.E. Schuyler 156

Chapter 14: THREATENED AND ENDANGERED FISHES OF PENNSYLVANIA
Charles E. Denoncourt and Jay R. Stauffer, Jr. 163

Chapter 15: FISHES OF THE DELAWARE ESTUARY IN PENNSYLVANIA
Richard J. Horwitz 177

Chapter 16: NEW PERSPECTIVES ON THREATENED AND ENDANGERED AMPHIBIANS AND REPTILES IN PENNSYLVANIA
C.J. McCoy 202

Chapter 17: AN OVERVIEW OF ENDANGERED AND DECLINING BIRDS OF PENNSYLVANIA AND ADJACENT STATES
Richard J. Clark and Daniel Klem 211

Chapter 18: CAUSES FOR SPECIES OF LARGE MAMMALS TO BECOME THREATENED OR ENDANGERED
Hugh H. Genoways 234

Chapter 19: SMALL MAMMAL SPECIES OF SPECIAL CONCERN IN PENNSYLVANIA AND ADJACENT STATES: AN OVERVIEW
Gordon L. Kirkland 252

Chapter 20: FACTORS INVOLVED IN THE DECLINE OF THE BOBWHITE QUAIL
W.D. Klimstra 268

Part Three: Natural Features and Specific Programs

Chapter 21: CROSSLEY AND THE ECOPOLITICS OF ENDANGERED SPECIES PROTECTION: A NEW JERSEY CASE STUDY
Robert A. Zampella 278

Chapter 22: NEW JERSEY'S ENDANGERED AND NONGAME SPECIES PROGRAM
Paul D. McLain and Lawrence Niles 294

Chapter 23: PENNSYLVANIA'S BALD EAGLE RECOVERY PROJECT
Robert C. Mitchell and John A. Byerly 301

Chapter 24: THE PRZEWALSKI HORSE (*EQUUS PRZEWALSKII*) ECOSYSTEM: PROGRAMS AND PROGRESS
Ronald R. Keiper 310

Chapter 25: DEVELOPMENT AND PROGRESS OF PENNSYLVANIA'S RIVER OTTER REINTRODUCTION PROGRAM
Thomas L. Serfass, Larry M. Rymon and Jerry D. Hassinger 322

Chapter 26: THE EFFECTS OF AGRICULTURE ON THE HISTORY AND FUTURE OF THE RING-NECKED PHEASANT (*PHASIANUS COLCHICUS*)
Keith W. Harmon 343

Chapter 27: A SUMMARY OF THE PENNSYLVANIA NATURAL DIVERSITY INVENTORY AND OTHER NORTHEAST NATURAL HERITAGE PROGRAMS
Thomas L. Smith, Lawrence L. Master, Jan Cassin and D. Daniel Boone 356

Chapter 28: THE ECOLOGY OF THE CHESAPEAKE BAY: ITS IMPORTANCE TO RARE AND ENDANGERED SPECIES
Christopher P. White 373

Chapter 29: ENDANGERED WILDLIFE MANAGEMENT IN OHIO
Denis S. Case 388

Chapter 30: VIRGINIA'S ENDANGERED SPECIES PROGRAM
John P. Randolph 395

Chapter 31: THREATENED AND ENDANGERED SPECIES IN WEST VIRGINIA
Kenneth B. Knight 410

Chapter 32: MARYLAND ENDANGERED SPECIES PROJECTS
Gary J. Taylor 428

Chapter 33: RECOVERY OF THE PEREGRINE FALCON IN THE EASTERN UNITED STATES
Martin J. Gilroy and John H. Barclay 437

Part Four: Atmospheric Stressors and Their Contributions to Species Change

Chapter 34: AIR POLLUTION STRESSORS AND FOREST DECLINE: A REVIEW
J.R. Halma, Denise Rieker, and S.K. Majumdar 455

Chapter 35: IMPACTS OF ACIDIFICATION ON TROUT AND BENTHIC INSECTS OF HEADWATER STREAMS: AN OVERVIEW
W.G. Kimmel 463

Chapter 36: IMPACT OF ACID PRECIPITATION AND LIMESTONE NEUTRALIZATION ON BACTERIAL AND DIATOM POPULATIONS IN TWO LAKES IN THE POCONOS, PENNSYLVANIA
S.K. Majumdar, P.M. Steed, G.F. Rall, O. DeLucia, R.W. Snyder, L. Mineo, R.L. Morris, C.A. Barthelmes, K.R. Berger and T.A. Baker 472

Chapter 37: ACID PRECIPITATION: A REVIEW OF THE POTENTIAL AND OBSERVED EFFECTS ON VEGETATION, WITH PARTICULAR REFERENCE TO FOREST COMMUNITIES
David R. Vann and Arthur H. Johnson 486

Subject Index 507

Academy Officers 519

CONTRIBUTORS

T. A. Baker, (Chapter 36), Department of Biology, Lafayette College, Easton, PA 18042.

John H. Barclay, (Chapter 33), The Peregrine Fund, Cornell Laboratory of Ornithology, 159 Sapsucker Woods Road, Ithaca, NY 14850.

C. A. Barthelmes, (Chapter 36), Department of Biology, Lafayette College, Easton, PA 18042.

Clark R. Bavin, (Chapter 3), Chief, Division of Law Enforcement, U.S. Fish and Wildlife Service, Washington, DC 20240.

K. R. Berger, (Chapter 36), Department of Biology, Lafayette College, Easton, PA 18042.

D. Daniel Boone, (Chapter 27), Coordinator, Maryland Natural Heritage Program, Maryland Department of Natural Resources, Tawes State Office Building, C-3, Annapolis, MD 21401.

George C. Boone, (Chapter 6), Department of Biology, Susquehanna University, Selinsgrove, PA 17870.

Fred J. Brenner, (Chapter 5), Biology Department, Grove City College, Grove City, PA 16127.

John A. Byerly, (Chapter 23), Chief, Division of Federal Aid & Public Access, Bureau of Land Management, Pennsylvania Game Commission, P.O. Box 1567, Harrisubrg, PA 17105-1567.

Denis S. Case, (Chapter 29), Ohio Department of Natural Resources, Division of Wildlife, Fountain Square, Columbus, OH 43224.

Jan Cassin, (Chapter 27), Eastern Regional Information Manager, Eastern Heritage Task Force, The Nature Conservancy, 294 Washington Street, Boston, MA 02108.

Franklin C. Cech, (Chapter 12), Forestry Division, College of Agriculture and Forestry, West Virginia University, Morgantown, WV 26506-6125.

Richard J. Clark, (Chapter 17), Department of Biology, Professor of Biology, York College of Pennsylvania (YCP), York, PA 17403-3426.

O. DeLucia, (Chapter 36), Department of Biology, Lafayette College, Easton, PA 18042.

Charles E. Denoncourt, (Chapter 14), The Pennsylvania State University, The School of Forest Resources, 8B Ferguson Building, University Park, PA 16802.

Jack Edmundson, (Chapter 2), Office of Endangered Species, U.S. Fish and Wildlife Service, Washington, DC 20240.

Frank H. Felbaum, (Chapter 4), Executive Director, Wild Resource Conservation Fund, P.O. Box 1467, Harrisburg, PA 17120.

Hugh H. Genoways, (Chapter 18), Section of Mammals, Carnegie Museum of Natural History, 4400 Forbes Avenue, Pittsburgh, PA 15213.

Martin J. Gilroy, (Chapter 33), The Peregrine Fund, Cornell Laboratory of Ornithology, 159 Sapsucker Woods Road, Ithaca, NY 14850.

J. Robert Halma, (Chapter 34), Department of Biology, Cedar Crest College, Allentown, PA 18104.

Keith W. Harmon, (Chapter 26), Wildlife Management Institute, R.R. #1, Box 122, Firth, NB 68358.

Jerry D. Hassinger, (Chapter 25), Pennsylvania Game Commission, P.O. Box 174, Elizabethville, PA 17023.

Richard J. Horwitz, (Chapter 15), Division of Environmental Research, Academy of Natural Sciences of Philadelphia, 19th and the Parkway, Philadelphia, PA 19103.

Judy Jacobs, (Chapter 8), U.S. Fish and Wildlife Service, 1825 Virginia Street, Annapolis, MD 21401.

Arthur H. Johnson, (Chapter 37), Professor of Geology, Department of Geology, University of Pennsylvania, Philadelphia, PA 19104.

Carl S. Keener, (Chapter 11), Department of Biology, The Pennsylvania State University, University Park, PA 16802.

Ronald R. Keiper, (Chapter 24), Department of Biology, Pennsylvania State University, Mont Alto, PA 17237.

William G. Kimmel, (Chapter 35), Department of Biological and Environmental Sciences, California University of Pennsylvania, California, PA 15419.

Gordon L. Kirkland, Jr., (Chapter 19), The Vertebrate Museum, Shippensburg University, Shippensburg, PA 17257.

Daniel Klem, Jr., (Chapter 17), Assistant Professor of Biology, Department of Biology, Muhlenberg College, Allentown, PA 18104.

W. D. Klimstra, (Chapter 20), Director, Cooperative Wildlife Research Laboratory, Distinguished Professor Emeritus, Southern Illinois University at Carbondale, Carbondale, IL 62901.

Kenneth B. Knight, (Chapter 31), Wildlife Biologist, West Virginia Department of Natural Resources, P.O. Box 67, Elkins, WV 26241.

Shyamal K. Majumdar, (Chapters 34, 36), Department of Biology, Lafayette College, Easton, PA 18042.

Lawrence L. Master, (Chapter 27), Director/Zoologist, Eastern Heritage Task Force, The Nature Conservancy, 294 Washington Street, Boston, MA 02108.

C. J. McCoy, (Chapter 16), Division of Life Sciences, Carnegie Museum of Natural History, Pittsburgh, PA 15213.

Paul D. McLain, (Chapter 22), Deputy Director, N.J. Division of Fish, Game and Wildlife, P.O. Box 1809, Trenton, NJ 08627.

L. Mineo, (Chapter 36), Department of Biology, Lafayette College, Easton, PA 18042.

Robert C. Mitchell, (Chapter 23), Assistant Editor, Pennsylvania GAME NEWS, Bureau of Information and Education, Pennsylvania Game Commission, P.O. Box 1567, Harrisubrg, PA. 17105-1567.

R. L. Morris, (Chapter 36), Department of Biology, Lafayette College, Easton, PA 18042.

Lawrence Niles, (Chapter 22), Principal Nongame Zoologist, N.J. Division of Fish, Game and Wildlife, P.O. Box 1809, Trenton, NJ 08627.

Marilyn M. Park, (Chapter 11), Department of Biology, The Pennsylvania State University, University Park, PA 16802.

G. F. Rall, (Chapter 36), Department of Biology, Lafayette College, Easton, PA 18042.

John P. Randolph, (Chapter 30), Assistant Executive Director, Virginia Commission of Game and Fisheries, Richmond VA, 23230-1189.

Ann F. Rhoads, (Chapter 10), Morris Arboretum, University of Pennsylvania, Philadelphia, PA 19118.

Denise Rieker, (Chapter 34), Department of Biology, Cedar Crest College, Allentown, PA 18104.

Larry M. Rymon, (Chapter 25), Department of Biology, East Stroudsburg University, East Stroudsburg, PA 18301.

Christine Schonewald-Cox, (Chapter 1), National Park Service, Ecology Institute, University of California, Davis, CA 95616.

Alfred E. Schuyler, (Chapter 13), Academy of Natural Sciences of Philadelphia, 19th and the Parkway, Philadelphia, PA 19103.

Thomas L. Serfass, (Chapter 25), Department of Biology, East Stroudsburg University, East Stroudsburg, PA 18301.

Thomas L. Smith, (Chapter 27), Coordinator/Plant Ecologist, Pennsylvania Natural Diversity Inventory-East, P.O. Box 1467, Harrisburg, PA 17120.

R. W. Snyder, (Chapter 36), Department of Biology, Lafayette College, Easton, PA 18042.

Jay R. Stauffer, Jr., (Chapter 14), The Pennsylvania State University, The School of Forest Resources, 8B Ferguson Building, University Park, PA 16802.

P. M. Steed, (Chapter 36), Department of Biology, Lafayette College, Easton, PA 18042.

Gary J. Taylor, (Chapter 32), Nongame and Endangered Species Program Manager, Maryland Department of Natural Resources, Wye Mills, MD 21679.

David R. Vann, (Chapter 37), Research Associate, Department of Geology, University of Pennsylvania, Philadelphia, PA 19104.

Jay F. Watson, (Chapter 7), Habitat Resources, U.S. Fish and Wildlife Service, 500 N.E. Multnomah Street, Portland, OR 97232.

Christopher P. White, (Chapter 28), The Mare Nostrum Foundation, 93 Main Street, Suite 400, Annapolis, MD 21401.

Paul G. Wiegman, (Chapter 9), Western Pennsylvania Conservancy, 316 Fourth Avenue, Pittsburgh, PA 15222.

Robert A. Zampella, (Chapter 21), New Jersey Pinelands Commission, P.O. Box 7, New Lisbon, NJ 08064.

SYMPOSIA

1. *Endangered Species* — 60th Annual Meeting of The Pennsylvania Academy of Science, Seven Springs Resort, Champion, PA, March 30, 1984. *Chairman:* Dr. Fred J. Brenner

2. *Management of Endangered Species in Pennsylvania.* — Third Annual PAS-PSTA Fall Symposium, Grantville Holiday Inn, November 2, 1984. *Chairman*: Dr. Fred J. Brenner

ACKNOWLEDGMENTS

The Pennsylvania Academy of Science published this book in association with the Pennsylvania Department of Environmental Resources (DER). Any opinions, findings, conclusions, or recommendations expressed are those of the author(s) and do not necessarily reflect the views of the DER or The Pennsylvania Academy of Science.

INTRODUCTION

George C. Shoffstall, Jr., Ph.D.
Immediate Past-President of The Pennsylvania Academy of Science
and
President, National Association of Academies of Science

Qualitatively and quantitatively we are living through a biological crisis with regard to endangered and threatened species, many species either are or have headed toward disaster.

The crisis has many causes, the unprecedented increase in population, the tremendous rate of urbanization, the unforeseen and non-systematic technological progress. Simply put, by allowing our settlements to expand as we currently do, we spoil values of greater importance, we spoil our natural heritage.

This is not only true from the aesthetic point of view. If we only remember how many forests have been cut down or burned and how many mountains and hillsides have lost their topsoil, we can realize the parallel to the aesthetic disaster; we are causing a loss of natural resources.

Concomitant with spoiling land, water and air in this manner, we are also destroying many other expressions of nature, such as plants, insects, fish, reptiles, birds, and mammals.

However, we do have a historic responsibility, and that is to understand the crisis and develop new approaches in order to adequately ameliorate the problem(s). It is obvious that we must act in a more efficient way and on a much larger scale with some expediency.

Many skeptics ask, "What is the quid pro quo"? Unwittingly, a human premise pervades rational thought—we have the right and obligation to interfere with nature in order to save Man.

Indeed, technology has always been doing the aforementioned, but now we must do it wisely. Since more is at stake, we need a more careful scientific approach. Granted, we are dealing with very complex ecosystems and it may be near impossible to control the multitude of factors in all their dimensions. It is more probable that we can and will control their relationships since many of these factors depend on us.

When we seek to explain why a particular species succeeds or fails in any given environment, we quickly come to realize that we must focus our attention on the population of individual species members, not just on the individuals themselves. Because individuals are inevitably lost through death, the critical question arises is whether the population can continuously produce new individuals fast enough to replace those that are lost. Our search therefore, must begin with factors that control whether a population will rise, decline, or remain the same size.

Congruent with the analysis of population growth, is the critical consideration of the availability of resources for growth and reproduction. Therefore, we must focus our attention on the role of the population within the community of populations in which it finds itself. Namely, which other populations will provide these resources, and how successful will they be? Which other populations will be competing for resources, and what will be the outcome of that competition? What other populations will be using the particular population we are interested in, etc.

Tatamount to these additional questions requires that we must understand the physical aspects of the environment—the availability of water, minerals, sunlight, and heat. Thus our attention is drawn to considerations of still broader scope—to the ecosystem in which our community interacts with other communities and with the physical environment of the surrounding areas. Further extrapolation would be to subdivide the earth's surface into biomes and ultimately revealing the fundamental unity and interdependence of all life into earth's biosphere.

Ironically, we see the task of deriving an answer from a simple question, "Why does a species succeed in one place and not another"? is not easy. Complexities are manifest but solvable.

In spite of the difficulties, we have to acquire the ability to foresee the future. Convinced as we are of the fundamental unity of life, we must look continuously for generalizations that simplify the tasks and diversities we see about us. We have to be concerned about the future because we will live in it, and we and our descendants will be committed by actions taken today regarding our threatened and endangered species.

Ecologists are understandably cautious, for in virtually all cases of threatened species, the actual factors maintaining community integrity are far more subtle than was initially supposed.

Active support by society as a whole on basic investigations of populations in community structure and function will not only provide useful insights into biological principles; they can be expected to be of material use in optimizing humanity's interaction with the rest of the natural world.

The Pennsylvania Academy of Science has for many years championed the cause and effect of sound management of our natural environs and is pleased to present this newest book — *Endangered and Threatened Species Programs in Pennsylvania and Other States: Causes, Issues and Management.*

Ergo, this important volume is stimulating and fascinatingly informative and should be regarded as an introduction to the total efforts which have to be made in the preservation and conservation of our Endangered and Threatened Species.

Endangered and Threatened Species Programs in Pennsylvania and other States: Causes, Issues and Management. Edited by S. K. Majumdar, F. J. Brenner and A. F. Rhoads. © 1986, The Pennsylvania Academy of Science.

Chapter One

FOUNDING POPULATIONS IN CONSERVATION: PROBLEMS AND CHARACTERISTICS OF SMALL POPULATIONS

Christine Schonewald-Cox
National Park Service, Ecology Institute
University of California, Davis, California 95616

INTRODUCTION

It is frequently the decline in population size that signals pending extinction for species. Consequently, the focus for most species-oriented conservation work is on small populations. Because the focus of this publication is "endangered species," most conservation planning and management dealt with here will revolve, of necessity, around the small population in recovery and restoration projects. In this chapter I address the issue of small population characteristics and survival. In the first section I review some of the definitions and theoretical background for small population management from two perspectives: (1) that of the influence of small population size on population survival, and (2) that of the predisposing influence that management has on herd survival. In the second section I review the planning process and extend the guidelines developed in Schonewald-Cox[1] to use in planning management options for a hypothetical population of elk. Most founding events that I have encountered for elk and other ungulates in North America are characterized by small population size and consequently by many of the problems discussed here.[2] Hopefully, this paper will illustrate how the incorporation of small population genetics into planning of population management can be used to determine population health and evolutionary potential.

It is striking that the techniques for small population management and restoration are still in their early developmental stages. If it were easy to rehabilitate every species on the brink of extinction by simply giving it protection, the task for protecting endangered species would be rather straightforward. We would stop the destruction, where possible, and allow remnant population fragments to restore themselves to former levels. Once the population recuperated, we would be able to assume that it would continue as if no decline had previously occurred and would no longer require assistance. Instead, if we take diploid animals for an example, we must still ask, "How do populations become restored?"; and "What are some of the difficult hurdles that small populations have to face?"

A valuable lesson can be gained from the international zoo community, which also has taken an active interest in conservation as an increasing number of species are extinct (or are essentially so) in the wild, and the only gene pools remaining are captive. Zoological parks that have research and conservation programs have made it their objective to maintain small populations in captivity for use in eventual restoration programs. While developing plans for conservation programs, it became apparent to the researchers and managers of these zoological parks that many captive populations suffered low fecundity and infant survival rates. In addition, numerous disorders suspected of being congenital appeared in the animals. Careful analysis of breeding records[3,4,5] revealed that captive populations which were inbred suffered losses at rates above normal. These rates are similar to those known for humans at large, livestock and laboratory species.[6,7,8] Ralls and her collaborators have obtained a significant correlation between survival of newborn animals in the first year and value of the inbreeding coefficient (f, defined as a measure of the proportion of homologus alleles derived by common descent). This discovery prompted a great deal of activity which has led to the use of innovative management techniques for captive populations. Foremost among the developments has been the avoidance of inbreeding (with the exception of last resort cases such as those described by Templeton and Read[9]) and the equalization of contributions by founders of the gene pool. Manipulations of gene flow and other modifications have also been developed to promote conservation of healthy populations that may one day be restored to habitats from which they have been extirpated.[10,11,12]

Choice of mates is not controlled in natural populations, as it is for captive populations, and matings that have been observed are no guarantee of insemination. Therefore, in order to determine actual inbreeding coefficients as opposed to estimates that are based upon population size, means need to be developed for determining the number of actual contributors to each generation, and the relationship (by descent) between individuals in the population. Such a determination of inbreeding levels has just begun for selected natural populations.[13,14,15] For cheetahs, for example, this study is being accomplished by such varied techniques as protein electrophoresis, histocompatability tests,[16] and electrophoresis of mitochondrial DNA (which is usually inherited through the mother[17]). However, until more progress is made, the connection of inbreeding to deleterious effects will continue to be difficult to substantiate. It is hoped that means will become available to circumvent the difficulty of tracing parental ancestry so that inbreeding coefficients can be determined for individuals in free roaming populations, and deleterious effects occurring disproportionately in inbred (versus non-inbred) populations can be adequately documented.

Those concerned with species in natural habitats are not without power of observation. While sometimes one is relegated to using estimates of inbreeding levels and can only suspect connections between inbreeding and survival (or difficulty of adaptation), one can use this information to bring about a more careful and success-prone management of small populations in the wild. In addition, the symptoms and outcomes of inbreeding are sufficiently similar across species to suggest that benefits will be gained by utilizing corrective measures whenever deleterious inbreeding is suspected.

There is one other problem of small population management, one for which we cannot turn to captive populations for insight. This the problem of allele loss, which is more likely to be manifested subtly as decreased environmental tolerance or decreased survival over decades, as opposed to months or a few years. We have found that some populations do not seem to recuperate from severe bottlenecks, and that some species do not respond to protection in ways we would hope (some tule elk and desert bighorn sheep populations, for example). It may be that no reproduction occurs in a population or, if it does, that fecundity is reduced, or infant survival is extremely low; and additionally, it is possible that survival to age of reproduction is reduced. We also may find that, while the reproductive rate does not suffer immediately, as soon as one or several environmental variables change, the population appears particularly fragile, with either a high mortality or low reproductive rate or both.

Any number of the conditions I have characterized here are symptomatic of most species that we are trying to save from pending extinction. Speke's gazelle, tule elk, sandhill cranes, Alala or Hawaiian crow, nene, and Pere David's deer are just a few of the considerable numbers of species.[18,19] While there are many factors which can contribute to this small population dilemma, there is one underlying factor, the adaptation to changes in the genome, that seems to be at the heart of the trouble.

The two subjects I will focus upon here are, (1) the definition of the small population and associated characteristics for diploid, typically outbreeding species; and (2) methods for coping and, it is hoped, predisposing managed populations (remnant or founder populations) to circumvent the genetic pitfalls of small population size.

IDEAL POPULATIONS, EFFECTIVE POPULATION SIZE (N_e) and INBREEDING COEFFICIENT (f)

First, some terms need defining. Because the field of conservation biology is very young, most applications, of necessity, are based on theoretical populations and predictions. Although the jump from theory to field may seem to be less than perfect, it is far better than pursuing conservation without considering the effect of genes on survival.

Many of the constructs and discussion of small populations are based upon the notion of an "ideal population," whose definition in Schonewald-Cox, et al.[20] is: a theoretical, diploid, sexually reproducing population that meets the following criteria: individuals mate at random; generations do not overlap; there is no migration into or out of the population; there is no selection; there is no mutation. Such a definition of "ideal population" permits certain manipulations of data and statistics that assist biologists in determining trends and effects in natural populations. The "ideal" population is the basis for much of the small population demographics and genetics discussed in conservation biology publications.

In order to make a connection between theory (the ideal population) and the real population in the field, the "effective population size (N_e)" of a natural population is generally used. The N_e is the size of an hypothesized ideal population that would cause it to have the same rate of genetic drift and decrease in genetic diversity as does the real population being observed. Because of its fixed statistical assumptions, the value of N_e conveys more information of value to modeling and statistical manipulations for small population genetics and demography. Wright[7] and later Franklin[21] discuss N_e in considerable detail. When minimum effective population sizes are recommended for species it is not unusual that the number, translated into actual population size, increases three, four, or five-fold, or even more. This is simply because individuals in a real population are not all necessarily of the same age. They do not mate necessarily at random and the generations frequently overlap. All of these factors may increase the potential for inbreeding and a reduction in the genetic diversity for small populations.

WHAT IS A SMALL POPULATION?

Colloquially, a small population of a species is a number of individuals which are noticeably few relative to expectations for the location, season and species. From a technical standpoint, however, "small" can be identified in several ways.

A population may be considered small if it is below the minimum effective population size—the population size necessary to preserve most rare alleles without severe risk of loss in the short or long term. A population below this level does not retain the natural frequency and diversity of alleles characteristic of the species at the locality, and has a high risk of further allele loss. Such populations may not be able to adjust to stresses which are typical of their historical ranges, and may suffer reduced phenotypic plasticity, which may result in the population not being able to survive environmental fluctuations that previous populations endured during the species' abundance. This latter condition is usually the result of the loss of alleles, and may be symptomatic of the loss of those rare alleles which change frequency in the population during cycles of environmental change.

A population also may be considered "small" if it is inbred when it is not naturally adapted to inbreeding. If, in addition, there are also overlapping generations with an uneven representation of contributions by each sex to each generation, the danger of inbreeding is high. When abnormal levels of inbreeding occur, two events (mentioned earlier) follow: (1) there is an increase in the expression of deleterious or lethal recessive alleles because two individuals carrying the same recessives as a result of common descent may mate; and (2) there is a rapid loss of alleles, particularly rare ones, as more and more related individuals contribute offspring. In species that typically inbreed, the primary risk is loss of alleles, and one must expect the genetic load to be comparatively small.

HOW DO POPULATIONS BECOME SMALL?

There are many causes of populations becoming small. Probably the most common reasons are habitat elimination and direct exploitation of the species. Frequently, during restoration efforts, populations are founded that are too small to begin with.[2] One certainty is that most populations of species which do not thrive when inbreeding fall rapidly once they cross a minimum threshold. Determining this threshold is especially critical for both monitoring endangered species and for initiating restoration programs that require founding populations.

WHICH SPECIES SUFFER MOST FROM SMALL POPULATION SIZE?

Not all species or populations are threatened by small population size. Selander[22] shows effectively how self fertilizing slugs do quite well and make successful colonizers, at least for a while. Self-fertilizing plants also make good colonizers and do not suffer the same deleterious effects as outbreeding species. But, as Selander also notes, each of the self-fertilizing slug species has a very close relative which is, in fact, outbreeding. This suggests that self-fertilization is a short-term evolutionary strategy, and that outbreeding and cross-fertilization provide for more than simple range expansion. They provide for greater variation in recombination, for adaptation to small or great environmental changes, and, it is hoped, for the slow or rapid change of one species into one or several others. Polyploidy, a characteristic common to both plants and invertebrates, is definitely advantageous in cases of self-fertilization and restricted gene pool size where inbreeding occurs. The allelic diversity otherwise lost in diploids that inbreed are preserved in the multiple genomes carried by each individual.

A reduced population is especially deleterious for species that do not typically inbreed or show low within-population diversity as their biological characteristics. Such species are not likely to develop the alternatives of self-fertilization and polyploidy. Reversal of a decline and threatened extinction for these species depends upon chance or applying careful management to those factors that will determine the choice of mates and simultaneously speed population growth. Continued management may also be necessary to encourage or manipulate both immigration and emmigration.

PREVENTION OF POPULATION FAILURE WITH LIMITED SPACE

What can be done now with available theory to protect species at the state or local level in situations where space is generally limited to 10,000 hectares or less (not including Federal lands and projects)? Frequently the difficulty of managing these lands is aggravated by marginal funding, and a highly localized interest and support group.

All species require space. The location and characteristics of the space together with its size will determine the number of individuals that can survive in the space. This is not to say that this is the only factor that will determine species survival, but that it is a critical one and a useful factor to focus upon in the context of small population management.[23,1] For species to survive on their own, space and associated resources must not be limiting. In examining an existing population of an endangered species or in planning for its restoration to a habitat, the space available will predetermine the extent to which the population will need active management. One factor associated with space, the shape of the reserve, including the existence of connected subdivisions within the reserve that can each sustain small populations, will affect the ability of the population to grow, divide, and store genetic diversity.[24]

How much space is necessary? This has yet to be determined on an absolute scale. Individual critical habitat analyses have suggested the amounts necessary for a few species in specific localities. A recent synthesis[1] indicated that certain mammals, regardless of specific qualities of species or habitat, tend to have predictable population sizes associated with specific area size. This gives us a first, generalized way (a first order indicator) of looking at what size populations local parks may be capable of supporting. The combined knowledge of a population's size and a species' biology will suggest whether genetic diversity is likely to be stored within or between populations and, further, for what sort of demographic structure the manager ought to strive. The structure may likely be a single large population for some species, while for others, it will be several subdivided groups (several populations and/or herds). The optimum demographic structure, and the degree of a species' tendency for sociality will assist the manager in determining how many animals, (tens, hundreds, thousands), will be necessary to create natural divisions when they are prescribed.[25,26]

PLANNING PROCESSES AND ASSESSMENT OF OBJECTIVES

Taking the simplest information most likely to be available, the size of a park or refuge, let us look at the first sorting levels for information and examine the objectives of management. Next let us find out the most likely procedures for planning conservation, say, of a large mammal, based upon development of this one major factor, space, and its related variables, population size and demographic complexity.

A priori, the species of concern is identified, and all known information is compiled pertinent to diet, sociality, reproduction, movement, development, pathology and environmental tolerance. No piece of information is too little. If, in a rare instance, nothing is known about the species' habits, one can look at close relatives, convergent niche types, and gross anatomy for the suggestion of pertinent bits of information.

Subsequently, the locality where the species is to remain or where the species is to be restored is identified and its size is recorded. Then answers are found for the following questions: Is the area limited by legal boundaries or by the extent of the area which the species will use? Is it subjected to multiple use or heavy impacts? Would the species be restricted by fencing or very severe demarcation? What is the species' distribution outside of the protected area? Or, does it survive outside?

In a manner similar to Schonewald-Cox,[1] the size of area necessary to support the minimum effective size of population is estimated and compared to the actual size of the space available in the park or reserve. The counter-estimate can also be made: What population size does the park's size actually suggest it can carry?

If the objective is to preserve this species into the future, but the size of the space suggests that only a small fraction of a typical population can be supported, it then becomes obvious that the objectives must be redefined or more space must be secured. If no additional space can be made available then one of these two choices is inevitable:

1. Let the species become extinct in the habitat. If it manages to survive by "letting nature take its course," fine.

2. Supply management to assist the population, realizing that the smaller the group size the area suggests, the more intense the management will have to be.

If one chooses to supply continuous management to assist the population, one then estimates the minimum population size equivalent to a minimum effective population size of 50. (This is a very conservative minimum based upon 1% increase in inbreeding coefficient per year, as considered tolerable by breeders of domestic species.) Can the area selected sustain a population of this size?

If the area cannot sustain the minimum effective population size equivalent, the objectives should be redefined once again or more space *must* be found. If the area can sustain the minimum effective population size then it is possible to proceed with the other aspects of planning that have to do with other equally important facets of population survival.

If one is ready to establish a population, this can be done all at once or gradually. If it must be done gradually (most likely) for logistical reasons, it is important to step aside and examine some of the species' biological data collected earlier for guidance.

When do males and females first breed? What is the average (or usual if average is not available) sex ratio among breeding adults (e.g. average number of *breeding* adult males, and average number of females bred by each male)? For selfing species or species that typically inbreed, found in several small pockets within available habitat, selection will determine which phenotypes are most suited. The less suited ones may not do as well but as long as they survive, they serve as a genetic reserve if habitat characteristics change and the formerly dominant genotypes are no longer suited. For typically outbreeding species, the founder or remnant population should be maintained so that inbreeding is discouraged and, if possible, prevented altogether.

A population can be established as a single unit or as several units which, as they grow, will encounter each other. Species behavioral predisposition and logistics will dictate which organization is better (e.g., separate units will be better for highly territorial species in which spacing between family groups is critical to success.) Also, consideration should be given to which option permits each of the founder genotypes a greater potential of reproducing rapidly at the outset and thereby preserving more of the rare alleles. When the separated groups (in the second option) meet in a generation or two, selection may favor one phenotype over another, but the loss of rarer characteristics will be comparatively slower.

If in some way, the numbers are a little short of the minimum effective population size and introduction of new members is to be made over time, then decisions must also be made as to when, which sex, and what developmental stages to introduce. For some species, those in which heavy competition occurs between males and familiarity of the males with the habitat is essential to the competition between males or defense of mates, it is not wise to bring in animals that have a low probability of mating. One can bring in several young males and overtake low probabilities of mating by having sufficient numbers introduced. A very dominant personality can be introduced or females can be brought in. The effect of new females brought into a polygynous system, for example, may be a slower way to introduce new alleles into the population and may not immediately override initial inbreeding, but it will be more certain to be effective in the long run *if* females are always mated. If, in the selected species, strange females are shunned and have difficulty in raising young, and if they have a significantly lower reproductive potential, then it may be better to introduce males or start an entire family group at the opposite end of the reserve with the hope that some assimmilation or joining of the two groups will occur in the future. There are many other ways in which the scenario could proceed, with the outcome depending upon the knowledge one has about the species' reproductive biology and social tendencies. Parallels exist with plants which also have their spacing mechanisms and controls over pollination.

To establish a population and predispose it to succeed (that is, to avoid deleterious inbreeding and critical allele loss, in addition to protecting from exploitation or other hazards) is only a first step. Until the population is established and begins to expand into the habitat and forms daughter populations, supervision will need to be intense, unless, of course, one has left the species' survival to chance.

There are some new means to monitor the progress of populations. Some of these techniques are labor intensive and some are not. Techniques common to population and evolutionary genetics can provide answers with regard to questions concerning specific levels of resolution for genetic diversity at the individual or population level, or for determining gross mutations or compatibility of gametes.

In the manner which I have just described one can make preliminary plans merely by asking and answering the questions. This scheme also informs one what studies will be especially important in increasing the probability of a population's success in restoration or recovery from an evolutionary or genetic standpoint. While what I suggest here is obviously biased for mammals, it does not take much more than energy to seek out and explore similar techniques for other taxa. The fact that many small population management procedures have met with myriad crises suggests that this process is as good as any other place from which to start.

For illustration purposes, I have selected one species with which I am familiar and a hypothetical site of 10,000 hectares to serve as an abbreviated example of the planning process I have described above.

ABBREVIATED PLANNING PROCESS AND GUIDELINES: A HYPOTHETICAL POPULATION

1. *What is the species?* Cervus elaphus (elk or wapiti)
2. *What is the purpose of the restoration?* To restore this species' population to a habitat where previously extirpated, and to maintain populations for the long term.
3. *What is the species' diet?* They are grazers primarily, and utilize forest edge and forest for cover.
4. *What is the species sociality?* Female herds with males scattered or in small groups of two or three; female herds (2-25 females) with juvenile males remaining with female herds up to 2 years; during calving, females seek isolation.
5. *What is the mode of reproduction?* One calf per year beginning when the female is 2-3 years of age; males not socially competitive until 5 years old although sexually mature at 2-3 years; male defends harem of one to many females (conservative average = 4/breeding male); number of females in a harem limited by number of females in herd and intensity of competition between males for females; outbreeding adapted, though source population has been previously bottlenecked.
6. *What types of daily and seasonal movements characterizes populations in this type of habitat?* No migration, though herd may engage in extensive daily movements, animals show wide temperature and other climatological tolerance; however, tolerance to new parasites and disease in the habitat selected for restoration is unknown, with one exception: there is known tolerance for brucellosis.
7. *What is expected mortality?* Female's first calf 20% mortality above annual average of 20% for all young born; differential mortality between sexes; adult sex ratio 1M:2.6F; expected sources of mortality in new habitat include climate, parasitism, killing because of trespassing onto agricultural lands (crop destruction), feral dogs (predation, no natural predators in new habitat), poaching, and accidental deaths by hunters when mistaken for white tail deer.
8. *What is the estimated capacity of the area?* Determination of carrying capacity to be made by use of ecological survey, or use of a regression, such as found in Schonewald-Cox! The first estimate is about 500. *But* habitat is suboptimal and is used for cultivated forest and hunting. Adjacent lands will not tolerate expansions or movements by elk into agricultural or residential lands. Therefore, reduction of the estimate for carrying capacity to about 200-300 is suggested. (Conservative estimate favoring success of planning effort to establish the population for the long term).
9. *What minimum population size does the elk require to survive (both short- and long-term)?* Franklin (1980) points to the fact that breeders of domestic livestock will tolerate up to 1% increase in inbreeding coefficient per generation. The effective population size (N_e) necessary to maintain this level or less is $N_e = 50$. Franklin[21] suggests tentatively that this amount is the minimum

necessary effective population size for large mammals for short-term management. What does this suggest as to the actual minimum number of male and female elk that would equal $N_e = 50$? First an assumption needs to be made about the average ratio of breeding males to females. For this scenario, it is assumed for practicality that, on the average and in this habitat, every breeding male has approximately 5 breeding females in his harem. Taking Wright's Formula,[7] and Franklin's demonstration:[21]

$$N_e = \frac{1}{\frac{1}{4N_m} + \frac{1}{4N_f}} \tag{1}$$

$$50 = \frac{1}{\frac{1}{4N_m} + \frac{1}{4(5N_m)}} \tag{2}$$

$N_m = 15$. Thus 15 breeding males, and 75 breeding females (that is, N_m x 5) (a sex ratio of 5:1) are necessary to establish $N_e = 50$. (This doesn't include juveniles or non-reproducing adults in the population.) For long-term conservation of the population, (with the hope that the population would not only sustain itself with little or no management assistance, but would have the potential to change with the environment and natural selection), the N_e recommended by Franklin for randomly mating populations is tentatively 500. Interestingly, in captivity or with domestic stock one can calculate N_e on the basis of breeding pairs when choice of mates is controlled. However, with free roaming populations this is not possible and adjustments need to be made for sex ratio as was done. The results suggest that 150 males and 750 females contributing offspring to subsequent generations (size of breeding population) are necessary for long term survival with $N_e = 500$. The inbreeding coefficient, f, under these circumstances ($f = .01\%$) indicates that inbreeding is no longer a threat.

In the short-term management objective, the principal threat is the expression of deleterious alleles resulting from inbreeding and the loss of rare alleles occurring by genetic drift. In the long-term objective, efforts are made to counteract loss of rare alleles due to genetic drift. In other words the population must overcome the full diversity of natural and novel selection pressures. The more options the population has in its genome (alleles and groups of interacting genes) the greater its potential to meet demands for long-term survival. In order for the hypothetical population to survive in the short term, presumably with protection from inbreeding-related mortality (to avoid inbreeding depression) and short-term selection pressures it would have to number at least 90 breeding adults. Including calves of the year, other immatures, non-breeding adult individuals and senile individuals, all occurring in natural populations, the population would have to number 150 to 200 animals minimum. For the population to be self-sustained for the long-term, it would have to number at least 900 adult breeding animals, include developing and other non-reproducing individuals, and would have to number between 1,500 and 2,000 animals.

10. *What sort of protected area size would a population of 2,000 individuals require?* Based upon the regression in figure 1 (taken from Schonewald-Cox and Bayless;[2] developed from Schonewald-Cox[1]), about 100,000 ha. of protected habitat (about 400 sq. mi.). If the habitat is subject to multiple use or if substantial portions of it are unuseable as I described earlier, one could easily double or quadruple the area required, or provide sustained gene flow (sacrificing some of the self-sustained advantage that the population should optimally have).

11. *What is the optimum demographic complexity for the elk that the habitat can accommodate?* The optimum demographic complexity that the elk require would be one in which allele diversity was reflected in differing frequencies between groups but with a presence of rare alleles in as many groups as possible, especially since the population being discussed is relatively small. With limited movement between groups, rare alleles could be maintained and inbreeding depression supressed even if a limited amount of inbreeding did occur within any one group. Some inbreeding is likely to occur, simply because primary female associations tend to be familial, and if a limited number of males succeed in mating with most females, daughter-father, daughter-uncle, and some sister-brother matings may be likely. It is hard to speculate how males will disperse in the habitat since elk socioecology is very much habitat specific.[27-32]

An insurance against lack of knowledge on how gene flow will occur is to spread diversity among as many groups as possible in the limited habitat, but to maintain multiple groups so that multiple opportunities occur to develop adaptive responses to local environmental stress. This size habitat (10,000ha.) can accommodate to multiple groups only at the herd level, i.e. sub-divided population! If some partially effective natural or artificial barriers exist that slow (without impeding) communication between, say, two major subdivisions, the potential exists for storing considerable diversity between as well as within groups.

12. *What sort of protected area size would a population of 150 to 200 elk require?* About 10,000 ha. of protected habitat (about 40 sq. miles). However, as above, multiple use of the habitat or serious deficiencies in availability of habitat could increase this significantly to 30,000 or more hectares.

CONCLUSIONS

All the foregoing brings the earlier topic of objectives forward once more. If conservation (or management) objectives are to restore endangered species or any other populations to evolutionary health, preventive measures need to be taken to emancipate the populations from human care other-than-classic protection from intrusions such as poaching. Every human interference, (that is, *any* manipulation) carries with it risks of alteration resulting from unknown changes in the natural genetic balance of not only the manipulated species, but all other species that somehow have contact with it. Populations that will never have the space to roam or will not have any source of gene flow, like some of the endangered birds or plants of Hawaii, will require continuous management,[12,18] and may actually benefit from short-term adaptation to inbreeding if they haven't done so already through repeated bottlenecks they have experienced. But for those species that have sources for gene flow and for which real hope exists for their reestablishment in self-sustained multiple populations, careful planning should be initiated to avoid unnecessary change in the reproductive system (inbreeding versus outbreeding) or loss of any significant portion of rare alleles.

At this point in time the state of knowledge about the amount of genetic diversity and evolutionary potential that is lost with specific population sizes is still somewhat theoretically based, yet it is conservatively and objectively derived. I believe that, when applied to management problems, it is much better than management with *no* knowledge. It pays to predetermine (1) estimates for the capacity of the area to maintain the species, (2) estimates for the species' optimum or minimum population size for long-term evolution, (3) whether space exists for optimum levels of demographic complexity, and (4) probable effective population sizes resulting from given sex ratios, and age structures in the population. In addition, calculations of or approximations of inbreeding coefficients could help the manager of a restoration avoid causing abrupt shifts in the ongoing mating regime to which the source population is adapted.

There is no doubt that more detailed analysis of available habitat and species physiology is important. Adapting to changes in one's genome is but one facet of survival. What is presented here is not intended as a substitute for what is currently being done in ecological and range analysis, but is intended to serve as an examination of one aspect of speceis survival—the species' internal capability to meet survival needs with suitable phenotypes for present as well as future conditions. This is especially important throughout North America, where acidification of the soil and slow climate change and other effects are causing vegetational distributions to shift. Species that are more or less confined to protected habitats are restricted. If the vegetation distribution shifts north, for example, the park boundaries will not automatically shift with it.[33,34] The objective of protection in the park or reserve must remain to give protection, and the species composing the ecosystem must be able to change to meet the new demands of environmental change if they are to survive. When both nature and humans place such unreasonable demands upon species, it becomes increasingly important to give the species the probabilistic advantages for survival or for the conservor to redirect funds to other projects and concede the probable loss ahead of time.

ACKNOWLEDGMENTS

I would like to thank J.W. Bayless and R. Baker for their reviews of this manuscript and Audrey Dixon for her editorial assistance. Statements made in this paper are solely those of the author and do not necessarily reflect the opinions or policies of the National Park Service.

LITERATURE CITED

1. Schonewald-Cox, C.M. 1983. Conclusions: Guidelines to management: a beginning attempt, pp. 414-445. *In* Schonewald-Cox, C.M., S.M. Chambers, B. MacBryde, and L. Thomas (eds.) *Genetics and Conservation.* Benjamin Cummings, Inc., Menlo Park, CA.
2. Schonewald-Cox, C. and J. Bayless. in prep. Survival predispositions of elk restorations: inbreeding and carrying capacity.
3. Ralls, K., D. Brugger, and J. Ballou. 1979. Inbreeding and juvenile mortality in small populations of ungulates. Science 206:1101-1103.
4. Ralls, K. and J. Ballou. 1983. Extinction: lessons from zoos, pp. 164-184. *In* Schonewald-Cox, C.M., S.M. Chambers, B. MacBryde, and L. Thomas (eds.) *Genetics and Conservation.* Benjamin Cummings, Inc., Menlo Park, CA.
5. Ballou, J. 1983. Calculating inbreeding coefficients from pedigrees. pp. 509-520. *In* Schonewald-Cox, C.M., S.M. Chambers, B. MacBryde, and L. Thomas (eds.) *Genetics and Conservation.* Benjamin Cummings, Inc., Menlo Park, CA.
6. Lasley, J.F. 1978. *Genetics of Livestock Improvement*, 3rd ed. Prentice-Hall, Englewood Cliffs, NJ.
7. Wright, S. 1969. *Evolution and the Genetics of Populations,* Vol. 2. University of Chicago Press, Chicago.
8. Wright, S. 1977. *Evolution and the Genetics of Populations,* Vol. 3. University of Chicago Press, Chicago.
9. Templeton, A.R. and B. Read. 1983. The elimination of inbreeding depression in a captive herd of Speke's Gazelle, pp. 241-266. *In* Schonewald-Cox, C.M., S.M. Chambers, B. MacBryde, and L. Thomas (eds.) *Genetics and Conservation.* Benjamin Cummings, Inc., Menlo Park, CA.
10. Foose, T.J. 1983. The relevance of captive populations to the conservation of biotic diversity. *In* Schonewald-Cox, C.M., S.M. Chambers, B. MacBryde,

and L. Thomas (eds.) *Genetics and Conservation.* Benjamin Cummings, Inc. Menlo Park, CA.
11. Benirschke, K. 1983. The impact of research on the propagation of endangered species in zoos. pp. 402-413. *In* Schonewald-Cox, C.M., S. M. Chambers, B. MacBryde, and L. Thomas (eds.) *Genetics and Conservation.* Benjamin Cummings, Inc. Menlo Park, CA.
12. Schonewald-Cox, C., R. Baker, and R.M. Nakamura. in prep. An alternate approach to restoration of nearly extinct Hawaiian birds: a case study, Hawaiian crow.
13. Templeton, pers. com., for lizards.
14. O'Brien, S.J., D.E. Wildt, D. Goldman, C.R. Merril, and M. Bush. 1983. The cheetah is depauperate in genetic variation. *Science* 221:459-462.
15. O'Brien, S.J., et al. submitted for cheetahs.
16. O'Brien, S.J., pers. com.
17. Powell, J.R. 1983. Molecular approaches to studying founder effects. pp. 229-240. *In* Schonewald-Cox, C.M., S.M. Chambers, B. MacBryde, and L. Thomas (eds.) *Genetics and Conservation.* Benjamin Cummings, Inc., Menlo Park, CA.
18. See also Templeton and Read,[9] Schonewald-Cox, et al.,[12] Foose,[10] Ralls and Ballou,[5] and Schonewald-Cox, C. in press. Genetics, minimum population size and the island reserve. *In* Stone, C. and M. Scott (eds.) spec. issue.*Pacific Science.*
19. Temple, S.A. (ed.). 1978. *Endangered Birds; Management Techniques for Preserving Threatened Species.* University of Wisconsin Press, Madison.
20. Schonewald-Cox, C.M., S.M. Chambers, B. MacBryde, and L. Thomas (eds.). 1983. *Genetics and Conservation.* Benjamin Cummings, Menlo Park, Ca.
21. Franklin, I.R. 1980. Evolutionary change in small populations, pp. 135-149. *In* M. Soule and B. Wilcox (eds.)*Conservation Biology.* Sinauer Associates, Sunderland, MA.
22. Selander, R.K. 1983. Evolutionary consequences of inbreeding, pp. 201-215. *In* Schonewald-Cox, C.M., S.M. Chambers, B. MacBryde, and L. Thomas (eds.) *Genetics and Conservation.* Benjamin Cummings, Inc., Menlo Park, CA.
23. Soule, M.E. and B.A. Wilcox (eds.). 1980. *Conservation Biology.* Sinauer Associates, Sunderland, MA
24. Schonewald-Cox, C. and J.W. Bayless. in review. The boundary approach: A geographic analysis of design and conservation of nature reserves. 24pp. ms.
25. See Schonewald-Cox[1] for a description of demographic units as they relate to planning.
26. For an illustration of the use of demographic units in planning see: Salwasser, H., S.P. Mealey, and K. Johnson. in press. Wildlife population viability—a

question of risk. Proc. Wildlife Soc.
27. Clutton-Brock, T.H., F.E. Guiness, and S.D. Albon. 1982. *Red Deer; Behavior and Ecology of Two Sexes.* University of Chicago, Chicago.
28. Darling, F.F. 1937. *A Herd of Red Deer.* Oxford University Press, London.
29. McCullough, D.R. 1969. The Tule elk, Its History, Behavior and Ecology. University of California Press, Berkeley.
30. Franklin, W.L., A.S. Mossman, and M. Dole. 1975. Social organization and home range of Roosevelt elk. J. Mammal. 56:102-118.
31. Houston, D.B. 1982. *The Northern Yellowstone Elk; Ecology and Management.* Macmillan, Inc., New York.
32. Thomas, J.W. and D.E. Toweill. 1982. *Elk of North America; Ecology and Management.* Stackpole Books, Harrisburg, PA.
33. Norse, E.A. 1983. From the Washington office. Bull. Ecol. Soc. Am. 64(4):247-248.
34. Norse, E.A. and R.E. McManus. 1980. Ecology and living resources- biological diversity. p. 69. *In* Environmental Quality; The 11th Annual Report of the Council on Environmental Quality, U.S. Government Printing Office, Washington, D.C.

Endangered and Threatened Species Programs in Pennsylvania and other States: Causes, Issues and Management. Edited by S. K. Majumdar, F. J. Brenner and A. F. Rhoads. © 1986, The Pennsylvania Academy of Science.

Chapter Two

INTERACTION OF FEDERAL AND STATE AGENCIES IN THE ENDANGERED SPECIES PROGRAM*

JACK EDMUNDSON
Office of Endangered Species
U.S. Fish and Wildlife Service
Washington, D.C. 20240

The current Endangered Species Act (Act) evolved from acts with similar intent which were passed in 1966 and 1969. Unlike the current Act, however, these earlier acts were relatively weak in that they expressed the importance of preventing the extinction of species, but provided no means by which to carry out their expressed philosophy. In 1973, the current Act was passed. This is a much stronger Act in that it requires Federal agencies to protect listed species. It also establishes the conservation of listed species as a goal and encourages States to do the same. In drafting this Act, Congress declared that: "...(1) various species of fish, wildlife, and plants in the United States have been rendered extinct as a consequence of economic growth and development untempered by adequate concern and conservation; (2) other species...have been so depleted...that they are...threatened with extinction; (3) these species are of esthetic, ecological, education, historical, recreational, and scientific value to the Nation and its people; (4) the United States has pledged itself in the international community to conserve...the various species...facing extinction...; (5) encouraging the States...through Federal financial assistance...to develop and maintain conservation programs...is a key to meeting the Nation's...commitments...." Congress also states that the purpose of the Act is "to provide a means whereby the

---

*Paper presented at 60th Annual Meeting, Pennsylvania Academy of Science, March 30-April 1,1984.

ecosystems upon which endangered species and threatened species depend may be conserved, [and] to provide for the conservation of such endangered species and threatened species...." The Act then declares it "to be the policy of Congress that all Federal departments and agencies shall seek to conserve endangered species and threatened species and shall utilize their authorities in furtherance of the purposes of this Act."

These excerpts from the Endangered Species Act demonstrate that (1) Congress is concerned about the extinction of species, (2) the policy of Congress is to conserve endangered species, (3) a conservation program is necessary and (4) that the States are recognized as vital components of any conservation attempt. This last point is the facet of the Act that will be discussed in this paper.

Section 6 of the Act is entitled Cooperation with the States and deals with the concept of cooperative agreements between State agencies and the Department of the Interior (as represented by the U.S. Fish and Wildlife Service) for the purpose of conserving endangered and threatened species (listed species). In order to qualify for a cooperative agreement, a State agency must "maintain an adequate and active program" for the conservation of listed species. Five criteria are applied to the State agency to determine if "an adequate and active program" exists. They are:

(1) Authority to conserve resident species which have been determined by the State and/or Federal government to be endangered or threatened. This test is met through a review of State law. It should also be noted that this test recognizes the State's right to develop their own list of endangered and threatened species in addition to the Federal list.
(2) A conservation program to protect all resident listed species of fish or wildlife for which a cooperative agreement is sought. This test is met by the agency providing evidence of a conservation program.
(3) Authorization to conduct investigations to determine the status and requirements for survival of resident species. This test is met through a review of State law.
(4) Authorization to establish programs, including land and aquatic habitat aquisition, for the conservation of listed species of fish or wildlife. This test is also met by a review of State law. The key here is the authority of the agency to purchase habitat (both terrestrial and aquatic) for the protection of animal species. There is, however, no requirement that authority exist for the purchase of habitat for plant species.
(5) A provision for public participation in designating resident species as endangered or threatened. Once again, this test is met through a legal review. It should be noted that this criteria reinforces the States' right to develop their own list of endangered and threatened species.

It has been recognized that any one State agency may not have authority over all species, therefore, an agency may only obtain agreements for those species over which it has authority. For example, many State wildlife agencies do not have authority for plant species, but can still qualify for a "limited authorities" agreement covering only fish and wildlife. Thus, many States have separate agreements for plants and animals. The limited authorities agreement can also exclude individual species from the cooperative agreement if the States' laws and/or management of that species is not consistent with its Federal status. For example, the grizzly bear, which is federally listed as threatened, is not included in Montana's cooperative agreement because State law does not allow the State agency to provide it with special consideration as would be required by its federal designation.

The most obvious advantage for a State to have a cooperative agreement is that its endangered species projects become eligible for financial assistance under Section 6 of the Endangered Species Act. Section 6 is administered in much the same way as the Pittman-Robertson (PR) and Dingell-Johnson (DJ) funding, that is, individual projects can receive Federal reimbursements of 75 percent of their cost or 90 percent, if two or more States are cooperating on the same project. But, unlike the PR and DJ Programs in which funds are divided among the States based on a formula, under the Endangered Species Act each individual State project must compete against the other projects for funding. This helps to insure that the most worthy projects receive Federal funding.

As stated in the Act, the reason behind providing Federal assistance for endangered species projects is to encourage States to develop conservation programs for listed species. Prior to the initiation of this program in 1976 only a handful of States (such as California, Florida, and New York) had programs for endangered species. Currently there are 41 States and territories with cooperative agreements and several others are in the process of developing agreements.** This program has obviously been successful in encouraging the development of endangered species programs at the State level. It has also added an immeasurable amount of public involvement and support for the endangered species program. Another less tangible benefit derived from the State cooperative agreement program is a raising of the general public's consciousness in the field of non-game wildlife biology and management.

Between 1977, when Section 6 allocations to the States were first made, and 1983, more than 25 million dollars of Federal money has been spent by the States for endangered species projects. An additional two million dollars (approximate figure) has been allocated for use in the current fiscal year. Over the years, the money has helped to fund a wide variety of studies including status surveys of State listed species, reintroduction of species, land acquisition for species, research on the biology of a species, and active management of listed species.

**As of January, 1986 there are 46 states and territories with cooperative agreements and several others which are in the process of developing agreements.

Among the many projects funded this year are a State black-footed ferret coordinator in Wyoming, monitoring the small whorled pogonia in Rhode Island, life history studies of the Plymouth red-bellied turtle (Massachusetts), reintroduction and monitoring of the Delmarva Peninsula fox squirrel in Delaware, gray and Indiana bat protection (several States), captive propagation of Morro Bay kangaroo rats (California), predator control for the protection of the Hawaiian goose (Hawaii), and habitat monitoring for the California condor (California).

The availability of Section 6 funding encouraged the State of New York to pioneer the technique of hacking bald eagles. Through their work, the State was able to develop the technique to the point where hacking no longer was considered merely a method of supplementing an existing eagle population. In 1981, New York began an ambitious program to utilize their hacking technique on a large scale to reestablish a large nesting population of eagles. Their program consists of five annual releases of 25-30 birds. The goal is to increase New York's nesting bald eagle population from two pairs to 50 pairs over the next several years. While it will be some time until the results are know, the technique appears to be very promising and a number of other States, including Pennsylvania, are now employing hacking methods in hopes of bolstering their bald eagle populations.

Pennsylvania's program for the reestablishment of bald eagles is a 7-year project aimed at releasing about 12 birds per year from two different sites: one on the Susquehanna River and one in the northeastern part of the State. When combined with the four known nests in western Pennsylvania, the State hopes to eventually have breeding eagles throughout Pennsylvania. This project received Section 6 support last year and will also receive money this year.

Since its initiation, the Section 6 program has produced a lot of good, biologically sound research on listed species. It has also provided funds to allow States to actively participate in the development and implementation of recovery plans for listed species. Probably most important of all, it has encouraged States to develop their own endangered species programs which have, in turn, raised the level of public consciousness about endangered species, and probably all non-game species. This has been an important program in stimulating the States to become involved in the conservation of endangered and threatened species. As Congress has recognized, the States must develop and maintain conservation programs if the Act is to be successful. The role of Section 6 in the State program has been recognized and we believe the program will continue to play an important role in endangered species conservation in the future.

Endangered and Threatened Species Programs in Pennsylvania and other States: Causes, Issues and Management. Edited by S. K. Majumdar, F. J. Brenner and A. F. Rhoads. © 1986, The Pennsylvania Academy of Science.

Chapter Three

MANAGEMENT OF UNDERCOVER OPERATIONS IN ENDANGERED SPECIES AND OTHER WILDLIFE LAW ENFORCEMENT

CLARK R. BAVIN
Chief, Division of Law Enforcement
U.S. Fish and Wildlife Service
Washington, D.C. 20240

A marked increase in the known incidence of commercial wildlife crime throughout the world has been recorded during the last several years. This is undoubtedly a result of increased enforcement as well as economic pressures and the profitability in large scale, commercially oriented operations involving fish and wildlife. The prices people are willing to pay for wildlife are astonishing. With the increase in profits, more money and resources are available to the criminal. Complex schemes are developed and executed to carry out illegal commercial transactions. In order to effectively meet these challenges, the U.S. Fish and Wildlife Service has refocused its law enforcement efforts. To the extent practicable, attention has been shifted away from large numbers of smaller violations having limited impact on wildlife resources, to fewer, large-scale violations often carried out by persons or organized groups intent on commercial gain through illegal exploitation of wildlife resources. These persons not only knowingly violate the law, but frequently and matter-of-factly assess the risk of doing so as part of their costs of doing business.

As part of this refocusing of limited law enforcement resources on large-scale or commercial violations, the use of undercover techniques has increased many fold. This has been necessitated because these crimes are usually committed in a clandestine manner or by secretive, organized groups and are difficult to detect by conventional law enforcement activities. The success of these efforts is best illustrated by some of the investigations themselves. For example:

In November 1982, State and Federal agents concluded "Operation Gillnet," an 18-month covert investigation involving illegal commercial dealings in Great Lakes fish, featuring the use of a Chicago wholesale fish business as a "cover." The cooperative investigation involved wildlife officers from Wisconsin, Illinois, Indiana, Michigan, and Tennessee. It revealed that as many as 27,000 kg of fish were illegally harvested from the Great Lakes and sold each year. The principal impact was on lake trout, but, in addition, brown trout, rainbow trout, salmon, black bass, crappie, and blue-gill were invlved in these illegal transactions. To date, 90 individuals have been convicted resulting in fines in excess of $120,000.

In June 1984, "Operation Falcon," a 3-year undercover investigation into the illegal taking and commercialization of birds of prey, was made public by the arrest of over 30 individuals in 14 states. Those arrested were charged with violating various federal wildlife statutes, as well as smuggling, conspiracy, mail fraud, and making false statements to the Government. In addition, 54 search warrants were executed and over 100 live raptors, pick-up trucks, sedans, an aircraft, 2.3 kg of marijuana, and $3,100 in counterfeit bills were seized. This is an on-going investigation which is international in scope (8 foreign nationals have been indicted and are currently fugitives from justice). To date, 55 persons have been convicted and sentenced to over $324,000 in fines and 2 years in jail.

In October 1984, "Operation Trophykill," a 3-year undercover investigation into illegal poaching and smuggling of native and exotic wildlife, culminated in the execution of 20 search warrants and the charging of 34 persons from 9 states. Violations included smuggling endangered species skins and illegal interstate transportatin of illegally killed North American wildlife, such as big horn sheep, mountain goats, elk, mule deer, black bear, antelope, mountain lions, bobcat, and lynx. Additional violations of the Eagle Protection and Migratory Bird Treaty Acts were charged. To date, 45 individuals have been convicted and sentenced to over $114,000 in fines and over 51 years in jail. Two of the defendants were sentenced to serve jail terms of 15 years and 10 years respectively for their involvement in the poaching and selling of protected wildlife, representing the most severe penalties ever handed down for wildlife offenses.

In January 1985, a 2-year East Coast undercover investigation involving illegal commerce in fish and wildlife culminated in the filling of charges by State and Federal wildlife agents against more than 130 individuals. A major segment of the investigation focused on the illegal taking of deer and other resident species and illegally transporting them for commercial purposes in interstate commerce. Another phase of the investigation involved illegal taking of "over-sized" striped bass from Chesapeake Bay and their illegal sale to fish markets and buyers in Philadelphia, New York, Maryland, Virginia, and the District of Columbia. To date, 127 persons have been convicted of State and Federal violations and sentenced to over $345,000 in fines and 8 years in jail.

In the Midwest the covert phase of a 2-year joint State/Federal investigation into illegal trafficking of furs such as fisher, bobcat, lynx and otter, was terminated. Under a cooperative agreement, Service agents and wildlife officers from Michigan, Minnesota and Wisconsin discovered a vast illegal market in furs. Large quantities of business records have been seized and several persons arrested. When the investigation is complete nearly 250 persons may be charged in State and Federal courts.

These investigations are representative of the types of cases that have been the focus of the Service, frequently in close cooperation with State wildlife agencies. While resident Special Agents conduct hundreds of undercover investigations on the local level each year, the Service also maintains a full-time undercover unit that during the last 5 years alone has engaged in seven major covert investigations resulting in the conviction of 428 individuals who were fined nearly $1,106,000 and sentenced to 145 years in jail. The Service firmly believes that such enforcement efforts have led to the successful prosecution of major, commercially-oriented wildlife criminals and have created a substantial deterrent, which is essential if the overall goal of preserving our wildlife resources is to be realized.

PUBLIC CONCERN

While there is no question that an undercover operation catches violators, it is an investigative technique that can be fraught with danger and is often surrounded by public misunderstanding and concern.

In February 1980, "Operation Abscam" was made public. This was the elaborate FBI undercover operation to present opportunities for a number of well-known politicians to be bribed by Federal agents posing as representatives of rich Arab sheiks. Early critics cried "foul", "unfair", "entrapment" and a violation of due process of law. Abscam created considerable interest in Congress. The House Subcommittee on Civil and Constitutional Rights conducted a 4-year review that included 21 hearings and produced an enormous amount of information.[1] Senate Resolution 350 established a select committee to study Department of Justice undercover activities. The select committee reviewed volumes of documents, conducted numerous interviews, and held hearings. The final report, nearly 800 pages, was issued in December 1982.[2] As a result of these inquiries several bills have been introduced in Congress to regulate Federal undercover operations, but none have been enacted into law.

There have also been numerous editorials and articles written concerning Abscam and other major FBI undercover investigations, and the use of undercover techniques in general.[3] The last major case to receive such attention involved John Z. DeLorean.[4]

Federal wildlife undercover investigations are, as they should be, also subject to Congressional inquiry and public concern. "Operation Falcon" was the most controversial undercover case in recent years and was the subject of Congressional testimony in both the House and Senate.[5] Numerous articles, both complimentary and critical, have appeared in major newspapers and magazines. Unfortunately, much of the criticism has not been based upon complete knowledge of the facts, as evidenced by an editorial in a national outdoor magazine.[6] Fortunately, this was answered by a letter to the editor from a Federal prosecutor.[7]

A major concern expressed by most writers, however, is not that violators get caught, but that innocent individuals may be induced to break the law. This danger, along with other dangers inherent in undercover operations, is discussed in more detail below.

In view of the increased use and effectiveness of undercover operations in State and Federal wildlife law enforcement agencies and in view of the public concern and misunderstandings about these operations, it is imperative that wildlife managers at the highest level have an understanding of the legal and policy ramifications of using this investigative technique. State wildlife administrators should promulgate written policies and procedures concerning undercover operations in order to protect the public, protect the resource, and insure that their officers are operating in a fair and legal manner.

TYPES OF UNDERCOVER OPERATIONS

In considering the management of undercover operations through policy development, it should be recognized that there are 5 distinct types of undercover activities. Each of these has different levels of intrusion and may need to be considered separately by supervisory and management personnel.

The first of these, the pretext interview or patrol, is probably used most frequently by wildlife officers. Here the officer operates in plain clothes and simply talks with potential violators or circulates in a hunting or fishing situation in such a manner that the public is unaware of his or her true identity. This often involves engaging sportsmen in conversation at public docks and parking areas, or participating in actual hunting or fishing activities so that potential violators can be observed. This type of undercover activity is least intrusive and generally does not cause concern for the administrator.

Secondly, undercover techniques are sometimes used to investigate previous crimes. This differs from the pretext interview or patrol because it is not a random or chance encounter, but a planned undercover investigative operation to infiltrate a group or become acquainted with specific individuals who are known to have previously violated the law. In these situations the officer must be careful not to pose as someone who could have a legal confidential relationship with the violator, such as an attorney, physician, or clergyman.

Buy-bust undercover cases are the third type and are also frequently used by wildlife undercover officers. These operations generally involve an officer working alone offering to illegally buy wildlife from someone that intelligence sources indicate has been known to sell in the past. A typical example may involve a guide, outfitter, tavern owner, or other local individual who is willing to sell an illegal deer to almost anyone who comes along. After the sale is made to the undercover officer, the violator is arrested. This is not the type of operation that involves several individuals or lasts for a long period of time.

The fourth type of undercover operation involves inserting an undercover officer into an on-going criminal activity. This is where officers have information about a particular criminal activity, such as a deer-poaching ring. The undercover officer gains the confidence of these individuals and becomes a member of the gang. In these situations the officer is generally passive and, while he can influence the activities of the group to some extent, he is merely there to observe what goes on and later testify in court.

Finally, the fifth and the most controversial and potentially most intrusive undercover method can be characterized as a "sting." This technique is also described as involving "creative" crimes, i.e., where the "criminal opportunity" has been fictitiously created by the undercover agent. Many large-scale operations conducted by the Service recently have involved this type of operation. For example, in "Operation Trophykill" the Service established a tannery offering services to guides, outfitters, and hunters. In "Operation Gillnet" State and Federal officers used a specially created seafood company as the base for the operation. These investigations typically involve numerous officers operating over a wide geographic area and generally evolve over a long period of time.

DANGERS OF UNDERCOVER OPERATIONS

Testimony before Congressional committees as well as the articles mentioned above identify the potential abuses and damage to individuals and society as a whole that can result from undercover activities. While many of these are somewhat theoretical, the risk of injury to individuals is real and should be recognized by wildlife administrators, particularly as policies are formulated. These dangers of undercover operations, as applicable to wildlife law enforcement, are summarized below in no particular order of importance.

If undercover operations are not closely controlled and monitored in selected cases, there is the potential danger of damage to public individuals and institutions. This can happen when undercover investigations implicate high public officials, such as State or Federal legislators, State or Federal cabinet officers and judges, governors, mayors, chiefs of police, heads of fish and game departments and other people appointed to positions of public trust. This does not mean that such individuals should not be investigated if there is information that they are engaged in illegal wildlife activities, but that approval for using undercover techniques should be at a high level. Policies should control undercover officers so that such covert investigations are carefully controlled and monitored, because when it is disclosed that public officials have been the target of an investigation, even if they are not charged with a crime, damage may be irreparable to not only the individual, but the institution itself.

The second area of potential harm is where an undercover officer poses as an attorney, physician, clergyman, or other person who is under the obligation of a legal privilege of confidentiality and the particular information discussed would ordinarily be privileged. This could occur when the undercover officer leads a person into a professional or confidential relationship as a result of this pose. Special controls and policy guidelines are necessary in this area not only to avoid the legal issues, but also keep from undermining long-established precepts of confidentiality.

The third area of potential danger in using undercover operations is to fish and wildlife resources themselves. In some undercover activities it may be necessary for the officer to kill animals to maintain his "cover." This may involve simply hunting with others in a legal manner or actually poaching trophy specimens. It could involve the need to take endangered or threatened species. This is an area where there are great philosophical differences and where the wildlife administrator should clearly enunciate policies to control undercover operations.

Potential damage to innocent and uninvolved third parties is the fourth area that should be of concern to the policy maker. While the Service and individual agents have had several damage suits filed as a result of undercover operations, no significant monetary awards have been made to date. However, as of last April, civil suits in excess of $466 million had been filed against the federal government as a result of FBI undercover operations. So the potential is real and special efforts must be taken to protect uninvolved third parties. Under this fourth category several examples of how damage could occur are summarized below.

There is the danger of injury caused to uninvolved third parties by cooperating informants. Often informants are or have been previously involved in various illegal activities, many times not even associated with wildlife. It is possible for informants to use their new cover to engage in illegal activities not associated with the operation that may cause third parties to sustain financial losses. Such illegal activities may not be known to the government, but even in situations where victims may become suspicious and inquire about the informant's status, he may be reassured that the informant is legitimate or at least not warned of the double dealing. This is often necessitated in order to not disclose the cover and destroy the undercover operation.

Injury to uninvolved third parties could also be caused by undercover officers themselves. For example, a cooperating individual may allow officers to use his particular business as a front and a loss or deterioration in such business may occur because of the undercover operation resulting in financial harm. As another example, if officers were to divert a substantial amount of business away from existing taxidermists in the area to their undercover taxidermy company, it could result in significant financial loss and possibly force innocent third persons into bankruptcy.

Risk to innocent and uninvolved third parties can also result where the undercover operation "creates" criminal opportunities. While this may be perfectly appropriate as related to the targets or the investigation, the creation of crime could cause potential damage to third parties in unusual situations. For example, where officers have created a deer poaching operation and livestock of innocent farmers are accidentally killed, the argument can be made that but for the creation of the crime by the government, such accidental killing would not have taken place.

The fifth category involves the possibility, although remote, that innocent individuals may be prosecuted and convicted as a result of undercover operations. This is most likely when the government sets up the illegal activity and possible opportunity for crime. While the entrapment defense discussed below theoretically protects these people, there is still a possibility of abuse. As Mel Weinberg, the key figure in the Abscam case said, "You put the big honey pot out there, all the flies come to it."

The government should make sure that there is reasonable information that the targeted individual has already participated in or is likely to engage in the criminal activity, and that the setting for the criminal activity is structured in such a way that only people who are predisposed are reasonably likely to engage in the contemplated activity. When the government supplies a commodity that is generally not available, such as a hard to obtain specimen or an endangered species, as an inducement to violate the law, this is particularly significant. Also, the number of specific times or the length of the period of time that indivduals are contacted by undercover officers, as well as the amount of money offered in the transaction, must be carefully controlled. All of these factors need to be considered in undercover operations and careful policy guidelines should be developed to make sure that otherwise innocent individuals are not induced to break the law by the operation.

THE LEGAL SAFEGUARD OF ENTRAPMENT

In our judicial system there are many legal safeguards to protect innocent people from being convicted of crimes. In undercover operations one of the most significant is what is known as the "entrapment defense." This is a word which is familiar to almost everyone since it is mentioned in television and newspaper accounts involving undercover operations. Most people know that it connotes something bad, some sinister conduct attributed to unethical, overzealous law enforcement officers attempting to trap innocent people, yet they have no idea of what does or does not constitute entrapment from a legal standpoint. It is important that wildlife administrators, as well as officers, know the legal distinctions and ramifications of the entrapment defense in order for policies and procedures to be written in accordance with legal guidelines.

The Federal entrapment defense has changed little since the Supreme Court created it in 1932 in *Sorrells v. U.S.*[8] Entrapment is not a constitutionally based doctrine, but is a limitation that the Supreme Court has found to be implicit in every federal criminal statute upon its belief that "Congress could not have intended that its statutes were to be enforced by tempting innocent persons into violations."[9] In other words, if a court finds that the defendant was induced to commit the crime by a government agent, the defendant may not be convicted of having violated a federal criminal statute unless he was previously disposed to engage in similar criminal activity. If the defendant produces evidence demonstrating that the undercover agent induced him to commit the crime, the government must establish beyond a reasonable doubt that the defendant was predisposed towards criminal conduct. To show predisposition the government may introduce evidence relating to the defendant's character, reputation, prior bad acts, and prior convictions.[10] Whether the defendant was predisposed is a question of fact to be resolved by the jury.[11] If a judge decides, however, that the evidence is clear that the defendant was entrapped he may rule as a matter of law that entrapment exists and take that question from the consideration of the jury.

The essense of the Federal entrapment defense is that it focuses largely on the defendant's state of mind and is called the subjective test. Government actions that "merely afford opportunities or facilities for the commission of the offense" do not constitute entrapment. Entrapment occurs only when the criminal conduct was "the product of the *creative activity* of law enforcement officials."[12] "To determine whether entrapment has been established, a line must be drawn between the trap for the unwary innocent and the trap for the unwary criminal.[13]

Some defendants in Federal criminal cases have claimed that entrapment should be found where law enforcement officers actually participate in the illegal conduct or provide essential products or services in connection with the alleged crime. The Supreme Court has consistently rejected that claim.[14]

The Federal "subjective" standard for entrapment is used by the majority of State courts. In 11 States, however, the courts use the due process standard where the conduct of the officer is examined to determine if an otherwise innocent person would have committed the crime. This is called the "objective" test. In other words, in these States a person can be entrapped even if predisposed to commit the crime if the officer's conduct would have induced an innocent person to commit the crime.

The Supreme Court has also recognized the due process concept in *Russell* and said in dictum that "...we may someday be presented with a situation in which the conduct of law enforcement agents is so outrageous that due process principles would absolutely bar the government from invoking judicial process to obtain a conviction, *cf. Rochin v. California*, 342 U.S. 165 (1952)."[15] The Court found however, that the facts in *Russell* did not reach that level of conduct. In *Hampton*, the Court noted that cases involving this principle would be "rare", and observed that "police overinvolvement in crime would have to reach a demonstrable level of outrageousness before it could bar conviction."[16] This possible application of the due process concept is different than used in the minority of States, because the Federal courts would only find entrapment of a predisposed person if the officer's conduct was truly outrageous.

In addition to the major Supreme Court cases defining the law of entrapment, there are hundreds of appellate and district court cases reflecting a wide variety of factual situations that need to be reviewed in order to have a complete understanding of the law of entrapment. It is obvious that undercover officers need a great deal of training in this area in order to avoid the entrapment defense. The area where training is particularly significant is for officers to be familiar with the techniques for recognizing and establishing evidence of a defendant's predisposition. While wildlife administrators do not need the same detail of knowledge, it is desirable for them to have a basic understanding of the law of entrapment in order to develop appropriate policies for the guidance of their officers, as well as informants or cooperators who are operating at the direction of their officers.

POLICY AND PROCEDURAL SAFEGUARDS

In addition to the legal safeguards surrounding entrapment, there are a number of policy and procedural safeguards which the wildlife administrator should consider. First, written policies should be promulgated that guard against all of the inherent dangers of undercover operations described above. Policies should also be established to guide officers in avoiding entrapment. These deal specifically with the length of the undercover operation, the type and quantity of inducements offered (including money) and the use of middlemen or cooperators. In these areas the guidance of legal counsel should be carefully considered.

In addition, written policies should be established dealing with each of the following areas: approval level for undercover operations, control and use of informants, participation in criminal activity by undercover operatives and informants, use and accountability of funds for undercover operations, recording of conversations, duration of undercover operations, monitoring and control of the undercover operations, evidence handling and storage, security, and dealing with the press upon public disclosure of the operation.

Each of these areas needs well thought out policy and procedural guidelines so that undercover officers can function with full knowledge that they are operating within the law and within the acceptable standards of the agency. Many of these subjects will require extensive analysis and fairly detailed policies depending on the organization of the agency and the types of wildlife crimes being investigated.

Another area that may need written guidelines, but if not, at least should receive the attention of wildlife administrators, deals with officer stress. Undercover operations, particularly where officers are working in fairly deep cover for long periods of time, are extremely stressful. Care should be taken to select undercover officers with the right temperament and ability to control stress.

The Service has had written policies dealing with undercover operations for several years; however, we are in the process of re-drafting some of these policies in light of recent court decisions and our experience in handling large-scale undercover operations. Once these revised policies are finalized a copy will be sent to any state wildlife agency upon request. Since many undercover operations are joint State/Federal projects, it is desirable that undercover policies be consistent.

TRAINING OF UNDERCOVER OFFICERS AND SUPERVISORS

It is axiomatic that undercover officers need thorough training in all phases of undercover tactics, procedures, and policies. In 1978 the Service initiated its training program for state officers specifically in undercover operations. This is a national training program offered at the Federal Law Enforcement Training Center in Glynco, Georgia. The first session in 1978 was designed for top level State law enforcement administrators and of the 36 students in attendance, 21 were State chiefs of wildlife law enforcement. Since 1978 the training has been conducted every year except 1980 and 1983. A total of 317 officers have been trained from 49 states, Guam, Puerto Rico, the Virgin Islands, Canada, and Australia.

The present one-week basic undercover training program is designed to train state wildlife officers to identify the legal, operational, physical and mental requirements of undercover operations and perform them in a successful manner, as well as to develop additional expertise in the use of specialized equipment. This program is of benefit to both line and supervisory personnel.

As a result of the continued interest in this training program by the states and at their suggestion, the Service is developing a two-week program that will incorporate practical exercices so that students will have an opportunity to actually apply the various concepts, techniques, and skills discussed in the classroom. The Service plans to continue to offer the one-week seminar for state officers next year and should have the new two-week program developed and tested by the following year. The one-week course will be redesigned for managers and supervisors.

CONCLUSION

Undercover operations are one of the most effective and successful investigative tools available today in the war against commercial wildlife crime. Most commercial violations are secretive in nature and performed by consenting parties so that no one is available to complain about the crime. Infiltrating these operations or setting up sting operations has been utilized with increasing success by state and federal wildlife agencies. In conducting such operations, however, there are several dangers which can create harm to innocent people. In order to safeguard the rights and privileges of innocent citizens, and to conduct effective and efficient undercover operations, it is essential that wildlife administrators are familiar with these problems, and with the legal safeguards concerning the law of entrapment. Written policies and procedures to guide the conduct of their undercover operations are essential. Wildlife administrators should also be certain that their undercover operatives are properly trained in all aspects of undercover work and are invited to participate in programs being offered by the U.S. Fish and Wildlife Service.

A high rate convictions usually occur with undercover operations because officers are participating in or observing the crime and can testify as to the details against each defendant. Furthermore, since conversations are often recorded, there can be no dispute as to what was said. However, the judicial system is not always predictable and a jury can render a decision against the government in spite of all precautions. In the DeLorean case the traditional entrapment defense was not the basis for acquittal. Instead, the defense was to confuse the jury, concentrate on the way the government conducted the investigation, and try to indict the agency for lack of policies and control of its agents. It really pointed out the need for agencies to develop policies and police themselves. Wildlife administrators should not be discouraged if a few cases are lost. As former Attorney General William French Smith said following the DeLorean case "an acquittal in one case will not affect our use of undercover operations." We feel the same way and plan to continue to use covert operations as a major tool against organized illegal crime.

ENDNOTES

1. FBI Undercover Operations, Report of the Subcommittee on Civil and Constitutional Rights of the House Committee on the Judiciary, April 1984, H.Doc. 98-267.

2. Final Report of the Senate Select Committee to Study Undercover Activities of Components of the Department of Justice, December 15, 1982, Report No. 97-682.
3. See for example: Marx, "Who Really Gets Stung? Some Issues Raised by the New Police Undercover Work," *Crime and Delinquency,* April 1982, pp. 165-193 and Blecker, "Beyond 1984: Undercover in America—Serpico to Abscam," *New York Law School Law Review.* 1984, pp. 823-1024.
4. See "The Debate: Entrapment, U.S.A. Today, August 21, 1984.
5. Endangered Species Act Authorizations: Hearings Before the Subcommittee on Environmental Pollution of the Senate Committee on Environment and Public Works, 99th Cong., 1st Sess., S. Hrg. 99-70, April 16 and 18, 1985. Hearings before the Subcommittee on Fisheries and Wildlife Conservation and the Environment of the House Committee on Merchant Marine and Fisheries were held on Endangered Species Act Authorizations on March 14, 1985, and H.R. 2767 on July 10, 1985, but have not yet been published.
6. Reiger, "Operation Falcon—The Anatomy of a Sting," *Field and Stream.* January 1985.
7. Rubin, letter to the Editor of *Field and Stream,* by an Assistant United States Attorney, Central District of California, February 25, 1985.
8. *Sorrells v. U.S.,* 287 U.S. 435 (1932).
9. *Sherman v. U.S.,* 356 U.S. 369, 372 (1958).
10. *Osborn v. U.S.,* 385 U.S. 323, note 1, at 332 (1966).
11. *Sherman v. U.S.,* supra, note 8, at 377.
12. *Sorrells v. U.S.,* supra. at 441, 451.
13. *Sherman v. U.S.,* supra, at 372-373.
14. *U.S. v. Russell,* 411 U.S. 423 (1973), and *Hampton v. U.S.,* 425 U.S. 484 (1976).
15. *U.S. v. Russell,* supra. at 431-432.
16. *Hampton v. U.S.,* supra. note 7, at 495.

Chapter Four

THE ROLE OF PENNSYLVANIA'S WILD RESOURCE CONSERVATION FUND IN ENDANGERED SPECIES MANAGEMENT

Frank H. Felbaum

Executive Director
Wild Resource Conservation Fund
P.O. Box 1467
Harrisburg, Pennsylvania 17120

Historically the management and protection of non-game wildlife and native wild plants were supported by sportsmens dollars. The support was not a direct expenditure of funds but in the form of spin-off management techniques of the game species habitat. If the habitat was managed correctly then all species benefited directly and indirectly, but certain species were still losing ground.

Many people saw the need for more specific management and protection for non-game wildlife and native wild plants. The question arose as to the funding source for the new demands being placed on the managing agencies.

Pennsylvania was the eighteenth state to adopt "Tax Check-Off" funding for non-game wildlife and native wild plants. Pennsylvania's law is unique because it includes native wild plants in its statutory charge to manage and protect the renewable natural resources of the Commonwealth.

The "Tax Check-Off" legislation created the Wild Resource Conservation Fund. Signed into law June 23, 1982 by Governor Richard Thornburgh and became effective January 1, 1983. This voluntary fund established a means for all citizens of the Commonwealth to support the management and protection of the states flora and fauna.

Pennsylvania Wild Resource Conservation Fund Logo.

The wild Resource Conservation Fund now makes it possible for the managing environmental agencies, Department of Environmental Resources, Pennsylvania Fish Commission and Pennsylvania Game Commission to expand their efforts in areas of non-game wildlife and native wild plants. The Wild Resource Conservation Fund provides funds that these agencies can gear up their activities in the protection and management of non-game wildlife and native wild plants.

The agencies will be collecting information on all the endangered or threatened species within the commonwealth. This research includes habitat evaluation, census of existing populations and recommendations on how to protect and manage the remaining population.

The major role of the Wild Resource Conservation Fund is to continue to supply the needed monies for the environmental agencies to carry out their non-game wildlife and native wild plant research. This research will further define additional species that are endangered and threatened within the "Keystone State" borders.

As of the date of this publication the Wild Resource Conservation Fund has funded approximately $800,000.00 in projects. Many of these projects support field surveys in attempting to gather as much data about a species.

Listed below are many of the projects that the Wild Resource Conservation Fund supported. The Wild Resource Conservation Fund was developed to help benefit all non-game and native wild plant species for a better management and protection program.

- Funded publication of the book *"Species of Special Concern"* in Pennsylvania by the Carnegie Museum of Natural History in Pittsburgh. The book should provide a blueprint and data for future actions by the Board of the Wild Resource Conservation Fund.
- Research potential wildlife sustaining shrubs that could be used in the reclamation of surface mined lands.
- Public education projects dealing with reptiles, amphibians and non-game fish.
- Co-sponsor "Operation Wildflower", a workshop on wildflower propogation conducted by the Garden Club Federation of Pennsylvania.
- Fund DER's Wild Plant Management Program. The Department is establishing a classification system designed to help protect special plant populations. A centralized computer data base containing information on all of Pennsylvania's plants and wildlife will be maintained by the Department. This is statutory mandated under the Act 170-82.
- Inventory of Wild Plants on Presque Isle. This will up-date 1908 survey.
- Updating the Pennsylvania Fish & Wildlife database. The first species to be updated are those which are listed as either endangered or threatened.
- Update 1950 publication, *"Pennsylvania Reptiles and Amphibians"*. This publication will be used as an educational tool which will be used in the classroom.
- Assessment and management of wildlife depredation at fish hatcheries.
- Extraction of useful data from organized snake hunts; rattlesnake populations and how individual snakes respond to the hunt and handling.
- The study intends to focus on the drainages in the Ohio River system (located in Pennsylvania) where 21 of the 29 undetermined status species are found in this watershed.
- Pennsylvania Breeding Bird Atlas Survey; the data gathered will provide a sound foundation for environmental planning at all levels of government. This study locates the breeding habitats of birds across the Commonwealth.
- Western Pennsylvania Conservancy to continue its database and field survey work on Pennsylvania Natural Diversity Inventory.
- Non-game wildlife Biologist, this individual will be responsible for all activities dealing with non-game wildlife programs within the Pennsylvania Game Commission.
- This survey will help monitor 32 species for use in up-dating the computerized inventory system for mammal research and management.
- The Nature Conservancy to continue its database and field survey work on Pennsylvania Natural Diversity Inventory.
- Pennsylvania River Otter reintroduction program.
- This study would investigate the legal status of small non-game mammals in all fifty states and Canada. It will be reviewing all pending laws and regulations that govern mammal protection.

- Field survey of Pennsylvania Natural Diversity Inventory in the Pymatuning Region.
- DER mini-grants for education and public awareness on wild native plants.
- "Wild Resource Conservation Fund Activity Storybook" will be developed to increase the public awareness about wild resources within the Commonwealth. This book will be used throughout the state school system network.
- Status surveys will be conducted by Carnegie Museum of Natural History on Endangered and Threatened Amphibians and Reptiles. A pressing need exists for surveys of the present occurrence and population of each species.
- Support for Osprey hacking, monitoring returns and documentation of nesting behavior in the Commonwealth.
- Field studies on Eastern Pennsylvania Plants of special concern to Morris Arboretum for input into Pennsylvania Natural Diversity Inventory.
- Field survey the populations and habitats of the Eastern Woodrat in Eastern Pennsylvania.
- Raptor identification workshop for District Game Protectors.
- Inventory and computerize the mosses of Pennsylvania.

All these projects have been funded by voluntary Tax Check-Off contributions by the taxpayers of the Commonwealth. This commitment speaks highly for the dedicated citizens across the state of Pennsylvania for their continuing financial support of all the wild resources.

Endangered and Threatened Species Programs in Pennsylvania and other States: Causes, Issues and Management. Edited by S. K. Majumdar, F. J. Brenner and A. F. Rhoads. © 1986, The Pennsylvania Academy of Science.

Chapter Five

HABITAT PRESERVATION AND DEVELOPMENT FOR RARE AND ENDANGERED SPECIES MANAGEMENT

Fred J. Brenner

Biology Department
Grove City College
Grove City, PA 16127

GENERAL HABITAT DESCRIPTIONS

Pennsylvania and surrounding states have a vast array of diverse aquatic and terrestrial habitats that are conducive to rare, threatened and endangered species management. Aquatic habitats are hereby defined as all magnitudes of streams as well as lakes and various types of wetlands, while terrestrial habitats include geological formations and areas in various stages of succession from bare ground to climax forest. In general, terrestrial habitats are based on the previous descriptions of Erdman and Wiegman[1] and aquatic habitats are based on the classification system devised by Cowardin *et al*[2] and subsequently used by Brenner.[3] Plant and animal communities have evolved over long periods of time in association with particular habitats and, therefore, any alteration—either natural or manmade—will result in a change in the size and composition of these communities. The overall objective of this chapter is to describe the general characteristics of the different habitats and to discuss the biological and ecological factors involved in the management and development of habitats for rare, threatened and endangered species.

AQUATIC HABITATS

Open water habitats include those areas of nonflowing or slowly flowing water greater than 2 m in depth with surface or near surface vegetation along the edges. These habitats are characterized by permanently flooded lands lying below the deep water boundary of wetlands. Hydrophytes are the dominant plants and the substrates are considered nonsoil because the water is too deep to support emergent vegetation.[4] Deep water habitats include the limnetic zone and those portions of the littoral zone where the water depth is 2 m or greater. Natural deep water habitats would include kettle-holes of the glacial physiographic provinces, dune lakes and man-made lakes created for flood control, recreation, or by surface mining.

RIVERINE SYSTEMS

Riverine systems include all aquatic habitats contained within a defined channel except those areas that are (1) dominated by trees, shrubs, persistent emergent vegetation or (2) water with a salinity greater than 0.5 percent.[2,3] Riverine systems originate where the channel leaves a lake, spring or marsh area and terminates when the salinity exceeds 0.5 percent or where the channel enters a lake. Riverine systems are divided into four subsystems (tidal, lower perennial, upper perennial, and intermittant) which are defined in terms of water permanence, gradient, water velocity, substrate and extent of flood plain development.

The tidal system is characterized by a low gradient (under 3m/km), well developed flood plain and water velocity fluctuating under tidal influences. The lower perennial subsystem has a low gradient, slow velocity, water flow throughout the year, and a substrate mainly of sand and gravel. The upper perennial lacks a well defined flood pain and is characterized by a high gradient (over 3m/km), swift velocity, water flow throughout the year and a substrate consisting of rock, cobbles, gravel and occasional patches of sand. In the intermittant subsystem, the channel contains flowing water part of the year which may remain throughout the remainder of the year in isolated pools or be entirely absent.

AQUATIC-TERRESTRIAL TRANSITION

These habitats are adjacent to bodies of water, and are subjected to periodic flooding. The vegetational patterns are generally not well developed, but are, however, characterized by specific types of vegetation. Some ecologists include these habitats as part of the Riverine System but Reid and Ward[5] proposed a separate classification since these areas are subjected to occasional flooding and in some cases may never be flooded. These habitats would include tidal mud flats and sandy lake shores, both of which contain distinctive and characteristic plant communities often containing rare, threatened and endangered species.

WETLANDS

According to the accepted classification system,[2,3] wetlands are transitional areas between aquatic and terrestrial systems where the land is covered by shallow water or where the water table is generally at or near the surface. Wetlands must have one or more of the following criteria: (1) the area must support hydrophytes predominantly, (2) the substrate is predominantly undrained hydric soil and (3) the area must be saturated with water or covered by shallow water at some time during the growing season each year. The upland limit of wetlands is designated as (1) the boundary between land with predominantly hydrophytic cover and land with predominatly mesophytic or xerophytic cover, (2) the boundary between predominatly hydric and non-hydric soil, or (3) if vegetation is lacking, the boundary between land that is saturated part of the time each year and land that is not.

Three principal wetland systems, Lacustrine, Palustrine, and Estuarine, occur in Pennsylvania and surrounding states (Fig. 1). The Lacustrine System includes wetlands and deep water habitats with the following three characteristics: (1) situated in a topographical depression or dammed river channel, (2) lacking trees, shrubs, persistent emergents, emergent mosses or lichens with greater than 30 percent coverage, and (3) total area exceeding 8 ha (20 acres). The Palustrine System includes all nontidal wetlands dominated by trees, shrubs, persistent emergents, emergent mosses and lichens or tidal wetlands where salinity is less than 0.5 percent. These systems are further subdivided into classes, subclasses and dominant types. Class is the highest taxonomic unit below subsystem and describes the general appearance of the habitat in terms of dominant vegetation life form or the physiography and composition of the substrate. "Subclass" defines the finer differences in life form, and "dominant type" determines the dominant plant species (Table 1).

ESTUARINE SYSTEM

Estuarine Systems (Fig. 1) consist of deep-water tidal habitats and adjacent wetlands that are generally partly enclosed by land but have open, partly obstructed, or sporadic access to the open ocean and are, at least occasionally, diluted by freshwater runoff. The salinity may be periodically increased above that of the open ocean by evaporation or reduced runoff. The Estuarine System extends (1) upward and landward to where ocean-derived salts measure less than 0.5 percent during the period of average annual low flow; (2) to an imaginary boundary closing the mouth of a river, bay, or sound; and (3) to the seaward limit of wetland emergents, shrubs, or trees.[2] Offshore areas with typical

TABLE 1

Subclasses and Dominant Types of Estuarine and Fresh Water Palustrine Wetlands.[2,3]

Subclass	Typical Dominant Vegetation
Emergent	
1. Persistent	
a. Estuarine	cordgrass (Spartina), cattails (*Typha angustifolia*)
b. Freshwater	bullrushes (*Scirpus*), cattails (*Typha*), sedges (*Carex*), purple loosestrife (*Lythrum salicaria*), dock (*Rumex mexicanus*), smartweeds (*Polygonum*)
2. Non-persistent	arrow arum (*Peltanda virginica*), pickerel (*Pontedaria cordata*), arrowheads (*Sagitaria*).
Scrub-shrub	
1. Broadleaf deciduous	
a. Estuarine	sea-myrtle (*Baccharis halimifolia*), marsh eider (*Iva frutescens*)
b. Freshwater	alders (*Alnus*), willows (*Salix*), buttonbush (*Cephalanthus occidentalis*) red-osier dogwood (*Cornus stolonifera*) red maple (*Acer rubrum*).
2. Needle-leaved Deciduous	tamarack (*Larix laricina*)
3. Broadleaf Evergreen	Labrador tea (*Ledum groenlandicum*), bog laurel (*Kalmia polifolia*)
4. Needle-leaved Evergreen	black spruce (*Picea mariana*), other conifers
5. Dead	
Forested—found in both estuarine and freshwater systems	
1. Broad-leaved Deciduous	red maple (*Acer rubrum*), ashes (*Fraxinus*), American elm (*Ulmus americana*), blackgum (*Nyssa sylvatica*), swamp white oak (*Quercus bicolor*), pin oak (*Q. palustris*).
2. Needle-leaved Deciduous	tamarack (*Larix laricina*)
3. Needle-leaved Evergreen	black spruce (*Picea mariana*) white cedar (*Thuja occidentalis*)
4. Dead	

estuarine plants and animals, such as red mangrove (*Rhizophore mangle*) and eastern oysters (*Crassostrea virginica*), are also included in the Estuarine System.

GEOLOGIC COMMUNITIES

These habitats are a result of unique geological formations, examples of which occur throughout the northeastern United States. These habitats would include rock outcrops and talus slopes that generally occur on steep or almost vertical slopes in mountainous regions. The vegetation on these areas is sparse with

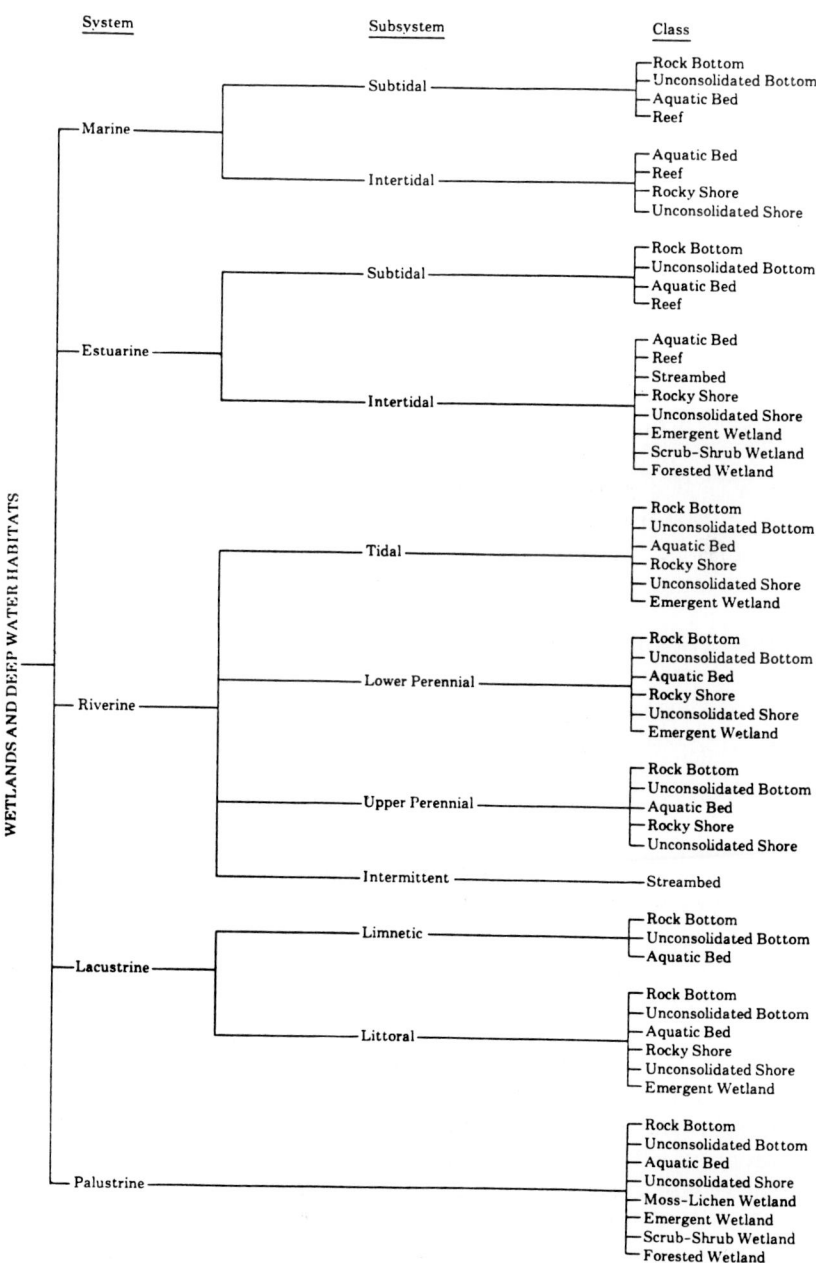

FIGURE 1. Classification hierarchy of wetlands and deepwater habitats, showing systems, subsystems, and classes. The Palustrine System does not include deepwater habitats [Cowardin, et. al. (2)].

an irregular distribution often restricted to small crevices. The geologic habitat often referred to "barrens" are a result of infertile soils which are derived from sandstone or shale formations. One such habitat is the "barren" located in the Nittany Valley in Center and Huntington Counties in Pennsylvania with it distinctive history in addition to its unique ecological characteristics.[3] Other types of barrens include the shale barrens occurring on outcrops of Brailler Shales of the Devonian Period and Serpentine outcrops both of which support prairie-like plant communities containing endemic species.[3]

The other major types of geologic communities that provide distinctive habitats are rock shelters and caves. A rock shelter is defined as an opening caused by the expansion of a joint or fracture in a sandstone formation. The caverns have a relatively shallow depth and should not be considered a true cave. Caves, on the other hand, are generally found in limestone formations as a result of the erosive action of an underground stream although caves may also occur in sandstone formations. These habitats may be extensive and are characterized by a fairly constant temperature (10 C) and high humidity. Many cave systems have been commercialized, often to the detriment of natural communities.

TERRESTRIAL HABITATS

Terrestrial habitats encompass diverse plant communities in various stages of succession from bare ground and cultivated fields to climax forests.

Grassland Communities

Old field communities are a common grassland habitat throughout the northeastern United States. These generally represent areas that have formerly been farmed and are in various stages of succession, reverting back to a forest community. A few native grassland or prairie communities do exist, however, often as a result of distinctive geologic formations such as the shale barrens in southeastern Pennsylvania. These areas include such endemic species such as the barren's ragwort (*Senecio antennariifolius*), Kate's mountain clove (*Trifolium virginicum*), barren's bindweed (*Convolvulus spithamaeus*), and barren's evening primrose (*Oenothera argillicola*). Another native prairie plant community that deserves mention is the Blazing Star meadows located in Beaver, Butler and adjacent counties in Pennsylvania. These areas are characterized by the presence of blazing star (*Liatris spicata*) communities and at least one area, Jennings Environmental Education Center in Butler County, PA, also supports the endangered Massasauga rattlesnake (*Sistrurus catenatus*). All these natural prairie communities are subjected to the continued invasion of woody vegetation and, therefore, in order to maintain these communities they must be intensively

TABLE 2
Forest Stand Classification in use by the U.S. Forest Service.[3,8]

Stand Classification	Characteristics
Sawtimber	Commercial species of minimum diameter breast height (DBH)—soft wood—22.5 cm; hardwood—27.5 cm and contains at least a 3.6 m merchantable saw log.
Pole-timber	Commercial species—DBH—soft wood—12.5 -22.5 cm; hardwood—12.5-27.5 cm.
Sapling-seedling	Commercial species less than 12.5 cm DBH

managed. For example, sections of the Blazing star communities on the Jennings Environmental Education Center are burned on a rotating basis in order to preserve the prairie community.

Forest Habitats

A forest stand as defined by the U.S. Forest Service is a growth of trees on a minimum of 7 ha (10 acres) that is at least 10 percent stocked by trees of any size. Sawtimber stands (Table 2) are defined as an area in which at least 10 percent or greater of the trees are growing stock and 50 percent or greater of the stand stocked with sawtimber that is at least equal to poletimber. Whereas, poletimber is defined as an area at least 10 percent stocked with growing stock and 50 percent or more in sawtimber and pole timber with poletimber exceeding the sawtimber. A sapling and seedling stand is defined as an area where at least 10 percent of the stand is stocked with growing stock and saplings and/or seedlings comprised the majority of the stocking. A non-stocked stand is then defined as forest lands that are less than 10 percent covered with growing trees (Table 2). The distinction and composition of these stands very among the forest communities within the northeastern United States.

The Eastern Deciduous Forest Biome of North America has been subjected to human disturbance that, along with variations in topography, climate, drainage patterns, geological formations and soil types, has resulted in a variety of primary and secondary forest communities. The basic forest regions described by Braun[6] have been redefined by Kuchler[7] and the U.S. Forest Service[8] according to the dominant species which constitute each forest type (Table 3). If no indicator species makes up the majority, the forest community is then defined on the basis of plurality of stocking.[8] It is not within the confines of this chapter to define the habitat requirements of wildlife species that inhabit forest communities but it should be remembered that these species will be affected by the management practices and successional stages of these communities.

TABLE 3

Comparison of the Three Classifications Systems Used To Describe Forest Habitats in Pennsylvania and Other States.

Braun[6]	Kichler[7]	U.S. Forest Service[6]
Beech-maple	Beech-maple	White Pine (< 50%) includes pitch or other pines
Mixed Mesophytic	Mixed Mesophytic	Virginia Pine (< 50%)
Hemlock-White Pine	Hemlock-Northern Hardwood	Oak-Pine (25-50%)
Oak-Chestnut	Appalachian Oak	Oak-Hickory
	Oak-Hickory-Pine	Oak-Gum
	Northern Hardwood Spruce	Elm-Ash-Red Maple
		Maple-Beech-Birch
		Aspen-Birch

HABITAT RELATIONSHIPS AND SPECIES MANAGEMENT

HABITAT USE BY SPECIES OF CONCERN IN PENNSYLVANIA

An examination of the Species of Concern in Pennsylvania[9] reveals some interesting data on the geographic distribution and the principal habitat use by these species. Of the 21 plant species listed as "endangered" in Pennsylvania by Weigman,[10] 52 percent are located primarily in southeastern Pennsylvania (Table 4) and 28.5 percent are located in mountainous regions of the south central portion of the state. The majority of the endangered plant species in Pennsylvania are found in wetlands (57 percent) with the next largest number (23.8 percent) occurring in barrens habitats (Table 5). Likewise, an examination of 40 invertebrate species listed as either threatened or endangered by Opler,[11] indicated that 65 percent are primarily wetland inhabitants with the next largest number (15 percent) being found in barrens habitats. Due to the mobility of animal species, it is difficult to assess the geographical distribution of many of these species. For example, a species may be a bog inhabitant and occur in these habitats throughout the northeastern and northwestern portions of the state. Likewise, a species that is a Riverine inhabitant may occur in limited numbers throughout the drainage area. It is of interest, however, that the majority of invertebrate species of concern are located in the eastern and northcentral portions of Pennsylvania (Table 4). This may be due to the fact that these regions have been sampled more intensely than other areas of the state.

An analysis of the geographical and habitat distribution of fish species that are of concern in Pennsylvania reveals that 52 percent are found in large or medium size rivers and of these 45 percent are located primarily in the Ohio River Basin and 7.2 and 29.5 percent are found within the Susquehanna and Delaware Basins (Table 6), respectively. Twenty fish species that inhabit lakes are either listed as being of concern or extirpated in Pennsylvania and of these 16 were found only in Lake Erie. The two factors that probably affect the size

TABLE 4
Regional Distribution of Species of Concern in Pennsylvania.

Region	Plants	Invertebrates	Fish	Amphibians-Reptiles	Birds	Mammals	Total
Southeast	11	16	8	7	22	14	78
Northeast	3	20	1	2	21	12	59
Southcentral	6	15	2	4	16	17	60
Northcentral	3	17	0	3	18	14	55
Southwest	3	9	6	6	18	12	54
Northwest	3	10	19	6	25	12	75

TABLE 5
Number of Species of Concern (Exclusive of Fish) Found in Different Habitats in Pennsylvania.

Habitat	Plants	Invertebrates	Amphibians	Reptiles	Birds	Mammals	Total
Wetlands							
Bogs	2	12		1			15
Palustrine	2		2	4	10	3	21
Intertidal	6						6
Riverine	2	10			1	3	16
Deepwater		4		1	1		6
SUBTOTAL	12	26	2	6	12	6	64
Grasslands	1	1			11	3	16
Woodlands							
Deciduous	2	2		5	6	7	22
Coniferous		4			1	1	6
SUBTOTAL	2	6		5	7	8	28
Barrens	5	6					11
Caves		1				4	5
Rock Outcrops	2		1			2	5
Others	1					3	3
TOTAL	22	39	3	11	30	26	132

and distribution of fish species within these drainage areas are the natural geographic range of the species and pollution of the major waterways.[12] Many of these species were probably always present in these drainage areas in low numbers but industrial and other types of pollution eliminated them from their former range. It is of interest to note that as pollution is abated, species such as the sauger (*Stizostedion canadense*) and possibly the freshwater drum (*Aplodinotus grunniens*) are returning to the Ohio River and its tributaries.

Only 3 species of amphibians are currently listed as either endangered or vulnerable in Pennsylvania. Of these, the New Jersey Chorus Frog (*Pseudacris triseriata kalmi*) and the Coastal Plain Leopard Frog (*Rana utricularia*) are wetland inhabitants and, the Green Salamander (*Aneides aeneus*) occurs only

TABLE 6

Number of Species of Concern Found in Different Habitats and Drainage Basins in Pennsylvania.

Major Habitat Preference	No. Species	Extirpated	Total
Large Rivers	6	9	15
Medium Large Streams	13	4	17
Small Streams	3	1	4
Lakes	11	7 (Erie) 2 (other)	20
Anadromous	2	0	2
Bogs—Acid Water	0	3	3
Total	35	26	
Ohio Drainage Basin	22	7	29
Susquehanna Drainage Basin	4	2	6
Delaware Drainage Basin	7	6	13
Lake Erie Basin	11	7	16
Total	44	22	

on outcroppings of the Homewood Sandstone in Fayette County along the Pennsylvania-West Virginia border. McCoy[12] listed 11 species of reptiles as either endangered or vulnerable and approximately 55 percent are wetland inhabitants while 5 percent are inhabitants of deciduous woodlands. The majority of these species occur in either the southeastern or western portions of the state.

As with many of the other taxonomic groups discussed, 40 percent of the 30 birds species of concern in Pennsylvania are wetland inhabitants, but in contrast to the other groups, 36.7 percent inhabit grasslands while the remainder occur primarily in woodlands. These species are fairly evenly distributed across the state with slightly larger numbers occurring in the east and northeast, probably because of the concentration of wetlands in these areas. On the other hand, the principal habitat of the 26 species of mammals currently of concern in Pennsylvania, only 23 percent are wetland inhabitants with approximately an equal number[8] occurring in woodlands. Six species of bats are of concern in Pennsylvania, and of these, 3 use caves for hibernation during the winter months. In addition to these species, the endangered eastern woodrat (*Neotoma floridana*) are also common cave inhabitants. Hence, the preservation of these geological habitats should be of prime concern by regulatory agencies.

Although this analysis was compiled for Pennsylvania, similar conditions exist throughout the northeast. It must be remembered however, that the management of habitats, especially wetlands, for these and other species may require maintaining habitats in the successional stage most advantageous to a particular species.

MANAGING HABITATS FOR RARE, THREATENED AND ENDANGERED SPECIES

PRESERVATION VS. MANAGEMENT

In the management of any species, the question exists as to whether we should develop single species management policies or a broad-based program that involves the entire ecosystem as has been proposed for the Pinelands National Preserve.[16] If the ecosystem approach is chosen as the overall management objective, then it must be realized that natural biological and ecological processes such as succession and interspecific interactions may result in the loss or decline of certain species. In the case of rare, threatened or endangered species, this could result in a genetic bottleneck[17] which may reduce the genetic diversity of the species.

One of the primary factors that has been proposed for the decline of certain species is the loss of critical habitat. This often results in legislation to preserve these critical habitats. In many cases, however, land is preserved without any attempt to develop sound management policies that incorporate the biological and habitat requirement of species with natural succession or other ecological changes in the environment. For example, if the overall management object is to encourage nesting populations of the bobolink (*Dolichonyx oryzovorus*) and other grassland species, then the area must be maintained as a prairie habitat which would require the discouragement of woody vegetation.

Wetlands are critical habitats that have been subjected to a variety of impacts, and the northeastern United States is no exception. Activities such as channelization, spoil deposition and urban development has resulted in losses of wetlands,[18] especially in coastal areas[19] but agriculture has been the principal cause of wetland reduction in the United States.[9] Reduction in the number of wetland habitats has resulted in loss of diversity and size of plant and animal communities dependent on these habitats. For example, 49 percent of the species of concern in Pennsylvania are dependent partly or entirely on wetland habitats.

In recent years, legislative action has been taken by federal, state and local governments to preserve these habitats. This has often resulted in conflict between industrial, urban development and agricultural interests as to the value of certain wetlands. In an attempt to resolve these conflicts, Nelson and Weller[20] proposed a rationale for wetland management that includes the scarcity of certain wetland habitats in an area, habitat diversity and carrying capacity, the degree of degradation from past development, and the increment losses already incurred within the same wetland ecosystem. They indicate that regulatory effects should be concentrated where these characteristics indicate high quality wetlands. Of course, additional benefits can result if rare, threatened or endangered species are using the area. These authors further state that wetland impacts appear to fit into five basic orders of magnitude which pertain to the relative cost and difficulty of impact mitigation.

Although wetlands appear to be one of the most critical habitats that affect the number and distribution of rare, threatened and endangered species, similar rationale and management objectives could be developed for other habitats that will significantly affect the future of these species of special concern.

Until recently, genetics has been a factor that has been given little attention by resource managers. The conservation ethic requires resource managers to maintain the natural characteristics of a species. This requires that the management of a species must employ methods to minimize loss of fertility, fecundity and vigor.[17] The management of a rare, threatened or endangered species often requires the founding of a population from small inbred natural or captive populations from zoos.[21] Although this appears to be intrinsically limited, natural cases of population founding from a few individuals are numerous and these populations do not appear to lack genetic diversity.[17,22]

The management of rare, threatened or endangered plants requires the evaluation of the response of the species to a founder event which will depend on the adaptive potential and demographic structure of the population, as well as the constraints imposed by the new environment.[23] Plants range from intense inbreeding of many annual species to the obligate outbreeding and genetic variability of many woody species. Moreover, the reservoir of genetic variation in polyploid species provides a buffer against genetic erosion often associated with the founder effect.[23] Perhaps in order to better understand the role of genetics in resource management we should capitalize on the numerous natural experiments on the founding and subsequent spread of Eurasian plant species introduced into North America since many of these species may exist in genetically distinct demes.[24]

Although many rare plants and animals have overcome bottle necks and founding events, there have been recent extinctions which are virtually all anthropogenic. In natural populations, the intrinsic factors which may contribute to extinction include: (1) demographic stockasticity; (2) social dysfunction, and (3) genetic deterioration. In general, the species that are most vulnerable to extinction are those with poor dispersal mechanisms and populations on natural or man-made islands.[25] Thus, a decrease in habitat size may result in either (1) the extinction of rare species as a result of decrease in population size and genetic diversity and/or (2) isolation and disappearance of essential resources or habitats and the subsequent extinction of species dependent on them.[25] These factors must be given careful consideration by resource managers if they are to safeguard the genetic resources and ultimately prevent the extinction of any given species.

The manager responsible for managing rare or endangered species must determine how realistic his or her objectives are for each local species, taking into account the types of protection, the space available, and the probable longevity of the demographic unit.[26] Managing wild populations requires maintaining the natural integrity of populations or taxonomic units and ultimately the dynamics of species evolution. If at all possible, this must occur within the confines of the diversity and stability of the ecosystem.

HABITAT DEVELOPMENT

Since the size and distribution of habitats appears to be a critical factor in the management of endangered species,[26] it appears desirable, therefore, to develop a program of habitat restoration especially designed for rare and endangered species. Based on the limited data available, some endangered species are using man-made habitats for at least part of their life cycle. For example, the only nesting colony of the endangered common tern (*Sterna hirundo*) in Ohio occurs on dredged material located in the Lucas County Port Authority Facility on Maumee Bay at Toledo[27] and endangered bat species have been shown to use abandoned mine shafts in Kentucky and Tennessee.[28] Although not endangered, the Pennsylvania elk (*Cervus canadensis*) herd has been shown to benefit from grasslands created by surface coal mining [29] and many grassland nesting bird species are either increasing, expanding or returning to their range because of prairie-like habitats developed on surface mined lands in both Pennsylvania [30] and West Virginia.[31] For example, the Dickcissel (*Spiza americana*) and the Upland Sandpiper (*Bartramia longicauda*) are currently nesting on grassland habitats on surface mined lands in Clarion County, Pennsylvania. Even though these species and other grassland species of concern in Pennsylvania such as the Bobolink (*Dolichonyx oryzivorus*) (Brenner, unpub. data) and the bobwhite quail (*Colinus virginianus*)[3] have been shown to be using grasslands on surface mines. In South Dakota, restored prairies have been shown to be beneficial to non-game species but the composition of bird communities will change through time as succession changes the composition of the plant communities.[32] It would appear desirable, therefore, to encourage the development of prairie habitats for rare and endangered species on certain surface mines and other devastated lands as proposed by Brenner[3] since at least 52 percent and 36.7 percent of the plant and bird species of concern in Pennsylvania, respectively, are found on grassland habitats.[9]

The development of wetland habitats during the reclamation of surface mines or other devastated lands would also be of benefit to a vast array of rare, endangered and other species as well. A variety of wetland bird species have been shown to be using wetlands created on surface mine lands in Pennsylvania, Indiana[34] and Illinois.[35] The development of wetlands on surface mines are not only beneficial to wildlife but this type of reclamation on mined lands has been shown to reduce reclamation costs by 80 percent in some cases[34] and their development should be encouraged by regulatory agencies.

In the development of habitats for rare and endangered species, all aspects of the life history of the species must be taken into account. Plant species must be able to complete their life cycle and, in addition, the habitat should include food, nesting, brood and escape cover for wildlife. Habitat size may be a critical factor. The spatial requirements of a given species in conjunction with the composition and biomass of vegetative cover determine the carrying capacity or species biomass that the area will support. The intensity with which these restored habitats will have to be managed depends on the type of habitat being developed and the stage of succession desired for the number and type of species being encouraged. In addition, management plans should include all the social and perceptual factors that might be desirable in the overall management of the species,[36] community or ecosystem.

REFERENCES CITED

1. Erdman, K.S. and P.G. Wiegman. 1974. Preliminary list of natural areas in Pennsylvania. Western Pennsylvania Conservancy Pittsburgh. 106 pp.
2. Cowardin, L.M., V. Carter, F.C. Golet, and E.T. Laroe. 1979. Classification of wetlands and deepwater habitats of the United States. U.S. Dept. of the Interior, FWS/OBS 79/81/ 103 pp.
3. Brenner, F.J. 1985. Aquatic and terrestrial habitats in Pennsylvania. pp 7-18. In H.H. Genoway and F.J. Brenner (eds.) Species of Special Concern in Pennsylvania. Carnegie Museum of Natural History. Special Publication No. 11. Pittsburgh, 430 pp.
4. U.S. Soil Conservation Service Soil Survey Staff. 1975. Soil taxonomy: a basic system of soil classification for making and interpreting soil surveys. U.S. Soil Conservation Service, Agric. Handbook. 436:1-754.
5. Reid, G.K. and R.D. Wood. 1976. Ecology of inland water and estuaries. D. Van Nostrand and Co. New York. 485 pp.
6. Braun, E.L. 1950. Deciduous forests of the eastern North America. Hafner, Publ. Co., New York. 596 pp.
7. Kuchler, A.W. 1964. Manual to accompany the map of potential natural vegetation of the conterminous United States. Amer. Geogr. Soc. Spec. Publ. 36:1-116.
8. Perguson, R.M. 1968. The timber resources of Pennsylvania. U.S. Forest Service Resources Bull. NE-8. 147 pp.
9. Genoways, H.H. and F.J. Brenner. 1985. Species of Special Concern in Pennsylvania. Carnegie Museum of Natural History. Special Publication No. 11. Pittsburgh, 430 pp.
10. Wiegman, P.G. 1985. Plants. pp. 39-80. In H.H. Genoways and F.J. Brenner (eds.). Species of Special Concern in Pennsylvania. Carnegie Museum of Natural History Special Publication No. 11. Pittsburgh. 430 pp.
11. Opler, P.A. 1985. Invertebrates. pp. 81-168. In H.H. Genoways and F.J. Brenner (eds.). Species of Special Concern in Pennsylvania. Carnegie Museum

of Natural History Special Publication No. 11. Pittsburgh. 430 pp.
12. Cooper, E.L. 1985. Fishes. pp. 169-258. *In* H.H. Genoways and F.J. Brenner (eds.). Species of Special Concern in Pennsylvania. Carnegie Museum of Natural History Special Publication No. 11. Pittsburgh. 430 pp.
13. Mc Coy, C.J. 1985. Amphibians and Reptiles. pp. 259-298. *In* H.H. Genoways and F.J. Brenner (eds.). Species of Special Concern in Pennsylvania. Carnegie Museum of Natural History Special Publication No. 11. Pittsburgh, 430 pp.
14. Gill, F.B. 1985. Birds. pp. 299-354. *In* H.H. Genoways and F.J. Brenner (eds.). Species of Special Concern in Pennsylvania. Carnegie Museum of Natural History Special Publication No. 11. Pittsburgh. 430 pp.
15. Genoways, H.H. 1985. Mammals. pp. 355-423. *In* H.H. Genoways and F.J. Brenner (eds.). Species of Special Concern in Pennsylvania. Carnegie Museum of Natural History Special Publication No. 11. Pittsburgh. 430 pp.
16. Good, R.E. and N.F. Good. 1984. The Pinelands National Reserve: an ecosystem approach to nanagement. Bioscience 34: 169-176.
17. Carson, H.L. 1983. The genetics of the founder effect. pp. 189-200. *In* C. Shonewald-Cox, S. Chambers, B. MacBryde, W. Thomas (eds.). Genetics and Conservation: a reference for managing wild animal and plant populations. The Benjamin/Cummings Publishing Co., Inc. Menlo Park. 722 pp.
18. Deegan, L.A., H.M. Kennedy, and C. Neill. 1984. Natural factors and human modification contributing to marsh loss in Louisiana's Mississippi river deltic plains. Environmental Manage. 8: 519-528.
19. Tiner, R.W., Jr. 1984. Wetlands of the United States: current status and recent trends. U.S. Dept. of Interior, Fish and Wildlife Service. Washington, D.C. 59 pp.
20. Nelson, R.W. and E.C. Weller. 1984. A better rationale for wetland management. Environmental Manage. 8:295-308.
21. Tangley, L. 1984. The zoo ark—charting a new course. Bioscience 34: 606-612.
22. Beardmore, J.A. 1983. Extinction, survival and genetic variation. pp. 125-151. *In* C. Schonewald-Cox, S. Chambers, B. MacBryde, W. Thomas (eds.). Genetics and Conservation: a reference for managing wild animal and plant populations. The Benjamin/Cummings Publishing Co., Inc. Menlo Park. 722 pp.
23. Clegg, M. and A.H. Brown. 1983. The founding of plant populations. pp. 216-228. *In* C. Schonewald-Cox, S. Chambers, B. MacBryde, W. Thomas (eds.). Genetics and Conservation: a reference for managing wild animal and plant populations. The Benjamin/Cummings Publishing Co., Inc. Menlo Park. 722 pp.
24. Brenner, F.J. 1984. Restoration of natural ecosystems on surface coal mined lands in the northeastern United States. pp. 211-225. *In* T.N. Vezuoglu (ed.). The biosphere: problems and solutions. Elsevier Science Publishers.

Amsterdam.
25. Soule, M.E. 1983. What do we really know about axtinction? pp. 111-124. *In* C. Schonewald-Cox, S. Chambers, B. MacBryde, W. Thomas (eds.). Genetics and Conservation: a reference for managing wild animal and plant populations. The Benjamin/Cummings Publishing Co., Inc. Menlo Park. 722 pp.
26. Schonewald-Cox, C. 1983. Conclusions guidelines to management: a beginning attempt. pp. 414-445. *In* C. Schonewald-Cox, S. Chambers, B. MacBryde, W. Thomas (eds.). Genetics and Conservation: a reference for managing wild animal and plant populations. The Benjamin/Cummings Publishing Co., Inc. Menlo Park. 722 pp.
27. Shields, M.A. and T.W. Townsend. 1985. Nesting success of Ohio's endangered common tern. Ohio J. Science. 85:45-49.
28. Barclay, L.A., Jr. and D.R. Parsons. 1983. An endangered species survey of abandoned mine shafts in the big south fork national river and recreation areas, Kentucky and Tennessee. U.S. Army Corps of Engineers. Nashville. 195 pp.
29. Brenner, F.J. 1983. Environmental aspects of coal production in Pennsylvania. pp. 405-424. *In* S.K. Majumdar and E.W. Miller (eds.). Pennsylvania Coal: Resources, Technology and Utilization. PA. Acad. Sci. 594 pp.
30. _____ and J. Kelly. 1981. Characteristics of avian communities on surface mined lands in Pennsylvania. Environmental Manage. 5: 441-449.
31. Whitmore, R.C. 1978. Managing reclaimed surface mines in West Virginia to promote non-game birds. pp. 381-388. *In* D.E. Samuel, J.R. Stauffer, C.H. Hocutt, and W.F. Mason, Jr. (eds.). Proc. Surface Mining and Fish/Wildlife Needs in the Eastern United States. FWS/OBS 78-81. 388 pp.
32. Brown, S.L. and D.E. Samuel. 1978. The effects of controlled burning on potential bobwhite quail habitat on surface mines. pp. 352-358. *In* D.E. Samuel, J.R. Stauffer, C.H. Hocutt and W.F. Mason, Jr. (eds.). Proc. Surface Mining and Fish/Wildlife Needs in the Eastern United States. FWS/OBS 78-81. 388 pp.
33. Blankes Poor, G.W. 1980. Prairie restoration: effects on nongame birds. J. Wildl. Manage. 44:667-672.
34. Brenner, F.J. 1985. Land reclamation after strip coal mining in the United States. Mining Magazine. September pp. 211-217.
35. Sandusky, J.E. 1978. The potential for management of waterfowl nesting habitats on reclaimed mined land. pp. 325-327 *In* D.E. Samuel, C.H. Hocutt and W.F. Mason, Jr. (eds.). Proc. Surface Mining and Fish/Wildlife Needs in the Eastern United States. FWS/OBS 78-81/388 pp.
36. Kellert, S.R. 1985. Social and perceptual factors in endangered species management. J. Wildl. Manage. 49: 528-536.

Endangered and Threatened Species Programs in Pennsylvania and other States: Causes, Issues and Management. Edited by S. K. Majumdar, F. J. Brenner and A. F. Rhoads. © 1986, The Pennsylvania Academy of Science.

Chapter Six

ENDANGERED HABITATS AND HOW THEY AFFECT RARE AND ENDANGERED PLANT SPECIES

GEORGE C. BOONE
Department of Biology
Susquehanna University
Selinsgrove, PA 17870

INTRODUCTION

The problem of plant species becoming endangered or extinct is often the result of habitat deterioration or destruction. Thus to help prevent the loss of plant species, we must have an understanding of the events occurring in their habitats.

Habitat, in this paper, is used in both a broad and narrow sense. In the broad sense, habitat includes the ecosystem containing the plant since factors that affect the ecosystem will directly affect the habitat. In the narrow sense, habitat is used to denote the specific set of conditions needed by a plant to survive. An ecosystem is a collection of unique habitats all the result of biotic and abiotic forces interacting at a given place and time. So when we talk about changes occurring in specific habitats this usually reflects a situation that results in a change in the whole ecosystem.

Habitat dynamics include the mechanisms that affect habitat stability and species diversity in an ecosystem. Stability is defined by Preston[1] as the persistence of an ecosystem which is the property of being resistant to internal and external perturbations. Increased species diversity helps maintain stability in that any perturbation (if not massive) will affect smaller numbers of organisms thus having a smaller effect on the whole ecosystem. Sources of ecosystem perturbation may be generated from within (autogenic) or originate outside the ecosystem (allogenic).

A knowledge of habitat structure alone is not sufficient to insure the survival of a plant species. The autecology of a species must also be understood if conservationists are to maintain environmental conditions conducive to the survival of rare and endangered species. Massey and Whitson[2] state that the key is "species biology", a holistic approach to the understanding of individuals, populations and population systems using evidence from many different disciplines.

There are many examples in the literature relating to the importance of habitat in species conservation. Jenkins[3] states that the present precarious state of many plant species is indirectly related to the destruction of their habitats. Roush[4] indicates that usually the easiest, most efficient, and surest way to conserve a species is habitat preservation. Likewise, Myers[5] suggests that what now constitutes the main form of threat (to threatened species) is habitat disruption. Because of the importance of habitats in species survival, the purpose of the chapter is to review autogenic and allogenic forces affecting habitats that may lead to the extinction of plant species.

The number of forces influencing an ecosystem and their affect on rare or endangered species is almost unlimited. Therefore, no attempt has been made to include all factors which can affect ecosystems. The forces discussed in this chapter are included to illustrate the diversity of factors that can impinge upon habitats.

AUTOGENIC FORCES—SUCCESSION

Succession is hereby defined as a progressive alteration in the structure and species composition in a given location over time. The concept applies equally well to plants and animals. In terrestrial plant succession the progressive changes in plant composition lead to corresponding changes in animal composition.[6,7] Succession can be subdivided into primary and secondary succession. The colonization of an area which previously lacked vegetation is termed primary succession. The revegetation of an area which previously contained plant growth that had been destroyed is termed secondary succession.

Succession is an orderly continuum of change in flora and fauna which is arbitrarily subdivided into seral stages by ecologists. A generalized sequence of seral stages that may occur in secondary succession in Pennsylvania include the following; 1) annuals (pioneer stage), perennials (old field stage), brush, coniferous forest, and deciduous forest (climax stage). These seral stages may be of short duration such as the pioneer stage (first seral stage to colonize an area) or of long duration such as the climax stage (the final, stable seral stage). The exact sequence of change varies from location to location and is somewhat dependent on the local abiotic factors such as soil type, climate, physiography, etc. and biotic factors such as seed sources, rates of plant colonization, rate of reproduction, etc. Each geographic location has its own unique successional history and only broad generalizations can be made about ecological succession in a given location.

Numerous authors have addressed the effects of succession on plant species in example. Massey and Whitson[2] indicate that the preponderance of rare species are successional and that conditions for maintenance of a rare species are quite different from conditions necessary for reproduction. While Woodwell[8] states that disturbing an ecosystem or habitat will shift species composition in a predictable pattern. First, the disturbance-sensitive species are totally eliminated or substantially reduced in abundance. Second, ubiquitous weedy species replace the disturbance-sensitive species. Diversity may initially decrease but will subsequently increase as weedy species accumulate. Obviously succession is a major consideration when attempting to understand why plant species become endangered.

The mechanism that drives succession is currently being debated by ecologists. A brief review of a few of the ecological hypotheses will illustrate that our understanding of succession is not complete and that additional data must be compiled before this topic is fully understood. Drury and Nisbet[9] base their succession model on inter-specific competition. They state "the appearance of successive replacement of one "community" or "association" by another results in part from interspecific competition which permits one group of plants temporarily to suppress more slowly growing successors". The recognition of the role of competition in succession is not new to the plant ecologist but Paine[10], and Pyke et al.[11] suggest that predation rather than competition is the major force driving succession. These authors feel that animal foraging behavior is the key to community structure.

Pickett[12] offers an evolutionary model of succession. He specifies four points to support his evolutionary population-based theory: 1) a population cannot be both generalist and specialist; 2) succession provides a complex gradient of physical and biotic environments analogous to spatial gradients; 3) evolutionary strategies and life cycle characteristics determine the position of a species in a successional gradient; and 4) patches of different successional environments are continuously changing, depending on disturbances, offering different opportunities and selective pressures.[12]

Another attempt at defining mechanisms that control succession was made by Connell and Slatyer.[13] Based on a review of the literature, they formulated three different mechanisms of succession that were based on effects that vegetation had on the habitat. Vegetation did nor did not modify the habitats so that the plants enhanced or inhibited future colonization of the habitat. The outcome of succession was the same in each model but the pathway the plant communities followed to arrive at the climax was different.

Van der Valk[14] proposed for the first time a Gleasonian model of allogenic plant succession in freshwater wetlands. In this model succession occurs whenever one or more new species become established, when one or more species already present are extirpated, or when both occur simultaneously in a wetland. An important feature of the model is the impact of the two environmental states (with standing water or without standing water) on the wetland plant species. Van der Valk[14] considers the model as a beginning framework for understanding and predicting the vegetation dynamics of wetlands.

From the number of different theories proposed to explain the mechanism of succession it is apparent that the final answer is not yet available. Regardless of this problem, succession is a dynamic process that can be observed in ecosystems. It is a process that can have a profound effect on rare and endangered plants.

MODIFICATION OF ABIOTIC AND BIOTIC COMPONENTS IN A HABITAT

The existence of a plant species in a given habitat depends upon the correct mix of abiotic and biotic factors. If that mix of factors is not present or is modified through plant succession the plants must either become extinct or adapt to a new set of environmental conditions.

Soil is an abiotic factor that is influenced by plant communities. Before soil is colonized by pioneer plants it is primarily mineral in composition and shows little or no stratification. When plants colonize soil several changes occur: 1) stratification begins, 2) organic material begins to collect from dead plant and animal remains, 3) the extremes of soil temperature decrease, 4) soil moisture content increases and is maintained at higher levels and 5) the nutrient level in the soil is increased by plants absorbing minerals from deep soil layers and then depositing them on the soil surface through the decomposition of plant material (nutrient cycling). After several years of vegetation cover soil properties are significantly changed.

Microclimate within the habitat is also influenced by vegetation. The amount of moisture in the air increases around plants by evapotranspiration and evaporation of water from litter on the soil surface. The increased air moisture in turn decreases temperature fluctuations. In addition, air flow at the ground surface in vegetation is almost nonexistent. The moderation of effect of these climatic forces creates a habitat that shows few climatic extremes. In other words, micro climate is moderated by the presence of plants.

Available light is also modified by the presence of plants. Shading becomes important in plant communities and a plant community will be composed of shade-intolerant plants (sun plants) and shade-tolerant plants (shade plants). Light availability will help determine the mix of plants present.

For example, a forest that has been clear cut and in direct sunlight will often be revegetated by conifers because they are shade intolerant. A forest that has been selectively cut (leaving some trees) is usually revegetated by deciduous species because they can grow in shade.

These three examples are but a few of the abiotic forces that help shape a plant community. It is apparent that any modification of these three factors or a multitude of other abiotic factors such as fire, topography, wind, north vs. slope exposure, etc. also affect the composition of a plant community.

BIOTIC FACTORS IN PLANT COMMUNITIES

Allelopathy, a production of chemical compounds by plants, is a biotic factor that will affect the growth and development of nearby plants[15] thereby, influencing community composition. Gant and Clebsch[16] discussed the allelopathic influences of *Sassafras albidum* in old field succession and Wilson and Rice[17] cited the allelopathic role of *Helianthus annuus* in old field succession—both examples of plant phenomena that may have an important role in determining the plant community composition. The properties of plants to restrict or inhibit the presence of other plants in a community can have an effect not only on the community composition but may also restrict the distribution of a plant species.

Competition among plants is another important factor in succession that determines community composition. As stated earlier competition is considered a major force in the mechanism of succession by many ecologists.

Competition for resources such as light, water, space, minerals, pollinators, etc. results in less competitive species being forced out of a community. It is a mechanism that leads to species becoming better adapted by selection in their gene pool or, if that fails, the species will become extinct. Competition also functions as a filter allowing only species adapted for certain environmental conditions to exist in habitats where these conditions prevail.

Disease, parasitism, and symbiotic interactions are other examples of biotic interactions which can influence the composition of plant communities. These types of interactions usually dictate the presence of at least two different plant species for the survival of both species. For example, the mutualist relationship of *Rhizobium* and legumes or the mycorrhizal association with roots of different species of trees illustrate the association and enhancement of survival of both species in the relationship. If these mutualist association are obligatory then the loss of one species will automatically lead to the loss of the other species.

When one considers the effect of succession including the abiotic and biotic modifications to the habitat it is not difficult to see why succession can be a natural cause of extinction of plant species. Since succession is a process of continual change any plant that lives in a seral stage other than the climax stage is in danger of extinction. For example, if a plant can only exist in a coniferous forest floor or in a Sphagnum bog the continued existence of the plant is in jeopardy because a coniferous forest, and the Sphagnum bog in many regions of the Northeast are transient stages in succession. Eventually plant species requiring "transient" habitats must become extinct because the abiotic conditions will change sufficiently to prohibit the further survival of such a plant species in that habitat. For example, the Swamp-Pink (*Arethusa bulbosa L.*) is found only in sphagnous bogs or peaty meadows. Such habitats are rare and represent brief seral stages in succession in moist areas. The Pennsylvania Dept. of Environmental Resources[18] lists both the Swamp-Pink and the Small-Whorled Pogonia on its proposed endangered plant list. *Isotria medeoloides* (Pursh Raf. Small-Whorled Pogonia) requires a dry woodland habitat. Again such a habitat is transient and generally short lived because as succession continues one of the abiotic trends is for increased soil moisture which would in time transform a dry woodland into a mesic woodland.

Plants living in a climax community should not be subjected to extensive changes in the habitat because the climax is considered to be self-perpetuating. Theoretically, habitat conditions should be stable and basically unchanged so long as that climax community exists.

ALLOGENIC FORCES

Air Pollution

Air pollution is affecting plants and their habitats in much of the world. It not only affects plants directly by reducing photosynthesis, growth, and reproduction but air pollution also affects plants indirectly by impacting on soil, consumers and decomposers. The continued stress imposed on habitats by air pollution can be a major force in the decline and loss of endangered species.

Ozone and sulfur dioxide are two of the prevalent air pollutants affecting plant communities, their effect has been described in numerous publications.[19,20,21] Although recognition of injury symptoms caused by single pollutants is essential to fully understand the effect of air pollution on plants and their habitats, injury to plant communities often represents the effects of mixtures of several pollutants. Since most gaseous pollutants are seldom completely absent from our contaminated atmosphere, they may exert additive effects and in some cases act synergistically in compounding the damage to plant life. Jaeger and Banfield[22] and Dochinger *et al.*[23] report that mixtures of ozone and sulfur dioxide result in macroscopically visible injury to white pine even when the concentrations of ozone and sulfur dioxide are too low to produce symptoms of injury independently. Boone[24] reports that white pine needles fumigated with mixtures of ozone and sulfur dioxide in concentrations considered to be below the threshold of injury will induce injury to mesophyll tissue after a brief exposure period of 15 min.

The fact that there is a direct relationship between air pollutants and damage to plant tissues means that plants under pollution stress will undergo changes and generally be less productive and be more sensitive to stresses that can kill plants. Guderian and Kueppers[21] reported that high doses of air pollution lead to a break-down in the plant community producing a less diverse community. In this case, succession was reversed—going from later seral stages such as a deciduous forest back to a shrub or herb stage. If pollution levels are sufficiently concentrated, a barren zone may be produced such as what occurred at Copperhill, Tennessee, where fumes from a copper smelter killed the vegetation surrounding the smelter. Even moderate or low levels of air pollution can induce changes in the plant communities but the process will be slower and the results are less obvious.[21]

In addition to gaseous pollutants damaging plants there is mounting evidence that heavy metals are also damaging plants in natural habitats. Wiersma et al.[25] present evidence of the occurrence of increased lead deposition at higher elevations of the Great Smokey Mountains National Park and similar evidence is reported for areas of New England by Schlesinger et al.[26] The deposition of lead is greater at higher elevations and may effect rare species residing in those habitats.[27] The direct effect of pollutants on plants and the indirect effect of pollutants on the plants via successional changes doubly threatens the existence of rare and endangered plants.

Introduced Plant Pests.

There have been many plant pests introduced into North America that have had a serious impact upon plants and, secondarily, the habitats they occupied. *Lymantria dispar* (Gypsy Moth), *Scolytus scolytus* and *S. multistriatus* which carry *Ceratocystis ulmi* causing Dutch Elm Disease, and *Endothia parasitica*, a fungus causing blight in the American chestnut (*Castanea dentata*) were introduced into habitats where no natural control devices existed. The pests have done irreparable damage to forests in Pennsylvania.

Chestnut blight has greatly altered the composition of the eastern deciduous forests of the United States. At one time over 50 percent of the trees in the forests in this region were American chestnut.[28] However, within 30 years after the discovery of the blight in 1904, all of the American chestnut trees in the east were either dead or infected and dying.[29]

Currently the American chestnut exists primarily as stump sprouts which grow to a certain age and may flower but soon die. Whether the American chestnut has a future is unclear at this time. Svetec,[30] in her review of the evolutionary history of the American chestnut, states that if the American chestnut is to survive it must evolve an immunity to the blight similar to the Japanese chestnut (*Castanea crenata*) and Chinese chestnut (*Castanea mollisima*) have done. (See chapter ⁰⁰ for a more complete discussion of the impact of chestnut blight on forest structure).

Gypsy Moth was introduced into the United States from Europe in 1869 by M.L. Trouvelet.[31] However, a few larvae escaped from his laboratory and by 1880 over 1000 km² were infested Medford, Mass.[31] Since 1880, the gypsy moth has migrated southward and westward through the deciduous forests until today it is approaching the southern and western borders of Pennsylvania.

The most commonly favored hosts of the larvae include: all species of oaks, especially white oak (*Quercus alba*) and chestnut oak (*Q. prinus*); alders (*Alnus spp.*); aspen (*Populus spp*); basswood (*Tilia americana*); black spruce (*Picea mariana*); sumac (*Rhus typhina*); willows (*Salix spp.*); and grey (*Betula populifolia*), white (*B. papyifera*), and river (*B. nigra*) birch. Older larvae will also attack beech (*Fagus grandifolia*), chestnut, eastern hemlock (*Tsuga canadensis*) and all species of pines and spruces.[32] In the 12 years between 1968-1980 over 12.5 million ha of forest have been defoliated.[32]

Gypsy moth itself may not kill oak tress directly but defoliated trees are more vulnerable to unfavorable rainfall and site characteristics. Secondary insect invasions by the two-lined chestnut borer (*Agrilus bilineatus*) and shoestring root rot (*Armillaria mella*) often kill weakened trees.[32]

The damage caused by gypsy moth can seriously alter natural habitats. Tree species, especially white pine and hemlock, are killed by a single defoliation while other tree species may be seriously weakened.[31] The loss of trees and the resultant succession will cause an earlier seral stage to develop on the site. The reversal of succession would be rapid, thus changing habitat conditions leading to local extinctions of sensitive plant species.

Historically we have seen the composition of the Oak-Chestnut Forest[33] on the mountain ridges of the Ridge and Valley Physiographic Province change to an Oak-Oak Forest. The removal of American chestnut by blight has lead to a reorganization of dominance of the forest with chestnut oak replacing American chestnuts as a dominant species in these forests. Habitats would also be modified or destroyed by change in species composition. The final effect of plant pests is unknown, the impact of the rapid loss of American chestnut is still not fully known. The forest is still in transition with the final species composition approaching a climax still several generations away.[34] The effect of gypsy moth on forest communities can not be determined at this time. Even without the final verdict it is apparent that the pests will alter habitats creating a ripple effect of plant species change.

DEMANDS ON LAND RESOURCES

Agricultural economics has indirectly lead to the destruction of plant habitats. The depressed prices paid to farmers for crops, the increased cost of energy and equipment and the opening of foreign markets for grain exports have put extreme pressure on farmers to cultivate land previously considered useless or marginal by the farmer. Hedge rows and hillsides earlier considered too steep to farm and 1.6 million ha of dry rangeland have been plowed.[35] Between 1975 and 1978, land planted for export crops increased 33 percent and since 1978 another 39 percent has been planted in wheat while pasture land decreased 40 percent between 1967 and 1977.[35]

Farmers are looking at nonproductive land as a liability because the land is not providing income to pay increased local and state taxes. Often this marginal land is bogs, marshes, woodland or other unique habitats. These unique habitats can often be cleared, filled, drained or destroyed thus eliminating special habitats and associated plants.

Agriculture is not the only force destroying sensitive habitats. Highway construction by state and local agencies; housing projects in urban and rural environments; and the development of recreational facilities such as ski slopes, public parks, recreation, flood control and water supply impoundments are activities by their nature destructive to native habitats and biota.

A major consequence of agricultural and construction activity is soil erosion. Estimates of soil loss in Pennsylvania range from 2 to 4 tons of soil per ha per year. In the United States 13.4 million ha of highly erosive land is being farmed and two-thirds of it is producing highly erosive crops such as corn and soybeans.[35]

The resulting displaced soil often carrying pesticides with it, fills waterways, clogs drains, destroys habitats, thereby creating serious economic consequences. Aquatic habitats such as springs, ponds, lakes, wetlands and streams are affected by soil erosion. The deposition of silt from agricultural land can destroy aquatic plants by burying them or indirectly by the the toxic effects of herbicides.

PROTECTION OF ENDANGERED HABITATS

With the recognition that there are forces that continually threaten fragile habitats, we must identify means to either prevent habitats from becoming endangered or to restore habitats for rare on endangered species.

Obviously the primary mechanism to prevent the loss or rare or endangered plants is to understand the biological factors involved. The more we understand how and where a particular species plant grows the more likely we will be able to preserve it.

In addition, we must have a better understanding of how habitats respond to perturbations. The disturbance of habitats shifts the array of species in a predictable pattern. First, the highly specialized members are eliminated or substantially reduced. Secondly, hardy weedy species replace them and the numbers of species per unit area may decrease initially but will subsequently rise as exotics accumulate.[8] Massey and Whitson[2] proposed a species information program that would include: 1) species general information; 2) species population, habitat and threat inventory status information; 3) species biology status information and 4) environmental factor status information. They feel that if the complete history of a plant can be established through such a procedure, the information will suggest the best strategy of species conservation.

Bratton and White[36] proposed a plan to manage rare plants on a preserve but a similar program should work for any type of rare plant management. Their proposal included: 1) establishing a basic policy as to what is to be preserved and why; 2) establish an inventory of plants and collect basic data for the species; 3) prioritize research and management issues based on the information gathered in step 2 in relation to the basic policy; 4) use the information in step 3 to answer critical questions and create an active management program and 5) integrate the management plan into the overall conservation philosophy of the management area.

Both of these management programs center around obtaining a substantial data base for the rare plants. Without basic information, a successful management plans cannot be developed. Massey and Whitson[2] and Woodwell[8] all demonstrated the value of a basic research program in their reporting on the role of succession in the fate of rare species.

STRATEGIES TO PRESERVE ENDANGERED HABITATS AND PLANTS

Current Strategies-Public. In 1973, Congress enacted the U.S. Endangered Species act thereby, protecting endangered species. This act provided that threatened or endangered species would not be killed nor would the destruction of habitats occur that might lead to the extirpation of listed species on Federally owned land. The act did not, however, protect endangered plant species on private land.

In 1981, the Pennsylvania Department of Natural Resources-Bureau of Forestry established a procedure for the conservation, management, enhancement and protection of wild flora native to Pennsylvania.[36] This program was established to: 1) determine the status of wild flora native to Pennsylvania, 2) establish and maintain regulations for the management of wild flora, 3) enforce rules and regulations established under the Wild Resource Conservation Act, 4) provide plant identification training sessions for interested persons, 5) promote a statewide system of private wild plant sanctuaries, 6) establish public wild plant sanctuaries to protect plants of special concern in Pennsylvania, 7) regulate wild plant removal and collection through a permit system, and 8) solicit research proposals for the preservation of endangered plants.[36] At the same time the Pennsylvania Natural Diversity Inventory, a computer-assisted ecological inventory was designed by the Department of Environmental Resources-Bureau of Forestry, the Nature Conservancy, and the Western Pennsylvania Conservancy. In February, 1985, the coalition published an updated list of Plants of

Special Concern in Pennsylvania[37] categorizing plants as to their status of endangerment.

The Wild Resources Conservation Act of January, 1983 created a voluntary fund to which citizens of Pennsylvania can contribute by designating a portion of their state income tax refund or by direct contributions. In its first year the fund generated $224,000 and in 1984 the amount was in excess of $406,000.[38] These monies were used to support research on endangered flora and fauna in Pennsylvania.

Private Organizations. In addition to the State and Federal efforts to protect endangered species, there are also private organizations that are acting to preserve endangered species and habitats. Prominent among these organizations in Pennsylvania, are the Western Pennsylvania Conservancy and The Nature Conservancy. Both are intent on identifying and conserving habitats and ecosystems for rare species. The State Natural Heritage Program of The Nature Conservancy concentrates on identifying areas exemplifying the full range of landscape types.[39] Once a prime example is identified the Nature Conservancy then attempts to protect it either by outright purchase or landowner agreements.

Field stations owned privately or by colleges and universities serve as a repository for endangered species. Usually field stations are large blocks of habitat protected from broad public use or development. As such they serve a vital purpose not only from the standpoint of conservation, but also by ongoing research into the life history and ecology of endangered species. Brussard[40] makes the point that field stations are usually large blocks of habitat, have a core of investigators to conduct research and can provide public education programs.

In summary, Pennsylvania has an extensive network for the protection of endangered flora and fauna from both the public and private sectors. The key to the success of protecting endangered species, however, lies with education. More people need to be educated to the implications of the potential loss of rare species. People also need to be encourage to support public and private organizations both financially and by involvement in conservation activities.

SUMMARY

Plants become endangered because habitats are altered or destroyed. Natural ecological processes can create habitats not conducive to the continued success of a plant species resulting in a decline in numbers or local extinction. Many rare plants exist only in transient habitats. Compounding the rate of extinction of rare plants are a broad diversity of intrusions by man including air pollution, introduced pests, soil erosion, etc. These and many other human activities increase the rate at which plants are lost. However, efforts on the federal, state and private levels are attempting to reduce the rate at which endangered plants are lost. Through federal and state legislation and private acquisition of rare or threatened habitats, plants may have a better chance of surviving the pressures of civilization. Education of the public to the plight of rare plants and their habitats must be strengthened at both the public and private levels. Public support is necessary to insure the success of programs to save rare plant species.

LITERATURE CITED

1. Preston, F.W. 1962. The canonical distribution of commonness and rarity: Parts 1 and 2. Ecology 43:185-215, 410-432.
2. Massey, J.R. and P.D. Whitson. 1977. Species biology: definition, direction, data and decisions. pp. 88-94. in Conference on Endangered Plants in the Southeast. USDA Forest Service Gen. Tech. Rep. SE-11. Southeastern Forest Experiment Station, Asheville, N.C. 104 pp.
3. Jenkins, R.E. 1975. Endangered plant species: a soluble ecological problem. The Nature Conservancy News 25:20-21.
4. Roush, G.J. 1977. Why save diversity? The Nature Conservancy News 27:9-12.
5. Myers, N. 1979. The Sinking Ark: A New Look at the Problem of Disappearing Species. Pergamon Press, N.Y. 307 pp.
6. Johnson, D.W. and E.P. Odum. 1956. Breeding bird populations in relation to plant succession on the Piedmont in Georgia. Ecology 37:50-62.
7. Shelford, V.E. 1913. Animal Communities in Temperate America. University of Chicago Press. Chicago. 368 pp.
8. Woodwell, G.M. 1977. The challenge of endangered species. pp. 5-10. in Extinction is Forever. G.T. Prance and T.S. Elias (Eds.). N.Y. Botanical Garden. Bronx, N.Y. 437 pp.
9. Drury, W.H. and I.C.T. Nisbet. 1973. Succession. The Arnold Arbor. J. 54:331-368.
10. Paine, R.T. 1969. The *Pisaster-Tequla* interaction: prey patches, predator food preference, and interdidal community structure. Ecology 50:950-961.
11. Pyke, G.H., H.R. Pullian and E.L. Charnov. 1977. Optimal foraging: a selective review of theory and tests. Quart. Rev. Biol. 51:137-154.
12. Pickett, S.T.A. 1976. Succession: an evolutionary interpretation. Am. Nat. 110:107-119.
13. Connell, J.H. and R.O. Slatyer. 1977. Mechanisms of succession in natural communities and their role in community stability and organizations. Am. Nat. 111:1119-1144.
14. van der Valk, A.G. 1981. Succession in wetlands: a Gleasonian approach. Ecology 62:688-696.
15. Muller, C.H. 1966. The role of chemical inhibition (allelopathy) in vegetation composition. Torrey Bot. Club Bull. 93:332-351.

16. Gant, R.E. and E.E.C. Clebsch. 1975. The allelopathic influences of *Sassafras albidum* in old-field succession in Tennessee. Ecology 56:604-615.
17. Wilson, R.E. and E.L. Rice. 1968. Allelopathy as expressed by *Helianthus annuus* and its role in old-field succession. Bull. Torrey Bot. Club 95:432-448.
18. Pennsylvania Department of Environmental Resources. 1984. Plants of Special Concern in Pennsylvania. Unpublished list. Pa. Dept. Environ. Res. Harrisburg, Pa. 14 pp.
19. Brandt, C.S. and W.W. Heck. 1968. Effects of air pollutants on vegetation. pp. 401-443. *in* Air Pollution and Its Effect. 2nd Ed. Vol. I. A.C. Stern (Ed.) Academic Press, New York. 694 pp.
20. Jacobson, J.S. and A.C. Hill, Eds. 1970. Recognition of Air Pollution Injury to Vegetation: A Pictorial Atlas. NAPCA, Pittsburgh, Pa. 109 pp.
21. Guderian R. and K. Kueppers. 1980. Response of plant communities to air pollution. pp. 187-200. *in* Effects of Air Pollutants on Mediterranean and Temperate Forest Ecosystems. P.R. Miller (Tech. Coord.) USDA Forest Service Gen. Tech. Rep. PSW-43. Pacific Southwest Forest and Range Experiment Station, Berkeley, Calif. 256 pp.
22. Jaeger, J. and W. Banfield. 1970. Responses of eastern white pine to prolonged exposure to atmospheric levels of ozone, sulfur dioxide or mixtures of these pollutants. Phytopath. 60:575. (Abstr.)
23. Dochinger, L.S., F.W. Bender, F.L. Fox and W.W. Heck. 1970. Chlorotic dwarf of eastern white pine caused by ozone and sulfur dioxide interaction. Nature 225:476.
24. Boone, G.C. 1980. Histological comparisons of white pine needles fumigated with ozone and sulfur dioxide singly and in mixtures. Proc. Pa. Acad. Sci. 54:128-130.
25. Wersma, G.B.K., W. Brown, and A.B. Crockett. 1978. Development of a pollutant monitoring system for Biosphere Reserves and results of the Great Smoky Mountain pilot study. pp. 451-455. *in 4th* Joint Conf. on Sensing of Environmental Pollutants. Am. Chem. Soc. 945 pp.
26. Schlesisnger, W.H., W.A. Reiners and P.S. Knupman. 1974. Heavy metal concentrations and deposition in bulk precipitation in montane ecosystems of New Hampshire, U.S.A. Environ. Pollut. 6:39:47.
27. Bratton, S.P. and P.S. White. 1980. Rare plant management—after preservation what? Rhodora 82:49-75.
28. Noyes, W. 1928. Wood and Forest. The Manual Arts Press. Peoria, Ill. 294 pp.
29. Hepting, G.H. 1971. Diseases of forest and shade trees of the United States. Agricultural Handbook No. 386. U.S. Dept. of Agriculture Forest Service. Wash. D.C. 658 pp.
30. Svetec, C. 1984. The evolution of a species: the American Chestnut example. Unpub. Honors Thesis. Susquehanna U. Selinsgrove, Pa. 24 pp.

31. Gerardi, M.H. and J.K. Grimm. 1979. The History, Biology, Damage, and Control of the Gypsy Moth (*Porthetria Dispar*) (L). Fairleigh Dickinson University Press. Rutherford, N.J. 233 pp.
32. Nichols, J.O. 1980. The Gypsy Moth. Dept. of Environmental Resources. Bureau of Forestry, Harrisburg, Pa. 34 pp.
33. Braun, E.L. 1950. Deciduous Forests of Eastern North America. Hafner Publ. Co., Inc. New York. 596 pp.
34. Smith, D.W. and N.E. Linnartz. 1980. The southern hardwood region. pp. 145-230. *in* Regional Silviculture of the United States. J.W. Barrett (Ed.). John Wiley and Sons. N.Y. 551 pp.
35. Steinhart, P. 1985. We can't grow when its gone. Natl. Wildlife 23:17-22.
36. Bratton, S.P. and P.S. White. 1980. Rare plant management—after preservation what? Rhodora 82:49-75.
37. Anon., 1982. Pennsylvania Native Plant Management Plan. Xerox. DER-Bureau of Forestry. Harrisburg. 3 pp.
38. Anon., 1985. Plants of Special Concern in Pennsylvania. Xerox. DER-Bureau of Forestry. Harrisburg. 13 pp.
39. Anon., 1985. Fact Sheet. Xerox. Wild Resource Conservation Fund. Harrisburg. 3 pp.
40. Sanders, R. 1978. A Partnership to Preserve Natural Diversity. The Nature Conservancy News 28:13-19.
41. Brussard, P.F. 1982. The Role of Field Stations in the Preservation of Biological Diversity. Bioscience 32:327-330.

Endangered and Threatened Species Programs in Pennsylvania and other States: Causes, Issues and Management. Edited by S. K. Majumdar, F. J. Brenner and A. F. Rhoads. © 1986, The Pennsylvania Academy of Science.

Chapter Seven

COMPUTER-GENERATED MAPPING OF RARE/ENDANGERED SPECIES

Jay F. Watson, Ph.D.

Habitat Resources
U.S. Fish and Wildlife Service
500 N.E. Multnomah Street
Portland, Oregon 97232

Resource mapping systems enhance the decision making capabilities of fish and wildlife biologists responsible for endangered species management. Maps and mapping systems available are of two types—manually drafted maps and computer-generated maps. Each process requires the same basic steps—data collection, data management, data analysis and displays. For any mapping system to be useful, it must be current, available, easily interpreted and cost-effective.

INTRODUCTION

Fish and wildlife management can be divided into 5 developmental stages. According to Leopold[1] these stages are: 1) restriction of hunting, 2) predator control, 3) reservation of game lands (as parks, forests, refuges, and other areas), 4) artificial replenishment (restocking and game farming) and 5) environmental controls (e.g. control of food, cover, special factors and disease).

Leopold's developmental stages also characterize the evolution of the application of the Endangered Species Act of 1973.[2] For example, (1) the Act restricts the taking of endangered and threatened species, (2) predators are controlled to prevent further destruction of breeding populations (e.g. fencing to protect least tern (*Sterna antillarum*) nests in southern California), (3) refuge areas provide protection for endangered species (e.g. salt marsh harvest mouse, San Francisco Bay National Wildlife Refuge, (4) the reestablishment of the whooping crane (*Grús americána*) at Bosque del Apache National Wildlife Refuge; and (5) protection of endangered species habitat (e.g. California condor (*Gymnogyps californianus*) habitat in southern California).

Traditionally, fish and wildlife managers have used a process that involves census, measurement of productivity, diagnosis, and control. First, abundance and productivity of the species are determined. Next diagnosis is made to determine if population numbers are controlled by hunting, predators, starvation and drought, diseases and parasites, mechanical accidents, and/or food, water, or coverts (geographical units of cover). Once diagnosis is completed, management decisions can be made.

Mapping is essential in all aspects of fish and wildlife management. In particular, maps are useful in defining species range, distribution of habitat and seasonal use patterns of fish and wildlife species. Maps and mapping systems available to fish and wildlife managers are of two types—manually drafted maps (e.g. U.S. Geological Survey quadrangle sheets) and computer-generated maps. Whether a map is manually drafted or computer-generated, the process of mapmaking involves the same basic steps—data collection, data management, data analysis and display.

MANUALLY DRAFTED MAPS (PACIFIC ECOLOGICAL INVENTORY)

A manually drafted mapping system useful for endangered species management is the Fish and Wildlife Service's Ecological Inventory Series (Pacific, Atlantic, and Gulf Coasts). The ecological inventories were compiled to (1) reduce conflicts between fish and wildlife resources and construction and energy-producing companies and agencies and (2) facilitate leasing processes for Outer Continental Shelf oil and gas leasing processes, oil spill contingency planning and other aspects of resource and coastal zone management.

The Pacific Coast Ecological Inventory,[3] was the first comprehensive series of natural resource maps of the west coast showing fish and wildlife and their habitats and major land use designations. The series consists of 30 maps at a scale of 1:250,000 extending from Mexico to Canada and including Puget Sound. The maps show important concentrations of 356 different important fish and wildlife species. The steps in development of this series are as follows.

DATA COLLECTION

Before data collection actually began, a collection strategy was developed that assisted in the compilation of information. The strategy consisted of several tiers of information cataloging. That is, the information was collected by state, zones, sections within the zones, coastal zone boundaries, groups of plants and animals, and by status (endangered, threatened, commercial, sport and/or biological/ecological significance). Within groups of plants and animals, further divisions were used to catalog information.

Once the classification system for the information had been determined, data collection was initiated. Although field trips were used to collect some of the data, existing information was used as much as possible to develop the ecological inventory.

DATA MANAGEMENT

Data management consisted of a manual listing of information by species, cataloging and reviewing, and a final field check of the information by site visits. The information was cataloged as species with special status (e.g. endangered or threatened), valuable resource, migratory routes, and seasonal habitats.

DATA ANALYSIS

Once the information was cataloged, it was reviewed to determine if it would be retained for mapping. Retention criteria included availability of reports, the proprietary nature of the information and reliability of the information. Some information rejected is retained by the states (e.g. bald eagle nest locations) and is not available for general use in resource publications. Finally, the source of the information had to be well documented and considered reliable by most users.

DISPLAY

The cartographic effort involved a series of coordinated tasks leading to the production of 30 color-coded maps showing the ecological resources of the Pacific coast. The tasks included negative engraving (scribing process), preparation of negative open windows (peel coat process), composition of type nomenclature, placement of type and photo laboratory processing.

COMPUTER-GENERATED MAPS

Computer mapping has been approached from two different directions—computer-assisted mapping (cartographic features and engineering modeling) and geographic information systems.[4]

COMPUTER-ASSISTED MAPPING (MAPIT)

Many of the tasks previously completed by cartographers can now be done by computer. These tasks include transforming data to common scales, registering overlays for common coordinate systems, and overlaying data. However, planimeters and other manual tools are required to analyze the mapped data. MAPIT is a map-composing system[5] supported by Control Data Corporation and used by the U.S. Fish and Wildlife Service. MAPIT makes maps from computations.

DATA COLLECTION

MAPIT uses x,y coordinate values which are obtained using traditional survey data gathering procedures.

DATA MANAGEMENT

Data management consists of entering the coordinate values for township range lines, county lines, section lines, fence lines, water, levees, monuments, and other features as contained in the survey field notes and other documents.

DATA ANALYSIS

Data analysis can consist of 100 overlay sheets which may be selectively displayed, 10 overlay sheets for map labeling, and 35 symbols that may be used for showing map features.

DISPLAY

Maps are produced at one of four scales or in a free-form with the size determined by the available plotting equipment and paper size. Any of the 100 overlay sheets can be selected for printing (e.g. surface water and fence lines). MAPIT has been used to produce maps for acquisition of endangered species habitat.

GEOGRAPHIC INFORMATION SYSTEMS (CNDDB)

The Federal Interagency Coordinating Committee on Digital Cartography[6] defines a Geographic Information System (GIS) as a system of computer programs used to acquire, store, manipulate, analyze, and display spatial data for use in decision making processes. That is,[4] a point location with a geographic information system (GIS) will describe the attributes of that location, what is located within a certain distance and "what is possible." GIS's make computations from maps as opposed to systems like MAPIT which make maps from computations.

Mead and Phelps[7] list 11 available geographic information systems: ARC/INFO, MOSS, INTERGRAPH, SYNERCOM, COMRAC, GEOBASED, AGIS/GRAM, BAUSCH & LOMB, ERDAS, IDIMS and INTERNATIONAL IMAGING SYSTEMS.

Geographic information systems can be further divided into two groups: systems with relational data base management and those systems without relational database management. A relational database management system (DBMS) makes it possible to create and manage georeferenced data.

It is important to note that although some systems may not contain a fully integrated DBMS, they can use DBMS's external to the GIS. For example, it is possible for a system to use an external DBMS such as ESIS (Endangered Species Information System, U.S. Fish and Wildlife Service). ESIS is a computerized system with 67 fields that is used to store, retrieve and disseminate endangered species information including detailed narratives and "keyword" fields.[8] This information can be manipulated on ESIS, used with a GIS and not have to reside in the GIS on a permanent basis. An example of this type of system is the California Natural Diversity Data Base (CNDDB) which uses the GIS INTERGRAPH.

The CNDDB is a statewide manual and computerized inventory of locational information on California's rare and endangered species and natural communities.[9] This system, patterned after similar programs in 34 states, was established by the state legislature in 1980. All of the programs were originally established by the Nature Conservancy, a national non-profit conservation organization.

DATA COLLECTION

CNDDB staff biologists obtain information from numerous sources including publications, literature, reports, museum specimens, herbaria, field surveys, maps and correspondence.

DATA MANAGEMENT

To date, 11,000 locations of species or communities (element occurrences) have been entered in the data base and are available for use. Since changes are inevitable, the inventory is updated on a continuous basis to keep the system current. Information concerning each element is organized into 33 fields.

DATA ANALYSIS

Species and communities (elements) are organized into three categories—special animals, special plants, and natural communities. An element occurrence is defined as the location record for a habitat or area which sustains or otherwise contributes to the survival of a population or self-sustaining example of the element.

The elements are further defined as: plants, animals with limited mobility, mobile animals, migratory animals, mobile aquatic animals and communities. Data analysis is by field (e.g. element name (scientific name), status, occurrence number, date site last observed, county, etc.).

DISPLAY

The information from this data base can be received as a computer text printout, computer-generated maps (transparent overlay or opaque paper) or printed on maps provided by the user at several scales including 1:24,000 and 1:62,500. In addition, information can be plotted manually on 8½ x 11 reduced U.S. Geological Survey topographic sheets.

MANAGEMENT DECISIONS

Excellent resource mapping enhances the decision making capabilities of resource managers responsible for endangered species. In order to be useful management tools, maps, whether generated by manual or computer systems, must be current, available, easily interpreted and cost-effective.

Maps must have direct application to current fish and wildlife management problems. They must be updated on a regular basis. Since maps are used for making decisions that in some cases involve millions of dollars (e.g. critical habitat determinations), it is extremely important that the information provided on the maps is current. Habitats and animal distributions change rapidly from year to year; resource maps need to reflect these changes.

Resurveying map area and reentering the data for both manual and computer systems is an expensive and time consuming process. In cases where the size of the study area is limited, the rate of change is minimal and the density of information (lines and/or symbols per square inch) on the map is low, it may be more appropriate to use manual mapping systems. For example, the manually drafted *Ecological Inventory Maps* completed in 1981 do not show any endangered species that have been listed since that date.

When study areas are large, change is frequent and density is high, computer systems offer an obvious advantage. For example, the CNDBB, which is continually updated, always contains current listings for endangered species.

It is important that maps are available to as many decision makers as possible—resource and construction agencies, developers and the public. They should be able to obtain maps quickly and for a reasonable price. Manually drafted maps distributed by the U.S. Geological Survey are probably the most easily obtained by a large group of users. GIS's with a formal distribution system like the CNDBB are the next most easily obtained maps. The specialized agency GIS's probably are the most difficult to obtain because the maps are very specific and may have to be printed at remote (to the user) computer centers.

Policymakers must be able to interpret maps easily. For maps to be appropriate for use by management biologists, water quality units should be expressed in ppm or mg/l, wetlands described using common terminology, organisms listed by common and scientific names, and maps scaled in standard units (e.g. 1:24,000). If a map is labeled using other systems, it probably will be rejected by many managers in favor of a map employing standard units.

For map systems to be useful in endangered species management, they must be cost effective. The annual costs for maintaining the different systems depend upon their frequency of updating. The Pacific Coast Ecological Inventory cost about $200,000 to complete in 1981. Individual maps are still available from the U.S. Geological Survey for $4.00 each. The MAPIT system costs approximately $75,000 per year to maintain and once the maps have been entered into the system cost approximately $50—$75 each to produce. The CNDDB has an annual operating budget of approximately $150,000—$200,000 per year and has a set fee schedule for map products (e.g. $30 for a computer-generated textual report and $6—$10 for each standard scale map overlay).

ACKNOWLEDGMENTS

I appreciate the assistance of D.G. Barton, C.A. Bohan, J. Compton, R.E. Ducret, W.A. Gill, S. Gude, D.J. Lenhart, D. Marshall, C. Soper, A. Newman, R. Swanson, A.F. Robinson, Jr., F. Stainer, M.A. Watson, W. White, and R. Wright.

REFERENCES CITED

1. Leopold, A. 1933. *Game Management*. Charles Scribner's Sons, New York, xii + 481 pp.

2. Smith, R.L. 1976. *Ecological Genesis of Endangered Species: The Philosophy of Preservation.* Ann. Rev. Ecol. Syst. 7:33-55.
3. Beccasio, A.D., J.S. Isakson, A.E. Redfield, et al. 1981. Pacific Coast Ecological Inventory: User's Guide and Information Base. Biological Services Program, U.S. Fish and Wildlife Service, FWS/OBS-81/30, vii + 159 pp.
4. Drinnan, C.H. 1985. Mapping Information Management Systems. DEC Professional. 4(6):17-28.
5. Ducret, R.E. 1984. MAPIT Manual, September 1, 1984, U.S. Fish and Wildlife Service, Portland, Oregon, 88 pp. (mimeo)
6. Federal Interagency Coordinating Committee on Digital Cartography. 1984. *Coordination of Digital Cartographic Activities in the Federal Government.* Washington, D.C. 72 pp. + app. (mimeo).
7. Mead, R.A., and W.R. Phelps. 1985. Strategy for Adopting and Implementing GIS Technology in Region 8. U.S. Forest Service, Atlanta, Georgia, 47 pp.
8. Gill, W.A. 1986. Personal Communication. Biologist. Endangered Species Program, U.S. Fish and Wildlife Service, Wasington, D.C.
9. California Department of Fish and Game. 1985. The California Natural Diversity Data Base. Sacramento, California var. pp.

Endangered and Threatened Species Programs in Pennsylvania and other States: Causes, Issues and Management. Edited by S. K. Majumdar, F. J. Brenner and A. F. Rhoads. © 1986, The Pennsylvania Academy of Science.

Chapter Eight

THE FEDERAL ENDANGERED SPECIES PROGRAM: HOW DO SPECIES GET LISTED AND THEN WHAT?

Judy Jacobs
U.S. Fish and Wildlife Service
1825 Virginia Street
Annapolis, Maryland 21401

1. THE ORIGINS OF ENDANGERED SPECIES LEGISLATION.

The early explorers and settlers in North America found a land teeming with wildlife and the air aswarm with birds! Who can blame the early trappers and settlers for helping themselves freely to this cornucopia of game? The supply seemed limitless. But as civilization pushed west, the effects of habitat alteration and over-hunting finally became noticeable.

The American bison (*Bison bison*) and the passenger pigeon (*Ectopistes migratorius*) are perhaps the classic symbols of mankinds' impressive ability to devastate wildlife. During the 19th century, the bison was reduced from an estimated 60 million to only a few hundred by the mid-1880's.[2] Fortunately, the bison's plight was recognized in time to save these magnificent beasts from extinction. This was not the case for the passenger pigeon. Once thought to number an incredible six billion, this bird was hunted to extinction during the 19th and early 20th centuries. The last passenger pigeon in the world—Martha—died in the Cincinnati Zoo on September 1, 1914.

Along with the demise of these and other species came the recognition that wildlife should be conserved. In 1900, Congress passed the Lacey Act, which authorized the Department of Agriculture to "regulate the introduction of American or foreign birds or animals" into new locations.[3] In 1903, President Theodore Roosevelt signed an executive order creating the Pelican Island Bird

Sanctuary in Florida, the start of the National Wildlife Refuge System. Since that time, other laws such as the Migratory Bird Treaty Act of 1918 and the Bald Eagle Act of 1940 have been passed to protect wildlife.[4]

The first legislation specifically for endangered species was the Endangered Species Preservation Act of 1966. This law required that an official list of endangered species be prepared and maintained. The 1966 Act also authorized the acquisition of endangered species habitat under the National Wildlife Refuge System. However, while this law authorized the Government to spend funds to manage listed species, it did not provide the authority to protect them off Refuge lands.

The Endangered Species Conservation Act of 1969 took a further step towards active protection of rare species. This law prohibited the importation, purchase or sale of any listed fish or wildlife species that had been taken illegally. However, it did not prohibit take *per se,* nor did it provide protection for the habitat of these species, or for rare plants or invertebrates.

2. OUR CURRENT LAW

The Endangered Species Act of 1973 as amended (referred to below simply as the Act) is far more comprehensive than previous legislation. It extends protection to plants and to all classes of animals, including invertebrates. It defines "species" to include subspecies of plants and animals and even populations of vertebrates. It recognizes "threatened" as well as "endangered" species, thus establishing Federal authority for protection before the danger of extinction becomes grave. The 1973 Act also authorizes Federal grant programs to the states for endangered species conservation, under the Section 6 Cooperative Agreement provisions, as discussed in Chapter 2 of this text. The authority for management of terrestrial, freshwater aquatic species, marine mammals (excluding whales, dolphins and seals) and sea turtles, when they are on land, is vested in the Secretary of the Interior, via the Fish and Wildlife Service; marine species are otherwise under the jurisdiction of the Secretary of Commerce, specifically, the National Marine Fisheries Service.

3. THE FISH AND WILDLIFE SERVICE'S ENDANGERED SPECIES PROGRAM

The Endangered Species Program of the Fish and Wildlife Service (hereafter referred to as the Service) is divided into three subprograms not including law enforcement. These are listing, consultation and recovery. Listing, the official addition of a species (including subspecies or population) to the List of Endangered and Threatened Wildlife and Plants, is a necessary first step towards protection. However, without the subsequent steps of consultation and recovery, this list would merely be a tabulation of man's progress in decimating the natural world around him. The purpose of the consultation process is to prevent Federal activities from pushing listed species further toward the brink of extinction. Recovery is the process through which we attempt to restore listed species to their former non-endangered status. Each of these subprograms is discussed below.

3.A. Listing

3.A.(1) Candidate Lists

The Fish and Wildlife Service maintains lists of vertebrates, invertebrates and plant species that are, or have been, under consideration for listings, referred to as candidate species. Updates of these lists are published periodically as notices of review in the Federal Register. The dates of the most recent publications of these lists are: Vertebrates—September 18, 1985; invertebrates—May 22, 1984; plants—September 27, 1985. Copies of these are available from the Office of Endangered Species, U.S. Fish and Wildlife Service, Interior Building, 18th and C Streets, NW, Washington, D.C. 20240. In publishing these notices, the Service is soliciting data on the status and distribution of any taxon in the notice, as well as information on any other organism that warrants inclusion as a candidate. Candidate species in the notice are divided into three categories. Category 1 species are those for which the Service has enough information to warrant listing and anticipates the publication of a rule proposing to list them as threatened or endangered. Category 2 species are those for which listing may be appropriate but existing status information currently is not sufficient to support listing. In other words, for Category 2 species, we need more information, to allow us to decide whether to elevate them to Category 1 or "demote" them to Category 3. Category 3 is reserved for those species that are no longer under consideration for listing, either because they have been found to be more abundant than previously believed (3C), they are no longer considered a good taxon (3B), or they have been become extinct (3A). Species in Categories 1 or 2 that are believed likely to be extinct are denoted in the Federal Register with an asterisk (*).

Candidate species extant or historically occurring in Pennsylvania are listed in Appendix II. At present, all are classified in Category 2. Information on the distribution and natural history of many of these species has been recently summarized.[5]

3.A.(2) Status Surveys
In order to gain new field data on distribution of Category 2 (or sometimes,

Category 1) species, the Service may let contracts for status surveys to biologists or organizations that have expertise in field work with specific taxonomic groups. Properly conducted status surveys will assess (or sample) the taxon's presence, viability and threats it faces at historical sites and other suitable habitat throughout its range. The status survey report should provide the Service with sufficient information to decide whether listing is warranted and, if so, whether the more appropriate status is endangered (= "in danger of extinction throughout all or a significant portion of its range")[6] or threatened (= "likely to become an endangered species in the foreseeable future"). According to the Act, this determination will be made solely on the basis of scientific and commercial (not economic) data.

3.A.(3) Obtaining Listed Status
i. The normal route

Once this determination has been made, the next step is to prepare a listing proposal for publication in the Federal Register. For U.S. species, this is usually accomplished at the field station or Regional Office level. The listing proposal summarizes the threats facing the species under the following categories:

(A) the present or threatened destruction or modification or curtailment of its habitat or range;
(B) over utilization for commercial, recreational, scientific or educational purposes;
(C) disease or predation
(D) the inadequacy of existing regulatory mechanisms; or
(E) other natural or manmade factors affecting its continued existence.

If critical habitat is proposed, an economic analysis must also be prepared. Subsequently, the proposal and associated documents are sent to the central Office of Endangered Species in Arlington, Virginia, for review and clearance by the solicitors. If the document passes inspection, it will be published as a proposed rule in the Federal Register. At the time of publication all potentially affected states, counties, Federal agencies and other interested parties are notified. Notices of this proposed action must also be published in newspapers of general circulation in the affected area. There follows a 60-day period during which written comments on the proposal are accepted. Also, from the date of publication, there is a 45-day period during which any interested party may request a public hearing concerning the listing.

Within one year of the date of publication, the proposal may be withdrawn or a final rule implementing the proposal should be published. Final rules must address all comments received during the comment period and summarize the content of any public hearings. Like proposals, final rules are again subjected to scrutiny within the Service prior to publication. Final rules generally become effective, thus imparting listed status to the species they address, 30 days after the date of publication.

ii. The petitioning process

The Endangered Species Act must be reauthorized by Congress every three years. This reauthorization process is usually accompanied by one or more amendments. The 1982 amendments included a clarification of the petitioning process. According to these amendments, any interested person may petition the Service to list a species. The petition must be accompanied by supporting biological data. Within 90 days after receipt of a petition, the Service must "publish a finding as to whether the petition presents substantial...information indicating that the petitioned action may be warranted".[7] If this is the case, the Service must initiate a status review of the petitioned species, and within one year publish a finding that the petitioned action is, or is not warranted. If the petition is found to be warranted, the listing proposal must be promptly published. Thus, the petitioning process provides an avenue for biologists or others with extensive knowledge of a species' biology to influence the listing process directly. However, with rare exceptions, it is equally effective to promote a needed listing through normal channels by communication with state non-game or heritage programs or with Service biologists.

iii. Emergency listing

The Act also provides for the extreme case in which a previously unprotected species is suddenly faced with imminent danger, "posing significant risk to (its) well-being".[8] Under such circumstances, the Service may publish an emergency regulation, effective immediately, providing listed status for the species of

TABLE 1

Annual number of U.S. Fish and Wildlife Service endangered species consultations, 1979 to present. (Source: Office of Endangered Species, Arlington, VA)

Fiscal Year	No. Informals	No. Formals	% Formal
1979	1585	968	37.9
1980	2374	707	22.9
1981	3535	504	12.5
1982	4334	338	7.2
1983	5249	283	5.1
1984	8165	301	3.5
1985 (first half)	3787	156	3.9

concern. Such an emergency rule is effective for 240 days, during which time a regulation must be published via the normal channels to make listed status permanent.

The listing process is dealt with in detail in Section 4 of the Endangered Species Act and associated regulations. The strict requirements of the law and regulations ensure that the official List of Endangered and Threatened Wildlife and Plants is maintained as a meaningful enumeration of true rarity and/or threat to the biotic elements of our environment. The remaining subprograms, consultation and recovery, provide a mechanism for saving these elements from obliteration and, ultimately, restoring their populations to safety from future extinction.

3.B. Consultation

The endangered species consultation process is addressed in Section 7 of the Act. This section requires all Federal agencies to ensure that any action they authorize, fund or carry out is not likely to jeopardize the continued existence of any endangered or threatened species.

Federal agencies control much of the development of our nation's resources. Millions of ha of public lands are leased for mineral exploration, logging and grazing. Federal agencies are also involved in building highways and dams and providing funds for the construction of housing, sanitation, energy, agriculture and other projects that permanently alter the environment. The requirement for Section 7 consultation reflects Congress' recognition that the major threat to most species results from destruction of their habitat through land and resource development.

Our current consultation process is an outgrowth of the 1978 amendments to the Act. Generally the process begins with informal consultation. The Federal agency or their designated representative (hereafter referred to as the action agency) requests from the Service a list of endangered, threatened or proposed species occurring or potentially occurring in the project area. If any listed species are known or believed to be present, the Service so informs the action agency and may work with them informally to avoid potential adverse impacts to these species. The action agency must then make a determination of effect of the project on listed species. For major Federal projects, the action agency must conduct a biological assessment, which can be incorporated into the NEPA process. The biological assessment reviews relevant literature and evaluates all project-related impacts to listed and proposed species. If necessary information is lacking, the agency may conduct surveys or further studies to determine these impacts. The biological assessment, which is normally completed within 180 days, concludes either that the action may affect, or will not affect the listed species of concern.

In the case of a "may-affect" determination, the Federal agency must submit to the Service a written request for formal consultation. During the formal consultation period, a Service biologist works further with agency representatives in exploring less harmful, or beneficial, project alternatives. Formal consultation is normally completed within 90 days and results in the Service's issuance of a biological opinion. This document concludes either that the action is, or is not likely to jeopardize the continued existence of the species addressed in the consultation. In the case of a "jeopardy" opinion, the Service must identify any "reasonable and prudent alternatives" that would avoid the jeopardy situation.

Over the years since 1978, the number of consultations per year has increased steadily, (Table 1), as endangered species staff has increased and other Federal agencies have incorporated endangered species considerations into their routine project procedures. However, note also from Table 1 that the percent of formal consultations has decreased, indicating that potential endangered species conflicts are being resolved through careful project planning, before the "may-affect" stage is reached.

3.C. Recovery

The goal of the endangered species program is to restore listed species to the point where they no longer require the protection of the Act. To achieve this goal, the Service develops recovery plans for U.S. species. The recovery plan outlines the tasks necessary for recovery and describes these tasks, including the responsible agency or agencies and the estimated costs. Recovery plans may be prepared by a Service biologist, by a State or private individual or institution on a contract basis, or by a recovery team appointed by the Service. Draft recovery plans are subjected to in-house and external review before they are approved and signed by the Director. Approved plans are reviewed annually and updated, if necessary. Recovery plans specify such techniques as periodic monitoring, studies of ecological requirements and aspects of life history, habitat acquisition, habitat manipulation and captive propagation, among others. Because of limited funding and the growing number of listed species, tasks are prioritized, so that the most critical species needs will be addressed first. Oftentimes, states with Section 6 cooperative agreements take the lead in carrying out recovery activities (see chapter 2 of this text).

As of September 1985, 215 of the 318 Endangered and Threatened Species in the U.S. have approved recovery plans. All of the currently listed endangered and threatened species in Pennsylvania (see Appendix I) have approved recovery plans. The goal of recovering listed species to safe levels requires cooperative efforts among State and local governments, private conservation groups and Federal agencies.

In summary, the three-part process of listing, consultation and recovery has proven an effective means of identifying species in danger of extinction and trying to reverse current downward trends in order to preserve and promote the natural diversity of life forms on this planet.

REFERENCES

1. Bruemmer, F. 1985. Where Father Charlevois found paradise. International Wildlife 15(3): 19-23.
2. Reynolds, H.W., R.D. Glaholdt and A.W.L. Hawley. 1982. Bison. pp. 972-1007 *In* J.A. Chapan and G.A. Feldhamer, eds. Wild Mammals of North America. Baltimore: Johns Hopkins Press, 1147 pp.
3. U.S. Fish and Wildlife Service. 1980. Selected list of Federal laws and treaties relating to sport fish and wildlife. U.S. Government Printing Office: Stock Number 024-010-00585-1, 22 pp.
4. U.S. Fish and Wildlife Service. 1981. Endangered Means There's Still Time. D.O.I. Publications. 32 pp. [This pamphlet is the source of much of the background information in this paper].
5. Genoways, H.H. and F.J. Brenner, 1985. Species of Special Concern in Pennsylvania. Carnegie Museum of Natural History Special Publication No. 11, Pittsburgh, 430 pp.
6. Definition (Section 3) in The Endangered Species Act as amended by Public Law 97-304 (The Endangered Species Act of 1982). 98th Congress, 1st Session. U.S. Government Printing Office. 53 pp.
7. Ibid, Section 4 (b)(3)(A). [Section 4 of the Act deals with the process of adding species to the List of Endangered and Threatened Wildlife and Plants].
8. Ibid, Section 4 (B)(7).

APPENDIX I
Federally Listed Endangered and Threatened Species in Pennsylvania

Common Name	Scientific Name	Status	Distribution
FISHES:			
Sturgeon, shortnose*	*Acipenser brevirostrum*	E	Delaware River and other Atlantic coastal rivers
BIRDS:			
Eagle, bald	*Haliaeetus leucocephalus*	E	Entire State
Falcon, American peregrine	*Falco peregrinus anatum*	E	Entire state—re-establishment to former breeding range in progress
Falcon, Arctic peregrine	*Falco peregrinus tundrius*	E	Entire state migratory—no nesting
Warbler, Kirtland's	*Dendroica kirtlandii*	E	Entire state—occasional migrant
MAMMALS:			
Bat, Indiana	*Myotis sodalis*	E	Entire state
Cougar, eastern	*Felis concolor couguar*	E	Entire state—probably extinct
MOLLUSKS:			
Mussel, pink mucket pearly	*Lampsilis orbiculata*	E	Historical records from Allegheny and Monongahela Rivers; probably extinct
Mussel, orange-footed pearly	*Plethobasus cooperianus*	E	(same as above)
PLANTS:			
Small-whorled pogonia	*Isotria medeoloides*	E	Most historical records in eastern half of state; extant population in Centre Co.

*Principal responsibility for this species is vested with the National Marine Fisheries Service.

APPENDIX II
Candidate Species in Pennsylvania

Plants

Common Name	Scientific Name	Family
sensitive joint vetch	(*Aeschynomene virginica*)	Fabaceae
serpentine aster	(*Aster depauperatus*)	Asteraceae
Barratt's sedge	(*Carex barrattii*)	Cyperaceae
long-hairy field chickweed[1]	(*Cerastium arvense var. villosissimum*)	Caryophyllaceae
Hill's thistle	(*Cirsium hillii*)	Asteraceae
Parker's pipewort	(*Eriocaulon parkeri*)	Eriocaulaceae
Darlington's spurge	(*Euphorbia purpurea*)	Euphorbiaceae
large-flowered Barbara's buttons	(*Marshallia grandiflora*)	Asteraceae
Canby's mountain-lover	(*Paxistima canbyi*)	Celastraceae
White-fringed prairie orchid	(*Platanthera leucophaea*)	Orchidaceae
(blue grass)	(*Poa paludigena*)	Poaceae
Van Brunt's jacob's ladder	(*Polemonium vanbruntiae*)	Polemoniaceae
Northeastern bulrush	(*Scirpus ancistrochaetus*)	Cyperaceae
Virginia spiraea	(*Spiraea virginiana*)	Rosaceae
Mountain pimpernel	(*Taenidia montana*)	Apiaceae
Steele's Meadow-rue	(*Thalictrum steeleanum*)	Ranunculaceae
Kate's Mountain clover	(*Trifolium virginicum*)	Fabaceae

Vertebrates

Common Name	Scientific Name	Family
Lake Sturgeon	(*Acipenser fulvescens*)	Acipenseridae
blue sucker	(*Cycleptus elongatus*)	Catastomidae
eastern sand darter	(*Ammocrypta pellucida*)	Percidae
longhead darter	(*Percina macrocephala*)	Percidae
hellbender	(*Cryptobranchus alleganiensis*)	Cryptobranchidae
green salamander	(*Aneides aeneus*)	Plethodontidae
bog turtle	(*Clemmys muhlenbergi*)	Emydidae
Kirtland's snake	(*Conophus kirtlandi*)	Colubridae
shortheaded garter snake	(*Thamnophis brachystoma*)	Colubridae
eastern massasauga	(*Sistrurus catenatus catenatus*)	Viperidae
Appalachian Bewick's wren	(*Thryomanes bewickii altus*)	Troglotydidae
migrant loggerhead shrike	(*Lanius ludovicianus migrans*)	Laniidae
Bachman's sparrow	(*Aimophila aestivalis*)	Emberizidae
southern water shrew	(*Sorex palustris punctulatus*)	Soricidae
long-tailed shrew	(*Sorex dispar*)	Soricidae
northeastern pygmy shrew	(*Microsorex hoyi thompsoni*)	Soricidae
eastern small-footed bat	(*Myotis subulatus leibil*)	Vespertilionidae
New England cottontail	(*Sylvilagus transitionalis*)	Leporidae
eastern woodrat	(*Neotoma floridana magister*)	Muridae
Pymatuning redbacked vole	(*Clethrionomys gapperi paludicola*)	Muridae
Kittatiny redbacked vole[1]	(*Clethrionomys gapperi rupicola*)	Muridae

APPENDIX II (continued)

Candidate Species in Pennsylvania

Plants

Common Name	Scientific Name	Family
Invertebrates		
Pennsylvania sponge[1]	(*Heteromeyenia longistylis*)	Spongillidae
Refton cave planarian[1]	(*Sphallopana pricei*)	Planariidae
Pennsylvania cave amphipod	(*Crangonyx dearolfi*)	Crangonyctidae
Pizzini's amphipod	(*Stygobromus pizzinii*)	Crongonyctidae
Stellmack's cave amphipod[1]	(*Stygobromus stellmacki*)	Crangonyctidae
Midget snaketail dragonfly	(*Ophiogomphus howei*)	Gomphidae
Six-banded longhorn beetle	(*Dryobius sexnotatus*)	Cerambycidae
Northeastern beach tiger beetle[2]	(*Cicindela dorsalis dorsalis*)	Cicindelidae
Cobblestone tiger beetle	(*Cicindela marginipennis*)	Cicindelidae
American burying beetle[2]	(*Nicrophorus americanus*)	Silphidae
black lordithon rove beetle[2]	(*Lordithon niger*)	Staphylinidae
Chestnut case-bearer moth[1,2]	(*Coleophora leucochrysella*)	Coleophoridae
Karner blue butterfly[2]	(*Lycaeides melissa samuelis*)	Lycaenidae
Albarufan dagger moth[2]	(*Acronicta albarufa*)	Noctuidae
Marbled underwing moth[2]	(*Catocala marmorata*)	Noctuidae
Tawny crescent butterfly[2]	(*Phyciodes batesi*)	Nymphalidae
Regal fritillary butterfly	(*Speyeria idalia*)	Nymphalidae
Chestnut clearwing moth[2]	(*Synanthedon castaneae*)	Sesiidae
Vannote's cheumatopsyche caddisfly[1]	(*Cheumatopsyche vannotei*)	Hydropsychidae
Dwarf wedge mussel	(*Alasmidonta heterodon*)	Unionidae

[1]Endemic to Pennsylvania
[2]Believed extirpated in Pennsylvania

Endangered and Threatened Species Programs in Pennsylvania and other States: Causes, Issues and Management. Edited by S. K. Majumdar, F. J. Brenner and A. F. Rhoads. © 1986, The Pennsylvania Academy of Science.

Chapter Nine

ENDANGERED PLANTS IN PENNSYLVANIA: PRESENT STATUS AND FUTURE PROTECTION

PAUL G. WIEGMAN
Western Pennsylvania Conservancy
316 Fourth Ave.
Pittsburgh, PA 15222

The United States has a rich and diverse flora of approximately 20,000 species. At the present time, approximately 3,000 of these are threatened, endangered or are in danger of becoming extinct.[1] This loss of native plants is a culmination of extensive modification of the natural landscape due to the development of an expanding society. The result is the loss of individual plants and plant habitats in general. Within the last decade a nationwide effort has been started to deal with the problem of loss of species, and to stem the tide of extinction. At the same time as the Federal initiative, Pennsylvania and other states have launched statewide efforts to protect native floras.

THE ENDANGERED SPECIES ACT OF 1973

To provide a nationwide mechanism for preventing the further loss of both plants and animals, the United States Congress passed the Endangered Species Act of 1973.[2] In accordance with the Act, the Smithsonian Institution was directed to prepare a list of threatened and endangered plant species of the United States. The initial report was transmitted to the House of Representatives on January 9, 1975. Species on the Smithsonian list were accepted by the U.S. Fish and Wildlife Service (USF&WS) and published in the Federal Register.[3]

The Smithsonian document included a list of more than 3,000 native taxa thought to be extinct, threatened, or endangered. In July 1975, USF&WS published a notice which announced that the Smithsonian list had been accepted as a petition under the terms of the Endangered Species Act. Because of a two-year limit provision for proposed rules in the Endangered Species Act amendments of 1978, the 1975 proposed list was mandatorily withdrawn in November 1979.[4] Withdrawal of the Smithsonian list was not due to biotic or conservation status of the plants listed, but due to the expiration of the deadline for rule-making concerning the plants on the list.

In the December 1980 Federal Register, the USF&WS republished all plant taxa that were included in previous notices, as well as other species on which information had become available.[5] In addition, the individual species were categorized to reflect accurately the USF&WS's evaluation of their status and establish priorities for final listing of the species.

The legal route for a plant to become a Federally Endangered or Threatened species begins with the species being recognized as a *candidate*. Then, information is gathered to support the appropriateness of assigning full legal status. Once sufficient information is obtained, the species is *proposed* for a final status and sent through the legislative process. If approved by the Congress, the species is *listed* as either *endangered* or *threatened*. Protection under that status is defined by the Endangered Species Act of 1973.[2]

Candidate categories (C1, C2, C3) recognize three levels of information concerning both the status and life histories of the species, the present taxonomic understanding as represented in published revisions and monographs, and the appropriateness of listing as endangered or threatened.[5] Environmental Impact Statements, the C1 and C2 candidate species, are treated the same as listed species.

Since the publication of the December 15, 1980 list, USF&WS has revised the candidate species list on November 28, 1983.[6] This is the most recent candidate list and is a considerable refinement from the original Smithsonian list of 1975. Presently there are still 2700 species awaiting sufficient information to propose them for listing.

After nine years of deliberation, only approximately 300, or 10% of the original 3,000 species have been listed or deleted. This painfully slow process attests to the lack of easily available information concerning rare plant species and the relative difficulty in getting species from the original list to official legislative status. Only 25 plants are currently proposed.[7] Fifty-seven species, with their range wholly within the U.S., have been listed as endangered or threatened. In comparison, 143 animals, including mammals, birds, herps, fishes, snails, clams, crustaceans and insects, have been listed.

At the federal level, plant listing is slow in coming. The problem is also compounded in that listing ultimately provides only a partial degree of protection for species so designated. This lack of complete protection is due to the difference in legal status between plants and animals. Under law, animals are the property of the Federal Government. This is reflected in various federal laws protecting migratory birds, as well as other animals. Most of the responsibility for wildlife is transferred to individual states and administered through fish and game agencies. On the other hand, plants are the property of individual landowners on whose land the plant grows. Plants are therefore beyond the legislative power of the Federal or State Governments.

Arguments have been made that in the case of rare or endangered species, the genetic materials of those unique species should not be considered the sole property of the landowner on whose land the plant is growing, but instead the property of the society in general and should be available for the benefit of society. It is further pointed out that the plants should be governed by laws similar to those regulating the taking or using of animals.[8]

Although a plant is listed on the Federal list of endangered or threatened species, the protection of that plant extends only to activities which are licensed or funded by the Federal Government. The most publicized case where the Endangered Species Act has resulted in actions to protect a listed plant is the case of the furbish lousewort (*Pedicularis furbishae* S. Wats.) on the St. John's River in Maine. Here a federally funded and licensed impoundment project would have inundated the only known populations of *P. furbishae* along the St. John's River.

Application of the Endangered Species Act provisions halted the project and stimulated research into the possibility of establishment of the species in other areas, the protection of those new locations, the life history of the plant, and search for additional populations of the plant. If *P. furbishae* had been on private property, and no federal funds were used for the project or a federal license was not necessary, the population could have been eliminated without any violation of established law. In short, private actions which might jeopardize a given occurrence of a Federally listed plant cannot be halted under the 1973 Endangered Species Act. Similarly, state initiated legislation carries no greater restrictions.

Only one species of the 57 now on the Federal list occurs in Pennsylvania, *Isotria medeoloides* (Pursh) Raf., Lesser Whorled Pogonia. Of the 14 collection localities reported in Pennsylvania over the last 100 years, a single population discovered in 1973 is extant near Port Matilda, Centre County. A new locality, with a population of three plants, was discovered in Venango County in 1983. Since the listing of this plant, concerted efforts have been made to understand habitat requirements, distribution, and occurrence of this poorly understood plant throughout its range. The result has been that in 1982 there were 495 known plants from 11 populations; in 1983 there were 1,556 individual plants known in 31 populations. Ten of these sites were newly discovered populations.[9]

ENDANGERED PLANT LIST IN PENNSYLVANIA

In Pennsylvania rare plant protection is a recent responsibility of the State Government. A portion of the present interest in plant protection stems from the Endangered Species Act of 1973. In 1978 the USF&WS sought to have each state prepare a list of rare and endangered vascular plants for use by the Service to better evaluate the 1975 Smithsonian list. The object was to make additions or deletions to the 1975 list, and to suggest species which should be given immediate attention as proposed species. In Pennsylvania there was no state agency which was legislatively mandated to oversee the protection of native plants and the USF&WS turned to a private conservation organization for the development of such a list. The Western Pennsylvania Conservancy was asked to review 17 candidate species from the Smithsonian list indicating which species should remain on the list and ultimately be proposed as endangered or threatened species, and which should be considered for deletion. A fourth aspect of the survey was to address species uncommon to Pennsylvania and prepare a list of endangered or threatened species for the state.

The first draft of the Pennsylvania rare plant list was compiled from original reports prepared by Keener and Wherry,[10] Buker,[11] and Henry and Buker,[12] as well as records from the Morris Arboretum, Carnegie Museum of Natural History Herbarium, Academy of Natural Sciences, and other references pertaining to the flora of Pennsylvania.

The original draft list focussed on plants occurring in four or less counties in Pennsylvania. Species of the genera *Rubus* and *Cratagus* were not included due to the complexity and taxonomic problems of the taxa.

From the first draft list, a second draft was prepared which included only those species generally occurring in two or less counties. Consideration was given in this process of deletion to species with limited ranges, the area and size of the counties of occurrence, and the extent of development and alteration within those counties. For example, species occurring in the counties of Philadelphia, Bucks, and Delaware might be retained on the list because of extensive development and small size of those counties combined. On the other hand, a species occurring in Tioga, Potter, and Clinton Counties, and with several localities in each, might be deleted. After further review, the list was completed in 1979 and published by the USF&WS.[13]

In 1982 the Wild Resources Conservation Act[14] was signed into law in Pennsylvania. The Act directed the Department of Environmental Protection (DER) to develop an official state rare plant list and authorized the promulgation of regulations to protect listed species. In May 1985 a list of 406 plants was submitted;[15] final approval is expected by early 1986. This list represents the input of botanists throughout the state who have met annually to review plant status reports on the basis new information and recent field studies. Of the 406 species listed, 62 are listed as extirpated, 25 as endangered, 44 as threatened, 2 as vulnerable, 158 as rare and 115 as tentatively undetermined. (see appendix A and B category definitions and full listings.)

In accord with the Act DER has also submitted regulations designed to protect plants listed as endangered or threatened in the state. Final approval of these regulations is also expected in early 1986.

PENNSYLVANIA NATURAL DIVERSITY INVENTORY

Another component of the Wild Resources Conservation Act was the establishment of a fund, based on a voluntary state income tax check-off, to support studies of rare species. A major emphasis of the fund, now entering its third year, has been support of the Pennsylvania Natural Diversity Inventory (PNDI) is a computer indexed database containing locational and baseline ecological information about Pennsylvania's *rare native plants, unique plant communities, special concern animals,* and *significant geologic features.* The system, covering all counties in Pennsylvania, contains accurate locational, and pertinent ecological information gathered from publications, museums, universities, colleges, and recent field work by professionals throughout Pennsylvania. The completed data base is expected to contain several thousand records of Pennsylvania's ecologic and geologic diversities. By combining a computer's capabilities and the specific information and accuracy of USGS 7.5' topographic maps, a search of the PNDI database can quickly and precisely show whether a plot of land, watershed, municipality, county, or physiographic region in Pennsylvania contains any significant biologic resource or geologic feature.

PNDI data has been gathered from acknowledged sources. The system combines the accumulated rare and endangered plant and animal field survey experiences of Pennsylvania's finest museums, universities and state institutions into a single database. The information represents actual occurrences of the biologic components of special concern, not generalized distributions or ranges described in secondary sources.

In 1981, PNDI began as an effort of the Western Pennsylvania Conservancy (WPC) to assemble a database covering the 31 counties in the western half of the state. This project was based upon the methodology developed by the Nature Conservancy, with significant modifications to make the system more finely tuned to specific localities, to better fit existing DER regulatory methods, and to pack more information into the computer record. The Pennsylvania Department of Environmental Resources, Bureau of State Forests and Bureau of Environmental Planning assisted by convening an advisory group of botanists, ecologists, zoologists and planners to help in the development of the plant and plant community classification schemes used in PNDI. In 1982 The Eastern Pennsylvania Chapter of The Nature Conservancy (TNC) joined the effort. At present, WPC is collecting and entering data from the western counties. TNC is doing the same for the remaining 36 eastern counties from approximately Franklin and Tioga Counties east.

ENDANGERED PLANTS IN PENNSYLVANIA

There are many reasons for the decline of species within Pennsylvania. The most obvious is the modification and destruction of habitat through extensive utilization of natural resources and expansion of human development. Countryman estimated that perhaps 90 percent of all endangered species have resulted from habitat loss.[16] The ubiquitous sprawl of road building, housing, extractive mineral recovery, land reclamation, and other modern activities contribute to the loss of plants and plant habitat. Most of the losses are inadvertant in that they are by-products of landscape alteration. Even governmental agencies responsible for the wise use of natural resources may alter critical habitats simply through ignorance of the presence of special populations. With the adaption of a state rare plant list and PNDI, we have the ability to screen activities which may affect plant populations. If applied early in the planning process, before permits are issued, the result should be a diminishment of inadvertant habitat loss. The value of timely and early intervention has been proven over the past decade with the use of Environmental Impact Statements for large and potentially destructive projects, habitat loss has been abated. Unfortunately, projects for which Federal Impact Statement are not required, and individual actions on private lands continue. The application of PNDI information through state regulatory and permitting agencies will help to stem losses at the local level.

Commercial exploitation of plants is another reason for the major decline of several selected species or families. Cacti in the southwestern states are being gathered by collectors and wholesalers who sell them to dealers and collectors in other parts of the country. Commercial trade in native plants is an expanding business as demonstrated by the variety of local and regional nurseries which advertise native orchids and other showy species. Sale of insectivorous plants from the southeastern coastal plain bogs at the local supermarkets is a prime example of wild plant extraction. Trade in wildflowers is an increasing problem and will continue as long as collectors are interested in the rare and unusual, and states allow sale or transportation without regulation.

Other problems are neither obvious or well-documented. These include excessive competition for introduced and naturalized species, diseases and insects pests introduced from other regions, loss or displacement of pollinators, acid precipitation, changes in groundwater chemistry and amount, increased stream turbidity, and changes in regional climatic cycles. Endangered plants are among our poorest known natural resources, and yet they may hold some of our most valuable genetic resources in their ability to adapt and survive in adverse environmental conditions.

Loss of specialized habitats accounts for a significant number of the entries on the Pennsylvania list. The number of state endangered species is 25 plants. Of these, 2 are endemic or at least restricted to specialized habitats:

Intertidal Freshwater Marsh - Philadelphia and Bucks Counties	*Bidens bidentoides* (Nutt.) Britt. *Sagittaria calycina* Engelm. var. *spongiosa* Engelm.
Eastern Serpentine Barrens - Delaware, Chester and Lancaster Counties	*Aster depauperatus* (Porter) Fern. *Cerastium arvense* (L.) var. *villosissimum* Pennell *Sporobolus heterolepis* (Gray) Gray *Talinum teretifolium* Pursh.
Appalachian Shale Barren - Bedford, Fulton and Huntingdon Counties	*Senecio antennariifolius* Britt. *Trifolium virginicum* Small *Taenidia montana* (Mackenzie) Cronq.
Bog/Fen Wetlands - Throughout NW & NE Pennsylvania	*Arethusa bulbosa* L. *Trollius laxus* Salisb. *Listera smallii* Wieg.

Although the problems of identification of rare and endangered plants and the loss of natural diversity in the state of Pennsylvania went unattended for many years, the present situation is brighter. The extent of the problem is more clearly addressed and mechanisms are now being developed or are in place to assist in the preservation of native flora. The essential ingredient of public acceptance and involvement is now the final step toward a viable program. Protection of plants is an effort that must combine the resources of both the state and the private individual or organization. The state provides the legal backing for the protection of private entities, the individual plants and populations.

REFERENCES

1. Federal Register, (Washington, D.C., Vol. XLV, No. 202, 15 December 1980).
2. *The Endangered Species Act.* (Washington, D.C.: U.S. Code, Vol. XVI, 1973) sec. 1531-1543.
3. Federal Register, (Washington, D.C. Vol. XL, No. 127, 1 July 1975).
4. *Endangered Species Act Amendments,* (Public Law 95-632, 1978).
5. Federal Register, (Washington, D.C., Vol. XLV, No. 202, 15 December 1980).
6. Federal Register, (Washington, D.C., Vol. XLVIII, No. 29, 28 November 1983).
7. *Endangered Species Technical Bulletin.* (Vol. IX, No. 2, February 1984) pp. 8.
8. Norman Myers, *The Sinking Ark* (New York: pergamon Press, 1979).

9. Leslie J. Mehrhoff, (Letter to P.G. Wiegman, Western Pennsylvania Conservancy, Pittsburgh, Pa., March 23, 1984).
10. E.T. Wherry and C.S. Keener, *A Preliminary List of Rare Species of Vascular Plants Native to Pennsylvania*. (University Park, Pa.: Pennsylvania State University, Unpublished Report, 1977).
11. W.E. Buker, *Rare Western Pennsylvania Plants* (Pittsburgh, Pa.: Carnegie Museum of Natural History, Unpublished List, 1975).
12. L.K. Henry and W.E. Buker. "Rare or Otherwise Noteworthy Plants of Western Pennsylvania," *Trillia*, 12 (1964-63).
13. Weigman, Paul G., Rare and Endangered Vascular Plant Species in Pennsylvania. U.S. Fish and Wildlife Service, November 1979.
14. Wild Resource Conservation Act, *Title 32-Purdon's Pennsylvania Statutes Annotated* (1982). sec. 32.
15. Department of Environmental Resources Environmental Quality Board, Conservation of Pennsylvania Native Wild Plants. Pennsylvania Bulletin, Vol. 15, No. 18, Saturday May 4, 1985. pp. 1659-1674.
16. William D. Countryman, "The Northeastern United States," in *Extinction is Forever*, ed. by G.T. Prance and T.S. Elias (New York: The New York Botanical Garden, 1977) p. 33.

APPENDIX A

PENNSYLVANIA CLASSIFIED PLANT CATEGORY DEFINITIONS

PENNSYLVANIA EXTIRPATED—A classification of plant species believed by the Department to be extinct within Pennsylvania. These plants may or may not be in existence outside Pennsylvania. If plant species classified as "Pennsylvania Extirpated" are found to exist, the species automatically will be considered to be classified as "Pennsylvania Endangered."

PENNSYLVANIA ENDANGERED—A classification of plant species which are in danger of extinction throughout most or all of their natural range within Pennsylvania, if critical habitat is not maintained or if the species is greatly exploited by man. This classification shall also include any populations of plant species that have been classified as "Pennsylvania Extirpated," but which subsequently are found to exist in Pennsylvania.

PENNSYLVANIA THREATENED—A classification of plant species which may become endangered throughout most or all of their natural range within Pennsylvania, if critical habitat is not maintained to prevent their further decline in Pennsylvania, or if the species is greatly exploited by man.

PENNSYLVANIA RARE—A classification of plant species which are uncommon within Pennsylvania. All species of native wild plants classified as "Disjunct", "Endemic", "Limit of Range" and "Restricted" are included within the "Pennsylvania Rare" classification.

"Disjunct" — A sub-classification of plant species, which is composed of plant species that are significantly separated from their main area of distribution. The "Disjunct" sub-classification is contained within the larger classification of "Pennsylvania Rare".

"Endemic" — A sub-classification of plant species, which is composed of plant species that have limited ranges and that are confined to a specialized habitat. The sub-classification of "Endemic" is contained within the larger classification of "Pennsylvania Rare".

"Limit of Range" — a sub-classification of plant species, which is composed of plant species that are uncommon in Pennsylvania because they are at or near the periphery of their natural distribution. Within the main body of their distribution, these species may or may not be common. The sub-classification of "Limit of Range" is contained within the larger classification of "Pennsylvania Rare".

"Restricted" — A sub-classification of plant species, which is composed of species that are found in specialized habitats or in habitats infrequent within Pennsylvania, although the species may be common outside of the state. The sub-classification of "Restricted" is contained within the larger classification of "Pennsylvania Rare".

PENNSYLVANIA VULNERABLE—A classification of plant species which are in danger of population decline within Pennsylvania because of their beauty, economic value, use as a cultivar, or other factors which indicate that persons may seek to remove these species from their native habitats.

SPECIAL CONCERN POPULATION—A classification that is composed of colonies, groups, or single individuals of a plant species that the Department has determined to be a unique occurrence deserving protection. Among the factors that may be used to classify a plant population within this category are the existence of unusual geographic locations, unisexual populations, or extraordinarily diverse plant populations.

TENTATIVELY UNDETERMINED—A classification of plant species which are believed to be in danger of population decline, but which cannot presently be included within another classification due to taxonomic uncertainties, limited evidence within historical records, or insufficient data.

UNLISTED—Plant species which are native to Pennsylvania, which are presently capable of sustaining their populations successfully, which are not in need or protection currently, and which currently are not included in classifications under this chapter.

APPENDIX B
Pennsylvania Classified Plants*
(*From Pennsylvania Bulletin, Vol. 15, No. 16, Saturday, May 4, 1985.)

Pennsylvania Extirpated

Scientific name	Common name
Aeschynomene virginica (L.) BSP	Sensitive Joint-Vetch
Asclepias rubra L.	Red Milkweed
Berberis canadensis P. Mill	American Barberry
Carex adusta Boott	Crowded Sedge
Carex chordorrhiza Ehrh. ex L.f.	Creeping Sedge
Carex hyalinolepis Steud.	Shore-Line Sedge
Carex mitchelliana M.A. Curtis	Mitchell's Sedge
Carex nigra (L.) Reich.	Black Sedge
Carex sartwellii Dewey	Sartwell's Sedge
Chamaecyparis thyodies (L.) BSP	Atlantic White Cedar
Coreopsis rosea Nutt.	Pink Tickseed
Crassula aquatica (L.) Schoenl.	Water Pigmy-Weed
Crotonopsis elliptica Willd.	Elliptical Rushfoil
Cyperus polystachyos Rottb.	Many-Spiked Flatsedge
Cypripedium candidum Muhl. ex Willd.	Small White Lady's-Slipper
Dichanthelium acuminatum var. *densiflorum* (Rand. & Redf.) Gould & Clark	Acuminate Dichanthelium
Distichilis spicata (L.) Greene	Sea-Shore Salt-Grass
Elatine americana (Prush) Arn.	Long-Stemmed Water-Wort
Eleocharis tricostata Torr.	Three-Ribbed Spike-Rush
Eleocharis tuberculosa (Michx.) R. & S.	Long-Tubercled Spike-Rush
Elodea schweinitzii (Planch.) Caspary	Schweinitz's Waterweed
Eriocaulon parkeri B. L. Robins.	Parker's Pipewort
Eryngium aquaticum L.	Marsh Eryngo
Eupatorium leucolepis (DC.) Torr & Gray	White-Bracted Thoroughwort
Helianthus angustifolius L.	Swamp Sunflower
Hypericum denticulatum Walt.	Coppery St. John's-Wort
Hypericum stans (Michx.) P. Adams & Robson	St. Peter's-Wort
Ilex glabra (L.) Gray	Ink-Berry
Juncus greenei Oakes & Tuckerm.	Greene's Rush
Lespedeza stuevei Nutt.	Tall Bush Clover
Limosella australis R. Br.	Awl-Shaped Mudwort
Lithospermum caroliniense (Walt. ex J.F. Gmel.) MacM.	Hispid Gromwell
Ludwigia sphaerocarpa Ell.	Spherical-Fruited Seedbox
Lycopodium sabinifolium Willd.	Fir Clubmoss
Lycopodium selago L.	Mountain Clubmoss
Micranthemum micranthemoides (Nutt.) Wettst.	Nuttall's Mud-Flower
Mitella nuda L.	Nakes Bishop's-Cap
Muhlenbergia capillaris (Lam.) Trin.	Short Muhly
Platanthera cristata (Michx.) Lindl.	Crested Yellow Orchid
Platanthera leucophaea (Nutt.) Lindl.	Prairie White-Fringed Orchid
Polemonium vanbruntiae Britt.	Jacob's-Ladder
Polygala lutea L.	Yellow Milkwort
Prenanthes racemosa Michx.	Glaucous Rattlesnake-Root
Proserpinaca pectinata Lam.	Comb-Leaved Mermaid-Weed
Ranunculus hederaceus L.	Long-Stalked Crowfoot
Rhododendron calendulaceum (Michx.) Torr.	Flame Azalea
Rhynchospora fusca (L.) Ait.f.	Brown Beaked-Rush
Rhynchospora gracilenta Gray	Beaked-Rush
Sabatia campanulata (L.) Torr.	Slender Marsh Pink

Scientific name	Common name
Sabatia stellaris Pursh	Sea Pink
Sagittaria stagnorum Small	Arrow-Head
Scirpus heterochaetus Chase	Slender Bullrush
Scleria reticularis Michx. var. *pubescens* Britt.	Reticulated Nutrush
Smilax pseudo-china L.	Long-Stalked Greenbrier
Sparganium minimum(Hartm.) Fries	Small Bur-Reed
Spiraea virginiana Britt.	Virginia Spiraea
Trifolium reflexum L.	Buffalo Clover
Triglochin maritima L.	Sea-Side Arrowgrass
Triglochin palustre L.	Marsh Arrowgrass
Utricularia fibrosa Walt.	Fibrous Bladderwort
Utricularia inflata Walt.	Floating Bladderwort
Utricularia resupinata B.D. Greene	Northeastern Bladderwort

Pennsylvania Endangered

Arethusa bulbosa L.	Swamp-Pink
Aster depauperatus (Porter) Fern.	Serpentine Aster
Bidens bidentoides (Nutt.) Britt.	Swamp Beggar-Ticks
Carex barrattii Schw. & Torr.	Barratt's Sedge
Cerastium arvense (L.) var. *villosissimum* Pennell	Mouse-Ear Chickweed
Euphorbia purpurea (Raf.) Fern.	Glade Spurge
Gymnocarpium robertianum (Hoff.) Newm.	Limestone Oak Fern
Isotria medeoloides (Pursh) Raf.	Small-Whorled Pogonia
Juncus gymnocarpus Cov.	Coville's Rush
Listera smallii Wieg.	Kidney-Leaved Twayblade
Montica chamissoi (Ledeb. ex Spreng) Greene	Chamisso's Miner's-Lettuce
Pachistima canbyi Gray	Canby's Mountain-Lover
Poa paludigena Fern. & Wieg.	Prairie Bluegrass
Potamogeton hillii Morong	Hill's Pondweed
Sagittaria calycina Engelm. var. *spongiosa* Engelm.	Arrow-Head
Scirpus ancistrochaetus Schuyler	Northeastern Bullrush
Scleria minor (Britt.) W. Stone	Minor Nutrush
Senecio antennariifolius Britt.	Cat's-Paw Ragwort
Sporobolus heterolepis (Gray) Gray	Prairie Dropseed
Taenidia montana (Mackenzie) Cronq.	Mountain Pimpernel
Talinum teretifolium Pursh.	Round-Leaved Fame-Flower
Trifolium virginicum Small	Kate's Mountain Clover
Triphora trianthophora (Sw.) Rydb.	Nodding Pogonia
Trollius laxus Salisb.	Spreading Globe-Flower
Viola brittoniana Pollard	Coast Violet

Pennsylvania Threatened

Aconitum reclinatum Gray	White Monkshood
Asplenium bradleyi D.C. Eat.	Bradley's Spleenwort
Carex aurea Nutt.	Golden-Fruited Sedge
Carex bebbii (Bailey) Fern.	Bebb's Sedge
Carex eburnea Boott	Ebony Sedge
Carex geyeri Boott	Geyer's Sedge
Carex polymorpha Muhl.	Variable Sedge
Carex wiegandii Mackenzie	Wiegand's Sedge
Cryptogramma stelleri (S.G. Gmel.) Prantl.	Slender Rock-Brake
Cypripedium parviflorum Salisb.	Small Yellow Lady's-Slipper
Dichanthelium leibergii (Vasey) Freckmann	Leiberg's Dichanthelium
Dodecatheon meadia L.	Common Shooting-Star

Scientific name	Common name
Eleocharis intermedia Schultes	Matted Spike-Rush
Eleocharis rostellata Torr.	Beaked Spike-Rush
Fimbristylis annua (All.) R. & S.	Annual Fimbry
Galium labradoricum (Wieg.) Wieg.	Labrador Marsh Bedstraw
Gaylussacia brachycera (Michx.) Gray	Box Huckleberry
Hemicarpha micrantha (Vahl) Britt.	Common Hemicarpa
Hottonia inflata Ell.	American Featherfoil
Iris prismatica Pursh	Slender Blue Iris
Juncus militaris Bigel.	Bayonet Rush
Listera australis Lindl.	Southern Twayblade
Listera cordata (L.) R. Br.	Heart-Leaved Twayblade
Lobelia kalmii L.	Brook Lobelia
Lonicera oblongifolia (Goldie) Hook.	Swamp Fly Honeysuckle
Marshallia grandiflora Beadle & F.E. Boynton	Large-Flowered Marshallia
Oenothera argillicola Mackenzie	Shale-Barren Evening-Primrose
Platanthera dilatata (Prush) Lindl. ex Beck	Leafy White Orchid
Potamogeton confervoides Reichenb.	Tuckerman's Pondweed
Potamogeton tennesseensis Fern.	Tennessee Pondweed
Potentilla tridentata (Soland) Ait.	Three-Toothed Cinquefoil
Pycnanthemum pycnanthemoides (Leavenw.) Fern.	Southern Mountain-Mint
Rhynchospora capillacea Torr.	Capillary Beaked-Rush
Ribes missouriense Nutt. ex Torr. & Gray	Missouri Gooseberry
Ruellia humilis Nutt.	Fringed-Leaved Petunia
Salix candida Flugge ex Willd.	Hoary Willow
Salix serissima (Bailey) Fern.	Autumn Willow
Scheuchzeria palustris L.	Pod-Grass
Scleria verticillata Muhl. ex Willd.	Whorled Nutrush
Sida hermaphrodita (L.) Rusby	Sida
Spiranthes magnicamporum Sheviak	Ladies'-Tresses
Spiranthes ovalis Lindl.	October Ladies'-Tresses
Thalictrum steeleanum Boivin	Steele's Meadow-Rue
Viola villosa Walt.	Hairy Violet

Pennsylvania Rare

Scientific name	Common name
Aconitum uncinatum L.	Blue Monkshood
Alisma plantago-aquatica L. var. *americana* Schultes & Schultes	Broad-Leaved Water-Plantain
Amaranthus cannabinus (L.) Sauer	Waterhemp Ragweed
Amelanchier bartramiana (Tausch) M. Roemer	Oblong-Fruited Serviceberry
Ammannia coccinea Rottb.	Scarlet Ammannia
Ammophila breviligulata Fern.	American Beachgrass
Arctostaphylos uva-ursi (L.) Spreng.	Bearberry Manzanita
Asplenium resiliens Kunze	Black-Stemmed Spleenwort
Aster spectabilis Ait.	Low Showy Aster
Astragalus neglectus (Torr. & Gray) Sheldon	Cooper's Milk-Vetch
Baccharis halimifolia L.	Eastern Baccharis
Boltonia asteroides (L.) L'Her.	Aster-Like Boltonia
Bouteloua curtipendula (Michx.) Torr.	Tall Gramma
Cakile edentula (Bigel.) Hook.	American Sea-Rocket
Camassia scilloides (Raf.) Cory	Wild Hyacinth
Carex aquatilis Wahlenb.	Water Sedge
Carex bicknellii Britt.	Bicknell's Sedge
Carex bullata Schk.	Bull Sedge
Carex complanata Torr. & Hook.	Hirsute Sedge

Scientific name	Common name
Carex oligosperma Michx.	Few-Seeded Sedge
Castanea pumila (L.) P. Mill	Allegheny Chinkapin
Chasmanthium laxum (L.) Yates	Slender Sea-Oats
Chrysogonum virginianum L.	Green-and-Gold
Commelina erecta L.	Slender Day-Flower
Commelina virginica L.	Virginia Day-Flower
Cyperus diandrus Torr.	Umbrella Flatsedge
Cyperus houghtonii Torr.	Houghton's Flatsedge
Cyperus refractus Engelm. ex Steud.	Reflexed Flatsedge
Cyperus retrorsus Chapm.	Retrorse Flatsedge
Cyperus tenuifolius (Steud.) Dandy	Thin-Leaved Flatsedge
Cypripedium reginae Walt.	Showy Lady's-Slipper
Desmodium sessilifolium (Torr.) Torr & Gray	Sessile-Leaved Tick-Trefoil
Diarrhena americana Beauv.	American Beakgrain
Dicentra eximia (Ker-Gwal.) Torr.	Wild Bleeding-Hearts
Dichanthelium scoparium (Lam.) Gould	Velvety Dichanthelium
Dichanthelium xanthophysum (Gray) Freckmann	Slender Dichanthelium
Digitaria cognatum (Schultes) Pilger	Fall Witch-Grass
Dodecatheon amethystinum (Fassett) Fassett	Jeweled Shooting-Star
Dryopteris campyloptera (Kunze) Clarkson	Mountain Wood Fern
Echinochloa walteri (Pursh) Heller	Walter's Barnyard-Grass
Eleocharis elliptica Kunth	Slender Spike-Rush
Eleocharis parvula (Roemer & Schultes) Link	Little-Spike Spike-Rush
Eleocharis quadrangulata (Michx.) R. & S.	Four-Angled Spike-Rush
Eleocharis robbinsii Oakes	Robbins' Spike-Rush
Equisetum variegatum Schleich. ex Weber & C. Mohr	Variegated Horsetail
Erianthus giganteus (Walt.) Muhl.	Sugar Cane Plumegrass
Eriophorum tenellum Nutt.	Rough Cotton-Grass
Euphorbia ipecacuanhae L.	Wild Ipecac
Euphorbia obtusata Pursh	Blunt-Leaved Spurge
Festuca paradoxa Desv.	Cluster Fescue
Gaultheria hispidula (L.) Muhl. ex Bigelow	Creeping Snowberry
Gaylussacia dumosa (Andr.) Torr. & Gray	Dwarf Huckleberry
Gentiana catesbaei Walt.	Elliott's Gentian
Glyceria obtusa (Muhl.) Trin.	Blunt Manna-Grass
Gymnopogon ambiguus (Michx.) BSP	Broad-Leaved Beardgrass
Hibiscus laevis All.	Showy Hibiscus
Hierochloe odorata (L.) Beauv.	Vanilla Sweet-Grass
Hordeum pusillum Nutt.	Little Barley
Hypericum adpressum Raf. ex Bart.	Creeping St. John's-Wort
Hypericum gymnanthum Engelm. & Gray	Clasping-Leaved St. John's Wort
Hypericum majus (Gray) Britt.	Larger Canadian St. John's Wort
Iodanthus pinnatifidus (Michx.) Steud.	Purple Rocket
Iris cristata Soland.	Crested Dwarf Iris
Itea virginica L.	Virginia Willow
Juncus alpinus Vill.	Richardson's Rush
Juncus balticus Willd.	Baltic Rush
Juncus brachycarpus Engelm.	Short-Fruited Rush
Juncus brachycephalus (Engelm.) Buch.	Small-Headed Rush
Juncus dichotomus Ell.	Forked Rush
Juncus filiformis L.	Thread Rush
Juncus longii Fern.	Long's Rush
Ledum groenlandicum Oeder	Common Labrador-Tea
Ligusticum canadense (L.) Britt.	Nondo Lovage
Lobelia dortmanna L.	Water Lobelia

Scientific name	Common name
Lobelia nuttallii R. & S.	Nuttall's Lobelia
Lobelia puberula Michx.	Downy Lobelia
Ludwigia polycarpa Short & Peter	False Loosestrife Seedbox
Luzula bulbosa (Wood) Rydb.	Common Wood-Rush
Lycopodium porophilum Lloyd & Underwood	Rock Clubmoss
Lygodium palmatum (Bernh.) Sw.	Hartford Fern
Lyonia mariana (L.) D. Don	Stagger-Bush
Lythrum hyssopifolia L.	Hyssop Loosestrife
Magnolia tripetala (L.) L.	Umbrella Magnolia
Megalodonta beckii (Torr. ex Spreng.) Greene	Beck's Water-Marigold
Monarda punctata L.	Spotted Bee-Balm
Muhlenbergia uniflora (Muhl.) Fern.	Fall Dropseed Muhly
Myrica heterophylla Raf.	Evergreen Bayberry
Myriophyllum farwellii Morong.	Farwell's Water-Milfoil
Myriophyllum heterophyllum Michx.	Broad-Leaved Water-Milfoil
Myriophyllum tenellum Bigel.	Slender Water-Milfoil
Nelumbo lutea (Willd.) Pers.	American Lotus
Nymphoides cordata (Ell.) Fern.	Floating-Heart
Oenothera pilosella Raf.	Evening-Primrose
Opuntia humifusa (Raf.) Raf.	Prickly-Pear Cactus
Oryzopsis pungens (Torr. ex Spreng.) A.S. Hitchc.	Slender Mountain-Ricegrass
Panicum amarum Ell. var. *amarulum* (A.S. Hitchc. & Chase) P.G. Palmer	Southern Sea-Beach Panic-Grass
Phyllanthus caroliniensis Walt.	Carolina Leaf-Flower
Pilea fontana (Lunnell) Rydb.	Lesser Clearweed
Poa autumnalis Muhl. ex Ell.	Autumn Bluegrass
Polygala cruciata L.	Cross-Leaved Milkwort
Polygala curtissii Gray	Curtis's Milkwort
Polygala incarnata L.	Pink Milkwort
Polygonum ramosissimum Michx.	Bushy Knotweed
Polystichum braunii (Spenner) Fee	Braun's Holly Fern
Potamogeton friesii Rupr.	Fries' Pondweed
Potamogeton gramineus L.	Grassy Pondweed
Potamogeton obtusifolius Mert. & Koch	Blunt-Leaved Pondweed
Potamogeton praelongus Wulfen	White-Stemmed Pondweed
Potamogeton pulcher Tuckerm.	Spotted Pondweed
Potamogeton vaseyi Robbins	Vasey's Pondweed
Potentilla anserina L.	Silverweed
Potentilla fruticosa L.	Shrubby Cinquefoil
Prunus maritima Marsh.	Beach Plum
Prunus pumila L.	Sand Cherry
Ptilimnium capillaceum (Michx.) Raf.	Mock Bishop-Weed
Pycnanthemum torrei Benth.	Torrey's Mountain-Mint
Pyrularia pubera Michx.	Buffalo-Nut
Quercus falcata Michx.	Spanish Oak
Quercus shumardii Buckl.	Shumard's Oak
Ranunculus micranthus (Gray) Nutt. ex Torr. & Gray	Small-Flowered Crowfoot
Rhexia mariana L.	Maryland Meadow-Beauty
Rhododendron atlanticum (Ashe) Rehd.	Dwarf Azalea
Rotala ramosior (L.) Koehne	Tooth-Cup
Ruellia carolinensis (Walt. ex J.F. Gmel.) Steud.	Carolina Petunia
Rumex hastatulus Baldw. ex Ell.	Heart-Winged Sorrell
Sagittaria subulata (L.) Buch.	Subulata Arrow-Head
Salix amygdaloides Anderss.	Peach-Leaved Willow
Scirpus acutus Muhl. ex Bigelow	Hard-Stemmed Bullrush

Scientific name	Common name
Scirpus fluviatilis (Torr.) Gray	River Bullrush
Scirpus smithii Gray	Smith's Bullrush
Scirpus torreyi Olney	Torrey's Bullrush
Scleria pauciflora Muhl. ex Willd.	Few Flowered Nutrush
Sedum rosea (L.) Scop.	Roseroot Stonecrop
Sedum telephioides Michx.	Allegheny Stonecrop
Senecio plattensis Nutt.	Prairie Ragwort
Shepherdia canadensis (L.) Nutt.	Canada Buffalo-Berry
Sisyrinchium albidum Raf.	Blue-Eyed Grass
Sisyrinchium arenicola Bickn.	Sand-Blue-Eyed Grass
Sisyrinchium atlanticum Bickn.	Eastern Blue-Eyed Grass
Solidago curtisii T. & G.	Curtis's Golden-Rod
Solidago erecta Pursh	Slender Golden-Rod
Spiranthes romanzoffiana Cham.	Hooded Ladies-Tresses
Sporobolus clandestinus (Biehler) A.S. Hitchc.	Rough Dropseed
Sporobolus cryptandrus (Torr.) Gray	Sand Dropseed
Stachys hyssopifolia Michx.	Hyssop Hedge-Nettle
Stachys nuttallii Shuttlw. ex Benth	Riddell's Hedge-Nettle
Strophostyles leiosperma (T. & G.) Piper	Slick-Seeded Wild-Bean
Thalictrum coriaceum (Britt.) Small	Thick-Leaved Meadow-Rue
Tipularia discolor (Pursh) Nutt.	Cranefly Orchid
Trautvetteria caroliniensis (Walt.) Vail	Carolina Tassel-Rue
Trichostema setaceum Houtt.	Blue-Curls
Trillium nivale Riddell	Snow Trillium
Triplasis purpurea (Walt.) Chapm.	Purple Sandgrass
Uvularia puberula Michx.	Mountain Bellwort
Viola renifolia Gray	Kidney-Leaved White Violet
Vitis rupestris Scheele	Sand Grape
Wolffiella gladiata (Hegelm.) Hegelm.	Bog-Mat
Zizania aquatica L.	Indian Wild Rice

Pennsylvania Vulnerable

Hydrastis canadensis L.	Golden-Seal
Panax quinquefolius L.	Ginseng

Tentatively Undetermined

Agalinis obtusifolia Raf.	False-Foxglove
Agrostis altissima (Walt.) Tuckerm.	Tall Bentgrass
Alnus viridis (Chaix) DC. ssp. *crispa* (Ait.) Turrill	Mountain Alder
Alopecurus carolinianus Walt.	Tufted Foxtail
Andromeda polifolia L.	Bog-Rosemary
Anemone cylindrica Gray	Long-Fruited Anemone
Anemone riparia Fern.	River Anemone
Antennaria solitaria Rydb.	Single-Headed Pussy-Toes
Aplectrum hyemale (Muhl ex Willd.) Nutt.	Puttyroot
Arabis missouriensis Greene	Missouri Rock-Cress
Aristida purpurascens Poir	Arrow-Feather Three-Awned Grass
Arnica acualis (Walt.) BSP	Leopard's-Bane
Aster ericoides L.	White Health Aster
Aster novi-belgii L.	Long-Leaved Aster
Aster solidagineus Michx.	Narrow-Leaved White-Topp Aster
Carex aenea Fern.	Fernald's Hay Sedge
Carex alata Torr.	Broad-Winged Sedge
Carex alopecoidea Tuckerm.	Foxtail Sedge

Scientific name	Common name
Carex atherodes Spreng.	Awned Sedge
Carex backii Boott	Rocky Mountain Sedge
Carex careyana Dewey	Carey's Sedge
Carex collinsii Nutt.	Collin's Sedge
Carex crawfordii Fern.	Crawford's Sedge
Carex diandra Shrank	Lesser Panicled Sedge
Carex formosa Dewey	Handsome Sedge
Carex garberi Fern.	Elk Sedge
Carex laricina Mackenzie	Larger Stellate Sedge
Carex paupercula Michz.	Bog Sledge
Carex pseudocyperus L.	Cyperus-Like Sedge
Carex schweinitzii Dewey ex Schwein.	Schweinitz's Sedge
Carex tetanica Schk.	Wood's Sedge
Carex viridula Michx.	Green Sedge
Chenopodium foggii Wahl	Fogg's Goosefoot
Chrysopsis mariana (L.) Ell.	Maryland Golden Aster
Cimicifuga americana Michx.	Mountain Bugbane
Cirsium horridulum Michx.	Horrible Thistle
Clematis viorna L.	Vase-Vine Leather-Flower
Clethra acuminata Michx.	Mountain Pepper-Bush
Collinsia verna Nutt.	Spring Blue-Eyed Mary
Corallorhiza wisteriana Conrad	Spring Coral-Root
Cuscuta corylii Engelm.	Hazel Dodder
Cuscuta polygonorum Engelm.	Smartweed Dodder
Cymophyllus fraseri (Andr.) Mackenzie	Fraser's Sedge
Cynanchum laeve (Michx.) Pers.	Smooth Swallow-Wort
Cyperus engelmannii Steud.	Engelmann's Flatsedge
Delphinium exaltatum Ait.	Tall Larkspur
Draba reptans (Lam.) Fern.	Carolina Whitlow-Grass
Eleocharis compressa Sulliv.	Flat-Stemmed Spike-Rush
Eleocharis obtusa var. *peasei* Svenson	Wright's Spike-Rush
Eleocharis tenuis var. *verrucosa* Svenson	Slender Spike-Rush
Elephantopus carolinianus Raeusch.	Elephant's-Foot
Erigenia bulbosa (Michx.) Nutt.	Harbinger-of-Spring
Euthamia tenuifolia (Pursh) Greene	Grass-Leaved Goldenrod
Fimbristylis puberula (Michx.) Vahl	Hairy Fimbry
Frasera caroliniensis Walt.	American Columbo
Froelichia floridana (Nutt.) Moq.	Florida Cotton-Weed
Galactia regularis (L.) BSP	Eastern Milk-Pea
Galactia volubilis (L.) Britt.	Downey Milk-Pea
Gentiana alba Muhl.	Yellow Gentian
Gentiana villosa L.	Striped Gentian
Goodyera tesselata Lodd.	Checkered Rattlesnake-Plantain
Hedyotis purpurea (L.) Torr. & Gray	Purple Bluet
Helianthemum bicknellii Fern.	Bicknell's Hoary Rockrose
Ilex opaca Ait.	American Holly
Iris verna L.	Dwarf Iris
Juncus torreyi Cov.	Torrey's Rush
Kalmia polifolia Wang.	Pale Laurel
Koeleria cristata (L.) Pers.	Junegrass
Lathyrus japonicus Willd. var. *glaber* (Ser.) Fern.	Beach Peavine
Leiophyllum buxifolium (Berg.) Ell.	Sand-Myrtle
Lemna valdiviana Philippi	Pale Duckweed
Liatris scariosa (L.) Willd. var. *novae-angliae* Lunell	Gay-Feather

Scientific name	Common name
Lilium michiganense Farw.	Michigan Lily
Lycopodium complanatum L.	Trailing Clubmoss
Magnolia virginiana L.	Sweet Bay Magnolia
Malaxis brachypoda (Gray) Fern.	White Adder's-Mouth
Matelea carolinensis (Jacq.) Woods.	Carolina Milkvine
Menziesia pilosa (Michx.) Juss.	Minniebush
Myrica gale L.	Sweet Bayberry
Nuphar luteum (L.) Sibthorp & Sm. ssp. *pumilum* (Timm) E. O. Beal	Yellow Cowlily
Onosmodium virginianum (L.) A. DC.	Virginia False-Gromwell
Parnassia glauca Raf.	Carolina Grass-of-Parnassus
Phlox subulata L. ssp. *brittonii* (Small) Wherry	Moss Pink
Phoradenron serotinum (Raf.) M. C. Johnston	Christmas Mistletoe
Platanthera peramoena (Gray) Gray	Purple-Fringeless Orchid
Populus balsamifera L.	Balsam Poplar
Potentilla paradoxa Nutt. ex Torr. & Gray	Bushy Cinquefoil
Prenanthes crepidinea Michx.	Crepis Rattlesnake-Root
Prunus nigra Ait.	Canada Plum
Ptelea trifoliata L.	Common Hop-Tree
Ruellia strepens L.	Limestone Petunia
Salix planifolia Pursh	Tea-Leaved Willow
Salvia reflexa Hornem.	Lance-Leaved Sage
Saxifraga micranthidifolia (Haw.) Steud.	Lettuce Saxifrage
Scutellaria saxatilis Riddell	Rock Skullcap
Scutellaria serrata Andr.	Showy Skullcap
Senecio anonymus Wood	Plain Ragwort
Solidago arguta Ait. var. *harrissii* (Steele) Cronq.	Harris' Goldenrod
Solidago purshii Porter	Pursh's Golden-Rod
Solidago roanensis Porter	Tennessee Golden-Rod
Solidago spathulata ssp. *randii* var. *racemosa* (Greene) Gleason	Sticky Golden-Rod
Spiraea betulifolia Pall. ssp. *corymbosa* (Raf.) Taylor & MacBryde	Dwarf Spiraea
Spiranthes cernua (L.) Rich. var *incurva* Jennings	Nodding Ladies'-Tresses
Spiranthes tuberosa Raf.	Little Ladies'-Tresses
Spiranthes vernalis Engelm. & Gray	Spring Ladies'-Tresses
Spirodela punctata (Mey.) C.H. Thompson	Eastern Water-Flaxseed
Stylophorum diphyllum (Michx.) Nutt.	Celandine Poppy
Trillium flexipes Raf.	Declined Trillium
Utricularia inflata Walt.	Floating Bladderwort
Utricularia purpurea Walt.	Purple Bladderwort
Vernonia glauca (L.) Willd.	Tawny Ironweed
Veronica catenata Pennell	Pennel's Speedwell
Viola appalachiensis Henry	Appalachian Blue Violet
Viola tripartita Ell.	Three-Parted Violet
Wolffia braziliensis Weddell	Pointed Water-Meal

Chapter Ten

RARE PLANTS OF EASTERN PENNSYLVANIA

Ann F. Rhoads
Morris Arboretum
University of Pennsylvania,
Philadelphia, PA 19118

Because of its diverse geology, physiography and geographic position, Pennsylvania has a large and varied flora. The total number of species native to the state is approximately 2,100. Some of this diversity results from the state's position between the northern hardwood forest type and the Appalachian oak forest of the mid-Atlantic area.[1] Consequently, the Pennsylvania flora contains a significant component of northern plants at or near the southern limit of their range and southern species reaching their northernmost extreme. Many species classified as endangered, threatened or rare fall into these categories.

Geological features which add to the floral diversity include outcrops of serpentine rock, limestone beds, shale barrens, coastal plain deposits and glacial lakes and bogs. Northern counties have been glaciated several times, most recently during the Wisconsin glaciation approximately 10,000 years ago. The eastern half of the state (37 counties) contains all of the features mentioned above with the exception of shale barrens. Many of the endangered, threatened and rare plants of eastern Pennsylvania are associated with these rare and specialized habitats. In some cases these habitats have been further threatened by human activity.

Other reasons for plant rarity include overcollecting of commercially valuable species and naturally sparse distribution of some species.

Note: The abbreviations following the names of plants refer to the official protection status of the species in Pennsylvania. PE = Pennsylvania Endangered, PT = Pennsylvania Threatened, PR = Pennsylvania Rare, TU = Temporarily Undetermined. In addition, species under consideration for federal listing are shown as C1, C2 or C3.

SOUTHERN LIMIT OF RANGE

Northern species which approach the southern limit of their range in Pennsylvania are found at high elevations, and in bogs and glacial lakes in the northeastern counties. Tucked in the crevices of mountaintop rock outcrops in Luzerne, Lackawanna and Monroe Counties, three-toothed cinquefoil, *Potentilla tridentata* (Soland) Ait. (PT), can be found. Moist limestone cliffs in Sullivan and Lehigh Counties are home to the slender rockbrake, *Cryptogramma stelleri* (S.G. Gmel.) Prantl. (PT), and the ebony sedge, *Carex eburnea* Boott (PT).

Glacial lakes and bogs which are concentrated in Wayne, Pike, Monroe, Susquehanna, Lackawanna, Luzerne, Carbon, and Sullivan Counties are home to a number of unusual Pennsylvania plants many of which are common further north. Species included in this category and for which current sites are known in eastern Pennsylvania are: bayonet rush, *Juncus militaris* Bigel (PT); Tuckerman's pondweed, *Potamogeton confervoides* Reichenb. (PT); few-seeded sedge, *Carex oligosperma* Michx. *(PR),* Robins' spike-rush, *Eleocharis robbinsii* Oakes (PR); creeping snowberry, *Gautheria hispidula* (L.) Muhl. ex Bigelow (PR); thread-rush, *Juncus filiformis* L. (PR); Labrador tea, *Ledum groenlandicum* Oeder (PR); water lobelia, *Lobelia dortmanna* L. (PR); slender water-milfoil, *Myriophyllum tenellum* Bigel. (PR); floating heart,*Nymphoides cordata* (Ell.) Fern. (PR); blunt-leaved pondweed, *Potamogeton obtusifolius* Mert. & Koch (PR); and Torrey's bullrush, *Scirpus torreyi* Olney (PR). Variable sedge, *Carex polymorpha* Muhl., which is listed as threatened in Pennsylvania and is under review for federal listing occurs at several northern bog sites in Monroe and Carbon Counties. It has apparently disappeared from a number of former stations in Chester and Delaware Counties.

Additional northern bog species under consideration for state listing include Collin's sedge, *Carex collinsii* Nutt.; bog sedge, *Carex paupercula* Michx.; pale laurel, *Kalmia polifolia* Wang.; sweet bayberry, *Myrica gale* L.; and purple bladderwort, *Utricularia purpurea* Walt. All are presently placed in the TU (Temporarily Undetermined) category.

Several bog species, which were collected in the past, have not been seen recently in eastern Pennsylvania including pod-grass, *Scheuchzeria palustris* L. (PT), and rough cotton grass, *Eriophorum tenellum* Nutt. (PR). *Scheuchzeria palustris* was collected from 13 sites in 10 eastern counties from 1836 to 1913. *Eriophorum tenellum* has been reported from 16 sites in 10 counties, most recently in 1947. However, despite the presence of apparently suitable habitat at several of the original locations, neither plant has been found during the current rare plant survey. There is one extant population of *Scheuchzeria* in Clinton County in northwestern Pennsylvania. The reason for its disappearance from eastern Pennsylvania is not known. Raised water levels caused by beaver activity may be involved, as according to Dr. A. E. Schuyler (personal communication), *Scheuchzeria* is intolerant of inundation. The role of acid precipitation in the decline of these and other bog species has not been investigated. *Scheuchzeria* occurs in New York State where it is not listed as rare. Its range extends from Newfoundland west to Manitoba and Washington.[2] *Eriophorum tenellum* has a similar range and occurs south to New York, Michigan and Illinois. There is one recent report from New Jersey where it is listed as rare.

Although many glacial lake and bog sites remain in relatively undisturbed condition, continuing pressure for vacation home sites and recreational use of lakes is a serious threat. Growing awareness of the importance of wetlands in biological and hydrological cycles is an encouraging trend. Wetland identification and protection programs of the United States Fish and Wildlife Service, the Environmental Protection Agency and Pennsylvania Department of Envirometed Resources should help prevent further habitat loss.

The northern section of the Delaware River corridor is another area which contains species with northern affinities. Chamisso's miner's lettuce, *Montia chamissoi* (Ledeb ex Spreng) Greene (PE), has been described as the "most disjunct species in Pennsylvania".[3] Originally collected along the river near Milanville in 1893, it was correctly identified by Wherry many years later. A second location was found in 1950. A recent attempt to relocate the plant was unsuccessful, however, two new stations a few miles north of the original sites were discovered in 1984.[4] The main range of *Montia chamissoi* is from Alaska to New Mexico, Arizona and California. The closest known occurrence to Pennsylvania is in Winona County, Minnesota, some 600 miles distant.[2]

Occurring on alluvial islands and bars in the river from the Delaware Water Gap north is the prostrate sand cherry, *Prunus pumila* var. *depressa*. This plant is well adapted to the frequent scouring by ice and flood waters which characterizes its environment. Populations of *Prunus pumila* var. *depressa* (Pursh) Gl. are also reported from the upper Susquehanna and Alleghany Rivers.

Roseroot sedum, *Sedum rosea* (L.) Scop. (PR), grows in two areas along the Delaware River clinging to moist crevices in sheer rock cliffs. The range of this species extends from the Arctic regions into New England and locally southward.

COASTAL PLAIN COMPONENT

The Atlantic Coastal Plain extends into the southeastern corner of Pennsylvania to the fall line marking the beginning of the Piedmont Province. The coastal plain area of Pennsylvania comprises portions of Philadelphia and the adjacent suburban counties of Bucks and Delaware. Intense urbanization in this part of the state has reduced natural habitat to a few isolated remnants of coastal plain forest and several areas of intertidal marsh along the Delaware River. Coastal plain species have suffered accordingly; 30 of the 62 species listed as extirpated in Pennsylvania are coastal plain plants (see chapter nine for complete list).

Several coastal plain species including sweetbay magnolia, *Magnolia virginiana* L. (TU), coast violet, *Viola brittoniana* Pollard (PE), and American holly, *Ilex opaca* Ait. (TU), occur in Bucks County and along the southern portion of the Susquehanna River Valley in Lancaster County. A grove of mature *Magnolia virginiana* is virtually all that remains of a once very diverse coastal plain outlier in Montgomery County.[5,6] Bull sedge, *Carex bullata* Schk. (PR), another coastal plain species is known from one site in Bucks County and at a glacial sand dune formation located near Montandon in Northumberland County.[7,8]

Within the coastal plain province the fresh water intertidal zone is a unique habitat. Alternately exposed to the sun and wind and covered with up to 2 m of water these marshes support a group of specially adapted plants.[7] Swamp beggar-ticks, *Bidens bidentoides* (Nutt.) Britt. (PE), was at one time being considered for federal listing, however recent discoveries in the Hudson River estuary have caused it to be placed on the inactive federal C3 list. Two low-growing species of arrow-head, *Sagittaria calycina* var. *spongiosa* Engelm. (PE) and *S. subulata* (L.) Buch. (PR) are found at several of the marsh areas remaining in Bucks and Philadelphia Counties. Smith's bullrush, *Scirpus smithii* Gray (PR), and river bullrush, *S. fluviatilis* (Torr.) Gray (PR), also occur at several sites. It is of interest, that the river bullrush also occurs on the Northumberland County sand deposits mentioned above.

Tinicum Marsh was once the site of a diverse coastal plain flora. Thirty-five species now considered rare in the state were collected in the Tinicum vicinity in the past.[10] The local flora has apparently become seriously degraded as recent botanical surveys have been able to locate only 4 of these plant species. Wild rice, *Zizania aquatica* L. (PR), occupies approximately a hundred hectares in the wildlife refuge, but much of the former tidal marsh has been impounded, filled or overgrown with reed grass, *Phragmites australis* (Cav.) Trin. ex Steud. Little Tinicum Island, purchased by the state in 1983, contains the best stand of Walter's barnyard grass, *Echinochloa walteri* (Pursh) Heller (PR), remaining along the Pennsylvania portion of the Delaware. A more thorough discussion of the status of intertidal plants is included in Chapter thirteen.

NORTHERN LIMIT OF RANGE

The southern areas of Lancaster, York and Franklin Counties are prime locations for a number of inland southern species that reach the northern limits of their natural range in Pennsylvania. Two ferns, Bradley's spleenwort, *Asplenium bradleyi* D.C. Eat. (PT), and black-stemmed spleenwort, *A. resiliens* Kunze (PR), are found in this part of the state but are more common in the southern mountains. Other southern species are Allegheny chinkapin, *Castanea pumila* (L.) P. Mill. (PR); umbrella magnolia, *Magnolia tripetala* (L.) L. (PR);

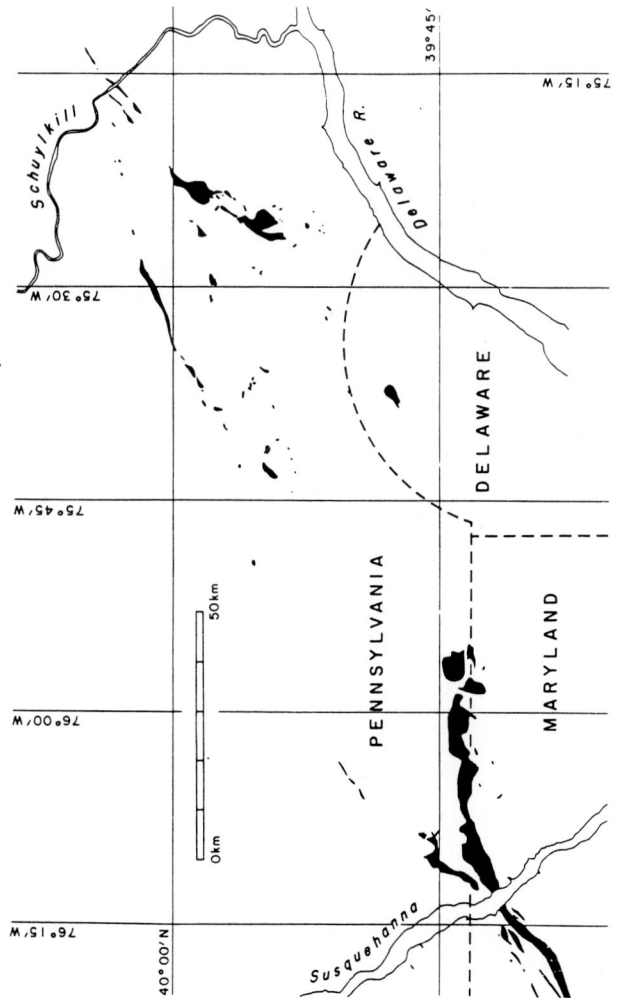

FIGURE 1. Serpentine Rock Outcrops of the Northern Piedmont.
Adapted from: Nancy C. Pearre and Allen V. Heyl, Jr. 1960. *Chromite and Other Mineral Deposits in Serpentine Rocks of the Piedmont Upland, Maryland, Pennsylvania and Delaware.* Geological Survey Bulletin 1082-K.

sida, *Sida hemaphrodita* (L.) Rusby (PT); green and gold, *Chrysogonum virginianum* L. (PR); aster-like boltonia, *Boltonia asteroides* (L.) L'Her. (PR).

SERPENTINE BARRENS

A cluster of endangered and threatened Pennsylvania plants is found on the serpentine barrens which lie in a band across Delaware, Chester and Lancaster Counties (Fig. 1).[11] The barrens, which result from the unusual mineral composition of serpentine rock—high chromium, nickel and magnesium and low nitrogen—constitute islands of grassland or pine woodland in the surrounding agricultural fields and deciduous forests of the Piedmont. Extensive surveywork during 1982 and 1983 resulted in the identification of 16 barrens ranging in size from less than an hectare to several hundred hectares.[12] Several barrens sites referred to by earlier botanists are gone, having fallen victim to suburban sprawl. Others have been reduced in size and species diversity.

Pennsylvania's only true endemic plant is found on the barrens. Mouse-ear chickweed, *Cerastium arvense* var. *villosissimum* Pennell (PE), was first described by Pennell in 1929 from the Goat Hill Serpentine Barrens.[13] That site, now part of a State Forest Natural Area,, remains the only known location for this species.

Other listed plants found on the barrens are serpentine aster, *Aster depauperatus* (Porter) Fern. (PE/C2); prairie dropseed, *Sporobolus heterolepis* (Gray) Gray (PE); round-leaved fame flower, *Talinum teretifolium* Pursh (PE); annual fimbry, *Fimbristylis annua* (All.) R & S (PT); tall gramma, *Bouteloua curtipendula* (Michx.) Torr. (PR), and Bicknell's sedge, *Carex bicknellii* Britt. (PR).

The serpentine aster is a true serpentine endemic and is currently found on 14 of the 16 extant barrens in Pennsylvania. Round-leaved fame flower, present on 11 of the barrens, also occurs on granite outcrops and other dry rocky sites south to Georgia and Alabama. The two grasses, prairie dropseed and tall gramma are more common farther west and reach their eastern limit of range on the serpentine barrens of Pennsylvania.

LIMESTONE WETLANDS

Limestone wetlands constitute another specialized plant habitat found in eastern Pennsylvania. Never abundant, they have been dangerously reduced in area by human activity. The best remaining examples are in Northampton and Monroe Counties at the southern edge of the glaciated area. Former sites in Lancaster, Bucks and Lehigh Counties have been destroyed.[11] The spreading globeflower, *Trollius laxus* Salisb., endangered in Pennsylvania and under consideration (C1) for federal listing, occurs at 5 sites in eastern Pennsylvania. Populations are small with 100 or fewer plants at each site. Three plants restricted to limestone wetlands are listed as threatened in Pennsylvania: brook lobelia, *Lobelia kalmii* L.; capillary beak-rush, *Rhyncospora capillacea* Torr.; and whorled nutrush, *Seleria verticillata* Muhl. ex Willd. Shrubby cinquefoil, *Potentilla fruticosa* L., listed as rare in the state is found at one site and Carolina grass-of-parnassus, *Parnassia glauca* Raf., is under review for possible state listing.

OVERCOLLECTING A THREAT

I have not made any attempt in this chapter to include all of the endangered, threatened, vulnerable and rare plants of eastern Pennsylvania, but rather to discuss those which illustrate the major habitat groupings. A complete list of extirpated, endangered, threatened, vulnerable, rare and temporarily undetermined plants of Pennsylvania is included in Chapter nine.

Additional field work is needed to document the current status of many of these plants in the state. It is very clear, from our experiences with *Montia chamissoi* and several other species, that verifying historical collection sites is not sufficient. Additional areas of appropriate habitat should also be identified and searched to provide a complete picture.

Several eastern Pennsylvania plant species are currently listed as vulnerable due to their economic value. Overcollecting threatens populations of ginseng, *Panax quinquefolia* L., and golden seal, *Hydrastis canadensis* L. Other native plants, including showy wildflowers and orchids face similar pressure. While some are included on present endangered, threatened and rare lists, others may have to be added if collecting continues. However, listing alone is no guarantee of protection, for the regulations proposed under the Wild Resources Conservation Act protect only endangered and threatened plants.

Protection of the biological diversity which still remains in the Pennsylvania flora will require educating the public to the significance of the resource and securing their assistance in saving it.

REFERENCES

1. Kuchler, A.W. 1964 *Potential Natural Vegetation of the Conterminous United States.* Special Publication No. 36. American Geographical Society New York, New York. 116 pgs.
2. Fernald, M.L. 1950. *Gray's Manual of Botany.* Eighth Edition. American Book Co., New York. 1632 pgs.
3. Wherry, E.T. 1964. The most disjunct species in Pennsylvania. Bartonia 34:7.

4. Rhoads, A.F., A. Newbold, R.H. Mellon and R.E. Latham. 1985. *Montia chamissoi* rediscovered along the Delaware River in Wayne County, Pennsylvania. Bartonia 51:77.
5. Stone, W. 1910. *The Plants of Southern New Jersey.* Annual Report of the New Jersey State Museum. Trenton, N.J. p. 46-47.
6. Tees, G.M. 1979. The Plants of Frazier's Bog, Montgomery County, Pennsylvania. Bartonia 46:43-44.
7. Manning, W.E. 1960. Some interesting ferns, fern allies, and woody plants of the Lewisburg. Pennsylvania region. Proc. Pennsylvania Acad. of Science. 34:15-16.
8. Peltier, L.C. 1949. *Pleistocene Terraces of the Susquehanna River Pennsylvania.* Bulletin 6-23 Pennsylvania Geological Survey. Harrisburg, PA. p. 48-51.
9. Ferren, W.R., Jr., and A.E. Schuyler. 1980. Intertidal vascular plants of river systems near Philadelphia. Proc. Acad. of Natural Sciences 132:86-120.
10. McCormick, J., R.W. Grant and R. Patrick. 1970. *Two Studies of Tinicum Marsh.* The Conservation Foundation. 85 pgs.
11. Pearre, N.C. and A.V. Heyl, Jr. 1960. *Chromite and Other Mineral Deposits in Serpentine Rocks of the Piedmont Upland Maryland, Pennsylvania and Delaware.* Geological Survey Bulletin 1082-K, United States Government Printing Office, Washington, D.C. 126 pgs.
12. Latham, R. 1983. Northern piedmont serpentine barrens as inland "islands". Swarthmore College Senior Thesis. Swarthmore, Pennsylvania. Unpublished. 22 pgs.
13. Pennell, F.W. 1929. On some critical species of the serpentine barrens. Bartonia 12:1-23.
14. Schuyler, A.E. 1980. Botanical degradation of Dillerville Swamp, Lancaster County, Pennsylvania. Bartonia 47:1-2.

Endangered and Threatened Species Programs in Pennsylvania and other States: Causes, Issues and Management. Edited by S. K. Majumdar, F. J. Brenner and A. F. Rhoads. © 1986, The Pennsylvania Academy of Science.

Chapter Eleven
AN OVERVIEW OF THE VASCULAR PLANT GEOGRAPHY OF PENNSYLVANIA

Carl S. Keener and Marilyn M. Park
Department of Biology
The Pennsylvania State University
University Park, PA 16802

Based on the *Atlas of the Flora of Pennsylvania*, the distribution patterns of the native vascular flora of Pennsylvania are classified into eight major groups: species common throughout, species confined to one or more of seven major physiographic provinces, regional species (e.g., western, eastern, southern, etc.), disjuncts within Pennsylvania, regional endemics due to specialized habitats (serpentine, shale), widespread disjunct endemics, and plants of special habitats (aquatics, bogs, calcareous marshes, limestone, and sandy dolomitic barrens). An attempt is made to correlate these patterns with climate, topography, and edaphic variables.

INTRODUCTION

This study aims to present a general perspective of the distribution patterns of the vascular flora native to Pennsylvania. Two principal objectives include 1) discerning the basic patterns, i.e., where, within Pennsylvania, the different groups of species occur, and 2) correlating these patterns with relevant topographic, edaphic, and climatic factors. The basic problem therefore is to ascertain why plants are distributed in certain recognizable patterns. Because the native flora is more likely to be in equilibrium with the regional topography, soils, and climate, naturalized or casual escapes were omitted. And, in general, native species rare to Pennsylvania were omitted also. Not that naturalized or such rare native plants are not of interest, but we believe that by focussing on patterns perceived in the native flora a more convincing case can be made that the vegetation within Pennsylvania reflects certain fundamental distribution patterns and that these are related to regional climatic regimes. To be sure, a study of both rare native and variously regionalized introduced species would be of interest, and could, perhaps, be undertaken as a study comparable to this one. At least 50 introduced species (e.g., *Poa compressa* L.) are common throughout Pennsylvania; many others, often casual escapes, are known from one or two sites. Likewise, a number of native species are extremely rare within the Commonwealth. Some, such as *Asplenium resiliens* Kunze are known from only one site; other species (e.g., *Trifolium reflexum* L.), once collected within Pennsylvania, are now believed to be extirpated. Such intrinsically rare plants, reaching, in some cases, their geographic limits within Pennsylvania, would have to be studied within the context of a generally broader-based regional biogeography, a consideration not attempted here.

No flora remains stable indefinitely. Certainly, in Pennsylvania, human activities have disturbed immensely the original forest flora. But to what extent such activities have led to a marked alteration in the distribution patterns of native species remains an open question. In an analysis such as this, one must work with known distribution patterns and on the basis of these discern possible correlations. We do not pretend to offer an exhaustive study, although for each major distribution pattern outlined below we do include nearly all native species illustrating a given pattern. But many of the roughly 2300 taxa native to Pennsylvania are rare, widely scattered, or seemingly fit into no discernible pattern, and these were omitted from this study.

There is no comprehensive review of the plant geography of Pennsylvania, although certain regional studies[1,2] included Pennsylvania in their comprehensive analysis. To be sure, various investigators have, over the years, studied certain regions of Pennsylvania largely from a phytosociological or ecological approach. Although our list is not exhaustive, such investigations include those by Cribbs,[3,4] Donahue,[5] Goodlett,[6] Harshberger,[7] Hough and Forbes,[8] Jennings,[9,10,11] and Keever.[12] In contrast to a plant community or ecological approach, our study is primarily floristic and comparative, i.e., we are asking whether there are any discernible patterns with respect to the plant distributions themselves and then whether or not these patterns can be correlated with any specific environmental variable.

METHODS

The *Atlas of the Flora of Pennsylvania*[13] provided the initial data-base for this study. Initiated in the 1930's, the *Atlas* presents, by means of dot maps, the results of an intensive floristic survey within Pennsylvania. Despite its being somewhat out-of-date (few "dots" have been added within the last decade to the master card file housed at the Morris Arboretum), the *Atlas* portrays quite accurately various distribution patterns because each "dot" indicates more or less the exact location for a given specimen (not one "dot" per county). Nomenclature follows that of the USDA *National List of Scientific Plant Names*, issued in 1982. Names in the *Atlas* differing from the USDA *List* are given in parentheses.

At least two problems beset this approach: 1) accuracy of specimen determination, and 2) completeness of the floristic survey. The latter problem, especially, is one that confronts all biogeographers, particularly if the database should be relatively comprehensive. But no floristic survey is ever complete in any ideal sense. For example, in a recent survey of the vascular flora of Blair County, Pennsylvania, over 500 taxa heretofore unrecorded were collected from the county.[14] Despite its incompleteness, the *Atlas* does suggest trends, e.g., whether or not a species is common, or confined to the Coastal Plain, the shale barrens, or the northeastern glaciated section of the Appalachian Plateaus Province.

Once the key distribution patterns are known, then these can be correlated with available data concerning climate, topography, and soils. Such fitting of patterns to relevant data is not, given our present information, subject to fine quantitative analysis. And in this sense, our analysis is a scenario: a portrayal of plant distribution patterns correlated with climate and topography, as based on our best judgement. Eventual autecological studies of key species such as those by Gunther[15] or intensive surveys covering the entire Commonwealth such as those by Goodlett[6] for Potter County, Pennsylvania, might lead eventually to a comprehensive statistical analysis of the distribution patterns of the entire vascular flora. But at present, a general approximation is the best we can accomplish. We hope, however, that this study will inspire others to undertake additional and more thorough analyses of the biogeography of the flora of Pennsylvania.

RESULTS

The vascular flora of Pennsylvania can be classified into 7 major patterns: 1) species common throughout, 2) species confined to the glaciated regions (Fig. 31), 3) species occurring chiefly in one of 7 major provinces (Fig. 31), 4) species occurring in several topographic regions, 5) disjuncts within Pennsylvania, 6) regional endemics, and 7) plants of special habitats. In general, we have attempted to list all native taxa illustrative of a given pattern. But, as pointed out above, many species (e.g., *Sanguinaria canadensis* L., Fig. 1), despite their relative frequency, seemingly fit no pattern. Only a critical autecological study can uncover the reasons for such distribution patterns. Each pattern is listed below, together with most of those species fitting that pattern.

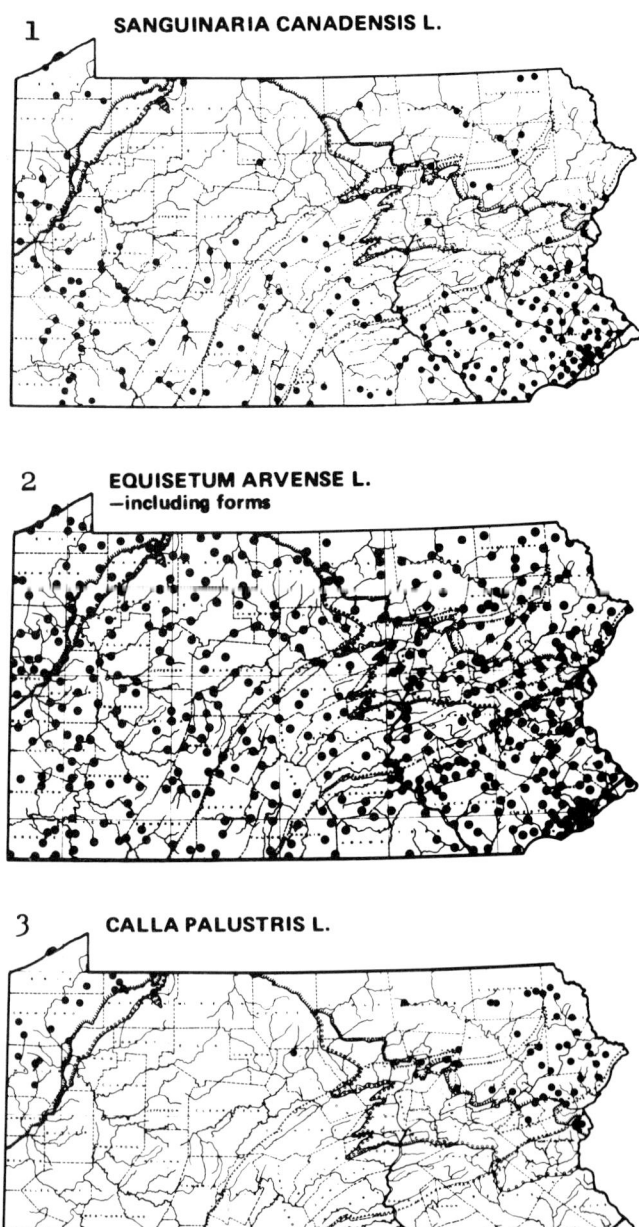

FIGURES 1-30. Distribution patterns of selected species. Maps reproduced (by permission) from the *Atlas of the Flora of Pennsylvania.*[13]

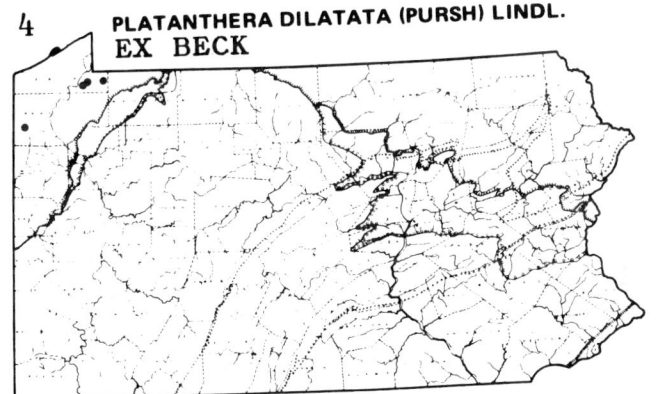

4 PLATANTHERA DILATATA (PURSH) LINDL. EX BECK

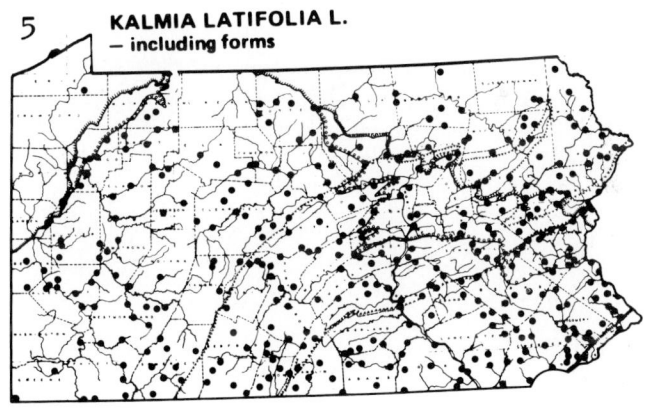

5 KALMIA LATIFOLIA L.
— including forms

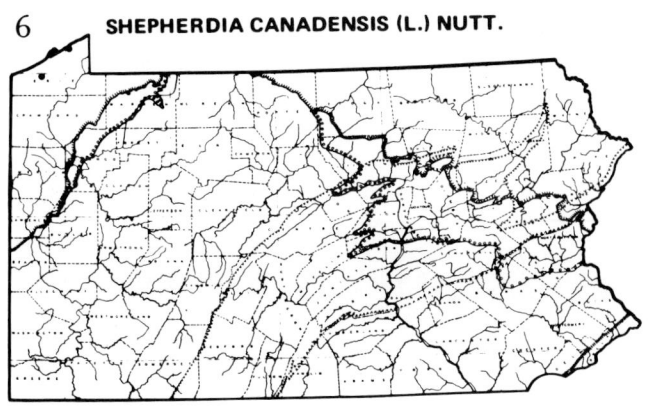

6 SHEPHERDIA CANADENSIS (L.) NUTT.

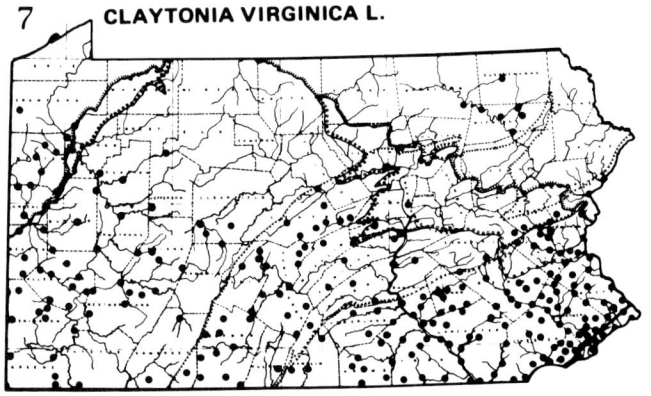

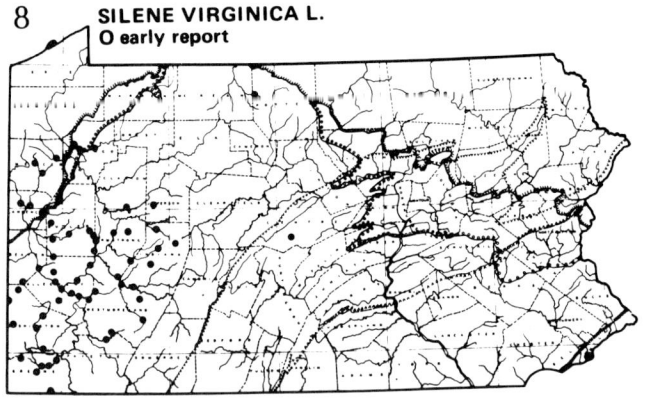

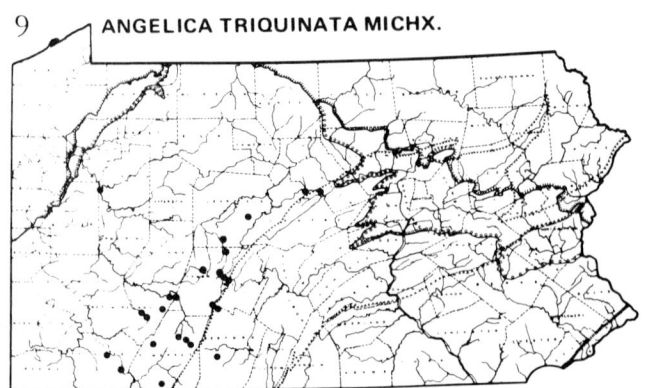

An Overview of the Vascular Plant Geography of Pennsylvania 117

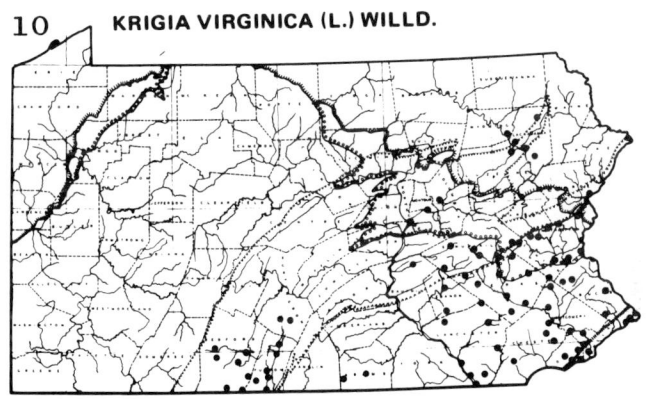

10 KRIGIA VIRGINICA (L.) WILLD.

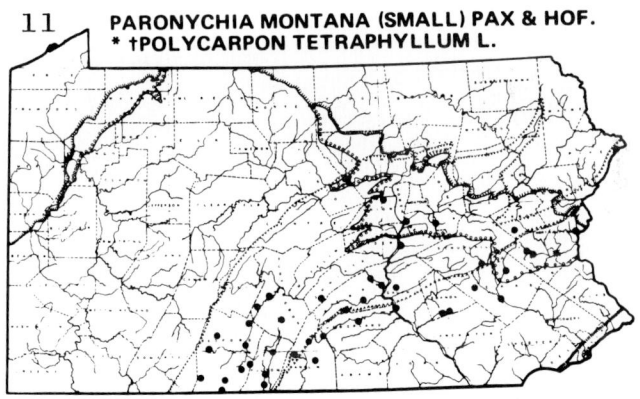

11 PARONYCHIA MONTANA (SMALL) PAX & HOF.
* †POLYCARPON TETRAPHYLLUM L.

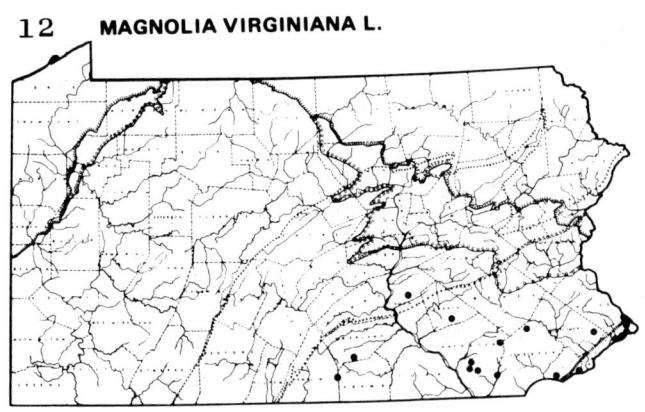

12 MAGNOLIA VIRGINIANA L.

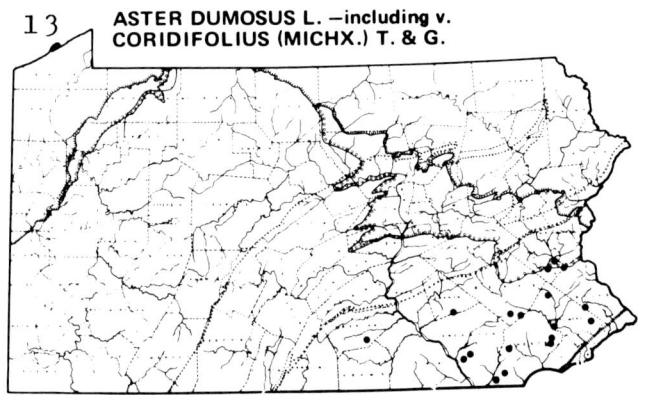

13 ASTER DUMOSUS L. —including v. CORIDIFOLIUS (MICHX.) T. & G.

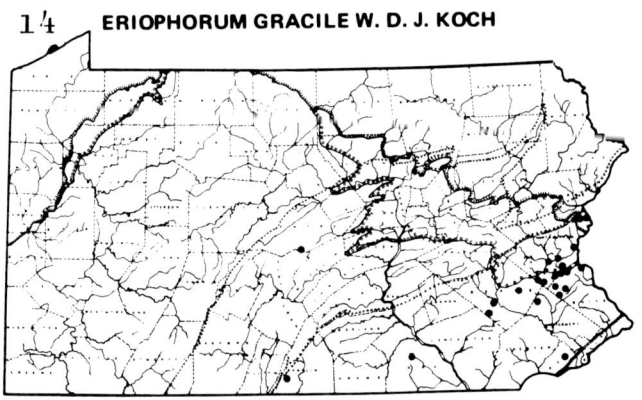

14 ERIOPHORUM GRACILE W. D. J. KOCH

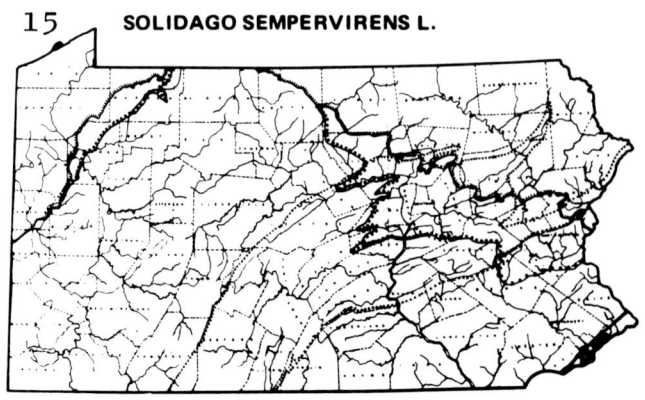

15 SOLIDAGO SEMPERVIRENS L.

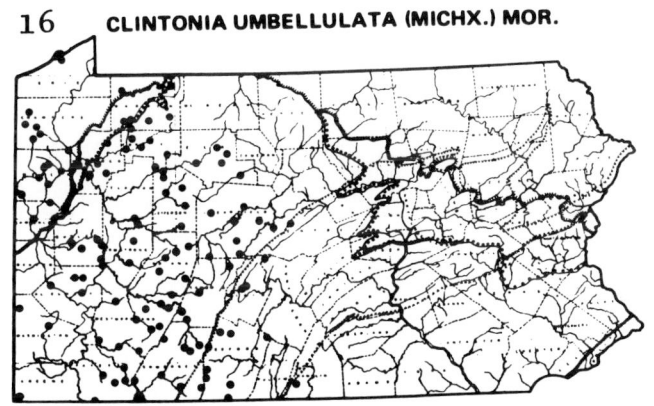

16 CLINTONIA UMBELLULATA (MICHX.) MOR.

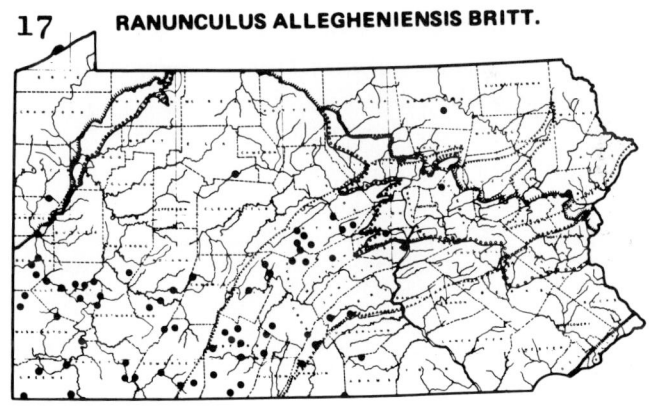

17 RANUNCULUS ALLEGHENIENSIS BRITT.

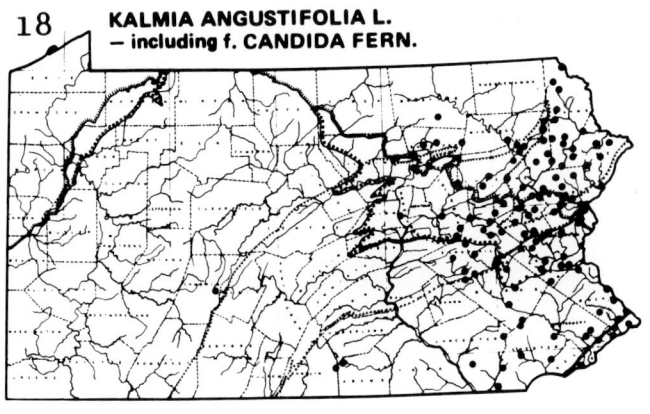

18 KALMIA ANGUSTIFOLIA L.
— including f. CANDIDA FERN.

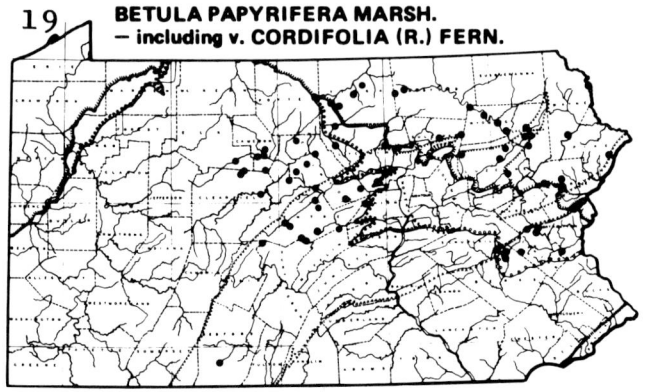

19 **BETULA PAPYRIFERA MARSH.**
— including v. **CORDIFOLIA (R.) FERN.**

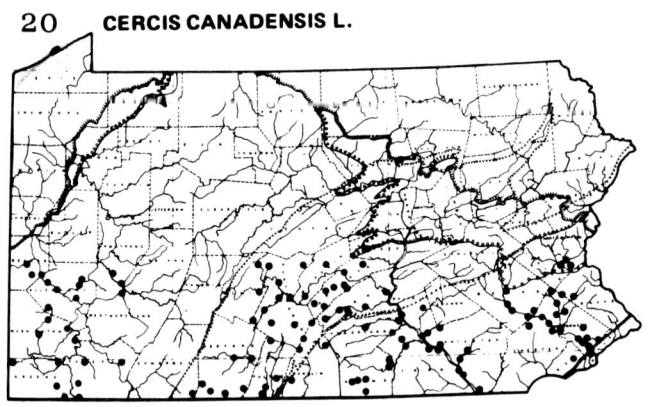

20 **CERCIS CANADENSIS L.**

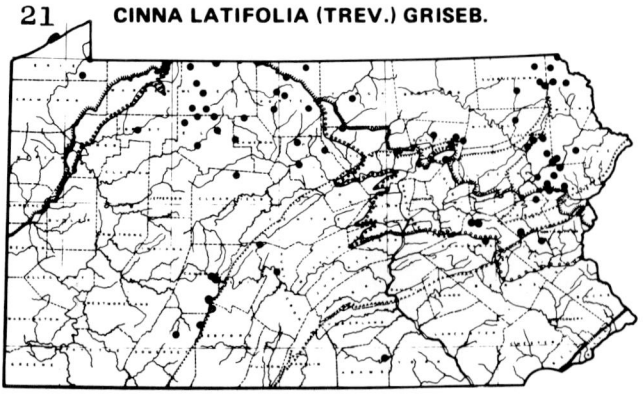

21 **CINNA LATIFOLIA (TREV.) GRISEB.**

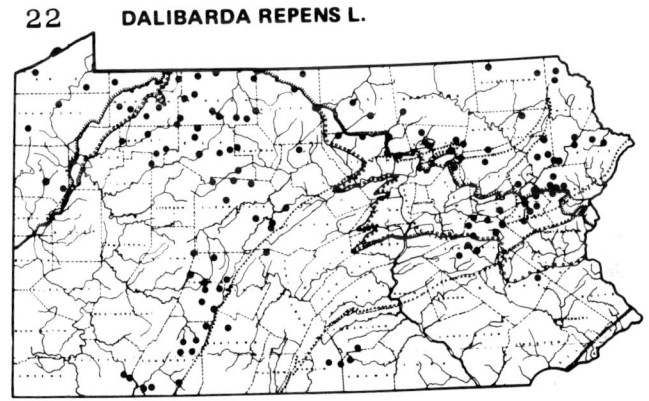

22 DALIBARDA REPENS L.

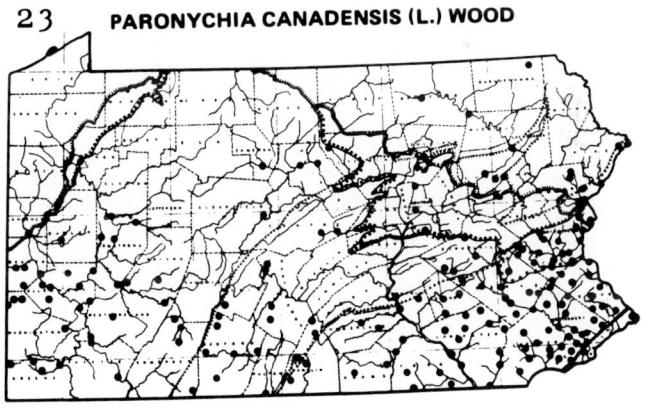

23 PARONYCHIA CANADENSIS (L.) WOOD

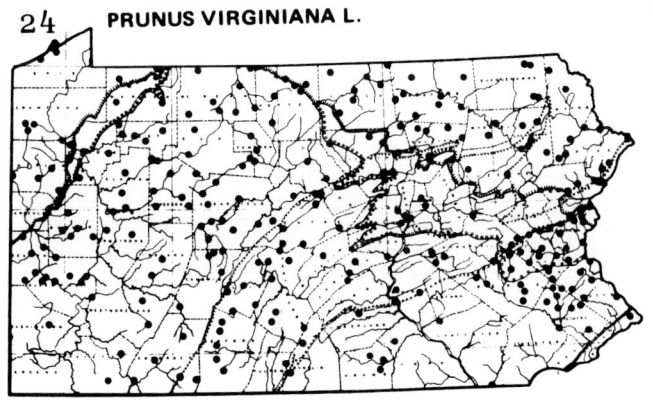

24 PRUNUS VIRGINIANA L.

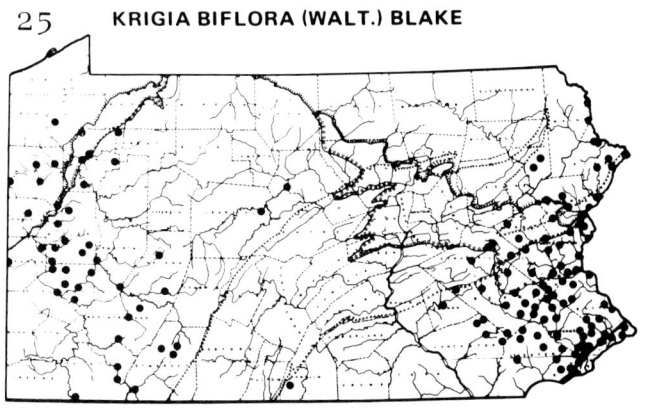

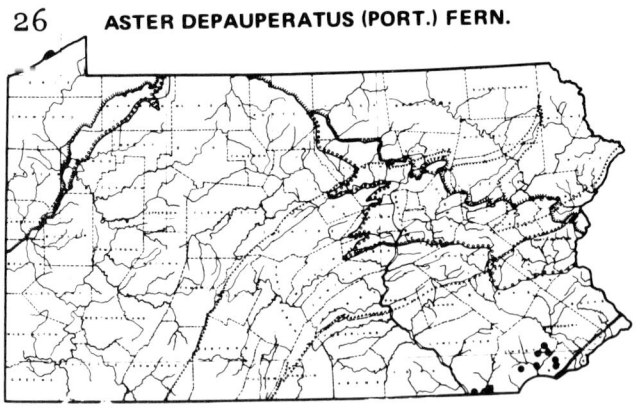

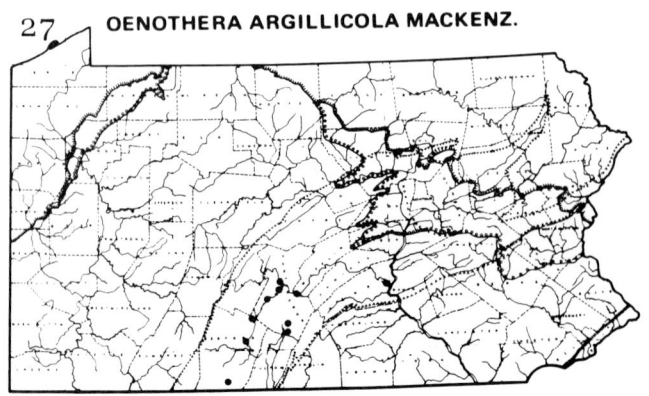

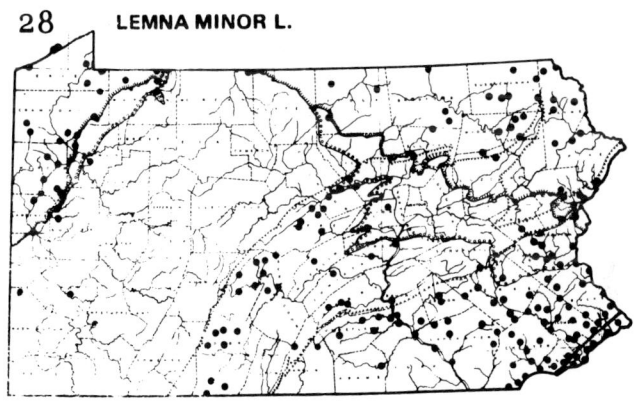

28 LEMNA MINOR L.

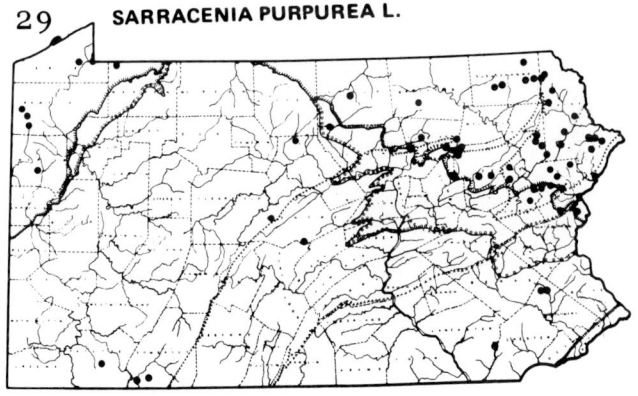

29 SARRACENIA PURPUREA L.

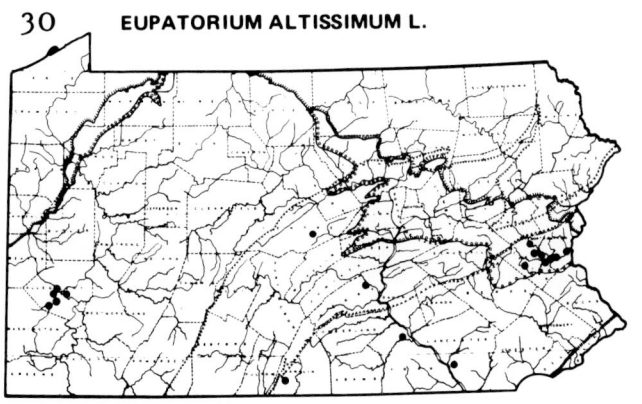

30 EUPATORIUM ALTISSIMUM L.

1. Common Native Species

At least 87 species are common or frequent throughout Pennsylvania. Some families (e.g., Apiaceae, Brassicaceae, Cyperaceae, Fabaceae, Juncaceae, Poaceae, Rosaceae) have relatively few widespread species, whereas other families (e.g., Polygonaceae, Ranunculaceae) have relatively more widespread common species. Exemplified by *Equisetum arvense* (Fig. 2), the widespread species include:

Acer rubrum L.; *A. saccharum* Marsh.; *Adiantum pedatum* L.; *Agrostis perennans* (Walt.) Tuckerm.; *Ambrosia artemisiifolia* L.; *Anemone virginiana* L.; *Aquilegia canadensis* L.; *Arisaema triphyllum* (L.) Schott; *Aster divaricatus* L.; *A. prenanthoides* Muhl. ex Willd.; *Botrychium virginianum* (L.) Sw.; *Cardamine pensylvanica* Muhl. ex Willd.; *Carex lurida* Wahlenb.; *C. vulpinoidea* Michx.; *Carpinus caroliniana* Walt.; *Castanea dentata* (Marsh.) Borkh.; *Clematis virginiana* L.; *Cryptotaenia canadensis* (L.) DC.; *Danthonia spicata* (L.) Beauv. ex Roem. & Schultes; *Dennstaedtia punctilobula* (Michx.) Moore; *Dichanthelium acuminatum* (Swartz) Gould & C.A. Clark var. *implicatum* (Scribn.) Gould & C A. Clark (= *Panicum implicatum* Scribn.); *Dryopteris intermedia* (Willd.) Gray; *D. marginalis* (L.) Gray; *Eleocharis obtusa* (Willd.) Schultes; *Epilobium coloratum* Biehler; *Equisetum arvense* L.; *Erigeron annuus* (L.) Pers.; *E. strigosus* Muhl.; *Eupatorium perfoliatum* L.; *E. rugosum* Houtt.; *Euthamia graminifolia* L. var. *nuttallii* (Greene) W. Stone (= *Solidago graminifolia* (L.) Salisbury var. *nuttallii* (Greene) Fern.); *Fagus grandifolia* Ehrh.; *Galium tinctorium* L.; *G. triflorum* Michx.; *Geranium maculatum* L.; *Geum canadense* Jacq. var. *canadense;* *Glyceria striata* (Lam.) Hitchc.; *Hamamelis virginiana* L.; *Hypericum mutilum* L.; *Impatiens capensis* Meerb.; *Juncus tenuis* Willd.; *Laportea canadensis* (L.) Wedd.; *Lobelia inflata* L.; *Lycopodium digitatum* Dill. ex A. Braun (= *L. flabelliforme* (Fern.) Blanch.); *Lycopus americanus* Muhl.; *Mimulus ringens* L.; *Mitchella repens* L.; *Mitella diphylla* L.; *Oenothera perennis* L.; *Onoclea sensibilis* L.; *Osmunda cinnamomea* L.; *O. claytoniana* L.; *Phytolacca americana* L.; *Pinus strobus* L.; *Plantago rugelii* Dcne.; *Polygonum pensylvanicum* L. var. *laevigatum* Fern.; *P. sagittatum* L.; *P. scandens* L.; *Polypodium virginianum* L.; *Polystichum acrostichoides* (Michx.) Schott; *Populus grandidentata* Michx.; *Potentilla simplex* Michx.; *Prunus serotina* Ehrh.; *Pteridium aquilinum* (L.) Kuhn var. *latiusculum* (Desv.) Underw. ex A. Heller; *Quercus alba* L.; *Q. rubra* L.; *Ranunculus abortivus* L.; *R. recurvatus* Poir.; *R. septentrionalis* Poir.; *Rudbeckia hirta* L.; *R. laciniata* L.; *Salix nigra* Marsh.; *S. sericea* Marsh.; *Sambucus canadensis* L.; *Scutellaria lateriflora* L.; *Sisyrinchium angustifolium* Mill.; *Solidago nemoralis* Ait.; *Smilacina racemosa* (L.) Desf.; *Thalictrum pubescens* Pursh; *Thelypteris noveboracensis* (L.) Nieuwl.; *Tsuga canadensis* (L.) Carr.; *Verbena hastata* L.; *Veronica americana* (Raf.) Schwein.; *V. officinalis* L.; *Viburnum acerifolium* L.; *Viola cucullata* Ait.; *V. sororia* Willd.

2. Glaciated Sections

In general, species confined for the most part to the glaciated regions (Fig. 32) inhabit acid bogs, cold swamps, and swampy thickets. Many are widespread northern species reaching their southern limits in Pennsylvania. Species of glaciated sections occur in one or both of these glaciated areas. Accordingly, a subclassification follows.

2.a. Species occurring in both the northwest and northeast glaciated sections (e.g., *Calla palustris*, Fig. 3).
Actaea rubra (Ait.) Willd.; *Andromeda glaucophylla* Link; *Calla palustris* L.; *Carex cryptolepis* Mackenz.; *C. flava* L.; *C. pauciflora* Lightfoot; *Decodon verticillatus* (L.) Ell.; *Elymus wiegandii* Fern.; *Eriophorum spissum* Fern.; *Ledum groenlandicum* Oed.; *Lonicera oblongifolia* (Goldie) Hook.; *Lysimachia thyrsiflora* L.; *Malaxis brachypoda* (Gray) Fern.; *Megalodonta beckii* (Torr.) Greene; *Nymphaea odorata* Ait.; *Platanthera hyperborea* (L.) Lindl. var. *huronesis* (Nutt.) Luer; *Potentilla palustris* (L.) Scop.; *Rumex orbiculatus* Gray; *Sarracenia purpurea* L.; *Smilacina trifolia* (L.) Desf.; *Utricularia minor* L.

2.b. Species occurring in the northwest glaciated section (e.g., *Platanthera dilatata*, Fig. 4).
Carex pseudocyperus L.; *Platanthera dilatata* (Pursh) Lindl. ex Beck; *Rumex verticillatus* L.; *Salix amygdaloides* Anderss.

2.c. Species occurring in the northeast glaciated section (e.g., *Kalmia polifolia*, Fig. 5).
Arceuthobium pusillum Peck; *Botrychium multifidum* (Gmel.) Rupr. var. *multifidum;* Carex cumulata (Bailey) Mackenz.; *C. mitchelliana* M.A. Curtis; *Chenopodium foggii* Wahl; *Drosera intermedia* Hayne; *Eleocharis olivacea* Torr.; *Eriocaulon septangulare* With.; *Eriophorum tenellum* Nutt.; *Kalmia polifolia* Wang.; *Lobelia dortmanna* L.; *Minuartia glabra* (Michx.) Mattf.; *Oryzopsis pungens* (Torr. ex Spreng.) Hitchc.; *Picea mariana* (Mill.) BSP.; *P. rubens* Sarg.; *Pinus resinosa* Ait.; *Polystichum braunii* (Spenn.) Fee; *Potentilla tridentata* Ait.; *Rhododendron canadense* (L.) Torr.; *Utricularia cornuta* Michx.; *U. purpurea* Walt.; *Viola selkirkii* Pursh ex Goldie; *Xyris montana* Ries

3. Major Physiographic Provinces

Seven major provinces of considerably unequal size occur within Pennsylvania (Fig. 31). Except for rare or infrequent species most native species occur in more

FIGURES 31-37. Physiographic, topographic, edaphic, and climatic features of Pennsylvania. Figs. 32-35 and 37 are used by permission courtesy of Ptolemy Press, Ltd., Grove City, Pa. Fig. 31 is based on a map produced by the Pennsylvania Topographic and Geologic Survey. Fig. 36 is based on data from *The National Atlas of the United States of America* (United States Department of Interior Geological Survey, Washington, D.C., 1970).

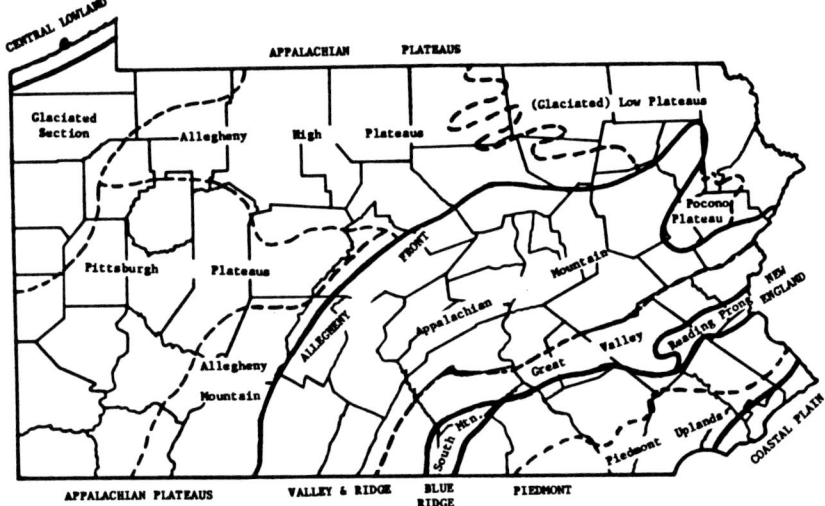

FIGURE 31. Physiographic Provinces of Pennsylvania.

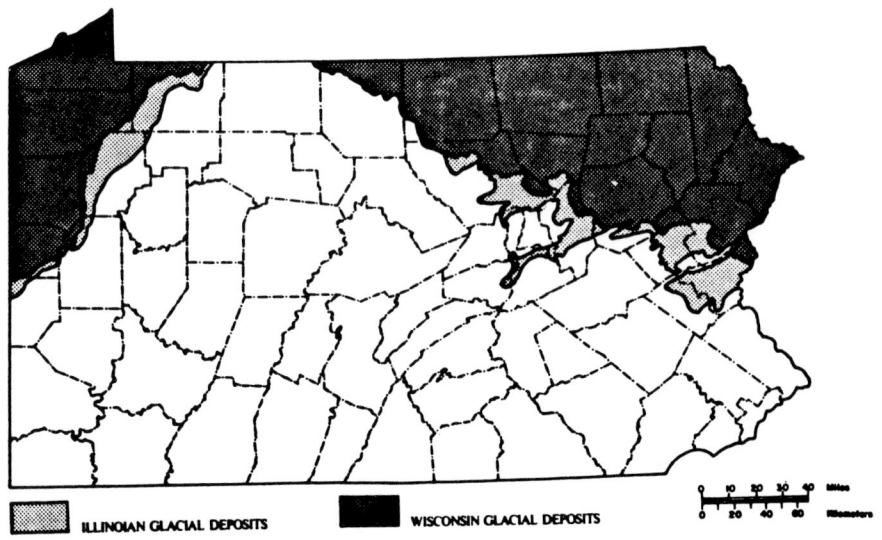

FIGURE 32. Glacial Deposits in Pennsylvania.

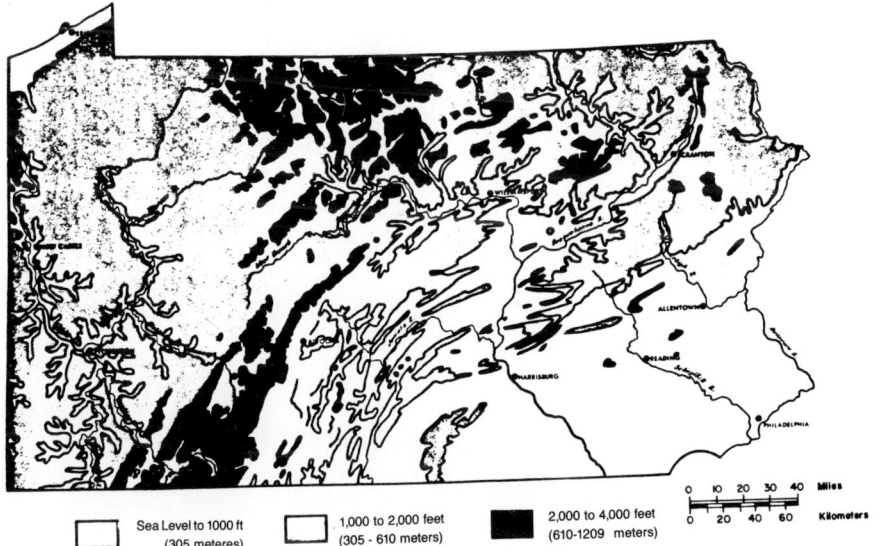

FIGURE 33. Generalized Elevations in Pennsylvania.

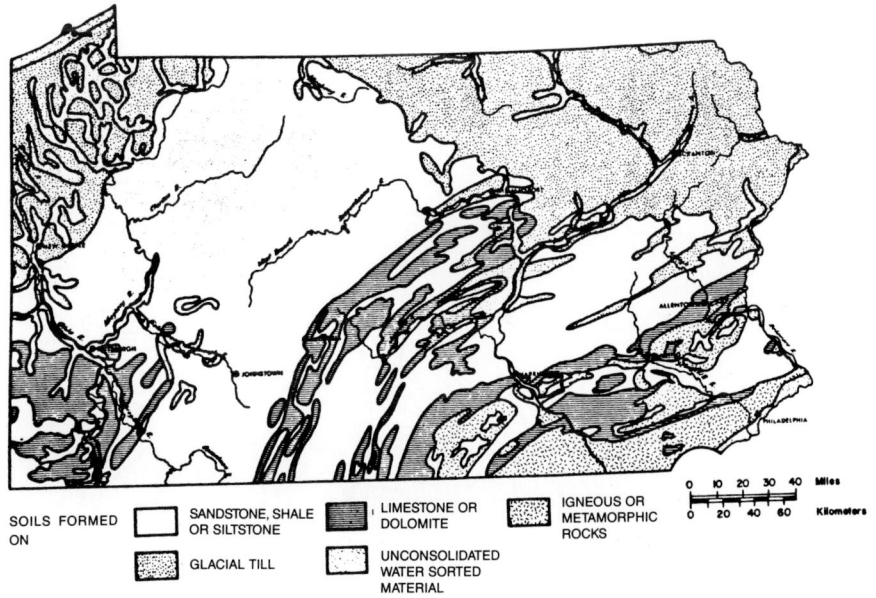

FIGURE 34. Parent Material for Soils in Pennsylvania.

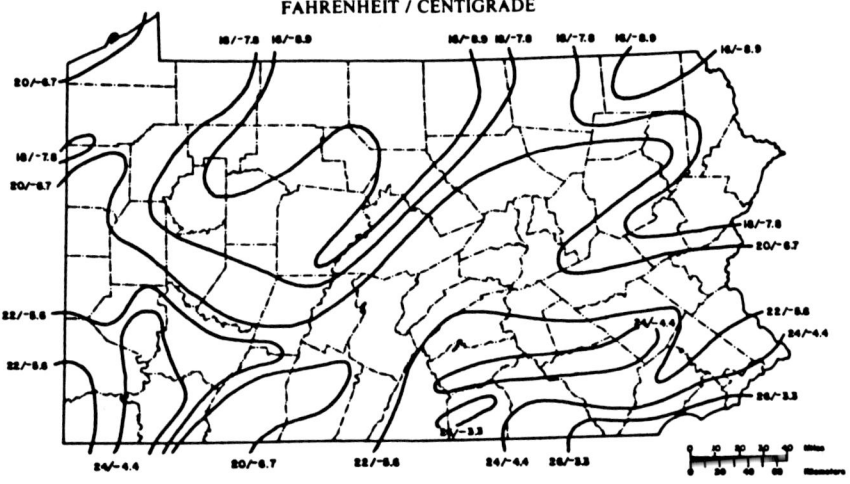

FIGURE 35. Mean Minimum January Temperature.

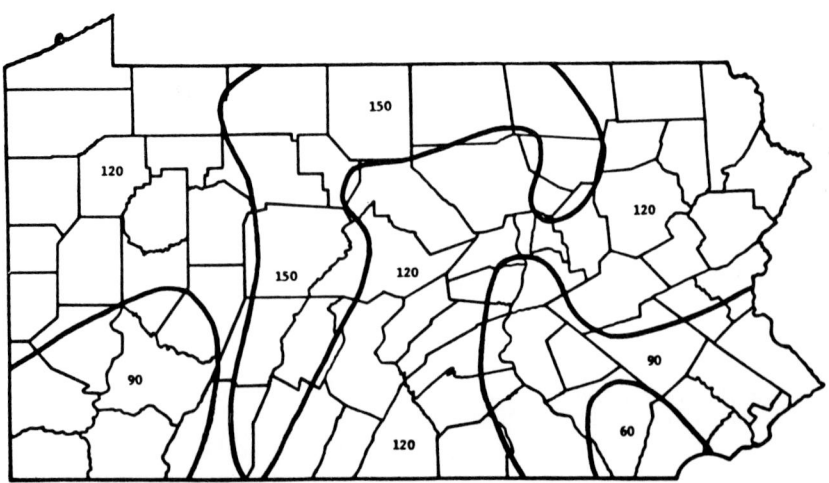

FIGURE 36. Mean Number of Days Below Freezing for Pennsylvania.

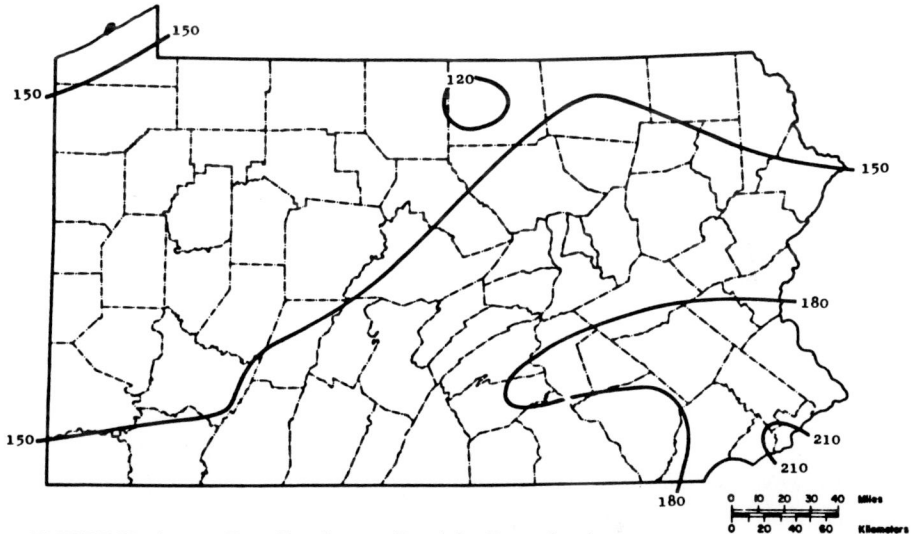

FIGURE 37. Average Frost-Free Season (Days) for Pennsylvania.

than one province. However, a number of species may be locally frequent, some of which are confined for the most part to a single province. Beginning at the northwestern corner and moving southeast, the patterns can be organized as follows.

3.a. Central Lowland Province. A few species (e.g., *Shepherdia canadensis*, Fig. 6) are confined to this Province, i.e., they border Lake Erie, and range, within North America, northeast and west of this region.
Ammophila breviligulata Fern.; *Carex laricina* Mackenz.; *C. substricta* (Kuek.) Mackenz.; *Equisetum variegatum* Schleich. ex F. Weber & D.M.H. Mohr; *Juncus alpinus* Vill. var. *rariflorus* Hartm.; *Potamogeton praelongus* Wulfen; *Prunus pumila* L.; *Shepherdia canadensis* (L.) Nutt.

3.b. Appalachian Plateaus Province. Consisting of 6 sections (Fig. 31), this Province is the largest within Pennsylvania. No species appears to be restricted chiefly to the Allegheny High Plateaus Section or the Pocono Plateau Section, but several species occur principally throughout the province and others are generally restricted to the Pittsburgh Plateaus Section or Allegheny Mountain Section; these are treated as subdivisions below.

3.b.1. Species (e.g., *Claytonia caroliniana*, Fig. 7) occurring generally throughout the Appalachian Plateaus Province and which range both north and south of Pennsylvania include:
Claytonia caroliniana Michx.; *Dentaria diphylla* Michx.; *Hepatica nobilis* P.

Mill. var. *acuta* (Pursh) Steyermark (= *H. acutiloba* DC.); *Ribes cynosbati* L.; *Tiarella cordifolia* L.; *Uvularia grandiflora* Sm. (absent northeastern Pa.)

3.b.2. Species (e.g., *Silene virginica,* Fig. 8) occurring in the Pittsburgh Plateaus Section are usually confined to the southwestern part and in general reach their northeastern North American limits here. They include:
Aconitum uncinatum L.; *Aesculus octandra* Marsh.; *Aster shortii* Lindl.; *Baptisia australis* (L.) R. Br.; *Clethra acuminata* Michx.; *Collinsia verna* Nutt.; *Delphinium tricorne* Michx.; *Helianthus microcephalus* T. & G.; *Hydrophyllum appendiculatum* Michx.; *Iodanthus pinnatifidus* (Michx.) Steud.; *Meehania cordata* (Nutt.) Britt.; *Oxydendrum arboreum* (L.) DC.; *Pyrularia pubera* Michx.; *Silene virginica* L.; *Trautvetteria caroliniensis* (Walt.) Vail; *Trillium nivale* Riddell; *T. sessile* L.

3.b.3. Species (e.g., *Angelica triquinata,* Fig. 9), restricted chiefly to the Allegheny Mountain Section, include the following seven species all of which reach their northeastern or northern limits in Pennsylvania.
Angelica triquinata Michx.; *Antennaria solitaria* Rydb.; *Cimicifuga americana* Michx.; *Cymophyllus fraseri* (Andr.) Mackenz.; *Hedyotis michauxii* Fosb.; *Phlox stolonifera* Sims; *Solidago roanensis* Porter

3.c. Provinces southeast of the Allegheny Front. A number of species such as *Krigia virginica* (Fig. 10), most commonly occurring in the central to southeastern regions, include:
Aronia prunifolia (Marsh.) Rehd.; *Asclepias amplexicaulis* Sm.; *A. verticillata* L.; *Asplenium ruta-muraria* L.; *Aster laevis* L.; *Betula nigra* L.; *Campanula rotundifolia* L.; *Carex conoidea* Schkuhr; *C. festucacea* Schkuhr ex Willd.; *C. lanuginosa* Michx.; *Celtis occidentalis* L.; *C. tenuifolia* Nutt. var. *tenuifolia* ; *Chenopodium standleyanum* Aellen; *Cuscuta compacta* Juss.; *Desmodium marilandicum* (L.) DC.; *Diodia teres* Walt.; *Helianthemum canadense* (L). Michx.; *Krigia virginica* (L.) Willd.; *Lechea puchella* Raf. (= *L. leggettii* Britt. & Holl.); *Minuartia michauxii* (Fenzl.) Farw. (= *Arenaria stricta* Michx.); *Pinus pungens* Lamb.; *Polygonum tenue* Michx.; *Prenanthes serpentaria* Pursh; *Ranunculus trichophyllus* Chaix; *Scutellaria integrifolia* L.; *Senecio pauperculus* Michx.; *Solidago rigida* L.; *Trillium cernuum* L.; *Verbena simplex* Lehm.; *Viola pedata* L.; *Zanthoxylum americanum* Mill.

3.d. Valley and Ridge Province. Several taxa are generally restricted to this Province, some occurring throughout while others are confined to the southwestern part, as subdivided below.

3.d.1. Taxa (e.g., *Paronychia montana,* Fig. 11) ranging largely throughout the VR Province include:

Arabis laevigata (Muhl.) Poir. var. *burkii* Porter; *Calystegia spithamaea* (L.) Pursh ssp. *purshiana* (Wherry) Brummitt; *Heuchera pubescens* Pursh; *Lithospermum canescens* (Michx.) Lehm.; *Paronychia montana* (Small) Pax & Hoffm.; *Rhus aromatica* Mill.; *Woodsia ilvensis* (L.) R. Br.

3.d.2. A number of species, many of which reach their northern limits in Pennsylvania, occur only in the southern part of the VR Province. These include the shale barren endemics (discussed below, 6.b—see also map for *Oenothera argillicola,* Fig. 27) and a number of other species such as:
Aristida curtissii (Gray) Nash; *Asplenium resiliens* Kunze; *Calamagrostis porteri* Gray; *Carex schweinitzii* Dewey; *Chrysogonum virginianum* L.; *Galium latifolium* Michx.; *Liatris scariosa* (L.) Willd. var. *scariosa; Ligusticum canadense* (L.) Britt.; *Paxistima canbyi* Gray; *Penstemon canescens* (Britt.) Britt.; *Polygala polygama* Walt.; *Prunus alleghaniensis* Port.; *Ruellia humilis* Nutt.; *Sedum telephioides* Michx.; *Spiraea betulifolia* Pallas ssp. *corymbosa* (Raf.) Taylor & McBryde (= *S. corymbosa* Raf.); *Thalictrum coriaceum* (Britt.) Small

3.e. Piedmont and Coastal Plain Province. Species (e.g.,*Magnolia virginiana,* Fig. 12) generally restricted to these two Provinces include:
Aletris farinosa L.; *Amelanchier canadensis* (L.) Medic.; *Andropogon elliottii* Chapm.; *Asclepias incarnata* L. var. *pulchra* (Ehrh.) Pers.; *Carex hirta* L.; *Cirsium horridulum* Michx.; *Crotalaria sagittalis* L.; *Cyperus lancastriensis* Porter; *C. odoratus* L.; *C. ovularis* (Michx.) Torr.; *Desmodium laevigatum* (Nutt.) DC.; *Digitaria filiformis* (L.) Koel.; *Eleocharis engelmannii* Steud.; *Eupatorium dubium* Willd.; *E. hyssopifolium* L.; *E. pilosum* Walt.; *Heteranthera reniformis* R. & P.; *Heterotheca mariana* (L.) Shinners; *Hieracium gronovii* L.; *Leucothoe racemosa* (L.) Gray; *Linum medium* (Planch.) Britt.; *Lycopodium adpressum* (Chapm.) Lloyd; *Lyonia mariana* (L.) D. Don; *Magnolia virginiana* L.; *Mikania scandens* (L.) Willd.; *Panicum anceps* Michx.; *Paspalum laeve* Michx.; *Quercus marilandica* Muenchh.; *Q. stellata* Wang.; *Sagittaria australis* (J.G. Sm.) Small; *Setaria geniculata* (Lam.) Beauv.; *Strophostyles helvola* (L.) Ell.; *S. umbellata* (Muhl. ex Willd.) Britt.; *Viburnum dentatum* L.; *V. nudum* L.; *Viola stoneana* House; *Zizania aquatica* L.

3.f. Piedmont Province. Relatively few species are generally restricted to the Piedmont Province. Some such as *Aster dumosus* (Fig. 13) and *Rudbeckia fulgida* are scattered throughout the Province, the latter occurring also in the Reading Prong area of the New England Province. The remaining species listed below are generally localized (SW, E, etc.) within the Piedmont; their localized areas are given in parentheses. All species in this group range southward, and a few northeastward, even to Maine or southern Ontario.
Aster dumosus L.; *Castanea pumila* (L.) Mill. (SW); *Elephantopus carolinianus* Raeusch. (SE); *Eupatorium aromaticum* L. (E); *Gaylussacia dumosa* (Andr.)

T. & G. (S-central, E); *Lobelia puberula* Michx. (S-central, E); *Phlox pilosa* L. (SW, E); *Polygala incarnata* L. (S-central); *Rudbeckia fulgida* Ait.; *Tipularia discolor* (Pursh) Nutt. (SE); *Tomanthera auriculata* (Michx.) Raf. (E); *Vernonia glauca* (L.) Willd. (SE)

3.g. New England Province. Three species, typified by *Eriophorum gracile* (Fig. 14) are concentrated in the Reading Prong area of the New England Province (Fig. 31). All are extralimital to the NE and W (SW) of Pennsylvania. *Eleocharis intermedia* J.A. Schultes; *Eriophorum gracile* W.D.J. Koch; *Scleria verticillata* Muhl. ex. Willd.

3.h. Coastal Plain Province. At least 22 species such as *Solidago sempervirens* (Fig. 15) are restricted to the Coastal Plain. These species occur regionally along the eastern coast, and occasionally inland (see Wherry[16] for a more detailed list). *Amaranthus cannabinus* (L.) Sauer; *Aster spectabilis* Ait.; *Bidens bidentoides* (Nutt.) Britt.; *Carex barrattii* Schwein. & Torr.; *Chasmanthium laxum* (L.) Yates (= *Uniola laxa* (L.) BSP.); *Echinochloa walteri* (Pursh) A. Heller; *Euphorbia ipecacuanhae* L.; *Euthumia tenuifolia* (Pursh) Greene (= *Solidago tenuifolia* Pursh); *Fimbristylis castanea* (Michx.) Vahl.; *Juncus dichotomus* Ell.; *Liquidambar styraciflua* L.; *Lobelia nuttallii* Roem. & Schultes; *Micranthemum micranthemoides* (Nutt.) Wettst.; *Quercus falcata* Michx.; *Q. phellos* L.; *Rhexia mariana* L.; *Scirpus smithii* Gray; *Sisyrinchium arenicola* Bickn.; *Solidago sempervirens* L.; *Spiranthes vernalis* Engelm. & Gray; *Triplasis purpurea* (Walt.) Chapm.; *Viola brittoniana* Poll.

4. Regional Species.

Many species occur in parts of 2 or more provinces. Although some of the following patterns are not sharply delimited (e.g., 4e from 4g), the regional species can be classified into 9 different patterns.

4.a. Species ranging in the western half (e.g., *Clintonia umbellulata*, Fig. 16). *Aralia spinosa* L.; *Clintonia umbellulata* (Michx.) Mor.; *Euonymus obovatus* Nutt.; *Magnolia acuminata* (L.) L.; *Phlox divaricata* L. ssp. *divaricata*; *Quercus imbricaria* Michx.; *Trillium grandiflorum* (Michx.) Sol.; *Vernonia gigantea* (Walt.) Trel.

4.b. Species ranging from central to southwestern Pennsylvania include *Aruncus dioicus* (Walt.) Fern. and *Ranunculus allegheniensis* Britt. (Fig. 17).

4.c. Species ranging in the eastern half (e.g., *Kalmia angustifolia,* Fig. 18). *Amianthium muscaetoxicum* (Walt.) Gray; *Aster linariifolius* L.; *Betula populifolia* Marsh.; *Carex emmonsii* Dewey; *C. vestita* Willd.; *Clethra alnifolia*

L.; *Gaylussacia frondosa* (L.) T. & G.; *Ilex laevigata* (Pursh) Gray; *Kalmia angustifolia* L.; *Lygodium palmatum* (Bernh.) Sw.; *Sagittaria graminea* Michx.; *Solidago odora* Ait.; *S. puberula* Nutt.; *Spiraea latifolia* (Ait.) Borkh.; *Stellaria alsine* Grimm; *Thelypteris simulata* (Dav.) Nieuwl.

4.d. Species ranging generally from central to northeastern Pennsylvania include *Betula papyrifera* Marsh. (Fig. 19) and *Cynoglossum boreale* Fern.

4.e. Species ranging across the southern part. Many species fit the *Cercis canadensis* pattern (Fig. 20) in that they are found generally in the southern half of Pennsylvania. In general, such species are absent or infrequent in the Allegheny Mountain Section, but otherwise they occur in the southwestern, south-central, and southeastern region.
Acalypha virginica L.; *Agastache nepetoides* (L.) Ktze.; *Aristolochia serpentaria* L.; *Ascelpias purpurascens* L.; *A. viridiflora* Raf.; *Aster patens* Ait. var. *phlogifolius* (Muhl. ex Willd.) Nees; *A. radula* Ait.; *Bidens bipinnata* L.; *Brickellia eupatorioides* (L.) Shinners; *Carex frankii* Kunth; *C. glaucodea* Tuckerm.; *C. leavenworthii* Dewey; *C. molesta* Mackenz.; *Cassia fasciculata* Michx.; *Celtis tenuifolia* Nutt. var *georgiana* (Small) Fern. & Schubert *(=C. georgiana* Small); *Cercis canadensis* L.; *Chaerophyllum procumbens* (L.) Crantz; *Cirsium altissimum* (L.) Spreng.; *Corydalis flavula* (Raf.) DC.; *Cuphea viscosissima* Jacq. *(=C. petiolata* (L.) Koehne*); Cynoglossum virginianum* L.; *Dentaria heterophylla* Nutt.; *Desmodium canescens* (L.) DC.; *Dioscorea quaternata* (Walt.) J. Gmel.; *Galium concinnum* T. & G.; *Geum vernum* (Raf.) T. & G.; *G. virginianum* L.; *Hybanthus concolor* (T. F. Forst.) Spreng.; *Hydrastis canadensis* L.; *Ipomoea pandurata* (L.) G. F. W. Mey.; *Jeffersonia diphylla* (L.) Pers.; *Morus rubra* L.; *Obolaria virginica* L.; *Parietaria pensylvanica* Muhl. ex Willd.; *Paronychia fastigiata* (Raf.) Fern. var. *fastigiata; Plantago virginica* L.; *Poa cuspidata* Nutt.; *P. sylvestris* Gray; *Quercus macrocarpa* Michx.; *Q. muhlenbergii* Engelm.; *Ranunculus micranthus* Nutt.; *Sabatia angularis* (L.) Pursh; *Scutellaria nervosa* Pursh; *Staphylea trifolia* L.; *Thalictrum revolutum* DC.; *Trichostema brachiatum* L.; *Verbesina alternifolia* (L.) Britt.; *Viburnum prunifolium* L.; *Vitis vulpina* L.

4.f. Species occurring chiefly in upland regions. A number of species occur usually in regions above 305m (1000 ft). In general, such areas are northwest of the Great Valley Section of the Valley and Ridge Province (Figs. 31 and 33). Although the distinctions are not clearcut, several subgroups can be recognized.

4.f.1. Regions above 610 m (2000 ft) (Fig. 33). Several species (e.g., *Cinna latifolia,* Fig. 21) appear confined to the highest elevations in Pennsylvania, including the following:
Carex brunnescens (Pers.) Poir. var. *sphaerostachya* (Tuckerm.) Kuek.; *C. plan-*

taginea Lam.; *Cinna latifolia* (Trev.) Griseb.; *Lycopodium annotinum* L.; *Poa saltuensis* Fern. & Wieg.

4.f.2. Regions above 305m (1000 ft).

4.f.2.a. A number of species (e.g., *Dalibarda repens,* Fig. 22) occur in the northern half of Pennsylvania and range southward to the Allegheny Mountain Section and (occasionally) South Mountain. These species are generally infrequent or absent in the Pittsburgh Plateaus Section.

Acer pensylvanicum L.; *Carex leptonervia* Fern.; *Circaea alpina* L.; *Clintonia borealis* (Ait.) Raf.; *Cornus canadensis* L.; *Dalibarda repens* L.; *Ilex montana* T. & G.; *Lonicera canadensis* Bartr.; *Nemopanthus mucronata* (L.) Trel.; *Oxalis montana* Raf.; *Poa alsodes* Gray; *Prunus pensylvanica* L.f.; *Streptopus roseus* Michx.; *Thelypteris phegopteris* (L.) Slosson (= *Phegopteris connectilis* (Michx.) Watt.); *Trillium undulatum* Willd.; *Trientalis borealis* Raf.; *Viburnum lantanoides* Michx. (= *V. alnifolium* Marsh.); *Waldsteinia fragarioides* (Michx.) Tratt.

4.f.2.b. Regions above 610 m (2000 ft) southward but ranging northward into Allegheny High Plateaus Section and the northwest Glaciated Section at elevations from 305-610 m (1000-2000 ft). These species are absent in eastern and northeastern Pennsylvania.

Carex woodii Dewey; *Disporum lanuginosum* (Michx.) Nicholson; *Phlox stolonifera* Sims; *Viola hastata* Michx.

4.f.2.c. Regions above 610 m (2000 ft) southward, but ranging northward into the Allegheny High Plateaus Section and the northeast Glaciated Low Plateaus Section at elevations from 305-610 m (1000-2000 ft). Two species, *Aster acuminatus* Michx. and *Carex baileyi* Britt., are absent from the northwest glaciated section and are uncommon in the west-central portion of the Pittsburgh Plateaus Section.

4.f.2.d. Regions above 305 m (1000 ft) in the northern half of Pennsylvania, but more or less absent in the southern upland regions. Two species, *Eupatorium maculatum* L. and *Poa palustris* L., are wide-ranging northern species occurring in the Appalachian Mountains south of Pennsylvania. Two other species, *Carex arctata* Boott and *C. deweyana* Schwein., apparently reach their southern limit in Pennsylvania.

4.g. Taxa generally south of the Glaciated Sections and Allegheny High Plateaus Section (Fig. 31), illustrated by *Paronychia canadensis* (Fig. 23), include a number of wide-ranging, well-known taxa. Many of these species have ranges approximating the *Cercis canadensis* pattern (4.e.; Fig. 20) but, at present, we believe both patterns are of biogeographic interest.

Agrimonia parviflora Ait.; *A. pubescens* Wallr.; *Alnus serrulata* (Ait.) Willd.; *Ambrosia trifida* L.; *Arnoglossum atriplicifolia* (L.) H. Robs. (= *Cacalia atriplicifolia* L.; *Asclepias quadrifolia* Jacq.; *A. tuberosa* L.; *Asplenium platyneuron* L. BSP.; *Aster lateriflorus* (L.) Britt.; *Aureolaria pedicularia* (L.) Raf.; *Campanula americana* L.; *Carex squarrosa* L.; *Cerastium nutans* Raf.; *Chenopodium missouriense* Aellen; *Claytonia virginica* L.; *Cornus florida* L.; *Epigaea repens* L.; *Eupatorium purpureum* L.; *Galium aparine* L.; *Heuchera americana* L.; *Hieracium venosum* L.; *Hypoxis hirsuta* (L.) Cov.; *Isotria verticillata* (Muhl. ex Willd.) Raf.; *Liparis liliifolia* (L.) Rich. ex Ker-Gawl.; *Paronychia canadensis* (L.) Wood; *Phryma leptostachya* L.; *Physalis subglabrata* Mackenz. & Bush; *Pilea pumila* (L.) Gray; *Polygonatum biflorum* (Walt.) Ell.; *Porteranthus trifoliatus* (L.) Britt. (= *Gillenia trifoliata* (L.) Moench); *Quercus montana* Willd.; *Q. prinoides* Willd.; *Ranunculus hispidus* Michx. var. *hispidus* ; *Rhododendron periclymenoides* (Michx.) Shinners; *Rosa carolina* L.; *Sanguinaria canadensis* L.; *Sassafras albidum* (Nutt.) Nees var. *albidum* & var. *molle* (Raf.) Fern.; *Sedum ternatum* Michx.; *Thalictrum thalictroides* (L.) Eames & Boivin (= *Anemonella thalictroides* (L.) Spach); *Vernonia noveboracensis* (L.) Michx.

4.h. Species absent from the southwestern Pittsburgh Plateaus Section and the Piedmont Uplands Section of Lancaster and York Counties (Fig. 31). A few species, generally common or frequent throughout Pennsylvania, appear to be absent or uncommon in the two areas indicated above. These lacunae may be due to incomplete sampling of the flora, but, at present, several species, such as *Prunus virginiana* (Fig. 24), appear to have this pattern.

Betula lenta L.; *Carex normalis* Mackenz.; *Gaultheria procumbens* L.; *Lycopodium lucidulum* Michx.; *Mianthemum canadense* Desf.; *Populus tremuloides* Michx.; *Prunus virginiana* L.; *Scirpus cyperinus* (L.) Kunth; *Scrophularia lanceolata* Pursh; *Veronica americana* (Raf.) Schwein.

4.i. Other patterns. Some species do not fit the patterns specified above. Though many other possible patterns could be recognized, only a few of these exceptional cases are singled out below.

1. *Commandra umbellata* (L.) Nutt.—common southeast of the Allegheny Front and western portion of the Pittsburgh Plateaus Section with scattered localities in the glaciated areas, but notably absent from the southwestern and central regions of the Pittsburgh Plateaus Section and most of the Allegheny High Plateaus Section.

2. *Eupatorium fistulosum* Barratt ex Hook.—common except in the northeastern Glaciated Low Plateaus Section.

3. All Lemnaceae (*Lemma, Spirodela, Wolffia* spp.) are generally absent from the Appalachian Plateaus Province.

4. *Orontium aquaticum* L.—frequent in the Allegheny Mountain Section,

eastern part of the Glaciated Low Plateaus Section, and southeast of the Allegheny Front but rare elsewhere.

5. *Sida hermaphrodita* (L.) Rusby—infrequent along the Juniata River (including Raystown Branch) and the Lower Susquehanna River (one locality elsewhere).

6. *Solidago juncea* Ait.—absent in the northwestern Glaciated Section, but generally common elsewhere.

5. Disjuncts within Pennsylvania.

The following species are separated distributionally, in most cases (e.g., *Krigia biflora,* Fig. 25) with a conspicuous gap between the areas indicated below, with illustrative examples given for each pattern.

5.a. Western/eastern regions
Cirsium pumilum (Nutt.) Spreng.; *Krigia biflora* (Walt.) Blake; *Spiraea tomentosa* L.; *Veronicastrum virginicum* (L.) Farw.

5.b. Southwestern/southeastern regions
Andropogon glomeratus (Walt.) BSP.; *Cyperus tenuifolius* (Steud.) Dandy; *Gentiana saponaria* L.; *Passiflora lutea* L.; *Phacelia purshii* Buckl.; *Stellaria pubera* Michx.; *Valeriana pauciflora* Michx.

5.c. Northwestern Glaciated Section/extreme east-central (esp. Reading Prong of the New England Province) regions
Cyperus schweinitzii Torr.; *Eriophorum viridi-carinatum* (Engelm.) Fern.; *Parnassia glauca* Raf.; *Peltandria virginica* (L.) Schott & Endl. (general throughout extreme eastern Pa.); *Trollius laxus* Salisb. (also one record in central Pa.)

5.d. Western (chiefly west-central)/southeastern regions
Liatris spicata (L.) Willd.; *Selaginella apoda* (L.) Spring; *Rudbeckia speciosa* Wender.; *Stenanthium gramineum* (Ker-Gawl.) Morong

5.e. Northwestern Glaciated Section/eastern (non-glaciated) regions
Bidens coronata (L.) Britt.; *Carex seorsa* Howe; *Quercus palustris* Muenchh.; *Ranunculus longirostris* Godr.

5.f. Northwestern Glaciated Section/northeastern Glaciated Low Plateaus Section and southeast of Allegheny Front
Carex comosa Boott; *Lemna minor* L. (cf. 4.i.3.); *Spirodela polyrhiza* (L.) Schleid.

5.g. Northwestern Glaciated Section/Centre County
Anemone cylindrica Gray

5.h. Southwestern Pittsburgh Plateaus Section/southeast of the Allegheny Front
Diospyros virginiana L.; *Hedyotis purpurea* (L.) T. & G. var. *longifolia* (Gaertn.) Fosb.; *Pinus virginiana* Mill.; *Tridens flavus* (L.) Hitchc.

5.i. Allegheny Mountain Section, adjacent southern Valley and Ridge Province/east-central Valley and Ridge Province
Juncus debilis Gray; *Menziesia pilosa* (Michx.) Juss.

5.j. Allegheny Mountain Section, adjacent southern Valley and Ridge Province/New England Province
Saxifraga micranthidifolia (Haw.) Steud.

5.k. Central Pennsylvania/New England Province
Phlox ovata L.

5.l. Allegheny Mountain Section/northeastern upland and glaciated areas
Gentiana linearis Froel.; *Gentianella quinquefolia* (L.) Small ssp. *quinquefolia* (= *Gentiana quinquefolia* L.)

5.m. Central Pennsylvania/Glaciated Low Plateaus Section
Carex oligosperma Michx.; *Liatris scariosa* (L.) Willd. var. *nieuwlandii* Lunnell (= *L. borealis* Nutt.)

5.n. Northwestern Glaciated Section/central Pennsylvania
Cypripedium reginae Walt.

6. Regional Endemics
Several species are restricted to two specialized habitats extending southward to adjacent states. Both support an endemic flora which is increasingly threatened by human activities. These include the serpentine and shale barrens of south-central and southeastern Pennsylvania.

6.a. Serpentine barrens of the southern Piedmont Uplands Section. A chain of roughly thirty outcrops ranges from Delaware County to southern Lancaster County and extends into adjacent Maryland.[17] According to Miller,[17] the mature forest communities developed on serpentine versus those on nearby schist substrata are only 7.1% similar. It appears that low levels of P, Ca, and K, coupled with high levels of Mg, Ni, and Cr and a shallow soil profile are restrictive parameters.[18] Those species (e.g., *Aster depauperatus,* Fig. 26) generally restricted (within Pennsylvania) to the serpentine barrens are listed below (see Wherry[19] for a more comprehensive list).
Aster depauperatus (Porter) Fern.; *Carex bicknelli* Britt.; *Cerastium arvense*

L. var. *villosissimum* Pennell; *Dichanthelium dichotomum* (L.) Gould (= *Panicum annulum* Ashe); *Fimbristylis annua* (All.) Roem. & Schultes (= *F. baldwiniana* (Schultes) Torr.), NE limits in SE Pa.; *Sporobolus heterolepis* (Gray) Gray, SE limits of range in SE Pa.; *Talinum teretifolium* Pursh

6.b. Mid-Appalachian Shale Barrens. Ranging from south-central Pennsylvania to southwestern Virginia and adjacent West Virginia, these Paleozoic shaly outcrops generally have a steep southern exposure, often a stream undercutting the base, weather resistant fissile shale fragments and a relatively sparse vegetation in contrast to the surrounding mesophytic forest.[20] The sparseness of the vegetation appears to be due chiefly to low moisture conditions at the bare soil surface plus the high insolation temperatures unfavorable to the successful development of competitive colonizers. The endemics appear to require adequate root space and high light intensity (i.e., the endemics are obligate heliophytes). Eighteen taxa are generally confined to the shale barrens,[20] and of these, 3 are strict endemics (denoted by an asterisk) illustrated by *Oenothera argillicola* (Fig. 27; no longer found at many of the sites shown in Fig. 21), and 5 preferential endemics occur in Pennsylvania.
Antennaria virginica Stebbins; *Calystegia spithamaea* L. ssp. *purshiana* (Wherry) Brummitt; *Oenothera argillicola* Britt.*; *Paronychia montana* (Small) Pax & Hoffm.; *Senecio antennariifolius* Britt.*; *Solidago arguta* Ait. var. *harrisii* (Steele) Cronq.; *Taenidia montana* (Mackenz.) Cronq. (= *Pseudotaenidia montana* Mackenz.); *Trifolium virginicum* Small*

7. Widespread Disjunct Endemics

At least 3 species in Pennsylvania represent wide disjuncts whose centers of range lie considerably distanced from this area.
Carex geyeri Boott (Centre Co., mountains of Colorado and westward); *Juncus gymnocarpus* Cov. (mountains of Lebanon and Schuykill Cos., mountains of North Carolina and Tennessee, and Walton Co., Florida); *Montia chamissoi* (Led. ex Spreng.) Greene (Wayne Co., Minnesota and westward)

8. Plants of Special Habitats

Numerous species are more or less restricted in range due to specialized habitats. For example, soils derived from limestone or dolomite occur in the southern half of Pennsylvania, and, consequently, obligate calciphiles will be found only in this region. Likewise, few natural bogs are found in the southern half; hence, acidiphiles requiring such habitats will occur chiefly in the northern half. In addition to the barrens treated above, some of these specialized habitats together with a few examples are listed here.

8.a. Aquatics. Many species occur in wetland areas, such as ponds, rivers and streams. Some are widespread, e.g., *Justicia americana* (L.) Vahl, *Lemna minor*

L. (Fig. 28), and *Sagittaria latifolia* Willd., while others, for obscure reasons, are rare (e.g., many species of *Potamogeton*). A comparative study of the distributional patterns of aquatics would be instructive.

8.b. Bogs and marshes. A number of bogs occur, especially in the glaciated regions, and like aquatic habitats, have a distinctive flora consisting of species belonging to many families. *Sarracenia purpurea* L. (Fig. 29) illustrates the general distribution of a bog species, though it no longer occurs in many of the recorded sites.

8.c. Calcareous marshes. Such marshes are scattered infrequently throughout the southern half of Pennsylvania (see Fig. 34 showing occurrence of limestone or dolomite). Species characteristic of this type of wetland include: *Carex lacustris* Willd.; *C. prairea* Dewey; *C. schweinitzii* Dewey; *C. tetanica* Schkuhr; *Juncus balticus* Willd.; *Ribes hirtellum* Michx.; *Trollius laxus* Salisb.

8.d. Limestone outcrops. Calciphiles occurring on limestone rock ledges or thin soils derived from limestone or dolomite (e.g., *Eupatorium altissimum*, Fig. 30) include:
Arabis lyrata L.; *Aster oblongifolius* Nutt.; *Camptosorus rhizophyllus* (L.) Link; *Carex oligocarpa* Schkuhr; *Cystopteris bulbifera* (L.) Bernh.; *Eupatorium altissimum* L.; *Paxistima canbyi* Gray; *Pellaea atropurpurea* (L.) Link; *P. glabella* Mett. ex Kuhn; *Staphylea trifolia* L.; *Zanthoxylum americanum* Mill.

8.e. Sandy Dolomitic Barrens. Although "The Barrens" of Nittany Valley in Centre and Huntingdon Counties support an unusual flora due chiefly to a deficiency of mineral nutrients, extreme acidity of the soil and markedly dry surface areas,[6] there are no known strict endemics to this region. Westerfeld[21] and Wherry[16] provide lists of typical plants, the latter noting similar species found also in the New Jersey Pine Barrens. Several distinctive species include *Calamagrostis porteri* Gray, *Liatris scariosa* (L.) Willd. var. *nieuwlandii* Lunnell (= *L. borealis* Nutt.; rare in Pennsylvania—occurs elsewhere in Pennsylvania only in Luzerne Co.), *Lindernia anagallidea* (Michx.) Pennell, and *Woodwardia virginica* (L.) Sm.

DISCUSSION

In the preceding section we outlined a number of distributional patterns perceived within the native flora of Pennsylvania. The biogeographical problem is to suggest reasonable explanations of these patterns. Obviously some distribution patterns can be correlated with specific and sharply delimited habitats, e.g., serpentine and shale barrens, acid bogs, and calcareous marshes.

But why some species are common while others are rare or infrequent poses a set of general problems we are unable to resolve on the basis of our present understanding of the precise autecological requirements of such species. And we scarcely know enough about the biohistory of the flora, especially the herbaceous flora, to speculate on the present distributional patterns based on biohistory alone. That is, we lack sufficient information concerning the precise impacts of Pleistocene glaciations to be able to explain the various restricted ranges treated in this paper. Aside from these broad disclaimers, however, a few general correlations seem to be relatively convincing.

Mean annual temperatures and mean maximum mid-summer temperatures within Pennsylvania appear too uniform to have any significant causal basis for the various distributional patterns already delineated above. Mean annual temperatures range from 7.8°C (46°F) in some of the northern tier counties to 12.2°C (54°F) in extreme southeastern Pennsylvania, whereas the mean maximum July temperature is 26°C (78°F) in the Pocono Plateau Section and 31°C (88°F) in the southeastern Piedmont and Coastal Plain areas. Likewise, the mean annual precipitation is fairly uniform, ranging from a low of 91 cm (36 in) in several areas to a high of 122 cm (48 in) in extreme east-central Pennsylvania.[22]

The key variables appear to be topography and elevation (Figs. 31, 33), soil (limestone, sandy loam, etc.), including glacial deposits (glacial till, Fig. 32), the mean minimum January temperature (Fig. 35), the mean number of days below freezing (Fig. 36), and, possibly, the length of the frost-free growing season (Fig. 37). The broad patterns emerging from correlating the various distributions with topography, climate, and edaphic features, appear to be the following.

1. The glaciated areas (Figs. 31, 32) have a number of cold acid peat bogs supporting a number of species generally restricted to this region (Results, 2). Because such habitats are infrequent elsewhere within Pennsylvania, this specialized habitat alone may explain the distributional patterns of many species in this group (cf. *Kalmia polifolia,* Fig. 5).

2. Considerable autecological work will be required to assess the factors underlying the distributional patterns associated with the major provinces. Species restricted to the Central Lowland and Coastal Plain Provinces appear to be influenced by hydrologic factors and possibly, temperature regimes. Temperature and biogeographic history may account for a number of species restricted to the southwestern part of the Appalachian Plateaus Province, although similar temperatures, elevations and soil types occur in southeastern Pennsylvania yet the species (listed in Results, 3.b.2) do not occur there! It could be suggested that those species restricted to southwestern Pennsylvania cannot migrate eastward due to the relatively lower temperature regimes in the central part (see Fig. 36). Indeed, this low temperature barrier, and the related shorter growing season, appear to be one of the best correlations of occurrence of species in the southwestern or southeastern parts of Pennsylvania. But why certain species that appear to be confined to the Allegheny Mountain Section (Results,

3.b.3) are unknown in north-central Pennsylvania where elevations and soil types are similar remains a puzzle. Possibly because these are southern Appalachian species reaching their northeastern limits in the Allegheny Mountain Section, the length of the frost-free season and mean minimum January temperature may be limiting factors. The numerous species confined to one or more provinces southeast of the Allegheny Front(see Fig. 31) may first be restricted by temperature (reflected also in the length of the growing season—see Figs. 36, 37), and second, by soil types (e.g., limestone) not found north of the Allegheny Front. Again, many of these species would appear compatible with environmental conditions in the southwestern areas of Pennsylvania but are absent in that region. The important causal factors may actually be biogeographical rather than intrinsic physiological tolerances to a given suite of environmental parameters. That is, the migratory routes (dispersal due chiefly to chance?) of many of these species did not result in colonizing all possible sites and therefore edaphic and climatic factors are not correlated necessarily with the distribution patterns of many species localized within Pennsylvania. If, for example, a species migrated northward along the Coastal Plain and Piedmont (e.g., *Magnolia virginiana*, Fig. 12), or inland along the Mississippi and Ohio River valleys, (e.g., *Silene virginica*, Fig. 8), such a species may very well reach its northern limits in either SE or SW Pennsylvania.

3. Regional species such as those confined to western or eastern Pennsylvania (Results, 4.a., e.g., Fig. 16; 4.c., e.g., Fig. 18) have distribution patterns not correlated with any apparent topographic, edaphic, or climatic variable. Again, the biohistory of these species may provide a clue to present distributional patterns, but we have insufficient data to construct a general pattern. A reasonable conjecture is that such species may have a biogeographical history reflecting whether the northward migration occurred *east* or *west* of the "upland wedge" stretching from the north-central counties to Somerset and Fayette Cos. (Fig. 31; see also discussion under "2", above). On the other hand, species confined to the southern part of Pennsylvania (the *Cercis canadensis* pattern, Fig. 20) appear to be correlated largely with the mean minimum January temperature of $-5.6°C$ ($22°F$). To what extent edaphic factors are involved is not known. One might observe, however, that although dolomite outcrops occur in Centre County, *Cercis canadensis* is not native to this county. The same overall correlation of distribution and temperature seems to hold for species found south of the Glaciated and Allegheny High Plateaus Section (Results, 4.g. and Figs. 23, 31).

4. Species confined for the most part to upland areas appear correlated with acid soils and the physiological tolerance for low temperatures (cf. distribution of *Dalibarda repens,* Fig. 22, with Fig. 33). In an intensive phenecological study of *Clintonia borealis* and *C. umbellulata,* Gunther[15] suggested that *C. umbellulata* is not well-adapted to northern regions (as compared to *C. borealis*) because of various phenodynamic distortions preventing successful reproduc-

tion, distortions "caused by early onset and rapid progression of senescence followed by the killing frosts of autumn." That is, the growing season may be too short for the successive stages of bud form, anthesis, fruit ripening and senescence of the aerial portions of the perennial plants. Nevertheless, even in a well-studied species pair as *Clintonia borealis* and *C. umbellulata,* little is known concerning the underlying factors limiting the range of each species.

5. The disjuncts within Pennsylvania provide some fascinating patterns for autecologists to disentangle. Some disjuncts may have specialized habitat requirements which explain their distribution. This appears to be the case with *Trollius laxus.* But why *Krigia biflora* (Fig. 25) would be relatively common in both the extreme eastern and western areas while rare elsewhere remains unexplained—no variable appears correlated, not even temperature (Why does this species not occur in Adams and York Counties?).

Otherwise, one might hypothesize that *Krigia biflora* and similar disjuncts migrated into Pennsylvania via the Coastal Plain/Piedmont and Ohio River corridors but did not migrate into the central regions due to relatively low temperature regimes (Fig. 36).

6. Species restricted to special (uncommon) habitats, e.g., shale barrens, serpentine barrens, acid bogs, and calcareous marshes will occur only where such habitats appear. Many of these species are rare or threatened and certainly deserve immediate conservation measures.

Despite these general patterns, key problems remain, all requiring additional research and new, testable hypotheses. Clearly, considerable research on the autecology of a diverse group of species remains to be completed before anyone can offer convincing correlations between present distributions with one or more environmental variables. Certainly such studies of rare species would be instructive, especially because human activities are destroying or altering many unique (or unusual) habitats and with them the rare species. We hope this overview of biogeographic distribution patterns of the vascular flora native to Pennsylvania will spur others to undertake the requisite investigations involving both fresh empirical data and testable hypotheses and that the outcome of such research will strengthen our ability to conserve this wonderfully diverse flora.

ACKNOWLEDGMENTS

We gratefully acknowledge permission from the Morris Arboretum to reproduce Figs. 1—30 from the *Atlas of the Flora of Pennsylvania* by E.T. Wherry, J.M. Fogg, Jr., and H.A. Wahl (Morris Arboretum, Philadelphia, 1979). Likewise, we are grateful to Ptolemy Press, Ltd., for permission to reproduce Figs. 32—35, and 37 taken from *Pennsylvania Atlas,* 2nd. ed., by P.F. Rizza and J.C. Hughes (Ptolemy Press, Ltd., Grove City, Pa., 1982). We deeply appreciate the careful criticism of an earlier draft of this paper by George Beatty, although we are responsible for all remaining errors of fact or judgement.

REFERENCES CITED

1. Braun, E.L. 1950. Deciduous forests of eastern North America. The Blakiston Co., Philadelphia.
2. Harshberger, J.W. 1958. Phytogeographic survey of North America, 2nd (reprint) edition. Hafner Publ. Co., New York.
3. Cribbs, J.E. 1917a. Plant association of western Pennsylvania with special reference to physiographic relationship. Plant World 20:97-120.
4. Cribbs, J.E. 1917b. Plant association of western Pennsylvania with special reference to physiographic relationship. II. Plant World 20:142-157.
5. Donahue, W.H. 1954. Some plant communities in the Anthracite region of Northeastern Pennsylvania. Amer. Midl. Nat. 51:203-231.
6. Goodlett, J.C. 1954. Vegetation adjacent to the border of the Wisconsin drift in Potter County, Pennsylvania. Harvard Forest Bull. No. 25, pp. 1-93.
7. Harshberger, J.W. 1904. A phyto-geographic sketch of extreme southeastern Pennsylvania. Bull. Torrey Bot. Club 31:125-159.
8. Hough, A.F. and R.D. Forbes. 1943. The ecology and silvics of forests in the high plateaus of Pennsylvania. Ecol. Monogr. 13:299-320.
9. Jennings, O.E. 1927. Classification of the plant societies of central and western Pennsylvania. Proc. Pennsylvania Acad. Sci. 1:23-55.
10. Jennings, O.E. 1939. A contribution towards a plant geography of western Pennsylvania. Trillia 10:46-81.
11. Jennings, O.E. 1943. The ecological plant geography of western Pennsylvania. Quart. Bull. Polish Inst. Arts and Sci. in Amer. 1:980-997.
12. Keever, C. 1973. Distribution of major forest species in southeastern Pennsylvania. Ecol. Monogr. 43:303-327.
13. Wherry, E.T., J.M. Fogg, Jr., and H.A. Wahl. 1979. Atlas of the flora of Pennsylvania. Morris Arboretum of the University of Pennsylvania, Philadelphia.
14. Kunsman, J. and C.S. Keener. 1986. New records of vascular plants from Blair County, Pennsylvania. Bartonia, in press.
15. Gunther, P. 1972. The phenodynamics of *Clintonia borealis* (Ait.) Raf. and *C. umbellulata* (Michx.) Morong (Liliaceae) as related to their general distributions. Ph.D. thesis, The Pennsylvania State University.
16. Wherry, E.T. 1964. Some Pennsylvania barrens and their flora. II. Bartonia 34:8-11.
17. Miller, G.L. 1977. An ecological study of the serpentine barrens in Lancaster County, Pennsylvania. Proc. Pennsylvania Acad. Sci. 51:169-176.
18. Hart, R. 1980. The coexistence of weeds and restricted native plants on serpentine barrens in southeastern Pennsylvania. Ecology 61(3):688-701.
19. Wherry, E.T. 1963. Some Pennsylvania barrens and their flora. I. Serpentine. Bartonia 33:7-11.

20. Keener, C.S. 1983. Distribution and biohistory of the endemic flora of the mid-Appalachian shale barrens. Bot. Rev. 49:65-115.
21. Westerfeld, W. 1961. An annotated list of vascular plants of Centre and Huntingdon Counties, Pennsylvania. Castanea 26:1-80.
22. Rizza, P.F. and J.C. Hughes. 1982. Pennsylvania atlas: A thematic atlas of the Keystone State, rev. 2nd ed. Ptolemy Press, Grove City, Pa.

Endangered and Threatened Species Programs in Pennsylvania and other States: Causes, Issues and Management. Edited by S. K. Majumdar, F. J. Brenner and A. F. Rhoads. © 1986, The Pennsylvania Academy of Science.

Chapter Twelve

AMERICAN CHESTNUT (*CASTANEA DENTATA*)—REPLACEMENT SPECIES AND CURRENT STATUS[1]

FRANKLIN C. CECH[2]

[2]Forestry Division
College of Agriculture and Forestry
West Virginia University
Morgantown, WV, 26506-6125

PRE-BLIGHT AMERICAN CHESTNUT

Little more than a half century has passed since American chestnut (*Castanea dentata* (Marsh.) Borkh.) was a major source of timber and wood products from the forests of eastern North America. This beautiful tree provided products that served mankind from birth to death. His cradle was often made from the easily worked chestnut wood, his home had chestnut siding, chestnut beams and rafters, chestnut shingles, chestnut furniture, and his coffin was made of chestnut. Chestnuts provided a staple food for wildlife and man (one railroad station in West Virginia shipped 155,000 pounds of nuts in 1911)!

Because chestnut was durable and rot resistant, it was used for telephone poles, railroad ties, and farm fencing. Extracts from chestnut provided tannin for the leather industry.

In the 1978 American Chestnut symposium held at West Virginia University in Morgantown, WV, Kuhlman[2] emphasized the pre-blight importance of chestnut in the forests of North America, noting that the American chestnut comprised approximately 25 percent of the early eastern hardwood forest. Its

---
[1]This paper is published as Scientific Article 1991, West Virginia Agricultural and Forestry Experiment Station.

natural range included over 80 million ha. Mature trees were between 18-36 m in height with straight boles up to 25 m in diameter. On good sites trees often grew 2.5 cm in diameter per year and could sometimes sustain this growth for more than 50 yrs. Growth of chestnut stands averaged 500 board feet per acre per year and chestnut had a faster growth rate than any of its associated species.[2]

The volume of chestnut in West Virginia alone was estimated at 10 billion board feet and in Pennsylvania there were an estimated 3 million ha of forest land with 21 percent of the growing stock in chestnut timber. In 1912, the total value of all chestnut products in Pennsylvania was estimated at 70 million dollars!

In 1904 officials of the Bronx Zoological Park of New York City noted that their chestnut trees were showing signs of deterioration and after the first evaluation they suggested that it was an environmental response—probably drought. However, Merkel in 1905 wrote that "an epidemic of a fungus disease has occurred throughout the parks of the Borough, which, but for the fact that it was confined to a single species of tree, might have overshadowed in deadliness and rapid spread all other enemies of tree life."[2]

His statement was unfortunately true and in spite of efforts to control the disease, by 1950 more than 80 percent of the chestnut trees throughout their range had been infected.[2] *Endothia parasitica* (Murr,) P.J. and H.W. And,* the chestnut blight fungus is an exceptionally efficient disease, and American chestnut has no genetic resistance. In less than 50 years, a species that was a major component of the eastern forest and major source of raw materials for several industries had disappeared as a canopy component. Since the chestnut root system is not killed by the blight, and because of its sprouting ability, this species lives on in the understory, sprouting, growing for a while and then being killed by the blight.

EARLY POST-BLIGHT SUCCESSION

In 1924 Frothingham noted three aspect of the result of the blight:
1. Destruction—of the mainstay of existing pole, tie, tanning, extract and other chestnut using industries.
2. Developmental—loss of varied products contributing to economic and social development.
3. Silvicultural—the disappearance of one of the most rapid growing, easily raised, abundant and worthwhile species of the region.[3]

With the loss of more than 90 percent of the canopy trees (via chestnut blight and logging), large areas were left with little or no advance reproduction and some attempts were made to replace the chestnut with various species of conifers.[4,5] Eastern white pine (*Pinus strobus*),** red pine (*P. resinosa*), and Scotch pine (*P. sylvestris*) were planted in areas of Pennsylvania and New Jersey. After

---
*Currently the *Endothia* genus is being taxanomically reevaluated and there is evidence suggesting that *parasitica* should be placed in the genus *Cryphonectria*.
**Nomenclature from Little.[6]

two years, pine survival ranged from 40 to 80 percent. However, hardwood sprouts, especially chestnuts, suppressed the pines. Without sprout removal (cleaning), the conifers were so badly suppressed that additional serious mortality occurred, but in most cases cleaning was not economically feasible. Thus, because of the nature of the ecosystem where chestnut had flourished, and the extensive areas concerned, natural succession rather than artificial regeneration dictated which species would replace chestnut, both on managed and unmanaged forest land.

Openings left after the demise of the chestnut (often followed or preceded by salvage logging operations) were reoccupied by three basic processes:[7]

1. Closure of the canopy by adjacent dominant and codominant trees in mature or nonmature stands.
2. Growth of advance reproduction.
3. Growth of seedlings established after the death of the chestnut.

The first process, canopy closure, was the most important where chestnuts occupied less than 30 to 40 percent of the canopy. The crowns of adjacent trees grew rapidly into the relatively small openings left by the dead chestnut. Since there was little change in the nature of the crown cover, light was limiting to the intolerant invader species, and probably insufficient for the release of any tolerant species in the understory. Except for the loss of the chestnut there was little, if any, change in the species composition of these stands and they changed from an oak-chestnut type to a mixed oak forest.

In larger openings, where stands had consisted of more than 40 percent chestnut, advance reproduction—suppressed saplings and seedlings present under the canopy—responded quickly to the release offered by the slowly dying chestnut. A period of slightly increased growth occurred as the chestnuts were dying, followed in order, by (1) a period of "greatly accelerated" growth (5-8 years), (2) a period of rapid decrease in growth (1-4 years), (3) a 2-4 year period of slightly increased growth, and then (4) the normal decrease in growth as the released trees increased in size and the canopies closed.[7]

Also in large openings, where dormant seed was present in the forest floor or where seed blew or was carried into the openings, germinating seeds provided seedlings that filled the gaps left by the dead chestnut. In such situations, early successional species dominated. This occurred generally where chestnut had been the predominant species and their crowns had overlapped or were contiguous.[7]

Since oaks were prominent associates of American chestnut (oak-chestnut forest region sensu Braun,[8]) it is not surprising that the early succession included a large oak component. Barnes in 1917 described the Nittany Forest in Pennsylvania, which was clearcut prior to planting pines, as 60 percent chestnut, 20 percent chestnut oak (*Quercus prinus*), with smaller amounts of white oak (*Q. alba*) and northern red oak (*Q rubra*).[4]

Early discussions concerning the successional events which occurred after the demise of canopy chestnut noted that the nature of replacement varied with locality, site, slope, elevation, forest type and species remaining.[9] Illick[9] listed the 10 most important species associated with chestnut on dry hillsides in Pennsylvania as chestnut oak, pitch pine (*Pinus rigida*), black locust (*Robinia pseudoacacia*), sweet birch (*Betula lenta*), black oak (*Quercus velutina*), red oak, white oak, white ash (*Fraxinus americana*), yellow-poplar (*Liriodendron tulipifera*), and white pine. On the better sites the major species were yellow-poplar, white ash, red oak, white pine, red maple (*Acer rubrum*), and white oak plus a few other species.

Natural replacement in Pennsylvania was better in quality and quantity and also more complete than had been anticipated. Replacement species on better sites were yellow-poplar, white ash, red oak, white pine, red maple and white oak and a few other species. On dry slopes, where open areas were larger, replacement species included less commercially valuable trees such as pitch pine, chestnut oak, black locust, sweet birch, black oak, pignut hickory (*Carya glabra*), table mountain pine (*Pinus pungens*) and Virginia pine (*Pinus virginiana*).[3,9]

Woods and Shanks[7] made a comprehensive study of the replacement species in the Great Smoky Mountains National Park. They noted that 50 species were found in the stands containing chestnut. The mesic nature of many of these stands was illustrated by the large number of hemlock (*Tsuga canadensis*), yellow-poplar, Fraser magnolia (*Magnolia fraseri*), silverbell (*Halesia carolina* var *monticola*), sweet birch, basswood (*Tilia americana*), red oak, and sugar maple (*Acer saccharum*). Chestnut had been an important member of the high quality mesic cove forests of this region. Three species (chestnut oak, hemlock and silverbell), comprised 46 percent of the replacement trees. However, the authors noted that 41 percent of all replacements were oaks and no other genus approached this degree of abundance. They suggested that this percentage was probably a fair representation of the association in the oak-chestnut region. When distribution was considered, chestnut oak (24%), red oak (24%), and red maple (22%) were present in the greatest number of openings. These three species were considerably more important than all others with regard to distribution and were separated from them by 12 percentage points. The species next in abundance was hemlock, present in 9 percent of the openings, followed in gradually descending order by the balance of the 24 species deemed to be major replacement species. With respect to aspect, they found three major groups—species more characteristic of northern exposures, species more characteristic of southern exposures, and species without a pronounced aspect affinity. Chestnut, red and white oaks were representative of species with no pronounced aspect affinity, whereas silverbell, yellow-poplar, hemlock, flowering dogwood (*Cornus florida*), and American beech (*Fagus grandifolia*) were characteristic of northern exposures. Only scarlet oak (*Quercus coccinea*) was confined mainly to southern exposures.

In the mountains of North Carolina, American chestnut had constituted 40 percent of the overstory. From 1934 to 1953, American chestnut was reduced by the blight from 41 percent of the basal area to less than one percent.[10,11] At the Coweeta Hydrologic Laboratory in western North Carolina, yellow-poplar was the most important replacement species, and all oaks increased in number, as did hickory and red maple. Of interest was the fact that sourwood (*Oxydendrum arboreum*), cucumber tree (*Magnolia acuminata*), sweet birch, yellow birch (*Betula alleghaniensis*) and hemlock were listed as invader species.

By the early 1950's, American chestnut was relegated to a component of the understory over its entire range, the former oak chestnut type had changed to a mixed oak type[7] and the mixed mesophytic forest of the lower slopes of the Ridge and Valley section no longer listed *Castanea* as a canopy component.[8]

LATE POST-BLIGHT SUCCESSION

The oak-chestnut forest of 80 years ago would not resemble the forest of today. In general, species characteristic of mesic sites have increased in importance in the cove hardwood areas, while the more xeric-site species have achieved greater importance on the ridge and hill tops. According to Good[12] it is expected that oaks will have less success in the future in the highlands of New Jersey and species such as beech, sweet birch and red maple will be much more important than in the early forest.

The canopy of the former oak-chestnut forest in western Pennsylvania might once have been as high as 70 percent chestnut with mixture of a few larger sized black cherry (*Prunus serotina*), red maple, black oak, sweet birch, sour or black gum (*Nyssa sylvatica*), white oak, beech, chestnut oak and hemlock. Today the canopy is dominated principally by black cherry, with an IV* of 145.8. It also includes red maple, sugar maple, black oak, sweet birch and sour gum. Less common canopy species are chestnut oak, white oak, sassafras (*Sassafras albidum*), beech, white ash, hickory, tulip poplar and hemlock.[13] Mackey and Sivec[13] quote Grizes who indicates that cherry is probably a transitional species in this complex. Grizes' conclusion is substantiated by the fact that cherry decreases to an IV of 23.6 in the understory as compared to sugar maple with an IV of 162.0. Other species (beech, sassafras, and dogwood) remain at about the same level.

Stephenson[14] surveyed 12 former oak-chestnut communities in southwestern Virginia, noting that these could currently be regarded as representative of an oak association complex. Using IV values,** he found that chestnut oak, red, scarlet and white oak and red maple were the most important tree species. On

---

*IV = importance value = percent density + percent relative frequency + percent dominance (basal area).[15]
**Base value = 100.

southern exposures, chestnut oak was the most dominant species, IV-41, and scarlet and white oak were next in importance with IV's of 14 and 13, respectively. On northern exposures red oak was dominant, IV-39, with chestnut oak also very important with an IV of 27. Red maple, scarlet oak and white oak were much less important.

In a second paper, Stephenson[16] presented the results of a survey of an area originally studied by Braun in 1932 and typed as an example of an oak-chestnut association.[8] He found that red oak was the most important species with an IV of 69.0. Red maple (IV = 7) and sweet birch (IV = 5) were the only important associates. Sugar maple, serviceberry (*Amelanchier arborea*), black cherry and yellow birch were relatively important on a few plots, but were not important overall. He concluded that this area in southwestern Virginia should also be included in the oak association complex.

To summarize, the original oak-chestnut association, with the advent of the blight and the loss of chestnut has become in general an oak association complex, dominated by red oak on the more mesic sites and chestnut oak on the more xeric sites. The loss of chestnut trees followed by salvage logging created a relatively open situation which permitted the invasion of mid-successional species which, together with the residual post-blight canopy species, make up today's forests. Often mesic sites have been invaded by more mesophytic types (hemlock, yellow-poplar, magnolia, silverbell and sugar maple), while xeric sites have been occupied by more xerophytic species (scarlet oak, sour wood and pitch pine). Other species (beech, sassafras, and dogwood) remain at about the same level. Several species not present in the original canopy have become more or less important components of the current forest. However, no single species has taken over the niche formerly occupied by chestnut.

THE CURRENT STATUS OF AMERICAN CHESTNUT

As a result of the blight, American chestnut has been relegated to an understory species. Chestnut sprouts prolifically from the stumps. The sprouts grow slowly in the subdued light of the understory until they are infected, and then die back. It was thought that succeeding sprouts would weaken until the root systems eventually died. This may have happened to a degree, yet after 50 years or more there are numerous sprouts existing, many of these growing into the canopy before succumbing to the blight.*

One approach to breeding disease resistant plants is to utilize partially resis-

---

*Dr. Ray Hicks, forest ecologist in the Division of Forestry, West Virginia University has observed that in northeastern West Virginia American chestnut is "all but gone" on the good sites, but where the canopy is less dense—in this case on the poorer sites—there are numerous sprouts. (Personal communication 8/13/85). Dr. Steven Stephensen indicates that this is also true in southwestern Virginia (personal communication 9/13/85).

tant individuals that are, or appear in the population. In the case of chestnut blight, it has been said that there was no resistance in the population. However, large trees are occasionally found that have been attacked by the blight and are still living.[17,18]

In response to a small notice which appeared in the woodworking magazine"Hands On" (Sept-Oct 1982), we have received numerous letters advising us of the location of large (>30 cm dbh) American chestnut trees, but unfortunately, circumstances have not permitted positive identification of many of these trees. A notable exception was two 35 cm diameter breast height (dbh) trees reported by a Pennsylvania correspondent who was unwilling to risk cutting scion material for grafting purposes. Unfortunately, we have recently heard that both trees have died—victims of the blight. The largest tree reported to us is in North Carolina. It is 76 cm dbh, has no cankers on the bole, and is very healthy (K.O. Summerville, personal communication 6/18/82). Scion material from this exceptional tree is in our chestnut breeding bank at West Virginia University.

Prolific sprouting can occur, and dense stands of chestnut appear whenever openings occur in areas where a high percent of the original canopy was in chestnut. One such area is in the vicinity of Marlinton, WV, where a storm ravaged stand of *ca.* 24 ha was clearcut as a salvage operation. This area now has an estimated 5000 to 12,500 chestnut stems per hectare[19] varying in size from 1-20 cm at 1.3 m above the ground. Another example is an area in southeastern West Virginia that has been patch clearcut (Dr. W.M. MacDonald, personal communication 7/15/85). The stand generally was mixed red, white, and chestnut oak. Chestnut sprouts had been numerous, but "reasonably" suppressed prior to the cutting. Now there are numerous trees in the 10-15 cm class approaching canopy height. Griffin *et al*[26] noted that sprout stands greater than 1000 clumps per ha may occur near Blacksburg, Virginia. Stephensen (unpublished data) has sampled stands in southwestern Virginia in which there were more than 1800 chestnut sprouts per ha.

Similar data for sites in Connecticut, Massachusetts, and Virginia have been published by Paillet[21] and Hebard *et al*[22]. In forest openings caused by clearcuts or by defoliation (especially by gypsy moth) the chestnut sprouts which are successful understory competitors react very quickly to the increased light, changing from a shrub form to a dominant stem sapling. Because the early bark form is smooth and unbroken, the sapling grows without infection until normal bark fissuring occurs. The newly fissured bark opens infection courts, *Endothia* inoculum builds up and a minor epidemic occurs, reducing the chestnut to the previous understory component.

HYPOVIRULENCE

In 1938 the chestnut blight was reported in Italy on European chestnut

(*Castanea sativa*) and 40 yrs later it had spread throughout most of Italy. In 1950 Professor Anthony Biraghi, a pathologist from the University of Florence, found trees with healing cankers in areas of early infection, and interestingly, 15 yrs after this discovery, blight in Italy was no longer a problem.[23] Cultures from the healing cankers were found to be weak parasites, and in addition, were white rather than the normal brown color. Further investigation showed that the hypovirulent hyphae were able to transform the virulent to the hypovirulent form. Hypovirulence spread naturally in Italy, and today there is again a thriving chestnut orchard industry, and coppice management for chestnut wood products is being practiced.

In France, Grente developed a method of inoculating blight cankers to extend the hypovirulent strain of *Endothia* to the French chestnut groves. There the hypovirulent strain spread naturally and the French chestnut industry is also currently viable.[24,25]

Jaynes and his coworkers at the Connecticut Agriculture Experiment Station imported inoculum of the European hypovirulent fungus and after careful testing on other species of the beech (*Fagaceae*) family and determining that it posed no danger to the close relatives of American chestnut, introduced it into the field. The European strain of the hypovirulent fungus did, in fact, cause remission of cankers on American chestnut, but there was no evidence of natural transmission to adjacent cankered individuals.[26,27,28]

Investigation of the French hypovirulent strain showed that it possessed double stranded (ds) RNA which contained virus like particles. Twenty eight mycelial isolates were then screened for ds RNA. None of the virulent types had ds RNA, but all of the hypovirulents tested positive for ds RNA, a characteristic of most fungal viruses.[29] Naturally occurring American hypovirulent strains have now been isolated, but these do not seem to spread naturally when tested on sprout clumps in the natural range of American chestnut.[27,30,31,32]

American chestnut groves were established in Michigan outside of the natural species range of the species. These flourished, but around 1928 the blight became established, slowly destroying these groves. However, a great number of trees have survived. Cankers abnormal in appearance have been tested for hypovirulence. Hypovirulent isolates have been identified from 7 separate areas, indicating that the survival of these trees is probably due to the widespread hypovirulent phenomenon. It is suggested that the hypovirulents are spreading naturally in the Michigan area, giving rise to the hope of a recovery similar to that in Europe.[33,34] A current theory of why the hypovirulent strains have been successful in Europe and Michigan, but not in the natural range of American chestnut suggests that it takes 10 to 15 yrs for the double stranded RNA to build up in the *Endothia* populations. The chestnut groves of Europe and Michigan are essentially pure stands, and there is no competition. The chestnut are free to grow and, therefore, develop rapidly from seed or sprouts. Additionally, the hypovirulent phenomenon has occurred before many of the larger trees have died, thus forming a reservoir of cankers for the hypovirulent form to colonize and develop. Such is not the case in the natural range of American chestnut and possibly it will take much longer for the hypovirulent reservoir to reach effective levels. Additionally the hypovirulent strains are weak competitors and may be lost before a reservoir can be built in the absence of large cankered chestnut trees.

Although some encouraging signs are present, hypovirulence is still a question with reference to the restoration of American chestnut.

Recently a new effort has been initiated in Minnesota utilizing standard breeding methods for breeding resistant American chestnut. With proper support and time, this effort may build on the earlier work in hybridization, utilizing extant forest-form hybrids and the suspected partial resistance in the lingering American chestnut population to develop a blight free or blight resistant form (C.R. Burnham personal communication 9/18/83). In the meantime vegetative propagation by means of micropropagation (tissue and stem culture) is being investigated at West Virginia University so that when new resistant forms are developed they can be utilized. Plantlets can be developed *in vitro* at this time, but the step from the test tube to soil has been minimally successful to date.[35]

With the renewed interest and efforts to restore the American chestnut it is not inconceivable that this highly desirable species may once again become a major component of our forests.

LITERATURE CITED

1. Detweiler, S.B. 1912. The Pennsylvania Programme. Pa. Chestnut Blight Conf. Harrisburg, PA. pp. 129-136.
2. Kuhlman, G.E. 1978. The devastation of American chestnut by blight. Proc. American Chestnut Symp. Jan. 4-5. Morgantown, WV. pp. 1-3.
3. Frothingham, E.H. 1924. Some silvicultural aspects of the chestnut blight situation. Jour. For. 22:861-872.
4. Barnes, L.C. 1917. Utilization and reforesting chestnut blight lands. Jour. For. 15:854-858.
5. Richards, E.C.M. 1917. A study of reforested chestnut cut-over lands. Jour. For. 15:609-614.
6. Little, E.L., Jr. 1979. Check list of United States trees. Agr. Handbook 541. USDA For. Ser. 375 pp.
7. Woods, F.W. and R.E. Shanks. 1959. Natural replacement of chestnut by other species in the Great Smoky Mountains Natural Park. Ecology 40:349-361.
8. Braun, E.L. 1950. Deciduous forests of eastern North America. The Blakeston Co. 596 pp.
9. Illick, J.S. 1921. Replacement of the chestnut. Jour. For. 19:104-114.

10. Keever, C. 1953. Present composition of some stands of the former oak-chestnut forest in the southern Blue Ridge mountains. Ecology 34:44-54.
11. Nichols, H.M. 1925. What trees are replacing our chestnuts. Forest Leaves 20:44-45.
12. Good, N.F. 1968. A study of the natural replacement of chestnut in the highlands of New Jersey. Bull. Torrey Bot. Club 95:240-253.
13. Mackey, H.E., Jr. and N. Sivec. 1973. The present composition of a former oak-chestnut forest of the Allegheny mountains of western Pennsylvania. Ecology 54:915-919.
14. Stephenson, S.L. 1974. Ecological composition of some former oak-chestnut communities in western Virginia. Castanea 39:278-286.
15. Curtis, J.T. and R.P. McIntosh. 1950. The interrelationship of certain analytic and synthetic photo-sociological characters. Ecology 31:434-455.
16. Stephenson, S.L. 1986. Changes in a former chestnut-dominated forest after a half century of succession. In press, Amer. Mid. Nat.
17. Hebard, F.V., J. Griffin and J.R. Elkins. 1982. Summary research on biology of hypovirulent and virulent *Endothia parasitica* on blight resistant and blight susceptible chestnut trees at Virginia Polytechnic Institute and State University. Proc. USDA For. Ser. American Chestnut Coop. Mtg. Morgantown, Jan. 5-7. pp. 49-67.
18. Thor, E. 1978. Breeding of American chestnut. Proc. American Chestnut Symp. Jan. 4-5. Morgantown, WV. pp. 7-9.
19. MacDonald, W.M. and M.L. Double. 1978. Frequency of vegetative compatibility types of *Endothia parasitica* in two areas of West Virginia. Proc. of American Chestnut Symp. Jan. 4-5. Morgantown, WV. pp. 103-105.
20. Griffin, J.S., F.V. Hebard, R.W. Wendt, and J.R. Elkins. 1983. Survival of American chestnut trees: evaluation of blight resistance and virulence in *Endothia parasitica.* Phytopathology 73(7): 1084-1092.
21. Paillet, F.L. 1982. The ecological significance of American Chestnut *Castanea dentata* (Marsh.) (Borkh) in the holicene forests of Connecticut. Bull. of the Torrey Bot. Club. 109(4): 457-473.
22. Hebard, F.V., G.J. Griffin and J.R. Elkins. 1981. Implications of chestnut blight incidence in recently clearcut and mature forests for biological control of blight with hypovirulent strains. USDA For. Ser. American Chestnut Coop Mtg. Morgantown, WV. For. Ser. Tech. Rep. NE-64. pp. 12-13.
23. Mittenperger, L. 1978. The present state of chestnut blight in Italy. Proc. American Chestnut Symp. Jan. 4-5. Morgantown, WV. pp. 34-36.
24. Chelminski, Rudolph. 1979. A fungus beats the chestnut blight at its own game. Smithsonian Mag., June 1979:97-102.
25. Grente, J. and S. Berthelay-Sauret. 1978. Biological control of chestnut blight in France. Proc. American Chestnut Symp. Jan. 4-5, Morgantown, WV. pp. 30-32.

26. Anagnostakis, S.L. 1982. Biological control of chestnut blight. Science 215:466-471.
27. Jaynes, R.A. and J.E. Elliston. 1978. Control of *Endothia parasitica* cankers on American chestnut sprouts with hypovirulent strains. Proc. American Chestnut Symp. Jan. 4-5. Morgantown, WV. pp. 110-113.
28. Van Alfen, N.K., R.A. Jaynes, S.L. Anagnostakis and P.R. Day. 1975. Chestnut blight: biological control by transmissable hypovirulence in *Endothia parasitica*. Science 89:890-891.
29. Dodds, J.A. 1978. Double stranded RNA and virus like particles in *Endothia parasitica*. Proc. American Chestnut Symp. Jan. 4-5, Morgantown, WV. pp. 108-109.
30. Anagnostakis, S.L. 1978a. American experience with hypovirulence in *Endothia parasitica*. Proc. American Chestnut Symp. Jan. 4-5, Morgantown, WV. pp. 37-38.
31. _____. 1978b. The American chestnut: new hope for a fallen giant. Conn. Ag. Exp. Sta. Bull. 777, 9 pp.
32. MacDonald, W.M. and M.L. Double. 1981. Effectiveness of slurry treatments in controlling individual *Endothia parasitica* cankers on American chestnut. USDA For. Ser. American Chestnut Coop Mtg. Morgantown, WV. For. Ser. Tech. Rep. NE-64, p. 6.
33. Brewer, L.G. 1982. The present status and future prospect for the American chestnut in Michigan. The Mich. Bot. 21:117-128.
34. Fullbright, D.W., W.H. Weidlich, K.Z. Haufler, C.S. Thomas, and C.P. Paul. 1983. Chestnut blight and recovering American chestnut in Michigan. Can. Jour. of Bot. 61(12): 3164-3171.
35. Keys, R.N. and F.C. Cech. 1982. Propagation of American chestnut *in vitro*. Proc. USDA for. Ser. American chestnut. Morgantown, WV. Jan. 5-7. pp. 106-110.

Endangered and Threatened Species Programs in Pennsylvania and other States: Causes, Issues and Management. Edited by S. K. Majumdar, F. J. Brenner and A. F. Rhoads. © 1986, The Pennsylvania Academy of Science.

Chapter Thirteen

RARE PLANTS OF THE DELAWARE ESTUARY IN PENNSYLVANIA[1]

ALFRED E. SCHUYLER
Academy of Natural Sciences of Philadelphia
19th and the Parkway, Philadelphia, PA 19103

The estuarine portion of the Delaware River in Pennsylvania extends for a distance of about 85 kilometers from Morrisville downstream to Marcus Hook with Philadelphia in between. This portion of the river and portions of its tributaries on the Coastal Plain of Bucks, Philadelphia, and Delaware counties are the only tidal waters in the state. Despite being tidal, the water is fresh, and the Delaware estuary is one of the most extensive areas having this combination in eastern North America. Many plant species of tidal freshwater habitats are rare in Pennsylvania and elsewhere because of the limited occurrence of these habitats. In addition, twelve species previously found in the Pennsylvania portion of the Delaware estuary are extirpated and four others have been eliminated from the portion below Philadelphia.

Rare plants of the Delaware estuary can be placed into two major groups: (1) those restricted to tidal habitats or rarely found outside such habitats and (2) those found in both tidal and non-tidal habitats but mostly not found outside of tidal habitats in Pennsylvania. Species in the first group are referred to as intertidal endemics. Most of them are rare (one presumed extinct) throughout their ranges. In contrast, most species in the second group are not rare in substantial portions of their ranges outside Pennsylvania. Also, some widespread species display structural variation correlated with tidal and non-tidal conditions and have varieties that mostly occur in tidal habitats.

---

[1] The official Pennsylvania status of species mentioned in the article may be found by consulting the appendix of chapter xx by Paul G. Wiegman.

INTERTIDAL ENDEMICS

Extirpated Intertidal Endemics. Three of the four species in this category, *Micranthemum micranthemoides* (Nutt.) Wettst., *Limosella australis* R. Br., and *Eriocaulon parkeri* B.L. Robins., are low-growing plants that were previously known from numerous localities on both sides of the Delaware River above and below Philadelphia! Early literature[2,3] and herbarium specimen data indicate that these species grew in similar shoreline habitats along with three other low-growing species: *Crassula aquatica* (L.) Schoenl., *Elatine americana* (Pursh) Arn., and *Sagittaria subulata* (L.) Buch. *Micranthemum micranthemoides* (Nutt.) Wettst. can no longer be found in any part of its range and is presumed extinct. The last Pennsylvania collection was in 1932 along the Delaware River above Philadelphia near Eddington. *Limosella australis* R. Br. was last collected in the Delaware estuary at the mouth of Poquessing Creek above Philadelphia in 1917. It is still found along many tidal rivers north and south of Pennsylvania as well as in ponds or depressions along the Atlantic Coast that probably are influenced by tides. The last collection of *Eriocaulon parkeri* B.L. Robins. in Pennsylvania was above Philadelphia near the mouth of Neshaminy Creek in 1932. Unlike *Micranthemum* and *Limosella, E. parkeri* presently occurs in numerous places along tidal rivers in southern New Jersey.

The fourth extirpated intertidal endemic, *Aeschynomene virginica* (L.) BSP, was known from numerous localities in the Delaware estuary below Philadelphia and Camden. It is a tall plant that grows along the upper portions of tidal shores and in high tidal marshes among other tall plants. This species is now eliminated from the Delaware estuary except for a few localities in New Jersey in the Maurice River system,[4] which is a tributary of Delaware Bay. It was only known from two or three localities in the Pennsylvania portion of the estuary and was last collected from Tinicum Island in 1865. The last collection along any portion of the Delaware River was from near Pennsville, New Jersey, in 1934. Although known from states south of Pennsylvania, this species is rare throughout its present range.[5,6,7,8]

Existing Intertidal Endemics. The three species in this category, *Bidens bidentoides* (Nutt.) Britt., *Sagittaria subulata* (L.) Buch., and *Amaranthus cannabinus* (L.) Sauer, are presently known from numerous localities in the Delaware estuary although the two former species have undergone range reductions. *Bidens bidentoides* (Nutt.) Britt. is mostly found in the upper portion of riverine intertidal zones that are often perturbed by man and harbor ruderal plants. It is locally abundant in some places along the Pennsylvania side of the Delaware River above Philadelphia, but despite its tolerance of man's perturbations, has not been collected in Pennsylvania below Philadelphia since 1868. *Sagittaria subulata* (L.) Buch. grows throughout much of the intertidal zone except for the upper portion where *Bidens bidentoides* (Nutt.) Britt. usually grows. Early literature[3] associates it with three intertidal endemics—*Micranthemum micran-*

themoides (Nutt.) Wettst., *Limosella australis* R. Br., and *Eriocaulon parkeri* B.L. Robins.—that are extirpated from Pennsylvania. Unlike these species, however, *S. subulata* is common and locally abundant along the river above Philadelphia. Below Philadelphia, the last Pennsylvania collection is from Tinicum in 1874. *Amaranthus cannabinus* (L.) Sauer is a common species in the Delaware estuary, occurring along river shores and in tidal marshes. There is no evidence that it has decreased or increased in abundance. It appears to be more tolerant of man's perturbations than most of the other plants considered here.

SPECIES OF TIDAL AND NON-TIDAL HABITATS

Extirpated Species. Of the eight species belonging to this category, five were previously known from only one Pennsylvania locality. *Carex hyalinolepis* Steud. is a southern species that reached the northern limit of its range in Pennsylvania (Philadelphia) and New Jersey (Salem) where it was last collected in 1898 and 1888, respectively. It is not rare in states farther south. *Sabatia stellaris* Pursh. and *Ptlimnium capillaceum* (Michx.) Raf., species presently found in brackish portions of the Delaware estuary, were both collected once in Lower Bucks County at or near Tullytown in 1904 and 1927, respectively. *Eleocharis quadrangulata* (Michx.) R.&S. and *Cyperus polystachyos* Rottb. are widespread species that are rare in the Delaware estuary. Although recently collected in tidal and non-tidal localities in Salem, Cumberland, and Cape May counties, New Jersey, both were last collected in Pennsylvania in 1863 and 1935, respectively. The only Pennsylvania locality for *Eleocharis quadrangulata* (Michx.) R.&S., was the shore of the Schuylkill below Gray's Ferry where it was first collected about 1825. *Cyperus polystachyos* Rottb. was collected once in a marsh along the Delaware River above Greenwich Point in 1935. Both localities are in industrial parts of Philadelphia where one would not expect to find rare plants today.

Elatine americana (Pursh.) Arn. and *Crassula aquatica* (L.) Schoenl. are low-growing plants that grew associated with or in similar habitats to *Micranthemum micranthemoides, Limosella australis* R. Br., and *Eriocaulon parkeri* B.L. Robins. *Elatine americana* (Pursh) Arn. was previously known from numerous localities in the Delaware estuary, and although recent collections have been made in the New Jersey and Delaware portion of the estuary, it cannot be found in many localities where it was previously collected. The last Pennsylvania collection was made in 1932 near Eddington. Collections of *Crassula aquatica* (L.) Schoenl. were only known from two localities in the Delaware estuary and both of these were in Pennsylvania. It was reported to be abundant above Kensington (now part of Philadelphia) in 1818[3] and was last collected at Andalusia in 1918 where, according to the collector, "only this one plant" could be found. This apparently was not the case in 1917 when numerous plants were collected from the same place.

Eryngium aquaticum L. is at the northern limit of its range that previously included five Pennsylvania localities along the Delaware River between Bristol and Chester. It is a comparatively tall species that occurs in the uppermost portions of intertidal zones on shores and in marshes. It was last collected in Pennsylvania at Tinicum in 1874. The last collection in the Delaware estuary was made along the Maurice River near Millville, New Jersey, in 1925. This species still occurs at other tidal and some non-tidal localities in southern New Jersey, and is not rare in states farther south.

Existing Species. Of the nine species in this category, two have had their ranges reduced below Philadelphia, two have had their ranges extended to Pennsylvania above Philadelphia, four appear to be distributed about as they've been in the past, and one is an Asiatic introduction that has become widespread in the Delaware estuary.

Scirpus smithii Gray and *Isoetes riparia* Engelm. are low-growing plants whose ranges in the Delaware estuary have become reduced. Both can be found at a few localities along the river shore above Philadelphia but are absent below Philadelphia where the last collections were made in the 19th century.

Sagittaria calycina Engelm. and *Eleocharis parvula* (Roemer & Schultes) Link are species that occur in brackish portions of the Delaware estuary well below Philadelphia that have recently been discovered[9,10] in the freshwater portion of the estuary above Philadelphia. The first collection of *Sagittaria calycina* Engelm. in Pennsylvania was made at Bristol in 1972. Both *Sagittaria calycina* Engelm. and *Eleocharis parvula* (Roemer & Schultes) Link were collected along the shore of Neshaminy Creek near its mouth in 1983, which is the first time that *Eleocharis parvula* (Roemer & Schultes) Link was collected in Pennsylvania. It seems unlikely that botanists who collected along Neshaminy Creek early in the 20th century would have overlooked both of these species. Therefore it is more likely that these plants arrived about or after the middle of the 20th century. *Sagittaria calycina* Engelm. has persisted for 13 years since first discovered. Whether or not *Eleocharis parvula* (Roemer & Schultes) Link persists remains to be determined. The factors responsible for the disjunct occurrence of these species in the Delaware estuary are unknown.

Four tall-growing species, *Zizania aquatica* L., *Scirpus fluviatilis* (Torr.) Gray, *Echinochloa walteri* (Pursh) Heller, and *Bidens laevis* (L.) BSP, are widespread in the Delaware estuary although the first two species no longer occur at many localities where they were found in the past. *Echinochloa walteri* (Pursh) Heller is comparatively rare and the scarcity of both old and recent collections preclude any comparison of past and present distribution. *Bidens laevis* (L.) BSP is a common plant in tidal marshes in the Delaware estuary and probably will remain so as long as tidal marshes exist.

An introduced species, *Cyperus brevifolioides* Thier. & Delahous. was first reported from the Philadelphia area in 1878 in Fairmount Park where it may have been introduced with other Asiatic plants for the centennial celebration. Its collecting history indicates it is more abundant now than it ever was; its frequent occurrence on or among debris near the limit of high tide indicates it is well adapted to habitats influenced by man's activity.

INFRASPECIFIC VARIANTS

Two wide-ranging species that occur in diverse habitats have infraspecific variants mostly found in tidal habitats. In both instances, the tidal variants have undergone similar modifications. *Bidens frondosa* var. *anomala* Porter ex Fern., occurs primarily in tidal habitats and differs from var. *frondosa* by having achenes with antrorsely instead of retrorsely barbed awns. *Eleocharis obtusa* var. *peasei* Svenson is locally restricted to tidal habitats and has achenes with bristles reduced or lacking in contrast to those of var. *obtusa* which have well-developed barbed bristles. These awn and bristle characteristics may be adaptations that prevent achenes from being dispersed by animals or from getting attached to litter in the upper portion of the intertidal zone. Thus the achenes of these tidal variants have a greater chance of remaining in tidal habitats with open moist substrates where they have the best chance for survival. These variation patterns give us a greater appreciation of the evolutionary importance of tidal habitats.

CONCLUSIONS

The portion of the Delaware estuary below Philadelphia has lost more rare species than the portion of the river above Philadelphia. The losses also occurred earlier below than above the city. All except one of the 13 species eliminated below Philadelphia were last collected in the 19th century. In contrast, all except one of the 8 species eliminated above Philadelphia were last collected in the 20th century between 1904 and 1932.

Of the 12 species extirpated from Pennsylvania, five (*Micranthemum micranthemoides,* (Nutt.) Wettst., *Limosella australis* R. Br., *Eriocaulon parkeri* B.L. Robins. *Elatine americana* (Pursh) Arn., and *Crassula aquatica* (L.) Schoenl. are low-growing plants that (A) were once common and/or locally abundant, (B) grew in similar habitats along tidal shores, and (C) were last collected along the river above Philadelphia in the early part of the 20th century. Three other low-growing species (*Sagittaria subulata* (L.) Buch., *Scirpus smithii* Gray, and *Isoetes riparia* Engelm.), which have some ecological affinity with this group, have been eliminated below Philadelphia but still occur above Philadelphia. These extirpations and reductions represent the most significant floristic changes in the Pennsylvania portion of the Delaware estuary.

What caused these extirpations and reductions? We don't know and may never know. We do know that the construction of bulkheads and the deposition of dredge spoil and land fill have altered many localities where these species used to grow. Unfortunately, we don't know how increased water pollution has affected these plants.

Our present knowledge of plant distributions in the Pennsylvania portion of the Delaware estuary is better than it has ever been. This knowledge can be put to good use as a way of judging environmental quality. If species continue to disappear, we must be doing something wrong. Because of the substantial efforts to preserve and protect Pennsylvania's estuarine wetlands, this should not happen. If it does happen, we should have a better idea of why it happened and be able to answer questions like *"whatever happened to Micranthemum?"*

ACKNOWLEDGEMENTS

I am grateful to Vincent Abraitys and Wayne R. Ferren, Jr., for sharing much information about intertidal plants with me. Florence M. Givens, Richard H. Mellon, Ann F. Rhoads, Marvin L. Roberts, Thomas L. Smith, Paul G. Wiegman, and Dorothy A. Viola also were helpful.

LITERATURE CITED

1. Ferren, W.R., Jr. and A.E. Schuyler. 1980. Intertidal Vascular Plants of River Systems near Philadelphia. Proc. Acad. Nat. Sci. Philadelphia 132:86-120.
2. Nuttall, T. 1817. An Account of Two New Genera of Plants, and of a species of *Tillaea* and *Limosella*, Recently Discovered on the Banks of the Delaware in the Vicinity of Philadelphia. J. Acad. Nat. Sci. Philadelphia 1:111-123.
3. Barton, W.P.C. 1818. Compendium Florae Philadelphicae. M. Carey & Son, Philadelphia. 2 v.
4. Ferren, W.R., Jr. 1976. Aspects of the Intertidal Zones, Vegetation, and Flora of the Maurice River System, New Jersey. Bartonia 44:58-67.
5. Snyder, D.B. and V.E. Vivian. 1981. Rare and Endangered Vascular Plant Species in New Jersey. United States Fish and Wildlife Service, Newton Corner. viii + 98 pp.
6. Tucker, A.O. et al. 1979. Rare and Endangered Vascular Plant Species in Delaware. United States Fish and Wildlife Service, Newton Corner. v + 89 pp.

7. Broome, C.R. et al. 1979. Rare and Endangered Vascular Plant Species in Maryland. United States fish and Wildlife Service, Newton Corner. vii + 64 pp.
8. Porter, D.M. 1979. Rare and Endangered Vascular Plant Species in Virginia. United States Fish and Wildlife Service, Newton Corner. v + 52 pp.
9. Ferren, W.R., Jr. 1974. Range Extensions of *Sagittaria montevidensis* in the Delaware River System. Bartonia 42:1-4.
10. Rhoads, A.F. 1985. Eastern Pennsylvania Rare Plant Survey Update. Bartonia 51:113-114.

Endangered and Threatened Species Programs in Pennsylvania and other States: Causes, Issues and Management. Edited by S. K. Majumdar, F. J. Brenner and A. F. Rhoads. © 1986, The Pennsylvania Academy of Science.

Chapter Fourteen

THREATENED AND ENDANGERED FISHES OF PENNSYLVANIA

Charles E. Denoncourt and Jay R. Stauffer, Jr.

The Pennsylvania State University
The School of Forest Resources
8B Ferguson Building
University Park, PA 16802

E.L. Cooper[1] listed 24 extant families of fishes currently present in Pennsylvania. R.F. Denoncourt[29] reported a total of 27 families of fishes recorded from Pennsylvania. Of the total 159 species reported in Cooper's book, 119 are considered primary freshwater species. The remaining 40 are either diadromous, salt tolerant, or freshwater representatives of marine groups.

These species are representatives of the 5 major drainage systems in Pennsylvania—the Delaware, Susquehanna, Potomac, Ohio and Great Lakes drainages (Figure 1).

In 1976, the Pennsylvania Fish Commission established an Advisory Committee on Fishes. This committee was comprised of four ichthyologists (E.L. Cooper, R.F. Denoncourt, C.H. Hocutt, J.R. Stauffer, Jr.) actively involved in sampling Pennsylvania waters, and one member of the Fish Commission's staff (C.N. Shiffer). The purpose of the committee was to determine the status of Pennsylvania fish species, particularly those considered "nongame" species.

Of the 159 species currently listed as found in Pennsylvania, four are afforded special status, along with one sub-species (Table 1). Three are considered officially endangered by the Committee. Only one of these, the shortnose sturgeon (*Acipenser brevirostrum* LeSueur), is listed as federally endangered.[2] The subspecies, the blue pike (*Stizostedion vitreum glaucum* Hubbs), is considered extirpated from Pennsylvania. The remaining species afforded special status is the eastern sand darter (*Ammocrypta pellucida* (Putnam)), which is considered threatened.

Historically, species have been considered for special status by political regions. It is much more realistic to consider their status from a geographical

TABLE 1
Status of Pennsylvanias threatened and endangered fish species in surrounding states.

	PA	NY	NJ	DE	MD	WV	OH
Acipenser brevirostrum shortnose sturgeon	EF[2]	EF[2]	EF[2]	EF[2]	EF[2]	EF[2]	EF[2]
A. fulvescens lake sturgeon	ES	T[5]	O[16]	O[16]	O[16]	T[5]	T[5]
Gasterosteus aculeatus threespine stickleback	ES	P[22]	P[22]	P[22]	P[22]	O[22]	O[22]
Ammocrypta pellucida eastern sand darter	T	T[5]	O[24]	O[24]	O[24]	T[5]	ES[6]
Stizostedion vitreum glaucum blue pike	EXTINCT IN NORTH AMERICA[30,31]						

Subscripts refer to literature cited section

Symbols used—
- EF - endangered status at federal level
- ES - endangered status at state level
- T - threatened
- O - outside species range
- P - present

perspective since these species do not recognize the arbitrary boundaries established by man. It is the purpose of this chapter to examine the question of protection or management of these threatened or endangered fishes from this geographic viewpoint.

Natural zoogeographic variations should be taken into consideration when determining the status of a questioned species. For example, the lake trout (*Salvelinus namaycush* (Walbaum)) has been recommended for vulnerable status in Pennsylvania.[3] However, it is well represented in more northern regions such as New York, Vermont, New Hampshire and Canada.[4] It is the opinion of the authors that this species should not be given special status in Pennsylvania, even though the populations within this state are declining, since Pennsylvania is on the extreme periphery of its range.

SHORTNOSE STURGEON
Acipenser brevirostrum LeSueur

Description:

The shortnose sturgeon is the smallest species in the genus *Acipenser*, reaching a length between 50 and 60 cm. As in other sturgeons, the head is covered by dermal armature. A total of 8-10 bony plates extend dorsally from the head to the dorsal fin, and 22-33 plates are located along each side.[7] It can be dif-

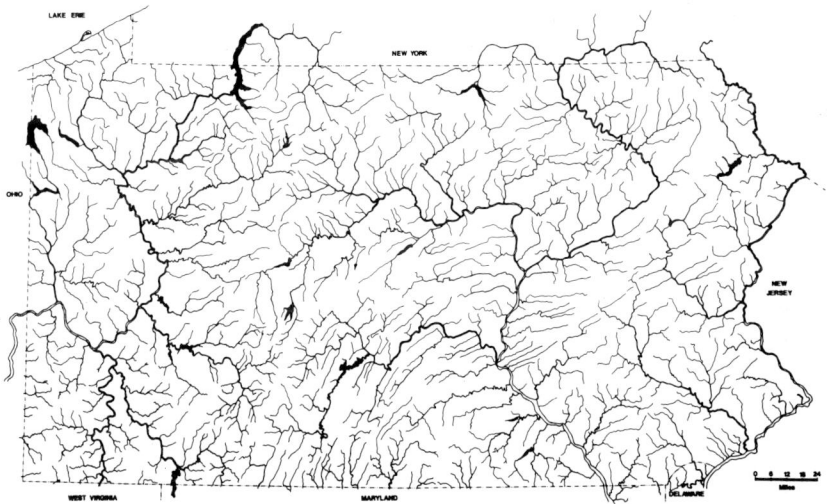

FIGURE 1. Stream systems of Pennsylvania.

ferentiated from smaller specimens of the sympatric species *Acipenser oxyrhynchus* Mitchell by its wider mouth, single row of lateral dermal shields, blackish viscera, and the pigment variation between the pale lateral scutes and the darker body.[8]

Range:

Acipenser brevirostrum is confined to the Atlantic slope drainages of North America from the St. John River, New Brunswick[8] south to the St. Johns River, Florida;[9] although most recorded specimens were collected from the waters between and including the Delaware and Hudson Rivers.[10] In Pennsylvania, the shortnose sturgeon has only been recorded from the Delaware River which still appears to contain a breeding population[8] (Figure 2). Music[11] reported that reproducing populations are believed to exist in the following river systems:

St. John River, New Brunswick
Kennebec River, Maine
Connecticut River, Massachusetts
Hudson River, New York
Altamaha River, Georgia

Habitat:

This sturgeon spends most of its life over sandy substrates in estuarine waters, ascending into large freshwater rivers to spawn.[8]

Life History and Ecology:

Maturity is reached between 5 and 6 years of age at a length of between 52 and 56 cm.[8] Reproduction is hypothesized to occur in large rivers over rocky substrate between April and June depending upon water temperature. The shortnose sturgeon forages in 1 to 2 m of water[12] on a variety of bottom invertebrates and plant material.[8] Gorham and McAllister[13] reported this species as regularly reaching an age of 27 years.

Status:

The shortnose sturgeon is the only federally listed species that occurs in Pennsylvania, it is also considered endangered by the Pennsylvania Fish Commission's Advisory Committee on Fishes.

Recommendations:

This species was consistently collected in the Delaware River between 1954 and 1979.[14] Despite recent extensive and consistent pollution of the lower Delaware River, recent collections (1984) at the Point Pleasant Power Plant indicate that this species is at least maintaining a population in the area (C. Shiffer, pers. comm.). Every effort should be made to maintain and improve water quality and all forms of water impoundment should be avoided. Damming of rivers has been hypothesized to cause the extirpation of this species from other rivers (James and Rappahannock rivers) by preventing it from reaching spawning habitats.[11]

LAKE STURGEON
Acipenser fulvescens Rafinesque

Description:

The lake sturgeon is one of the largest members of the sturgeon family, reaching a length of 370 cm and 140 kg in weight.[15] Most specimens do not exceed a size of 150 cm and 36 kg.[16] The adult lake sturgeon is pentagonal in cross section.[16] It possesses the 5 rows of dermal armature characteristic of the sturgeon family.[7] The only other syntopic species of sturgeon belongs to the genus

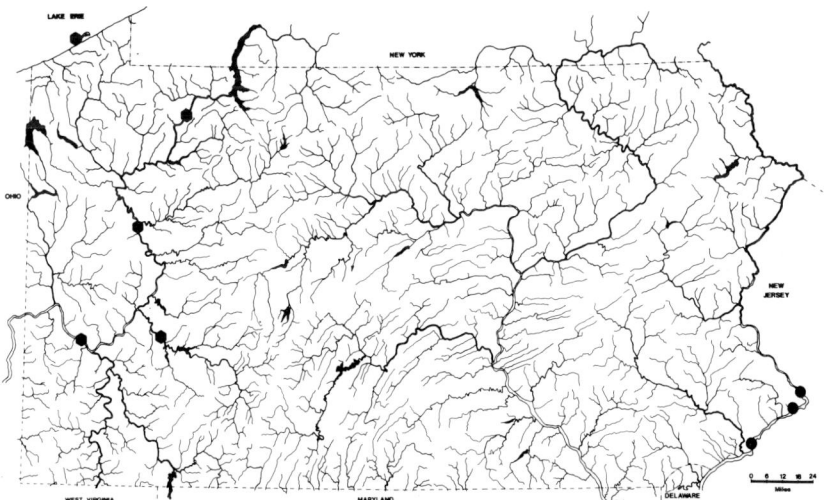

FIGURE 2. Occurrences of *Acipenser brevirostrum* LeSueur (circles) and *Acipenser fulvescens* Rafinesque (hexagonals) in Pennsylvania waters.

Scaphirhynchus,[16] and can be differentiated from the lake sturgeon by its fringed barbels.[15]

Range:

This species is found in rivers of the Mississippi Drainage system as far west as the Saskatchewan River in Alberta and as far east as southern Quebec.[16] In the northern part of its range, it occurs in parts of the Hudson Bay Drainage system, and it is distributed south to areas in northern Mississippi and Alabama.[17] Historically, the lake sturgeon has been collected in the main channel of the Ohio, Allegheny, and Kiskiminetas rivers[16] (Figure 2).

Habitat:

Although primarily an inhabitant of large rivers and lakes with sand, rock, or gravel substrate,[15] the lake sturgeon is sometimes found over mud bottoms or in brackish water in the Hudson Bay area and the St. Lawrence Seaway.[17]

Life History and Ecology:

Reaching maturity at an age of 20 years,[15] this species spawns from early May through June[17] when water temperature reaches about 11.6 C.[19] Spawning occurs in shallow rapids (0.6 to 5 m), swift waters of smaller streams,[16] or on rocky shoals of lake shores.[15] Females are capable of producing over 500,000 adhesive eggs, which are laid rather indiscriminately over rocky substrate.[15] Females do not reproduce every year, usually spawning every 4 to 6 years, while males spawn at 2 or 3 year intervals.[7] Females are reported to live longer and attain a larger size than males.[15]

The lake sturgeon feeds in areas of clean sand, gravel, and small rocks where mollusks, small crustaceans, and insect larvae can be found in abundance.[6]

Status:

Lake Sturgeon populations have declined significantly since 1885, when 2.27 million kg was reported harvested in Lake Erie alone. There was a single recent specimen collected in Lake Erie (M. L. Hendricks, pers. comm.) by the Pennsylvania Fish Commission, but no other reported specimens. The lake sturgeon is considered endangered by the Advisory Committee on Fishes.

Recommendations:

Interruption of spawning movements by dams and increased siltation caused primarily by runoff probably have affected the Pennsylvania population of the lake sturgeon. Maintenance of water quality and minimization of obstructions could enhance the possibility of recolonization by the lake sturgeon, but artificial introductions may be necessary to re-establish this species in Pennsylvania rivers.

It is also the recommendation of the authors that this species be considered as an addition to the list of federally endangered species of the United States. Extreme declines in range-wide populations[6,15,18,19,20] would appear to warrant federal consideration for this species which was historically a valuable commercial fish.

THREESPINE STICKLEBACK
Gasterosteus aculeatus Linneaus

Description:

Gasterosteus aculeatus, the threespine stickleback, is one of the most studied species of fishes in the world because of hardiness, small size, and adaptability to laboratory environments. Wootton[21] has consolidated the available literature into two books dealing with the biology of the stickleback family, although most of the data are specifically related to the threespine stickleback. Unless otherwise referenced, all information contained herein comes from Wooten.[21]

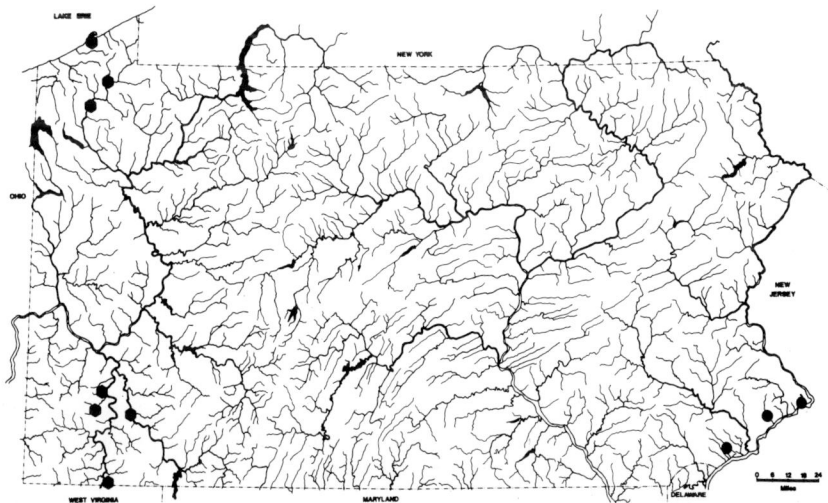

FIGURE 3. Occurrences of *Gasterosteus aculeatus* Linnaeus (circles) and *Ammocrypta pellucida* (Putnam) (hexagonals) in Pennsylvania waters.

The threespine stickleback is one of the smallest North American fishes, reaching an adult size of 10 cm. The body is laterally compressed, spindle shaped, and tapers to a slender caudal peduncle possessing a truncate caudal fin.

The dorsal and anal fins are located far back on the body. Three spines occur anterior to the dorsal fin, although some members of this species have 2 or 4 dorsal spines. Two of these spines are approximately equal in height to the dorsal fin and one is approximately half that size. There is also a pectoral spine that is slightly longer than the dorsal spines located posterior and ventral to the pectoral fins.

This species can be separated from other Gasterosteidae of North America by the fact that its gill membranes are joined separately to the isthmus, and it possesses lateral dermal armature in the form of bony plates.[7]

Range:

Gasterosteus aculeatus is nearly circumpolar and is widely distributed between 35 and 70 degrees N latitude in Europe, North America, and parts of Asia.[22] It is present in fresh, salt, and brackish waters, and is generally restricted to coastal or near coastal areas.

On the eastern half of North America, this stickleback occurs west of the Chesapeake Bay and north into the Hudson Bay area. It occurs from Rio Rosario, Baja, California, up the Pacific coast, along the Aleutian Islands, and into the southwestern coast of Alaska.[22] In Pennsylvania, it has been reported from 3 sites in the lower Delaware River drainage system[!]

Habitat:

This species is generally found in slow-flowing backwaters, tributaries of rivers, ditches, sheltered bays and harbours. It can also be found in lakes and ponds where emergent or submerged vegetation occurs.

Life History and Ecology:

Outside of the breeding season, sticklebacks are schooling fish, except in times of low food supply. In the spring, sticklebacks migrate to spawning areas, either from salt to freshwater, or from deep to shallow areas within freshwater. Females continue to school, while the males become territorial. Within their territory, the males build nests of cemented vegetation and sand. Gravid females move into the territories and a series of courtship movements follow, until the female enters the nest, lays her eggs, and leaves. The male then enters the nest and fertilizes the eggs. He then settles the eggs in the bottom of the nest, drives the spent female away, and begins another courtship ritual. The male may fertilize up to seven clutches before ceasing his courtship behavior.

The male tends the nest, fans the eggs, and drives away predators until the eggs hatch. He then dismantles the nest, protects, and herds the fry until they become too active for him to control. Several days after dispersal of the fry, the male may build another nest and begin the cycle again. Males have been known to complete five cycles of nesting within a season.

High mortality of males is common at the end of these breeding cycles. At the end of the breeding season, surviving adults and young migrate back to their wintering habitat.

For females, maturity may occur within 4 to 5 months of hatching. They are capable of producing several clutches of eggs during the breeding phase depending upon light, temperature, and food supply.

Status:

Of the three Pennsylvania sites in the lower Delaware River reported to have yielded *Gasterosteus aculeatus*, only one has yielded a voucher specimen for verification (PSU 1200). This specimen comes from Pennypack Creek in Philadelphia County, and was collected in 1969[!]

Considering this species questionable historical record in Pennsylvania, and the probability that collected specimens may have been isolated individuals dispersing into unsuitable habitat, it does not appear to warrant classification as an endangered species in Pennsylvania. An additional point of consideration is its abundance in other surrounding regions.[22]

Recommendations:

It is the authors' opinion that the threespine stickleback be removed from the list of endangered species of Pennsylvania.

EASTERN SAND DARTER
Ammocrypta pellucida (Putnam)

Description:

The eastern sand darter is a very slender, elongated darter. The standard length ranges between 7.0 and 11.2 times the body depth. As in all *Ammocrypta*, there is one short, soft, anal spine, and the ventral portion of the body is scaleless, except for several rows below the lateral line.[6] The frenum is wide, dividing the upper lip groove.

Live specimens are particularly colorless, reflecting the latin roots of its name "pellucidus", which means transparent or clear.[23] There are 9 to 14 small oblong dark spots along the midline of the side, and 12 to 16 saddle-like spots along the dorsal midline.[6]

It is the only member of the genus *Ammocrypta* found in Pennsylvania, and is easily distinguished from other syntopic darters (Etheostomatini) by its elongated body shape and pale coloration.[1]

Range:

Ammocrypta pellucida is distributed from the southern tip of Lake Huron, around Lake Erie and south through most of the Ohio River basin to western Kentucky. There is also disjunct population which exists in the St. Lawrence—Lake Champlain drainage.[23]

In Pennsylvania, this darter occurred in the lower Youghiogheny and Monongahela Rivers, further north at two sites in French Creek, and in Presque Isle Bay of Lake Erie[1] (Figure 3).

Habitat:

Occurring primarily in low gradient lotic habitats with moderate to high flows,[6] this species is occasionally found in wave-protected areas of lake shores.[24] It usually occurs over silt free sandy substrates,[6] but can be found over a variety of other substrates ranging from sand to a mixture of mud, clay, silt, gravel, and sand.[24]

Life History and Ecology:

Spawning takes place between early June in the Ohio River basin and early August in the St. Lawrence River and Great Lakes region.[25] Very little is known about the biology of the eastern sand darter, but its close relative, the western sand darter, *Ammocrypta clara* Jordan and Meek, has been observed to produce an average of 200 eggs and reaches an age of 3 years.[9]

An interesting behavior of *A. pellucida* is that of burying themselves in soft sand with only their eyes and mouths exposed.[6,25,26] Williams[25] hypothesized that this is a means of protection from predators, or more probably energy conservation, as they occur in areas that rarely support a population of predators. Trautman[6] described this burial behavior as part of a feeding mechanism associated with ambushing prey items.

Status:

The eastern sand darter is officially considered threatened in Pennsylvania. Lake Erie has yielded only 2 specimens since 1907,[23] and may not contain a viable population to date. A population was located in French Creek near Venango, Pa. However, the last specimen obtained from this site was collected in 1977. Recent (1985) extensive collections in this area by the authors have yielded no additional specimens, indicating that this population may be extirpated.

Recommendations:

It is the recommendation of the authors that the eastern sand darter be elevated to endangered status in Pennsylvania. This reommendation is based on the absence of this species from recent collections in the French Creek and Presque Isle Bay areas, and on its special status in all adjoining states that consider it a portion of their indigenous fauna (Table 1).

The minimization of siltation loads in the French Creek area is of major importance as there may still exist a small population capable of reasserting itself in the local fauna. Trautman[6] reported the decline of the eastern sand darter in Big Darby Creek, Pickaway Co., Ohio, where its decline was directly related to the loss of clean, sandy substrate.

BLUE PIKE
Stizostedion vitreum glaucum Hubbs

Description:

The blue pike, a subspecies of *Stizostedion vitreum*, is a slender, elongated fish with two well separated dorsal fins and a moderately forked tail. The terminal mouth possesses many large sharp canine teeth on the jaws and palatines. The free edges of the preopercle are strongly serrated. The spinous dorsal fin has a large dark spot that covers the webbing between the last 3 spines.[6]

It can be differentiated from the walleye by its whitish-blue pelvic fins and grayish-blue body. The walleye has yellowish pelvic fins and a brassy-yellow body. The eyes of the blue pike are larger and closer together than those of the walleye.[6]

Range:

The blue pike was believed confined to Lake Erie,[6] but Cooper[27] reported its apparent presence in Lake Ontario and possibly in Lake Nipissing, Ontario.

Habitat:

Stizostedion vitreum glaucum inhabited the deeper, clearer waters of Lake Erie[6] and Lake Ontario[27]. Their numbers were greatest in the eastern two-thirds of Lake Erie, although a general migration to the western third of the lake occurred in fall and early winter.[6]

Life History and Ecology:

The blue pike reached a size between 23 and 41 cm and a weight up to 0.7 kg, and was thus much smaller than the walleye which often grows to 66 cm and 2.5 kg.[6] The blue pike was preferred by commercial fishermen because of its smaller size, soft flesh, and blue coloration. In 1885, U.S. commercial fishermen harvested almost 1.5 million kg. This catch declined in the early 1900's, but until 1959, the industry still harvested large catches (900,000 to 11,800,000 kg between 1950 and 1957).[28]

Little is known of the ecology of this fish as a subspecies. It was considered a color morph of the walleye until described by Hubbs in 1926.[6]

Status:

The blue pike is considered endangered in Pennsylvania, and until recently, it was considered a Federally endangered subspecies. However, it has recently been reclassified as extinct in the United States[30] and Canada.[31]

Recommendations:

The blue pike is officially recognized by the Pennsylvania Fish Commission's Advisory Committee on Fishes as an extinct subspecies in Pennsylvania.

LITERATURE CITED

1. Cooper, E.L. 1983. Fishes of Pennsylvania and the Northeastern United States. The Pennsylvania Univ. Press, University Park, vii + 243pp.
2. Federal Register, March 11, 1967.
3. Cooper, E.L. 1985. Lake trout, *Salvelinus namaycush* (Walbaum), pp. 187-189 *in:* Fishes, E.L. Cooper, pp. 169-256 in Species of Special Concern in Pennsylvania, H.H. Genoways and F.J. Brenner (eds) Carnegie Mus. of Nat. Hist., Pittsburgh, PA, vi + 430pp.
4. Martin, B., S.P. Platamia and D.E. McAllister. 1978. *Salvelinus namaycush* (Walbaum), lake trout, pp. 117-118 in Atlas of North American Freshwater Fishes, D.S. Lee et al. (eds) all editors N.C. State Mus. Nat. Hist., Raleigh, NC., x + 854pp.
5. Deacon, J.E., G. Kobetich, J.D. Williams, S. Contreras. 1979. Fishes of North America endangered, threatened, or of special concern. Fisheries 4(2): 29-44.
6. Trautman, M.B. 1981. The Fishes of Ohio, with illustrated keys. Ohio State Univ. Press, Columbus, xxv + 782pp.
7. Eddy, S. and J.C. Underhill, 1978. How to Know the Freshwater Fishes. W.C. Brown Co., Dubuque, IO, viii + 215pp.
8. Gilbert, C.S. 1985. Shortnose sturgeon, *Acipenser brevirostrum* Lesueur, pp. 171-174 *in* Fishes, E.L. Cooper pp. 169-256 in Species of Special Concern in Pennsylvania. H.H. Genoways and F.J. Brenner (eds). Carnegie Mus. of Nat. Hist., Pittsburgh, PA, vi + 430pp.
9. Grunchy, C.G. and B. Parker. 1979. *Acipenser brevirostrum* Lesueur, shortnose sturgeon, p. 38 in Atlas of North American Freshwater Fishes, D.S. Lee et al. (eds.) N.C. State Mus. Nat. Hist., Raleigh, x + 854pp.
10. Lee, D.S., A.W. Norden and C.S. Gilbert. 1984. Endangered, threatened and extirpated freshwater fishes of Maryland, pp. 287-328 *in* Threatened and Endangered Plants and Animals of Maryland, A.W. Norden et al. (eds.) Maryland Dept. Nat. Res., Baltimore, iv + 475pp.
11. Music, J.A. 1979. Shortnose sturgeon, pp. 335-337 in Proceedings of the Symposium on Endangered and Threatened Plants and Animals of Virginia, D.W. Linzey. (ed) Virginia Polytech. Inst. and State Univ., v + 665 pp.
12. McCleave, J.D., S.M. Fried and A.K. Towt. 1977. Daily movements of shortnose sturgeon, *Acipenser brevirostrum*, in a Maine estuary. Copeia (1):149-157.
13. Gorham, S.W. and D.E. McAllister. 1974. The shortnose sturgeon *Acipenser brevirostrum*, in the Saint John River, New Brunswick, Canada, a rare and possible endangered species. Syologeus, 518 pp.
14. Brundage, H.M. and R.E. Meadows. 1982. Occurrence of the endangered

shortnose sturgeon. *Acipenser brevirostrum*, in the Delaware River Estuary. Estuaries 5:203-208.
15. Pfleiger, W.L. 1975. The Fishes of Missouri. Missouri Dept. Conserv., Western Publ. Co., St. Louis, vii + 343 pp.
16. Cooper, J.E. 1985. Lake sturgeon, *Acipenser fulvescens* Rafinesque, pp. 174-176 in: Fishes, E.L. Cooper, pp. 169-256 in Species of Special Concern in Pennsylvania, H.H. Genoways and F.J. Brenner (eds). Carnegie Mus. of Nat. Hist., Pittsburgh, PA, vi + 430 pp.
17. Grunchy, C.G. and B. Parker. 1980. *Acipenser fulvescens* Rafinesque, lake sturgeon, p. 38 in Atlas of North American Freshwater Fishes, D.S. Lee et al. North Carolina State Mus. of Nat. Hist., Raleigh, x + 854 pp.
18. Harkness, W.J. and J.R. Dymond. 1961. The lake sturgeon. The history of its fishery and problems of conservation. Ontario Dept. Lands and Forests, Fish and Wildl. Branch., 121 pp.
19. Becker, G.C. 1983. Fishes of Wisconsin. The University of Wisconsin Press, Madison, xii + 1052 pp.
20. Van Meter, H.D. and M.B. Trautman. 1970. An annotated list of the fishes of Lake Erie and its tributary waters exclusive of the Detroit River. Ohio J. Sci. 70:65-78.
21. Wootton, R.J. 1976. The Biology of the Sticklebacks. Academic press, New York, x + 387 pp.
22. Burgess, G.H. and D.S. Lee. 1978. *Gasterosteus aculeatus* Linneaus, three spine stickleback, p. 563-564 in Atlas of North American Freshwater Fishes, D.S. Lee et al (eds. include all editions), N.C. State Mus. of Nat. Hist., Raleigh, x + 854 pp.
23. Hendricks, M.L. 1985. Eastern sand darter, *Ammocrypta pellucida* (Putnam), pp. 182-184 in Fishes, E.L. Cooper, pp. 169-256 in Species of Special Concern in Pennsylvania, H.H. Genoways and F.J. Brenner (eds). Carnegie Mus. of Nat. Hist., Pittsburgh, PA, vi + 430pp.
24. Hocutt, C.H. 1980. *Ammocrypta pellucida* (Agassiz), eastern sand darter, p. 620 in Atlas of North American Freshwater Fishes, D.S. Lee et al. North Carolina State Mus. Hist., Raleigh, x + 854pp.
25. Williams, J.D. 1975. Systematics of the percid fishes of the subgenus Ammocrypta, Genus *Ammocrypta*, with descriptions of two new species. Bull. of the Alabama Mus. of Nat. Hist. 1:1-56.
26. Linder, A.D. 1953. Observations on the care and behavior of darters, Etheostominae, in the laboratory. Proc. of the Oklahoma Acad. of Sci. 43:28-30.
27. Cooper, J.E. 1985. Blue pike, *Stizostedion vitreum* glaucum Hubbs, pp. 254-255 in Fishes, E.L. Cooper, pp. 169-256 in Species of Special Concern in Pennsylvania, H.H. Genoways and F.J. Brenner. Carnegie Mus. of Nat. Hist., Pittsburgh, PA, vi + 430 pp.

28. Applegate, V.C. and H.D. Van Meter. 1970. A brief history of commercial fishing in Lake Erie. Fishery Leaflet 630, U.S. Fish and Wildl. Ser., Bur. of Comm. Fish., 28 pp.
29. Denoncourt, R.F. 1975. Key to the families and genera of Pennsylvania freshwater fishes and the species of freshwater fishes of the Susquehanna River drainage above Conowingo Dam. Proc. PA Acad. Sci. 49:82-88.
30. Federal Register, September 2, 1983.
31. U. S. Fish & Wildlife Service, 1983. Endangered Species Technical Bulletin 8(10):3.

Endangered and Threatened Species Programs in Pennsylvania and other States: Causes, Issues and Management. Edited by S. K. Majumdar, F. J. Brenner and A. F. Rhoads. © 1986, The Pennsylvania Academy of Science.

Chapter Fifteen

FISHES OF THE DELAWARE ESTUARY IN PENNSYLVANIA

Richard J. Horwitz
Division of Environmental Research
Academy of Natural Sciences of Philadelphia
19th and the Parkway
Philadelphia, PA 19103

The Delaware Estuary is formed by rising sea levels drowning the lower portions of the river channel, tributary channels and floodplain.[1] It starts at the Fall Line, represented by Scudder's Falls, at Trenton, N.J. (opposite Yardley, Pa.) and extends 222 km seaward to its mouth, bordered by Capes May and Henlopen (fig. 1). The average tidal range is 2 m at Trenton, and 1.8 m at Philadelphia, with a maximum range up to 4.2 m.[2] The upper estuary is fresh, with salinities typically less than 400 mg/l from Marcus Hook up and less than 100 mg/l at Paulsboro (seawater has a typical salinity of 33000 mg/l) (data of Philadelphia Water Department and Delaware River Basin Comission). Thus, the Pennsylvania portion is typically fresh water, although the salt line moves upstream in periods of low freshwater input (fig 2). In the rest of this chapter, the estuary will be defined as the tidal portions of the river and its tributaries; the portion of the estuary upstream of the Pennsylvania-Delaware state line will be referred to as the upper estuary. Unless specific localities are mentioned, records from the New Jersey and Pennsylvania sides of the river will not be differentiated. The Schuylkill River is the only major tributary; There are also a number of smaller tributaries, some forming small bays at their mouths. Naturally, the Pennsylvania tributaries are tidal up to the Fall Line, which is generally only a few km above their mouths. Tidal sections of the New Jersey tributaries reach much farther upstream. Dams, e.g., the Art Museum Dam on the Schuylkill, now form the upper limit of tidewater on a number of tributaries.

FIGURE 1. Map of Upper Delaware Estuary and lower courses of major tributaries.

Before settlement, the river in the upper estuary contained a meandering channel, with pools separated by shoals 1 to 2.4 m in depth.[2] The shores of the river contained extensive freshwater, intertidal marshes. Dominant plants in the deeper parts of these marshes included many species still present in remaining marshes: several species of *Sagittaria* and *Pontederia,* and *Peltandra virginica, Zizania aquatica,* and *Nuphar advena*.[3] (A. Schuyler, pers. comm.). The lower estuary was (and is) fringed by extensive saltwater marshes.[3] There is less historical data on submerged vegetation; it is likely that in places there were extensive beds of species of *Potamageton, Najas, Elodea* and *Vallisneria* (A. Schuyler, pers. comm.).

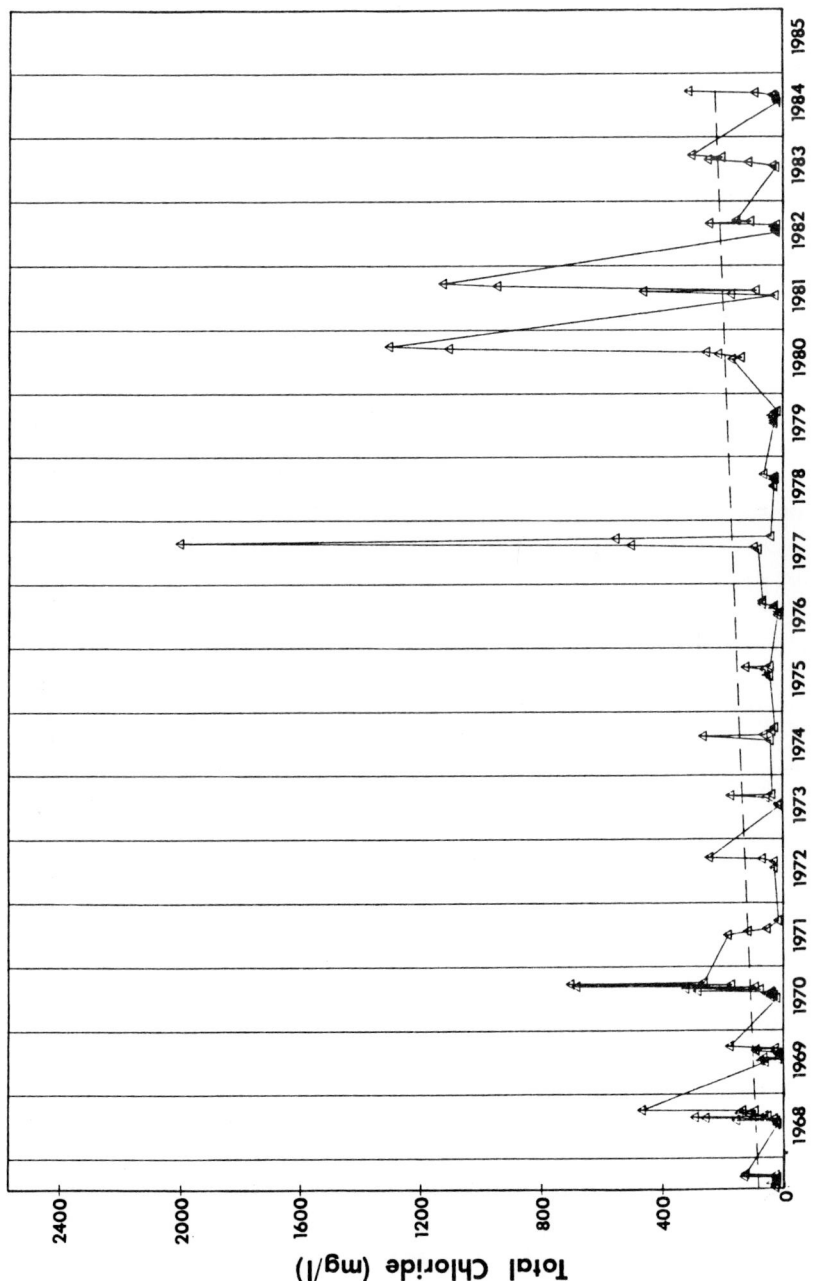

FIGURE 2. Summer chloride concentrations (mg/l) at Marcus Hook, Pennsylvania. Values are for surface samples taken between June and September. Data are from the Delaware River Basin Commission.

180 Endangered and Threatened Species Programs in Pennsylvania and other States

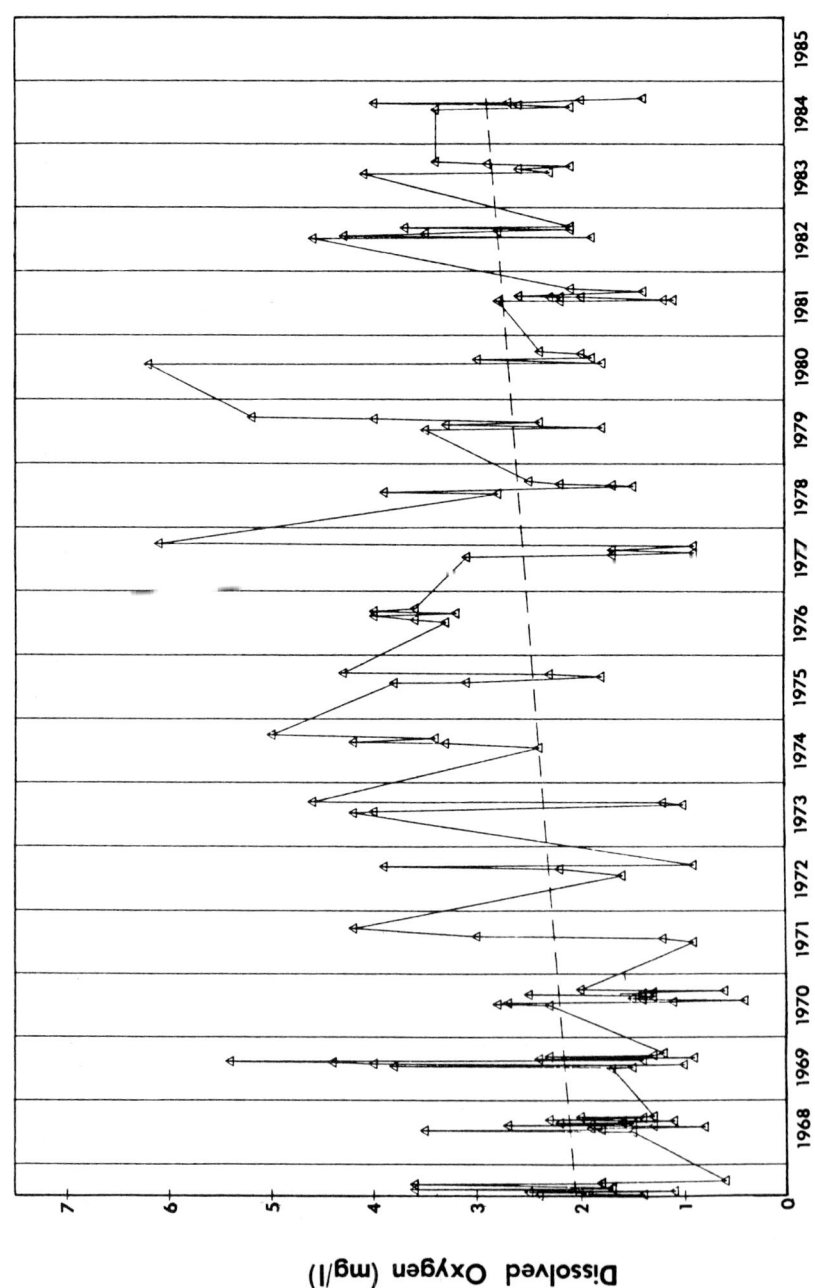

FIGURE 3. Summer dissolved oxygen concentrations (mg/l). Data are from the Delaware River Basin Commission. Values are for samples taken between June and September.
   a. Bottom (49 feet depth) concentrations at the Benjamin Franklin Bridge, Philadelphia, Pennsylvania.

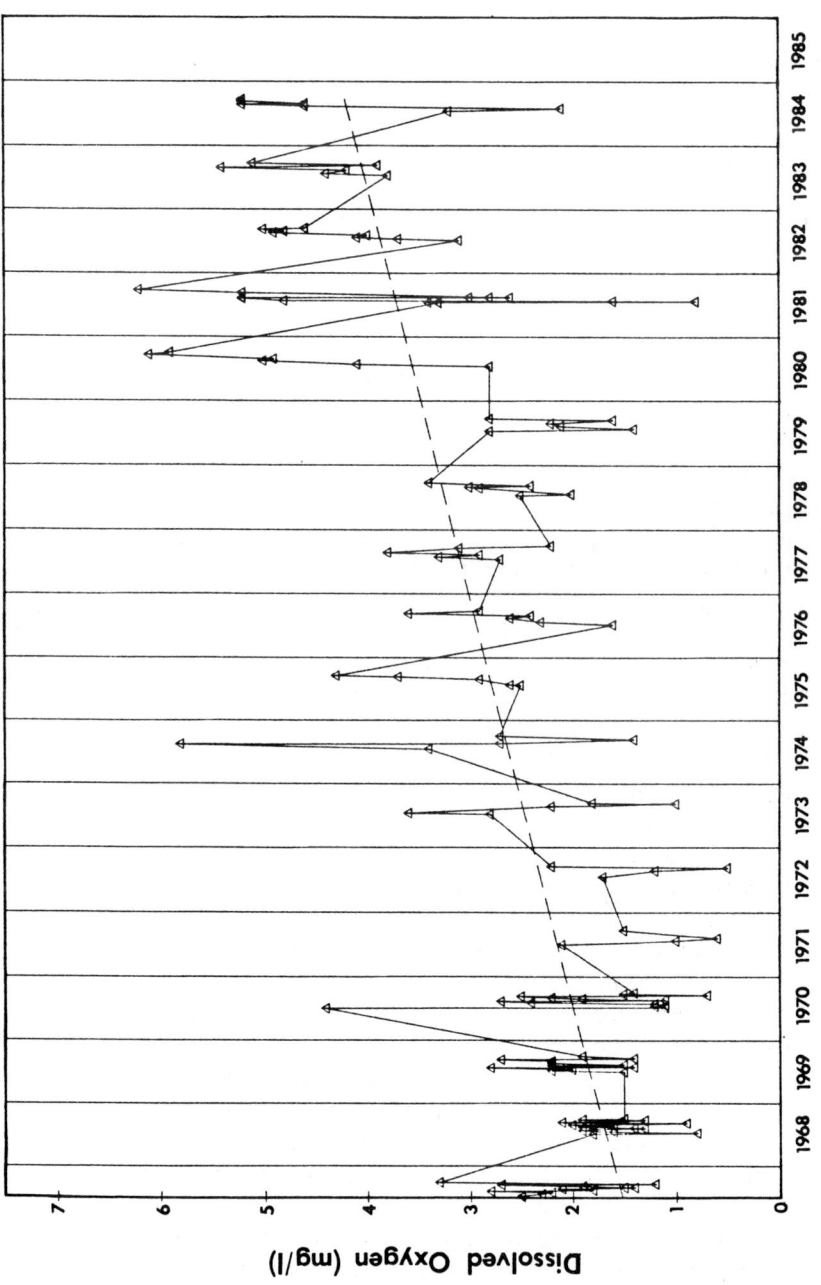

b. Surface concentrations at Marcus Hook, Pennsylvania.

There have been tremendous anthropogenic changes in the estuary. Dredging of a navigational channel (started in 1836; the current design implemented from 1930 on) has produced typical cross sections of shallow shore zones of soft substrates and a deep (7.5-12 m below the Trenton Marine Terminal) channel of gravel or sand substrate.[2] Development of land adjacent to the river and dumping of dredge spoil has resulted in filling of much of the marshland in the upper estuary, although marshes are still present along mouths of tributaries and along backwaters.[3, 4] While many of the original plant species have persisted in these marshes, a number of species, especially intertidal species, have become much less common.[5] There is less recent information on submerged vegetation, but it appears that there are fewer areas of extensive submerged vegetation; remaining areas may consist largely of the alien species *Myriophyllum spicatum*.[2] (A. Schuyler, pers. comm.).[6] Construction of boat slips and extensive areas of pilings have provided novel habitats along the industrial portions of the river. In addition to changing the channel form, periodic maintenance of the channels may remove benthic fauna and increase the suspended solid load in and near areas being dredged.[2] In several places, especially near Bristol and Tullytown, small lakes have been created near the river; the fish communities of these ponds may be somewhat different from those in the main rivers.[7]

Diversions from the upper Delaware River, e.g., to parts of New Jersey and New York City, and consumptive uses within the basin decrease the total freshwater input to the estuary and may affect the position of the salt line, especially during dry years. Regulation of flow from dams on tributary streams controls the inflow to some extent. The Chesapeake and Delaware Canal reaches Delaware Bay at Delaware City, about 30 km south of the Pennsylvania-Delaware state line. The canal provides a net input of freshwater to the Delaware Estuary, although the direction and magnitude of flow is highly variable. The input of freshwater is particularly significant during low flow periods, when the canal may provide as much net freshwater input as the main river.[8, 9]

Historically, one of the most severe impacts on the river came from inputs of sewage and organic industrial waste into the estuary, leading to severe depletions of dissolved oxygen. During summer and early fall, a region between Philadelphia and Marcus Hook, a reach of about 35 km, often contained virtually no dissolved oxygen.[10] In addition to rendering the areas uninhabitable to fishes and other aquatic groups, this produced a block to the downstream movement of postspawning adults and juvenile anadromous species in summer and early fall [11, 12] (fide).[13] Mortality sometimes occurred on upstream runs as well.[11] In recent years, increased processing of wastes has led to decreased organic inputs, and increased summer DO levels have been noted (fig. 3), although periods of low DO still occur. Areas of higher DO may occur along the New Jersey shore even during periods of low DO across the rest of the channel (C. Emory, pers. comm.).

While treatment has decreased the oxygen demand associated with organic enrichment, the nutrient input from processed water and non-point sources remains high. There have also been considerable inputs of metals (e.g., lead, zinc, nickel), hydrocarbons (from oil spills, refineries, etc.), and other organic contaminents (e.g., PCBs). Although inputs of many of these have decreased, substantial amounts remain in sediments. While high concentrations of several pollutants have been detected in tissues of fish from the estuary, toxic effects are poorly known.

Other conditions which may effect fish populations include thermal effluents, which may limit fish distribution. For example, movement into Marcus Hook Creek from the river has at times been prevented by high temperature water at the mouth (ANSP).[14,15,16] Impingement and entrainment of organisms at water intakes may also affect fish populations.

The changes in the environment of the Delaware estuary have been matched by extensive changes in the fish fauna of the system, including extirpation of several speceis, decreases of a number of native species, and introduction and increase of many non-native species. These changes must be discussed in the context of the ecology and biogeography of the native fauna.

The fauna of the Delaware Estuary consists of a mix of species typical of freshwater, brackish, and saltwater habitats. There are no natural barriers to movement within the estuary, and many species use different portions of the system at various life stages. Species characteristic of one part of the estuary may stray into areas of higher or lower salinity. There are a number of anadromous species (species which are mainly resident in estuarine or marine waters, but which spawn in freshwater) and one catadromous species (species which are mainly resident in freshwater, but which spawn in saltwater). The Delaware River system has a relatively low number of principally freshwater species of fish, due to glaciation and restricted opportunities for movement from other drainage basins (cf.)[17] (cf).[18] As a result, anadromous and catadromous species are especially important in the river and estuary.

The Delaware estuary system represents not only a transition between fresh and salt water, but represents the boundary between Piedmont and Coastal Plain provinces. The upper limit of the estuary on the main river at Trenton and along the smaller tributaries in Pennsylvania is the Fall Line, the boundary between the two provinces. The main river, the lower courses of the Pennsylvania tributaries and most of the New Jersey tributaries flow through the Coastal Plain. Within the Coastal Plain are boggy areas, with acid, brownwater streams and ponds. Most of these are located in the Pine Barrens (on the Outer Coastal Plain), but pockets of similar habitat occur within the Inner Coastal Plain near the Delaware River, e.g., near Bristol. Also, the larger tributaries on the New Jersey side extend into the Outer Coastal Plain. As a result, some species typical of the Pine Barrens occur in or near the Delaware estuary. Historically, Mill Creek, near Bristol, was one of the most important areas for these species; recent collecions indicate that most of the local Coastal Plain species no longer occur in the area.

Thus, the native fish fauna of the upper Delaware estuary has a number of anadromous species, as well as elements of the typical faunas of brackish estuaries, brackish marshes, larger freshwater rivers, small Piedmont streams, and small Coastal Plain streams (including some species typical of the Pine Barrens waters of the Outer Coastal Plain). The Delaware estuary is also near the northern or southern boundary of the range of a number of species. Because of this mix of species, many of the rarer species of the Delaware estuary occur as marginal populations or strays, with the species occurring commonly in other areas; changes in the Delaware estuary populations may have relatively small effects on total species abundance. In a few cases, however, the estuary may provide habitat for a species declining in other parts of its range.

The low number of native sport species in the Delaware river led to the introduction of a number of species to the river and upper estuary: bowfin (scientific names of all species mentioned in this paper are given in Table 1), muskellunge (primarily the hybrid "tiger muskie"), brown trout, carp, goldfish, channel catfish, walleye, largemouth bass, smallmouth bass, black crappie, white crappie, rock bass, bluegill, and green sunfish. The spotfin shiner also appears to be a recent, natural colonist.[18] The carp, goldfish, spotfin shiner, channel catfish, walleye, largemouth bass, black and white crappies, and bluegill are well established in the upper estuary; the bowfin is established but rare; the muskellunge is maintained as a common species by stocking. There are records of smallmouth bass [2,20] and brown trout (observed in the Schuylkill River fishway, presumably from fish stocked in upstream tributaries) from the estuary; the rock bass and green sunfish are more common in tributaries of the estuary but do occur in tidewater. A few other species were introduced but did not become established (e.g., the Atlantic salmon), or are occassionally encountered as "bait-bucket" releases (e.g., fathead minnow, which may be established in the Schuylkill River). The mosquitofish was reported to be common in the Tinicum march area.[21] A record of the warmouth from the Delaware River [22,20] presumably derives from an introduction.

The most significant change in the fish fauna created by these introductions is the increase in the diversity of piscivorous fish. Among native fishes, the chain pickerel and striped bass are the only strongly piscivorous species; the American eel, yellow perch and white perch are also piscivorous to some extent. Virtually all the introduced species (and especially the bowfin, muskellunge, walleye, and basses) are piscivorous. This change is greatest in the upper river, above the main range of the striped bass and white perch, but is present in the estuary as well. It seems likely that these introductions of piscivorous species would lead to decreases of the native piscivorous species and/or increases in predatory pressure on other species. However, these effects are difficult to document and could be counterbalanced by human harvest of the larger, most strongly predatory

TABLE 1

Scientific and common names of species reported from the upper Delaware estuary (defined as the portion of the estuary upstream of the Pennsylvania-Delaware boundary). Names not in quotation marks from Robins et al.[61]

Scientific name	Common name		Special status*		Occurrence and Records	
		U.S.	Pa.	N.J.		
Petromyzon marinus	sea lamprey	NA	I		R	1,13
Acipenser brevirostrum	shortnose sturgeon	NA	E	E	R	3
Acipenser oxyrhynchus	Atlantic sturgeon	NA	V	T	R	3
Amia calva	bowfin	IF	I		R	13,16
Lepisosteus osseus	longnose gar	NF	I		X	
Alosa aestivalis	blueback herring	NA			R	1,3,6,13-17
Alosa mediocris	hickory shad	NA	I		see text	
Alosa pseudoharengus	alewife	NA			R	3,6,9,13-17
Alosa sapidissima	American shad	NA		T	R	13-17
Dorosoma cepedianum	gizzard shad	NF			R	3,9,13-17
Brevoortia tyrannus	menhaden	NE			R	4,13,14,16,17
Anchoa mitchilli	bay anchovy	NE			R	4,13,14,17
Salmo salar	Atlantic salmon	IA			X	
Salmo trutta	brown trout	IP			see text	
Osmerus mordax	American smelt	NA			X	
Umbra pygmaea	Eastern mudminnow	NF			R tPN	2,5,8
Esox americanus	redfin pickerel	NF			R	6,13,17
Esox masquinongy and	muskellunge	IP				
Esox masquinongy x lucius	"tiger muskie"	IP			R	3,9
Esox niger	chain pickerel	NF			R	3,16
Carassius auratus	goldfish	IE			R	3,6,13,14,16,17
Cyprinus carpio	carp	IE			R	3,6,13-17
Exoglossum maxillingua	cutlips minnow	NF			H	2
Hybognathus regius	Eastern silvery minnow	NF			R	1,3,6, 13-17
Notemigonus crysoleucas	golden shiner	NF			R	1,3,6,13,14,16,17
Notropis amoenus	comely shiner	NF			R	1,2
Notropis analostanus	satinfin shiner	NF			R	1,3,6
Notropis bifrenatus	bridle shiner	NF	V		see text	
Notropis chalybaeus	ironcolor shiner	NF	X		X	
Notropis cornutus	common shiner	NF			R	13
Notropis hudsonius	spottail shiner	NF			R	1,3,6,13-17
Notropis procne	swallowtail shiner	NF			R	1,6
Notropis spilopterus	spotfin shiner	NF			R	1
Pimephales notatus	bluntnose minnow	NF			R tN	8
Pimephales promelas	fathead minnow	IF			R	13
Rhinichthys atratulus	blacknose dace	NF			R	1,6
Rhinichthys cataractae	longnose dace	NF			R	13
Semotilus atromaculatus	creek chub	NF			R	1
Semotilus corporalis	fallfish	NF			H	2
Carpiodes cyprinus	quillback	NF			R	3,13
Catostomus commersoni	white sucker	NF			R	3,6,9,14-17
Erimyzon oblongus	creek chubsucker	NF			R	1
Ictalurus catus	white catfish	NB			R	3,6,9,13-17
Ictalurus natalis	yellow bullhead	NF			R	3
Ictalurus nebulosus	brown bullhead	NF			R	3,6,9,13-17
Ictalurus punctatus	channel catfish	IE			R	3,6,9,13-17
Noturus gyrinus	tadpole madtom	NF	V		H	2
Noturus insignis	margined madtom	NF			H	2
Anguilla rostrata	American eel	NC			R	1,3,6,13-17
Strongylura marina	Atlantic needlefish	NE			R	1,2
Cyprinodon variegatus	sheepshead minnow	NE			R tN	10
Fundulus diaphanus	banded killifish	NB			R	3,6,13-17
Fundulus heteroclitus	mummichog	NE			R	3,6,13-17

Scientific name	Common name	Special status* U.S.	Special status* Pa.	Special status* N.J.	Occurrence and Records
Fundulus luciae	spotfin killifish	NE			R 5
Gambusia affinis	mosquitofish	IF			R 5
Merluccius bilinearis	silver hake	NE			R 1
Microgadus tomcod	Atlantic tomcod	NE	T		R 1
Pollachius virens	pollack	NE			R 1
Urophycis chuss	squirrel hake	NE			R 1
Apeltes quadracus	fourspine stickleback	NB	I		R 1,3,6
Gasterosteus aculeatus	threespine stickleback	NB	E		R 1,13,17
Syngnathus fuscus	Northern pipefish	NE			R 1
Aphredoderus sayanus	pirate perch	NF	X		X 2
Opsanus tau	oyster toadfish	NE			R 13
Morone americana	white perch	NB			R 3,6,9,13-17
Morone saxatilis	striped bass	NA			R 3,4,13-17
Acantharchus pomotis	mud sunfish	NF	X		X 2,11
Ambloplites rupestris	rock bass	IE			R 2,13
Enneacanthus chaetodon	blackbanded sunfish	NF	X		X 2
Enneacanthus gloriosus	bluespotted sunfish	NF			R tN 6,12
Enneacanthus obesus	banded sunfish	NF	V		R 13 (see 7)
Lepomis auritus	redbreast sunfish	NF			R 3,9,13,15,17
Lepomis cyanellus	green sunfish	IP			R 1,13,15-17
Lepomis gibbosus	pumpkinseed	NF			R 3,6,9,13-17
Lepomis gulosus	warmouth	IF			R 13 (see 7)
Lepomis macrochirus	bluegill	IE			R 3,6,13-17
Micropterus dolomieui	smallmouth bass	IE			R 3
Micropterus salmoides	largemouth bass	IE			R 3,6,9,13,15-17
Pomoxis annularis	white crappie	IE			R 3,13,14,16,17
Pomoxis nigromaculatus	black crappie	NF			R 3,6,13,14,16,17
Etheostoma fusiforme	swamp darter	NF	X		X 2
Etheostoma olmstedi	tesselated darter	NF			R 3,6,13,14,16,17
Perca flavescens	yellow perch	NF			R 3,13-17
Stizostedion vitreum	walleye	IE			R 3,9
Pomatomus saltatrix	bluefish	NE			R 1,13,14
Trachinotus carolinus	Florida pompano	NE			R 1
Bardiella chrysura	silver perch	NE			R 1
Cynoscion regalis	weakfish	NE			R 1,2
Leiostomus xanthurus	spot	NE			R 1,2,3,13-17
Micropogonias undulatus	croaker	NE			R 4,13,14
Gobiosoma bosci	naked goby	NE			R 4,13,14
Mugil cephalus	striped mullet	NE			R 4
Menidia beryllina	tidewater silversides	NE			R 2,4,13,17
Paralichthys dentatus	summer flounder	NE			R 13
Pseudopleuronectes americanus	winter founder	NE			R 1
Trinectes maculatus	hogchoker	NE			R 2,3,13,14

Species recorded from nontidal portions of tributaries of the upper estuary, but not recorded from estuary:

Scientific name	Common name	Special status* U.S.	Special status* Pa.	Special status* N.J.	Occurrence and Records
Lampetra appendix	American brook lamprey	NF			2
Salvelinus fontinalis	brook trout	NF	T		
Percina peltata	shield darter	NF		2	

Distribution: IE Introduced, established in upper estuary;
　　　　　　　IP Introduced, maintained by stocking, or as strays from established non-estuarine populations
　　　　　　　NF Native, primarily freshwater
　　　　　　　NE Native, primarily estuarine or marine　　NB Native, freshwater or estuarine
　　　　　　　NA Native, anadromous　　　　　　　　　　NC Native, catadromous

Status: E endangered; T threatened; V vulnerable; I status undetermined; X extirpated.

Occurrence: R records from main river known after 1950; H records known before 1950, none known after 1950, but species still present in adjacent nontidal tributaries; X records known before 1950, none known after 1950, species not known in adjacent nontidal tributaries; tP records from tidal tributaries in Pennsylvania known after 1950; tN records from tidal tributaries in New Jersey known after 1950.

Representative records: References or specimens of species in upper estuary. Not all records of species are listed. 1 Ichthyological Associates collections from Bordentown area (specimens in ANSP); 2 Other ANSP specimens; 3 Hastings,[2] O'Herron and Hastings;[32] 4 Pennsylvania Fish Commission; 5 McCormick;[21] 6 ANSP;[4] 7 Cooper;[20] 8 Hastings and Good;[33] 9 ANSP;[7] 10 Walton and Patrick;[3] 11 Fowler;[58] 12 Graham and Hastings;[46] 13 PECO;[22] 14 PECO;[34] 15 PECO;[35] 16 PECO;[36] 17 PECO;[37]

individuals (cf. Trautman,[23] for a discussion of changes in predator and prey abundance and age structure induced by fishing) or by increased productivity of prey species.

The American eel is the only catadromous species in the estuary. It has been an abundant species throughout the period of record.[24,20] The native anadromous fish of the Delaware estuary include four species of river herrings (the American shad, hickory shad, blueback herring and alewife), the shortnose and Atlantic sturgeons, the sea lamprey, the smelt, the white perch and the striped bass. These vary in the extent of upstream movement. The hickory shad typically moves short distances into freshwater [25,26] and is rarely reported from the upper estuary.[20] On the other hand, the sea lamprey and American shad move upstream as far as New York. The other herrings also move into the Delaware River above Trenton. Historically, the species moving into the upper river and into tributaries were adversely affected by dams, notably a dam at the mouth of the Lackawaxen River (built 1823, a fishway built 1891, dam broached a few years after)[27,11] While no dams now occur on the main river, dams limit spawning habitat in a number of tributaries, especially the Schuylkill River and Lehigh River. A fishway has been built on the Art Museum Dam on the Schuylkill, but there are still several upstream dams without fishways. It is expected that fishways will be built in the near future on the two lowermost dams on the Lehigh River (L. Young, J. Miller, pers. comm.). Overfishing probably decreased populations of some of these species, especially the Atlantic sturgeon. As noted above, the oxygen block in the Philadelphia area has had a major adverse effect. The area of low DO encompassed major parts of the spawning grounds of several species, including the striped bass, Atlantic sturgeon and the American shad. The DO block may also have lead to reduced populations of species (e.g., the white perch) which would normally have used the area as adults. As noted above, the severity of the oxygen block appears to have decreased in recent years, which may lead to reversal of some of the historical trends. However, one of the anadromous species, the smelt, is extirpated in the estuary.[20] Although known from specimens and reported as common in the Schuylkill and Delaware Rivers in the nineteenth century,[28] I know of no twentieth century records. Because of the commercial and sport interest in most of these species, there is a great deal of information on them; their status will be discussed in greater detail below.

American shad. Historically, the American shad was the primary commercial species in the upper estuary and the Delaware River. The Delaware was one of the most important shad rivers in the country. The shad decreased in abundance in the nineteenth century, presumably because of dams and overfishing. For example, records of a fishery at Woodbury, NJ, showed the following average catch: 1818-1822 131,000/year; 1845-1849 66,890/year; 1865-1869 60,739; 1870-1873 less than 25,000/year.[29] Increases were noted in the late nineteenth century, attributed to removal of dams, increased protection, and stocking.[28] The total catch from the Delaware was estimated to be between 800,000 and 1,150,00/year for the years 1885-1892.[27] Subsequently, the shad decreased again, with apparent sharp decreases between 1901 and 1904 and between 1913 and 1920.[11] This trend is demonstrated by the average annual catches over time: 1880-1892 12,400,000 pounds, 1893-1901 15,900,000 pounds, 1904-1916 3,600,000 pounds, 1917-1930 400,000 pounds, 1931-1945 260,000 pounds, 1946-1954 118,000 pounds.[11] Toward the end of the period, many of the fish were caught in Delaware Bay and may not have been part of the Upper Delaware stock. The development of the oxygen block has been considered the major factor in this decline,[11,13] although the contributions of various factors and the cause of the major declines cannot be determined. Sykes and Lehman[11] and Chittenden[13] found a very low proportion of repeat spawners in the Delaware River shad relative to other stocks, which suggests high postspawning mortality. Although probably never in imminent danger of extirpation, the shad has been listed as threatened in New Jersey.[30]

With improving water quality in the Philadelphia area and restoration of shad fisheries in other rivers (e.g., the Connecticut), there has been increased interest in shad management and restoration. Currently, the Delaware River Basin Commission, the U.S. Fish and Wildlife Service and the state fish departments are cooperating in a program to monitor and manage the American shad population in the Delaware. Programs include estimation of adult population sizes, fishing mortality, and year class strength using capture-recapture methods, abundance surveys of juveniles, regulation of fishing, implementation of fish ladders at dams on tributaries, and stocking of eggs, larvae and/or adults in the Lehigh and Schuylkill Rivers to develop populations which will be able to use the fish ladders. The effects of this program will not be fully apparent for several years, because of the four to five year lag between larval production and upstream spawnings movements, natural variability in year class strength, high statistical variability of population estimates, and because several elements (e.g., opening of fish ladders, improvements in water quality) are not finished. Recent population estimates of the adult population range from 106,000-233,000 for 1975-1979 and 182,000-546,000 for 1980-1983.[31]

Other herrings. The alewife has been, and continues to be, a common species in the Delaware estuary. It is likely that it has been affected by many of the same factors which caused declines in the American shad. While declines have not been noted in historical accounts, this may be due to the relative lack of interest in the alewife resulting from its lower commercial value. There is no reference to the hickory shad or blueback herring in early accounts; these species may have been confused with the alewife or other species at times. Both species were noted by Fowler.[22] Recent collections show the blueback to be fairly common in the Delaware.[4,20,2,32,33,22,34,35,36,37] As noted above, the hickory shad rarely occurs in the upper estuary.

Striped bass. The striped bass has been one of the most important commercial and sport species in the Hudson River and the Chesapeake Bay. After 1934, there were a number of strong year classes in these areas. Recently, there have been major declines in the Chesapeake Bay, with no strong year class since 1970. As a result, there has been increasing research and management interest in the striped bass. The striped bass has not received as much attention in the Delaware River, although it has been consistently recorded from the river and upper estuary.[24,28,32,20] The development of the oxygen block may have prevented an increase in the Delaware River in the period after 1934 comparable to the increase in the Chesapeake. Murawski[31] (fide)[28] noted that spawning occurred in the low salinity portions of the Delaware Bay and tributaries, but that no eggs and larvae occurred in the 45 km region near Philadelphia, presumably due to low oxygen conditions; above Philadelphia, larvae were noted up to Newbold Island. In contrast to the upper estuary, the Chesapeake and Delaware Canal has been a major spawning area. Adults and juvenile striped bass have been captured fairly commonly in the upper estuary in recent years (C. Emory, PFC, pers. comm.), although there has been some question whether these juveniles derive from spawning in the Chesapeake and Delaware Canal or the upper estuary (J. Miller, pers. comm.).

Shortnose sturgeon. The shortnose sturgeon was described from the Delaware River in 1818. It was relatively common in the nineteenth century, but declined after about 1910; there are no documented collections between 1913 and 1964.[2] There was no major commercial fishery on the smaller shortnose sturgeon as there was on the larger Atlantic sturgeon; because of the large mesh used in the Atlantic sturgeon gill net fishery, not many shortnose sturgeon were caught.[39] However, as large Atlantic sturgeon became rare, smaller mesh sizes may have been used, leading to greater catch of shortnose sturgeon: Smith[40] reported that many of the sturgeon caught in 1914 were shortnose sturgeon. Shortnose (and small Atlantic sturgeon) were taken in the shad seine fishery in the upper estuary and were often killed.[39] The shortnose sturgeon has been protected and given Endangered status by the Fish and Wildlife Service, New Jersey, and Pennsylvania. Ongoing studies of the species in the Delaware [2,41,32] have found the species to be relatively common inthe deep channel of the river, particularly in the region between Trenton and Newbold Island. In the Delaware, it does not appear to forage in shallows, as has been noted in other rivers. Because of its restricted habitat, it is not vulnerable to conventional fishing gear, and Hastings conjectured that the paucity of records after 1920 may be due to the lack of appropriate fishing effort; if so, the apparent decrease after 1920 and the apparent increase to current levels would be due to sampling artifacts rather than real changes in abundance. However, it is plausible that the apparent trends are real and reflect the response of the sturgeon to changes in water quality and food supply. Bivalves form a major part of the diet of the shortnose sturgeon. In the Delaware, its main food appears to be the introduced clam *Corbicula,* which is by far the dominant mollusc in the river. Based on its pattern of spread, McMahon[42] concluded that *Corbicula* colonized the Atlantic coastal drainages only after about 1965. The earliest records for the Delaware are from 1971.[43] Historically, there was an important native mussel fauna in the river; these species have disappearred or declined in most of the upper estuary, probably due to dredging, siltation and oxygen depletion. Thus, it is possible that there was a period of very low bivalve abundance between the decline of the native fauna and the arrival and increase of *Corbicula* (alternatively, the decrease in some native species may have been due to the increase of *Corbicula*). The current abundance of the shortnose sturgeon may reflect increased food resources.

Virtually all the shortnose sturgeon recently collected have been large juveniles or adults. The smallest fish were estimated to be three to four years old, despite efforts to collect larvae and small juveniles. O'Herron and Hastings[32] conjectured that no successful spawning occurred in the study years, possibly because of high river flows (the species is thought to spawn in the high gradient areas near and possibly above Scudder's Falls). If successful recruitment is dependent on occasional years with favorable spawning conditions, the species may be more vulnerable than the current population size would otherwise indicate. Thus, although recent studies indicate a sizeable population in the upper estuary, the history and population dynamics of the population is still uncertain.

Atlantic sturgeon. Early records describe large populations of the Atlantic sturgeon.[24,28,44,39] Adults occurred primarily in the estuary, moving upstream to spawn. Spawning was thought to occur mainly in the region 30 km above and below Delaware City;[39] this region includes part of the upper estuary, so that spawning would have been affected by pollution below Philadelphia. Juveniles were common upstream to Trenton[39] and were reported as far upriver as Port Jervis.[28] A large commercial fishery developed around 1870.[44,24,39] Annual catches of 4,200,000-5,000,000 pounds were taken in Pennsylvania, New Jersey and Delaware in 1890-1892;[45] most of this was in the middle estuary, but there were active fisheries in the upper estuary. The populations subsequently declined, likely as a result of fishing pressure: by 1901, the annual catch was only 275,000 pounds, in 1921 58,000 pounds, 1929-1935 18,000 pounds, 1937-1938

5900 pounds (figures from various annual reports of the Commissioner of the U.S. Bureau of Fisheries). Between 1890 and 1899, the average catch per net fell from 60 to 8.[39] A number of recent records exist for the upper Delaware, although it does not appear as common in the area as the shortnose sturgeon.[2,41,32] It is plausible that protection and improvements in water quality would lead to increasing populations, but there are not enough data to document any trend.

In contrast to the anadromous species, there are a number of estuarine species which spawn in the ocean; the larvae and juveniles of these species move up into estuaries and may move into or near freshwater. Several of these species (spot, croaker, menhaden, bluefish, Florida pompano, squirrel hake, pollack, and summer flounder) have been recorded in the upper Delaware estuary, especially during low flow years. Juveniles and adults of other species which are resident in estuaries (bay anchovy, tidewater silverside, northern pipefish, Atlantic needlefish, tomcod, naked goby, striped mullet, oyster toadfish, silver hake, silver perch, weakfish, winter flounder) also occur in the upper Delaware estuary, also most commonly during low flow years;[22,34] (also IAB, ANSP and PFC collections). Although these species are more common in more saline parts of estuaries, some (e.g., needlefish and mullet) may be resident in freshwater reaches. The periods of greatest upstream abundance of these species coincides with the greatest severity of low DO conditions; historically, many of these species may have been excluded from Pennsylvania waters by the oxygen block. For example, the needlefish was considered to be common in the upper estuary,[24] and there are a number of records from the period 1908-1911. Although there are some recent records (e.g., 1957) and reports of catches in Pennsylvania (C. Emory, pers. comm.), the needlefish appears to be less common recently. These estuarine species are generally common to abundant in other parts of the estuary, so the exclusion may not have been very significant to the species in general.

Several resident estuarine species are most common in tidal marshes. These environments often have great temporal variation in salinities and these species are usually very tolerant of a range of salinities. Many occur in freshwater; landlocked populations of some of these species are common. Several of these are recorded in marshes, shallows or associated with submerged vegetation throughout the upper Delaware estuary. For example, the mummichog is one of the commonest species throughout the estuary.[3,33,46] The sheepshead minnow was not reported from the upper estuary in early surveys; however, there is a specimen from a Piedmont locality, Trumbauersville, Bucks County (1917). The sheepshead minnow was one of the commonest species in samples from Lower Rancocas Creek in 1972.[3] The spotfin killifish was reported from the vicinity of Tinicum marsh in 1966.[21]

The four-spine and the three-spine stickleback are both uncommon in the upper estuary. Both are near the southern limit of their range,[26] although they do occur in Chesapeake Bay. They are listed as species of uncertain status in Pennsylvania by the PFC and may be declining. The three-spine stickleback was reported to be "abundant in ponds and ditches along the Delaware";[28] however, there is only one historical record (a tributary of the Delaware River at Holmesburg; taken in 1905). Three-spine sticklebacks were also collected at intake screens at several places in the area in the 1970s (IAB, PECO).[22,37] The four-spine stickleback was reported to be abundant in tidewater streams along the Delaware[24] and there are number of specimens from the Delaware River and tributaries from Trenton to Camden taken between 1899 and 1919. There is a 1970 record from the Burlington area (IAB) and several records from tidal parts of Crosswicks Creek and marsh.[14] Hastings[2] reported 1 specimen taken in the upper estuary in 1983 (exact locality not given). (The species was also collected in 1951 in Wissahickon Creek, above the Fall Line; Cooper[20] shows localities from the central Delaware River, also above the Fall Line.)

There are several species which are most common in the low salinity or freshwaters of upper estuaries and the lower courses of large coastal rivers. The white catfish and the hogchoker are common in the upper Delaware estuary (the white catfish was commonly referred to as the Schuylkill catfish because of its abundance in the Schuylkill River.[24,47]) The tomcod is much rarer in the Delaware estuary. Declines in the Hudson River populations have led to its classification as a threatened species in New Jersey.[30] It is near the southern limit of its range in the Delaware.[26] It was not recorded in early accounts of the Delaware fauna, and has been unreported in most surveys of the river, upper and lower estuary. However, it is known from recent specimens (e.g., IAB specimens from the Bordentown area collected in 1970-1972). It is not possible to document trends in its abundance, except that it has apparently been rare throughout the period of record.

There are a number of species in the upper estuary which are widely distributed and typical of large eastern rivers, lakes and/or ponds, e.g., gizzard shad, golden shiner, spottail shiner, brown bullhead, silvery minnow, pumpkinseed, and yellow perch. With a few exceptions, there are no clear trends in the abundance of these species. However, the longnose gar, which was known from a specimen and early accounts (Cope[24] and Bean[28] reported it to be abundant in the lower Delaware River) is now extirpated. This species was at the northern limit of its range along the coast; its disappearance may have been caused by loss of spawning marshes or other factors. The chain pickerel, recorded as common ("abounds in Delaware";[28] is uncommon in the estuary now, although recent records exist.[2]

There are a number of species which are most common in Piedmont streams where they are usually associated with riffles or areas with sand substrates. Several of these, e.g., the blacknose dace, common shiner, creek chub, fallfish, comely shiner, swallowtail shiner and margined madtom, were reported from the upper estuary (largely Fowler specimens in ANSP collections). Although rare in the estuary,[48] most of these species have been recorded recently (see table 3). The early records of these species may have been strays from small tributaries; they may also have been resident in small side channels of the main river with appropriate habitat. It is unlikely that the estuary was ever a significant habitat for these species. Changes in occurrence (if real) may be due to pollution, damming of the lower stretches of tributary streams and/or loss of appropriate habitat in the main river because of dredging and filling. In contrast, species like the satinfin shiner, banded killifish and tesselated darter, which are not as dependent on clean substrates for spawning (they lay adhesive eggs on hard substrates off the bottom), remain common in parts of the estuary. The bluntnose minnow was reported from the tidal portion of Woodbury Creek.[33] The white sucker, which is common as an adult in the estuary (e.g.),[7,2] moves into the small tributaries to spawn.

The bridle shiner is most often recorded from Piedmont streams with vegetation, but it is also known from estuaries (Delaware[49] Chesapeake.[25,50]) There are also a number of records from Coastal Plain streams in New Jersey and Pennsylvania. The bridle shiner has decreased or been extirpated from many small streams[51] in Pennsylvania, New Jersey and the remainder of its range. Thus, occurrence in vegetated areas of the upper estuary could be significant to the population of the species. There are historical records from the Delaware River near Philadelphia from 1908 and 1911; there are a number of records from tributaries in the Tullytown and Bristol area between 1898 and 1917. There are no recent records from these areas. Bridle shiners were taken in the lower Delaware River in Delaware and New Jersey (near Pea Patch Island, Salem and Augustine Beach) in 1958-1960 (ANSP specimens).[49] Thus, the species may continue to exist in the estuary.

Like the bridle shiner, the yellow bullhead and grass pickerel occur in both Piedmont and Coastal Plain streams, particularly in clearer and/or more vegetated habitats. Fowler reported the grass pickerel from the upper estuary; recently, specimens were caught on impingement screens in Philadelphia and Chester[22,37] and in tidal parts of Crosswicks marsh.[4] The yellow bullhead was not reported from the upper estuary in early surveys; Hastings[2] reports 2 specimens from the upper estuary taken in 1983 (exact localities not given).

The greatest changes in distribution of species in the upper estuary are in species typical of vegetated Coastal Plain habitats[20,51,48]: tadpole madtom, ironcolor shiner, pirateperch, Eastern mudminnow, swamp darter, mud sunfish, banded sunfish, most bluespotted sunfish and blackbanded sunfish (some of these species occur outside the Coastal Plain in other parts of their range). The Delaware estuary and associated tributaries was the major area of occurrence of several of these in Pennsylvania, so that loss of these is equivalent to extirpation from the state, although most are common in parts of New Jersey.

The ironcolor shiner was described from a tributary of the Schuylkill River[52] above the Fall Line and was recorded from several areas in Pennsylvania. Two of these were near the Delaware, one in the lower parts of Neshaminy Creek and the other in Mill Creek, near Bristol. A record from Trenton could have come from the Delaware or a tributary. It was also recorded at several areas in or near the Pine Barrens. There are no Pennsylvania records after 1917. It has also disappeared from most areas in New Jersey, although there are recent records from a few localities.

Cope[24] noted the occurrence of the tadpole madtom in tributaries of the Delaware River. Specimens were taken from the Delaware River and from tributaries in both Pennsylvania and New Jersey from 1899-1917. Although still common in places in the Pine Barrens, I know of no recent records from the Delaware River or nearby areas. (There is a 1957 record from the East Branch of Brandywine Creek. In Pennsylvania, the species has also been recorded from near Lake Erie.)

The Eastern mudminnow was stated to be very common near Philadelphia.[24] However, Pennsylvania specimens (taken mainly between 1899 and 1917) are mainly from the Bristol to Tullytown area; these were taken from the river and from tributaries. The species has been recently reported from at least one of these areas (a tributary of Mill Creek), in tidal portions of Woodbury Creek in New Jersey,[33] in the Tinicum area[21] and in several Piedmont areas in Pennsylvania. It is abundant in many nontidal areas in the New Jersey coastal plain.

There are two old records of the pirateperch from Pennsylvania, one from the Delaware River (at Holmesburg, near Philadelphia) and one from Tullytown Creek, a Coastal Plain tributary. There are no recent records of the species from Pennsylvania. It is abundant in parts of New Jersey, especially in the Pine Barrens.

The swamp darter was known from Pennsylvania from Mill Creek near Bristol (specimens from 1905, 1911); there are also records from the Delaware River at Trenton. There are no recent records from the Delaware River or from Pennsylvania. The species is common in parts of the Pine Barrens.

There are four species of small sunfishes which primarily occur in Coastal Plain waters. All have been recorded from the Delaware estuary area, but have decreased in abundance. All continue to occur in the Pine Barrens, and some are common in other areas as well. The bluespotted sunfish is the most widely distributed, occurring in the Poconos and Piedmont as well.[20] It was reported as common in Southeastern Pennsylvania[24] and there are a number of records from the Delaware River and nearby tributaries from 1899-1917; the Delaware River records range from Trenton to League Island. Although apparently less common now, there are recent records in several tidal tributaries in New Jersey;[4,46] it is common in some of these localities. The banded sunfish was reported less commonly. It was considered rare in Southeastern Pennsylvania by Cope[24] and there are only 6 records by Fowler from the estuary[53] (ANSP specimens). These include river sites (some of the records give the town name, but do not indicate whether the fish came from the river or from tributaries). PECO[22] records 3 recent specimens taken on impingement screens on the Delaware River near Chester (this record is repeated by Cooper[20]). Graham and Hastings[46] reported one New Jersey locality near Salem. Thus, although rare, the species continues to occur in the Delaware estuary. The blackbanded sunfish is currently the species most restricted to acid Coastal Plain waters, although pH may not be the direct cause of the restriction.[54,46] There are 3 Delaware estuary records, from the Delaware River at Bristol (1898), from "Bristol" and from "Trenton". There are no recent records and it is probably extirpated from the estuary and Pennsylvania.[20] The mud sunfish is known from one Pennsylvania record, a Bucks County record by Fowler.[53] It was also reported from "Trenton" and from Crosswicks Creek, near Trenton (1903-1906). There are no recent records from the estuary or Pennsylvania. Recent records exist from the Pine Barrens and other parts of New Jersey.[62]

In summary, most of the freshwater species of the lower Delaware Drainage and many Delaware estuary species have been recorded from the upper estuary. While many of these species remain common in the upper estuary, decreases in the occurrence and abundance of a number of species have been noted. Decreases are most evident in anadromous species and species associated with vegetated habitats. The longnose gar and smelt are extirpated from the estuary and consequently from the Delaware drainage. The ironcolor shiner, pirateperch, mud sunfish, blackbanded sunfish, and swamp darter are apparently extirpated from the estuary. Although known from nontidal areas in New Jersey (some in the Delaware Drainage), localities in or near the estuary were the only known sites for Pennsylvania, so these species are presumably extirpated from Pennsylvania as well. The tadpole madtom has not been recorded recently from the estuary, although it is still present in other parts of Pennsylvania and New Jersey. The bluespotted sunfish has not been reported recently in Pennsylvania portions of the estuary, but is known from the estuary in New Jersey and from nontidal areas in both Pennsylvania and New Jersey. Several other species characteristic of vegetated Coastal Plain and/or Piedmont habitats are less common in the estuary now. One of these, the bridle shiner, is becoming uncommon in many other parts of its range, so that the estuarine habitat may be important to the distribution of the species. Most of the anadromous species certainly or probably declined in abundance in the period between 1820 and 1950, as a result of dams, overfishing, and pollution in the Philadelphia area. Most of these species remain below historical levels of abundance, but there are indications of recent population increases. Continuing protection and management, improvements in water quality, and construction of fishways on tributaries may lead to further population increases of these and other species. A number of introduced species have become well established in the estuary; some, like the channel catfish, are among the most common species in the estuary. Recent occurrences of a number of estuarine species in the upper estuary are compiled; many of these were not reported in historical synopses of the fuana of the upper estuary. The occurrence of these species reflects the intensive sampling in the 1970s and 1980s associated with environmental studies, improvements in water quality, and the occurrence of several years of low freshwater flows in the period.

ACKNOWLEDGEMENTS

I would like to thank Joe Miller, Arthur Lupine, Leroy Young, Jerry Pasquale, Clark Shiffer, Robert Hastings, Charles Emory and Ruth Patrick for supplying information on the status of various species; Faith Douglas and Dan Otte for help with the preparation of the figures; Barbara Bloomfield for information on water quality; and Alfred Schuyler for information on aquatic vegetation.

LITERATURE CITED

1. Sharp, J. H., C. H. Culberson and T. M. Church, 1982. The Chemistry of the Delaware estuary. General Considerations. Limnol. Oceanog. 27(6):1015-1028.
2. Hastings, R. W. 1983a. A Study of the Shortnose Sturgeon (*Acipenser brevirostrum*) Population in the Upper Tidal Delaware River. Initial Draft Report for the U.S. Army Corps of Engineers, Philadelphia District. 130 p.
3. Walton, T. E., and R. Patrick, ed. 1973. Delaware River Estuarine Marsh Survey. A Report to the National Science Foundation RANN Program. The Academy of Natural Sciences of Philadelphia. 172 p.
4. Academy of Natural Sciences of Philadelphia. 1975. Ecological analysis of Crosswicks Creek marsh and surrounding areas 1974 for Louis Berger Incorporated. Acad. Nat. Sci. Phila. 117 pp.
5. Ferren, W. R., Jr. and A. E. Schuyler. Intertidal vascular plants of river systems near Philadelphia. Proc. Acade. Nat. Sci. Phila. 132:86-120.
6. Davis, F. W. 1985. Historical changes in submerged macrophyte communities of Upper Chesapeake Bay. Ecology 66(3):981-983.
7. Academy of Natural Sciences of Philadelphia. 1985. Studies to Assess Accumulation of Target Compounds by Fishes of Schmidt's Lake and Lake Idaline and the Delaware River for the Rohm and Haas Company. 328 pp.
8. Pritchard, D. W. and L. E. Cronin. 1971. Chesapeake and Delaware Canal Affects Environment. American Soc. Civ. Engineers Nation Water Resources Engineering Meeting. 26 p.
9. Natural Resources Institute, University of Maryland. 1973. Hydrographic and ecological effects of enlargement of the Chesapeake and Delaware Canal. Final Report, Summary of Research Findings, to the U.S. Army

Corps of Engineers, Philadelphia District. 137 p.
10. Kiry, P. R. 1973. An historical look at water quality of the Delaware River Estuary to 1973. Cont. Dept. Limnology, Acad. Nat. Sci. Phila. no. 4. 76 pp.
11. Sykes, J. E. and B. A. Lehman. 1957. Past and present Delaware River shad fishery and considerations for its future. U.S. Fish and Wildlife Serv. Res. Rep. 46. 25 p.
12. Chittenden, M. E., Jr. 1969. Life history and ecology of the American shad, *Alosa sapidissima,* in the Delaware River. Rh.D. Thesis, Rutgers Univ., New Brunswick, N.J. 458 pp.
13. Chittenden, M. E., Jr. 1974. Dynamics of American Shad, *Alosa sapidissima* runs in the Delaware River. Fishery Bull. 73(3):487-494.
14. Academy of Natural Sciences of Philadelphia. 1977. Marcus Hook Creek studies for B. P. Oil Co., Inc. Report no. 77-26. Acad. Nat. Sci. Phila. 60 pp.
15. Academy of Natural Sciences of Philadelphia. 1980. 1980 Marcus Hook Creek Studies for the Sun Petroleum Products Co. Rept no. 80-21. Acad. Nat. Sci. Phila. 143 pp.
16. Academy of Natural Sciences of Philadelphia. 1981. 1981 Marcus Hook Creek Studies in the Vicinity of Marcus Hook Refinery for the Sun Refining and Marketing Company. Rept. 82-7F. Acad. Nat. Sci. Phila. 97 pp.
17. Bailey, R. M. 1945. Review of "Some Considerations on the distribution of fishes in Ontario". Copeia 1945(2): 125-126.
18. Sepkoski, J. J. Jr. and M. A. Rex. 1974. Distribution of Freshwater Mussels: Coastal Rivers as Biogeographic Islands. Syst. Zool. 23(2): 165-188.
19. Horwitz, R. J. 1982. The range and co-occurrence of the shiners *Notropis analostanus* and *N. spilopterus* in southeastern Pennsylvania. Proc. Acade. Nat. Sci. Phila. 134: 178-193.
20. Cooper, E. L. 1983. Fishes of Pennsylvania and the Northeastern United States. 243 pp. Pennsylvania State University Press. University Park.
21. McCormick, J. 1970. The Natural Features of Tinicum Marsh with Particular Emphasis on the Vegetation. pp 1-94 in Two Studies of Tinicum Marsh, Delaware and Philadelphia Counties, Pennsylvania. The Conservation Foundation.
22. Philadelphia Electric Company. 1977a. Eddystone Generating Station. Materials Prepared for the Environmental Protection Agency. 316(b) Report.
23. Trautman, M. B. 1981. The Fishes of Ohio. The Ohio State University Press. 782 pp.
24. Cope, E. D. 1881. The Fishes of Pennsylvania. pp. 60-145 in Report of the State Commissioners of Fisheries for the Years 1879 and 1880. Harrisburg.
25. Hildebrand, S. F. and W. C. Schroeder. 1928. Fishes of Chesapeake Bay. Bull. U.S. Bureau of Fisheries. 1927. vol. 53, part 1. 388 pp.

26. Lee, D. S., C. R. Gilbert, C. H. Hocutt, R. E. Jenkins, D. E. McAllister, and J. R. Stauffer, Jr. 1980. North American Freshwater Fishes. North Carolina State Museum of Natural History. 854 p.
27. Gay, J. 1892. The Shad Streams of Pennsylvania. pp. 151-187, appendix to Report of the State Commissioners of Fisheries for the Years 1889-1890-1891. Harrisburg.
28. Bean, T. H. 1892. The Fishes of Pennsylvania. pp. i-viii and 1-149, appendix to Report of the State Commissioners of Fisheries for the Years 1889-1890-1891. Harrisburg.
29. Slack, J. H. 1874. Notes on the shad, as observed in the Delaware River. pp. 457-460 in Report of the Commissioners of Fish and Fisheries of Pennsylvania for the Years 1872-1873.
30. New Jersey Department of Environmental Protection and U.S. Department of Agriculture. 1980. Endangered and Threatened Species of New Jersey. 44 pp.
31. Murawski, W. S. 1969. The distribution of striped bass, *Roccus saxatilis*, eggs and larvae in the lower Delaware River. N.J. Bui. Fish. Misc. Rept. no 1 M. 14 pp.
32. O'Herron, J. C. and R. W. Hastings. 1985. A Study of the Shortnose Sturgeon (*Acipenser brevirostrum*) Population in the Upper Tidal Delaware River: Assessment of Impacts of Maintenance Dredging (Postdredge Study of Duck Island and Perriwig Ranges). Draft Report for the U.S. Army Corps of Engineers, Philadelphia District. 100 p.
33. Hastings, R. W. and R. E. Good. 1977. Population analysis of the Fishes of a freshwater tidal tributary of the Lower Delaware River. Bull. New Jersey Acad. Sci. 22(2): 13-20.
34. Philadelphia Electric Company. 1977b. Chester Generating Station. Materials Prepared for the Environmental Protection Agency. 316(b) Report.
35. Philadelphia Electric Company. 1977c. Southwark Generating Station. Materials Prepared for the Environmental Protection Agency. 316(b) Report.
36. Philadelphia Electric Company. 1977d. Richmond Generating Station. Materials Prepared for the Environmental Protection Agency. 316(b) Report.
37. Philadelphia Electric Company. 1977e. Delaware Generating Station. Materials Prepared for the Environmental Protection Agency. 316(b) Report.
38. Smith, B. A. 1971. The Fishes of Four Low-Salinity Tidal Tributaries of the Delaware River Estuary. Part v in Ichthyological Associates, ed., An Ecological Study of the Delaware River in the Vicinity of Artificial Island. Ichthyological Associates, Bull. no. 5.
39. Cobb, J. N. 1900. The sturgeon fishery of Delaware River and Bay.

pp. 369-380 in U.S. Comission of Fish and Fisheries, Report of the Commissioner for the year ending June 30, 1899.
40. Smith, H. M. 1915. Sturgeon fishery of Delaware River. Bureau of Fisheries, Report of the U.S. Commissioner of Fisheries for 1914.
41. Hastings, R. W. 1983b. A Study of the Shortnose Sturgeon (*Acipenser brevirostrum*) Population in the Upper Tidal Delaware River: Assessment of Impacts of Maintenance Dredging (Pre-dredge Study of Duck Island and Perriwig Ranges). Draft report for the U.S. Army Corps of Engineers, Philadelphia District. 29 p.
42. McMahon, R. F. 1982. The Occurrence and spread of the introduced Asiatic freshwater clam, *Corbicula fluminea* (Muller), in North America: 1924-1982. The Nautilus. 96(4): 134-141.
43. Fuller, S. L. H. and C. E. Powell, Jr. 1973. Range Extensions of *Corbicula manilensis* (Philippi) in the Atlantic Drainage of the United States. The Nautilus 87(2): 59.
44. Meehan, W. E. 1897. Fish, Fishing and Fishes of Pennsylvania. pp. 313-459 in Report of the State Commissioners of Fisheries for the Year 1896. State of Pennsylvania. Harrisburg.
45. Smith, H. M. 1895. A Statistical Report on the Fisheries of the Middle Atlantic States. Bull U.S. Fish Commission 14: 339-467.
46. Graham, J. H. and R. W. Hastings. 1984. Distributional patterns of sunfishes on the New Jersey coastal plain. Env. Biol. Fishes 10(3): 137-148.
47. Jordon, D. S., B. W. Evermann, and H. W. Clark. 1930. Check List of the Fishes and Fishlike Vertebrates of North and Middle America. Appendix X. Report of the U.S. Commissioner of Fisheries for the Fiscal year 1928. 670 pp.
48. Schier, A. and P. Kiry. 1973. A Discussion of the Effects of Certain Potential Toxicants on Fish and Shellfish in the Upper Delaware Estuary. A Report to the National Science Foundation RANN Program. The Academy of Natural Sciences of Philadelphia. 54 p.
49. de Sylva, D. P., F. A. Kalber, Jr., and C. N. Shuster, Jr. 1962. Fishes and Ecological Conditions in the Shore Zone of the Delaware River Estuary, with Notes on Other Species Collected in Deeper Water. Univ. Del. Mar. Lab. Information series, Publ. no. 5 Delaware Board of Game and Fish Commissioners. 164 pp.
50. Mansueti, A. J. and J. D. Hardy, Jr. 1967. Development of fishes of the Chesapeake Bay Region, Part 1. An Atlas of egg, larval and juvenile states. Natural Resources Institute, University of Maryland. 202 pp.
51. Genoways, H. H. and F. J. Brenner. 1985. Species of Special Concern in Pennsylvania. Carnegie Museum of Natural History Spec. Publ. 11. 430 p.

52. Cope, E. D. 1869. Synopsis of the Cyprinidae of Pennsylvania. Trans. Amer. Phil. Soc. 13:351-399.
53. Fowler, H. W. 1940. A List of the Fishes Recorded from Pennsylvania. Commonwealth of Pennsylvania Board of Fish Commissioners. Bull. no. 7. 25 pp. Harrisburg.
54. Jenkins, R. E., L. A. Revelle and T. Zorach. 1975. Records of the Blackbanded Sunfish, *Enneacanthus chaetodon* and Comments on the Southeastern Virginia Freshwater Aichthyofauna. Va. J. Sci. 26(3): 128-134.
55. Abbott, C. C. 1874. Notes on the cyprinoids of central New Jersey. Amer. Natur. 8:326-338.
56. Fowler, H. W. 1906. Fresh and Salt Water Fish found in the Waters of New Jersey. Part 2 of the Annual Report of the New Jersey State Museum. 1905. Trenton.
57. Fowler, H. W. 1919. Notes on New Jersey, Pennsylvania, and Virginia Fishes. Proc. Acad. Nat. Sci. Phila. 71:292-300.
58. Fowler, H. W. 1939. Notes on Pennsylvania Fishes 1928-1935. pp 101-108 in Report of the Board of Fisheries Commissioners of Pennsylvania.
59. Greeley, J. R. 1936. Fishes of the area with annotated list. pp. 76-88 in: A biological survey of the Delaware and Susquehanna watersheds. Suppl. 25th Annual Report N.Y. State Conservation Dept. (1935).
60. Schuler, V. J. 1974. An Ecological Study of the Delaware River in the Vicinity of Artificial Island. Progress report for the Period January-December, 1973. Ichthyological Associates. Ithaca, N.Y. 571 pp.
61. Robins, C. R., R. M. Bailey, C. E. Bond, J. R. Brooker, E. A. Lachner, R. N. Lea, and W. B. Scott. 1980. A List of Common and Scientific Names of Fishes from the United States and Canada (Fourth Edition). American Fisheries Society. Spec. Pub. no. 12. 174 pp.
62. Mihursky, J. A. 1962. Fishes of the Middle Lenapewihittuck (Delaware River) Basin. Ph.D. thesis. Lehigh University. 208 pp.

APPENDIX: Sources of Information

Anecdotal information on the Delaware estuary fishes dates to the seventeenth century.[44] The development of major commercial fisheries and of scientific studies (e.g., by Le Sueur, Cope and Abbott) in the nineteenth century led to major increases in knowledge of the fish fauna; a number of species of fish were scientifically described from the Philadelphia area. Cope[24,52] and Abbott[55] published synopses the fauna; Bean[28] took most of his information from Cope's work, but added some newer information. In the period 1897-1921, H. W. Fowler made a number of collections in the Philadelphia area, including in the Delaware River. Fowler[32,53,56,57,58] summarizes some of these results. Although exact collecting localities and relative abundance of various species collected were often not recorded in these various studies, they provide useful indications of historical occurrence. There is relatively little information for the period 1921-1950, although major studies were done in the headwaters of the Delaware in this period[59]. After 1950, there was increasing research, often associated with the evaluation of the effects of industrial development, pollution, dredging, etc. Studies in the upper estuary include tabulations of fish impinged on power plant intake screens),[22,34,35,36,37] collections by the Academy of Natural Sciences in 1957-1960 and 1968-1970 (e.g., INCODEL and RANN Delaware River studies), and collections by Ichthyological Associates in the Bordentown area in 1970-1973 (in the text, these are referred to as IAB collections); these are particularly useful in providing records of estuarine species in the upper estuary. Studies in the Middle estuary (cf.)[49,60] and upper river[62] which were made in this period are also useful. Many of the Cope, Fowler, ANSP and IAB specimens are currently in the permanent collections of the Academy of Natural Sciences of Philadelphia; these specimens (most of which have been examined to verify identifications) provide the basis for many of the records mentioned in this paper. Cooper[20] compiled many records in his monograph. The Pennsylvania Fish Commission (PFC), the New Jersey Department of Fish and Game, the U.S. Fish and Wildlife Service, and the Delaware River Basin Commission have been conducting studies, primarily aimed at evaluation and management of major commercial and sport species. The U.S. Army Corps of Engineers has sponsored studies of the shortnose sturgeon.[2,32,41] Other relevant studies are cited in the text.

Endangered and Threatened Species Programs in Pennsylvania and other States: Causes, Issues and Management. Edited by S. K. Majumdar, F. J. Brenner and A. F. Rhoads. © 1986, The Pennsylvania Academy of Science.

Chapter Sixteen

NEW PERSPECTIVES ON THREATENED AND ENDANGERED AMPHIBIANS AND REPTILES IN PENNSYLVANIA

C.J. McCOY
Division of Life Sciences
Carnegie Museum of Natural History
Pittsburgh, PA 15213

The 18 species on the Pennsylvania list of threatened and endangered amphibians and reptiles are analyzed from historical, biogeographic, and ecological perspectives. Extirpated species (historical perspective) were eliminated during the initial phase of European colonization (1850-1900), and are probably not good candidates for re-introduction. Eight peripheral species (biogeographic perspective) warrant protection in Pennsylvania, but not extensive allocation of management resources. The 6 declining species should be analyzed from the ecological perspective, factors responsible for the decline identified, and resources allocated accordingly.

INTRODUCTION

The intense concern for the welfare of endangered species that accompanied the environmental revolution of the 1960's and 1970's was a reaction to an urgent problem! Species and populations of organisms whose continued existence was in jeopardy became the focus of attention for wildlife managers, legislators, and a public that was newly sensitized to environmental issues. In the resulting glare of publicity endangered species frequently became the objects of philosophical and rhetorical "tug-of-war" games between vested interests: interests too often represented only by their most outspoken and inflexible proponents. But despite the controversy, and persistent attacks on endangered species programs, the listing of threatened and endangered species proved to be an appropriate and effective response to the urgent problem of protecting species in jeopardy. Listing served to identify and publicize the species at greatest risk, and has given direction to subsequent action such as designation of critical habitat, and propagation and reintroduction programs. Now that the task of initial listing is largely completed, a more analytical approach to endangered species is appropriate. Each endangered species or population should be viewed from historical and biological perspectives, to ensure that future efforts at preservation are both adequate and appropriate.

The native amphibian and reptile fauna of Pennsylvania consists of 73 species.[2] Each of these species has been collected at least once in Pennsylvania during historic times, and for each a specimen of undoubted Pennsylvania provenance exists. Of the 73 species, 18 have been listed as "species of special concern".[3] These 18 species, and their status categories, are listed in Table 1. The status categories are defined as follows:[4]

Endangered — Species in imminent danger of extirpation throughout their range in Pennsylvania.

Vulnerable — Species which may become endangered because they, 1) exist in restricted geographic areas or habitats; 2) occur in low numbers, or 3) are particularly susceptible to exploitation or environmental modification.

Status Undetermined — Species that probably should be listed in one of the first three categories, but for which insufficient data are available.

Extirpated — Species that have disappeared from Pennsylvania, but still exist elsewhere.

In the volume "Species of Special Concern in Pennsylvania"[5] the reasons for listing these 18 species are fully reviewed and documented. On the basis of current information on distribution and population status these are the amphibians and reptiles at greatest risk in the Commonwealth.

This analysis, however, will view the list from three different perspectives. First, how the historical evidence affects the status of a species, second, how the distribution of Pennsylvania populations relates to the overall distribution of the species, and third, what are the ecological factors that may contribute to the decline of a species. These three perspectives—historical, biogeographic, and ecological—provide a different interpretation of the endangered species list, an interpretation that can be used to make decisions on future action and resource allocation.

EXTIRPATED SPECIES: THE HISTORICAL PERSPECTIVE

The process of extirpation, like most evolutionary processes, is a gradual one, but it has a fixed end point. This end point is the starting place for consideration of the extirpated amphibian and reptile species of Pennsylvania from the historical perspective. Four species of amphibians and reptiles have been extirpated from the fauna of Pennsylvania. Two of them, *Pseudotriton montanus* and *Ambystoma tigrinum*, are Coastal Plain forms, each recorded in Pennsylvania from a single collection made before 1900. *Pseudotriton montanus* was described from type-specimens collected on "South Mountain, Cumberland County".[6] The species has not been found again in Pennsylvania.[7] *Ambystoma tigrinum* was collected at Londongrove, Chester County around 1850.[8] Although this isolated record outside the Coastal Plain has been questioned,[9] *A. tigrinum* occurs in adjacent parts of New Jersey and Maryland, and habitat in the Londongrove area may have been suitable for the species.[2] The other two extirpated species, *Trionyx muticus* and *Emydoidea blandingii* are slightly better documented as former members of the Pennsylvania fauna. *Trionyx muticus* is a common riverine turtle in the lower reaches of the Ohio River System,[10] but was found only twice in Pennsylvania. Both records are from the Allegheny River, and both date from before 1901.[2] *Emydoidea blandingii*, a species of the midwestern prairies and Great Lakes area, was collected twice in Crawford County around the turn of the Century. Netting[11] hypothesized that these specimens were accidentally introduced in, or migrated through the Beaver and Lake Erie Canal (1844-1871). Whether that is the case, no population of *Emydoidea* now exists in Crawford County. Occasional waif individuals of *Emydoidea* are found along the Lake Erie shore, particularly at Presque Isle, but there is no evidence that a resident population exists, or ever existed, at that site.

Having established the end point of existence for these four species in Pennsylvania as sometime between 1850 and 1900, we can put them into historical perspective. Knowledge of the modern herpetofauna of Pennsylvania is based on a record that spans about 12,000 years. The earliest published reports, however, date roughly from the time of the American Revolution,[12] so documented first-hand observations cover only the most recent 200 years of this period. One may question how accurately this relatively brief record portrays the herpetofauna, and whether the apparent coincidence of extirpations in the period 1850-1900 is an artifact of insufficient data. Fortunately, both of these questions can be answered by study of the large and detailed body of faunistic data available from Paleo-indian sites in Pennsylvania. The most complete of these is the long sequence of cultural and associated faunal remains from the Meadowcroft Rockshelter, Washington County.[13] The occupation at this site dates from about 19,000 years B.P. (Before Present), and faunal remains extend back to about 11,300 years B.P. The fauna recovered from the lowest level implies that temperate Carolinian conditions prevailed at the site at that

TABLE 1

Pennsylvania amphibians and reptiles of special concern.

Endangered
  New Jersey Chorus Frog (*Pseudacris triseriata kalmi*)
  Coastal Plain Leopard Frog (*Rana utricularia*)
  Eastern Mud Turtle (*Kinosternon s. subrubrum*)
  Red-bellied Turtle (*Pseudemys rubriventris*)
  Bog Turtle (*Clemmys muhlenbergii*)
  Eastern Massasauga (*Sistrurus c. catenatus*)

Vulnerable
  Green Salamander (*Aneides aeneus*)
  Broad-headed Skink (*Eumeces laticeps*)
  Eastern Kingsnake (*Lampropeltis g. getulus*)
  Rough Green Snake (*Opheodrys aestivus*)
  Timber Rattlesnake (*Crotalus horridus*)

Status Undetermined
  Northern Coal Skink (*Eumeces a. anthracinus*)
  Kirtland's Snake (*Clonophis kirtlandii*)
  Eastern Hognose Snake (*Heterodon platyrhinos*)

Extirpated
  Eastern Tiger Salamander (*Ambystoma t. tigrinum*)
  Eastern Mud Salamander (*Pseudotriton m. montanus*)
  Blanding's Turtle (*Emydoidea blandingii*)
  Midland Smooth Softshell (*Trionyx m. muticus*)

time, and the herpetofauna was not different from that at the site today. The indian inhabitants of Meadowcroft Rockshelter, and elsewhere in Pennsylvania, at least up to the time of European colonization of Pennsylvania, utilized many species of amphibians and reptiles for food and other purposes. At some localities they may have largely subsisted, at certain seasons, on turtles and *Cryptobranchus alleganiensis*.[14] Although there is some evidence for localized extirpations of heavily utilized species,[15] no species of amphibian or reptile was extirpated from the Pennsylvania fauna before European colonization.

To summarize, a historical perspective on the herpetofauna of Pennsylvania indicates that it has been stable for the past 11,000-12,000 years. The modifications of habitat, both subtle and overt, that accompanied the European colonization of North American resulted in an episode of extirpation that eliminated 4 species of amphibians and reptiles from the Pennsylvania fauna between 1850 and 1900. The 4 extirpated species probably were particularly vulnerable. The populations of these species in Pennsylvania were at or near limits of the species' geographic ranges, and probably existed in small numbers in marginal habitats. The pervasive environmental changes during the earlier phases of colonization,[16] had the effect of extirpating these vulnerable marginal populations.

PERIPHERAL SPECIES—THE BIOGEOGRAPHIC PERSPECTIVE

The criterion for designation of amphibian and reptile species to be listed and protected in Pennsylvania is necessarily narrow and rigid. Listing of a species and placement in a status category are based on a single determination—the current population status of the species within the boundaries of the Commonwealth. The total range of the species, and status throughout that range, are not taken into consideration. From the legal standpoint this is a desirable approach to the recognition of endangered species. The mandate of the Pennsylvania Fish Commission is to protect and enhance the amphibian and reptile fauna of Pennsylvania, and their legal jurisdiction coincides with the boundaries of the Commonwealth. But animal species rarely recognize political boundaries, and no species of amphibian or reptile has its entire geographic range within Pennsylvania. From a biogeographic standpoint the rigid application of this narrow criterion results in a paradox: listings that have no relevance to the status of the species as a whole.

The term applied to species that narrowly overlap the boundaries of a political unit is "peripheral species." The term has no biological significance, but is useful in referring to these geopolitical artifacts. The list of endangered and threatened amphibians and reptiles in Pennsylvania includes eight forms that can be considered peripheral. Four of these (*Pseudacris triseriata kalmi, Rana utricularia, Kinosternon subrubrum,* and *Pseudemys rubriventris*) are Coastal Plain species that occur, in Pennsylvania, primarily in the narrow strip of Coastal Plain habitat in the Lower Delaware Valley.[2] Unfortunately for their survival, and the principal reason for their listing as endangered, that same strip of land is also occupied by the Philadelphia metropolitan area. Outside Pennsylvania, however, these species all have extensive geographic ranges. *Pseudacris triseriata kalmi* is a Coastal Plain subspecies (of a widespread species) that occurs throughout New Jersey and the Delmarva Peninsula.[17] The range of *Rana utricularia* extends throughout the Coastal Plain from New Jersey to Texas, and into the Mississippi Valley.[8] *Kinosternon subrubrum* is a widespread eastern and southern species that occurs in the Coastal Plain (and Piedmont farther south) from Long Island to eastern Texas.[17] *Pseudemys rubriventris* ranges from New Jersey to North Carolina in the Coastal Plain, and in the Potomac Drainage into southern Pennsylvania.[2, 17] Thus outside Pennsylvania all of these Coastal Plain species have extensive geographic ranges and are neither threatened nor endangered.

Four additional peripheral species, all listed in Pennsylvania as vulnerable because of their limited geographic range within the Commonwealth, occur along the southern border. *Eumeces laticeps* and *Lampropeltis getulus* are known from one or two localities each from the Susquehanna Valley eastward. *Opheodrys aestivus* is recorded from both the southwestern corner of Pennsylvania (Greene County), and the Susquehanna Valley. *Aneides aeneus* is known from a few localities along Chestnut Ridge, Fayette County.[19,20] Of these four, *Aneides aeneus* has the smallest range outside Pennsylvania, extending southward in the Appalachians to northern Georgia.[21] The other three species are widespread in eastern and southern United States.

The listing and status of peripheral species can be controversial. From a legal standpoint, an equally good case can be made for either considering them especially significant and worthy of protection as the only representatives of a species in the state fauna, or for regarding them as less worthy of protection and management than better-established members of the fauna. From the biological viewpoint maintenance of the species as a whole supercedes in importance the protection of peripheral populations. But at the periphery of its range a species is under greater selective pressure, and the pioneering or retreating populations can provide insight into the evolutionary history or future of the species. In any case, consistent application of the status category criteria adopted for Pennsylvania demands that the peripheral species be listed and protected.

DECLINING SPECIES—THE ECOLOGICAL PERSPECTIVE

The third perspective on the Pennsylvania list of endangered and threatened amphibians and reptiles is the ecological perspective. This perspective applies to 6 listed species that are neither peripheral in distribution, nor extirpated from the fauna. These are species for which the evidence indicates a decline in population size, or distribution, or both over the past 200 years. Wilson[22] has pointed out that the ecological factors contributing to a species' decline fall into 4 general categories: habitat change, direct killing, pollutants or introduced competitors, and predators or disease organisms. Factors in several categories have contributed to the decline of 3 of these species.

Clemmys muhlenbergii and *Sistrurus catenatus* are both wetland species, that require a specific type of habitat. *Clemmys muhlenbergii* inhabits marshy meadows at a particular seral stage that includes both flowing rivulets and grass tussocks.[23] *Sistrurus catenatus* hibernates below the water table in crawfish burrows, which must be available near the preferred old field summer habitat.[24] Habitats for both species have been decimated by draining of wetlands, both intentional and inadvertent. Moreover, both species also suffer from the factor of direct interference. *Clemmys muhlenbergii* is particularly desirable as a pet, and commercial collectors have extirpated some local populations by over-collecting. *Sistrurus catenatus* is a venomous species that is commonly destroyed by those who encounter it in the field.

Although *Crotalus horridus* is listed only as vulnerable, it has shown a precipitous decline throughout Pennsylvania and the northeastern states.[25] Historical records indicate a more extensive geographic range in Pennsylvania, and information from long-time rattlesnake hunters suggests a pervasive decline in abundance. Some of the ecological factors responsible for this decline are obvious. The increased recreational use of the mountainous portions of Pennsylvania brings people into contact with rattlesnakes, almost always resulting in destruction of the snake. Persistent collecting at known "dens" for sport or commercial purposes usually leads to extirpation of the local population. Less well documented, but equally important as causes of the long-term decline in rattlesnake populations, are natural ecological processes such as successional shading of basking sites. All of these factors suggest that *Crotalus horridus* is a legitimate candidate for listing as endangered in Pennsylvania.

Although it is possible to cite some of the ecological factors responsible for the declines of the three preceeding species, there are other declining species for which the responsible factors are not known. *Eumeces anthracinus, Clonophis kirtlandii,* and *Heterodon platyrhinos* are listed as "status undetermined" in Pennsylvania, because a decline in the populations of each species has been documented.[3] The most productive approach to management of these species is through ecological study, identification of the ecological factors responsible for the declines, and appropriate action to reverse the impact of those factors.

CONCLUSIONS

Endangered species listing is a valid first step in providing protection to the most vulnerable members of a fauna. The list should be assembled from the best available data, which for many species may be inadequate or inconclusive. Nevertheless, the initial step of listing provides legal protection for species at risk, and serves to focus attention on the species and problems most in need of study.

The second step requires viewing the endangered species list from three perspectives: historical, biogeographic, and ecological. Extirpated species must be seen in historical perspective to understand the causes responsible for their extirpation. This understanding will ensure that resources are not wasted on inappropriate re-introduction programs. The biogeographic perspective should be used to assess the status of peripheral species. Although peripheral species may be of unusual biological interest, they achieve listing status only as geopolitical artifacts. Extensive management or recovery programs for peripheral species may be neither feasible nor desirable, and all management of such populations should be appropriate to the welfare of the species as a whole. The ecological perspective should be applied to all listed species, but especially to those for which substantial declines in populations or geographic range can be documented. The first effort should be to identify and categorize the factors responsible for the decline, and management action focused on eliminating or mitigating these factors. As species for which the detrimental environmental factors can be identified and reversed have the best chance for survival, resources should be concentrated on those species.

REFERENCES

1. McCoy, C.J. 1982. Endangered species and the museum. Carnegie Mag. 56:28-31.
2. _____. 1982. Amphibians and reptiles in Pennsylvania. Carnegie Mus. Nat. Hist., Spec. Publ. 6:1-89.
3. _____. 1985. Amphibians and reptiles, Chapter 4, pp 259-295. *In* H.H. Genoways and F.J. Brenner, eds., Species of Special Concern in Pennsylvania. Carnegie Mus. Nat. Hist., Spec. Publ. 11: vi-430pp.
4. Dunstan, F. 1985. Definitions of status categories, p 35. *In* H.H. Genoways and F.J. Brenner, eds., Species of special concern in Pennsylvania. Carnegie Mus. Nat. Hist., Spec. Publ. 11: vi-430pp.
5. Genoways, H.H., and F.J. Brenner (eds.). 1985. Species of special concern in Pennsylvania. Carnegie Mus. Nat. Hist., Spec. Publ. 11: vi + 430 p.
6. Baird, S.F. 1850. Descriptions of four new species of North American salamanders, and one new species of skink. J. Acad. Nat. Sci. Philadelphia (2)1:292-294.
7. Conant, R. 1957. The eastern mud salamander, *Pseudotriton montanus montanus*: a new state record for New Jersey. Copeia 1957:152-153.
8. Cope, E.D. 1859. On the primary divisions of the Salamandridae, with descriptions of two new species. Proc. Acad. Nat. Sci. Philadelphia 11:122-128.
9. Dunn, E.R. 1940. The races of *Ambystoma tigrinum*. Copeia 1940:154-162.
10. Webb, R.G. 1962. North American Recent softshell turtles (Family Trionychidae). Univ. Kansas Publ., Mus. Nat. Hist. 13:429-611.
11. Netting, M.G. 1932. Blanding's turtle, *Emys blandingii* (Holbrook), in Pennsylvania. Copeia 1932:173-174.
12. Schoepff, J.D. 1792. *Historia testudinum*. Io. Iac. Palmii, Erlangen. Part 1:xii + 32p.
13. Adovasio, J.M., et al. 1984. Meadowcroft Rockshelter and the Pleistocene-Holocene transition in southwestern Pennsylvania pp 347-369. *In* H.H. Genoways and M.R. Dawson, eds., Contributions in Quaternary vertebrate paleontology. Carnegie Mus. Nat. Hist., Spec. Publ. 8: v + 538 p.
14. Lang, R.W. 1968. The natural environment and subsistence economy of the McKees Rocks village site. Pennsylvania Archeol. 38:50-80.
15. Adler, K.K. 1970. The influence of prehistoric man on the distribution of the box turtle. Ann. Carnegie Mus. 41:263-280.

16. Sears, P.B. 1942. History of conservation in Ohio. *In* The history of the state of Ohio. Ohio State Archeol. Hist. Soc., Columbus. 6:219-240.
17. Conant, R. 1975. A field guide to reptiles and amphibians of eastern and central North America. Houghton-Mifflin Co., Boston. xviii + 429 p.
18. Pace, A.E. 1974. Systematic and biological studies of the leopard frogs (*Rana pipiens* complex) of the United States. Misc. Publ. Mus. Zool. Univ. Michigan 148:1-140.
19. Richmond, N. D. 1952. First record of the green salamander in Pennsylvania, and other range extensions in Pennsylvania, Virginia and West Virginia. Ann. Carnegie Mus. 32:313-318.
20. Bier, C.W. 1985. Geographic distribution: *Aneides aeneus*. Herpet. Rev. 16:60.
21. Gordon, R.E. 1967. *Aneides aeneus*. Catalogue Amer. Amphib. Rept.: 54.1-54.2.
22. Wilson, G.R. 1983. Endangered animals—an overview. Aust. Ranger Bull. 2:76-78.
23. Ernst, C.H., and R.W. Barbour. 1972. Turtles of the United States. Univ. Press of Kentucky, Lexington. x + 347 p.
24. Reinert, H.K., and W.R. Kodrich. 1982. Movements and habitat utilization by the Massasauga, *Sistrurus catenatus catenatus*. J. Herpetol. 16:162-171.
25. Martin, W.H. 1982. The Timber Rattlesnake in the northeast: its range past and present. Herp (Bull. New York Herpetol. Soc.) 17:15-20.

Endangered and Threatened Species Programs in Pennsylvania and other States: Causes, Issues and Management. Edited by S. K. Majumdar, F. J. Brenner and A. F. Rhoads. © 1986, The Pennsylvania Academy of Science.

Chapter Seventeen

AN OVERVIEW OF ENDANGERED AND DECLINING BIRDS OF PENNSYLVANIA AND ADJACENT STATES

Richard J. Clark[1], Ph.D. and
Daniel Klem, Jr.[2], Ph.D.

[1]Professor of Biology
Department of Biology
York College of Pennsylvania (YCP)
York, PA 17403-3426
and
[2]Assistant Professor of Biology
Department of Biology
Muhlenberg College
Allentown, PA 18104

The text from the pictured memorial (*on next page*) built within the Pigeon Hills of York County, Pa. reads as follows:

> *In the interest of the preservation of wild life we here dedicate this memorial to the ill-fated passenger pigeon which from earliest pioneer days until the 1880's flocked to these pigeon hills this migratory bird now extinct was once so plentiful its numbers darkened the skies.*

A species derives infinitely more from man's effort to save it from extinction than from memorials dedicated to it after it is gone!

How will our children know wildlife?

Photo by R.J. Clark

"We have not inherited the Earth from our parents, we have borrowed it from our children." —IUCN, World Conservation Strategy, Introduction!

The auctioneer's old familiar phrase "going...going...GONE!" has an analogy in the "threatened...endangered...EXTINCT!" scenario of bird species whose numbers are dwindling drastically. The era when man became concerned with the survival of his fellow species on the only planet within our universe known to support life as we know it, has, on a large scale, only recently begun. The Bald Eagle Act of 1940 addressed a symbol but also gave special protection to that species. We might use the U.S. Endangered Species Act of 1966 to mark its beginning. Since that time a majority of states, actually 45,[2] have enacted legislation dealing with endangered species with 19 (including Delaware and Pennsylvania) subscribing to the Federal list of endangered species for their protection.

Our purpose is to focus attention on the bird species reported or suspected of suffering serious population declines in Pennsylvania and the adjacent states of Delaware, Maryland, New Jersey, New York, Ohio, and West Virginia. We have emphasized breeding birds, but a few non-breeding species are also considered. The principal emphasis of this chapter is on those species found in Pensylvania, but data on birds of adjacent states are included to provide a regional overview. More specifically, our objective is to draw attention to, and increase, the special emphasis given to select species needing or suspected of needing protection, and to reinforce and encourage additional studies designed to quantify the status of all birds in the 7 state region. Published accounts of the ornithology of Pennsylvania are substantial and contain valuable historical records.[3,4,5,6,7,8,9,10,11,12,13] This literature is decidedly biased toward the eastern and western portions of the state with similar information wanting for the central portion of Pennsylvania.

Pennsylvania's varied physiography includes representation within the Central Lowlands, Appalachian Plateau, Valley and Ridge, Blue Ridge, New England, Piedmont and Coastal Plain Provinces.[14,15] A variety of aquatic and terrestrial habitats occur in the state.[16] Aquatic habitats consist of tidal mud flats restricted to the lower Delaware River, Lake Erie with its sandy shore areas, scattered swamps, marshes and bogs, major rivers and streams, and various sized natural and man-made open water lakes. Pennsylvania is primarily terrestrial habitat in various stages of succession, but dominated by the Oak-Chestnut, Mixed Mesophytic and Northern Hardwood Climax types of the Eastern Deciduous Forest Biome[17] which provides a variety of habitats for avian species.

STATUS DESIGNATIONS

It is important to provide a frame of reference for the terms used in describing the status of species populations. Although similarities are clearly evident, federal and state agencies and various other institutional and individual authorities have used the same terms with various meanings. Moreover, some states have not yet officially adopted standardized definitions describing the species they protect. For this reason we list and reference the source of commonly accepted definitions for terms used to denote the status of designated species (Table 1). Unless operationally defined, the status designation "rare" is subject to relative interpretation. For example, Northern Cardinals with a population density of 10 pairs per 40.5 ha (100 acres) of field in the early shrub stage of vegetational succession could logically be thought of as common while that same density in a field of the late shrub stage might be considered rare. A density of three pairs of American Kestrels per 40.5 ha (100 acres) might warrant a label of very common while the same density for Field Sparrows would justify the designation of rare. Rare can only be a useful designation if we identify the range of an individual species population densities for optimum to marginal habitats for each species (DeGraff et al.[21] is a useful work which provides this sort of information from the literature). In spite of its shortcomings the rare designation is still used in the ICBP Red Data Book.[9]

The term species is misunderstood enough to warrant special attention also. The species is to the biological world as the atom is to the chemical world. It is a basic "kind," and considered to be a naturally occurring and, under most circumstances, a readily identifiable living unit. Relatively speaking, however, the atom is easily and objectively defined and it is relatively static whereas the species is typically considered to be a dynamic unit. Mayr[22,23] defines species as "groups of actually or potentially interbreeding natural populations which are reproductively isolated from other such groups," it thus represents a community of gene pools that are reproductively isolated. Others[24,25] point out some criticisms of the definition but the above will suffice for our discussion.

The Endangered Species Act also protects select subspecies because of their value to the overall health and survival of the entire species. When recognizable differences exist between geographically separate populations of species, these populations are considered to carry unique gene complexes adapted for survival over their specific range. These populations are the subspecies or races of species. Mayr[22,23] formally defines subspecies as "an aggregate of local populations of a species, inhabiting a geographic subdivision of the range of the species, and differing taxonomically from other populations of the species." The fact that subspecies are taxonomically different is indicated by a formal trinomial designation; for example, *Asio flammeus flammeus* refers to the type race of the Short-eared Owl white *Asio flammeus sandwichensis* refers to the insular (= island living) race of the Short-eared Owl of the Hawaiian Islands,

TABLE 1

Status Category Definitions of Pennsylvania and Adjacent States

Status/Definition.

Endangered[1,2] (E). Species is in imminent danger of extinction or extirpation throughout its range in Pennsylvania if the deleterious factors affecting it continue to operate. This is a species whose numbers have already been reduced to a critically low level or whose habitat has been so drastically reduced or degraded that immediate action is required to prevent its extirpation from the Commonwealth. (Similar designation has been adopted by New Jersey. New York and Ohio's legislation further require that the species be native or that it be designated as endangered by the U.S. Department of Interior. Delaware and Maryland honor the federally designated endangered species only and West Virginia, while having no current legislation dealing with endangered species does designate various status categories for listing "Special Animals" within its Wildlife/Heritage Data Base).

Threatened[1] (T) (= Vulnerable[2], = Rare[3]) A species that may become endangered within the foreseeable future throughout its range in Pennsylvania unless the causal factors affecting the organism are abated. This is a species in which: 1) most or all populations within the Commonwealth are decreasing or whose populations have been heavily depleted by adverse factors—and while not actually endangered, is still in critical condition; or 2) populations which may be relatively abundant but are under severe threat from serious adverse factors that have been identified and documented. (Similar designation utilized by New Jersey. New York further requires that the species also be either native or federally listed as with the endangered category. Delaware, Ohio and West Virginia have no similar designation).

Vulnerable[1] (V) A species not currently endangered or threatened but which may become endangered because: 1) it exists only in one or a few restricted geographic areas or habitats within Pennsylvania; or 2) it occurs in low numbers over a relatively broad area of the Commonwealth; or 3) although relatively abundant, it is particularly susceptible to certain types of exploitation or environmental modification.

Status Undetermined[1] (SU) (= Indeterminate[2]) A species that may be included in one of the above categories but there is insufficient data available to provide an adequate basis for its assignment to a specific category. New information is required to determine the status of this species.

Extirpated[1] (EP) A species that has disappeared from Pennsylvania since 1600 but continues to exist elsewhere.

Extinct (EX) A species for which no current, valid records of its existence occur anywhere on the planet Earth.

[1]Dunstan (18). (With slight modification in some cases).
[2]King (19). (Conceptually similar or the same but for different geographic locations).
[3]Smith, Burnard, Good and Keener (20) included to show a shift in terminology usage.

Asio flammeus sandfordi refers to the race occurring on the Falkland Islands, etc. When you can differentiate characteristics of a group, i.e., some are consistently and noticeably different, it suggests that there may be a diminution of gene flow between that group that is different from the main body and the main body of the species gene pool. The race may then represent a unit of evolution, i.e., represent a stage in the evolution of another species. Protecting races hence may be safeguarding a new species (= speciation) in the making. Conversely preventing the expression of this change in the species, in the making, may condemn it to extinction. Furthermore, it is necessary to protect subspecies to maintain the genetic diversity of species; for example, Cade[26] provides an excellent argument for using hybridization to preserve the unique genetic components of the Dusky Seaside Sparrow (*Ammospiza maritima nigrescens*). Thus, genetic diversity is critically important to species in that it represents the source from which new life forms evolve and it contributes to the species ability to adapt to varying environmental changes. As a practical matter, races are seldom readily identifiable in the field and can be misidentified even with the bird in hand (White 27); hence, the species as a whole must be protected in those areas where races may geographically overlap.

LEGISLATION

Birds, more than any other taxa, have enjoyed formal protection under federal and state law. Reviews of the history, development, and current status of these laws and other governmental rulings are comprehensively documented in Bean,[28] Eno and Di Silvestro,[29] Johnson[30] and Nilsson.[2] Wood[31] provides an excellent working bibliography on the literature of endangered species. Here we present an abstracted overview of the wildlife laws as they pertain to birds in general, and endangered and threatened bird species in particular.

The first formal legislation protecting birds was the Lacey Act passed by the U.S. Congress in 1900. Its purpose was to prevent the imminent extinction of various bird species being killed in large and uncontrolled numbers by plume hunters for the millinery trade. The Lacey Act prohibited interstate commerce of wildlife killed in violation of state laws. In 1903, President Theodore Roosevelt established the first national wildlife refuge at Pelican Island, Florida to protect the Brown Pelican (*Pelecanus occidentalis*). The Migratory Bird Act passed by Congress in 1913 was the first federal legislation with the specified purpose of conserving and managing migratory birds. Court challenges to the act were swift and argued that it violated the states' constitutional power to manage wildlife. Supporters of federal authority over wildlife encouraged the use of treaty powers to protect migratory birds, and in 1918 Congress passed the Migratory Bird Treaty Act with Great Britain on behalf of Canada. Although additional court challenges were brought, the Supreme Court upheld the supremacy of federal over state authority in the regulation of migratory birds. Subsequently, and with similar purpose, Congress passed additional migratory bird protection treaties with Mexico in 1936, Japan in 1972, and the Soviet Union in 1976. These treaties protect all birds species found in geographic areas under the jurisdiction of the U.S. government except: (1) game birds during prescribed hunting seasons, (2) individuals authorized by special federal and state permit to kill specified species for select purposes such as prevention of damage, or scientific collecting, and (3) the killing of select non-native species—Rock Dove (*Columba livia*), European Starling (*Sturnus vulgaris*), and House Sparrow (*Passer domesticus*). Other than these exceptions, an individual caught or found responsible for killing any bird anywhere in the U.S. is subject to a substantial fine and possible imprisonment. Although birds and many other forms of wildlife have long enjoyed federal protection, those needing the most protection received added legal attention when Congress passed the Endangered Species Preservation Act in 1966. The evolution of protective legislation for endangered and threatened species began with a key meeting, the Convention on International Trade in Endangered Species of Wild Fauna and Flora (CITES) which 86 nations signed. Congressional acts replacing or modifying the 1966 legislation resulted in the present Endangered Species Act of 1973 as amended in 1978 and 1982. The act must be reauthorized periodically by Congress. Reauthorization usually occurs every three years, and is occurring at the time of this writing (1985). The congressional committees responsible for reauthorizing the act are the House Committee on Merchant Marine and Fisheries and the Senate Committee on Environment and Public Works. Moreover, both House and Senate appropriations committees annually determine the amount of money to be allocated for the endangered species program. With some exceptions and overlap, the federal agencies having jurisdiction to protect listed endangered species are the Fish and Wildlife Service (FWS) in the Department of Interior for terrestrial species, and the National Marine Fisheries Service (NMFS) in the Department of Commerce for most marine species.

Three major contributions to conservation are attributable to the Endangered Species Act: (1) the recognition of species-specific *critical habitat* that serve as identifiable natural resources requiring protection and as an operational tool used by law enforcement agencies to protect these vital resources, (2) providing added protection for endangered birds, but more important, substantially increasing the amount of protection to other endangered wildlife taxa, and (3) affording protection to endangered wildlife of other nations through CITES. Of these, the first is the most important because extinctions caused by man and his activities are primarily associated with habitat destruction.[32]

Another complimentary piece of legislation whose potential merit lies in supporting additional research to identify and manage endangered and threatened birds is the Fish and Wildlife Conservation Act, originally passed by Congress in 1980. The act, also known as the Nongame Act, has never been funded by Congress, but it again passed the House of Representative this year (HR 1406, 29 July 1985). Although the FWS has a Nongame Migratory Bird Management Plan for the United States, the service has taken no formal action to implement it.[33]

From the founding of our nation, the history of wildlife law clearly documents the states' claim to ownership of wildlife living within their borders.[28] Current federal legislation has accepted authority over state laws, but federal laws in no way restrict the rights of states to enact additional and enhancing protective legislation. Such state laws are common, and existing or new laws have been modified or enacted to conform to federal authority. The majority of states have passed legislation and sponsored specific programs for the protection of endangered species.[2] For Pennsylvania and its surrounding states, only West Virginia lacks a formal state law addressing endangered and threatened species (Table 2). In general, state laws protecting endangered species carry lesser penalties for violations than do federal laws, and do not prohibit human activity that would adversely alter or destroy the critical habitat of endangered species.[2]

PROGRAMS

At least for birds, the Office of Endangered Species within the Fish and Wildlife Service of the Department of Interior is responsible for the overall FWS management of the endangered species program. Three other federal agencies—the National Park Service (NPS), the Bureau of Land Management (BLM) in the Department of Interior, and the U.S. Forest Service (USFS) in the Department of Agriculture[34] also have responsibility under the Endangered Species Act. Federal agencies other than the FWS participate in the endangered species program by enacting recovery plans for listed species or conducting studies and instituting management plans in an attempt to prevent the need for subsequent listing of a declining species population.

Federal endangered species research conducted by the FWS is directed by the FWS Patuxent Research Center in Laurel, Maryland, and is generally set up on a Recovery Team basis.[35] It consists of ecological and captive breeding studies. The ecological studies attempt to determine and correct the major limiting factors affecting endangered species. The captive breeding studies attempt to compensate for the low breeding or contribute to the diversity of the species gene pool. Where and when it is practical to do so, captive breeding programs ultimately seek to reintroduce individuals into geographic ranges formerly occupied by the species, and compliment and add to depressed and declining wild populations.[36] Supplementing this effort is information gathered by the North American Breeding Bird Survey (BBS) program coordinated by the FWS Migratory Birds and Habitat Research Laboratory at Laurel, Maryland.[37] BBS's are used to try to identify possible future candidates for endangered species listing. Using BBS data, in 1982 the FWS formally identified 28 species with unstable or declining U.S. population trends during the previous 10 to 15 years. Five of these were formally designated as National Species of Special Emphasis (NSSES) needing increased research and management attention; they were

TABLE 2
State Endangered Species Legislation and Programs.[1]

State	USWS Cooperator[2]	Endangered Species Law	Federal Endangered List Only	No. Federally Endangered Spp.	No. State End. Spp.	Natural Heritage Coop.[3]	Breeding Bird Atlas Prog.	Income Tax Return Revenue Prog.
Pennsylvania	FW	+		3[4]	3	+	1983-1988	+
Delaware	FW	+	+	2	0	*[5]	1983-1988	+
Maryland	FW	+		4	0	+	1983-1988	+
New Jersey	FW	+		2	14[6]	+	1981-1986	+
New York	FW	+		3	4	+	1980-1984	+
Ohio	P	+		3	4	+	1983-1987	+
West Virginia	FW		+	3	0	+	1984-1988	+

[1] Table is modified from Nilsson (2) and was updated by information from individual state agencies.
[2] FW = full cooperative agreement with the United Sates Fish and Wildlife Service (USFWS) on fish and wildlife; P = full cooperative agreement with USFWS on plants.
[3] Nature Conservancy cooperator.
[4] For Pennsylvania: The Pennsylvania Game commission lists (18 June 1983) an additional 6 Threatened, 12 Species of Concern, 7 Status Undetermined, 8 (including Greater Prairie-chicken race [Health Hen]) Extirpated and 1 Extinct species.
[5] State maintains Natural Areas Preservation System.
[6] In the case of five species only the breeding population endangered.

Trumpeter Swan (*Olor buccinator*), Piping Plover (those species listed in Tables 3 and 4 have their binomials listed there), Roseate Tern, Least Tern (interior population), and Spotted Owl (*Strix occidentalis*).[33] Although not determined to be declining in numbers, the FWS report also listed the western populations of Golden Eagle and Osprey as NSSES. The other 23 nongame birds species with unstable or declining population trends were: Common Loon, Reddish Egret (*Dichromanassa rufescens*), Least Bittern, American Bittern, Wood Stork (*Mycteria americana*), White-faced Ibis (*Plegadis chihi*), Red-shouldered Hawk, Ferruginous Hawk (*Buteo regalis*), Northern Harrier, Black Rail, Snowy Plover, Long-billed Curlew, Upland Sandpiper, Gull-billed Tern (*Gelochelidon nilotica*), Black Tern, Common Barn-Owl, Loggerhead Shrike, Bell's Vireo (*Vireo bellii*), Golden-cheeked Warbler *(Dendroica chrysoparia),* Baird's Sparrow *(Ammodramus bairdii),* Henslow's Sparrow, Seaside Sparrow, and Bachman's Sparrow.

In addition to federal programs, national private organizations contribute substantially to the conservation of endangered and threatened species. Among others, a few noteworthy and valuable efforts are: the National Heritage Program by the Nature Conservancy, the eagle census by the National Wildlife Federation, the raptor reintroduction program by the Peregrine Fund at Cornell University, and the publication of the Blue List of potentially declining bird species and the sponsorship of the Breeding Birds Censuses, Winter Bird Population Studies, and Breeding Bird Atlases by the National Audubon Society and their affiliated chapters.

The Endangered Species Act requires the maximum cooperation between federal and state wildlife agencies. To date, cooperative efforts in which the states maintain the majority of responsibility consist of joint agreements and research projects involving endangered species within state borders.[32] Moreover, many states maintain their own endangered and threatened species listing species additional to those protected by the federal listing (see Table 3 listing PA species and Table 4 for species of adjoining states). Many states have separate but the same or similar programs providing attention to endangered and threatened wildlife in a more general sense. These include: (1) revenue generating state programs typically associated with income tax refund contributions such as the Pennsylvania Wild Resource Conservation Fund, (2) formal cooperative endangered species program agreements with the FWS, (3) Natural Heritage Programs coordinated by the Nature Conservancy and designed to create inventories of all wildlife in unique ecosystems, and (4) Breeding Bird Atlas Programs that are statewide surveys of confirmed, probable, and possible nesting resident species (Table 2). The Breeding Bird Atlas program underway in a number of states is a valuable first step in assessing the existence and distribution of local populations.[42] Of critical importance is the determination of the abundance and breeding status of all bird species throughout their geographic range. Atlas projects attempt to determine the breeding distribution of bird species throughout a state.[43] They are characteristically coordinated by natural history organizations affiliated with state government or private institutions, rely primarily on volunteer efforts, and generally cover a 5-year period. The purpose of the project is to collect and publish breeding status information and to identify species composition and additionally, respective associated habitats requiring needed protection, preservation, and management. Furthermore, federal agencies such as the FWS component charged with managing federal wildlife refuges and the U.S. Forest Service overseeing the National Forest lands have management plans that directly and indirectly include listed endangered and threatened species.

Frankel[44] specifically addressing wildlife management, describes three strategies for conserving living resources: (1) provide enough space to permit continued survival and evolution of the species, (2) accept extinction or the removal of threatened species to protected zoological and botanical gardens, or (3) to the best of our knowledge and ability, manage the population size and structure of endangered species in balance with the environmental resources available to them. He further defines three fundamental elements of any conservation effort: (1) the identification of a target species or higher order of association such as a community or ecosystem, (2) the time of a program from short term single acts requiring a single seasonal intervention to actions having

TABLE 3
Status of Designated Avian Species in Pennsylvania.

Common Name[+]	Scientific Name	AOU[+]	PGC	F&W	T&T	DE	MD	NJ	NY	OH	WV	Comments
American Bittern	*Botaurus lentiginosus*	190	T		BL						U/HR	BR, A FEW WINTER (7)
Least Bittern	*Ixobrychus exilis*	191	T		BL				SC			RARE T, LOC BR S RES (5)
Great Blue Heron	*Ardea herodias*	194	SC					T				PER RES, FEW IN WINTER (5)
Osprey	*Pandion haliaetus*	364	T					T*	T		SI	*CHANGED FROM E 4/85
Bald Eagle	*Haliaeetus leucocephalus*	352	E	E		E	E	E	E	E	FE	RARE BR. CASUAL W-V (7)
Northern Harrier	*Circus cyaneus*	331	SC		BL			E BR ONLY	T		U	REG T, BR (5)
Sharp-shinned Hawk	*Accipiter striatus*	332	SU/I		BL					E		REG T BR AND W (5)
Cooper's Hawk	*Accipiter cooperii*	333	SC					E	SC		U	REG T, UNC RES
Northern Goshawk	*Accipiter gentilis*	334	SU/I								SI	REG T, BR (7)
Red-shouldered Hawk	*Buteo lineatus*	339	SC		BL			T	T			REG T, BR AND WINTERS (7)
Peregrine Falcon	*Falco peregrinus*	356	EP	E		E	E	E	E	E	FE	REG T, FORMER BR (5)
Greater Prairie-Chicken	*Tympanuchus cupido*	305	EP*	E				EP*				*RACE *CUPIDO* EXTINCT (2)
Northern Bobwhite	*Colinus virginianus*	289	SC									REG RES (7)
King Rail	*Rallus elegans*	208	E		BL					E		RARE T, COC BR S RES (5)
Piping Plover	*Charadrius melodius*	277	EP		BL			E	T			FORMER BR PRESQUE ISLE (7)
Upland Sandpiper	*Bartramia longicauda*	261	T		BL			E	SC	E	U/HR	REG T, LOCAL BR (7)
Common Tern	*Sterna hirundo*	070	EP						T	E		F C T, BR PRESQUE ISLE (5)
Black Tern	*Chlidonias niger*	077	T		BL				SC			BR CRAWFORD & ERIE CO (3)
Common Barn-Owl	*Tyto alba*	365	SC						SC		U	REG RES (7)
Long-eared Owl	*Asio otus*	366	SU/I								U	RARE AN PER RES (
Short-eared Owl	*Asio flammeus*	367	E		BL			E BR ONLY	SC			REG T, CAS (7)

Endangered and Threatened Species Programs in Pennsylvania and other States

Species	Scientific Name	#	PGC	F&W	BL	MD	NJ	DE	NY	OH	WV	COMMENTS
Whip-poor-will	Caprimulgus vociferus	417	SU/I									REG T, BR S RES (7)
Red-headed Woodpecker	Melanerpes erythrocephalus	406	SC				T					REG T, LOC BR (5)
Yellow-bellied Sapsucker	Sphyrapicus varius	402	SU/I									REG T, BR S RES, OCC W V (7)
Least Flycatcher	Empidonax minimus	467	SU/I									REG T, BR S RES (5)
Purple Martin	Progne subis	611	SC									REG T, S R (7)
Bewick's Wren	Thryomanes bewickii	719	E		BL							LOC BR S RES, CASUAL W V (7)
Sedge Wren	Cistothorus platensis	724	T							SC		RARE T, IRR BR S R (5)
Marsh Wren	Cistothorus palustris	725	SC				E			U/HR		RARE T, LOC BR S RES (5)
Eastern Bluebird	Sialia sialis	766	SC		BL							REG T, OCC RES
Loggerhead Shrike	Lanius ludovicianus	622	EP		BL						SC	REG T, FORMERLY CASUAL BR (7)
Dickcissel	Spiza americana	604	EP		BL							CASUAL TO RARE V OR RES (5)
Bachman's Sparrow	Aimophila aestivalis	575	EP		BL					SI/HR		ACC LOC S R, LAST SEEN 1973 (7)
Vesper Sparrow	Aimophila aestivalis	540	SC				E BR ONLY			SC		REG T, BR S RES, RARE W V (5)
Lark Sparrow	Chondestes grammacus	552	EP							SI/HR		ACC, VERY RARE BR S RES (5)
Grasshopper Sparrow	Ammodramus savannarum	546	SC		BL		T				SC	REG T, LOC BR S RES (5)
Henslow's Sparrow	Ammodramus henslowii	547	T				E			SI/HR	SC	RARE T, LOC B S RES (5)
Bobolink	Dolichonyx oryzivorus	494	SU/I				T					BR FIELDS, TALL GRASS (7)

Column Titles: **F&W** = U S Fish and Wildlife Service; **PGC** = Pennsylvania Game Commission; **DE** = Delaware Dept of Natural Resources and Environmental Control; **MD** = Maryland Dept of Natural Resources; **NJ** = New Jersey Dept of Environmental Protection; **NY** = New York State Dept of Environmental Conservation; **OH** = Ohio Dept of Natural Resources; **WV** = State of West Virginia Dept of Natural Resources; **T&T** = Tate and Tate, (38).

Status Descriptors: **BL** = Blue Listed, **E** = Endangered, **EP** = Extirpated, **EX** = Extinct, **E BR ONLY** = Endangered (only breeding population (NJ)), **FE** = Federally Endangered (WV), **HR** = Habitat Restricted (WV), **P** = Peripheral (WV), **SC** = Species of Concern (PA) or Species of Special Concern (NY), **SI** = Scientific Interest (WV), **SU/I** = Status Undetermined/Indeterminate (PA), **T** = Threatened, **U** = Undetermined Status (WV), * = see COMMENTS

Comments Documentation: (1) = Beck;[4] (2) = Greenway,[39] (3) = Jackson,[40] (4) = Nilsson,[2] (5) = Poole,[4] (6) = Turnbull[11] and (7) = Wood.[13]

Comments Status: Unless otherwise noted comments deal with the species in Pennsylvania. **Acc** = Accidental, **Br** = Breeds, **C** = Common, **Dist** = Distribution, **F** = Fairly, **Irr** = Irregular, **Loc** = Local, **Occ** = Occasional, **Per** = Permanent, **Reg** = Regular, **Res** = Resident, **S** = Summer, **T** = Transient, **Unc** = Uncommon, **V** = Visitor, **W** = Winter.

*AOU (41).

TABLE 4

Status of Designated Avian Species in States Adjoining Pennsylvania.

Common Name	Scientific Name	AOU	F&W	T&T	DE	MD	NJ	NY	OH	WV	Comments
Common Loon	Gavia immer	007						SC*			*NY ONLY: REG T, RARE BR (5)
Pied-billed Grebe	Podilymbus podiceps	006					E BR ONLY				F COM LOCAL BR S RES (5)
Western Grebe	Aechmophorus occidentalis	001		BL							ACC 6 PA RECORDS (7)
Yellow-crowned Night-Heron	Nycticorax violaceus	203					T*				*NJ ONLY: RARE OCC BR S RES (7)
Hooded Merganser	Lophodytes cucullatus	131									R (5), BR LOC (7)
Black Vulture	Coragyps atratus	326								U/P*	*WV ONLY, BR ADAMS & YORK CO (7)
Swainson's Hawk	Buteo swainsoni	342		BL							ACC 1 RECORD (5)
Golden Eagle	Aquila chrysaetos	349	E					E		U	FORMER RARE RES (5)
Merlin	Falco columbarius	357					T				MAY BREED (?), (5)
Spruce Grouse	Dendragapus canadensis	298						T*			*NY ONLY
Black Rail	Laterallus jamaicensis	216						SC			FORMERLY BRED PA? (5)
Whooping Crane	Grus americana	204	E				EP*				*BR CAPE MAY (6)
Snowy Plover	Charadrius alexandrinus	278		BL							ACC 1 RECORD (5)
Eskimo Curlew	Numenius borealis	266	E			E		E			PROBABLY EXTINCT? (2)
Long-billed Curlew	Numenius americanus	264		BL							ACC (7)
Roseate Tern	Sterna dougallii	072					E	E			ACC 3 RECORDS (5)
Least Tern	Sterna antillarum	074	E*				E	E			*RACE BROW/NJ ONLY (4)
Black Skimmer	Rynchops niger	080		BL			E				ACC 5 RECORDS (5)
Passenger Pigeon	Ectopistes migratorius	315									EX (2), LAST PA RECORD 1906 (5)
Carolina Parakeet	Conuropsis carolinensis	382	EX								FORMERLY IRR V (1)
Barred Owl	Strix varia	368					T				RES, IRR DIST (5)
Common Nighthawk	Chordeiles minor	420						SC*			*NY ONLY; REG T, LOC C S RES (5)
Ruby-throated Hummingbird	Archilochus colubris	428		BL							REG T, BR S RES (5)
Hairy Woodpecker	Picoides villosus	393		BL							PER RES (5)
Red-cockaded Woodpecker	Picoides borealis	395	E			E					BR MD (3), ACC PA (5,6)
Olive-sided Flycatcher	Nuttallornis borealis	459								SC*	*WV ONLY; RARE T, POSS BR (5)

Species		#				
Willow Flycatcher	*Empidonax traillii*	466		BL		REG T, LOC BR S RES (7)
Cliff Swallow	*Hirundo pyrrhonota*	612				BREEDS PA (7)
Common Raven	*Corvus corax*	486			SC*	*NY ONLY; RARE RES, IRR T (5)
House Wren	*Troglodytes aedon*	721	E*	E BR ONLY		*Guadeloupensis & Mesoleucus (4)
Golden-winged Warbler	*Vermivora chrysoptera*	642		BL	U	UNC T, LOC BR S RES (5)
Yellow Warbler	*Dendroica petechia*	652		BL		REG T, BR S RES (7)
Kirtland's Warbler	*Dendroica kirtlandii*	670	E		E	ACC, 2 RECORDS (7)
Sutton's Warbler	*Dendroica potomac**	—			FE U	**D. Potomac* X *Parula Americana*
Savannah Sparrow	*Passerculus sandwichensis*	542		T*		*BOTH RACES *Savanna* & *Princeps*
Seaside Sparrow	*Ammodramus maritimus*	550		T		ACC 2 PA RECORDS (7)
Eastern Meadowlark	*Sturnella magna*	501		BL		REG T, BR AND WINTERS (7)

Column Titles: **F&W** = U S Fish and Wildlife Service; **PGC** = Pennsylvania Game Commission; **DE** = Delaware Dept of Natural Resources and Environmental Control; **MD** = Maryland Dept of Natural Resources; **NJ** = New Jersey Dept of Environmental Protection; **NY** = New York State Dept of Environmental Conservation; **OH** = Ohio Dept of Natural Resources; **WV** = State of West Virginia Dept of Natural Resources; **T&T** = Tate and Tate.[38]

Status Descriptors: **BL** = Blue Listed, **E** = Endangered, **EP** = Extirpated, **EX** = Extinct, **E BR ONLY** = Endangered (only breeding population (NJ)), **FE** = Federally Endangered (WV), **HR** = Habitat Restricted (WV), **P** = Peripheral (WV), **SC** = Species of Concern (PA) or Species of Special Concern (NY), **SI** = Scientific Interest (WV), **SU/I** = Status Undetermined/Indeterminate (PA), **T** = Threatened, **U** = Undetermined Satus (WV), * = see COMMENTS.

Comments Documentation: (1) = Beck;[4] (2) = Greenway;[39] (3) = Jackson;[40] (4) = Nilsson;[2] (5) = Poole;*[6] = Turnbull[11] and (7) = Wood.[13]

Comments Status: Unless otherwise noted comments deal with the species in Pennsylvania. **Acc** = Accidental, **Br** = Breeds, **C** = Common, **Dist** = Distribution, **F** = Fairly, **Irr** = Irregular, **Loc** = Local, **Occ** = Occasional, **Per** = Permanent, **Reg** = Regular, **Res** = Resident, **S** = Summer, **T** = Transient, **Unc** = Uncommon, **V** = Visitor, **W** = Winter.
*AOU.[41]

no recognizable end, and (3) actual management techniques influencing population size and structure. With specific attention to management, Schonewald-Cox[45] provides guidelines based on: (1) the size of protected areas, (2) the relationship of species population size to habitable area, and (3) what she describes as demographic protection referring to levels of protection from individuals in captivity to complexes of large reserves capable of sustaining stable long term populations.

The natural history information required to decide on a responsible strategy to conserve declining avian populations is largely unknown for nearly all species. We are hopeful that the information currently existing in the literature, and the summary herein provided will encourage amateurs and professionals alike to join in an effort to safeguard the species presently within our Commonwealth. The Breeding Bird Atlas Projects provide an excellent opportunity to add to the meager knowledge that we must now use to plan conservation/management strategies.

Following, and Table 2, is an overview of the current or planned species-specific programs in the state of Pennsylvania and its six neighboring states of Delaware, Maryland, Ohio, New Jersey, New York, and West Virginia.

Pennsylvania. — The Pennsylvania Breeding Bird Atlas Project encompasses the period from 1983 to 1988, and is sponsored by the state, the Academy of Natural Science of Philadelphia, the Carnegie Museum of Pittsburgh and the Pennsylvania Audubon Council. In Pennsylvania, the Breeding Bird Atlas follows the publication of a list of species of special concern.[46] This work has provided attention to select species suspected of having low or declining populations and those having an undertermined status. Additional and more quantitative studies addressing the general natural history, population biology, habitat requirements, and management will be required for those species identified as endangered, threatened, or vulnerable. Moreover, the historical distribution of species and their current status needs special attention,[46] e.g. the Bachman's Sparrow is listed as extirpated, however it has been shown[47] that this species extended its range into Pennsylvania from Ohio and West Virginia in the latter nineteenth and early twentieth century and receeded in the early 1920's. From the beginning of the colonial period to the present, human alteration of habitat resulted in the extirpation of some species while facilitating the range extension of others. Detailed studies of the history of state habitats and probable species-specific distribution is needed. Should states protect and manage declining or satellite populations if it is determined that the species is not or may not have been endemic to the state? The state of Pennsylvania is presently sponsoring recovery projects for the federally listed endangered Bald Eagle[48,49] and the state listed threatened Osprey.

Delaware. — The state has a formal endangered species program coordinated by the Division of Fish and Wildlife in the Department of Natural Resources and Environmental Control. A Breeding Bird Atlas project is underway and encompasses the period from 1983 to 1988. Formal state supported research and management projects exist for the Bald Eagle and Peregrine Falcon. In 1978 the state established the Natural Areas Preservation System to inventory and register unique areas and is dedicated to permanently and legally protecting the valuable natural areas of the state.

Maryland. — The state sponsors and conducts formal studies on resident endangered species coordinated by the Maryland Forest, Park and Wildlife Service in the Department of Natural Resources. A Breeding Bird Atlas project is underway and encompasses the period from 1983 to 1988.[50] State supported research and management projects exist for the Bald Eagle[51,52] and Peregrine Falcon. Studies on the history, habitat and status of the Red-cockaded Woodpecker in Maryland have been published.[53,54]

New Jersey. — The state sponsors and conducts formal studies on resident endangered species within their Endangered and Nongame Species Program coordinated by the Division of Fish, Game and Wildlife in the Department of Environmental Protection. A Breeding Bird Atlas project is currently underway in the state, but it has no formal state agency support. The atlas project is coordinated by the Raccoon Ridge Bird Observatory and encompasses the period 1981 to 1986. State supported research and management projects currently exist for colonial water birds in general[55,56,57,58] and the Great Blue Heron, Osprey,[59] Bald Eagle, Northern Harrier, Peregrine Falcon, Upland Sandpiper, Piping Plover, Least Tern, Black Skimmer,[60] and Cliff Swallow.[61] In cooperation with the Office of Natural Lands Management, the Bureau of Wildlife Management within the Division of Fish, Game and Wildlife is conducting an environmental review for the purpose of identifying critical habitat needing protection and preservation. Wildlife management plans have been or are being developed for Higbee Beach Wildlife Management Area in Cape May County, Pequest Wildlife Management Area in Warren County, High Point State Park in Sussex County, and Delaware Gap National Recreation Area in Warren and Sussex Counties.

New York. — The state sponsors and conducts an Endangered Species Program on resident endangered species which is coordinated by the Division of Fish and Wildlife in the Department of Environmental Conservation. In cooperation with the Federation of New York State Bird Clubs, the Division of Fish and Wildlife has conducted a Breeding Bird Atlas program encompassing the period 1980 to 1984 and is currently in preparation for publication (Andrle, pers. comm.). State supported research and management projects currently exist on the status of endangered avian species the Common Loon in the Adirondack Park and the Osprey,[62,63] Bald Eagle[64] and Peregrine Falcon.

Ohio. — Smith *et al*[20] published an early, extensive list which should be consulted for Ohio. The state sponsors and conducts an endangered species program coordinated by the Division of Wildlife in the Department of Natural Resources. The Division of Natural Areas and Preserves in cooperation with other life science and conservation organizations is conducting a Breeding Bird Atlas program encompassing the period 1983 to 1987. The Division of Wildlife is engaged in a Bald Eagle Restoration project. The Ohio Biological Survey, an inter-institutional research group, has plans to publish a book on rare, endangered and extirpated species of Ohio (Peterjohn, pers. comm.). Osborne and Peterson[65] have documented the status of the Upland Sandpiper in Ohio. The Division operates a program of land wildlife management that is offered to private landowners requesting assistance. A number of metropolitan park districts in, among others, the cities of Columbus, Dayton, and Cincinnati maintain select lands in various successional stages to encourage breeding bird abundance and diversity (Rice, pers. comm.)

West virginia. — The state sponsors and conducts studies on a list of special animals categorized as Species of Special Concern, of Scientific Interest, and Undetermined Status. These efforts are coordinated by the Wildlife Resources Division of the Department of Natural Resources. The Wildlife Resources Division is sponsoring a Breeding Bird Atlas program encompassing the period 1984 to 1988. Hall[66] has provided a treatment of West Virginia birdlife. State supported research and management projects currently exist for the Osprey, Bald Eagle and Peregrine Falcon. LeFranc *et al.*[67] provided evidence for the breeding of the Bald Eagle in that state. The state is in the early planning stages for a major statewide nongame program (Knight, pers. comm.).

FACTORS LEADING TO EXTINCTION

While it should be obvious to all that extinctions have occurred naturally in the past, Soule[68] has pointed out that "virtually all recent extinctions are anthropogenic," and has devised a scheme for predicting a species vulnerability to extinction (see Table 5). He considers two major factors: (1) those that involve some kind of environmental change and (2) those that are intrinsic characteristics for the species or bear a constant relationship between the species and its environment. Left out of this vulnerability analysis are terms that Soule[68] refers to as (1) demographic stochasticity (random fluctuation in population variables such as the distribution of age classes or sex ratio), and (2) dysfunction of social behavior (such as extreme sociability coupled with some decimating factor). An example of demographic stochasticity is the sex ratio extinction of

TABLE 5

Factorial Interactions Relating to the Survivability of a Species.

ENVIRONMENTAL	BIOLOGICAL Rarity (clumped)	Rarity (dispersed)	Low Reproductive Potential	High Sociability	Island Living	Low Dispersal Ability
Competition				X		
Predation				X	X	X
Disease	X		X	X	X	X
Hunting/Collecting	X	X	X	X	X	X
Loss of mutualists						X
Catastrophe	X			X	X	X
Succession	X					X
Environmental variation						X
Long term trends					X	X
Disturbance	X	X	X	X	X	X

An X indicates that particular interaction is probable (after Soule[68]).

the Dusky race of the Seaside Sparrow (*A. m. nicgrescens*). Currently the population of this race consists of three males. These three males have been mated with a closely related subspecies in captivity. The parental males are then mated with the female offspring of that first mating (geneticists refer to this as backcrossing). Subsequent backcrossing of the parental males with their female progeny increases the proportion of Dusky genes in the captive population. The "reconstructed" Dusky race has been carried through three generations and the resulting female genome is about 75% Dusky genes. Theoretically six generations will yield approximately 98% Dusky genes and the males are already 8 or 9 years old. Can they survive through three more generations?[69] It can be seen that the greater the number of interactions that characterize a species and its environment the more susceptible it is to extinction; e.g., a species that has low dispersal ability and is prized by collectors is most susceptible to extinction. What factors are actually influencing the decline of birds in Pennsylvania and surrounding states is largely unknown and needs responsible attention.

ACKNOWLEDGMENTS

We are grateful to the following individuals and the associated agencies that they represent for assistance in obtaining information on respective state agency programs: Janis Thomas (Delaware—Nongame and Endangered Species Coordinator), Gary J. Taylor (Maryland—Nongame and Endangered Species Program Manager), Denis S. Case (Ohio—Assistant Administrator, Wildlife Management and Research), Jo Ann Frier-Murza (New Jersey—Manager, Endangered and Nongame Species Program), Peter Nye (New York—Endangered Species Unit, NYSDEC), Dale E. Sheffer (Director, Bureau of Game Management, PGC), and Kenneth B. Knight (West Virginia — Wildlife Biologist, WV Wildlife Resources Div.). We also thank Robert M. Schutsky and Francis D. Watson for calling our attention to references. Last, but not least, the senior author gratefully acknowledges a grant from the Research and Publications Committee of York College of Pennsylvania's Faculty Senate and thanks his wife Joan for proofreading the manuscript of this chapter.

LITERATURE CITED

1. International Union for Conservation of Nature and Natural Resources. 1980. Unipub., New York, 70pp.
2. Nilsson, G. 1983. The endangered species handbook. The Animal Welfare Institute, Washington, 244pp.
3. Baird, S.F. 1845. Catalogue of birds found in the neighborhood of Carlisle, Cumberland County, Pa. Literary Record and Journal Linnaean Assoc. of Penn. College. 1:249-257.
4. Beck, H.H. 1924. A chapter on the ornithology of Lancaster County, Pennsylvania with supplementary notes on the mammals, pp. 1101-1126. *In*: H.M.J. Klein. Lancaster County, Pennsylvania—A history. The Lewis Historical Publishing Co., Inc., New York, 1172pp. (Two volumes)
5. Burns, F.L. 1919. The ornithology of Chester County, Pennsylvania. The Gorham Press, Boston, 122pp.
6. Frey, E.S. 1943. The centennial checklist of the birds of Cumberland County, Pennsylvania and her borders. Pub. Privately, 63pp.
7. Grube, G.E. 1959. The breeding birds of Adams County, Pennsylvania. Lock Haven Bull. Ser. 1, No. 1:45-57.
8. Poole, E.L. 1964. Pennsylvania birds. Delaware Valley Ornithological Club, Livingston Publishing Co., 94pp.

9. Stone, W. 1894. Birds of eastern Pennsylvania and New Jersey. Delaware Valley Ornithological Club, Livingston Publishing Co., 185pp.
10. Todd, W.E. 1940. Birds of western Pennsylvania. U. Pittsburgh Press, Pittsburgh, 710pp.
11. Turnbull, W.P. 1869. The birds of east Pennsylvania and New Jersey. Printed for private circulation, Glasgow, 62pp.
12. Warren, B.H. 1890. Report on the birds of Pennsylvania with special reference to the food habits based on over four thousand stomach contents. Harrisburg, 434pp.
13. Wood, M. 1979. Birds of Pennsylvania. The Pennsylvania State University, University Park, 148pp.
14. Fenneman, N.M. 1928. Physiographic divisions of the United States. Assoc. Am. Geog. Annals 18:261-353.
15. Guilday, J.E. 1985. The physiographic provinces of Pennsylvania, pp. 19-29. *In*: Genoways, H.H. and F.J. Brenner (Eds). Species of special concern in Pennsylvania. Carnegie Mus. Nat. Hist., Spec. Pub. No. 11, Pittsburgh, 430pp.
16. Brenner, F.J. 1985. Aquatic and terrestrial habitats in Pennsylvania, pp. 7-17. *In*: Genoways, H.H. and F.J. Brenner (Eds). Species of special concern in Pennsylvania. Cargenie Mus. Nat. Hist., Spec. Pub. No. 11, Pittsburgh, 430pp.
17. Dansereau, P. 1957. Biogeography: an ecological perspective. The Ronald Press Co., New York, 394pp.
18. Dunstan, F. 1985. Definitions of status categories, p. 35. *In*: Genoways, H.H. and F.J. Brenner (Eds). Species of special concern. Carnegie Mus. Nat. History, Spec. Pub. No. 11, Pittsburgh, 430pp.
19. King, W.B. 1981. Endangered birds of the World: The ICBP Bird Red Data Book. Smithsonian Institution Press, Washington, 624pp.
20. Smith, H.G., R.K. Burnard, E.E. Good and J.M. Keener. 1973. Rare and endangered vertebrates of Ohio. Ohio J. Sci. 73:257-271.
21. DeGraff, R.M., G.M. Witman, J.W. Lanier, B.J. Hill and J.M. Keniston. 1980. Forest habitat for birds of the northeast. USDA, For. Ser., Northeast Forest Exp. Sta. and Eastern Reg., GPO (Washington), 598pp.
22. Mayr, E. 1963. Animal species and evolution. The Belknap Press of Harvard University Press, Cambridge, 797pp.
23. Mayr, E. 1970. Populations, species, and evolution. Harvard University Press, Cambridge, 453pp.
24. Jonsell, b. 1984. The biological species concept reexamined, pp. 159-168. *In*: Grant, W.F. (Ed). Plant biosystematics. Academic Press, New York, 674pp.
25. Wagner, W.H., Jr. 1984. A comparison of taxonomic methods in biosystematics, pp. 159-168. *In*: Grant, W.F. (Ed). Plant biosystematics. Academic Press, New York, 674pp.

26. Cade, T.J. 1983. Hybridization and gene exchange among birds in relation to conservation, pp. 111-124. *In*: Schonewald-Cox, C.M., S.M. Chambers, B. MacBryde, and W.L. Thomas (Eds). Genetics and conservation, a reference for managing wild animal and plant populations. Benjamin Cummings Publishing Co., Menlo Park, 722pp.
27. White, C. 1972. *Falco peregrinus pealei* in Ohio—an error. Ohio J. Sci. 72:153-154.
28. Bean, M.J. 1983. The evolution of national wildlife law. Praeger, New York, 449pp.
29. Eno A.S., (Dir) and R.L. Di Silvestro (Ed). 1985. Audubon Wildlife Report. National Audubon Society, New York, 671pp.
30. Johnson, M.K. 1979. Review of endangered species: policies and legistation. Wildl. Soc. Bull. 7:79-93.
31. Wood, D. 1981. Endangered species—concepts, principles and programs: a bibliography. Florida Game and Fresh Water Fish Commission, Tallahassee, 228pp.
32. Drabelle, D. 1985. The endangered species program, pp. 72-90. *In*: A.S. Eno, (Dir.) and R.L. Di Silvestro (Ed). 1985. Audubon Wildlife Report. National Audubon Society, New York, 671pp.
33. Chandler, W.J. 1985. Migratory bird protection and management, pp. 26-70. *In*:A.S. Eno, (Dir) and R.L. Di Silvestro (Ed). Audubon Wildlife Report. National Audubon Society, New York, 671pp.
34. United States Department of Agriculture. 1979. Management of north central and northeastern forests for nongame birds. Workshop Proc. USDA, Forest Service; Gen. Tech. Rep. NC-51, 268; North Central For. Exp. Stn., St. Paul, (MN). 268pp.
35. Porter, R.D. and D.B. Marshall. 1975. The recovery team approach to restoration of endangered species. World Conference on Birds of Prey, Vienna. 1975:314-319.
36. Wiemeyer, S.N. 1981. Captive propagation of Bald Eagles at Patuxent Wildlife Research Center and introductions into the wild, 1976-80. Raptor Res. 15:68-82.
37. Bystrak, D. 1981. The North American Breeding Bird Survey. Studies in Avian Biology. 6:34-41.
38. Tate, J. and D. Jean Tate. 1982. The Blue List for 1982. Am. Birds. 36:126-135.
39. Greenway, J.C., Jr. 1967. Extinct and vanishing birds of the world. Second revised edition, Dover Publication, Inc., New York, 520pp.
40. Jackson, J. 1971. The evolution, taxonomy, distribution, past populations and current status of the Red-cockaded Woodpecker, pp. 4-29. *In*: Thompson, R.L. (Eds). Symposium on the Red-cockaded Woodpecker, Proceedings. USDI, BSF&W., 181pp.
41. American Ornithologists' Union. 1983. Check-list of North American birds. 6th ed. Allen Press, Lawrence (Ka), 877pp.

42. Laughlin, S.B., D.P. Kibbe and P.F.J. Eagle. 1982. Atlasing the distribution of the breeding birds of North America. Am. Birds 36:6-19.
43. Laughlin, S.B. and D.P. Kibbe (Ed). 1985. The atlas of breeding birds in Vermont. Univ. Press of New England, Hanover (NH), 478pp.
44. Frankel, O.H. 1983. The place of management in conservation, pp. 1-14. *In*: Schonewald-Cox, C.M., S.M. Chambers, B. MacBryde, and W.L. Thomas. (Eds). Genetics and conservation, a reference for managing wild animal and plant populations. Benjamin Cummings Publishing Co., Menlo Park. 722pp.
45. Schonewald-Cox, C.M. 1983. Conclusions: guidelines to management: a beginning attempt, pp. 414-445. *In*: Schonewald-Cox, C.M., S.M. Chambers, B. MacBryde, and W.L. Thomas (Eds). Genetics and conservation, a reference for managing wild animal and plant populations. Benjamin Cummings Publishing Co., Menlo Park, 722pp.
46. Gill, F.B. 1985. Birds, pp. 299-351. *In*: Genoways, H.H. and F.J. Brenner (Eds). Species of special concern. Carnegie Mus. Nat. History, Spec. Pub. No. 11, Pittsburgh, 430pp.
47. Brooks, M. 1938. Bachman's Sparrow in the north-central portion of its range. Wils. Bull. 50:86-109.
48. Mitchell, B. 1983. Eagles across the state. Pennsylvania Game News. 54:7-13.
49. Mitchell, B. 1984. Bald Eagle recovery project. Pennsylvania Game News 55:40-41.
50. Klimkiewicz, M.K. and J.K. Solem. 1978. The breeding bird atlas of Montgomery and Howard Counties, Maryland. Maryland Birdlife 34:3-39.
51. Andrew, J.M. and J.A. Mosher. 1981. Maryland's Bald Eagles. Maryland Conserv. 57:4-7.
52. Andrew, J.M. and J.A. Mosher. 1982. Bald Eagle nest site selection and nesting habitat in Maryland. J. Wildl. Manage. 46:382-390.
53. Devlin, W.J., J.A. Mosher and G.J. Taylor. 1980a. Potential Redcockaded Woodpecker habitat in Maryland. Nat. Hist. Miscellanea 212:1-7.
54. Devlin, W.J., J.A. Mosher and G.J. Taylor. 1980b. History and present status of the Red-cockaded Woodpecker in Maryland. Am. Birds 34:314-316.
55. Buckley, P.A. and F.G. Buckley. 1978. Guidelines for protection and management of colonially nesting birds. North Atlantic Regional Office, National Park Service, Boston, Mimeographed, 52pp.
56. Burger, J. and F. Lesser. 1978. Selection of colony sites and nest sites by Common Tern in Ocean County, New Jersey. Ibis 120:433-449.
57. Erwin, R.M. 1980. Breeding habitat use by colonially nesting water birds in two mid-Atlantic regions under different regimes of human disturbance. Biol. Conserv. 18:39-52.
58. Erwin, R.M., J. Galli and J. Burger. 1981. Colony site dynamics and habitat use in Atlantic coast seabirds. Auk 98:550-561.
59. Henny, C.J., M.A. Byrd, J.A. Jacobs, P.D. McLain, M.R. Todd and B.F.

Halla. 1977. Mid Atlantic coast Osprey population, present numbers, productivity, pollutant contamination, and status. J. Wildl. Manage. 41:254-265.
60. Burger, J. 1981. Aggressive behavior of Black Skimmers. Behaviour 76:2-7, 222.
61. Dunne, M. (Comp). 1984. The tenth year: endangered and nongame species research and management in 1984. N.J. Dept. Environ. Prot., Div. Fish, Game and Wildl., Endangered Species and Nongame Species Program, Mimeographed. 32pp.
62. Jurczak, T. and M. Forness. 1981. Operation Osprey. Conservationist (New York). 36:40.
63. Spitzer, R. and A. Poole. 1980. Coastal Osprey between New York City and Boston: a decade of reproductive recovery 1969-1979. Am. Birds 34:234-241.
64. Nye, P.E. and L.H. Suring. 1978. A wintering population of Bald Eagles on an area in southeastern New York. N.Y. Fish and Game J. 25:91-107.
65. Osborne, D.R. and A.T. Peterson. 1984. Decline of the Upland Sandpiper (*Bartramia longicauda*) in Ohio: an endangered species. Ohio J. Sci. 84:8-10.
66. Hall, G.A. 1983. West Virginia birds, distribution and ecology. Carnegie Mus. Nat. Hist., Spec. Pub. No. 7, Pittsburgh, 180pp.
67. LeFranc, M.N., Jr., T.A. Pierson and M.G. May. 1982. First record of a Bald Eagle nest in West Virginia. Wils. Bull. 94:316.
68. Soule, M.E. 1983. What do we really know about extinction? pp. 111-124. *In*: Schonewald-Cox, C.M., S.M. Chambers, B. MacBryde, and W.L. Thomas (Eds). Genetics and conservation, a reference for managing wild animal and plant populations. Benjamin Cummings Publishing Co., Menlo Park, 722pp.
69. Iker, S. 1985. Endangered Species: Can we live up to the law? Nat. Wildl. 23:8-15.

Endangered and Threatened Species Programs in Pennsylvania and other States: Causes, Issues and Management. Edited by S. K. Majumdar, F. J. Brenner and A. F. Rhoads. © 1986, The Pennsylvania Academy of Science.

Chapter Eighteen

CAUSES FOR SPECIES OF LARGE MAMMALS TO BECOME THREATENED OR ENDANGERED

Hugh H. Genoways
Section of Mammals
Carnegie Museum of Natural History
4400 Forbes Avenue
Pittsburgh, PA 15213

ABSTRACT

Sixteen species of large mammals are identified as being threatened or endangered in Pennsylvania and the surrounding states or are extirpated from this region (Pennsylvania, those states contiguous with Pennsylvania, and the New England states). The species included in this list are two rodents (beaver and porcupine), 10 carnivores (coyote, gray wolf, black bear, badger, fisher, river otter, wolverine, lynx, bobcat, and mountain lion), and four artiodactyls (wapiti, moose, caribou, and bison). The causes for these species being classified as threatened or endangered or extirpated can be grouped into four categories—control, exploitation, habitat alterations, and biological factors.

INTRODUCTION

The causes for animals becoming threatened or endangered are many and varied! Many of these causes can be directly related to man's activities. However, we must remember that decline and extinction are as much a part of the life of a species as are decline and death a part of the life of an individual. The objective of conservation is to identify those declines of species that are the result of human activity and distinguish them from natural decline.Conservation programs must be geared toward alleviating the effects of human activities while allowing natural causes to run their course. Larger mammals are generally more vulnerable to overexploitation because of their low reproductive rate. Many have but a single young per year and the litter size of the other species are small. It takes considerable time therefore for these species to recover from any lowered population levels.

Before attempting to identify unifying causes resulting in large mammals becoming threatened or endangered, several questions must be addressed. First, it must be determined which are the large mammals. For this paper, large mammals are those that normally weigh over 5 kg as adults.[2] Second, it must be determined which large mammals in Pennsylvania and the surrounding states (the states contiguous with Pennsylvania and the New England states) should be considered as being threatened or endangered and which have disappeared from the region completely. I have chosen to classify 16 species in these categories—2 rodents, 10 carnivores, and 4 artiodactyls. There may be disputes over some of the species selected for this paper. For example, the beaver is now quite abundant throughout these states; however, by about 1900 this species was nearly exterminated in the northeastern U.S. and was then reintroduced from Canada and Wisconsin. I believe that the beaver belongs on this list because the unique gene pool or germplasm represented by the original beaver populations from this area is now lost. It is not enough to have a species present in these states; it is important that we strive to conserve the unique genetic information that these animals possess as a result of evolving in the climatic and environmental conditions found in the northeastern U.S.[3] It is not important to have river otters in Pennsylvania if these represent Louisiana or Michigan gene pools, when we still have the opportunity to conserve the Pennsylvania gene pool. The white-tailed deer *(Odocoileus virginianus)* might have been included on this list because it also underwent severe population reductions around 1900, and individuals were stocked from several states.[4] However, the data are unclear at the present time as to exactly what the current populations of white-tailed deer represent;[5] therefore, I have not included it here.

In this paper, the past and present distributions of the threatened or endangered large mammals are discussed. Based upon the changing patterns of the distribution of these species, I have identified four major causes for these taxa becoming extirpated, extinct, threatened, or endangered.

PAST AND PRESENT DISTRIBUTION

Castor canadensis — Beaver

The pre-Columbian geographic range of the beaver was believed to have included those areas of North America where there was water and plant materials suitable for winter food.[6] However, by 1900 the beaver had been nearly exterminated in the northeastern U.S. In New Jersey, it most likely was extirpated by 1820[7] and in Ohio the beaver was probably gone by 1830.[8] The last reported native beaver in Pennsylvania was one killed in Union County in 1912.[5] The beaver was originally common throughout West Virginia, but was extirpated within 100 years of the arrival of the first European settlers.[9] By 1899, Miller[10] believed the beaver was "nearly exterminated if not quite extinct in New York".

Starting in 1917 and again in 1919, 1922, and 1924, beavers were reintroduced in Pennsylvania. These beavers came from Wisconsin, New York, and Canada.[4,5] This pattern of extermination followed by reintroduction was common throughout the eastern U.S. The beaver has now reclaimed most of its former range.

Erethizon dorsatum — Porcupine

The porcupine is known from Pennsylvania northward into New York and New England.[11,12] South of Interstate 80 in Pennsylvania it becomes rare and is probably not found in the southeastern and southwestern corners of the Commonwealth. Gottshang[8] stated that the porcupine was once fairly common in northeastern and northwestern Ohio, but it is now extirpated from the state. The porcupine evidently originally occurred in the mountainous western counties of Maryland because there are a number of records prior to 1881.[13] Since 1881, there are only five records of porcupines in the state with the last from Allegany Co. in extreme western Maryland in 1981;[14] these probably represent transient individuals from Pennsylvania. The porcupine was exterminated in New Jersey prior to 1900,[15] but it has been seen in increasing numbers in northern New Jersey since 1951.[7] In West Virginia, the porcupine was confined to the coniferous forests of the high mountains. It was considered rare in West Virginia by 1912 and probably was extirpated from the state about 1929 with the removal of the spruce forest from Spruce Knob.[9]

Canis latrans — Coyote

The history and relationships of the coyote in the northeastern U.S. are unclear at this time, but is it apparent that the coyote has only entered the area in this century. Hilton[16] reviewed the available data about the eastern coyote and concluded that this coyote dispersed from Ontario into New York in the late 1920s. From New York, the coyote moved into other areas of New England, arriving in Vermont and New Hampshire in the 1930s, Maine about 1936, Massachusetts in 1957, and Connecticut in 1958.[17]

Records from earlier dates in New York and New England are probably the result of escaped or released western coyotes. This is also true in Pennsylvania[5,8] New Jersey, Maryland,[13] and West Virginia.[9] The numbers of coyotes appeared to increase substantially in Pennsylvania in the 1960s and 1970s. At the same time, the geographic range of the species in Pennsylvania appears to have expanded from the northern third of the Commonwealth toward the southeastern corner. Whether this represents a natural dispersal of the coyote from the north or west or expansion of introduced populations is unknown at this time.[5] Therefore, even though the coyote is known from over half the counties in Pennsylvania, it is still considered to be of undetermined status.[9] The coyote in Ohio apparently entered the state from the west. The first valid record in Ohio was from Preble County in 1947 and subsequent records indicate that the species has reached as far east as Harrison County.[8]

Canis lupus — Gray Wolf

When European colonists arrived in North America, the gray wolf ranged throughout Pennsylvania and the remainder of the northeastern U.S. However, with the arrival of colonists, the range of the gray wolf began to recede from areas of settlement. The gray wolf was eliminated along the east coast by the 1880s,[20] Van Gelder[7] records that the wolf was exterminated from New Jersey by 1854 or 1855. The wolf was also eliminated from the shore and Piedmont regions of Maryland at a very early date, but they may have persisted in the western mountains until early in this century.[13]

The geographic range of the gray wolf receded in Pennsylvania from the southeast and southwest to make their final stand in the north-central part of the Commonwealth. The last verifiable record of a wolf taken in Pennsylvania was in Clearfield County in 1892.[5] By 1918, the last wolves had been killed in New England and New York.[17,20] The last wolf may have been killed in western Massachusetts in December 1918. Gottschang[8] considered the wolf as extirpated in Ohio by the mid-1880s. The gray wolf was common in West Virginia until just before the Civil War. McKeever[9] (1954) believed the last wolf was killed in West Virginia in January 1900 at the Junction of Pocahontas, Randolph, and Webster counties.

The species is now extirpated throughout the eastern U.S. It seems unlikely that any effort will be made to reintroduce the gray wolf to this area because it conflicts with human activities.

Ursus americanus — Black Bear

The primitive geographic range of the black bear encompassed the forested areas of North America; however, black bears are now confined to less settled, forested regions.[21] The black bear is still reported as being abundant in much of Maine, northern Vermont and New Hampshire, and eastern New York.[1] In Pennsylvania, the black bear is abundant in mountainous areas of northeastern and north-central parts of the state and is being reintroduced in south-central areas. No black bears are known in the southwestern and southeastern corners of the Commonwealth.

Historical records indicate that the black bear was widespread in Ohio prior to 1850; however, the last native bear was killed in Paulding County in 1881.[8] Black bears are still known in the mountainous areas of eastern West Virginia and western Maryland. It is believed to be on the verge of extirpation in Maryland, being found only in restricted areas.[13] The black bear once occurred in all counties of New Jersey, but persists only in the northwestern corner of the state.[7] If black bears still exist in Connecticut, it is only in the extreme northwestern corner of the state.[11] Black bears are reported as surviving only in enclaves of inaccessible habitat in western Massachusetts.[2] The species is extirpated from Rhode Island and Delaware.

Taxidea taxus — Badger

The badger probably has been a resident of the fauna of Ohio since at least the early or mid-1800s. Since that time, the badger has been extending its range south and east in the state with the easternmost known record from Geauga County.[8] The records from New York and western Connecticut are probably the result of released captive animals. Badgers were raised in this area for the fur trade in the 1930s and 1940s, but when this was no longer profitable, the remaining stocks were released in some cases.[22] The records of the badger in Pennsylvania between 1946 and 1955 are probably the result of escaped captives as well. However, if the eastern movement of the badger continues in Ohio, naturally occurring individuals can be expected in the western counties of Pennsylvania.[5] The badger was classified by the Pennsylvania Biological Survey as Status Undetermined.[23]

Martes pennanti — Fisher

The original geographic range of the fisher covered the northeastern U.S. and possibly extended as far south as northern Georgia along the Appalachian Mountains.[24,25] There are still breeding populations of the fisher in Maine, New Hampshire, Vermont, and the Adirondack Mountains of New York.[11] Fishers have been reintroduced into Massachusetts and the Catskill Mountains of New York in 1976[11] and West Virginia in 1969.[24]

The population in New York was on the decline as early as 1850 and was probably restricted to the Adirondacks by the 1890s.[10,24] Two specimens were taken in Ashtabula County, Ohio, in 1837, but Gottschang[8] estimated that the fisher was extirpated from the state by 1850. The historical records of the fisher in Pennsylvania are absent from the southeastern and southwestern parts of the Commonwealth. The last record of an individual of the original populations in Pennsylvania was probably from Lancaster County in 1921. The recent records from northeastern Pennsylvania and adjacent New Jersey are undoubtedly dispersing individuals from the reintroduced population in the Catskills.[5,7,26] This has led to the fisher being classified in Pennsylvania as a species of undetermined status.[26]

Lutra canadensis — River Otter

Originally the river otter occurred throughout Pennsylvania and the surrounding states, but it has been extirpated from many areas. They were residents of all major waterways of the United States until at least the eighteenth century.[27] The river otter probably still occurs throughout New England, eastern New York, Delaware, and Maryland.[13,17] Rhoades[15] considered the river otter to be rare in New Jersey, but Van Gelder[7] lists it as increasing in numbers. Although the river otter was probably common in Ohio at one time, it is now rare and has been designated as an endangered species. There are probably no established breeding populations in Ohio; the most recent sightings were in Monroe, Coshocton, and Ashtabula counties in 1951.[8] The otter has been considered rare in West Virginia since just after the Civil War. It may have been extirpated from the state, but in the early 1950s individuals were sighted in the eastern part of the state, which were presumably migrants from Virginia.[9] In Pennsylvania, the river otter now occurs in only 11 counties in the Pocono Plateau region of the northeastern part of the Commonwealth. Based upon this restricted distribution, the river otter was recently classified as Vulnerable in Pennsylvania.[28]

Gulo gulo — Wolverine

The primitive range of the wolverine extended as far south as northern Pennsylvania, but the species is now extirpated from the entire northeastern U.S.[29] The records for Pennsylvania are centered in McKean, Potter, Tioga, and Clinton counties, with the most reliable record being Portage Township in Potter County. If all available records are authentic, the wolverine may have existed in Pennsylvania until the early 1870s.[5]

Gottschang[8] listed the wolverine as one of the first mammals to disappear from Ohio, with the last record being from Toledo in 1842. The last records for New York (Rensselaer County) and Vermont appear to be from about 1811.[10,29] The last wolverines taken in New England appear to be two young animals from the Diamond region east of the Connecticut Lakes, New Hampshire, trapped in January 1918.[29]

Lynx canadensis — Lynx

Historically, the lynx was probably distributed as far south as northern Pennsylvania and Ohio; however, there are no valid records in New Jersey.[7] In Pennsylvania, the lynx was probably never common based upon paleontological and historical records.[5] There is a specimen in the Reading Public Museum, which was taken in Tioga County in 1923. The last reports in the Commonwealth are from Monroe County in 1926.[5] The current status of the lynx in Pennsylvania is considered to be undetermined.[30]

Gottschang[8] reported that there are no precise records of the lynx in Ohio, but it was probably extirpated there by the mid-nineteenth century. In New England, the lynx is currently uncommon to rare.[17] The species is still found from northern Maine to the White Mountains of New Hampshire. Before the bounty was removed from the lynx in 1965, the state of New Hampshire paid out the following bounties over the preceding 15 years: 1951-55, 10; 1956-60, 9; 1961-65, 5.[11] The most recent record for Vermont seems to be a specimen taken on 5 November 1937, at Ripton.[11] Godin[17] believed that the lynx could be encountered in Massachusetts and Connecticut, although no current records are available. Hamilton and Whitaker[11] stated that the lynx was scarce in the Adirondacks of New York, but was found nowhere else in the state.

Lynx rufus — Bobcat

The bobcat occurs throughout Pennsylvania and the surrounding states except Ohio and parts of West Virginia, but nowhere is it abundant. The bobcat is extirpated in Ohio, but there are no authenticated records to document the time of disappearance.[8] In 1954, McKeever[9] reported that the bobcat was found only in the extensive deciduous and coniferous forests of the high mountains of West Virginia, although it once occurred throughout the state. The unprecedented rise in the price of bobcat furs in recent years has caused concern for the species throughout its range.

The bobcat was recently classified as Vulnerable in Pennsylvania.[11] There was a bounty on the bobcat from 1810 to 1938 in the Commonwealth, but the bounty was repealed in 1938 because of a drastic decline in numbers. This can be seen in the steady decline in the number of bounties paid between 1927-28 and 1937-38.[5] In the period 1915 to 1938, the highest number of bounty claims were paid in 1915-1916 (792) and 1923-1924 (617); the latter occurred when the bounty was raised from $8.00 to $15.00. In the final year that bounties were paid, 1937-1938, only three claims were presented.[32] After 1938, the bobcat received complete protection in Pennsylvania. In New Jersey and Delaware, the bobcat is rare, but it is being reintroduced into New Jersey from Maine.[7,33] In Maryland, the species was formerly statewide in distribution, but it is now primarily confined to the mountains in the western portion of the state.[13] There has been a decline in the bounties paid in New Hampshire in recent years similar to what happened earlier in Pennsylvania: 1951-55, 1699; 1956-60, 1750; 1961-65, 1908; 1966-70, 386.[11]

Felis concolor — Mountain Lion

The eastern mountain lion formerly occurred throughout Pennsylvania and the surrounding states. However, the mountain lion is now extirpated in all of these areas and, in fact, the eastern subspecies, *Felis concolor cougar*, may now be extinct.[34]

In Pennsylvania, the last substantiated record was two individuals taken in Clinton County in 1871; however, there seem to be reliable records as late as 1914 when individuals were killed in Union and Centre counties. After that time there are only sight records, which have persisted to as late as the 1970s.[5] It was on this basis that the mountain lion was listed as Status Undetermined in Pennsylvania.[35] The specimen taken in Crawford County in 1967 is believed to be an individual from Central America, which escaped from a roadside zoo or circus.[18]

The last individuals were killed in New Jersey between 1830 and 1840 in Atlantic, Cape May, and Ocean counties.[7] At a later date, about 1850, the mountain lion was extirpated in Ohio.[8] The mountain lion, which was once found statewide in West Virginia, was beginning to disappear from some sections of the state by the mid-19th century. It was probably extirpated from the state by 1900 with the last individuals being from Webster and Logan counties.[9] Paradiso[13] was unable to document the date of extirpation of the mountain lion in Maryland, but he believed it was probably sometime toward the end of the 19th century.

The last stronghold of the mountain lion in the northeast may have been the Adirondacks, although the most recent record from there was 1903.[11] In New England, the most recent record of a mountain lion is from near Little Saint John Lake, Somerset County, Maine, where an individual was killed in January 1938. It appears that mountain lions persisted in remote areas of other New England states until the late 1920s or 1930s[36] with the exception of Rhode Island where the last lion was killed in 1847 or 1848.[17]

Cervus elaphus — Wapiti

At the beginning of colonization of North America, the wapiti was the most widely distributed hoofed mammal, being found throughout temperate areas of Canada, United States, and into northern Mexico. The eastern elk is now extinct and the deciduous hardwood portions of the original range are no longer occupied[37] except by small herds introduced from Minnesota and the Rocky Mountains.

Records of the wapiti in Pennsylvania showed that the range of the species retreated from the southwestern and southeastern corners of the Commonwealth to make its final stand in the mountains of the north-central region. The last wapiti was killed in Pennsylvania in either 1877 or 1878 in Centre or Union counties.[5] The last elk killed in West Virginia was taken on Middle River, Pocahontas County, in 1867.[9] In New Jersey, the wapiti was probably never abundant and they were exterminated before the 19th century,[7] and the last wapiti killed in Ohio was in Ashtabula County around 1840.[8] A wapiti was killed along the north branch of the Saranac in New York in 1836.[10,38] Elsewhere in New England there are early records, but the exact dates of disappearance are unclear.[17]

Alces alces — Moose

In the northeastern U.S., the moose originally occurred as far south as Pennsylvania during the 18th century, but retreated to northern New York in the 18th century. The moose is now limited to Maine and northern New Hampshire and Vermont.[17,39] There have been a few records of moose from the Adirondacks of New York in the past 30 years.[11]

All reports of the moose are from the northeastern and north-central parts of Pennsylvania. The dates for the last moose in Pennsylvania center around 1790 to 1805, although a set of "fresh" antlers was reported from McKean County in 1819.[5] In New Jersey, moose remains are known from Indan middens, but no historical records are available.[7] The moose was still present in several counties of northern New York when DeKay wrote his report in 1842, but by 1874, the moose was considered rare and a request was made to stop moose hunting in the state.[5] Some reports place the extirpation of the moose from the Adirondacks in 1861.[10]

Rangifer tarandus — Caribou

The caribou was probably never abundant in the northeastern U.S. and probably was already retreating northward when European man arrived in North America. There is no evidence that the caribou occurred in Pennsylvania during historic times, but several Pleistocene records confirm the presence of the caribou in the Commonwealth at an earlier time.[5] The caribou has occurred in Maine, northern New Hampshire, and Vermont, and possibly reached the Adirondack region of New York in modern times.[17] The caribou in Vermont and New Hampshire were not permanent residents, but were wandering herds. The last caribou sighted in New Hampshire was in Coos County around 1900. In Maine, where a permanent herd existed, the last caribou was seen in the Mount Katahdin area in 1905 or 1908 depending upon the report that is accepted. Attempts to reestablish the caribou in Maine have failed. This species is now extirpated throughout the northeastern U.S.[17]

Bison bison — Bison

The bison is one of the most enigmatic mammals of the northeastern U.S. Considerable legend and folklore have sprung up about the bison in the East. The species disappeared early during colonization, leaving us with only cloudy historical accounts and a few scraps of bones to argue over. There are reports of herds numbering as high as 12,000 migrating along the Susquehanna Valley of Pennsylvania in 1773[4] by early authors, whereas Guilday[40] questioned the presence of the bison in Pennsylvania based upon his study of archaeological and paleontological evidence. As Guilday[40] indicated, many of these early accounts were vague as to geographic references, written as romantic adventure, or were prepared for special political reasons.

The last historical reports of the bison in Pennsylvania concerned individuals from Northumberland and Somerset counties in 1810. The map of records presented by Williams et al.[5] shows the bison was probably confined to the western two thirds of Pennsylvania. However, there is considerable doubt about the abundance and distribution of the species in the Commonwealth.

The bison was numerous and widespread in Ohio as settlement began, but according to Gottschang[8] the last bison was killed in the state in Lawrence County in 1803. The settlers moving into western West Virginia also found the bison to be abundant along the large rivers. The bison occurred primarily near open areas where grass was abundant and the Indians burned the clearings and surrounding forest every year.[9] The bison occurred throughout West Virginia and into the mountains of western Maryland,[13] but the large herds were confined to western West Virginia. The last herd in Maryland was probably four bison sighted southeast of Grellin, Garrett County, in 1774.[13] The last bison for which there was a record in West Virginia was an individual killed 12 miles from Charleston in 1815 and a cow and a calf killed at Valley Head about 1825.[9]

Miller[10] reviewed the scanty evidence available for the bison in New York and concluded that the bison probably occurred in low numbers along the eastern shore of Lake Erie. These may have been transient individuals that moved into the state along the dune areas bordering the lake shore.

CAUSES FOR SPECIES BECOMING THREATENED OR ENDANGERED

The reasons that large mammals have become threatened or endangered, or have become extirpated or extinct, can be divided into four major categories—control, exploitation, habitat alteration, and biological factors. The first three of these categories are directly related to man's activities. Under the last factor, however, are listed natural causes for the decline of species.

Control

Control means the active destruction of a species of mammal by man because the species is believed to be a direct threat to man or his enterprises. Among the species that have occurred in the northeastern U.S., the extermination of the gray wolf and the mountain lion can be directly attributed to control measures. The decline of the black bear, lynx, and bobcat is certainly the result, at least in part, of control programs.

Control programs have included the hiring of federal and state hunters and trappers. The federal programs have been primarily in the western U.S., but the states in the Northeast have had their own control programs. As early as 1705, Pennsylvania was soliciting professional wolf-killers to spend at least three days per week hunting.[4] The other primary control method has been the bounty system in which cash is paid for proof that an undesired animal has been killed. The bounty system was instituted very early by individual states. For example, Pennsylvania began a bounty on wolves in 1683 and added the red fox in 1724;[41] Massachusetts began a bounty system in 1630 and Ohio in 1795.[42] This system was particularly effective; Pennsylvania alone paid $1,880,290 in bounties between 1915 and 1935.[41] Bounties are still paid on some species in the northeastern U.S., but not on any of the five species listed above. Finally, species that were considered to be a threat were simply killed on sight, no matter whether a control program was in effect or not.

These five species were believed to be, an undoubtedly were, threats to livestock. They are predators on medium-to large-sized mammals and birds. Livestock was just a new, and very plentiful, food source. Young and Goldman[43] in discussing the mountain lion state: "these animals are so destructive to man's interests that they cannot be tolerated except in the wildest areas". Mountain lions have been known to kill cattle, horses, pigs, sheep, and goats. Bears were believed to be notorious pig killers and the lynx and bobcat were known to kill smaller livestock such as sheep, goats, and poultry.[42]

Another reason for controlling populations of gray wolves, mountain lions, lynx, and bobcat is that they are predators on game species. Many people believe that the competition between hunter and predator can be confirmed by simple observations in which these predators are seen killing species which man hunts for food and sport. However, predator-prey relationships are not that simple and there is no definitive proof that a game animal taken by a predator would be available to a hunter. In fact, data from Minnesota presented by Mech[44] showed that the hunter success ratio was higher in areas where wolves were present than in areas where wolves were absent.

Finally, man has controlled these species, particularly wolves and mountain lions, out of fear that they would attack and kill humans. This can be termed the "Little Red Riding Hood" syndrome.[44,45] There are no confirmed reports of healthy wolves attacking humans in North America.[44] Young and Goldman[43] reviewed the records of mountain lion attacks on humans. One of the earliest attacks of a mountain lion on a human that they recorded occurred near Lewisvile, Chester County, Pennsylvania. Young and Goldman[43] believed that attacks have occurred, but they admitted "it is difficult to segregate facts from fiction". They also admitted that the role of rabies in attacks was not understood in early times. Although some attacks by these large predators on humans may have occurred, the frequency of these attacks would certainly not justify our uncontrolled fear of them.

Also under control could be listed the shooting of large artiodactyls as they eat and damage crops.[4] This would serve a dual purpose because undoubtedly the meat and hide were utilized (see below). The wapiti was probably the species considered herein that was affected most by this type of control. In fact, many elk in the introduced herd in Pennsylvania have been killed because they were damaging crops.

Exploitation

By exploitation, I mean the active acquisition of mammals by man for financial or other gain. One form of exploitation is the trapping of furbearing mammals. However, in the days before trapping seasons and bag limits, some species were driven to the edge of extinction by over-trapping. Certainly the classical case of overexploitation of a furbearer in the northeastern U.S. was the beaver. In the 1860s the American fur companies were exporting 150,000 beaver pelts annually, but this had dwindled to just over 11,600 by 1891.[46] Seton[46] estimated that the total death rate for beaver throughout North America from all causes may have reached 1,000,000 per year between 1860 and 1870. Beavers were nearly exterminated from the northeastern U.S. by 1900. The subsequent reintroduction of the species has been highly successful and beaver are currently being trapped in many states. The river otter, because of its beautiful pelage and because it shares an aquatic habitat with the beaver, was also overexploited. These species are still taken in the same trap lines where they occur sympatrically. The decline of the fisher undoubtedly occurred, at least in part, because of trapping.[24] The recent rise in the price of bobcat and lynx fur has caused some concern about the status of these species, although the situation in the northeastern U.S. appears to be stable.

The other reason for exploitation was obtaining food and hides. This was particularly important during colonization and during the spread of settlements. The species that were particularly affected by hunting for food and hides were the bison and wapiti and, to a lesser extent, the black bear, moose, and caribou. The bison was probably exterminated from the northeastern U.S. by 1825 and the last wapiti was probably gone by 1880. The other three species were probably declining for other reasons, but were probably shot for food whenever encountered. Bear meat was a favorite because it was juicy and could be picked for the winter. Bears also were taken because oils could be extracted from their fat for cooking and lighting dwellings.[4] Hunting certainly hastened the overall decline of these three species.

Habitat Alterations

Habitat alterations include those changes in the environment brought about by man as he changes his surroundings for his own benefit and carries on the activities of commerce. These alterations are not usually directed at the destruction of wildlife or its habitat, but are a by-product of these activities. Many of these alterations are subtle and are difficult to detect.

The first changes in the habitat of Pennsylvania and surrounding states were those associated with colonization. Patches of the forest were opened for farming purposes, and homes were built from felled logs.[4] Towns and cities were established, which led to the large metropolitan areas of today. These cities now occupy areas that were once wildlife habitat. These changes really resulted in the breaking up of the forest and the intrusion of permanent human presence in areas where it had not occurred previously. Lumbering of the forests of the East had a major effect on many of the species of mammals considered here. The major effects were felt in Pennsylvania at the end of the 19th century and the beginning of the 20th century. In a 15-year period from 1896 to 1910, over 225,000 acres were logged in the Upper Allegheny River Basin alone. The forests of Pennsylvania reached their low point of 12 million acres in 1900.[5] Many of these species, but particularly the fisher,[24] porcupine,[9] beaver, and black bear, were directly affected by logging activities because their primary habitat was disappearing. The beaver prefers wooded areas adjacent to water with no more than a 5 percent incline. Some species such as the wapiti may have impacted by an indirect as well as a direct effect. The disappearance of the forest may have concentrated these species in the remaining forest blocks where other factors such as hunting hastened their disappearance.

Many of the rivers and streams of the northeastern U.S. were polluted by industrial development. Semi-aquatic species such as the beaver and river otter may have disappeared from some areas as the result of this pollution which may have affected them directly or have affected their food sources. Water pollution certainly has slowed the reappearance of these species to some parts of their former range.

Biological Factors

Under this heading are grouped those natural factors that result in species being classified as threatened or endangered. Species do not occur uniformly over their geographic ranges; generally, as species approach the peripheries of their ranges, they become rarer. This is because the habitat and environmental requirements of the species are not being fully met. These changes in conditions eventually become so extreme that the species is no longer present. The bison, a species primarily of the grasslands of the Great Plains, reached the limits of its range in Pennsylvania, New York, West Virginia, and Maryland. It was never abundant in the woodlands east of the grassy areas of Ohio and West Virginia. This is certainly one of the reasons that the bison disappeared so quickly under early hunting pressure. The badger, another grassland species, becomes rare in Ohio at the eastern edge of the grassland habitat. The badger has been expanding its range eastward partly in response to the development of its preferred grassy habitat along highway rights-of-way. The porcupine is a species of the northern forests, and probably was never abundant near the southern edge of its range in West Virginia, Maryland, and southern Pennsylvania. Other pressures such as logging probably extirpated the porcupine from these peripheral areas, but this extirpation occurred very quickly because the porcupine was already rare in these areas.

Species that are invading new areas originally occur in low numbers and only later build up their numbers if conditions permit. The movement of the coyote into New York and New England and subsequently into Pennsylvania is a classical example of an invading species. The species is fairly abundant in New York and parts of New England, but is rare near the edge of its expanding range in Pennsylvania. However, records indicate that the numbers of coyotes are increasing in some areas of the Commonwealth.

Pennsylvania and the surrounding states have experienced some dramatic climatic and environmental changes over the last 25,000 years. This period saw the last great advance of the Pleistocene ice sheets and the accompanying environmental changes. As these great glaciers moved southward, they caused plant and animal life to shift southward. Then about 10,000 to 12,000 years ago, these ice sheets began to recede to the north and the plants and animals slowly shifted their ranges northward again. Some species, such as the moose, caribou, wolverine, and lynx, were affected by these changes; at least three of these species lingered as far south as Pennsylvania as colonization of North America began. However, the ranges of these four species were probably naturally receding to the north at the time of colonization, and the effects of colonization probably only hastened the disappearance of these species.

An interesting relationship between the biology of one large mammal and how it can affect other species is illustrated by the white-tailed deer and the brain worm parasite (*Parelaphostrongylus tenuis*). This parasite seems to be tolerated by white-tailed deer under normal conditions; however, it has a great effect on other large cervids such as moose and wapiti in which it is not well tolerated.[47,48] The decline of the moose population in Minnesota as the result of this parasite has been documented.[49,50] The decline of the introduced Pennsylvania wapiti herd has been related to the high incidence of this brain worm.[51,52] We can only speculate on the effect that the increasing white-tailed deer population had on the declining herds of other cervids via this parasite. However, such intricate biological interrelationships should not be ignored[5] when searching for causes of species becoming endangered and threatened.

DISCUSSION

Although the factors causing species to be classified as threatened, endangered, or extirpated are listed one by one above, they probably never affect a species in that manner. The decline or low numbers of individuals of a species is usually the result of two or more of these factors acting in concert. Powell[24] listed both trapping and logging as primary causes of the fisher decline, for example. The bison was at the edge of its range in the East so that hunting pressure quickly eliminated it from the area. The decline of the mountain lion was primarily because of control efforts by man, but the breaking up of the forest probably also contributed to the decline.

Those species of large mammals which declined and were extirpated were primarily eliminated from the northeastern U.S. before 1900. Some species lingered into the early 20th century but only in low numbers. This places the causes for these declines at a time when it is now difficult to assess exactly what the contributing factors were. However, with the institution of conservation programs in the early 20th century and with the development of modern wildlife management techniques, these species have faired much better. In many cases, it was the decline of these large species of mammals that stimulated the institution of these conservation programs. The Pennsylvania Game Commission was created in 1895, for example, just as many of these large mammals were disappearing or reaching a low point. The success of conservation programs with the increase in numbers of some of these species indicates that conservation programs can overcome the effects of man's earlier activities. However, some species such as the wolf, mountain lion, and bison will never reappear in the northeastern U.S. because their habits are incompatible with our modern civilization. However, as many of our remaining rare and endangered large mammals as possible must be preserved for our future enjoyment and benefit.

Of the larger mammals remaining in the northeastern United States, the bobcat and lynx probably should be monitored most closely. The increased price for the fur of these species has resulted in much larger harvests in recent years. The species may not be able to sustain this increased pressure for an extended period. A problem that is of increasing concern is the maintenance of the integrity of the gene pool or germplasm of the large mammals of the northeastern United States. This is threatened primarily by the introduction of the same species from elsewhere in North America as is currently occurring in the river otter, for example. The large mammals occurring in the northeastern U.S. represent the unique end products of a long evolutionary process. They have been shaped by the local environment and climate and this unique genetic information has been encoded into the genetic makeup of each species. In a very real sense, we are the custodians of this genetic information. The management plans that we devise must not only strive to preserve the species in the northeastern U.S., but also the unique features of their gene pools.

ACKNOWLEDGMENTS

Support for research on the status of Pennsylvania mammals has been generously given by the R. K. Mellon Family Foundation. S. B. McLaren, M. A. Burgwin, and S. L. Williams read a draft of the manuscript. M. A. Schmidt typed the final manuscript. I wish to express my appreciation to each.

REFERENCES CITED

1. Thornback, J., and M. Jenkins. 1982. The IUCN mammal red data book. Part 1. Threatened mammalian taxa of the Americas and the Australasian zoogeographic region (excluding Cetacea). IUCN, Gland, Switzerland, xl + 516 pp.
2. Doutt, J. K., C. A. Heppenstall, and J. E. Guilday. 1967. Mammals of Pennsylvania. Pennsylvania Game Comm., Harrisburg, 381 pp.
3. Oldfield, M. L. 1984. The value of conserving genetic resources. National

Park Service, U. S. Dept. Interior, Washington, DC, xii + 360 pp.
4. Eveland, T. 1985. Of white men and wildlife. Pennsylvania Game News, 56:21-24.
5. Williams, S. L., S. B. McLaren, and M. A. Burgwin. 1985. Paleoarchaeological and historical records of selected Pennsylvania mammals. Ann. Carnegie Mus., 54:77-188.
6. Hill, E. P. 1982. Beaver: *Castor canadensis.* pp. 256-281, *in* Wild Mammals of North America (J. A. Chapman and G. A. Feldhamer, eds.), Johns Hopkins Univ. Press, xiii + 1147 pp.
7. Van Gelder, R. G. 1984. The mammals of the state of New Jersey: A preliminary annotated list. Occas. Papers, New Jersey Audubon Soc., 143:1-20.
8. Gottschang, J. L. 1981. A guide to the mammals of Ohio. Ohio State Univ. Press, Columbus, vi + 175 pp.
9. McKeever, S. 1954. Ecology and distribution of the mammals of West Virginia. Unpublished Ph.D. dissert., North Carolina State Univ., Raleigh, 335 pp.
10. Miller, G. S., Jr. 1899. Preliminary list of the mammals of New York. Bull. New York State Mus., 6:273-390.
11. Hamilton, W. J., and J. O. Whitaker, Jr. 1979. Mammals of the eastern United States. Cornell Univ. Press, Ithaca, New York, 2nd ed., 346 pp.
12. Dodge, W. E. 1982. Porcupine: *Erethizon dorsatum.* pp. 355-366, *in* Wild Mammals of North America (J. A. Chapman and G. A. Feldhamer, eds.), Johns Hopkins Univ. Press, xiii + 1147 pp.
13. Paradiso, J. L. 1969. Mammals of Maryland. N. Amer. Fauna, 66:iv + 1-193.
14. Feldhamer, G. A., D. R. Gillespie, and W. B. Taliaferro. 1981. Recent record of a porcupine in western Maryland. Proc. Pennsylvania Acad. Sci., 55-199.
15. Rhoads, S. N. 1903. The mammals of Pennsylvania and New Jersey. Privately published, Philadelphia, 266 pp.
16. Hilton, H. 1978. Systematics and ecology of the eastern coyote. pp. 209-288, *in* Coyotes: Biology, Behavior, and Management (M. Bekoff, ed.), Academic Press, New York, xx + 384 pp.
17. Godin, A. J. 1977. Wild mammals of New England. Johns Hopkins Univ. Press, xii + 304 pp.
18. McGinnis, H. J. 1982. On the trail of a Pennsylvania cougar. Pennsylvania Game News, 53(2):2-8.
19. Enders, J. E. 1985. Coyote, *Canis latrans.* pp. 406-408, *in* Species of Special Concern in Pennsylvania (H. H. Genoways and F. J. Brenner, eds.), Spec. Publ., Carnegie Mus. Nat. Hist., 11:vi + 1-430.
20. Paradiso, J. L., and R. M. Nowak. 1982. Wolves: *Canis lupus* and allies. pp. 460-474, *in* Wild Mammals of North America (J. A. Chapman and G. A. Feldhamer, eds.), Johns Hopkins Univ. Press, xiii + 1147 pp.
21. Pelton, M. R. 1982. Black bear: *Ursus americanus.* pp. 504-514, *in* Wild

Mammals of North America (J. A. Chapman and G. A. Feldhamer, eds.), Johns Hopkins Univ. Press, xiii + 1147 pp.
22. Nugent, R. F., and J. R. Choate. 1970. Eastward dispersal of the badger, *Taxidea taxus,* into the northeastern United States. J. Mamm., 51:626-627.
23. Genoways, H. H. 1985. Badger, *Taxidea taxus*. pp. 408-409, *in* Species of Special Concern in Pennsylvania (H. H. Genoways and F. J. Brenner, eds.), Spec. Publ., Carnegie Mus. Nat. Hist., 11:vi + 1-430.
24. Powell, R. A. 1982. The fisher: life history, ecology, and behavior. Univ. Minnesota Press, Minneapolis, xvi + 217 pp.
25. Strickland, M. A., C. W. Douglas, M. Novak, and N. P. Hunzinger. 1982. Fisher: *Martes pennanti*. pp. 586-598, *in* Wild Mammals of North America (J. A. Chapman and G. A. Feldhamer, eds.), Johns Hopkins Univ. Press, xiii + 1147 pp.
26. Cunnigham, H. N., Jr. 1985. Fisher, *Martes pennanti pennanti*. pp. 413-416, *in* Species of Special Concern in Pennsylvania (H. H. Genoways and F. J. Brenner, eds.), Spec. Publ., Carnegie Mus. Nat. Hist., 11:vi + 1-430.
27. Toweill, D. E., and J. E. Tabor. 1982. River otter:*Lutra canadensis*. pp. 688-703, *in* Wild Mammals of North America (J. A. Chapman and G. A. Feldhamer, eds.), Johns Hopkins Univ. Press, xiii + 1147 pp.
28. Woolf, A. 1985*a*. River otter, *Lutra canadensis*. pp. 375-378, *in* Species of Special Concern in Pennsylvania (H. H. Genoways and F. J. Brenner, eds.), Spec. Publ., Carnegie Mus. Nat. Hist., 11:vi + 1-430.
29. Wilson, D. E. 1982. Wolverine: *Gulo gulo*. pp. 644-652,*in* Wild Mammals of North America (J. A. Chapman and G. A. Feldhamer, eds.), Johns Hopkins Univ. Press, xiii + 1147 pp.
30. Dalby, P. L. 1985. Lynx, *Lynx canadensis*. pp. 418-421,*in* Species of Special Concern in Pennsylvania (H. H. Genoways and F. J. Brenner, eds.), Spec. Publ., Carnegie Mus. Nat. Hist., 11:vi + 1-430.
31. Woolf, A. 1985*b*. Bobcat, *Lynx rufus*. pp. 378-381, *in* Species of Special Concern in Pennsylvania (H. H. Genoways and F. J. Brenner, eds.), Spec. Publ., Carnegie Mus. Nat. Hist., 11:vi + 1-430.
32. Anonymous. 1939. Summary of annual bounty payments since 1915. Pennsylvania Game News, 10(3):22.
33. McCord, C. M., and J. E. Cardoza. 1982. Bobcat and lynx: *Felis rufus* and *F. lynx*. pp. 728-766, *in* Wild Mammals of North America (J. A. Chapman and G. A. Feldhamer, eds.), Johns Hopkins Univ. Press, xiii + 1147 pp.
34. Dixon, K. R. 1982. Mountain lion: *Felis concolor*. pp. 711-727, *in* Wild Mammals of North America (J. A. Chapman and G. A. Feldhamer, eds.), Johns Hopkins Univ. Press, xiii + 1147 pp.
35. Zegers, D. A. 1985*a*. Mountain lion, *Felis concolor cougar*. pp. 416-418, *in* Species of Special Concern in Pennsylvania (H. H. Genoways and F. J. Brenner, eds.), Spec. Publ., Carnegie Mus. Nat. Hist., 11:vi + 1-430.
36. Jackson, C. F. 1922. Notes on New Hampshire mammals. J. Mamm., 3:13-15.

37. Peek, J. M. 1982. Elk: *Cervus elaphus.* pp. 851-861, *in* Wild Mammals of North America (J. A. Chapman and G. A. Feldhamer, eds.), Johns Hopkins Univ. Press, xiii + 1147 pp.
38. DeKay, J. E. 1842. Zoology of New York, or the New York fauna; Part I. Mammalia. W. and A. White and J. Visscher, Albany, New York, 146 pp.
39. Coady, J. W. 1982. Moose: *Alces alces.* pp. 902-922, *in* Wild Mammals of North America (J. A. Chapman and G. A. Feldhamer, eds.), Johns Hopkins Univ. Press, xiii + 1147 pp.
40. Guilday, J. E. 1963. Evidence for buffalo in prehistoric Pennsylvania. Pennsylvania Archaeologist, 33:135-139.
41. Gerstell, R. 1936. The Pennsylvania bounty system. Pennsylvania Game News, 7(9):3-5, 16.
42. Young, S. P. 1958. The bobcat of North America. The Stackpole Co., Harrisburg, Pennsylvania, xiv + 193 pp.
43. Young, S. P., and E. A. Goldman. 1946. The puma: mysterious American cat. Dover Publs., Inc., New York, xiv + 358 pp.
44. Mech, L. D. 1970. The wolf: the ecology and behavior of an endangered species. Univ. Minnesota Press, Minneapolis, xxiii + 384 pp.
45. Zegers, D. A. 1985*b.* Eastern timber wolf, *Canis lupus lycaon.* pp. 421, *in* Species of Special Concern in Pennsylvania (H. H. Genoways and F. J. Brenner, eds.), Spec. Publ., Carnegie Mus. Nat. Hist., 11:vi + 1-430.
46. Seton, E. T. 1929. Lives of game animals: rodents, etc. Doubleday, Doran & Co., Inc., Garden City, New York. 4(2):441-949.
47. Forbes, S. E., L. M. Lang, S. A. Liscinsky, and H. A. Roberts. 1971. The white-tailed deer in Pennsylvania. Pennsylvania Game Commission, Harrisburg, 40 pp.
48. Dougherty, E. C. 1945. The nematode lungworms (suborder Strongylina) of North American deer of the genus *Odocoileus.* Parasitology, 36:199-208.
49. Karns, P. D. 1967. *Pneumostrongylus tenuis* in deer in Minnesota and implications for moose. J. Wildlife Mgmt., 31:299-303.
50. Kearney, S. R., and F. F. Gilbert. 1976. Habitat use by white-tailed deer and moose on sympatric range. J. Wildlife Mgmt., 40:645-657.
51. Eveland, J. F., J. L. George, N. B. Huner, D. M. Forney, and R. L. Harrison. 1979. A preliminary evaluation of the ecology of the elk in Pennsylvania. pp. 145-151, *in* North American Elk: Ecology, Behavior, and Management (M. S. Boyce and L. D. Hayden-Wind, eds.), Univ. Wyoming, Laramie, v + 294 pp.
52. Mitchell, B. 1982. Pennsylvania's elk herd. Pennsylvania Game News, 53(12):14-18.

Endangered and Threatened Species Programs in Pennsylvania and other States: Causes, Issues and Management. Edited by S. K. Majumdar, F. J. Brenner and A. F. Rhoads. © 1986, The Pennsylvania Academy of Science.

Chapter Nineteen

SMALL MAMMAL SPECIES OF SPECIAL CONCERN IN PENNSYLVANIA AND ADJACENT STATES: AN OVERVIEW

Gordon L. Kirkland, Jr.

The Vertebrate Museum
Shippensburg University
Shippensburg, Pennsylvania 17257

Small mammals of special concern in Pennsylvania and adjacent states are surveyed in the context of the factors that cause species to become threatened and endangered. Habitat disturbance and destruction are the most important factors impinging upon small mammals. Overharvesting by man is potentially important to the larger species of small mammals, such as rabbits and hares. Environmental pollution generally is not a major factor, except in bats, which can be adversely affected by the ingestion of pesticides used to control insects on which they feed. Several small mammal species of special concern occur at the peripheries of their geographic ranges in Pennsylvania and adjacent states. Such peripheral species frequently exist in low numbers and in small disjunct populations. As a consequence, these species are natural candidates for threatened or endangered status.

INTRODUCTION

Species may become threatened or endangered for a number of reasons. These include overharvesting by man, habitat disturbance and destruction, competition from or predation by exotics, environmental pollution, hybridization, and natural causes (e.g. inability to adapt to long-term climatic and habitat changes).[1,2] In assessing the impact of these factors on small mammals, it is important to remember that just as small mammals differ from large mammals in their physiology and exploitation of their environments (e.g. coarse vs. fine-grained exploitation),[3] they also may differ from larger species in how they are affected by factors that cause species to become threatened and endangered. For example, their small size endows them with the ability to exploit habitats which are too small to support viable populations of larger species. Their generally higher reproductive rates mean that their populations have the ability to increase in numbers more rapidly than those of larger species. These inherent advantages of small mammals suggest that they might be less likely to become threatened and endangered. Nevertheless, small mammals constitute a considerable list of species of special concern in Pennsylvania and adjacent states (Table 1). In this chapter, I shall examine how small mammal species of special concern in Pennsylvania and adjacent states may be affected by factors that contribute to declines in the abundance of species. I shall also discuss the role of biogeography in determining the status of species of small mammals within individual states.

WHAT ARE SMALL MAMMALS?

Before proceeding, it is appropriate to define the term "small mammal" as used in this paper. The lower size limit in mammals is about 2 g body mass.[4] This lower limit is dictated by the relationship between surface area and body mass in endotherms. Below this size, mammals are unable to maintain a constant high body temperature owing to their very large surface area compared to body mass.[5] In contrast to this biologically determined minimum size, the upper size limit for "small mammals" is arbitrary. In his restrictive definition, Delany[4] chose 120 g as the upper size limit for small mammals, thus limiting the group primarily to insectivores and small rodents. The Small Mammals Working Group of the International Biological Programme (IBP) defined small mammals as encompassing species weighing up to 5 kg, thereby including lagomorphs (rabbits and hares) and small carnivores (e.g. weasels) among the small mammals.[6] I have adopted the IBP definition for use in this paper. Accordingly, I shall deal with representatives of five orders: Insectivora (shrews and moles), Chiroptera (bats), Lagomorpha (rabbits and hares), Rodentia (mice, voles, and squirrels), and Carnivora (only weasels and skunks).

SOURCES OF LISTS OF SPECIES OF SPECIAL CONCERN

The term species of special concern, as used herein, includes species classified as being endangered, threatened, vulnerable, rare, of special concern, status

TABLE 1

Small mammals of special concern in Pennsylvania and five adjacent states. The status designations for species are as follows: E (endangered), EX (extirpated), T (threatened), V (vulnerable), R (rare), SC (special concern), SH (historical occurrence; may be rediscovered – Nature Conservancy), SI (scientific interest – West Virginia Dept. Nat. Res.), SU (status undetermined), S1 (critically imperiled owing to extreme rarity – Nature Conservancy), and S2 (imperiled because of rarity – Nature Conservancy).

Species	Habitat Specialist	PA	NY	NJ	MD	WV	OH
Sorex dispar Rock Shrew	+			SU	SU	SI	
Sorex fontinalis Maryland Shrew		SU					
Sorex fumeus Smoky Shrew				SU			
Sorex hoyi Pygmy Shrew		SU			R	SI	
Sorex longirostris Southeastern Shrew				SU			
Sorex palustris Water Shrew	+	SU		SU	SU	SI	
Cryptotis parva Least Shrew		SU	SH	SU			
Condylura cristata Star-nosed Mole				SU		SI	
Scalopus aquaticus Eastern Mole						SI	
Parascalops breweri Hairy-tailed Mole				SU			
Myotis keeni Keen's Myotis	+	V		SU		SI	
Myotis liebii Small-footed Myotis	+	T	SC	SU	T	SI	
Myotis sodalis Indiana Bat	+	E	E		E	E	E
Lasiurus seminolis Seminole Bat		SU					
Lasiurus cinereus Hoary Bat				SU			
Lasionycteris noctivagans Silver-haired Bat		SU		SU			
Nycticeius humeralis Evening Bat		SU					
Plecotis rafinesquii Rafinesque's Big-eared Bat	+					SI	
Plecotis townsendii Townsend's Big-eared Bat	+					E	
Pipistrellus subflavus Eastern Pipistrelle	+			SU			
Lepus americanus Snowshoe Hare	+?	V		EX			
Sylvilagus transitionalis New England Cottontail	+	SU	SC	EX?	SC	SI	
Sciurus niger vulpinus Fox Squirrel		SU					

TABLE 1 (continued)

Species	Habitat Specialist	PA	NY	NJ	MD	WV	OH
S. niger cinereus Delmarva Fox Squirrel				E			
Glaucomys sabrinus Northern Flying Squirrel	+?					SI	
Ochrotomys nuttalli Golden Mouse						SI	
Oryzomys palustris Rice Rat	+	SU					
Neotoma floridana Eastern Woodrat	+	T	T	SI	T		E
Reithrodontomys humeralis Eastern Harvest Mouse					R	SI	
Microtus chrotorrhinus Rock Vole	+	V				SI	
Microtus ochrogaster Prairie Vole						SI	
Clethrionomys gapperi rupicola		SU					
C. gapperi paludicola Southern Red-backed Vole		SU					S2
Synaptomys cooperi Southern Bog Lemming				SU			
Zapus hudsonius Meadow Jumping Mouse						SI	
Mustela nivalis Least Weasel		SU	SI	SU	R	SI	
Mustela erminea Ermine				SU	SU		
Spilogale putorius Spotted Skunk		V			R	SI	

undetermined, recently extirpated, or extinct.[7,8] The list of small mammal species of special concern from Pennsylvania was prepared by the Mammal Committee of the Pennsylvania Biological Survey, chaired by Dr. Hugh H. Genoways.[9] Information on species of special concern for the six states adjacent to Pennsylvania was obtained principally from three sources. Recent publications provided information on species of special concern in Maryland,[10] New Jersey,[11] and New York.[12] A second source was a computer-generated list provided by Dr. Lawrence L. Master of the Nature Conservancy (Eastern Regional Office, 294 Washington St., Room 740, Boston, MA 02180). I should note that this list was not equally specific for all states. For example, it included only the rarest species from MD, WV, and OH. A third source of information was correspondence with representatives of conservation/wildlife agencies in neighboring states. Table 1 represents an amalgam of the information obtained from these various sources. One difficulty in developing the list was that the various states differ in the extent to which they have assessed the statuses of their small mammals. Accordingly, in some instances, I was obliged to make value judgements as to the status accorded to individual species.

FACTORS AFFECTING SMALL MAMMAL SPECIES OF SPECIAL CONCERN

Exploitation by Man

In contrast to larger mammals, most species of small mammals are not considered to represent a harvestable resource by man. Accordingly, mortality from this source generally is not an important factor in reducing populations of small mammals to the point that they are considered either threatened or endangered. Some sciurids (squirrels) and lagomorphs (rabbits and hares) are game species and may be subjected to considerable mortality from hunting. However, these species generally are small enough to have correspondingly high reproductive capacities to balance losses from hunting. Also, these small game species are managed by the individual states, through the regulation of bag limits and the length of open seasons, so as to maintain viable populations.

The New England cottontail (*Sylvilagus transitionalis*) presents an unusual problem in this regard. The numbers and distribution of this species appear to be declining throughout its geographic range.[13] Externally, this species is nearly indistinguishable from the eastern cottontail (*S. floridanus*), which is a principal game species in the United States and whose present geographic range totally overlaps that of *S. transitionalis*.[14] Thus, the New England cottontail represents a potentially threatened species which cannot easily be distinguished in the field from an intensively hunted species. One ameliorating factor is that the habitat preferences of these two species differ somewhat. The New England cottontail is a species of forests and boreal habitats,[13] whereas the eastern cottontail is more of an "edge" species, requiring at least some relatively open land.[15] Thus, hunters seeking cottontails in "typical" cottontail habitat should be unlikely to encounter New England cottontails.

Among the species listed in Table 1, the least weasel (*Mustela nivalis*), ermine (*M. erminea*), and spotted skunk (*Spilogale putorius*) may be subjected to incidental mortality from harvesting by man when they are accidentally taken in traps set for other furbearers. In general, however, factors other than exploitation by man are responsible for causing species of small mammals to become threatened and endangered.

Destruction or Loss of Habitat

Habitat or a "place to live"[16] is essential to the survival of species in the wild. It is axiomatic among wildlife biologists that the size and health of wildlife populations are dependent upon the quality and extent of suitable habitat. The International Union for the Conservation of Nature and Natural Resources[2] considers habitat destruction and disturbance to be the principal threat to species. Although loss or degradation of habitat has a negative impact on all species, this problem is particularly acute for habitat specialists. In contrast to habitat generalists, which may successfully invade other adjacent habitats, species with specialized habitat requirements (stenotopic species; Udvardy[17]) may suffer local extinction if their habitats are destroyed or sufficiently degraded.

A review of the species listed in Table 1 reveals that many are habitat specialists. Prominent in this list are species of bats dependent upon caves for hibernating, maternity, and/or roosting sites. Owing to the generally limited number and extent, and highly dispersed distribution of caves, such cave-dwelling species of bats are prime candidates to become threatened or endangered as a result of the destruction and disturbance of their cave habitats. Tuttle and Stevenson[18] describe the fragile nature of cave environments and the adverse impact that even small changes can have on the survival of resident species of bats. The thermal microclimates of caves are quite variable,[18] and individual species of bats may have preferred thermal zones and microhabitats within caves.[19,20] Changes in a thermal environment can make a cave uninhabitable to stenothermic species (those having narrow limits of tolerance for temperature). The disruption of normal air-flow patterns caused by installing gates at entrances to exclude humans has led to significant changes in the thermal environments of some caves, thereby making them unsuitable for the species of bats supposedly protected by such gates.[21,22]

Of Pennsylvania's 11 species of bats,[23] 6 are dependent upon caves,[9] and 3 of these, *Myolis keeni, M. liebii,* and *M. sodalis,* are considered to be vulnerable, threatened, and endangered, respectively.[24] Although 3 of the commonwealth's 5 species of tree bats (*Lasionycteris noctivagans, Lasiurus seminolis,* and *Nycticeius humeralis*) also are listed among the commonwealth's Species of Special Concern, all are classed as Status Undetermined.[24] The 3 species of cave-dwelling bats listed above have evinced substantial declines in numbers in recent years.[22,25,26,27] Such population declines are not suggested as the basis for listing the 3 non-cave dwelling bats,[28,29,30] 2 of which are peripheral species in Pennsylvania (see below).

Two other habitat specialists listed in Table 1 are the rock shrew (*Sorex dispar*) and the rock vole (*Microtus chrotorrhinus*). As their common names suggest, both species are geophilous (rock-loving) and are restricted in their ecological distributions principally to rocky and boulder-strewn sites.[31,32] Because the preferred habitats of these species are often remote and not prime sites for development (residential, recreational, or industrial), these species are not as subject to loss of habitat as some other habitat specialists. In fact, the rock shrew successfully has exploited man-made talus in the form of road fills[33] and open-pit mine wastes (Kirkland, unpublished data), indicating that in some instances this species may benefit from man's activity. Although *M. chrotorrhinus* has been reported to respond positively to clearcutting of spruce forests at higher elevations in West Virginia,[34] this species is probably less tolerant of habitat change than *S. dispar*. In general, the habitat requirements of the rock vole appear to be more exacting than those of *S. dispar*. Throughout most of its range the rock vole exists in discrete, disjunct populations.[32] In Pennsylvania, the rock vole is absent from many sites which appear to have suitable habitat for this species. This suggests that the rock vole may not be successful in dispersing across suboptimal habitats in order to colonize disjunct patches of suitable habitat. For this reason, it is important to maintain the integrity of those habitats in which it is known to occur.

Habitat specialization in a species frequently is associated with a limited geographic distribution and small populations. Species having such characteristics are not only prime candidates for extinction because of habitat loss, but they may be subject to extinction caused by stochastic events.[35]

Competition From or Predation by Introduced Species

Competition from introduced species has generally not been a major factor in influencing the status of small mammals in Pennsylvania and surrounding states. One exception might be the possible negative impact of the introduced Norway rat (*Rattus norvegicus*) on the rice rat (*Oryzomys palustris*) in Pennsylvania. Although remains of rice rats have been found at Indian archaeological sites in southwestern Pennsylvania,[36] more recently the distribution of the rice rat in Pennsylvania presumably was limited to the Tinicum marshes adjacent to the Delaware River in Philadelphia and Delaware counties.[37] For many years, a large landfill was located adjacent to this habitat (northwest of Darby Creek on land which is now part of the Tinicum Marsh National Educational Center). If *Oryzomys palustris* is now extirpated in Pennsylvania, loss of habitat was undoubtedly the principal factor responsible, witness the substantial (est. ⅔) reduction in the extent of Tinicum marsh as represented on 1894 and 1943 editions of U.S. Geological Survey topographic maps (Philadelphia, PA-NJ and Chester, PA-NJ-DEL quadrangles, 15 minutes series); however, competition from and/or predation by Norway rats from the landfill may have been a factor as the Tinicum marshes gradually became limited to the area immediately adjacent to the landfill.

Hybridization

The genetic integrity of a local population of a species can be lost as a result of the introduction of genes from other populations of that species or from closely related species. Intra- or interspecific hybridization is generally not a problem in small mammals, except in some of the larger species that are of economic value as game animals. In these species, the pressure to maintain high populations for hunting can lead private individuals/organizations and governmental agencies to import stocks from other regions of a species' range. Among Pennsylvania's small mammals, introductions of non-native stocks have been carried out for the eastern cottontail, the snowshoe hare, and the fox squirrel.[23] In the case of the eastern cottontail, the introduction of genetic information from populations (subspecies) throughout many portions of this species' extensive geographic range apparently has produced a genetically altered rabbit which exploits a broader spectrum of habitats than it did prior to such introductions. Chapman and Morgan[38] refer to this phenomenon as the niche width-introduction hypothesis, and they believe that the resultant increased contact and competition between eastern and New England cottontails has been a key factor in the decline in the abundance and distribution of the latter species. Chapman and Morgan[38] do note, however, that there apparently has been little hybridization between these two rabbits.

There has been a concerted effort by the Pennsylvania Game Commission and others to stock the snowshoe hare in regions of the commonwealth where it originally occurred.[39] In recent years, these stocks have come from New Brunswick and represent a different subspecies (*Lepus americanus struthopus*) from Pennsylvania native *L. a. virginianus*.[40] The impact of the infusion of non-native genes on snowshoe hare populations in Pennsylvania is not known.

The swamping of the native gene pool by introductions of individuals from different subspecies is suggested for the fox squirrel, *Sciurus niger vulpinus*, in southcentral Pennsylvania.[41] The extensive individual variation in pelage commonly found in fox squirrels, coupled with the fact that *S. n. vulpinus* is poorly represented in museum collections, make it difficult to assess the current taxonomic status of *S. n. vulpinus;* however, individuals recently collected within its historic range closely resemble *S. n. rufiventer*, a western subspecies which has been introduced in the range of *vulpinus*.[41]

Environmental Pollution

A recent problem faced by wildlife species is human-caused environmental pollution. Among small mammals, this problem has been identified as a possible factor in the population declines of insectivorous bats.[42,43] Because these bats feed upon the target species of modern insecticides, it is not surprising that substantial concentrations of these toxic substances or their metabolites have been found in bat tissues.[20,42,43] Mortality from pesticides can be especially critical in cave-dwelling species of bats whose populations have already been reduced as a result of habitat destruction or disturbance.

Another small mammal species potentially affected adversely by pollution is the water shrew (*Sorex palustris*). This species is closely associated with aquatic habitats. Much of its food consists of the larvae and nymphs of aquatic insects, such as Mayflies, caddisflies, and stoneflies.[44] Water pollution can pose a threat to the water shrew if the species of aquatic insects utilized by this species are reduced or eliminated.

Natural Causes

All species are subject to mortality from natural causes. The impact of natural catastrophies, such as fires and floods, will have a greater impact on species having limited geographic distributions and highly specific habitats. A case in point is the mortality in colonies of the endangered Indiana bat (*Myotis sodalis*) caused by flooding of their hibernacula,[22,45] including the presumed total loss of the largest known population, estimated at 300,000 individuals, at Bat Cave, Edmondson Co., Kentucky.[46]

INTERACTION OF FACTORS

As I have suggested in the preceding sections, the various factors impinging upon species of special concern do not necessarily act independently. Species often are subjected to mortality from several factors simultaneously. Species of bats, whose populations have declined as a result of habitat destruction or disturbance, may experience additional mortality from the toxic effects of insecticides.[42] The decline in the abundance of the Delmarva fox squirrel, *Sciurus niger cinereus,* is attributed to the combined effects of hunting pressure, habitat destruction, and increased competition from gray squirrels, *S. carolinensis*, which benefitted from the same habitat changes that adversely affected the Delmarva fox squirrel.[2] The snowshoe hare (*Lepus americanus*) has similarly been adversely affected by the same three factors, but in this case, the competitor is the white-tailed deer (*Odocoileus virginiana*).[23,38]

In the case of the New England cottontail, the clearing of Northeastern forests diminished its habitat, while at the same time, greatly expanding the habitat of the eastern cottontail, thereby facilitating ecological contact between these two species. This contact was further enhanced by massive introductions of eastern cottontails into regions of the eastern United States where *S. transitionalis* previously was the only cottontail species.[15] Some authors attribute the decline of the New England cottontail to its inability to compete with the more aggressive eastern cottontail.[38]

UNKNOWN FACTORS

A most frustrating problem in dealing with species of special concern are species whose numbers and distribution are decreasing for no obvious reason. The eastern woodrat (*Neotoma floridana*) is such a species. It apparently has disappeared from New England,[47] where it was known to occur in western Connecticut as late as the 1930s.[48] In New York State, the eastern woodrat appears to be undergoing a precipitous decline in numbers (Alan Hicks, personal communication), such that it is classed as Threatened in that state.[2] The Nature Conservancy considers *Neotoma floridana* to be critically imperiled in New Jersey, while the Ohio Department of Natural Resources lists this species as endangered (Denis S. Case, in litt.). It is now classed as threatened in Pennsylvania[49] and Maryland[10] but is not listed among the species of special concern in West Virginia. This suggests that the significant decline in the numbers of *N. floridana* is limited to the northern- and easternmost portions of its range, and that it continues to "do well" in the central and southern Appalachians. Data from the Pennsylvania Mammal Survey,[50,51,52,53,54,55] provide some perspective on the current status of the eastern woodrat in the commonwealth and elsewhere. Seventy-three woodrats from 17 different Pennsylvania counties were taken during the survey (1946-51). Woodrats were collected in all sections of the commonwealth but the northeast. These data indicate that 30 to 40 years ago, the eastern woodrat was widespread and reasonably abundant, at least locally, in Pennsylvania. The fewest specimens were taken in the NE (N = 0), NW (N = 9), SE (N = 10) and NC (N = 13) regions; the most were taken in the SC (N = 17) and SW (N = 24) regions. These data indicate a pattern of abundance for this species in Pennsylvania during the period 1946-1951 that conforms to the current pattern, which finds this species least abundant in the northern- and easternmost portions of its range. However, these data do not answer the question, why should *Neotoma floridana* be declining in abundance over such a large area? Is it responding negatively to some long-term environmental change or to some parasite or disease? In view of its rapid population decline in recent years, the answer must be found quickly before the eastern woodrat becomes extirpated in additional states.

One possible clue to the decline in the abundance of the eastern woodrat may be found in descriptions of this species by Rhoads[56] and Goodwin.[48] Both of these authors noted that woodrats prefer sites uninhabited by man. According to Goodwin,[48] woodrats disappear whenever man permanently encroaches upon their territory. Could the decline in abundance and distribution of the eastern woodrat represent a negative response to human encroachment? The decline in the abundance of this species has been most pronounced in portions of its range having the densest human populations. Also, might woodrats have responded negatively to the increased frequency and intensity of human contact brought about by the growth in the popularity of spelunking in recent years? Although it would be difficult to document a direct cause and effect relationship between the decline of the woodrat and its intolerance of human contact, any management efforts to preserve the eastern woodrat should at least consider this possibility and incorporate into recovery plans safeguards to minimize contact between humans and woodrats.

THE PROBLEMS OF PERIPHERAL AND ENDEMIC SPECIES

For the purposes of this chapter, I have defined peripheral species as those whose geographic distributions barely extend into a state or whose distribution within a state lies at the outermost 10% of their geographic ranges. The geographic range of a species can be envisioned as consisting of a core area and peripheral regions. Each species should be most abundant in the core area of its range because the biotic and abiotic environments there should be optimal or nearly so. Within the environmental mosaic of this core area, preferred habitats of the species should be abundant and relatively extensive. At the periphery of each species' geographic range, the physical environment should be less optimal, and preferred habitats should be considerably less common and more widely dispersed in the environmental mosaic. Accordingly, at the periphery of their geographic ranges, species should occupy smaller, relatively isolated patches of preferred habitat. For this reason alone, species should be less common at the periphery of their ranges than at the core. Species not considered to be habitat specialists in the core areas of their geographic ranges often are confined to small, isolated habitats at the peripheries and therefore function as habitat specialists in these peripheral regions.

The limited extent of habitats occupied by many species at the peripheries of their ranges will of necessity limit the size of their populations within individual habitat patches. Such small, isolated populations are prone to local extinction.[35] If preferred habitats at the periphery of a species' range are sufficiently isolated, their successful reinvasion through dispersal should be rare. Peripheral species should therefore be prime candidates for designation as endangered, threatened and vulnerable species. Thus, it is obvious that peripheral species pose special problems to states seeking to deal effectively with their species of special concern. Almost by definition, peripheral species will tend to be rare. The isolated and spatially limited nature of their habitats will dictate that management efforts must focus on preservation of critical habitats. Because biotic communities tend to be integrated systems and not random assembledges of species, critical habitat for one peripheral species of special concern will probably represent critical habitat for other ecologically associated species, which are likewise peripheral and potentially of special concern. As a consequence, management of the critical habitat for one species of special concern should be viewed in the broader perspective of all the species which are associated with or restricted to that habitat.

The extent of the problem of peripheral species in individual states will vary depending on the geographic locality of each state. States which are located in the centers of major biotic provinces or biomes should have fewer peripheral species represented in their biotas than states which coincide with the boundaries between biotic provinces and biomes. Based on the distributional maps in Hall,[40] peripheral species are well represented among the small mammals listed as species of special concern in Pennsylvania,[24] as follows: 1 of 2 Threatened species (*Neotoma floridana*), 3 of 4 Vulnerable species (*Lepus americanus, Microtus chrotorrhinus,* and *Spilogale putorius*) and 6 of 12 Status Undetermined species (*Sorex palustris, Sorex hoyi, Lasiurus seminolis, Nycticeius humeralis, Oryzomys palustris,* and *Mustela nivalis*). This high number of peripheral species in Pennsylvania's small mammal fauna is indicative of Pennsylvania's "keystone" position biogeographically. Rhoads[56] notes that Pennsylvania lies in a transitional region between the Canadian and Austral life zones. Dice[57] depicts the Canadian biotic province as extending southward into Pennsylvania and separating the western and southeastern regions, which are included within the Carolinian biotic province. Hagmaier[58] portrays Pennsylvania as lying principally within the Alleghenian mammal province, but with the Carolinian mammal province represented in the southeast corner and the Illinoian approaching the western border of the state. The distributions of Pennsylvania's 10 peripheral species of small mammals reflect this general pattern with 4 having their ranges principally to the north, 5 to the south, and 1 to the west.

In terms of having to deal with endemic species or subspecies, Pennsylvania and adjacent states are not faced with major problems. No species and only two subspecies of mammals are endemic to any of these 7 states.[40] This contrasts with the situation in Florida, where over half of the subspecies of mammals are endemic to the state, as are two species.[59] Such taxa are of necessity limited in geographic distribution and often are confined to specialized habitats. They are prime candidates for extinction, witness the fact that in 1978, Florida had 19 endangered or threatened taxa of land mammals,[59] compared to a current list of only nine endangered or threatened taxa for the combined states of Maryland, New York, Ohio, Pennsylvania, and West Virginia, which have an aggregate land area nearly three times that of Florida.

CONCLUDING REMARKS

I would to conclude by commenting on the conspicuous gaps in our knowledge of the status of small mammal species of special concern in the states covered by this review. This point is evident in the data presented in Table 1, which reveal that of the 78 status listings, 31 (39.7%) are Status Undetermined. Also, 24 of the 38 species listed (63.2%) are classed as Status Undetermined in at least one state. These data are indicative of how little we know about the biology of many of our native species of small mammals. They should also provide a focus for research on small mammal species of special concern in the individual states. Certainly, management plans for species of special concern will be incomplete until the ambiguity represented by the undetermined status of so many species is reduced.

REFERENCES CITED

1. Fisher, J., N. Simon, and J. Vincent. 1969. Wildlife in Danger. Viking Press, Inc., New York. 368 pp.
2. International Union for the Conservation of Nature and Natural Resources. 1982. The IUCN Mammal Red Data Book. Part 1. Threatened mammalian taxa of the Americas and the Australasian zoogeographic region (excluding Cetacea). (compiled by J. Thornback and M. Jenkins). I.U.C.N., Gland, Switzerland. 516 pp.
3. Pianka, E.R. 1982. Evolutionary ecology. 3rd Edition, Harper & Row Publ., New York. 416 pp.
4. Delany, M.J. 1974. The ecology of small mammals. Studies in Biology No. 51. Edward Arnold Publishers, Ltd., London. 60 pp.
5. Van Gelder, R.D., 1969. Biology of Mammals. Charles Scribner Son, New York. 197 pp.
6. Bouliere, F. 1975. Mammals small and large: the ecological implications of size. pp. 1-8 *in* Small mammals: their productivity and population dynamics. International Biological Programme 5 (Golley, F.B., K. Petrusewicz, and L. Ryszknowski, eds.). Cambridge Univ. Press, Cambridge, England. 451 pp.
7. Cooper, J.E. 1984. Vanishing species: the dilemma of resources without price tags. pp. 7-32 *in* Threatened and endangered plants and animals of Maryland. (A. W. Norden, D.C. Forester, and G.H. Fenwick, eds.). Maryland Nat. Heritage Prog. Spec. Publ. 84-I., Maryland Dept. Nat. Res., Annapolis. 475 pp.
8. Dunstan, F. 1985. Definitions of status categories. p. 35 *in* Species of Special Concern in Pennsylvania. (H.H. Genoways and F.J. Brenner, eds.). Spec. Publ. Carnegie Mus. Nat. Hist., 11:1-430.
9. Genoways, H.H. and F.J. Brenner, eds. 1985. Species of Special Concern in Pennsylvania. Spec. Publ. Carnegie Mus. Nat. Hist., 11:1-430.
10. Feldhamer, G.A., J.E. Gates, and J.A. Chapman. 1984. Rare, threatened, endangered, and extirpated mammals from Maryland. pp. 395-438 *in* Threatened and endangered plants and animals of Maryland. (A.W. Norden, D.C. Forester, and G.H. Fenwick, eds.). Maryland Nat. Heritage Prog. Spec. Publ. 84-I, Maryland Dept. Nat. Res., Annapolis. 476 pp.
11. Van Gelder, R.D. 1984. The mammals of the State of New Jersey: a preliminary annotated list. Occas. Paper No. 143, New Jersey Audubon Soc. 20 pp.
12. Nye, P.F. 1984. Managing the bottom 12 percent: New York's endangered species program. The Conservationist, 39(3): 26-34.
13. Chapman, J.A. 1975. Sylvilagus transitionalis. Mamm. Species. 55: 1-4.
14. Chapman, J.A., J.G. Hockman, and W.R. Edwards. 1982. Cottontails *Sylvilagus floridanus* and allies. pp. 83-123 *in* Wild Mammals of North

America (Chapman, J.A. and G.A. Feldhamer, eds.). Johns Hopkins Univ. Press, Baltimore. 1147 pp.
15. Fay, F.H. and E.H. Chandler. 1955. The geographic and ecological distribution of cottontail rabbits in Massachusetts. J. Mamm., 36: 415-424.
16. Dasmann, R.F. 1981. Wildlife Biology. 2nd Edition, John Wiley & Sons, New York. 212 pp.
17. Udvardy, M.D.F. 1969. Dynamic Zoogeography. Van Nostrand Reinhold Co., New York. 445 pp.
18. Tuttle, M.D. and D.E. Stevenson. 1978. Variation in the cave environment and its biological implications. pp. 108-121 *in* National Cave Management Sympos. Proc. 1977. (R. Zuber, J. Chester, and D. Rhodes, eds.) Adobe Press, Albuquerque, N.M.
19. Barbour, R.W. and W.H. Davis. 1969. Bats of North America. Univ. Kentucky Press, Lexington. 286 pp.
20. Hill, J.E. and J.D. Smith. 1984. Bats, a natural history. Univ. Texas Press, Austin. 243 pp.
21. Tuttle, M.D. 1977. Gating as a means of protecting cave dwelling bats. pp. 77-82 *in* Proc. Nat. Cave Manage. Symposium, 1976. (T. Aley and D. Rhodes, eds.). Speleobooks, Albuquerque, N.M.
22. Humphrey, S.R. 1978. Status, winter habitat, and management of the endangered Indiana bat, *Myotis sodalis*. Florida Sci., 41: 65-76.
23. Doutt, J.K., C.A. Heppenstall, and J.E. Guilday. 1973. Mammals of Pennsylvania. 3rd edition, Pennsylvania Game Comm., Harrisburg, 282 pp.
24. Genoways, H.H. 1985. Mammals. pp. 353-423 *in* Species of Special Concern in Pennsylvania. (H.H. Genoways and F.J. Brenner, eds.). Spec. Publ. Carnegie Mus. Nat. Hist., 11: 1-430.
25. Hall, J.S. 1985a. Indiana bat *Myotis sodalis* (Miller and G.M. Allen). pp. 357-359 *in* species of Special Concern in Pennsylvania. (H.H. Genoways and F.J. Brenner, eds.). Spec. Publ. Carnegie Mus. Nat. Hist., 11: 1-430.
26. _____ 1985b. Small-footed bat *Myotis liebii* (Audubon and Bachman). pp. 360-362. ibid.
27. _____. 1985c. Keen's little brown bat *Myotis keenii* (Merriam). pp. 365-367. *ibid.*
28. Schlitter, D.A. 1985a. Seminole bat *Lasiurus seminolus* (Rhoads). pp. 390-391 *in* Species of Special Concern in Pennsylvania. (H.H. Genoways and F.J. Brenner, eds.). Spec. Publ. Carnegie Mus. Nat. Hist., 11: 1-430.
29. _____. 1985b. Silver-haired bat *Lasionycteris noctivagans* (Le Conte). pp. 391-394. *ibid.*
30. _____. 1985c. Evening bat *Nycticeius humeralis humeralis* (Rafinesque). pp. 394-396. *ibid.*
31. Kirkland, G.L., Jr. 1981. Sorex dispar and Sorex gaspensis. Mamm. Species, 155: 1-4.

32. _____ and F.J. Jannett, Jr. 1982. Microtus chrotorrhinus. Mamm. Species, 180: 1-5.
33. Conaway, C.H. and D.W. Pfitzer. 1952. *Sorex palustris* and *Sorex dispar* from the Great Smoky Mountains National Park. J. Mamm., 33: 106-108.
34. Kirkland, G.L., Jr. 1977. The rock vole, *Microtus chrotorrhinus* (Miller) (Mammalia: Rodentia) in West Virginia. Ann. Carnegie Mus., 46: 45-53.
35. Brown, J.H. and A.C. Gibson. 1983. Biogeography. C.V. Mosby Co., St. Louis. 645 pp.
36. Gilmore, R.M. 1946. Mammals in archeological collections from southwestern Pennsylvania. J. Mamm., 27: 227-234.
37. Ulmer, F.A., Jr. 1951. Notes on the rice rat in New Jersey and Pennsylvania. J. Mamm., 32: 121-122.
38. Chapman, J.G. and R.P. Morgan, II. 1973. Systematic status of the cottontail complex in Western Maryland and nearby West Virginia. Wildl. Monogr., 36: 1-54.
39. Dalby, P.D. 1985. Snowshoe hare *Lepus americanus* Erxleben. pp. 367-370 *in* Species of Special Concern in Pennsylvania. (H.H. Genoways and F.J. Brenner, eds.). Spec. Publ. Carnegie Mus. Nat. Hist., 11. 1-430.
40. Hall, E.R. 1981. The mammals of North America. 2nd Edition, 2 vols. John Wiley & Sons, New York. 1181 + 89 pp.
41. Zegers, D.A. 1985. Eastern fox squirrel *Sciurus niger vulpinus.* pp. 399-402. *in* Species of Special Concern in Pennsylvania. (H.H. Genoways and F.J. Brenner, eds.). Spec. Publ. Carnegie Mus. Nat. Hist., 11: 1-430.
42. Clark, D.R., Jr., R.K. LaVal, and D.M. Swineford. 1978. Dieldrin-induced mortality in an endangered species, the gray bat (*Myotis grisescens*). Science, 199:1357-1359.
43. Clark, D.R., Jr. 1981. Bats and environmental contaminants: a review. U.S. Dept. of Interior, Fish and Wildlife Serv., Spec. Sci. Rept., Wildlife 235: 1-27.
44. Van Zyll de Jong, C.G. 1983. Handbook of Canadian mammals. 1. Marsupials and Insectivores. National Museums of Canada, Ottawa. 210 pp.
45. DeBlase, A.F., S.R. Humphrey, and K.S. Drury. 1965. Cave flooding and mortality in bats in Wind Cave, Kentucky. J. Mamm., 46: 96.
46. Hall, J.S. 1962. A life history and taxonomic study of the Indiana bat, *Myotis sodalis.* Reading Publ. Mus. and Art Gallery Sci. Publ., 12: 1-68.
47. Godin, A.J. 1977. Wild mammals of New England. Johns Hopkins Univ. Press, Baltimore. 304 pp.
48. Goodwin, G.G. 1935. The mammals of Connecticut. Connecticut State Geol. and Nat. Hist. Surv. Bull. 35: 1-221.
49. Hall, J.S. 1985d. Eastern woodrat *Neotoma floridana* (Ord). pp. 362-365. *in* Species of Special Concern in Pennsylvania. (H.H. Genoways and F.J. Brenner eds.). Spec. Publ. Carnegie Mus. Nat. History 11: 1-430.
50. Gifford, C.L. and R. Whitebread. 1951. Mammal survey of South Central Pennsylvania. Pennsylvania Game Comm., Harrisburg. 75 pp.

51. Grimm, W.C. and H.A. Roberts. 1950. Mammal survey of Southwestern Pennsylvania. Pennsylvania Game Comm., Harrisburg. 99 pp.
52. Grimm, W.C. and R. Whitebread. 1952. Mammal survey of Northeastern Pennsylvania. Pennsylvania Game Comm., Harrisburg, 82 pp.
53. Richmond, N.D. and H.R. Roslund. 1949. Mammal survey of Northwestern Pennsylvania. Pennsylvania Game Comm., Harrisburg and U.S. Fish and Wildlife Serv. 67 pp.
54. Roberts, H.A. and R.C. Early. 1952. Mammal survey of Southeastern Pennsylvania. Pennsylvania Game Comm., Harrisburg. 70 pp.
55. Roslund, H.R. 1951. Mammal survey of Northcentral Pennsylvania. Pennsylvania Game Comm., Harrisburg. 55 pp.
56. Rhoads, S.N. 1903. The mammals of Pennsylvania and New Jersey. Privately printed, Philadelphia. 266 pp.
57. Dice, L.R. 1943. The biotic provinces of North America. Univ. Michigan Press, Ann Arbor. 78 pp.
58. Hagmaier, E.M. 1966. A numerical analysis of the distributional patterns of North American mammals. II. Re-evaluation of the provinces. Syst. Zool., 15: 279-299.
59. Layne, J.L. 1978. Rare and endangered biota of Florida. Vol. 1—Mammals. Univ. Presses of Florida, Gainesville. 52 pp.

Endangered and Threatened Species Programs in Pennsylvania and other States: Causes, Issues and Management. Edited by S. K. Majumdar, F. J. Brenner and A. F. Rhoads. © 1986, The Pennsylvania Academy of Science.

Chapter Twenty
FACTORS INVOLVED IN THE DECLINE OF THE BOBWHITE QUAIL

W.D. Klimstra
Director, Cooperative Wildlife Research Laboratory
Distinguished Professor Emeritus
Southern Illinois University at Carbondale
Carbondale, Illinois 62901

The early literature suggests the bobwhite quail (*Colinus virginianus*) occurred rather widely in many states of Northeast United States.[1,2,3,4,5,6,7,8,9,10] There appeared to be a uniform pattern of population levels and trends in response to land use and weather. Accompanying the significant population increment and range extension, there was initial activities of man in clearing of "spaces" to accommodate subsistence.[11] For several years bobwhite quail flourished in major segments of many Northeast states. Although historically at 10 to 15 yr intervals adverse winter weather greatly reduced quail numbers over much of its range, there was recovery. However, by the late 1800's and early 1900's, recovery was not to previous levels and certain segments of ranges were not reoccupied.[12,13,14,15] The consequence was the development in the late 1800's of a wide range of quail management programs by private individuals and subsequently by state agencies.[11] Initially, primary emphasis was on introduction of quail purchased from South/Midwest/Southwest United States and Mexico. However, by the early 1900's, because of cost and availability of birds, this activity was replaced by extensive efforts to produce birds in game farms. Unquestionably, the magnitude of stocking pen-reared quail was significant; but, it was not without many problems which required detailed study, as evidenced by the extensive literature on housing, diseases, parasites and release techniques.[16,17,18] Evidenced too was recognition that inbreeding might occur and that in fact, the old original bobwhite was being "replaced" as a result of the "influence" of smaller birds and those of different color.[11] By the early 1900's there was an awareness of habitat needs resulting in widespread interest in special quail management programs by private individuals and state agencies addressing inadequate habitat.[9] Several studies addressed land use changes resulting from intensification of agricultural associated activities, quail management demonstration projects and the life history and ecology of the bobwhite quail.[20,21,22,23,24,25] However, by the late 1940's, there was no success story[26] as there was clear indication of significant decline in populations in the Northeast and complete disappearance of quail from major portions of the range documented during the mid 1800's to early 1900's.

According to Latham and Studholme[26] prior to the 1935-36 unprecedented winter, bobwhite quail prospered in Pennsylvania. It is suggested that there were "immense" numbers which accommodated "marketing" of birds and later, when laws constrained such, sport shooting was productive. Latham and Studholme[26] opinioned that the "blow" of the severity of weather started a "near-continuous" decline, not typical of all northern states. Such a deduction may be with due cause; however, the decline of quail numbers was probably general for most if not all states within the northern latitudes of the quail range. In the Midwest before 1900, changes as a result of land use practices suggest that these negative impacts initiated a decline in quail numbers that continues today[27]. It is with some certainty that a similar population trend[28] had already been in place in the northeast portion of the bobwhite's range. According to Leopold[29] changing land use in the Midwest and not gunning pressure was the cause for population declines observed in the 1920's. Because the message for other states is similar, it seems reasonable to believe a basic factor prevailed, namely, the incompatibility of bobwhite quail to the changes in quality and occurrence of essential habitat. However, there is reason to believe that rates of decline, the role of selected factors and their level of impact, probably varied markedly within given states, between states, and between major segments of the quail range.

Latham and Studholme[26] reasoned that Pennsylvania probably experienced some constraining factors on quail populations somewhat unique for that state. It was their opinion that two changes had occurred, in the bird (intrinsic) and in its environment (extrinsic). They believed there was gene pool degeneration as a result of "exotic stocks" from other states and Mexico resulting in quail with reduced physiological stamina when subjected to stress. They further postulated that diseases and parasites were a potential consequence of massive introductions; and, that loss of innate behaviors necessary for survival and population increment due to native stock contamination by game farm birds was a potential. These deductions, on the surface at least, appear reasonable; but, one must weigh their effectiveness in light of the ability of wild populations to endure, to overcome the intrusion of small transfusions. However, there is no good measure of the impact of a chronic situation over time among native populations as well as the significance of an impact that occurs during a period of high susceptibility to the effects of "exotic factors." Unfortunately there is no clear indication as to the role of potential individual factors, the sum of all factors, or the interaction of factors in population declines in spite of our sophistication in research and data analysis. However, "weighing" the known requirements of a species with changes in habitat and man's myriad activities, loss of essential habitat repeatedly surfaces as the principal problem. Although species of low mobility, and even those a product of diversity, have reasonable tolerance for change, there is a point when the challenges inherent in change and maladjustment cannot be biologically met. This truism must be accepted and addressed if there is to be understanding of the bobwhite quail plight. Further, it must be the foundation for addressing its future.

The decline of the bobwhite quail is widely documented through most of its North American range.[30] Although studies suggest a myriad of factors believed contributors, a common thread is habitat change and/or deficiency resulting from efforts to maximize food and fiber for national and international interests.[30] Unfortunately, the shortsightedness inherent in "mining" the soils, in monoculture, in bureaucratic economic decisions, in ignorance in natural courses of events, and in the folly of robbing Peter to pay Paul have lulled society into accepting in good faith erroneous scenarios regarding the foundation for the perpetuity of man.[31] Although the point of no return may well have passed, biologists must continue to address questions for possible answers that may be available to affront the challenges of the future. It is appropriate then to rationalize and opinion the state of the art and knowledge as they relate to the bobwhite quail, initially so benefited yet subsequently so victimized by man-related intrusions.

Although declining populations are largely a consequence of a multiplicity of both intrinsic and extrinsic forces, the latter generally sets the stage for exasperating the intrinsic, hence declines. Unless there is "genetic deterioration" the reproductive capability of the quail is not being challenged so as to result in a continuing decrease in numbers. However, catastrophic events such as diseases, parasites and elements can reduce to a level of inability to recover locally (on its own); but, on statewide or regional bases verification is often difficult, if not impossible. Obviously a declining breeding population and lowering survival of young yields a declining population overtime. Clearly then, the quality and quantity of places to live become the focal point as these factors set the stage, both short and long term. Relating these deductions to the biology of the bobwhite permits identifying several factors with adequate documentation as to their individual and collective roles in population decline.

Throughout the quail range there has occurred this century dramatic change in land use[32] as associated with an expanding human population in pursuit of greater affluency as afforded by advancing technology. Except for local communities, this change has reflected monoagriculture with significant loss in land use diversity originally associated with a variety of farming interests that included livestock, cash grain, crop rotation, woodlots, and specialty cropping.[33,34]

Even in the writings of Stoddard[35] over 50 years ago regarding the heart of premier quail range, and subsequently delineated by Rosene[36], such change has been evidenced. Probably most significant in its negative impact was the movement towards larger field size managed as a single unit; the consequence was loss of edge, idle areas, and riparian settings.[27,30] In addition, strips of cover between diverse habitats were eliminated resulting in isolation of habitat units, and in turn, the evolution of patchiness rather than a network. Combinations of these changes contributed to loss of year round needs in close proximity. In some cases, croplands yielded an enhanced food supply but an absence of protective cover from elements and predators and/or nesting cover. Invariably these conditions lacked one or more important ingredients essential to quality quail habitat.

The isolation of acceptable quail habitat creating patches has contributed yet another serious problem for the bobwhite. These settings, often with excellent quail numbers in some regions, have become so isolated that such populations become victimized by hunters as well as predators; we must appreciate that both are opportunists and each is similar in the desire to harvest. The consequence is the potential for complete elimination, or nearly so, of island populations; this is not unique for the quail. We learned the hard way that efforts to protect wetlands for breeding waterfowl in pothole regions through setting aside individual, isolated units created a unique opportunity for predators to impact reproduction.[37,38] The efficient predator concentrates on one to a few sites and/or moves from one island of habitat to another, and without much energy virtually annihilates reproduction, if not the breeding population.

Brought into very close association is a variety of interacting forms without provision of opportunity for escape or wide distribution and dispersal so prey has the potential of avoiding effectively predators and competitors. Island settings at best are invariable dangerous; this has been observed where efforts to preserve and perpetuate the Illinois prairie chicken (*Tympanuchus cupido*) through a checkerboard of habitat may well have resulted in different and more problems than before the protective efforts.

With remnants of habitat occurring in a patch-type distribution opportunity for recovery of a population impacted by extrinsic factors is poor at best. The expanse of low quality or nonexistent habitat between "habitat islands" does not permit movement and in turn inhibits not only genetic interchange[39] but supplementing low populations by higher ones through dispersal mechanisms. This scenario reflects a common occurrence throughout the bobwhite range and there is no indication that the trend will change. The exception is if public demands not only proper soil management and land use but also diversity of environment as created in the best interests of our soil, water, fauna, and flora.

One cannot address declining wildlife populations without suggesting that chemicals in agricultural programs have negative impacts. Chemicals contribute to reduced diversity and food supply and drastically interrupt natural checks and balances. They create a sterile environment because they limit types and quantities of food available, types and quantities of habitat, and in turn quality of space where fauna are expected to exist. In a variety of ways many current land use practices are in pursuit of simplicity rather than complexity; a major segment of our fauna is a product of the complex and cannot survive the simple. Unfortunately too, there are species among our fauna and flora widely and readily adapted to the simple; these, often with a competitive advantage, must be dealt with. The question must be raised as to in the long run which practices are the more economical, the more profitable to follow by farming as well as other land use interests.

Everywhere throughout the bobwhite range are classic examples of human intrusion, not associated with farming, reflecting a myriad of interests that result in widely dispersed, widely scattered and intensively concentrated populations of people. Such have resulted in extensive loss, malignant, and pollution of habitats once important for quail. In some situations, advancing city and metropolitan areas create isolated subdivisions with lands taken out of agriculture or other uses reserved for future development. Clearly in some instances there has been significant enhancement for wild animals and in some cases specifically the bobwhite quail. But, these must be viewed temporary havens as human populations are expected to continue growth and expansion. It is not suggested there are not development plans, urban management plans, that address enhancement of wildlife. Certainly such concepts of protection and management require public support, but they are not answers to deterioration of quail habitats; hence, they will not be effective in inhibiting decline in populations and their distribution.

It needs to be appreciated that major portions of the northeast United States historically have always been and will continue to be rather marginal for bobwhite quail even under best of conditions because of factors associated with weather and habitat. Long term studies in the Midwest establish the rise and fall of quail populations, many of which were directly associated with severity of winter. The same sequence of events as documented in 1935-36 in Pennsylvania[26] also occurred in the Midwest.[40] In examining such data and relating to that which has taken place in land use over time, only rarely did quail populations recover in total from the blow of bad weather. Generally, these devastating impacts over time reflect a decreasing ability of a population to revive due to continuing deterioration of habitats. Any species that occupies the fringe of its range has a greater susceptibility to change, whatever it may be, and likewise a lesser ability to recover. But, even in such situations, studies during the past 50 or more years indicate there may be segments of marginal range in which quail populations are essentially unscathed by bad weather or other events near catastrophic in nature. When there was opportunity as a result of continuity of a quality habitat, repopulation and rapid recovery has occurred. Where rapid recovery is not in place, populations tend to deteriorate over time for a variety of biological reasons rather than habitat reasons. In this context then, in marginal habitats there is inherently and historically a patchiness as it relates to quality. This is similar to that which has taken place due to massive land disturbance through agricultural activities.

There is no question that the future of the bobwhite quail is bleak in many segments of its range; the Northeast is no exception, nor is the prime segment of its range in the South. In addressing land use, probably the best that we can hope for is recognition that monoculture in the long run may have serious consequences. There are varieties of actions and activities that can serve in different settings to mitigate the extent of problems related to incompatible land use practices. There is much effort to capitalize on other programs that protect a variety of natural habitats through preservation of segments of our environment (i.e. natural areas, nature preserves, protected riparian zones). Although little research addresses the impact of these programs on bobwhites, there has been emphasis on special practices, i.e. minimum tillage, set aside and/or retirement of rowcrop lands including such practices as conservation easement, conservation reserve, sodbuster and swampbuster; and maximizing incorporation of known best land use practices based upon land capabilities. Although several of these were proposed in the early 1930's, only recently has there been some motivation to pursue some of them as well as additional ones. Seemingly, the new initiative has been prompted by the realization that after 35 billion dollars of enticements over nearly 50 yrs, serious soil erosion continues and at least twice that of the dust bowl experience. But, even with some such as minimal tillage, there is great concern that to accommodate control of soil erosion, which may contribute some habitat for our diminishing fauna, the long term use because of chemicals is a questionable farming effort. No one knows the potential, if not actual, damage to the biosystem from use of chemicals.[41] Past experience with land retirement, soil banking, and set aside efforts indicated modest results for some wildlife populations; there is little evidence that the bobwhite was benefited. Generally, the practices did not address precise needs of fauna of low mobility and products of a diverse setting. Also, management practices of natural areas, nature preserves, wilderness, as well as their often isolated setting, contribute little to the needs of any fauna largely associated with early to mid successional states except under special conditions. One cannot be encouraged that efforts emphasizing special land use practices will contribute much to the habitat needs of the bobwhite. Our greatest hope and probably rather minimal, is that agriculture will recognize its future is vested in working with land capabilities as a guideline and in providing that essential to ensure soil erosion is brought to a minimum. It needs to be appreciated that the United States Department of Agriculture is suggesting that by the year 2000, 50,000 farm businesses will control 50% of the agricultural production.[42] The small farm is already approaching being only a memory; we cannot then rationalize there being anything but very large farm enterprises managed to accommodate the most efficient and highest return for dollar spent; and unfortunately, I suspect, the investment will continue to be viewed on a short term rather than a long term basis. In addition, there is emphasis on the fact that up to 1.2 million ha per year will be converted from rural land to urban use and in "a buckshot pattern".[42] Place this setting in the context of that projected for the not too distant future; an almost continuous land use pattern from the East to the Midwest that emphasizes urban interests and needs along the Great Lakes to Chicago and the Ohio River to St. Louis. Although such projections are frequently in error in terms of intensity and time, rarely are they in error in terms of actual trends that will take place.

In forest management practices over the years there has been a general negative impact even though the bobwhite is not necessarily an inhabitant of a well-managed forest. There will be some contribution where quail have access to selective and clearcut areas; but, these are only temporary. Where management is emphasizing mono forest culture, attractiveness for quail will be far less. There is evidence that national forest plans recognize responsibility for wildlife;[43] they include efforts to enhance quail. But, even in southern United States there is less and less emphasis on management of forested areas primarily for wildlife except in very special cases where it represents an important thrust of a given holding by a major industry or an affluent private individual. Immensely devastating is the loss of woodlots and major segments of riparian forests. There is little reason to hope these will return; but, there is reason to expect there may be effective programs to protect and maintain many that still exist.

As already indicated, the urban settings have the potential for offering limited habitat for quail. Unfortunately, promotion of this interest and its effectiveness is not felt outside of a few large metropolitan areas and these largely in the East. But clearly, the concept of greenbelts and trailways is a step in the right direction. In segments of the Northeast there may be opportunities to capitalize quail habitat through addressing management associated with lands that have been impacted by mineral extraction, primarily coal.[44] One should guard jealously that which addresses the abandoned mined lands as these in some areas may hold the best opportunities for incorporating wildlife management concepts. In recent years as a result of efforts in the Midwest primarily, roadside management has been widely advocated; even under best of conditions, it will contribute little to enhancement of quail populations. There are those that would argue such strips are all that is left, they are inherently difficult to manage, but more importantly they represent death traps for whatever they might produce because of maintenance and automobile traffic.

There must be caution exercised where hunting prevails as the quail resource is immensely vulnerable because of its declining population, its patch type distribution and the inhibitions for dispersal. Consideration must be given to ensuring length and time of hunting seasons accommodate the best interests of the quail and not the hunter. Further, there must be in place the provision that permits immediate decision on closing a season when inclement weather occurs. The resource simply cannot provide for negative impacts that artificially reduce its numbers. Most of our quail populations of the northern segment of the range have little or no resiliency as the population size is now such there is virtually no reserve to respond to significant loss.

Invariably there appears in discussion with regard to the plight of the bobwhite quail the role of transplantation and propagation. Pros and cons of these are widely disseminated, and other than transplantation, probably offer nothing for the future of wild populations. Certainly the potential of repopulating habitats depopulated by catastrophic events rather than natural processes of loss can be emphasized as sites for transplants. Such a decision is not readily materialized because of the complication of factors involved, not the least of which is cost along with monitoring requirements to evaluate the effort. The reestablishment of native species such as ruffed grouse (*Bonasa umbellus*)and wild turkeys (*Meleagris gallopavo*) through transplants into some original ranges has been enormously successful. One must be dubious as to experiencing that kind of success with the bobwhite quail; we have few if any large tracts of land with the potential quality sufficient for survival of this bird. The required setting is quite different because it is so intimately entwined in diversity that was so characteristic of early agricultural activities. In many regions large tracts of forested land persist due to public and private ownerships; and some can and will be subjected to timber management of value in reestablishing and perpetuating wildlife populations. Because this is not characterized by most other types of land use, one cannot be encouraged there will be adequate contribution to the needs of the bobwhite.

LITERATURE CITED

1. Allen, F.H. 1895. Notes on the summer birds of central Berkshire County, Mass. Auk 12:87-89.
2. Allen, F.H. 1908. Summer birds of the Green Mountain region of southern Vermont. Auk. 25:56-64.
3. Miller, R.F. 1910. Summer residents of Philadelphia County, Pa. Oologist 27:116-119.
4. Miller, R.F. 1914. Summer residents of Pensauken Creek, New Jersey. Oologist 31:123-128.
5. Rhoads, S.N. 1899. Notes on some of the rarer birds of western Pennsylvania. Auk 16:308-313.
6. Rhoads, S.N., and C.J. Pennock. 1905. Birds of Delaware: A preliminary list. Auk 22:194-205.

7. Stone, W. 1894. Summer birds of the Pine Barrens of New Jersey. Auk 11:133-140.
8. Titcomb, J.W. 1982. Vermont quail. Forest and Stream 39:513.
9. Todd, W.E.C. 1893. Summer birds of Indiana and Clearfield counties, Pennsylvania. Auk 10:35-46.
10. Witherbee, W.C. 1892. Those Vermont quail. Forest and Stream 39:536.
11. Christy, B.H. 1926. Bob-white in Pennsylvania. Cardinal 1:7-18.
12. Burleigh, T.D. 1923. Notes on the bird life of Allegheny County, Pennsylvania. Wilson Bull. 35:79-99.
13. Cobb, S. 1945. A comparison of the summer resident birds today and forty years ago in a small area in Massachusetts. Auk 62:606-610.
14. Nelson, E.W. 1926. Results of the quail investigation. Md. Conserv. 3:9, 18, 20.
15. Titcomb, J.W., J.W. Stuber, W.B. Mershon, T.G. Pearson, H.C. Bryant, D.H. Madsen, and K. McCanse. 1929. Resolutions adopted by the sixteenth annual American Game Conference. Trans. Am. Game Conf. 16:211-214.
16. LeCompte, E.L. 1932. Bob-white quail propagation and some of its problems. Md. Conserv. 9:1 4, 27 29.
17. Wetmore, A. 1930. Investigation of introduced quail. Md. Conserv. 7:4-6.
18. Nestler, R.B., and A.T. Studholme. 1945. The future of pen-reared quail in post-war restocking programs. Pa. Games News 16:3, 26-27, 30.
19. Palmer, C.M. 1932. Want more quail? Here's how. Am. Game 21:60-61.
20. Brumback, L.H. 1936. Quail conservation. Md. Conserv. 13:15-16.
21. Burlington, H.J. 1939. Land clearing for wildlife in southern New Jersey. Trans. N. Am. Wildl. Conf. 4:546-548.
22. Gerstell, R. 1937. Practical management of the bobwhite quail on the northern range. Pa. Game News 8:10-11, 28, 29.
23. Wilson, K.A. 1938. Quail management in Maryland. Trans. N. Am. Wildl. Conf. 3:709-718.
24. Wilson, K.A., and E.A. Vaughn. 1942. Quail management in Maryland. Md. Conserv. 19:16-20.
25. Wilson, K.A., and E.A. Vaughn. 1944. The bobwhite quail in eastern Maryland. Game and Inland Fish Comm. of Md. 138 pp.
26. Latham, R.M., and C.R. Studholme. 1952. The bobwhite quail in Pennsylvania, Pa. Game News, Spec. Issue 4. 95 pp.
27. Roseberry, J.L. and W.D. Klimstra 1984. *Population ecology of the bobwhite*. South. Ill. Univ. Press, Carbondale. 259 pp.
28. Ripley, T.H. 1957. The bobwhite in Massachusetts. Mass. Div. Fish Game, Bur. Wildl. Res. Manage. Bull. 15. 20 pp.
29. Leopold, A. 1931. *Report on a Game Survey of the North Central States*. Sporting Arms and Ammunition Manufacturer's Institute. 299 pp.
30. Klimstra, W.D. 1982. Bobwhite quail and changing land use. Pp. *In* F. Schitoskey, Jr., E.C. Schitoskey, L.B. Talent (Eds.). Proc. Second Natl. Bob-

white Quail Symp., Oklahoma State Univ., Stillwater, Okla. 96 pp.
31. Clark II, E.H., J.A. Haverkamp and W. Chapman 1985. Eroding soils the off-farm impacts. The Conservation Foundation, Wash. D.C. 252 pp.
32. Soil Conservation Society. 1977. Land use: tough choices in today's world. Soil Conservation Soc. of Amer. Special Publ. No. 22. 454 pages.
33. Dumke, R.T., G.V. Burger, and J.R. March (eds.) 1981. Wildlife Management on private lands. Wisconsin Chapter of The Wildlife Society, Madison. 568 pp.
34. National Research Council 1982. Impacts of emerging agricultural trends on fish and wildlife habitat. National Academy Press, Wash. D.C. 303 pp.
35. Stoddard, H.L. 1931. The Bobwhite Quail: Its Habits, Preservation and Increase. C. Scribner's Sons, New York. xxix + 559 pp.
36. Rosene, W. 1969. The Bobwhite Quail, Its Life and Management. Rutgers Univ. Press, New Brunswick, New Jersey. xxv + 418 pp.
37. U.S. Fish and Wildlife Service 1978. High nesting success of ducks in an area of reduced predation. P. 98 In T.G. Scott, H.C. Schultz, D.H. Eschemeyer (Eds.). Fisheries and Wildlife Research and Development 1977, U.S. Govt. Printing Office, Denver, Colo. 170 pp.
38. _____ 1984. Seventeen-year history of waterfowl nest success in central North Dakota. Pp. 120-121 In D.H. Eschemeyer, D.K. Harris (Eds.). Fisheries and Wildlife Research and Development 1983, U.S. Govt. Printing Office, Denver, Colo. 220 pp.
39. Shaffer, M.L. 1981. Minimum population sizes for species conservation. Bioscience 31:131-134.
40. Errington, D.L. 1936. The winter of 1934-35 and Iowa bobwhites. Am. Midl. Nat. 17:554-568.
41. Steffen, S.L. 1985. Biological preserves on farms? J. Soil and Water Conserv. 40:395-396.
42. Little, C.E. 1984. What's happening to the countryside? Country Jour. 3 11:82-89.
43. Nelson, R.D. and H.C. Black 1985. Wildlife and fish management in the USDA Forest Service. Paper presented at First International Wildlife Symposium, Mexico City. 11 pp.
44. Brown, S.L., and D.E. Samuel. 1978. The effects of controlled burning on potential bobwhite quail brood habitat on surface mines. Pages 352-357 in D.E. Samuel, J.R. Stauffer, C.H. Hocutt, and W.T. Mason. Surface mining and fish/wildlife needs in the eastern United States. U.S. Fish Wildl. Serv. FWS/OBS-78/81. 386 pp.

Chapter Twenty-One

CROSSLEY AND THE ECO-POLITICS OF ENDANGERED SPECIES PROTECTION: A NEW JERSEY CASE STUDY

Robert A. Zampella
New Jersey Pinelands Commission
P.O. Box 7
New Lisbon, N.J. 08064

"It was Bill Hassler and 'Doc' Noble who 'discovered' Crossley quite by accident about 1933. At that time it was inaccessible except by sand roads."
Snakes and Snake Hunting, C.F. Kauffeld!

C.F. Kauffeld popularized the "town" of Crossley in his book "Snakes and Snake Hunting"[1] When his snake hunting "brotherhood" first came upon Crossley in the early 1930's, it was little more than a collection of clay mining company cabins situated along the Penn Central Railroad in the backwoods of the New Jersey Pinelands. Here, Kauffeld collected or reported on the occurrence of several species of reptiles and amphibians, but his interest in the locality was due mainly to the presence of two species, northern pine snake (*Pituophis melanoleucus melanoleucus*) and corn snake (*Elaphe guttata guttata*).

Today, Crossley is merely a place name on a map. The railroad tracks, frequented by Kauffeld in his search for "Crossley pines and corns", have been removed. No longer inaccessible, the area is becoming enveloped by development. Due to a reduction in the distribution and abundance of corn snake and pine snake, both species have been placed on New Jersey's threatened and endangered animal species list. One thing, however, remains unchanged. Corn

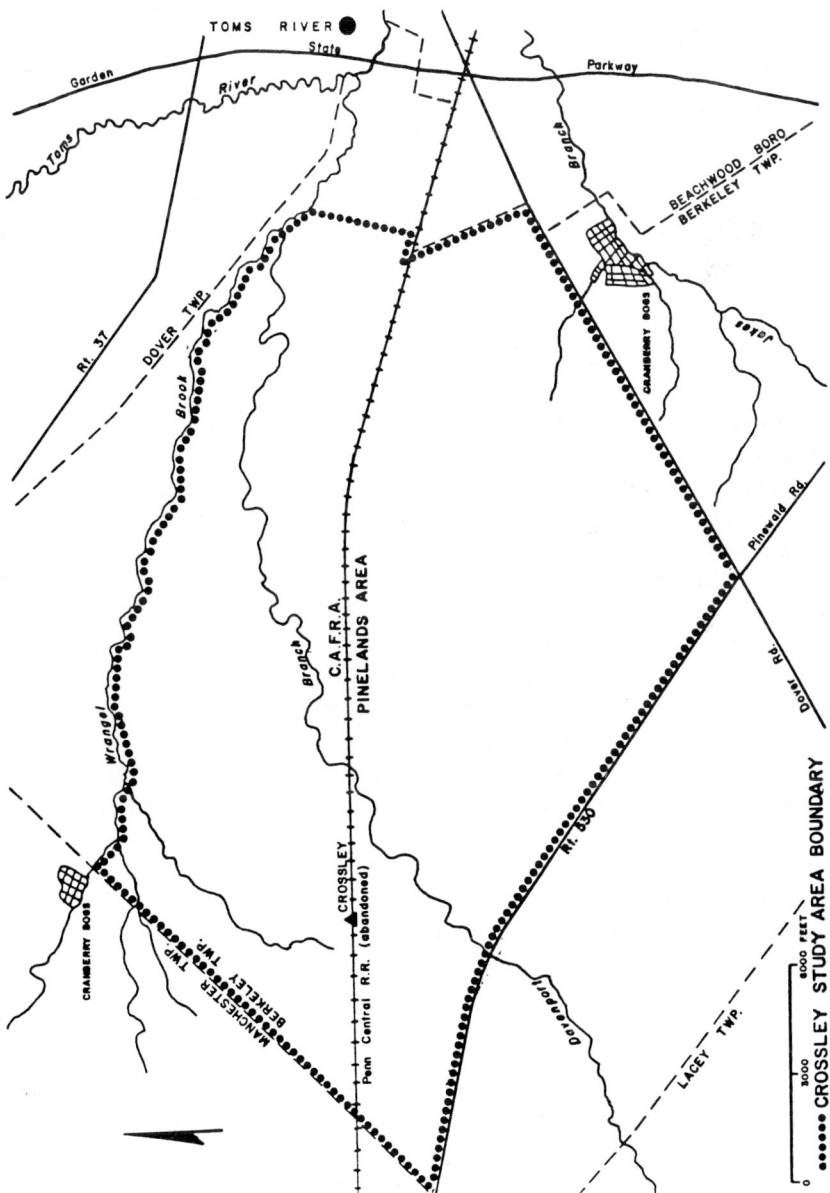

FIGURE 1. The Crossley Study Area, located in Berkeley Township, Ocean County, New Jersey. The entire study area lies within the Pinelands National Reserve. The area south of the abandoned railroad right-of-way is in the state designated Pinelands Area while the northern portion lies within the CAFRA area.

snakes and pine snakes still occur in the Crossley area, and in fact, the area is considered to be critical to the survival of these species in New Jersey.[2]

In recent years, the Crossley area has been the scene of a significant and complex conflict between development pressure and threatened and endangered species protection. The players in this land use conflict include state agencies with overlapping jurisdictions, county and local governments, developers, environmentalists, agricultural interests, and senior citizens. In this chapter I will describe the events that have taken place in this endangered species protection controversy.

STUDY AREA DESCRIPTION

Although the ecological and political issues associated with the species protection/development conflicts are regional in scale, for the purpose of this discussion study area boundaries have been delineated (Fig. 1). This 2830 ha study area is located in the western section of Berkeley Township, Ocean County, New Jersey.

The predominant vegetation in the undeveloped portions of the study area is upland pine-oak forest, composed of pitch pine (*Pinus rigida*), blackjack oak (*Quercus marilandica*), and scrub or bear oak (*Q. ilicifolia*). The forest is in various stages of succession resulting from fire and timber harvesting. Wetland vegetation includes pitch pine dominated lowlands, Atlantic white cedar (*Chamaecyparis thyoides*) swamps, hardwood swamps, and bogs (see McCormick,[3] for a description of Pinelands vegetation). The area is drained by the Wrangel Brook, Davenport Branch, and Jakes Branch, three tributaries of the Toms River.

The areas to the north, west, and east of the study area are predominantly developed, while an extensive, relatively unbroken forest exists to the south. Senior citizen housing comprises the majority of the existing development.

SPECIES ACCOUNTS

In addition to corn snakes and northern pine snakes the Pine Barrens treefrog (*Hyla andersoni*), a state designated endangered species, also occurs in the Crossley study area. In New Jersey, all three species are confined to the Pinelands.[4] Habitat destruction has contributed to the decline of each of these species, while collecting has further jeopardized the survival of corn snake and northern pine snake.[5]

Pine Barrens treefrog occurs as scattered populations extending from New Jersey to Florida.[4] Colonies of this species are found in wetlands habitats throughout the study area. Northern pine snake, which has been designated as threatened by New Jersey, is principally an upland species. It also occurs as scattered populations throughout its range, which extends along the Atlantic Coastal Plain from New Jersey to South Carolina.[4] Locality records compiled by the New Jersey Division of Fish, Game, and Wildlife indicate that compared to other areas of the Pinelands, a disproportionate number of northern pine snake sightings and collections has been reported from the Crossley area and general vicinity. Although this may reflect the popularity of the area as a snake collecting locality, it does suggest that the region is an important population center for the species. Like the northern pine snake, the corn snake is principally an upland species. The decline of this species in New Jersey is notable; recent occurrences have been limited to relatively few localities. It has been suggested that the Crossley area is the last known breeding site in Ocean County, New Jersey.[2] Because of the suspected decline, the New Jersey Division of Fish, Game, and Wildlife has recently changed the species' status from threatened to endangered.

THE ROLE OF STATE REGULATORY AGENCIES

Three state agencies, the Division of Fish, Game, and Wildlife, the Division of Coastal Resources, and the Pinelands Commission, afford a certain level of protection to each of the three species. The Division of Fish, Game, and Wildlife regulates the taking, possession, and transportation of state designated threatened and endangered species. The Pinelands Commission, a regional planning and regulatory agency with jurisdiction over the 378,000 ha state designated Pinelands Area, prohibits development "unless it is designed to avoid irreversible adverse impacts on habitats that are critical to the survival of populations of designated threatened and endangered species".[6]

Although the Pinelands Commission, created in 1979, was authorized by state and federal legislation (Pinelands Protection Act, 1979 and National Parks and Recreation Act of 1978, respectively) to develop a plan for both the Pinelands Area and the larger (445,000 ha), federally designated Pinelands National Reserve, the agency's authority to regulate development is limited to the Pinelands Area. Another state agency, the Division of Coastal Resources, has jurisdiction in most of the area where the federal boundary extends beyond the state designated area. This agency was established prior to the creation of the Pinelands Commission. Its regulatory authority within the study area is derived from the New Jersey Coastal Area Facility Review Act approved by the State Legislature in 1973. The Division, which is often referred to locally as CAFRA, the acronym of the enabling legislation, has a policy which prohibits development that would adversely affect the habitat of an endangered or threatened species, unless an area that is considered suitable to ensure the local survival of the species is set aside and properly managed.[7] The railroad bed, which Kauffeld frequented, forms one of several boundaries between the Pinelands Area and the Pinelands National Reserve. This line was established because it coincided with the preexisting boundary of the Division of Coastal Resources' area of jurisdiction.

THE CROSSLEY CASE STUDY

The Pinelands Commission and CAFRA have made several land use decisions that affect the study area and its populations of corn snake, northern pine snake, and Pine Barrens treefrog. In the following sections, I have presented four of the major decisions along with a description of the events that preceded them. Two cases address what are principally regional land use planning issues affecting the entire study area, while two involve the site specific review and regulation of residential development projects. An analysis of the decisions and the strategies employed to resolve the threatened and endangered species protection issues is also presented.

THE WESTERN BERKELEY CONTROVERSY

The New Jersey Pinelands Comprehensive Management Plan[6] provides the framework that guides development in the Pinelands region. Among the strategies that it employs to accomplish the goal of Pinelands protection is the allocation of varying levels of land use intensities among discrete management areas. This allocation, ranging from preservation to high density development, is based on the ecological value and sensitivity of an area and its ability to support development, along with its relationship to existing development patterns (see Good and Good, this volume for a summary of the Comprehensive Management Plan).

The Comprehensive Management Plan established three management areas within the 2830 ha study area. The 1210 ha located north of the Pinelands Area/Pinelands National Reserve boundary was designated as a high growth zone (1 residential unit/0.2 ha of upland). This was done for several reasons. Local development approvals had been granted in much of the area prior to the establishment of the Pinelands Commission, and both the Division of Coastal Resources, the state agency responsible for implementing the intent of the Comprehensive Management Plan within the area, and the Ocean County Planning Board, a local planning agency, identified the area as part of a growth region. The area represented a logical extension of adjacent growth, and in fact, a large portion of it had already been developed.

The Pinelands Area portion of the study area was divided into two management areas. Approximately 1215 ha were classified as a low growth zone (1 residential unit/6.4 ha of upland). This rather restrictive zoning was based on the high environmental quality and sensitivity of the area. Several factors such as water quality, the presence of wetlands, and other critical areas were used in this assessment. The presence of Pine Barrens treefrog, corn snake, and northern pine snake populations was principal among these factors.

The only existing land use within the low growth zone was a 31 ha developing industrial park located along the southern boundary. This industrial park, which was initiated prior to 1979, was approved by the Pinelands Commission under interim rules and regulations which were in effect during a development moratorium imposed while the Comprehensive Management Plan was being developed. The Commission initially denied the project because it affected the habitat of the northern pine snake. This decision was challenged by the project applicant, became the subject of an administrative law hearing, and was upheld by the hearing officer. However, once the Commission decided that the surrounding area would be classified as a low growth zone in the Comprehensive Management Plan, it reversed both its initial decision and that of the hearing officer. This reversal was based on the conclusion that even though habitat in the immediate area of the industrial park would be destroyed, the low growth classification would ensure that sufficient habitat to protect the pine snake population would be preserved. This action and its justification was an important consideration in blocking subsequent attempts to reclassify the area as a high growth region.

The remaining 405 ha of the study area, located in the eastern portion of the Pinelands Area, were designated as a moderate growth zone (1 residential unit/1.3 ha of upland). This area represented what the Pinelands Commission classified as a conflict area.[6] It displayed environmental qualities similar to those of the low growth area, especially with regard to the presence of populations of the three threatened or endangered species. However, it also possessed certain characteristics that made it an appropriate candidate as an area that could support additional development. Most importantly, it was the site of a development project, called the Davenport Cluster, that was initiated prior to the establishment of the Pinelands Commission. Local development approvals had been obtained, cul-de-sacs and roadways had been cleared, and a sewer line connection had been constructed. The proposed development, which involved the construction of approximately 1400 residential units on 228 ha (1 residential unit/0.2 ha), was halted by the Pinelands building moratorium in 1979. More will be said about the Davenport Cluster in a subsequent section.

The Comprehensive Management Plan was developed with the objective that it be implemented at the local level. Local county and municipal governments are required by the Pinelands legislation to revise their land use plans and ordinances to conform with the Comprehensive Management Plan's regional land allocation and environmental standards programs. During this conformance process, the Commission is able to provide flexibility in interpreting the Plan to reflect local needs. This can involve minor changes in management area boundaries. Once it is certified, a local government is responsible for implementing the Plan within its area of jurisdiction. The Pinelands Commission can, however, overrule local decisions which it deems to be substantially inconsistent with the Plan. Politically, conformance is a critical test of the Commission's effectiveness in implementing the Plan. Because home rule is an important issue in New Jersey, the number of counties and towns that are certified by the Commission provides one measure of the agency's success as a regional planning entity.

Ocean County encompasses 165,270 ha in southern New Jersey. Forty five percent of this area (74,060 ha) lies within the Pinelands Area. As the county planning agency, the Ocean County Planning Board has the primary responsibility of conforming to the Comprehensive Management Plan. When the process began in 1981, several differences between the Planning Board's existing county master plan and the Comprehensive Management Plan had to be resolved. The most substantial one involved the classification of the Pinelands Area of western Berkeley Township. The Planning Board identified the entire area as a high growth region. The County had already made a significant economic commitment to the area with the prior development of an air park/industrial park complex located directly south of the study area. Although Berkeley Township initially accepted the Pinelands Commission's designations, it reversed this position in favor of that held by the County.

During the conformance process, the County Planning Board challenged the environmental basis used by the Pinelands Commission to designate the area as a low and moderate growth region. This challenge involved the full spectrum of environmental factors presented by the Pinelands Commission, but concentrated on the issue of threatened and endangered species protection. The County identified this issue as the most important one which, if addressed, could open the area for development.

The County Planning Board pursued this issue by initiating a study of the habitat requirements of the corn snake and the pine snake which was partially funded by local, development oriented landowners. The objective of the study was to determine the minimum size of the area needed to maintain the existing populations of these species. The assumption made by the Planning Board was that once the critical habitat requirements were determined, sufficient land could be set-aside to accommodate these needs, and the remaining lands could be developed. The results of this study, which included a radio tracking study, field surveys, a review of available locality records, and an analysis of habitat features, were reported in a publication entitled "Critical Habitat Requirements of Two Threatened Species in the Davenport Basin".[8]

In the report, the Planning Board concluded that a properly managed wildlife preserve, totalling approximately 385 ha and consisting of the abandoned railroad bed, an adjacent buffer, and wetland areas, would provide sufficient habitat to support and maintain the existing populations of northern pine snake and corn snake. The railroad bed was identified as critical habitat and was the focal point of the County's protective strategy. The Planning Board recommended that the remainder of the study area be reclassified as a high growth zone with an overall density of approximately 1 unit/0.1 ha.

The technical staff within the Pinelands Commission questioned certain aspects of the methodology used in the study, and disagreed with the conclusions of the report. They found that the evidence presented did not support the County's conclusion regarding the adequacy of the proposed wildlife preserve. The preserve was viewed as an isolated, elongated island that except for stream/wetland corridors would eventually be totally surrounded by development. Commission staff suggested that designation of the railroad bed as critical habitat was influenced by biased sampling techniques and that there was an insufficient basis for associating this habitat with the minimum area required to support viable snake populations. They recommended that to provide maximum protection to the existing snake population no further encroachments be permitted in the low density zone. Similar conclusions were reached by an independent panel of scientists[9] and by the New Jersey Division of Fish, Game, and Wildlife. The Pinelands Commission accepted the reviews provided by its staff, the panel of scientists, and the Division of Fish, Game and Wildlife, and disallowed the findings of the County in any consideration of reclassifying the study area. Reclassification was also impeded by the U.S. Department of the Interior which concluded that acceptance of the County proposal would constitute a significant modification of the Comprehensive Management Plan. Such a change would require the approval of the Secretary of the Interior.

An impasse was reached. In an attempt to arrive at a compromise, the Ocean County Planning Board and the Pinelands Commission agreed to develop a plan that would accommodate what both agencies considered to be an accurate estimate of projected population growth for the area. The Commission concluded that this projected need could be met if an area similar in size to the moderate growth zone was reclassified as a high growth zone when adjacent areas became fully developed. Such a change in density allocation was provided by the Comprehensive Management Plan. The moderate growth zone appeared to be the logical choice for the redesignation, but this approach raised a new concern: the southern part of the moderate growth zone drained toward a cranberry bog complex, and because cranberry production is dependent on large quantities of high quality water, a valid concern regarding the impact of high density development on the cranberry operation was brought to the forefront. The Commission resolved this issue by recommending that the lower portion of the moderate density zone be reclassified as an agricultural production zone (1 residential unit/4.1 ha when associated with an agricultural operation), a more restrictive management area, and that in its place a comparable area within the low density zone be redesignated to accommodate future growth. The latter was located adjacent to both the northern section of the existing moderate growth zone and existing and approved development in the CAFRA area. While this decision was made with agricultural interests in mind, it provided an alternative designed to meet the needs of the County while maintaining a large, contiguous land mass that was considered essential to protecting the corn snake and pine snake populations.

The County found this proposal unacceptable, and suggested an alternative that affected a much larger area in the low density zone. The Commission concluded that there was no ecological basis for this alternative, and that the integrity of the low density zone would be excessively compromised if it were pursued. In the winter of 1983, the Commission found the County to be in noncompliance with the Comprehensive Management Plan, and retained the responsibility of implementing the County's role as it related to the Plan. Berkeley Township accepted the Commission's compromise, and the municipality's master plan and zoning ordinance will soon be certified by the Commission. As of this writing, the County has not been certified by the Commission. The controversy is, however, not over. Reclassification of western Berkeley Township remains an important item on the agenda of Ocean County.

THE CRESTWOOD INTERCEPTOR

The Ocean County Utilities Authority is a public agency responsible for administering the regional sewer service system. In 1982, it reinitiated long standing plans to construct a sewer interceptor line to service western Berkeley Township and areas within Manchester Township, an adjacent municipality. The proposal was presented principally as a means of correcting ground and surface water contamination problems associated with existing development in Manchester Township, but was also designed to accommodate future development. Because the project affected both the Pinelands Area and the CAFRA portion of the Pinelands National Reserve, it was jointly reviewed by the Pinelands Commission and CAFRA.

The Ocean County Utilities Authority identified several alternate interceptor routes. Both CAFRA and the Pinelands Commission limited their final review to two of these alternatives. One paralleled the northern side of the abandoned railroad bed, while the other followed the banks of the Wrangel Brook for much of its length. The Ocean County Utilities Authority concluded that the first route, referred to as the Crestwood Interceptor, was the preferred alternative. Among the reasons for this conclusion was that it would have less impact on existing development, wetlands, stream corridors, and the survival of northern pine snake, corn snake, and Pine Barrens treefrog. Both CAFRA and the Pinelands Commission agreed that the Crestwood Interceptor was the best overall alternative, but the Commission disagreed with the conclusion regarding the impact on threatened and endangered species. The Commission considered the impact to these species to be comparable along both routes.

A major issue raised by the Pinelands Commission and CAFRA was the growth generating potential of an interceptor that would parallel the northern boundary of the low density zone. Several strategies were cooperatively developed and employed to reduce this potential secondary impact to the low density zone. The size of the interceptor was reduced to more closely meet the needs of approved development areas and lateral connection points were strategically placed to limit the possibility of future tie-ins from the low density zone. The Utilities Authority agreed to transfer title of sections of the right-of-way to the State of New Jersey. These lands would be managed for the protection of the northern pine snake and corn snake, and would further limit the probability of additional tie-ins to the interceptor. Site specific approaches employed in this project were the avoidance of Pine Barrens treefrog habitats and known snake nesting areas, the construction of snake hibernacula, and the prohibition of construction activities during those periods when northern pine snake and corn snake were most active.

THE DAVENPORT CLUSTER

Halted by the Pinelands building moratorium in 1979, development of the 1400 unit Davenport Cluster was again pursued in 1982 under the provisions of the Comprehensive Management Plan. The major impediments to receiving an approval from the Pinelands Commission were (1) the proposal was inconsistent with the residential densities assigned to the moderate density zone and (2) the project would result in the destruction of northern pine snake and corn snake habitat, and therefore violated the threatened and endangered species protection standard included in the Comprehensive Management Plan.

Because local approvals were granted before the Pinelands Commission was established, the Commission was legally obligated to consider issuing a waiver from the density and threatened and endangered species provisions of the Comprehensive Management Plan. Such a waiver would be necessary to allow the developers to realize a reasonable rate of return on their investment. However, this could only be done if the Pinelands Commission found that this decision would not result in a "substantial impairment of the resources of the Pinelands".

The Pinelands Commission concluded that granting the waivers would not result in a substantial impairment if certain conditions were imposed on the project. Development would only be permitted on 137 ha located in the northern section of the parcel and representing about 60 per cent of the total project area. This area, located in the Davenport Branch drainage basin, coincided with what the Commission had previously suggested be converted to a high growth zone as part of the resolution to the western Berkeley controversy. A deed restriction would be required on the remaining 91 ha of the parcel located in the Jakes Branch drainage basin. This area, which drains towards the previously noted cranberry complex, would be managed as a northern pine snake and corn snake preserve. A management plan for the preserve and a two year snake capture and off-site release program for the northern section of the parcel would be developed and implemented, subject to the approval of the Division of Fish, Game, and Wildlife. Finally, development would not occur within 31 m of the abandoned railroad bed.

A critical element of the decision to grant a waiver was similar to the premise used in approving the permit for the industrial park. The assumption made by the Pinelands Commission was that the low density zone and the southern portion of the project area was required to support the existing snake populations. Development of the Davenport Cluster would not be permitted to proceed if the low density zone was further reduced in size unless it could be demonstrated that a less extensive low density zone could ensure the continued maintenance of the existing snake population.

The Pinelands Commission's decision was accepted by the project developers, but it was challenged by the New Jersey Sierra Club. The matter was referred to an administrative law hearing, and the hearing officer upheld the Pinelands Commission's decision. The Sierra Club subsequently agreed not to pursue the matter further. In return, the developers agreed to a settlement that included the donation of an off-site mitigation area.

As of this writing, construction of the Davenport Cluster has not begun. A management plan for the snake preserve, involving the conversion of four previously cleared 0.8 ha wooded areas to sand and sedge covered fields and the construction of artificial hibernacula, has been approved by the Division of Fish, Game and Wildlife, and is currently being implemented. The capture and release program has also begun. Nine adult northern pine snakes and 4 adult corn snakes have been captured in the Davenport Branch portion of the Davenport Cluster (R.T. Zappalorti, per. com.). These snakes have been marked and released on state preserves. Prior to their release, several gravid females of both species were included in a captive breeding program supervised by the Division of Fish, Game, and Wildlife. Eggs have been obtained and all hatchings will be released in the deed restricted Jakes Branch portion of the Davenport Cluster.

THE CAFRA EXPERIENCE

From 1981 through 1983, the Division of Coastal Resources (CAFRA) issued permits for three housing developments within the Pinelands National Reserve portion of the study area. A total of 3760 residential units were approved for development on 417 ha, including approximately 89 ha of designated open space located within the areas to be developed. The latter includes wetlands, buffers, and recreational lands. Construction has begun on all three developments, and they are in varying stages of completion.

Among the conditions included in the CAFRA permits were measures intended to mitigate the impact of the proposed development on corn snake, northern pine snake, and Pine Barrens treefrog populations. These mitigation measures, which were approved in cooperation with the Division of Fish, Game and Wildlife, included the creation of a 28 ha off-site wildlife management area located on the southern side of the railroad bed, the establishment of a 23 m buffer zone between the proposed development and the railroad bed, the construction of artificial snake hibernacula, the transfer of snakes collected on site to a protected area, and the preservation of known Pine Barrens treefrog wetland habitats.

Most of the CAFRA portion of the study area has been developed. When issuing the last development permit, CAFRA implied that no further approvals would be granted in the area until more was known about the critical habitat needs of the northern pine snake and corn snake. Recently, in an unrelated action, 100 ha of the undeveloped area were donated to the New Jersey Natural Lands Trust, a program administered by the Department of Environmental Protection. This land, which represents a majority of the remaining undeveloped area, will be managed as a natural preserve.

ANALYSIS

Several strategies have been employed to protect threatened and endangered species habitat in the Crossley study area. These include regional planning, use of environmental performance standards, and mitigation. The experience suggests that regional planning can have the greatest positive, long term effect. This was highlighted by the western Berkeley controversy, where protection of the Crossley area was viewed as an element of an overall strategy to preserve the Pinelands region, rather than as an attempt to protect a specific site based solely on a single issue. The arguments for endangered species protection were supported and enhanced by larger, regional issues.

The use of zoning in regional planning often provides the first line of defense against habitat destruction. Because the CAFRA area was designed to accommodate a given amount of development by both the Pinelands Commission and CAFRA, it was more difficult, both legally and politically, for the regulatory agency to restrict development there. CAFRA was also hindered by the management strategy that it is employs. Unlike the Pinelands Commission, CAFRA has not assigned specific building densities on a regional basis. Instead, it reviews individual development projects within the context of a general land use classification system and according to a set of development potential criteria. As with the western Berkeley controversy, zoning can be used to direct development away from more sensitive lands, thereby avoiding individual development project conflicts.

The Crestwood Interceptor case also demonstrated the greater effectiveness of a regional perspective compared to site specific development review. The assessment of secondary regional impacts associated with the construction of the Crestwood Interceptor was far more important to the survival of the threatened and endangered species than the review of the local, temporary disturbance of the railroad bed.

The Crossley experience emphasized the basic lack of knowledge regarding the minimum area requirements of endangered species populations, and the impact of landscape fragmentation on these species. In each of the cases discussed, the railroad bed was identified as critical habitat, and this designation was associated with the minimum critical area required for a functioning biological reserve. The Division of Fish, Game and Wildlife initially accepted this association, and the approach influenced CAFRA's decisions in the area. During the western Berkeley controversy the Pinelands Commission took a much broader approach to the definition of critical habitat, one which extended beyond a given site where locality records were collected. This reassessment was accepted and supported by the Division of Fish, Game and Wildlife. Although the solution of the Pinelands Commission was based on biological principles, it was a subjective decision that was tempered by legal and political considerations. The question regarding the minimum size of a biological reserve still remains unanswered.

Environmental performance standards can provide a second level of protection for natural resources if they are applied consistently and if the cumulative impact of individual development projects is assessed. This strategy has been successfully used to prevent the destruction of Pinelands wetlands in both low growth and high growth areas.[10] Wetland protection efforts have been effective, in part, because the resource can be identified as discrete critical areas, and development can be prevented from encroaching on these areas. As previously noted, no acceptable method for determining critical area boundaries for Pinelands threatened and endangered species populations has yet been developed. Performance standards are generally used to protect specific sites such as known nesting area. This approach can be effective in areas zoned for low growth, where the planning process has ensured that large areas of open space will be preserved. However, the events that have occurred in the Crossley area suggest that only isolated habitats may be preserved when such a strategy is employed in high growth areas. Here, the value of performance standards is overshadowed by the much greater impact of regional zoning.

Habitat enhancement, such as the construction of hibernacula, and land trades are mitigation techniques that were employed in both the state Pinelands Area and the CAFRA portion of the Pinelands National Reserve. Follow-up surveys of the artificial hibernacula constructed as part of CAFRA permit conditions have shown that they are used extensively by both corn and northern pine snakes as overwintering and nesting sites (R.T. Zappalorti, per. com.). However, such enhancement measure have only been successfully employed on off-site areas. Attempts by CAFRA to establish on-site snake management areas as part of one development project were met with substantial opposition by the senior citizen community. Comments from this community led CAFRA to conclude that endangered species management was not compatible with residential development. This confrontation resulted in press coverage which reflected negatively on the state's endangered species protection efforts.

Both CAFRA and the Commission have required that wildlife preserves be established as permit conditions. A notable distinction between the two is that the Commission required a more substantial *on-site* commitment of land. Once again, the regional plan and the many issues, e.g. protection of agricultural lands, associated with it contributed to the Commission's ability to make this decision. All the mitigation techniques used, however, have one important similarity: they do not prevent the destruction of habitat. These measures merely provide a means of developing a workable compromise between regulators and developers.

The cumulative effects of individual policy and regulatory decisions deserve attention. One of CAFRA's project development decisions contributed to the issuance of a permit for a subsequent project. CAFRA concluded that the earlier project had affected the integrity of an adjacent, undeveloped parcel where a second development was proposed, and mitigation measures required in the earlier project were counted towards approval of the later one. The Pinelands Commission's recognition of the cumulative effect of approving the industrial park and the Davenport Cluster will at least require that this factor be considered in any subsequent development projects proposed in the area. Also, because of its prior planning decisions, it will be difficult for the Commission to reduce the size of the low growth zone without new evidence being presented that indicates such a change will not adversely affect the existing northern pine and corn snake populations. A record has been established which will be difficult to reverse.

The process employed in developing the protective strategies for the Crossley area is of special significance. The planning and regulatory decisions made by the Pinelands Commission and CAFRA were based on the available scientific and resource management information, but the final outcome, which reflected both the state's primary goal of protecting natural resources and secondary social and economic demands and pressures, was determined through legal avenues and countless public meetings.

SUMMARY

The events that have occurred in the 2830 ha Crossley study area highlight the issues associated with efforts to protect threatened and endangered species on private lands and the strategies that can be employed to resolve these issues. Here, protection goals conflicted with local and private development plans and, to some degree, with regional growth need. Several strategies were employed to protect critical habitat while attempting to accommodate other land uses and provide a reasonable beneficial use of private lands. The most effective strategy was a regional planning approach which addressed threatened and endangered species protection as a component of a comprehensive resource management program. In all the cases presented here the resolution of the development vs. protection conflict involved the consideration of scientific, legal, and political factors.

ACKNOWLEDGEMENTS

I wish to thank Alice D'Arcy, Terrence D. Moore, William Harrison, Michael Bolan, Robert Piel, and Robert T. Zappalorti for their helpful review comments. My appreciation is also extended to Sharon Griffin for typing the original manuscript and to Robert Kirwan for preparing the graphics.

REFERENCES CITED

1. Kauffeld, C. 1957. Snakes and Snake Hunting. Hanover House, Garden City, N.Y., 266 pp.
2. Zappalorti, R.T. 1982. Forgotten Town of Crossley, in New Jersey's Endangered and Threatened Plants and Animals, W.J. Cromartie (ed.). Stockton State College, Pomona, N.J., pp. 263-264.
3. McCormick, J. 1979. The Vegetation of the New Jersey Pine Barrens, in Pine Barrens—Ecosystem and Landscape, R.T.T. Forman (ed.). Academic Press, N.Y., N.Y., pp. 229-243.
4. Conant, R. 1979. A Zoogeographical Review of the Amphibians and Reptiles of Southern New Jersey, with Emphasis on the Pine Barrens, in Pine Barrens—Ecosystem and Landscape, R.T.T. Forman (ed.). Academic Press, N.Y., N.Y., pp. 467-488.
5. New Jersey Department of Environmental Protection and United States Department of Agriculture. 1980. Endangered and Threatened Species of New Jersey. Trenton, N.J., 44 pp.
6. New Jersey Pinelands Commission. 1980. Comprehensive Management Plan for the Pinelands National Reserve (National Parks and Recreation Act, 1978) and Pinelands Area (New Jersey Pinelands Protection Act, 1979). New Lisbon, N.J., 446 pp. and maps.

7. New Jersey Department of Environmental Protection. 1982. Coastal Resource and Development Policies. Trenton, N.J., 196 pp.
8. Ocean County Planning Board. 1982. Critical Habitat Requirements of Two Threatened Species in the Davenport Basin. Toms River, N.J., 95 pp. and appendices.
9. Hastings, R.W., E.W. Stiles, and T. Uzzel. 1982. A Critique of Reports by Herpetological Associates and the Ocean County Planning Board on Two Threatened Snake Species in Berkeley Township, Ocean County. Center for Coastal and Environmental Studies, Rutgers—The State University, New Brunswick, N.J., 17 pp.
10. Zampella, R.A. and C.T. Roman. 1983. Wetlands Protection in the New Jersey Pinelands. Wetlands. 3:124-133.

Endangered and Threatened Species Programs in Pennsylvania and other States: Causes, Issues and Management. Edited by S. K. Majumdar, F. J. Brenner and A. F. Rhoads. © 1986, The Pennsylvania Academy of Science.

Chapter Twenty-Two

NEW JERSEY'S ENDANGERED AND NONGAME SPECIES PROGRAM

Paul D. McLain[1] and Lawrence Niles[2]

[1]Deputy Director
[2]Principal Nongame Zoologist
N.J. Division of Fish, Game and Wildlife
P.O. Box 1809
Trenton, N.J. 08627

New Jersey is the third smallest state comprising about 19,500 km^2. It is also the most populated state with about 2,600 people/km^2. In spite of its small size and large urban and suburban population, the Garden State has a diversity of habitats from the Appalachian Mountain ridges, to the rolling hills of the Piedmont, to the Pinelands of the Coastal Plain, and the tidal marshes and saltwater estuaries along the coast of the Atlantic Ocean, the Delaware River and Bay. Within these habitats resides over 600 vertebrate species of which about 60 are listed as game animals for which there is a legal hunting season.

Since 1903, legislation has charged the Division of Fish, Game and Wildlife as the state agency responsible for ALL the wildlife in New Jersey. From the early game protector working on horseback, the Division has grown steadily to a staff of over 250 individuals and an annual budget of over 10 million funded by hunting and fishing licenses and related fees.

From the inception of the Division, these license fees have protected the wildlife populations and acquired over 4,000 ha of wildlife management areas. Until the early 1970's, the primary concern of the division was for "consumptive" or hunted wildlife. This was due primarily to the sportsmen providing the funding base, and the specific training of the professional biologists in wildlife management to produce more public hunting and fishing opportunities. However, while the major management programs were directed at game species, there was a spin-off to nongame. Conservation officers protect all wildlife; land acquisition and management programs directly affect many nongame species;

and environmental reviews and habitat protection programs benefit both game and nongame wildlife.

With the environmental movement of the 1970's, the division expanded its scope of responsibilities to place greater emphasis on environmental assessments and reviews, land-use planning etc.; the term "nongame" became more familiar.

At this point, Director Russell A. Cookingham saw a need to develop a nongame and endangered wildlife program within the Division of Fish, Game and Wildlife. In 1972, he asked Deputy Attorney General, Lewis Goldshore, to draft legislation establishing an Endangered and Nongame Species Program. The legislation was introduced in the fall of 1973 by State Senator Walter Foran, Hunterdon County, and Josephine Margetts, Assemblyperson from Morris County.

At that time, Federal Aid Coordinator, Paul D. McLain, was assigned the responsibility of promoting the program and selecting a staff. There were no trained nongame biologists and McLain was successful in hiring a young woman, the first woman to graduate in Wildlife Management from the West Virginia University and the first woman to be hired as a biologist with the division. Her specialty was exotic wildlife and zoo animals, but she had an active interest in falconry and nongame wildlife.

Working together in 1973, they made legislative contact, prepared news releases, talked to conservation groups and generated public interest in the need to do something about wildlife species which were decreasing in number, and also for many nongame wildlife species.

In December, 1973, both houses of the New Jersey Legislature passed Assembly Bill A-2151, "The Endangered and Nongame Species Conservation Act" with only one abstaining vote. This legislation called for an appropriation of $100,000 a year to conduct research, management and protection for endangered and nongame species and their habitats. The legislation also called for establishing a citizens' advisory committee to recommend nongame programs and management to the Director of the Division.

In 1974, the legislature appropriated $60,000. Paul D. McLain wrote the first "Cooperative Agreement" with the U.S. Fish and Wildlife Service to qualify New Jersey for Federal Aid to Endangered Species funding under the 1973 Endangered Species Act. Through this agreement, New Jersey purchased Higbee Beach using $700,000 in federal funds and $300,000 in state Green Acres funding. This was one of the few, and largest, state acquisitions under the federal Endangered Species Act.

Between 1974 and the advent of the Tax Check-Off for Wildlife funding base in 1981, the Division of Fish, Game and Wildlife received funding for nongame and endangered species from the state legislature ranging up to $60,000 but with no funding in 1977. Program personnel developed emergency funding programs such as selling window decals and T-shirts and sought public donations. In 1977, the State Federation of Sportsmen's Clubs voted to fund the Endangered and

Nongame Species Program for one year with $25,000 of sportsmen's license money when the legislature failed to appropriate any money to operate or pay salaries.

Thanks to the Federal Aid to Endangered Species Act of 1973, the small amount of state money, usually less than $50,000 a year, resulted in New Jersey receiving about $45,000 a year of federal aid which was spent for research and management of only federal endangered species in New Jersey. This federal aid allowed the program a small budget to manage the nongame resource. The entire program never exceeded $100,000 a year prior to the 1981 Tax Check-Off for Wildlife Program.

The Endangered and Nongame Species Program between 1974 and 1984 was composed of a staff of three biologists and a program supervisor. The project developed a broad-based endangered and nongame species program, and also a captive nongame and exotic regulations section which was administered as part of the program.

New Jersey was one of the first 5 states to pass Tax Check-Off for Wildlife legislation modeled after Colorado. Opposition was encountered from the State Treasurer, and there was no administrative support at the Department level. Through public interest and the efforts of dedicated conservationists, Governor Brendan Byrne signed the New Jersey Check-Off for Wildlife Program into law in June, 1981.

The first year, 1981, about 80,000 citizens checked off $350,000 for endangered and nongame wildlife in New Jersey. By 1984, over 110,000 citizens donated about half million dollars from their state income tax refunds.

During this period, federal aid to endangered species funding was greatly reduced and tax check-off funding supported most of the program. Increased permit fees provided funds to support the exotic wildlife program.

Between 1981 and 1985, the program was expanded under an energetic Program Manager, JoAnn Frier-Murza, who came with the program in 1975, which included three regional biologists, an exotic wildlife biologist, a biologist at the Higbee Beach Management Area, a supervisor of research, and two full-time secretaries. Contractual research was done on every endangered species and a number of priority nongame species. At the present time, the staff of the Endangered and Nongame Species Program consists of a bureau chief, 2 principal biologists, four senior biologists, a wildlife technician, two full-time secretaries, and six seasonal biologists.

The legislative mandate to maintain and enhance all species must be interpreted in action through the program's research and management projects. This work is supervised by Larry Niles who joined the program in 1982. Projects are carried out by all program staff depending on their expertise and time constraints. Many projects are contracted out to individuals or organizations in New Jersey.

Our method for the restoration or protection of species in New Jersey starts

TABLE 1

Status and Prospect of Survival for Endangered and Threatened Species in New Jersey

Species	Status	Number	Trend	Problem	Solution	Feasibility of Survival
Shortnose Sturgeon	e	u	u	k	k	f
Atlantic Sturgeon	t	u	u	u	u	f
American Shad	t	l	e	k	k	f
Brook Trout	t	l	s	k	k	f
Atlantic Tomcod	t	u	u	u	u	u
Blue Spotted Salamander	e	c	d	k	i	p
Tremblays Salamander	e	c	d	k	i	p
E. Tiger Salamander	e	l	s	k	i	f
Longtailed Salamander	t	u	u	k	u	f
Pine Barrens Treefrog	e	l	s	i	i	g
Southern Grey Treefrog	t	l	u	u	u	f
Bog Turtle	e	l	d	k	i	f
Wood Turtle	t	l	u	u	u	f
Corn Snake	t	l	s	k	i	f
Northern Pine Snake	t	l	s	k	k	f
Timber Rattle Snake	e	c	u	i	i	p
Pied-billed Grebe	t	c	s	u	u	p
Great Blue Heron	t	l	e	k	k	g
Coopers Hawk	e	u	u	u	u	p
Red Shouldered Hawk	t	u	u	u	k	p
Bald Eagle	e	c	s	k	i	f
Northern Harrier	e	l	e	k	k	g
Osprey	t	l	e	k	k	g
Peregrine Falcon	e	c	e	k	k	g
Upland Sandpiper	e	c	d	k	i	p
Roseate Tern	t	c	u	u	u	p
Least Tern	e	c	d	i	i	p
Black Skimmer	e	c	d	i	i	p
Barrel Owl	t	u	u	k	u	f
Red-headed Woodpecker	t	u	u	u	u	f
Cliff Swallow	e	l	s	i	i	g
Sedge Wren	e	c	u	u	u	p
Bobolink	t	l	s	k	i	g
Savannah Sparrow	t	l	i	k	i	p
Henslows Sparrow	e	c	i	u	i	p
Vesper Sparrow	e	c	i	u	i	p
Grasshopper Sparrow	t	l	i	u	i	f

Status   e = endangered   t = threatened
Number   u = unknown   c = critical   l = low
Trend   u = unknown   i = under investigation   d = declining   s = stable   e = increasing
Problem   u = unknown   k = known   i = under investigation
Solution   u = unknown   k = known   i = under investigation
Feasibility of survival (in NJ)   p = poor   f = fair   g = good

with the endangered and threatened species list. A species is listed upon recommendation of staff biologists of the ENSP after review by the Citizen Nongame Species Advisory Committee, the Department of Environmental Protection and the general public through a state register. Listing a species is in itself a management action since it can then be considered for research, management, and environmental impact review.

Usually listing is only a first step (Table 1). The next step is to determine the size of the population, distribution throughout the state, and population trends. All three aspects are crucial for an accurate understanding of it present and future status listed species. This is particularly true in New Jersey where wild habitats are rapidly changing to human habitats. Priorities differ with species: for the wood rat (*Neotoma floridana*), pine barrens treefrog (*Hyla andersoni*), and the bog turtle (*Clemmys insculpta*), distribution is priority; for colonial waterbirds, cliff swallows (*Petrochelidon pyrrhonota*), and the beachnester species, trend is the priority; and for the peregrine (*Falco peregrinus*), and bald eagle (*Haliaeetus leucocephalus*), the size of the population is the priority (Table 2).

The decline in numbers of distribution of a species may be attributed to habitat loss, as in the piping plover sides, or competition with another species, as in the loss of nest by cliff swallows to house sparrows. Most often the cause of a species decline is a complex of problems, as is the case with the upland sandpiper. The most obvious cause is the loss of habitat, but, because of a home range requirement of over 260 ha, saving small groups would require purchasing large areas of the most expensive land in the state. Last, but not least, are the problems of all grassland species, such as early mowing when the birds are on eggs or the young have recently hatched.

Once the problem is recognized the job is to implement a management strategy to reverse or stabilize the decline. In the Bald Eagle the problem was pesticide accumulation. The species is now being reintroduced into their formerly occupied range. In the case of beachnester species, they must be protected from human disturbance by fencing and patrols.

But the solutions to some problems are difficult to understand, and the possibility exists that there may not be a solution with a reasonable chance of implementation. For example, until recently there has been little change in land use around the 22 historic Bald Eagle nest sites, but if the Bald Eagle hacking and nest management project is successful there will be approximately 10 nests in the historic nesting area. However, as the land changes rapidly, there will be a problem in maintaining land as eagle habitat without eagles actually using it.

One objective of New Jersey is to restore the Bald Eagle. We hope to precisely determine the habitat needs based on other Bald Eagle populations and the historic New Jersey population, as well as coordinating public land and private wildland management to avoid conflicts. The plan will also identify land that is important to eagles and at the same time vulnerable to development. This will focus upon land acquisition priorities for the state and private groups in-

TABLE 2

1985 Research and Management Projects of the Endangered and Nongame Species Program

Project	No. of Projects	Distribution	Trend	Habitat Problem	Population Problem	Habitat Management	Population Management
Grassland birds	1	x	x				
Upland sandpiper	1	x	x	x			
Colonial waterbird	1	x	x	x	x		
Least Tern/ Black Skimmer	4	x	x	x	x	x	x
Piping Plover	2	x	x	x	x	x	x
Bald Eagle	4	x	x	x	x	x	x
Peregrine Falcon	1	x	x			x	x
Osprey	2	x	x	x	x	x	x
Woodland raptors	1	x	x				
Migratory raptor songbirds	2			x	x		
Cliff Swallow	1	x	x	x			
Shorebirds	1	x	x		x		
Blue Spotted Salamander	1	x	x	x	x		
Tiger Salamander	1					x	x
Timber Rattlesnake	1			x			
Corn Snake	1						x
Bog Turtle	1						x
Woodrat	1	x	x		x		
Small mammal	1	x					
Area mapping	1					x	
Higbee Beach	1					x	
Bear Swamp	1					x	
TOTALS	31	14	13	10	9	9	8

terested in restoring the eagle to its former range in New Jersey. Activist groups can then be aware of land important not only to their community but also to the Bald Eagle.

New Jersey has a rapidly changing environment. This particularly impacts endangered species since they most often occur in undeveloped land. There are tremendous pressures to utilize what remains of this land. New Jersey is the most densely populated state in the nation, and, although the growth rate is barely positive, there is massive movement from urban environments to newly created rural developments. It is conceivable and actually the wish of many developers to turn New Jersey into a completely urban and suburban environment. A serious case should be made, therefore, that most of New Jersey species are in some way threatened.

As a result, New Jersey stands out among other states because of the very real possibility of species extinction within the state. In New Jersey the study and management of threatened and endangered species is not just a matter collecting data for the future or managing wildlife for the sake of managing wildlife. For many species currents rates of decline of both land and numbers will end in the loss of populations within the foreseeable future.

Our problems are immediate, and developing a long term strategy for the maintenance of species is made difficult by continually changing circumstances. An example comes from our surveys on the 18 colonial waterbird species nesting on New Jersey's Atlantic Coastline completed in 1977, 1978, 1979, 1983, and 1985. The 1983 data revealed declines in many species, although not statistically significant. But a repeat survey in 1985 revealed continued declines in many species and significant declines in a few of the heron species. Although the data is still being analyzed, the situation may deserve priority status that was not anticipated a few years ago.

Other more technical problems obstruct our understanding of the problems causing declines in New Jersey wildlife because nongame wildlife management is a relatively recent science, therefore, techniques for fieldwork and analysis must often be improvised. In many cases, new techniques or little used techniques must be tested extensively before use and then used only with caution. For example, determining trend and distribution of tree nesting bats practically demands an entirely new technique involving the perception and identification of high frequency species specific calls. The technology exists but has not been applied in a standardized population indexing scheme. Much work remains and in the meantime there is virtually no information available to decide whether summer bat species in New Jersey are safe or seriously endangered.

Obviously the successful management of endangered and threatened species in New Jersey depends on availability and good data on number, trend, and distribution of the different species. It will depend on a correct assessment of the problems causing species declines and the development of feasible alternatives to reverse these declines. But many species are in trouble in New Jersey and the answer will have to be more than putting in nesting structures or reintroducing new breeders.

The problems are extensive and the solutions must include coordinated actions by all conservationists working as a unit on specific programs. The strategy to restore or protect a species must include a meaningful analysis of all the different tasks necessary to understand its plight and/or appropriate action to restore it. The strategy must include a determination of which tasks are best suited to the state and which to private organizations.

The evolving strategy of New Jersey nongame research and management programs is to better integrate the work of those many individuals and groups doing research on New Jersey wildlife. The entire task is beyond the time and funding constraints of biologists within the Nongame Program. The Program must envision itself as playing a role within a team in protecting the states nongame wildlife and wildlands.

Endangered and Threatened Species Programs in Pennsylvania and other States: Causes, Issues and Management. Edited by S. K. Majumdar, F. J. Brenner and A. F. Rhoads. © 1986, The Pennsylvania Academy of Science.

Chapter Twenty-Three

PENNSYLVANIA'S BALD EAGLE RECOVERY PROJECT

Robert C. Mitchell[1] and John A. Byerly[2]

[1]Assistant Editor, Pennsylvania GAME NEWS
Bureau of Information and Education
and
[2]Chief, Division of Federal Aid and Public Access
Bureau of Land Management
Pennsylvania Game Commission, P.O. Box 1567, Harrisburg, PA 17105-1567

The future of the bald eagle (*Haliaeetus leucocephalus*) in Pennsylvania appears more secure with the successful beginning of a seven-year project designed to re-establish our endangered national emblem throughout the state.

In each of the past two summers, twelve nestling bald eagles were taken from nests along the Churchill River in Saskatchewan and placed on artificial nests in central and eastern Pennsylvania, and cared for until able to fly and fend for themselves.

This marks the initial step in "Pennsylvania's Bald Eagle Recovery Project," a long-range program designed to establish breeding populations of bald eagles in the Susquehanna and Delaware river watersheds. The Pennsylvania Game Commission adopted the hacking technique which was proven by New York Department of Conservation biologists to be a viable method for reestablishing bald eagles.

Falconers originally developed the method as a means to obtain birds for their sport. Young were fed in their natural nests, or on artificial towers until fully developed, at which point falconers would retrap and train them for hunting.

In recent years this technique has been modified and successfully employed by conservation organizations to reintroduce other endangered and threatened birds of prey, such as peregrine falcons, ospreys and golden eagles.

Paper presented at Endangered Species Symposium
November 2, 1984, Grantville, PA

The technique essentially involves obtaining young birds from either captive breeding stock or natural populations where the particular species is abundant, and raising them on artificial nests until they're able to fly, at which point they are released.

It has been demonstrated that when hacked birds reach breeding age, they return to nest at the hack site rather than their original hatching site.

New York biologists began experimenting with bald eagle hacking in 1976, and in five years hacked a total of 22 eagles. The procedure looked promising when birds were observed returning to hack site areas in subsequent years. In 1981, two birds hacked five years earlier were found breeding in northern New York, 84 miles from the hack site.

They successfully raised one eaglet. Further support of the technique occurred after the male of the only native breeding pair in New York was killed, and the female mated with a previously hacked male. A third female eagle, taken as a nestling in northern Minnesota and hacked in New York in 1979, was discovered nesting in Pennsylvania at the Pymatuning Wildlife Management Area in 1984, 225 miles from the tower where it had been released.

With eagles returning and breeding successfully, New York proceeded with a second five-year project, during which a projected 125 Alaskan bald eagles—22 to 25 per year—are to be raised and released. This level of hacking should result in 40 to 50 nesting pairs of bald eagles in the state. In view of successes in New

FIGURE 1. Young eaglets are taken from their natural nests along the Churchill River in Saskatchewan and brought to Pennsylvania where, it is hoped, they will ultimately return as nesting adults.

FIGURE 2. The young birds are helpless when they arrive at hacking towers in Pennsylvania.

York, similar bald eagle hacking programs have been initiated in several other states.

In order to improve the status of the endangered bald eagle in Pennsylvania, the Pennsylvania Game Commission decided to use the hacking technique to establish nesting bald eagles around the state. To complement the four nesting pairs of native bald eagles in the northwestern part of Pennsylvania, it was decided to concentrate hacking efforts in the Susquehanna and Delaware river watersheds, which should establish nesting bald eagles across the state.

Initial planning for the project began in 1982, a year before the birds were received. Original plans called for the Game Commission to receive eight eaglets from the Province of Manitoba, Canada in a cooperative agreement with the U.S. Fish and Wildlife Service, New Jersey and Massachusetts. Federal officials were coordinating arrangements with Canada, and the three states were to coordinate their activities and share preliminary survey, capture and transportation expenses to make the project cost effective.

Sites were selected and towers erected in Susquehanna and Delaware River watersheds where a readily available food supply exists, human access is easily controlled, and where eagles have reasonably good chances of surviving the critical first few weeks after release from the towers.

It was determined during the initial nesting survey in 1983 that because of low eagle production in Manitoba, only two eaglets would be available for the

FIGURE 3. For two months the young birds are atop 30-foot hacking towers where they are fed and protected.

FIGURE 4. On their release, the birds quickly begin to develop their flying skill.

hacking program in Pennsylvania. The actual projected cost per fledged bird therefore would be extremely costly since expenses, such as building towers, transporting birds and maintaining surveillance over the developing birds, are not proportional to the number of birds hacked.

Fortunately, arrangements for eaglets were subsequently made with the Wildlife Branch of the Saskatchewan Department of Parks and Natural Resources. Since this Province has an estimated 1500 pairs of breeding bald eagles, between eight and twelve eaglets could be provided for the Pennsylvania recovery project in each of the next several years.

This arrangement however, required that the Game Commission finance an eagle survey along the Churchill River near La Range, Saskatchewan. The nesting eagle population had been surveyed along the river a few years earlier, and the biologist who coordinated the original study was engaged by the Game Commission to do an aerial survey of the area and locate nest in areas where eaglets could be obtained.

Plans were then made for Game Commission personnel to go to Saskatchewan when young eagles would be between five and seven weeks of age and still easy to handle but old enough to survive without parental care.

Two recovery teams, each consisting of a pilot, climber, rope attendant, and support attendant were used to remove eaglets from the nests. The agreement with Saskatchewan stipulated one eaglet had to be left in each nest, therefore

FIGURE 5. After release the birds are completely free. It is hoped enough of these transplanted eagles will survive to age five when they can be expected to return to Pennsylvania and establish nesting territories here.

all nests containing only one eaglet were not disturbed. If a nest contained two eaglets, only one was removed and if the nest contained three eaglets, two were removed.

Once a nest was located and number of eaglets determined, the plane landed on the river, taxied to shore, and the climbing crew disembarked. Nests were often located 10-24m (35-80 ft) in spruce (Picea spp) or poplar trees (Populus spp).

One nest containing two eaglets was found in a dead tree which could not be safely climbed. In this instance, Climber Dennis Jones, Land Management Supervisor in the Southwest Region, climbed an adjacent white spruce, threw a rope over the nest and down to the ground. The support attendant then pulled Dennis over to the nest tree and the eaglet was captured.

After the climber reached the nest, the eaglet was placed in a cloth sack and lowered to the ground, placed in a carrying crate and, in order to minimize stress, flown back to a central holding area for feeding and banding.

While eaglets were being captured, parent birds usually flew to nearby perches, waited until the capture crew left, and then returned to their nests. In only one instance did an eagle demonstrate any form of aggression; a female flew in circles over the nest while an eaglet was being removed.

A total of 10 eaglets were captured on the first day and two the second morning. The following day the eaglets were flown from Saskatchewan, went through customs and veterinarian checks in Winnipeg, Manitoba and again in St. Paul, Minnesota.

In just under 85 hours, Game Commission personnel travelled over 4000 miles and moved 12 eaglets from their natural nests in northcentral Saskatchewan to hacking towers in Pennsylvania.

A great deal of credit must be given to the representatives of the Saskatchewan government who were extremely cooperative. If it were not for the time and effort extended by Saskatchewan officials, this entire project would not have been possible.

Six eaglets were placed on a hack tower located near Shohola Falls, in Pike County; the remaining six were placed on a tower on Haldeman Island in the Susquehanna River. The towers are approximately 9m (30 ft) in height and contain two compartments separated by a narrow observation corridor. Each compartment contained a natural-looking stick nest and larger sticks for perching. Three eaglets approximately the same size and age were put in each compartment.

Once on the tower the eaglets were under constant surveillance. Three hack site attendants were assigned to each location, with the responsibilities of feeding and watching them through to the fledging stage. Birds were provided with all the food they could eat, consisting of carp (*Cyprinus carpio*), suckers (*Catostomus*) and meat from roadkilled deer (*Odocoileus virginianus*). In 1983, immediately prior to release, each bird was tagged with a green wing marker sporting a red keystone, so it could be identified as a Pennsylvania-hacked bird.

The wing markers proved to be extremely difficult to see, and they didn't permit identification of individual birds. Eight eaglets were equipped with radio transmitters to monitor their movements once they left the tower. Each of the 1984 eagles, however, was tagged with a yellow leg band with prominent black letters, and all 12 birds were equipped with transmitters.

When eagles were ready to fledge they began stretching and exercising their wings, thus, birds were released according to feather development and behavior.

On the day eaglets were to be released, the barred gates on the front of each cage were opened before sun rise, in order not to unnecessarily disturb the birds. Because they were older, the six eagles at the Shohola site were released a week ahead of the Susquehanna River birds.

Behavior of the two groups upon release was surprisingly different between the two sites. The Shohola birds left the tower immediately and by 11:15 a.m. all six birds had made flights from the tower and one bird left for good.

Birds at Haldeman Island on the Susquehanna River did not leave the tower as quickly. As daylight arrived, five birds left their cages and perched around the platform moving from perch to perch, stretching and exercising their wings. The sixth bird, however, flew from the cage, similar to the eagles at the Delaware site, and flew around the tower. After one swing it attempted to land in a nearby perch, but landed in a pond. A team immediately tried to retrieve the bird, but upon approach, the bird paddled to shore using its wings, where it took refuge in tall grass. The eagle was left in the weeds for several hours before it was retrieved and placed back on the tower. Throughout the day, all six eagles spent most of the day jumping from perch to perch on the tower. Occasionally, a bird would make a short circular flight, alighting either on the tower or the ground.

On this and subsequent days, the birds gradually made longer and more frequent flights, apparently developing their flying skills.

Shootings, electrocutions, poisonings, disease, automobiles and other accidents take an especially heavy toll on birds less than one year of age. Past research on wild eagle populations indicate that only 50 percent live to be a year old. But, more optimistically, only 7 of the 44 eagles (16 percent) hacked by all states between the years 1976-81 are known to have died.

Mortality rates for birds over a year old are lower, but the birds do not reach adulthood until they are 4 to 5 years of age when they attain their distinctive white heads and tails, and begin nesting. Despite these low odds, only two of the twelve birds released in 1983 are known to have died. One was electrocuted on a powerline transformer soon after release from the Shohola Falls site. Another, from the Haldeman Island site, was found in downtown Harrisburg nearly three months after release. The bird died within 24 hours after it was found. It appeared undernourished, but the specific cause of death was not determined. As of this writing all 12 of the 1984 birds are thought to be alive.

Pennsylvania's Bald Eagle Recovery Project will continue over the next several years. Tentative plans are calling for hacking and releasing approximately 40 birds into each of the two major watersheds. Depending on the rate at which eaglets are obtained from Saskatchewan, this project should last six or seven years. At that time, some of the eagles will have reached breeding age, and the entire project can be evaluated.

New York biologists are also studying the effects of eagle removal on the donor nests in Alaska. Preliminary results of these studies indicate the removal of a nestling does not adversely effect the survival of the remaining sibling(s), and in the following year, pairs which had a nestling removed actually increased production in some sort of compensatory response.

First year expenses exceeded original expectations for a number of reasons, primarily because of the shift from Manitoba to Saskatchewan as source for eaglets, and the associated loss of cost sharing opportunities with the other states. The Working Together for Wildlife funds and federal endangered species allocations were used to finance the 1983 effort. Expenses over the next few years will be substantially lower, because many costs, such as the construction of the hacking towers, will not be repeated. In addition, in 1984, the Game Commission received a three-year grant totalling $108,000 from the Richard King Mellon Foundation.

The endangered bald eagle, our national emblem, was sent to the brink of extinction when water pollution made many areas uninhabitable and DDT caused a thinning of egg shells thereby reducing reproduction. The use of DDT has since been banned in this country and water pollution is under control, making many areas again suitable eagle habitat.

The Game Commission has embarked on an ambitious effort to re-establish nesting bald eagles throughout the Commonwealth so that our national emblem can once again be observed across the state.

Endangered and Threatened Species Programs in Pennsylvania and other States: Causes, Issues and Management. Edited by S. K. Majumdar, F. J. Brenner and A. F. Rhoads. © 1986, The Pennsylvania Academy of Science.

Chapter Twenty-Four

THE PRZEWALSKI HORSE (*EQUUS PRZEWALSKII*) ECOSYSTEM: PROGRAMS AND PROGRESS

Ronald R. Keiper
Department of Biology
Pennsylvania State University
Mont Alto, Pa. 17237

When the Polish-born Russian explorer Colonel Nikolai Przewalski returned from a journey through central Asia in 1878, he brought with him a skull and hide of a wild horse shot by hunters in the Mongolian district of Kobdo. These materials were examined by the Russian zoologist Poliakov in 1881, who concluded they did not come from a domestic horse (*Equus caballus*) but instead from another horse species which he named *Equus przewalskii* — the Przewalski, Mongolian, or Asiatic wild horse (IUCN, 1981).

There are some striking differences between the Przewalski and the domestic horse. Przewalski horses have an upright or standing mane and no forelock, while all breeds of the domestic horse have both a falling mane and a forelock. The tail of the Przewalski horse is also different, resembling that of a donkey. In domestic horses, the tail hairs start directly from the underside of the back. In Przewalski horses, a short piece of short-haired tail grows before the real tail hairs begin. Przewalski horses have a dark dorsal stripe on the back, like the wild asses, and dark, zebra-like stripes on the lower legs (Bouman, 1978).

Chromosomal studies reveal another difference: domestic horses have a diploid chromosome number of 64, whereas Przewalski horses have 66 chromosomes. Crosses of Przewalski and domestic horses produce fertile hybrids having body cells with a diploid chromosome complement of 65 (Waring, 1983).

In prehistoric times, Przewalski horses apparently had a range extending throughout Europe and much of Asia. Ancient cave paintings, like those at Lascaux, depict dun-colored horses with bulky heads, an upright mane, and other morphological features characteristic of *E. przewalskii* (Mohr, 1959).

By the end of the glacial period, Przewalski horses apparently lived over a broad area east of the Volga River, while other varieties with somewhat different external features scattered over the forests and steppes of Europe. The steppe tarpan lived on the grasslands of southwest Russia, and domestication of these animals, which led to the formation of the modern domestic horse, apparently began here in the third millennium B. C. (Waring, 1983). All wild populations of the steppe tarpan were either absorbed into domestic stock or exterminated by 1850.

All wild populations of the forest horse, living in western Europe, and the forest tarpan, which roamed the woods of central and eastern Europe, became extinct in the Middle Ages, although some scientists believe the cold-blooded breeds of the domestic horse, such as the Belgian draught breed, are descendants of the former horse type (Bouman, 1980).

Extirpation of the tarpans and the forest horse left Przewalskii horse as the only remaining truly wild, never domesticated, horse. In historic times, the size of populations of *E. przewalskii* and its range were greatly reduced by human predation for meat and skins and for elimination of their depredation on agricultural crops and covetry of domestic mares, by competition with domestic livestock, and by incorporation into domestic horse herds (Waring, 1983). By the 1900's, the species was represented by only a few scattered bands in inaccessible, barren locations along the border between Mongolia and northwest China. The last confirmed sighting was made in 1969, although recent unconfirmed sightings have been reported from the Chinese province of Xinjiang. Even if true, the wild population of *Equus przewalskii* probably numbers less than fifty animals, and these horses continue to be threatened by human encroachment. The best hope for preserving this species lies not in the few surviving wild horses but rather in the captive population of over five hundred Przewalski horses scattered over eighty zoos and private collections in Europe, the Soviet Union, and North America (Table 1). This chapter focuses on the contributions made by zoos and preserves in Pennsylvania and in the neighboring states of New York, Ohio, and Virginia and the District of Columbia toward preservation of these horses.

Captive breeding

The first living Przewalski horses brought out of the wild were captured in 1899-1901, not because they were endangered but because they were novel. A pair arrived at the Bronx Zoo (in New York City) in late 1902, but the zoo director, not satisfied with the mare, who had a forelock and a falling mane rather than an upright one, immediately ordered another pair. The original pair (called Bysk 7 and Bysk 8 after the Russian town where the captured animals were loaded onto Trans-Siberian railroad cars) were sent to the Cincinnati Zoo, where they produced their only foal, a colt (Cincinnati 1) in 1912 (Bouman, 1980).

TABLE 1.

The distribution of captive Przewalski horses as of January 1, 1984. The first figure denotes the number of stallions, the second the number of mares (Bouman, 1984).

Place	Number	Place	Number	Place	Number
Adelaide	1.1	Keokuk	1.0	Rostov/Don	2.1
Antwerp	3.4	Kiev	3.2	Rotterdam	1.1
Armorique	1.0	Kingussie	7.0	Sababurg	1.6
Arnhem	9.4	Kisinev	1.1	Salzburg	1.1
Askania Nova	20.26	Cologne	2.6	San Diego	1.2
Barcelona	2.0	Kurgan	1.1	San Pasqual	6.13
Port Lympne	12.21	Leipzig	3.10	Springe	3.5
Berlin-East	3.8	Lelystad	1.3	Stendal	1.0
Berlin-West	1.4	Leningrad	2.4	Stuttgart	1.2
Bern	5.3	Lodz	1.0	Tallinn	1.1
Bernburg	1.1	London	1.2	Taskent	1.0
Budapest	1.0	Los Angeles	1.2	Thot á Thonac	1.0
Cardigan	1.0	Marwell	6.15	Tokyo	2.2
Catskill	6.10	Memphis	1.3	Topeka	5.3
Cavriglia	1.0	Midway Manor	1.5	Warsaw	3.6
Chester	1.3	Minnesota	11.10	Whipsnade	3.7
Colombo	1.1	Montpellier	1.2	Vienna	4.2
Colwyn Bay	1.1	Moscow	6.7	Woburn	5.0
Denver	2.3	Munich	8.13	Lymington	2.0
Dubbo	4.9	Neumünster	1.0	Münster	1.1
Duisburg	2.1	Neuwied	1.0	Jersey	3.0
Edmonton	2.2	New York	4.11	Kraków	1.2
Fr£os£o	0.1	Nikolaev	2.3	Noorderheide	1.3
Gdansk-Oliva	1.0	Nürnberg	3.10	Schwerin	1.1
Genk	4.2	Oberwil	2.4	Front Royal (NZC)	1.2
Havana	2.3	de Ooij	5.0	Cèvennes	4.0
Halle/S	1.2	Paignton	1.0	Herberstein	1.2
Helsinki	1.2	Paris	2.2	Hohenstadt	1.0
Hilvarenbeek	2.5	Peking	1.1	Gramat	1.1
Karaganda	1.1	Pforzheim	1.1	Termez	1.0
Karl-Marx-Stadt	1.0	Praha	4.8		
Karlsruhe	2.1	Riga	2.1		
					242.310

The replacement couple reached New York in 1905 and produced six foals. The stallion also bred two of his daughters, producing seven other offspring. In 1916-17 the Bronx Zoo sold a stallion and two mares to the Sydney (Australia) Zoo. Although this population only produced five foals, two of these contributed vitally to the present Przewalski population. The mare (Sydney 3, Mira) was sold to Hellabrunn Zoo in Munich, where she became part of that important breeding population. A stallion (Sydney 4) went to Paris, where he sired a son that became part of the Praha line (see below).

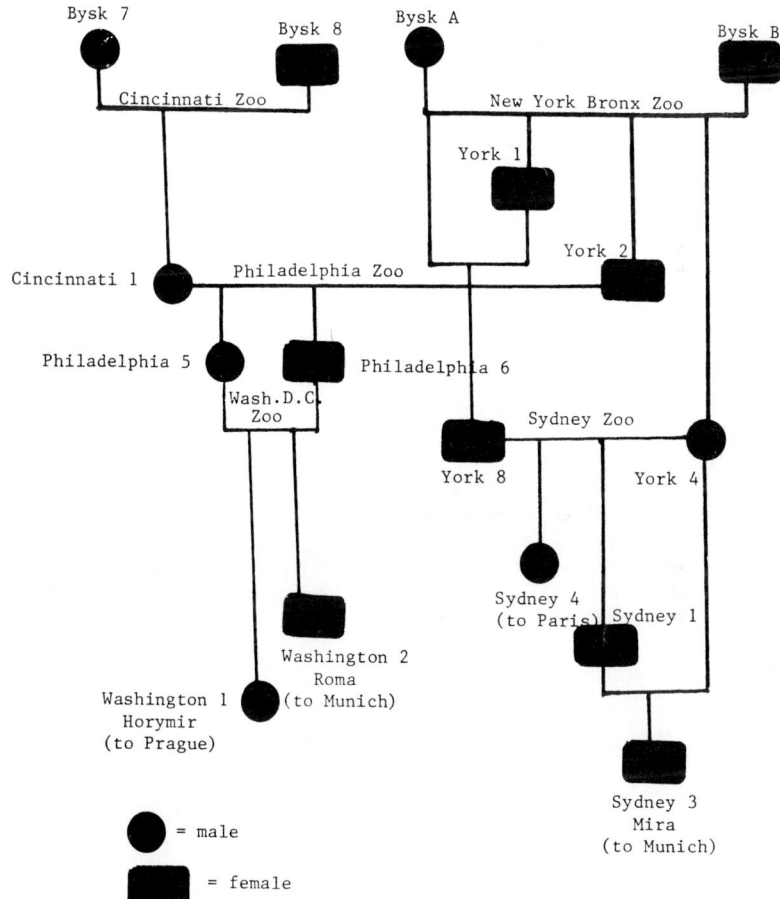

FIGURE 1. Structure of the U. S. line (after Bouman, 1980).

The lone offspring from Cincinnati was sent in 1913 to the Philadelphia Zoo, where, with a mare from New York, it produced six foals. The herd, however, died out in 1956.

The Washington, D.C. Zoo bought a brother and sister pair from Philadelphia in 1927-28, and this couple produced four foals before the line ended. One offspring, the stallion Horymir (Wash. 1), was sent to Prague where he became the father founder of the Praha line from which most of the European animals and about two-thirds of the current world population of Przewalski horses derive. Another Washington offspring, the mare Roma (Wash. 2), traveled first to Rome than to Munich where she became one of the founders of the Munich line, which produced virtually all the present U.S. Przewalski horses and the other third of the world population (Bouman, 1980). A summary of the structure of the U.S.A. line is presented in Figure 1.

Although more than fifty young wild horses were delivered into captivity from Mongolia at the start of the Twentieth Century, most failed to breed or died at a young age. Similarly, so many animals perished during World War II that in 1945 the captive stock of *Equus przewalskii* had been reduced to only three stallions and seven mares (Bouman, 1977). The population greatly increased in the next thirty years as the result of successful but isolated breeding of the Praha and Munich lines. Horymir and sons Uran and Oscar (in Prague) produced almost seventy foals, most of which were sold as breeding parts to zoos throughout Europe. In Munich the founder stallion Neville and his sons Severin, Sidor, and Simon were equally productive. Severin sired seven foals in Munich before he was sold to the Catskill Game Farm in New York state in 1956. There he fathered another thirty offspring before being succeeded by Bertold, another Munich stallion. Altogether, five stallions and eight mares moved from Munich to Catskill in the period 1956-63, and their offspring can be found today in Boston, Chicago, Denver, Los Angeles, Memphis, New York, San Diego, and Topeka, as well as in Edmonton, Canada.

The captive breeding program accomplished a goal important to the successful preservation of any endangered species; it dramatically increased the size of the captive population and allowed horses to spread over a number of widely dispersed sites. These changes made the species less vulnerable to disease or accident.

Controlling inbreeding

While captive breeding has allowed *Equus przewalskii* to continue as a species in spite of the decline and probable extinction of the wild population, there is cause for concern for its future. All Przewalski horses in captivity trace their ancestry to eleven animals captured in the wild at the turn of the century plus a single mare brought out of Mongolia in 1947 (Mohr, 1959). Such a small founder population probably means a small initial gene pool.

In contrast, two lines of evidence suggest a considerable genetic variation in the wild population of *E. przewalskii* which provided the founder animals. Photographs of early captives show clear differences in the external shape of the head, eye color, tail structure, and coloration of the coat (IUCN, 1981). More recent biochemical evidence from studies of blood groups and electrophoresis of proteins and plasma enzymes demonstrates marked variability (Putt and Fisher, 1979; Ryder et al, 1979).

Many management practices applied to the captive animals, such as the isolation of small breeding groups and the overemployment of certain stallions, further reduced the limited captive genetic variability. The isolation of the Munich and Praha lines came after a domestic horse mare was bred in 1906 to a Przewalski stallion and produced a male hybrid. This male then bred a Przewalski mare, whose offspring joined the Praha line (Mohr, 1959). Munich-line owners, reluctant to introduce the domestic horse background into their herds, kept them isolated.

Initial isolation of the two lines created few problems. The founder stallions (Horymir in Prague and Neville in Munich) were unrelated to their mares and showed an .000 inbreeding coefficient, but their sons increasingly bred their sisters, half-sisters, daughters, and even their mothers, leading to inbreeding coefficients as high as .410 (Bouman, 1980).

Because the captive breeding program had successfully increased the number of Przewalski horses, many people ignored the increasing inbreeding. However, in 1976, at the Third International Symposium on the Preservation of the Przewalski Horse in Munich and the Second World Conference on Breeding Endangered Species in Captivity in London, Bouman (1977) presented evidence that increased inbreeding accounted for decreased fertility, greater juvenile mortality, and shorter life spans. He also documented congenital defects characteristic of the present captive Przewalski population, including stunted growth and a hip weakness which reduced the chances of a successful mating.

One of the most foresighted actions for controlling inbreeding and most noteworthy achievements of the captive breeding period was the initial compilation and continued record-keeping of an international studbook (IUCN, 1981). Begun by Dr. Erna Mohr, the studbook has been published since 1960 by Dr. Jiri Volf of the Prague Zoo. The studbook records for each captive Przewalski horse its studbook number, name, sex, house or common name, date of birth, studbook and common names of its father and mother, and site of birth. Each year an annual addendum details the movement of horses during that year, foals born and the older horses dead, and places all living Przewalski horses by location.

While the Przewalski studbook is clearly valuable, some scientists felt that additional information was needed to combat inbreeding. Future breeding required knowledge of their blood line and inbreeding coefficient. Data on abortions and stillborn or premature foals, as well as data on live foals, needed recording. Breeders needed the data quickly, but Dr. Volf needed more than a year to prepare the studbook for publication. Information on new foals was not available. As most foals are bought and sold before their second year, studbook information often arrived too late to help breeders dispose of or acquire new stock with the lowest inbreeding coefficients and the maximum breeding potential.

The Foundation for the Preservation and Protection of the Przewalski Horse, founded on March 21, 1977, cooperated with Dr. Volf by publishing biannually a bulletin for keepers of Przewalski horses immediately announcing the latest births and providing blood line and inbreeding coefficient information on new foals. The Foundation also organized a conference on "Genetics and Hereditary Diseases of the Przewalski Horse" and subsequently provided all breeders with a copy of the conference proceedings. Finally, the Foundation developed a more extensive record system with data on individual horses, on details of identification, ancestry, and breeding, on collections maintaining Przewalski horses, their husbandry and breeding management, on herd composition at each location and such characteristics of the breeding lines as fertility, inbreeding coefficients, and blood composition (Bouman, 1977). Unfortunately, these data were not computerized and cannot yet be retrieved and made available quickly on a computer printout.

The most effective counteraction to inbreeding would be to use studbook information to reorganize present breeding units, mixing the Praha and Munich lines to promote outcrossing. There are, however, strong feelings against and several practical problems to such a mixing. It would disrupt present successful breeding units, involve risk of injury during transfer, and prove extremely costly in time and money (IUCN, 1981). While inbreeding has produced some negative effects, most foals survive to breeding age and the captive population is increasing in size. The danger to the survival of the species is most likely over the long term (the next fifty generations), requiring long-term planning to reduce inbreeding coefficients rather than drastic, immediate action (IUCN, 1981). Consequently, the most practical approach for the management of the captive population over the next decade involves a program of stallion exchange and continued breeding within the isolated Munich and Praha lines. Recently, an important exchange should maintain the isolation of the Munich line yet introduce new blood into it. In January 1984, Simon, the breeding stallion in Munich, was sent to Prague in exchange for the Prague stallion Bars. Bars is a son of Orlica III, the last wild mare, captured in 1947. The minimal relationship between Bars and the Munich mares should dramatically reduce inbreeding coefficients.

Inbreeding in other Munich line populations can be minimized by choosing least-related animals for breeding (based on their inbreeding coefficients) and by stallion rotation so that more males could contribute to subsequent generations and thus maximize the effective population size and minimize genetic drift. The sale of closely related breeding pairs must also end. This biologically unsound procedure, common in the past as a way of removing excess males from limited zoo space, contributed greatly to inbreeding. The establishment of new breeding units would promote outcrossing by combining animals from both Praha and Munich lines. In 1978, the Minnesota Zoological Garden became the first zoo in the U.S. to mix lines, combining European (Praha) mares with the American, Munich-line stallion George, born at Catskill. Subsequently the Bronx Zoo acquired the stallion Vulkan from the Russian Przewalski horse reserve at Askania Nova as stud for their American mares.

Coordinating the management of over five hundred Przewalski horses scattered over three continents and in some eighty institutions requires good communication and international cooperation. An important milestone was reached when the International Union for Conservation of Nature and Natural Resources

(IUCN) in Switzerland established the Przewalski Horse Committee within its Captive Breeding Specialists Group to look after the captive Przewalski population on an international scale. That group first met June 22, 1980, and endorsed a stallion-exchange program. The Committee also requested funds for the transportation of stallions between countries. Unfortunately, that funding was never provided.

Demographic management

As larger captive populations preserve more genetic diversity than smaller ones, the Committee recommended that the population be increased to a carrying-capacity level of about seven hundred animals, evenly divided between males and females to create the possibility of future reintroduction into the wild (IUCN, 1981). Because zoo space and resources are limited, this carrying capacity represented a compromise between preserving genetic *E. przewalskii* diversity and providing sanctuary for as many other endangered species as possible.

A demographic analysis performed by Foose (1977) projected that the Przewalski horse population will increase by five-to-ten percent a year. At such a growth rate, the female carrying capacity level will be attained in seven to ten years, the male level in ten to twelve years.

Once the recommended carrying capacity is reached, the population should be stabilized through manipulation of survivorships and fertilities, i.e., required removal of animals from certain age classes and/or regulation of reproduction, and management of age distribution and total numbers (IUCN, 1981). The exact parameters depend on objectives desired, e.g., one could devise a stabilization plan that maximized demographic security, minimized genetic drift or produced surplus horses (IUCN, 1981).

The present carrying capacity of zoological institutions has been crudely estimated, based on the assumption that one male to four female Przewalski horses represents the optimal-breeding group size and that zoos maintaining fewer than five horses should be able to accommodate that number. This would require zoos with only one or two to renovate facilities for a breeding group of five. More than fifty institutions have fewer than four females but could absorb more than one hundred and fifty additional animals. This modification alone would provide all of the female horses needed to expand to the carrying capacity level of three hundred and fifty.

Stallion depots

Because some of these institutions have more than one male, over twenty males would have to be removed to establish the one-male breeding groups. A few stallions could be transferred to zoos presently lacking them, and some zoos might be willing to maintain an extra male or two in a separate facility, but most excess stallions should be moved to stallion depots. These depots are important in maintaining a large, effective breeding population by holding "rotation breeders". Depots need to be accessible for transfer to surrounding zoos and able to handle both the introduction and removal of breeders (IUCN, 1981).

At present, two stallion depots have been established. The first, located on Ooij polder near Nijmegen in the Netherlands, was opened in spring 1983 and currently houses four young males owned by the Foundation for the Preservation and Protection of the Przewalski Horse: Sampsa, a gift from the Helsinki Zoo; Tello, bought from the Bern Zoo; Reep, acquired from Leipzig; and Askan, from Cologne. Unfortunately, as Sampsa got older, he displayed ataxic movements of the hindquarters, a common disorder of Przewalski horses, which made him unusable for breeding. Two other young stallions, acquired from Leipzig by the Foundation and released in the depot, subsequently died, Romanus from parasitic infestation and Rondo from unknown causes.

The second stallion depot has been operating since June 1983 in Parc National des Cèvennes in southeastern France. Four young males lived there originally, but Occitan, on loan from the Montpellier Zoo, died of an infection. The surviving stallions include Octavien, also on loan from Montpellier, and the Foundation-owned Piotr and Igor, both born in Bern.

Reintroduction

At the first meeting of the Przewalski Horse Committee in 1980, the members requested that the IUCN endorse the establishment of breeding groups to produce offspring for reintroduction into the wild (IUCN, 1981).[*] Reintroduction, while a lofty goal, is not an easy task. Przewalski horses have lived in captivity for over eighty years and eight generations. Most live in small enclosures without grass and remain stabled, and often separated, during the night. All receive supplemental food. Comparison of skeletal material from wild-caught Przewalski horses and animals born in the Prague Zoo conclusively indicated that the process of domestication has resulted in a decreased size of the lower jaw and its associated musculature (Volf, 1975). Fundamental changes have also occurred in their reproductive biology. The original Przewalski horses brought from the wild did not attain sexual maturity before four years of age. Captive animals commonly breed and successfully produce foals at an age of less than three (Volf, 1975). Early sexual maturity is common in animals kept in captivity and may provide a way of dispensing energy accumulated from the calorie-rich food which captive animals obtain without adequate effort (Volf, 1975). Domestication has also effected the distribution of births. In the wild, foals were born during a limited period of the year, probably from the end of April to the middle of June. Among captive breeding stocks, more than one-third were born outside the natural breeding season, and these foals would have had little or no chance of survival in the wild (Volf, 1975).

---

[*]In 1982 the IUCN officially accepted the stallion exchange and reintroduction proposals as project number 3077.

The Foundation for the Preservation and Protection of the Przewalski Horse has drawn up a detailed reintroduction program and has begun independent implementation. The strategy recommends establishing six breeding groups on "semi-reserves" of about seventy-five acres. Each group would consist of a stallion and four to five mares, and would produce offspring for release into the wild in other larger reserves of 80-100km^2. One group would consist of a stallion from Askania Nova with mares from the rest of Europe. Group two would pair an Askania Nova stallion with mares from the U.S.A. The third semi-reserve would house a stallion from the U.S.A. with mares from Askania Nova, and so on. By making up the breeding groups in this manner, the offspring would have the lowest inbreeding coefficients. Members of the breeding groups would never be reintroduced into the wild, but their offspring would be formed into social units that would gradually be released into the large reserves.

The Foundation began acquiring suitable young horses for the breeding groups, and in June 1982 established the first two groups at Lelystad and Noorderheide, both in the Netherlands (Bouman, 1982). The Lelystad group presently consists of the stallion Apollo from Cologne and the mares Lola and Laura from England, Nora from Bern, and Lory from Memphis. Apollo is from the Munich breeding line, while all the mares but Lory derive from Praha-line ancestors. The second group mixed the European mares Mira and Meta from Leipzig and Inge from Bern with the American stallion Boyce from San Diego. Unfortunately, Boyce died only a few months after being introduced in the fall of 1983, and has not yet been replaced.

The transition from life in the zoo to that in a semi-reserve has proven difficult. Horses in both the stallion depots and the breeding groups have died, and the surviving animals in winter showed coats in poor condition and drooping manes, a result of the reduction in the size of the fat deposit under the mane. The Foundation, during the 1983-84 winter, decided to provide supplemental food and worm medicine to both its breeding groups, an unfortunate step that will prolong the transition.

The Przewalski Horse Committee of the IUCN, although accepting the basic concepts of the Foundation reintroduction plan, recommended a number of modifications. They suggested that some zoological institutions, whose populations were managed to produce surplus offspring, act as the breeding units rather than establishing separate ones. This strategy has the advantage of not creating another ownership group of Przewalski horses, which may impede rather than promote international cooperation. Implicit in this proposal is the maintenance of genetic exchange between groups to promote genetic diversitiy (IUCN, 1981).

The Committee also felt it was desirable to place horses under more natural conditions as quickly as possible. By eliminating the separate breeding groups, offspring from zoos, after a period of isolation, could proceed immediately into the larger reserves.

Initially, several young females would be released into a natural area isolated from other bands to allow formation of social bonds. After a period of time, a stallion of similar age would then be introduced into the group. Aggression during the period of stallion introduction could be minimized by introducing the male outside of the breeding season or by using an immature stallion.

Eventually several one-male bands would be allowed to occupy the same large area. Inclusion of bachelor males into the reserve is strongly encouraged to improve reproductive competition and the potential for additional genetic diversity. Differences in the competitive abilities of the stallions could result in band of different sizes and a disproportionate number of young per male. Inbreeding could also increase and the reproductive potential of all animals vary. Some males will be genetically underrepresented (the less successful ones) and others over represented (the more successful ones). This situation might be desirable in that reproduction in nature provides changes in gene frequencies through time—natural selection prevails (IUCN, 1981).

The Committee recommended that the semi-reserves or the larger reserves be placed in location aas similar in climate, soil, and vegetation as possible to the original range of the Przewalski horse (IUCN, 1981). A suggested reserve on the island of Curacao was rejected because of its oceanic climate and too-mild winters. In such a climate (similar to that of San Diego) the horses fail to develop a heavy winter coat, a most unnatural situation.

Perhaps the most logical place to develop a Przewalski horse reserve would be Mongolia. The Mongolian People's Republic in 1976 created the Dzungarian National Park in the region where the last wild populations were observed and pledged to reintroduce horses there from a population acquired from Askania Nova. However, winter grazing by cattle and yaks is allowed on the area, and thousands of goats, camels, and domestic horses migrate across the park and compete for food. Domestic horses also bring the threat of contagious disease and cross-breeding (Bouman, 1984). Fencing to isolate and protect the Przesalski horses will take a tremendous amount of time and money. A Mongolian reserve is probably not feasible at present. Sites in the U.S.A., western Europe, and/or the U.S.S.R. seem more liekly. A New Mexico site was offered as a potential reserve site but was rejected by the Przewalski Horse Committee when the owner insisted on private ownership of the horses. However, a semi-refuge was established in 1984 on an area of about ten acres at the Conservation and Research Center of the National Zoo and the Smithsonian Institute in Front Royal, Virginia. Within two years, the size of that area will hopefully increase to about one hundred acres. The young mares Tracy, Marge, Misha, her 1983 foal Misty, Tasha, and her 1983 foal, Tara, were transported from the Minnesota Zoological Garden and released into the area. Several weeks later, the young stallion Bektair from Topeka was added as the breeding stallion. This breeding group mixes mares from the Praha line with a Munich-line stallion.

The long, slow road to reintroduction has begun. More semi-reserves need to be established, and larger protected reserves must be found. Perhaps by the year 2000, about one hundred years after the first Przewalski horses were brought into captivity, their descendants will have the opportunity to roam freely forever on a permanent range.

LITERATURE CITED

Bouman, J. 1977. The future of Przewalski horses in captivity. *Internat. Zoo Year.,* 17:63-68.
Bouman, J. 1978. The difference between the Przewalski horse and the domestic horse. *Przewalski Horse,* 1:10-11.
Bouman, J. 1980. The history of the Przesalski horse.*Przewalski Horse,* 5-60:11-19.
Bouman, J. 1982. Moving all seven of the foundation horses.*Przesalski Horse,* 10:4-6.
Bouman, J. 1984. The Gobi—a protected area. *Przesalski Horse,* 13:3-6.
Foose, T. Demographic models for management of captive populations. *Internat. Zoo Year.,* 17:70-76.
IUCN, 1981. Guidelines for the development of a captive management and reintroduction plan for *Equus przewalskii.* 52 pp.
Mohr, E. 1959. Das Urwildpferd. A. Ziemsen Verlag. 144 pp.
Putt, W. and Fisher, R. 1979. An investigation of some 36 genetically determined enzyme and protein markers in Przewalski and domestic horses. In: Genetics and Hereditary Diseases of the Przewalski Horse. Rotterdam Foundation for the Preservation and Protection of the Przesalski Horse. Rotterdam. 176 pp.
Ryder, O., Sparkes, M., Sparkes, R., and Clegg, J. 1979. Hemoglobin polymorphism in *Equus przewalskii* and *E. caballus* analyzed by isoelectric focusing. *Comp. Biochem. Physiol.,* 62B:305-308.
Volf, J. 1975. Breeding of Przewalski wild horses. In: Breeding Endangered Species in Captivity (eds. R. Martin). Academic Press, London, 270 pp.
Waring, G. 1983. Horse Behavior. Noyes Pub., Park Ridge, N.J. 292 pp.

Endangered and Threatened Species Programs in Pennsylvania and other States: Causes, Issues and Management. Edited by S. K. Majumdar, F. J. Brenner and A. F. Rhoads. © 1986, The Pennsylvania Academy of Science.

Chapter Twenty-Five

DEVELOPMENT AND PROGRESS OF PENNSYLVANIA'S RIVER OTTER REINTRODUCTION PROGRAM

Thomas L. Serfass[1], Larry M. Rymon[1] and Jerry D. Hassinger[2]

[1]Department of Biology
East Stroudsburg University
East Stroudsburg, PA 18301
and
[2]Pennsylvania Game Commission
Box 174, Elizabethville, PA 17023

The river otter (*Lutra canadensis*) was historically found in every major watershed in Pennsylvania. Water pollution and unregulated trapping eliminated it in all but the Pocono Mountains of northeastern Pennsylvania. Improved water quality throughout the state leads us to believe that certain areas which once supported river otters could, with proper management, do so again. Between 1979-82, research on the northeastern population investigated feeding relationships, habitat use, field sign, and developed effective capture and handling techniques. From May 1983 through July 1984, the program was expanded to include the introduction of 22 river otters into Pine Creek drainage in northcentral Pennsylvania. These otters were obtained from northeastern Pennsylvania, Louisiana, Michigan, and New York. Success of initial releases was determined by radio tracking and locating field sign. Radio tracking data indicate that otters survived at the relocation site and Louisiana otter did adapt to northcentral Pennsylvania winters. Instrumented otters are known to have travelled up to

80 km from the release site, but they have more typically remained within the general relocation area. An analysis of otter scats collected in the study areas indicates that fish and crayfish are the most commonly occurring food items in their diet. Otters have established several frequently used den sites, including undercut banks, rock formations, backwater sloughs, and flood debris.

River otter populations declined during the 1800's and early 1900's due to unregulated trapping and pollution from toxic substances into inhabited waterways. Many extensive tracts of formerly suitable otter habitat were polluted by tanneries, mines, oil wells, chemical works, factories, and foundries[1]. Since 1952, there has not been an open season on otters in Pennsylvania. This legal protection proved extremely valuable in saving the species from possible extirpation.

Eveland[2] evaluated the size and distribution of the Pennsylvania population by means of a questionnaire to game protectors throughout the state. His estimates indicated that otter numbers ranged from 285 to 465, averaging 375. Over 90 percent of the population was found to reside in the 7 counties of the northeast, with the remainder representing occasional sightings from 4 other counties. Almost 70 percent of the population in a 7 county concentration area was found in 3 counties: Pike, Wayne, and Monroe. This northeastern population is bounded by development and metropolitan areas, which largely block westward extension into the Susquehanna River drainage.

Recent improvements in water quality and management techniques have provided renewed potential for otters to regain portions of their former range. In 1983, efforts were began to determine whether a breeding population of introduced otter could be established within Pine Creek in northcentral Pennsylvania.

This project and continuing otter research at East Stroudsburg University is funded by the Pennsylvania Game Commission's Working Together for Wildlife Program, the Wild Resource Conservation Act (non-game tax checkoff), and the Pennsylvania Trappers Association. We thank D.E. Sheffer, J. Beard, and A. Hayden of the Pennsylvania Game Commission, F. Dissinger and V. Megargel of the Pennsylvania Trappers Association, and W.E. Askins of the Woodstream Trap Corporation for their cooperation and assistance.

INITIAL RESEARCH

Prior to initiating reintroduction efforts, between 1979-82 data basic research was compiled on the remaining otter population in northeastern Pennsylvania. This research evaluated otter feeding relationships, habitat use, field sign, and developed effective capture and handling techniques. Results and experience obtained were applied to the formulation and implementation of the reintroduction program.

TABLE 1
Overall Food of River Otter Based on the Analysis of 452 Scats Collected from Northeastern Pennsylvania

Food Items	124 Spring Scats N	%	115 Summer Scats N	%	105 Fall Scats N	%	108 Winter Scats N	%	452 Total Scats N	%
Fishes	121	98	98	85	97	92	107	99	423	94
Centrarchidae	92	34	62	54	67	64	86	80	307	68
Cyprinidae	25	20	17	15	25	24	11	10	78	17
Catostomidae	35	28	11	10	15	14	38	35	99	22
Percidae	13	10	10	9	14	13	29	27	66	15
Esocidae	36	29	4	3	7	7	24	22	71	16
Salmonidae	14	11	11	10	6	6	9	8	40	9
Cyprinodontidae	2	2	0	0	6	6	4	4	12	3
Ichtaluridae	0	0	2	2	3	3	1	1	6	1
Crayfish	52	42	72	63	40	38	30	28	194	43
Amphibians	6	5	19	17	4	4	1	1	30	7
Insects	8	6	12	10	3	3	1	1	24	5
Mammals	3	2	7	6	4	4	2	2	16	4
Molluscs	0	0	1	1	1	1	0	0	2	0.5
Birds	0	0	2	2	0	0	0	0	2	0.5

TABLE 2
Food of River Otter Based on the Analysis of 221 Scats Collected from the Saw Creek Lake Study Site

Food Items	72 Spring Scats N	%	44 Summer Scats N	%	41 Fall Scats N	%	64 Winter Scats N	%	221 Total Scats N	%
Fishes	69	96	37	84	40	98	63	98	209	95
Centrarchidae	67	93	36	82	38	93	62	97	203	92
Cyprinidae	22	31	0	0	13	32	26	41	61	28
Percidae	25	35	1	2	1	2	21	33	47	21
Esocidae	8	11	2	5	6	15	22	34	38	17
Cyprinodontidae	1	1	0	0	6	15	4	6	11	5
Salmonidae	6	8	0	0	1	2	3	5	10	5
Catostomidae	0	0	1	2	1	2	0	0	2	1
Crayfish	40	56	43	98	27	66	28	44	138	62
Amphibians	3	4	10	23	1	2	0	0	14	6
Insects	4	6	3	7	0	0	0	0	7	3
Mammals	2	3	0	0	0	0	1	2	3	1
Molluscs	0	0	1	2	0	0	0	0	1	0.5

TABLE 3
Food of River Otter Based on the Analysis of 131 Scats from the Tunkhannock Creek Study Site

Food Items	38 Spring Scats		49 Summer Scats		23 Fall Scats		21 Winter Scats		131 Total Scats	
	N	%	N	%	N	%	N	%	N	%
Fishes	38	100	39	80	21	91	21	100	119	91
Centrarchidae	19	50	10	20	6	26	15	71	50	38
Castostomidae	17	45	10	20	4	17	0	0	31	23
Salmonidae	7	18	11	22	5	22	5	24	28	21
Cyprinidae	10	26	9	18	1	4	5	24	25	19
Percidae	10	26	3	6	2	9	2	10	17	13
Esocidae	2	5	2	4	o1	4	0	0	5	4
Cyprinodontidae	1	3	0	0	0	0	0	0	1	1
Crayfish	11	29	26	53	7	30	2	10	42	32
Amphibians	2	5	2	4	1	4	1	5	6	5
Insects	1	3	3	6	2	9	0	0	6	5
Mammals	0	0	4	8	0	0	0	0	4	3
Birds	0	0	2	4	0	0	0	0	2	2

FEEDING RELATIONSHIPS

Otter food habits were compared at 3 dissimilar aquatic habitats in Monroe and Pike counties of northeastern Pennsylvania: Saw Creek Lake—a 28 ha manmade impoundment, Upper Tunkhannock Creek—a heavily stocked private trout stream, and Long Pond—an inland freshwater marsh. Comparison of research data from these habitats was useful in evaluating the suitability of aquatic habitats elsewhere in the state as reintroduction sites and for predicting the diet of otters.

Feeding information was gathered by analyzing scales, exoskeletons, and other undigested prey remains in 452 otter scats collected from the study areas in all seasons during 1981 and 1982.[3] The sample included 221 scats from Saw Creek, 131 from Tunkhannock Creek, and 55 from Long Pond. An additional 45 scats were collected from several impoundments having fisheries similar to that at Saw Creek. Food items were recorded by frequency of occurrence and data from all scats analyzed were tabulated and classified by season and study site.

Fish and crayfish (*Cambarus sp.*) were the most common prey of otters in northeastern Pennsylvania, occurring respectively in 93 percent and 43 percent of the 452 scats analyzed. Next in importance were amphibians (7%), aquatic insects (5%), mammals (4%), birds (0.5%) and molluscs (0.5%) (Table 1).

Although the fisheries and habitats varied significantly, fish were of nearly equal importance at the three study sites. The fish groups preyed upon most frequently at each study site tended to be taken in relation to their abundance

TABLE 4

Food of River Otter Based on the Analysis of 55 Scats from the Long Pond Study Site

Food Items	55 Total Scats	
	N	Percent
Fishes	51	93
Catostomidae	29	60
Centrarchidae	18	38
Esocidae	13	27
Ichtaluridae	10	21
Cyprinidae	9	19
Percidae	2	4
Salmonidae	1	2
Mammals	6	11
Insects	5	9
Amphibians	3	5
Crayfish	1	2

and swimming abilities (Tables 2,3,4). This supports the contention of Ryder[4] that fish are captured in proportion to their abundance and in inverse proportion to their swimming abilities. Otter predation was not considered a threat to game fish populations at any study site. Predation on trout (21%) at Tunkhannock Creek ranked third behind sunfishes (38%) and suckers (23%) even though trout were the most common species at this site due to extremely heavy stocking.

Otter predation at the Saw Creek Lake site appears to have had a positive affect on the fishery by controlling sunfish. MacNamara and Lippincott[5] commented that this lake was becoming "sunfish bound" and sunfishes were "somewhat stunted". They believed that the over abundance of sunfish caused them to prey heavily on the spawn of the other fish, and was a significant limiting factor for many species including largemouth bass. Sunfish were still the most commonly encountered species when the lake was resurveyed in 1982, but their growth rate increased and many large individuals were collected.

Results of a questionnaire indicated that most sportsmen were reasonably well informed regarding otter food habits and had positive attitudes toward otters. While only 11 percent considered the otter a threat to game fish, a portion of this minority was very vocal in condemning otter food habits.

It was determined therefore that a strong educational effort was needed to prevent a few vocal opponents from influencing public opinion at reintroduction areas. To accomplish this a slide series, based on otter food habits and emphasizing the otter's role as a positive factor in aquatic management, was prepared.

This educational approach was especially important at Pine Creek where initial opposition came from sportsmen concerned that the otters would harm trout populations. Local newspaper headlines read: "Pine Creek Sportsmen Oppose Otter Stocking." Following a public education session the paper read: "Sportsmen Back Otter Stocking Project."

Another public relations concern at reintroduction areas is potential otter depredation at fish hatcheries. Questionnaire surveys and interviews with northeastern Pennsylvania hatchery owners indicated that they had suffered fish losses from otter depredation.

Most otter visits lasted only a few days but old and sick otters often remained longer. One example was an adult female accidentally caught by a trapper at one of the hatcheries. She was in poor health having a large, malignant basal-cell epithelial tumor on her neck. Her condition indicated that she probably could not have foraged effectively in a natural aquatic habitat.

To prevent otter-hatchery conflicts at reintroduction sites local hatcheries are given an assessment of potential depredation problems and offered funds from the Pennsylvania Game Commission for materials to screen their facilities.

CAPTURE AND HANDLING TECHNIQUES

As part of the Pennsylvania otter reintroduction project, techniques were developed to safely live capture and handle river otters. Proper techniques are particularly important for minimizing stress and injury during capture and initial periods in captivity when otters often display violent escape behavior.

In this study Hancock livetraps and experimental #11/2 softcatch leg-hold traps were modified for use on river otters. Both were useful in live trapping river otters and each had advantages in given trapping situations.

The experimental #11/2 softcatch leg-hold traps were provided for this study by the Woodstream Trap Corporation. This trap is designed to minimize injury of trapped animals. The striking face of each jaw is cushioned by a 1.25 cm (0.5in) wide, grooved special rubber insert and the springs are weaker than in normal #11/2 leg-hold traps. Otters are powerful animals and larger ones frequently pulled free from this trap. The holding capacity was increased by replacing the trap springs with regular #11/2 springs. Improved results were also obtained by replacing one trap spring with a #2 spring.

Otters caught in traps were restrained and anesthetized by an intramuscular injection of ketamine hydrochloride.[2,7] Restraining techniques were developed for each type of trap or trapping technique used.

Otters trapped in Hancock traps are easily drugged while in the trap by pinning them against the wire mesh. Prior to drugging, Hancock traps containing otters were removed from the water and placed on the shoreline. This prevented the otter from ingesting water as muscular control is lost during anesthesia.

A hold-down device was developed to restrain otters captured in leg-hold traps.

FIGURE 1. Otter Restrained Prior to Being Anesthetized.

The device incorporated chain link fencing attached to a surrounding wooden frame (approximately 0.65 m x 1 m) (Fig. 1). Those caught in land sets were pinned under this device and drugged. A large fish landing net was used to entangle otters captured in long chained water sets. Once entangled, otters were brought to shore, pinned, and drugged.

After being anesthetized otters were weighed, measured and ear tagged and all scars, abnormalities and the general health of each animal was recorded.

After processing was completed, otters were placed in well ventilated wooden holding boxes, which also served as a drugging box for captive otters. The box is closed for transporting otter by attaching wooden caps to its open ends. For drugging, a wooden cap end was replaced with a screen cap end (fig. 2) Otters were pinned against the screen with a push block inserted through the opposite end of the box. A sliding wooden door was inserted when changing caps to prevent the otter from escaping. The box provided a dark environment free of any stressful external stimuli during recovery from the drug. Safely inside, the recovered otter could bite the soft wooden box without causing teeth damage.

This specialized equipment: softcatch trap, hold-down device and wooden holding box were developed during this project and further details concerning their use can be found in Serfass.[3]

Otters were transported in these boxes to holding facilities at East Stroudsburg University where captive behavior and requirements were studied. They were

FIGURE 2. Captive Otter Being Drugged in Holding Box.

held in two 5 m x 5 m climate controlled rooms with cement floors and walls, drains, and a water supply to facilitate cleaning.

Otters were allowed to move freely in the room. The wooden holding box remained in the room to serve as a nest box. A small plastic swimming pool filled with water was also placed in the room. Strips of carpeting were placed in the nest box and room for the otters to rub on and dry themselves. While in captivity otters were fed a diet of fish (1-1.5 kg daily) supplemented with Nutrical (high calorie dietary supplement manufactured by Evsco Phar-

FIGURE 3. Carrying Box with Cage Attachment for Longer Transportation.

maceuticals, Buena, N.J.) and Multi-Prime (B-complex vitamin—iron supplement manufactured by Burroughs Wellcome Co., Kansas City, MO.).

Despite the advantages of the wooden holding box during anesthesia recovery, it was not initially suitable for the 3 to 4 hr trips to reintroduction sites. Several otters displayed violent escape behavior including biting and clawing when so confined and became exhausted in a short period of time. Otters which were allowed to become accustomed to using holding boxes as refuges for several days prior to longer transportation times fared better. This transportation system was modified when a small cage (1 m x 0.5 m x 0.3 m) (Fig. 3) was attached to the front of the holding box in place of the front door. This provided an open area in the front of the box which, in most instances, resulted in a calming ef-

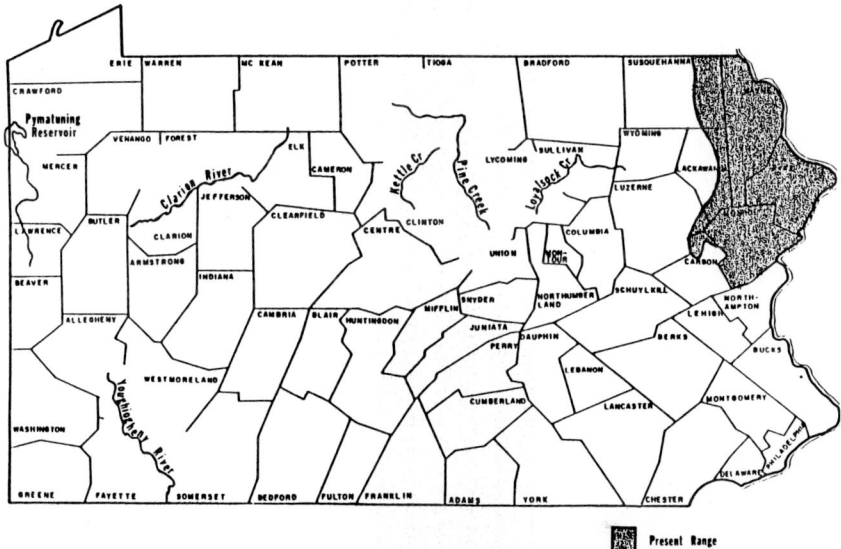

FIGURE 4. Location of Watersystems Ranking Favorably for Selection as Initial River Otter Reintroduction Sites.

fect as the otters remained in the security of the rear portion of the box during transport. Even animals which demonstrated violent activity in closed boxes were calmed when the cage was attached. A moistened strip of carpeting placed in the box further prevented otters from overheating during transport.

REINTRODUCTION SITE SELECTION

An evaluation of potential introduction sites was conducted through a questionnaire sent to the superintendents of state parks located outside the otters present range. The parks surveyed were associated with portions of most of the major watersheds located outside the northeast. The survey provided basic information regarding water quality, fisheries, land use, recreational use, and other factors from which the potential as an introduction site could be judged.

From survey results, certain sites were selected for closer evaluations. Each of these sites were visited and interviews were conducted with local Game commission, Fish Commission, and Bureau of Forestry employees to further assess their potential for otter introduction. A comprehensive examination of the water quality and fisheries was accomplished through a review of data provided by the Pennsylvania Fish Commission.

Based on these evaluations; Pymutuning Reservoir, Clarion and Youghiogheny Rivers, Kettle, Pine and Loyalsock Creeks all ranked favorably as initial sites for receiving otter (Fig. 4). Kettle Creek was selected as the first release site and four otters were released during 1982 (Serfass, Unpubl. rep.). Trapping pressure and an unwillingness of local trappers to accept trapping regulations led to a reevaluation of this site and a decision to move the project to neighboring Pine Creek.

The Pine Creek served as the principal release site during 1983-84. Lake habitat at the headwaters of the Loyalsock Creek in Sullivan County will serve as the next release site during 1985-86. This habitat contrasts the "big stream" into which otter were released along Pine Creek. A comparison of research data, gathered from released otter at these dissimilar habitats, should provide a basis for evaluating the potential of most aquatic habitats that will be encountered in Pennsylvania as prospective reintroduction sites.

PINE CREEK REINTRODUCTION AREA

STUDY AREA

Pine Creek is the largest tributary to the West Branch of the Susquehanna River. It flows approximately 125 km from the town of Galeton in Eastern Potter County entering the River at the town of Jersey Shore in Lycoming County. The Pine Creek Gorge Natural Area (Grand Canyon of Pennsylvania) occupies both sides of Pine Creek. Rafting and canoeing are popular on Pine Creek during the spring. Fishing, hunting, and trapping are also popular in the area, attracting sportsmen from throughout the state. Access to the gorge is restricted to foot travel, mainly along a railroad bed wich parallels the eastern bank.

Pine Creek Gorge is a rugged area with depths in excess of 300 m from Pine Creek to the rim and widths in excess of 1.6 km. The bottom lands are scoured during flooding when ice on Pine Creek breaks up each spring. Sycamore (*Platanus occidentalis*), Yellow Birch (*Betula alleghaniensis*), and Hemlock (*Tsuga canadensis*) predominate in the lowlands.

The shoreline is rocky and steeply sloped with few undercut banks or backwater areas. The stream is characterized by intermittent stretches of riffles and slow moving pools with a rocky substrate. The stream supports a healthy fish population. Common species are white sucker (*Catostomous commersoni*), fallfish (*Semotilus corporalis*), smallmouth bass (*Micropterus dolomieui*), and rock bass (*Ambloplites rupestris*). Brown trout (*Salmo trutta*) and rainbow trout (*Salmo gairdneri*) are stocked each spring. Crayfish are abundant in Pine Creek and its tributaries which also contain native brook trout (*Salvelinus fontinalis*).

METHODS

A total of 22 otter (11 M, 11 F), obtained through purchases from Louisiana

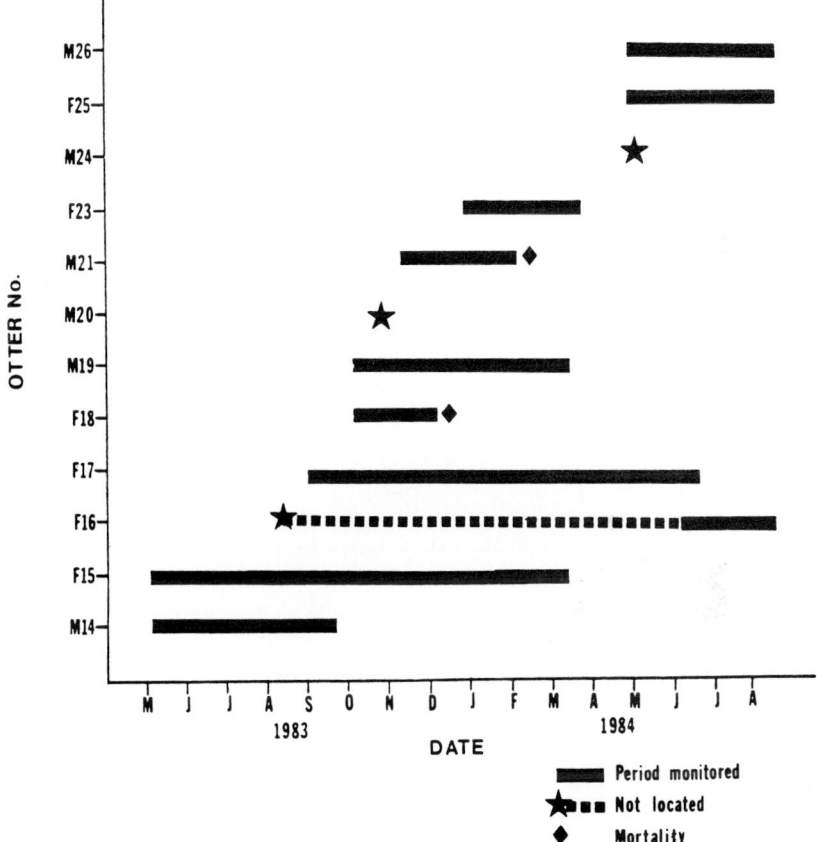

FIGURE 5. Summary of Radio Tracking (1983-84).

(17) and New York, (1), an exchange with Michigan (1), and live trapping in northeastern Pennsylvania (3) were released into Pine Creek. Between May 1983 and January 1984, 10 otter (group 1) were released at a single location on Pine Creek. This was followed by a second release of 12 animals (group 2) from May through July 1984.

The ability of relocated otter to survive, interact, and locate den sites was investigated through radio tracking. Radio transmitters were surgically implanted[7] in 9 of the first 10 otter released (Table 5). These otter were held at the university and given antibiotics for at least one week after implant surgery. Each individual was ear tagged in both ears using a size #1 metal fingerling fish tag.

As otters became available, usually individually or in small groups (2-3), they were released near one central point in the Pine Creek Gorge. Otters were radio traced on a weekly basis from the time of the first release (May 1983) through

TABLE 5

Summary of Otter Releases on Pine Creek

	Group I					Group II			
Otter No.	Age Class	Source	Release Date	Telemetry Equipped (x)	Otter No.	Age Class	Source	Release Date	Telemetry Equipped (x)
M13	Adult	La.	5/9/83		M24	Adult	La.	5/16/84	x
M14	Adult	La.	5/9/83	x	F25	Adult	La.	5/16/84	x
F15	Adult	La.	5/9/83	x	F26	Adult	La.	5/16/84	x
F16	Adult	Pa.	8/6/83	x	F27	Adult	La.	5/16/84	
F17	Juv.	Pa.	9/12/83	x	M28	Adult	La.	5/16/84	
F18	Adult	La.	10/10/83	x	F29	Adult	La.	5/16/84	
M19	Adult	La.	12/10/83	x	F30	Adult	La.	6/1/84	
M20	Juv.	Pa.	10/19/83	x	M31	Juv.	La.	6/1/84	
M21	Juv.	Mich.	11/12/83	x	F32	Adult	La.	6/1/84	
F23	Adult	N.Y.	1/12/84	x	F33	Juv.	La.	7/2/84	
					M34	Juv.	La.	7/2/84	
					M35	Adult	La.	7/2/84	

the spring beaver trapping season (March 1984).

Feeding information was gathered by analyzing otter scats collected along Pine Creek. Methods for analysis and tabulation were mentioned earlier in the text for the food study of otters in northeastern Pennsylvania.

RESULTS AND DISCUSSION

The movements of 8 of the 9 radio-tagged otter were successfully monitored for extended periods after their release (Fig. 5). These otters were known to feed, locate den sites, and stay within the drainage during the periods they were tracked.

The ability of otters to survive winter releases was tested when female otter (F23) was released (January 1984). At this time large portions of Pine Creek were ice covered but she was released in an open section of riffles. Mid-winter conditions produced evening temperatures averaging between $-20 - -30C$ through the next week. This otter was obtained from New York where she was held in outdoor facilities throughout the early winter. She had little difficulty adapting to release conditions and was monitored through mid-March when her transmitter began to fail. Fish placed along the shoreline, as a precautionary supplement during the first 2 days after the release, were utilized by the otter as evidenced by tracks in the snow. Although Louisiana otters were known to survive through northcentral Pennsylvania winters, their pelage was noticeably thinner than that northern otters and there is a question as to whether they could survive a winter release without being acclimatized.

Winter survival was evaluated by monitoring 6 radio-tagged otters until after ice break up in Pine Creek. The two Louisiana otters which were tracked adapted well to winter conditions and were known to survive through the ice out. The only mortality occurring as a result of winter conditions was that of an immature male (M21) from Michigan. This otter was apparently trapped in the ice flow that occurred (2/13/84). Its carcass was found washed approximately 25 km downstream from where it denned the previous week.

The other known death was that of a female otter (F18) from Louisiana. This otter died while denned in a large natural rock formation approximately 40 days after being released. The carcass could not be retrieved from the den to verify the cause of death but because of teeth damage suffered during her capture in Louisiana (she was missing each upper incisor and each canine was broken to varying degrees), it was assumed she may have starved. It is difficult to assess when teeth damage is too severe to permit survival, but scats collected near her dens indicated she had a certain degree of feeding success. Louisiana otter with all their cannines broken to incisor level survived after their release in Missouri (Erickson, pers. comm.).

Female otter (F16), was believed to have raised a litter on Pine Creek in the spring of 1984 the year following her release. She had been leg-hold trapped

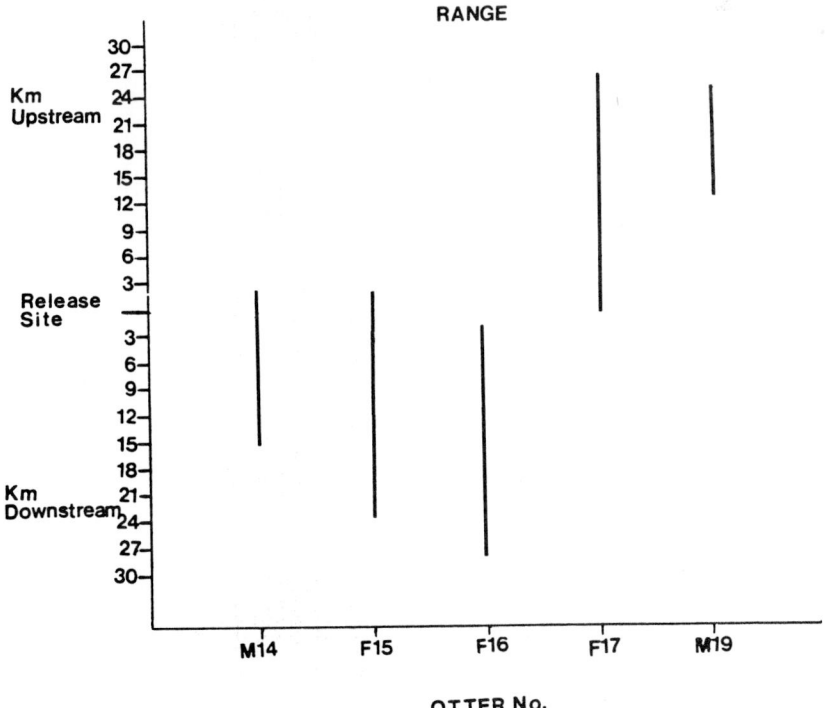

FIGURE 6. Ranges of Otter after Settling into a Regular Pattern of Den Use.

by hatchery personnel in northeastern Pennsylvania in August 1983. Her dead cub was located in a trap nearby indicating she had given birth that year and probably had bred for the coming year.[8] In March and April (1984) she was located regularly at a particular den site approximately 24 km south of the release site. Although researchers never observed young otters, several area sportsmen reported seeing a family group near this den during the summer. Following these reports, two juvenile males were illegally taken in a conibear trap and presumed to be the cubs of this otter. Their skinned carcasses were found along the shore approximately 28 km downstream from the suspected natal den in mid-October 1984.

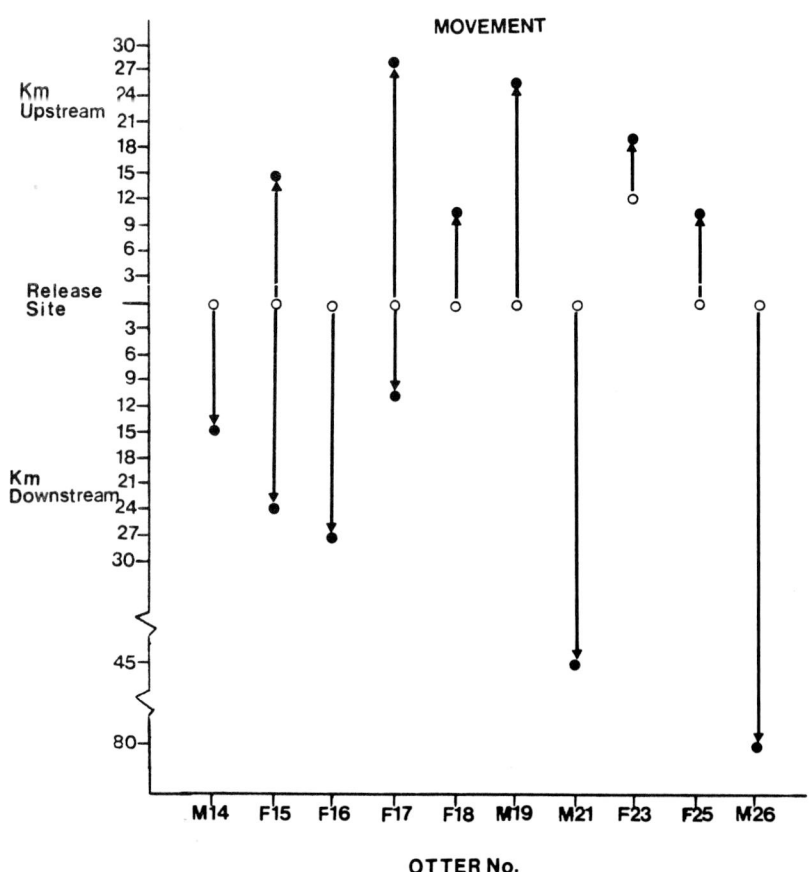

FIGURE 7. Furthest Upstream and Downstream Movement of Otter in Relation to the Release Site.

MOVEMENT

Radioed otter established ranges within Pine Creek drainage. Movement from the release site was related to the presence of established otter. The initial pair of radioed tagged otters (F14, M15) shared a similar range which included the release site. As others were released they usually moved further and beyond the range of the original pair. After initial dispersal otters tended to settle into a more specific range and pattern of movement (Fig. 6). For example, otter M19 gradually moved 25 km upstream during the two months after his release. At this point he adopted a range limited to 7 km through the remainder of this tracking (3/19/84).

Movement from the release area varied substantially between individuals (Fig. 7). The furthest known movement was that of otter M26 which was located nearly 80 km downstream 30 days after his release. Two otters were not located since shortly after their release. One of these may have been the badly decomposed carcass of an otter identified by a game protector along Bald Eagle Creek in December 1984. This site was approximately 100 km by the shortest water route from the release area.

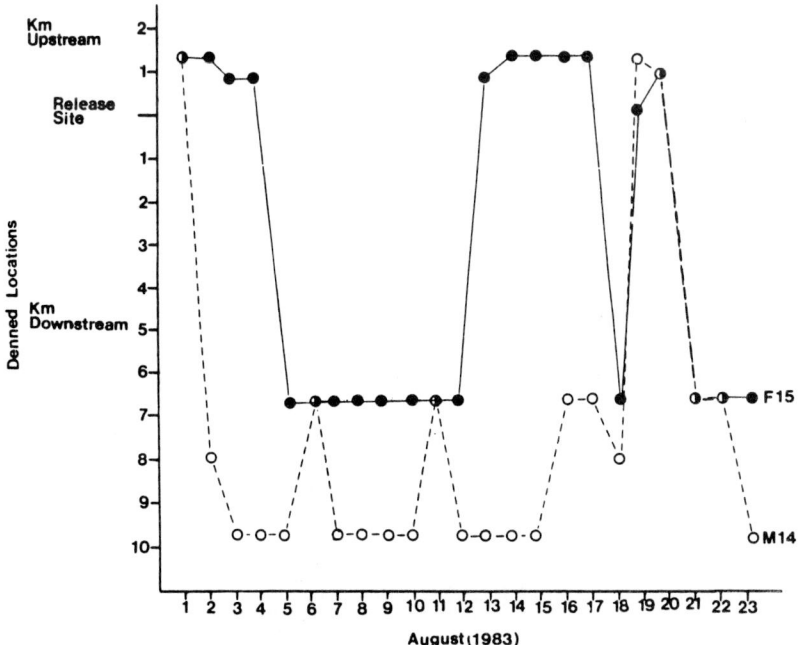

FIGURE 8. Regular Pattern of Den Use and Interaction of Otters (M14 and F15) During 23 Day Constant Monitor Period During August 1983.

INTERACTIONS

As mentioned earlier, otters were released during two periods; those in 1983 were group one and in 1984 group two. Group one releases demonstrated an ability to readily locate each other as was illustrated by movements of M14 and F15 (the first telemetered animals introduced) (Fig. 8). These animals were located 30 km apart 11 days after release but 16 days later were found together near the original release site. They continued to share a common range for the next 4 months. Otters released later in the group one introduction either made contact with earlier released animals or located their sign, and often occupied dens used previously. For example, one female (F17) was found within the range of M14 and F15 3 weeks after her release. She associated with them and used dens that they also had occupied.

Otters (M14, F15) established several latrines or spraints[9] throughout their range. Such areas serve as sign posts and were apparently easily detected by newly released otter. A male otter (M19) located one spraint minutes after his release and spent 45 min. thoroughly investigating the spot.

During the winter of 1983-84 Pine Creek was frozen over and snow covered. During this time tracks of paired otters were seen on 4 separate occasions. Through radio tracking, F15 was located twice in the area of paired tracks. Similar radio tracking associated F17 with other paired tracks in his area. Because only one animal was sending radio signals from the area in each case it was assumed the partners were previously released animals with failed transmitters.

The activities of radio-tagged otters in 1983 provided confidence that the otters released in 1984 will probably follow a similar pattern of dispersal and interaction.

DEN SITES

Although denning opportunities along Pine Creek appeared to be limited because of the rocky shoreline, otters proved to be very adaptive and used a variety of dens (Table 6). Sites recorded were those used after otters settled into an established denning pattern during the summer and fall of 1983. Ice cover

TABLE 6

Den Use Based on 142 Morning Denned Locations of Otters (M14, F15, F17, F18, M19) During the Summer and Fall (1983)

Den Type	Percent of Times Used
Undercut Banks (Tree Roots)	42
Rock Formations	32
Backwater Sloughs	25
Flood Debris	1

prevented accurate location and description of most winter den sites. The most common sites were those located near the stream including undercut banks, rock formations, backwater sloughs, and flood debris.

FOOD HABITS

The success of released otters as determined from telemetry data, indicates that Pine Creek provides suitable prey abundance. Specific feeding information was determined by analyzing 82 scats collected along the shoreline (Table 7).

Fish and crayfish were the most important prey, occurring in 96 and 45 percent of the scats, respectively (Fig. 9). The importance of these food items was similar to that observed from the native population in northeastern Pennsylvania with the exploitation of crayfish being related to seasonal abundance. This food item was taken more frequently during summer months than fish. Catostomidae (49%) and Cyprinidae (33%) were the fish groups most frequently utilized.

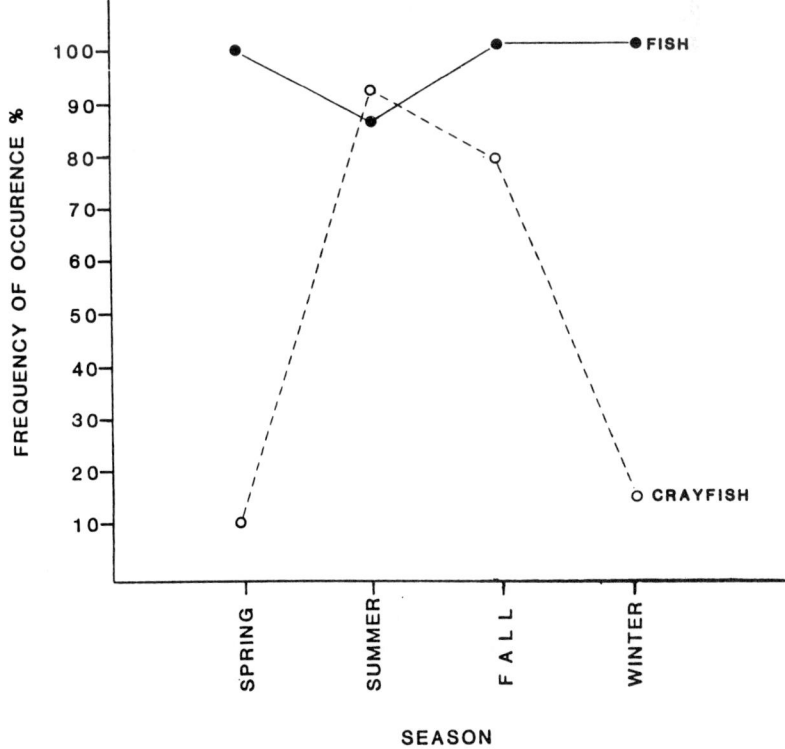

FIGURE 9. Seasonal Importance of Fish and Crayfish Based on 82 Scats Collected Along Pine Creek.

TABLE 7

Food of Introduced River Otter Based on the Analysis of 82 Scats Collected Along Pine Creek

Food Items	21 Spring Scats		25 Summer Scats		10 Fall Scats		26 Winter Scats		82 Total Scats	
	N	%	N	%	N	%	N	%	N	%
Fish	21	100	22	88	10	100	26	100	79	96
Catostomidae	13	62	10	40	7	70	10	38	40	49
Cyprinidae	2	10	10	40	5	50	10	38	27	33
Centrarchidae	3	14	2	8	3	30	9	35	17	21
Salmonidae	3	14					1	4	4	5
Crayfish			10	23	92	8	80	4	15	37	45
Mammals	1	5	1	4					2	2
Amphibians			1	4			1		1	

CONCLUSIONS

A total of 22 otter (Louisiana 17, northeastern Pennsylvania 3, New York 3, and Michigan 1) were released within Pine Creek drainage from May 1983 through July 1984. Data obtained through radio tracking and scat analysis indicates that otters successfully fed, located den sites, and remained within the drainage. Louisiana otters adapted well to the cold winter weather in northcentral Pennsylvania. Canoeing and fishing pressure appeared to have little consequence on otter movement. One otter (F16) was believed to have reared young at a popular fishing hole on Pine Creek.

Dispersal of released otter appeared related to the presence of previously released otter. The first pair of radioed otters released along Pine Creek established a home range that included the release site. Otters released later at this site tended to travel greater distances and usually did not include the release site in their range.

Mortality occurred in two of the radio-tagged otters. Environmental factors relating to severe flooding and ice flow (2/13/84) was apparently responsible for one mortality. The other mortality was probably caused by the inability of the otter to properly feed due to teeth damage which occurred when it was trapped in Louisiana.

The vulnerability of otters to heavy trapping pressure in low diversity aquatic habitat is evidenced by the fate of the four otter released along Kettle Creek in 1982. Since their release trappers have caught and freed otters on four occasions during the last two years thereby proving that otters are vulnerable to trapping. This evidence also indicates that otters have remained and are surviving in Kettle Creek habitat for over two years.

Trapping is more difficult along Pine Creek due to its rocky shoreline and fluctuating water levels but the potential for incidental and intentional capture is of great concern. Two juvenile otters have already been taken illegally in a conibear type trap in mid-October (1984) prior to the opening of trapping season.

The carcasses of the two juvenile otters found along Pine Creek in mid-October substantiated our belief that otter (F16) had given birth. This otter would have bred prior to being relocated on Pine Creek, but her apparent success in rearing young along this stream is encouraging. Adult female otter from Louisiana are not available from the supplier until after parturition. Considering the reproductive cycle,[8] it will be at least one year after their first spring in the introduction area before otters can be expected to reproduce. The interactions observed during radio tracking suggest otters will have little difficulty locating one another for breeding. Erickson et al.[10] has also drawn such conclusions in his study of a similar reintroduced population in Missouri.

This investigation has demonstrated that otters from various states and those livetrapped within the state can adapt well to selected watersheds presently outside their natural range. Given adequate protection and further study such translocated animals may form the nucleus of new and diverse sub-populations throughout the state.

LITERATURE CITED

1. Rhoads, S. 1903. Mammals of Pennsylvania and New Jersey. Mem. Mus. Compar. Zool. Cambridge, Mass. pp. 137-139.
2. Eveland, T. 1978. The staus, distribution, and identification of suitable habitat of river otters in Pennsylvania. Unpublished Master's Thesis. East Stroudsburg University. 54 pp.
3. Serfass, T.L. 1984. Ecology and feeding relationships of river otter in northeastern Pennsylvania. Unpublished Master's Thesis. East Stroudsburg University. 115 pp.
4. Ryder, R.A. 1955. Fish predation by the otter in Michigan. J. Wildl. Manage. 19:497-498.
5. MacNamara, E.E. and B. Lippincott. 1971. Fishery survey of Saw Creek Lake. Unpublished Report. Lehigh University, Allentown, PA. 13 pp.
6. Northcott, F.H. and D. Slade. 1976. a live-trapping technique for river otters. J. Wildl. Mgmt. 40:163-164.
7. Melquist, W.E. and M.G. Hornocker. 1979. Methods and techniques for studying and censusing river otter populations. Idaho Cooperative Wildlife Research Unit Forest, Wildlife, and Range Exp. Sta. Tech Report. No. 8, 17 pp.
8. Liers, E.E. 1958. Early breeding in the river otter. J. Mammal. 39:438-439.

9. Mowbray, E.E., D. Pursley, and J.A. Chapman. 1979. The status, population characteristics and harvest of the river otter in Maryland. Wildlife Ecology, Maryland Wild. Admin., Maryland Dept. of Nat. Res. No. 2, 16 pp.
10. Erickson, D.W., C.R. McCullough, and W.R. Porath. 1984. River otter investigations in Missouri. Unpubl. final rep., Missouri Fed. Aid Proj., W-13-R-38, Study No. 63, Job No. 2.

Chapter Twenty-Six

THE EFFECTS OF AGRICULTURE ON THE HISTORY AND FUTURE OF THE RING-NECKED PHEASANT (PHASIANUS COLCHICUS)

Keith W. Harmon
Wildlife Management Institute
R.R. #1, Box 122
Firth, Nebraska 68358

The role the ring-necked pheasant has played in weaving the social, political and economic fabric of many northern-latitude states is scattered throughout various and often unrelated forms of literature. Any attempt to better establish that role must therefore draw upon these disconnected sources. This leaves considerable literary license.

What follows is not a treatise on the biology and life history of the pheasant. It is rather an attempt to intertwine the host of events of a new and emerging nation that created an environment favorable for the pheasant.

From the moment the first white immigrants came ashore on the Atlantic coast, the North American continent would never again be the same. Primitive tools and limited numbers of people in the beginning brought imperceptible change; but this was only because of the vastness of the new land. On a local basis, change was dramatic.

The settlers encountered wilderness, a landscape foreign to a people from nations that had been settled and groomed for centuries. Their purpose was not to live and prosper in accord with a new environment but rather it was to shape and mold the land to conform to their European concept of village and farm.

The colonials by 1700 numbered about 250,000 souls[1] and all were found within 50 miles of the seashore, where they created forest clearings and expanded those made earlier by Indians.[2] To enhance their small farming operations, they imported crops such as wheat, oats, barley, clover and legumes[3] along with domestic livestock—cattle, goats, sheep and horses.[4]

For over 150 years, the Appalachians restricted westward settlement. Then military roads began pushing through the newly located mountain passes, and the potential farmland available with the Louisiana Purchase, Mexican War and Oregon Settlement fueled the growing westware movement. Pioneers spread over the land that would become Kentucky, Tennessee, Indiana and Ohio. Within 25 years, these lands, as well as those of the Gulf Plains, were settled following the War of 1812.[4] The eastern half of the continent was settled by 1850 with an estimated population of 23 million that grew to 32 million in just 10 years.[5]

As important as the settlement throughout these lands was the rapidly changing farming methods and equipment. The federal Swampland Acts of the mid-1800's conferred approximately 26 million ha of swamp and floodplain lands to the states for the purpose of reclaiming them for agriculture.[6] In Ohio alone, 32,000 km of public ditches drained 4.4 million ha by 1884. Through the 1800's, new farming equipment was developed to till the land which included among others the cast-iron plows, gang plows, mechanical reapers and threshing machines.[7]

As the eighth decade of the 1800's emerged, agriculture had advanced to the northern prairies. By 1900, in just 20 short years, farming pushed past the 100th meridian and into the arid grasslands.[2] The large cattle empires of the free-grass era, despite their often violent resistance, succumbed to the farmers and their barbed wire. More than the rancher fell before this avalanche of settlement. The volatile plains Indians abdicated to the greater resources of the whites. The great herds of buffalo, once numbering in the 10's of millions, were reduced to a few survivors sequestered in newly established national parks. The proghorn, formerly present in equally impressive numbers, dwindled to a few thousand.

At the same time the northern states were being redesigned to accommodate a new immigrant—the pheasant—an important social movement was underway and growing. Shocked by the decimation of species after species of wildlife, an ever-larger number of people became determined to reverse the abuses.

As sentiment for wildlife expanded, developments took place on 2 fronts—private and government. Prior to the Civil War, no central authority with responsibilities for wildlife existed. The first came in 1871 when the Congress established the United States Fishery Commission and over the next 9 years, nearly all states followed the federal lead and established their own fish commissions.[3] The perceived success of these fisheries commissions (stocking carp, for example) stimulated later demands for similar efforts with game birds.

The few embryonic wildlife management endeavors were conducted by the early fish commissions. Maine, the first state with paid game wardens, placed its officers under its Fish Commission in 1880. The New Hampshire legislature bestowed wildlife responsibilities upon its Fisheries Commission, renaming it the Commission on Fisheries and Game.[3]

The new fish and game departments were poor, meagerly staffed and largely ineffective. Most, when financed at all, were funded from the general fund. For example, the 1910 budget for the Colorado Game and Fish Department was $50,000 for all activities.[8]

A new, more reliable source of income was, however, gaining acceptance—the hunting license. In 1895, North Dakota required all hunters to purchase a license. Such a license was proposed in Pennsylvania that same year but did not become law until 1913. As late as 1922, 14 states did not require resident hunters to purchase a license.

As the United States moved toward the close of the 19th century, the stage was set for one of the most spectacular introductions of an exotic species. The land was settled, forever changed. Except for the industrial northeast, once almost wholly bucolic itself, the U.S. was predominantly a rural culture. Along with the change in the land, a mounting concern for wildlife was evident. That concern took the form of protection and propagation stimulated by pioneering work in fish stocking. Emerging state fish and game departments rounded out the equation.

Even prior to the culmination of these seemingly unrelated events, private pheasant introductions had been attempted. In 1733, Governor John Montgomerie reportedly released English pheasants on Nutten Island in New York.[9] There is little evidence that this effort met with success, and thus history credits the first successful introduction to Judge Denny of Oregon,[10] who liberated 28 Chinese ring-necked pheasants near his home in the Willamette Valley.

Most of the initial stocking of pheasants was carried out by individuals and sportsmen organizations. As more state fish and game departments came into being, however, they assumed an ever-increasing role. Many of the early state fish hatcheries had been transferred to the new fish and game agencies, and it was a natural step to expand into game farms.

Scientific wildlife management was unknown at the time, and agencies were searching for any meaningful endeavor. The raising and releasing of the newly introduced ring-necked pheasant was a natural to fill the void in programs.

Demand was high for pheasants, especially in the states east of the 100th meridian and north of the Mason-Dixon line. Here agriculture continued to negatively impact native game birds. Releases by private parties occurred in South Dakota in 1891 and 1898, and by the South Dakota Department of Game, Fish and Parks in 1911.[11] The Minnesota Department of Conservation first attempted stocking in 1905.[12] In Iowa, stocking began by accident when high winds leveled fences at the Wm. Benton game farm in 1900 or 1901, setting free about 2,000 birds.[13]. Then the Iowa Conservation Commission initiated a stocking program in 1910 with the distribution of eggs and adult birds. Other prairie states followed suit. However, the success of pheasants in that region resulted from limited stocking in suitable habitat and subsequent trapping and releasing wild birds.

The sequence of events in the Great Lakes region followed those in the plains.

Private pheasant hatcheries were noted in the vicinity of VanWert and Celina, Ohio before the turn of the century. In Michigan, a Holland-based sportsman club is credited with releases in 1895 with questionable results. Following these private efforts, state introductions were begun in Indiana in 1908, Michigan in 1918, Ohio in 1919, Illinois in 1928 and Wisconsin in 1929.[14] Unlike the plains states, however, where limited stocking took place, the Great Lakes area went full bore. According to McCabe et al.,[14] a minimum of 2,400,000 pheasants were stocked in the region prior to 1950, and in many areas stocking undoubtedly continued long after birds in the wild had reached a satisfactory huntable population.

The pheasant craze was not to be denied in the Northeastern states. Here, unlike northern-latitude states to the west, the pheasant never reached spectacular densities. While agricultural expansion throughout the Great Lakes and plains regions coincided with the introduction of the pheasant, the reverse was true in the Northeast. The cheaply produced farm products of the expanding agriculture in the Ohio and Mississippi Valleys were shipped to the eastern markets via the Erie Canal. Thousands of New England farmers, unable to cope with dropping prices, sold out and moved west.[5] Also, expanding wool production in Ohio caused New England wool output to decline 50 percent between 1840 and 1850.[5] Abandoned farms reverted to forests unsuitable as pheasant habitat.

Although time has shown that the only good pheasant range in the Northeast is the fertile agricultural lands of New Jersey, Pennsylvania and New York, first attempts to establish the pheasant were region wide. Initial stocking efforts were again by private parties and later the evolving game and fish agencies expanded these programs. Private releases were made in New York between 1886 and 1891 in the Hudson Valley, on Gardiner's Island in 1892 and 1893 and in western New York between 1897 and 1904. Populations were well established in the Ontario Lowlands by 1905.[9]

Private stockings also were made in Pennsylvania from the 1890's to 1915. Following that period, the state Game Commission began releasing game farm birds. Likewise, the pattern of private stocking with eventual assumption by state Commissions occurred in New Hampshire, Maine and Rhode Island.[9]

The events of several centuries of settlement—clearing a wilderness, expanding and changing agriculture, evolving state fish and wildlife agencies and pheasant introductions—culminated in pheasant hunting mania that gripped the northern states. This activity fueled the economy of many rural communities. The total dollar expenditure in pursuit of a single game bird species exceeds the imagination.

The first open pheasant hunting season occurred in the area of the first successful introduction—the Williamette Valley of Oregon—in 1891.[15] Others followed: Pennsylvania, 1902; Massachusetts, 1906; Idaho, 1916; South Dakota, 1919; Minnesota, 1924; and Michigan, 1925.[13,14,15] In 1931, the harvest in Pennsylvania was estimated at 294,000 birds, increasing to about half a million in 1941.[9] In better pheasant range, Kimball et al.[13] estimated that between 1940 and 1950 more than 82 million pheasants had been harvested by hunters in North Dakota, South Dakota, Nebraska, Iowa and Minnesota. For South Dakota alone, nonresident pheasant hunters' expenditures were estimated at nearly $10 million in 1959.[6]

Agriculture as it existed during the 20's, 30's and 40's when pheasant numbers flourished is today little more than a memory. Regardless of how, expanding crop production has been persistent in U.S. agriculture. What changed was the availability of advanced technology and fossil fuel-powered equipment that permitted farmers to impact larger acreages with ever-greater intensity.

High yields were, are and will continue to be a source of pride to the individual farmer, a status symbol. In most cases, it has provided financial rewards. That prevailing attitude cleared the forests and turned under the prairies, making conditions nearly ideal for the introduction and expansion of pheasants. It was rather by chance than design that pheasants profited. It would, as time passed, be equally devastating, even eliminating once-abundant populations in many locales.

Between 1870 and 1920, total acreage under the plow increased threefold. The expanding acreage of cropland was from two major sources, the westward expansion and the reclamation of land unsuitable for cropping in established farm areas. In the latter case, improved land in organized drainage enterprises increased by more than 16 million ha from 1890 to 1920, much of that in the Corn Belt.[17]

Although the amount of land under cultivation had stabilized, there were notable shifts between 1920 and 1940 on a regional basis. In essence, crop production in the New England and Mid-Atlantic regions shifted west and south.

Technology in agriculture continued to change. Slowed temporarily by the drought and depression of the 30's, major changes took place after 1940, spurred on by the more favorable economic conditions stimulated by World War II. Commercial fertilizer application more than tripled between 1940 and 1955. Hybrid corn which increased yields per acre by 20 percent was being planted on 90 percent of the corn hectarage in 1955 compared to 30 percent in 1940.[17] Pesticides came into increasingly widespread use.

Johnson[11] referred to these changes as they affected the landscape of North Dakota. He stated that the change in environment the past 20 years is almost beyond comprehension and must be considered a major limiting factor as far as pheasants are concerned. Johnson[11] further elaborated by stating that in the 1930's a peak of 5.2 million ha of idle land was reached. This was nearly half of the 11 million ha of cropland in North Dakota and much of it was sweet clover, a crop considered to be ideal for pheasants. Through the years this ideal land was gradually utilized for crops and grazing.

The agricultural revolution left no area occupied by the now well-established pheasant untouched. Wood County in northwestern Ohio was reported to have 480 + pheasants per km² in 1940.[18] A section of land in Wood County that year, as described by Leite,[18] might have small fields of oats, wheat, sweet clover, beans, corn, red clover and pasture. In 1967, the same section had large fields of corn and beans and some wheat. Gone were the clovers, oats and pastures. In a mere 27 years, the rural scene had changed from one of diversity to a row-crop monoculture. The limited acreage of legume crops that remained were harvested early for livestock feed with highly detrimental effects on nesting birds. Prior to that, many legumes were raised for seed production and remained undisturbed during the pheasant nesting season.

The 1968 fall survey in northwestern Ohio, once prime pheasant range, showed an average of 8 pheasants per 400 km, and Wood County was one of the lowest.[18] The impact of intensive agriculture on pheasants elsewhere did not go unnoticed. Declines in the Northwest were noted by Lauckhart and McKean,[15] in Nebraska by Baxter and Wolfe[19] and for the major pheasant states of the Midwest by Harmon and Nelson.[20]

On a relative scale, fish and wildlife agencies were not equipped to engage in pheasant management except for stocking programs for nearly half a century following introduction. Their meager funds were initially obtained from general revenues until such time as the states instituted hunting licenses. Here as well, however, income remained small compared to management needs, and might in some cases be directed to programs unrelated to wildlife. Had more money been available, it likely would not have been expended for what is today considered "state-of-the-art" management. Wildlife management as a science did not exist.

As agriculture intensified and pheasant populations declined, an earlier event at the federal level would aid in advancing wildlife management. The event, described by Trefethen,[3] was precipitated not by the pheasant but by a growing national concern for waterfowl as continental populations dwindled in the face of the 1930's drought. In 1929, Frederic C. Walcott of Connecticut became a U.S. Senator. He, along with Hawes of Missouri, successfully guided a resolution through the Senate to create a new Senate committee on wildlife. The committee immediately addressed the worsening waterfowl situation, and in succeeding years passed important legislation such as the Duck Stamp.

Later the Senate committee was expanded and chaired by Senator Key Pittman of Nevada. A companion committee was established in the House with A. Willis Robertson of Virginia as chairman. At this time, a portion of President Roosevelt's New Deal program was being financed by reinstated excise taxes, including those on sporting arms and ammunitions. Pittman and Robertson each introduced legislation to have the excise tax on those products dedicated to wildlife. The Federal Aid in Wildlife Restoration Act (P-R) became law in 1937.

The P-R Act not only provided a new and sizable infusion of funds into state wildlife agencies but it also required that in order for a state to be eligible for funds legislation had to be enacted to prevent diversion of game and fish funds for inappropriate programs. One can only speculate on the impact that the P-R Act has had in safe guarding state license revenues for the past 48 years.

P-R funding was modest at first. During the 1939 fiscal year, the first year after enactment, $890,000 were apportioned to the states. Ten years later, for fiscal year 1949, the states received $10.8 million. The pheasant became the focal point for these monies in many states. According to the Wildlife Management Institute[21], Ohio leased parts of 340 farms totaling 24,800 ha of which some 20,000 ha were established as seed-stock refuges for pheasants and rabbits. To develop these areas, more than 5,000 rods of fence have been constructed and 625,000 trees and shrubs planted. In addition to 1200 ha of nesting cover left by interested farmers, the State has contracted for 3120 ha of nesting cover, 120 ha of winter cover and 56 ha of standing crop for food. Such efforts were typical of state agencies throughout the pheasant range.

The pheasant also became the center of many research efforts with the aid of P-R funding.[21] Wisconsin in fiscal year 1949 funded an $18,511 pheasant-quail research project. Pheasant research that same fiscal year in other states included: California, $8,538; Illinois, $11,837; Main, $6,987; Michigan, $22,807; New York, $27,282 and South Dakota, $41,350 (included furbearers).

Following a 2-year investigation by the Ohio Cooperative Wildlife Research Unit[21], it was concluded that twice as many pheasants (were found) on Pittman-Robertson developed areas as on the unimproved check areas. However, while such findings were impressive, the overall impact on pheasants on a regional basis was slight. In Indiana, Bushong[22] found that while in some cases, prescribed development was excellent, too much attention had been given to quantity rather than quality. Not enough attention had been given to use of surrounding lands. He further stated that where the limiting factors in a region were of sufficient magnitude to keep farm-game populations low, development of small areas on land obtainable through this program did not cause an appreciable increase in populations.

On land around the areas however, the agricultural revolution continued unabated, and despite the efforts of state wildlife agencies, pheasants declines persisted. The presence of a new cadre of university-trained biologists in state agencies following World War II along with substantial increases in funding did not influence agriculture to any significant degree.

Not only did technology change agriculture, the increased involvement of the federal government negatively impacted farm wildlife. The Hugh Bennett era of soil conservation born of the "Dirty 30's" had emphasized that every farm have field borders, woodlots, wet areas, etc. that should be devoted to wildlife. The Soil Conservation Service advocated anchoring the soil and keeping the raindrop where it fell! However, as the higher echelons of the U.s. Department of Agriculture (USDA) became dominated by engineers and as the need for production of food and fiber for U.S. and allied troops increased, soil conservation took a back seat.

The 1936 Soil Conservation and Domestic Allotment Act had authorized federal financial assistance to farmers for installing soil and water conservation practices. Prior to 1940, no cost-shared drainage had been provided. Then, in 1941, USDA cost shared drainage on 22 ha in Vermont[23] and the floodgates were opened. The acreage drained increased dramatically during and after World War II, and in 1947, USDA provided cost sharing for open-ditch drainage on 2 million ha of which more than one million ha (49.5%) were in 17 important pheasant states. That same year cost sharing was provided for drainage on 236,274 ha with tile systems of which 222,112 ha (94%) were in those same 17 states.

The drainage and conversion of wetlands in pheasant states played a role in population declines. According to the Minnesota Division of Game and Fish,[12] Marsh edges provided pheasants with good cover and nesting sites, but as marshes are being drained for more crop production along with them goes pheasant cover. Wagner et al.[24] found in Wisconsin that between 1942-47 the decline in pheasant was less in counties with the highest percentage of land in wetlands. They also found that when those populations began to recover, the greatest increases occur in counties with the highest wetland acreage.

The ever-increasing capacity of U.S. agriculture to produce commodities beyond market demands brought the federal government into the act in an attempt to bolster farm income. Surplus crops simply depressed farm prices. There were too many resources devoted to food and fiber production. The federal government, reluctant to restrict landowner free choice for the inputs of capital and labor,[25] opted to use land retirement as a means of controlling production.

Fifty years of federal land retirement programs have taken two basic forms, each with a different but distinct impact on pheasants. The Crop Adjustment Act removed 8.2 and 6.8 million ha from production in 1934 and 1935, respectively. Planting cover on these lands was not a program requirement.[26] The Agricultural Conservation Program retired 11.4 million ha in 1936. This program peaked with 17 million ha out of production in 1941, but rapidly declined to 1.2 million ha in 1943. It ended in 1947 with only 0.6 million ha retired. Landowners participating in the program from 1936 to 1942 were required to seed a grass and/or legume cover crop which spurred an increasing pheasant population.[27] The small acreage remaining in the Agricultural Conservation Program after 1942 was used for legume seed production.

From 1948 to 1950, no land was retired through federal programs.[27] During the Korean conflict, only token acreages were out of production in 1951, 1952 and 1953 (73,200 ha average). Then for another 2 years (1954 and 1955) no land was retired.

The need for all-out production during the 2 war efforts was short lived, and in 1956, the Soil Bank program came on line;[20] this program contained 2 different features. The Acreage Reserve consisted of annual contracts with no vegetative cover requirement. This portion of the program retired 4.9 million ha in 1956, 8.6 million ha in 1957, 6.9 million ha in 1958 and none thereafter. The second feature, the Conservation Reserve, provided for up to 10-year contracts and required a protective cover crop. Enrolled acreages peaked in 1960 at 11.5 million ha, thereafter declining until less than 40,000 ha were retired in 1971.

Pheasants began a textbook recovery that coincided with the increasing land under contract in the Conservation Reserve portion of the Soil Bank. That response, for example, was evident in South Dakota. According to Dahlgren,[28] the value of good habitat to the pheasant population can be seen by comparing the population of the mid-fifties, 4 to 6 million birds, with that at the height of the Soil Bank, 8 to 11 million. In South Dakota, good cover nearly doubled pheasant numbers and similar responses were experienced throughout the pheasant range.

The reprieve was short lived. Practically to the year that Soil Bank lands began to decline as contracts expired, pheasants began to experience a reduction in numbers in South Dakota[29] and other Midwest states.[26] The intensity of agriculture had continued to increase on those fields in production during the Soil Bank era. When the last Soil Bank contracts expired (1970), pheasants in South Dakota, for example, were below pre-Soil Bank levels.

The irony of the situation was that federal land retirement programs had not ceased but had in fact increased.[20] What had changed was the approach. During the second highest enrollment (11.4 million ha) in the Soil Bank in 1961, the newly authorized Feed Grain Program retired an additional 10.1 million ha. The next year (1962) Soil Bank acreage declined to 9 million ha while 15.6 million ha were out of production under the Feed Grain Program and the new Wheat Program. Although retired cropland more than doubled, the decline of pheasants continued. In 1970, at the demise of the Soil Bank, 21.2 million wheat and feed grain ha were idled and pheasants were at an all-time low.

Lands in the Wheat and Feed Grain Programs were contracted on an annual basis. There were no requirements for seeding a cover crop as in the Soil Bank. The regulation requirement for "devoted to a conserving use" was bureaucratic jargon for fallow if the landowner wished, and most did. Faced with complete uncertainty relative to next year's program, if any, the farmer opted to maintain retired cropland in a condition that permitted planting the following year.

Numerous surveys documented the lack of cover on lands idled under annual contracts. According to Harmon and Nelson,[20] the results of a 13-state survey of wheat and feed grain fields retired in 1972 indicated that 57 percent lacked cover. For the remaining 43 percent they stated that about half had cover crops of grasses and/or legumes that had been established the previous year, and about half was in new seedings often small grains. They further stated new seedings commonly were sown in late May or early June after the cash crops were planted. Cover elimination by mowing and plowing began in late June and early July on both new and established seedings and over 25 percent was destroyed by July 15th. Similar findings—low value to farm wildlife relative to potential—were obtained in the same states on three subsequent surveys.[27] In fact, Berner[27] concluded that in Minnesota for the period 1958-83 the number of pheasant chicks per 100 km was greater during years without land retirement programs administered under annual contracts.

With the information in hand on the value of, and the potential for, retired land to wildlife, the Midwest state fish and wildlife agencies and private organizations launched an effort to realign the upcoming 1973 farm bill. They were later joined by a number of Southeastern states. Their actions resulted in the 1973 Agricultural and Consumer Protection Act containing provisions potentially beneficial to pheasants. Among them, the most important was the authority for USDA to conduct a "multi-year" set-aside program that required protective cover. Then, almost simultaneously, the devalued U.S. dollar increased European buying power for American farm products, the Middle East oil embargo was imposed and crops failed in several countries. These events stimulated demand for U.S. exports and aided and abetted an Administration determined to get the government out of agriculture. Instead of "multi-year" land retirement, then-Secretary of Agriculture Butz instituted his infamous "fence row to-fence row concept."

The net result was 22.6 million ha of wheat and feed grain land out of production with no cover requirement in 1972, 6.7 million ha in 1973 and none in 1974. It was not until 1978 that USDA again took wheat and feed grains out of production (7.2 million ha), still under annual contracts.

Habitat reductions continued. In two study areas in Indiana, 50 percent of the good nesting cover and 71 percent of the prime winter cover were lost between 1971 and 1978.[32] For 14 pheasant states, Farris and Cole[32] stated, in general, the indicators of farmland wildlife habitat change are increased urbanization of agricultural land; increased farm size; increased total acres in crops; significantly greater acres devoted to row crops; significantly decreased acres devoted to small grains, hay (wild and tame), and pasture; larger fields; and lost edge, fence rows, old farmsteads, wetlands, and idle fields.

As USDA ignored long-range solutions for adjustments in production, and as farmers responded to what they were told was the golden age of foreign marketing, pheasants numbers continued to decline. According to Farris and Cole,[32] declines ranged from 34 percent in Illinois (1957-77) to 96 percent in Ohio (1960-79). Other notable declines were: Colorado—70 percent, Indiana—91 percent, North Dakota—85 percent, Minnesota—86 percent and South Dakota—78 percent during comparable time periods.

With road ditch-to-road ditch cropping and only token land out of production—7.2 million ha, 5.2 million ha and 3.6 million ha in 1978, 1979 and 1982, respectively—surpluses mounted. The demise of the golden age of agriculture, cut adrift by USDA to operate in the free market, ushered in the now infamous Payment-in-Kind program. This 32.2 million ha land retirement program cost the taxpayer $12 billion.[31] In another survey, there was 62 percent cover on PIK acres than on retired acres in 1978, 83 percent less than in 1973 and 75 percent less than in 1972.

Congress is presently engaged in debating a new farm bill. To date, a 10-year, multi-million ha conservation reserve with a cover crop has survived. It seems certain this important feature will be contained in the final bill. If so, some semblance of the "ole days" of pheasant abundance may be enjoyed again, at least for awhile.

Without this long-term land retirement program, there is little reason to believe the pheasant will do more than persist in reduced numbers. However, with a 10-year conservation reserve in place, a multitude of benefits would be generated. In addition to regulating surpluses to increase farm commodity prices, pheasants would reach more acceptable population levels. At those levels, rural communities would experience additional economic activity. The general public would benefit, not only from more pheasants, but from soil erosion control and higer water quality.

USDA's single-minded insistence on annual land retirement programs has failed to capture these benefits. Agriculture needs a program with stability. The public needs the benefits that long-term land retirement can produce. The presence of abundant pheasant populations and other forms of game and non game wildlife would be an indication that these values are in fact being achieved.

REFERENCES CITED

1. McConnell, C.A., and K.W. Harmon. 1976. Agricultural effects on wildlife in America: a brief history. Proc. Soil Conserv. Soc. of Amer. 31:35-44.
2. Borland, H. 1975. The history of wildlife in America. Natl. Wildl. Fed., Wash., D.C. 197 pp.
3. Trefethen, J.B. 1975. An American crusade for wildlife. Winchester Press, New York, N.Y. 409 pp.
4. Rasmussen, W.D. 1975. A documentary history of American agriculture. Random House, New York, N.Y.
5. Billington, R.A. 1967. Westward expansion. The MacMillan Co., New York, N.Y. 933 pp.
6. Wooten, H.H., and L.A. Jones. 1955. The history of our drainage enterprises. Pages 478-491 *in* Water. The 1955 Yearbook of Agric. U.S. Dep. of Agric., Wash., D.C. 751 pp.
7. Schlebecker, J.T. 1975. Whereby we thrive. Iowa State Univ. Press, Ames. 342 pp.
8. Colorado Game, Fish and Parks. n.d. A look back: a 75 year history of the Colorado Game, Fish and Parks Division. Denver. 64 pp.
9. Studholm, A.T., and D. Benson. 1956. The pheasant in the northeastern states. Pages 388-430 *in* D.L. Allen, ed. Pheasants in North America.

Stackpole Co., Harrisburg, Pa. total pages 490 pp.
10. Einarsen, A.S. 1945. The pheasant in the Pacific Northwest. Pages 254-274 *in* W. L. MacAtee, ed. The ring-necked pheasant and its management in North America. Stackpole Co., Harrisburg, Pa. total pages 330 pp.
11. Johnson, M.D. 1964. Feathers from the prairie. N.D. Game and Fish Dep., Bismarck. 240 pp.
12. Minnesota Department of Conservation. 1967. The rugged ringneck of Minnesota. Minn. Dep. Conser., Div. of Game and Fish. St. Paul.
13. Kimball, J.W., E.L. Kozicky, and B.A. Nelson. 1956. Pheasants of the plains and prairies. Pages 204-263 *in* D.L. Allen, ed. Pheasants in North America. Stackpole Co., Harrisburg, Pa. 490 ppg.
14. McCabe, R.A., R.A. MacMullan, and E.H. Dustman. 1956. Ringneck pheasants in the Great Lakes Region. Pages 264-356*in* D.L. Allen, ed. Pheasants in North America. Stackpole, Co., Harrisburg, Pa. 490 pp.
15. Lauckhart, J.B., and J.W. McKean. 1956. Chinese pheasants in the northwest. Pages 43-89 *in* D.L. Allen, ed. Pheasants in North America. Stackpole Co., Harrisburg, Pa.
16. Matson, A.J. 1964. An analysis of economic factors and institutions affecting the productivity of South Dakota land and water resources for upland game birds and migratory waterfowl. Agric. Econ. Pamphlet 123. South Dakota State Univ., Brookings. 249 pp.
17. Barton, G.T. 1958. How our production has expanded. Pages 460-465 *in* Land. The 1958 Yearbook of Agric. U.S. Dep. of Agric., Wash., D.C.
18. Leite, E.A. 1971. Pheasant densities and land management practices in Ohio. Pages 19-26 *in* Status of the ring-necked pheasant in Ohio: a symposium. Ohio Game Monogr. Ohio Div. of Wildl., Columbus.
19. Baxter, W.L., and C.W. Wolfe. 1973. Life history and ecology of the ring-necked pheasant in Nebraska. Neb. Game and Parks Comm., Lincoln. 58 pp.
20. Harmon, K.W., and M.M. Nelson. 1973. Wildlife and soil considerations in land retirement programs. Wildl. Soc. Bull. 1:28-38.
21. Wildlife Management Institute. 1949. Federal aid in wildlife restoration, an annual report of the Pittman-Robertson program for the fiscal year ending June 30, 1949. Wash., D.C. 48 pp.
22. Bushong, C. 1961. Evaluation of farm-game habitat restoration efforts in Indiana. Ind. Dep. Conserv., Indianapolis. 104 pp.
23. U.S. Department of Agriculture. 1971. Agricultural Conservation Program: 35 year summary—1936 to 1970. Wash. D.C. 250 pp.
24. Wagner, F.H., C.D. Besadny, and C. Kabat. 1965. Population ecology and management of Wisconsin pheasants. Wisc. Conser. Dep. Tech. Bull. No. 34. 168 pp.
25. Shepherd, S. 1964. Farm policy: new directions. Iowa State Univ. Press, Ames. 292 pp.
26. Edwards, W.R. 1984. Early ACP, pheasants, boom and bust!—A historic

perspective with rationale. Proc. of Perdix III. (In press).
27. Berner, A.H. 1984. Federal land retirement program: A land management albatross. Trans. North Am. Wildl. and Nat. Resour. Conf. 49:118-130.
28. Dahlgren, R. 1967. The pheasant decline. S.D. Dep. Game, Fish and Parks, Pierre. 44 pp.
29. Erickson, R.E., and J.E. Wiebe. 1973. Pheasants, economics and land retirement programs in South Dakota. Wildl. Soc. Bull. 1:22-27.
30. Farris, A. L., and S. H. Cole. 1981. Strategies and goals for wildlife habitat restoration on agricultural lands. Trans. North Am. Wildl. and Nat. Resour. Conf. 46:130-136.
31. Cook, K. 1983. Soil Conservation: PIK in a poke. J. Soil and Water Conserv. 38:475-476.

Endangered and Threatened Species Programs in Pennsylvania and other States: Causes, Issues and Management. Edited by S. K. Majumdar, F. J. Brenner and A. F. Rhoads. © 1986, The Pennsylvania Academy of Science.

Chapter Twenty-Seven

A Summary of the Pennsylvania Natural Diversity Inventory and Other Northeast Natural Heritage Programs

Thomas L. Smith[1], Lawrence L. Master[2], Jan Cassin[3] and D. Daniel Boone[4]

[1]Coordinator/Plant Ecologist
Pennsylvania Natural Diversity Inventory-East
P.O. Box 1467
Harrisburg, Pennsylvania 17120

[2]Director/Zoologist and [3]Eastern Regional Information Manager
Eastern Heritage Task Force
The Nature Conservancy
294 Washington Street
Boston, Massachusetts 02108

[4]Coordinator, Maryland Natural Heritage Program
Maryland Department of Natural Resources
Tawes State Office Building, C-3
Annapolis, Maryland 21401

The Pennsylvania Natural Diversity Inventory is a comprehensive, computer-assisted, statewide ecological inventory designed by the Department of Environmental Resources-Bureau of Forestry, The Nature Conservancy, and the Western Pennsylvania Conservancy. The Pennsylvania program employs standardized methods and identical terminology as used by Natural Heritage Programs operating in 42 states, 3 interstate regions, 1 federal agency, and 5 Latin American countries. This list includes all northeastern states except Delaware and Virginia, i.e., Maryland, West Virginia, Ohio, New York, New

Jersey, Rhode Island, Connecticut, Massachusetts, New Hampshire, Vermont, and Maine (see appendix for names and addresses). These inventories are ongoing, continuously updated, systematic, scientific surveys to collect and store, in a centralized data management system, site specific information on rare, native plants, animals, and exemplary natural communities in a state. This information is readily available for making sound decisions on land use planning and protection. The goals, methods, and uses of the Heritage Programs will be discussed in general, including their role in the development of The Nature Conservancy's national databases, and the Pennsylvania Natural Diversity Inventory in particular.

ORIGIN OF NATURAL DIVERSITY INVENTORY (HERITAGE) PROGRAMS

The Nature Conservancy, a private, nonprofit conservation organization founded in 1951, has as its central goal the preservation of natural diversity. A difficult task facing the Conservancy has always been how to identify lands which, through their preservation, will do the most towards accomplishing this goal.

Generally, there are three ways in which conservation groups have chosen the lands to which they direct their preservation efforts. These are:

1. Preserve all the unspoiled lands, although this often means preserving all the mountaintops and nothing in the valleys;

2. Respond to immediate threats of destruction of well-known and not so well-known areas, thereby preserving a variety of lands, some significant and some not so significant; and

3. Accept miscellaneous gifts of land from people who want to see their favorite places preserved, and/or are taking a tax break for it.

The Nature Conservancy has used all the above methods, but in recent years has adopted a fourth approach more in keeping with its goals; this is to concentrate time and money on locating and preserving the biologically most critical and significant portion of the landscape, i.e., that portion which, when taken together, contains the maximum amount of diversity of natural habitats, species, processes, and relationships. Since such areas can only be identified through the comprehensive accumulation, organization, and analysis of ecological information, the Conservancy, with state government assistance in most cases, designed and implemented the State Natural Heritage Programs to initiate and carry out this process throughout the country.

In addition, a vital function of state governments is the protection of natural resources. This function includes land preservation programs such as dedicated natural areas, as well as developmental and environmental reviews. As state governments have been finding for the past ten years, natural heritage programs provide reliable, up-to-date, site specific data on the ecological features within the state and make its retrieval utilitarian and cost effective, thus expediting the environmental review process.

PROGRAM METHODOLOGY

The Elements of Natural Diversity

The first task of a program is to decide which "elements of natural diversity" need to be inventoried. An *element* is a "type" of entity, and an *element occurrence* (EO) is an individual "example" of such an element in the real landscape. For instance, an acidic rocky summit community is an *element*, but an individual acidic rocky summit community in Lackawanna County, Pennsylvania (such as, an exposed summit of shale bedrock dominated by grasses and ericaceous shrubs), is an *element occurrence*. The green salamander (*Aneides aeneus*) is an *element*, but an actual green salamander breeding site is an *element occurrence*. Plants, animals, and natural communities generally constitute the elements of natural diversity.

A program proceeds by developing lists of elements, assigning a rank to each element that describes how secure (rare) it is, and then inventories all available literature, collections, and consults experts for location and natural history data on those elements that are in danger of disappearing from the state. This information is then processed into the data management system, and the program conducts field surveys to verify the element's existence at a site.

It is impossible and unnecessary to inventory for every species in the state; thus we use an approach referred to as a coarse filter and a fine filter for capturing natural diversity through our list of elements. The coarse filter consists of a list of natural communities; we assume that by protecting exemplary occurrences of each persistent natural community in the state (such as freshwater intertidal marsh, Appalachian oak-hickory forest, calcareous seepage swamp, eastern serpentine barren, high-gradient clearwater stream, etc.) at least 85 percent of the species native to the state will be preserved, as they are common components of these communities. The identification and protection of examples of common as well as uncommon natural communities in the state, including such rare habitats as serpentine barren or pitch pine/scrub oak barren, also assures protection of the species (e.g., most invertebrates) and interactions of which we have little knowledge. As Frank Egler observed, "Ecosystems are not only more complex than we think, they are more complex than we can think". Heritage ecologists are currently working throughout the country to devise a common classification system to assure identification and protection of all natural community types in the region.

However, since some rare species are not found in examples of habitats that seem ideal for them (which may be a quite common community type), or are

(7/20/83) **STATE ELEMENT RANKING FORM** Date: 2/15/85

Element Code: PDRAN0P022   Element Name: *Trollius laxus* ssp *laxus*
Common Name: Spreading Globe Flower   State/Program: PA
Class: Plant, Dicot, Ranunculaceae   Prepared by: Tom Smith

HABITAT OR COMMUNITY DESCRIPTION: Wetlands influenced by cold highly alkaline groundwater seepage such as wet meadows, sloping calcareous fens, and calcareous seepage swamps.

EO SPECIFICATIONS: Individual plant most often a contiguous population

EXEMPLARY EO IN STATE: Northampton Co. PA Element Occurrence No. 501

TAXONOMIC DISTINCTNESS: One north American species. Two subspecies which are not considered taxonomically distinct, ssp *albiflorus* in Rocky Mountains and ssp *laxus* in NE.

PERMANENCE OF EOs: Long-lived perennial, appears stable with unchanging habitat.

STATE STATUS: Pennsylvania Endangered
Comments: will officially be listed in PA in 1985/86 with adoption of regulation for wild plant conservation legislation.

DEGREE OF LEGAL PROTECTION: will be unlawful to in any way disturb plant, other than by the landowner, fine is $100

STATE RANKING CRITERIA

Estimated State EOs: A **B** C D
Comments: extant sites; Lawrence Co.—1; Northampton Co.—4; Monroe Co.—1.

Estimated State Abundance: A **B** C D
Comments: about 3400 individuals but 2000 in one population so other pop. much smaller

State Range: **A** B C D
Comments: Lawrence, Monroe, Northampton Counties only extant sites.

Estimated Adequately Protected EOs in State: U **A** B C D
Comments: no protected EO's in state, all on private land

Relative Threat of Destruction: **A** B C D
Comments: only 6 sites, all in wetland habitat subject to draining and clearing and high threat from quarrying in PA

Ecological Fragility: A B **C** D
Comments: plants produce abundant fertile seeds, and seedlings reported. Occurs from open wet meadows to shaded seepage swamps.

Other Ranking Criteria: A conspicuous and attractive wildflower subject to collection by diggers also sometimes cultivated. The wildflower club is reprod. & selling individuals.

STATE ELEMENT PRIORITY RANK:S1 S2 S3 S4 S5 SA SE SH SU SX
Summarize reasons: only six extant EO's and 2000 of states. 3400 individuals area one site, high threat from habitat destruction by draining and clearing an quarrying.

NUMBER OF PROTECTED EOs NEEDED IN STATE (include reasons): three, Lawrence Co. pop. in WPA and two eastern populations to plants and habitat.

INVENTORY/RESEARCH NEEDS: research on taxonomic distinctness of *T. laxus* ssp. *laxus* needed and monitoring of populations to determine effect of shading.

OTHER PROTECTION/STEWARDSHIP NEEDS: none known

FIGURE 1: State Element Ranking Form
*See Heritage Operations Manual for field specifications and explanations of codes.

denizens of very rare habitat types, we also compile lists of plant and animal species of special concern (rare, threatened, endangered, extirpated). The identification and protection of the habitats in which the species occur constitute our fine filter approach.

In all states these lists are constructed with the assistance of all the available professional and amateur expertise. Many states have a committee that oversees the development of the lists and meets annually to make additions and deletions based on the past year's fieldwork. Pennsylvania's special concern lists, which are typical for the region, contain 406 plant species, 169 vertebrates, 144 invertebrates, and 90 natural communities.

Phase II — Element Priority Ranking

Once the element lists have been developed, and/or adopted from existing state lists, the program staff prioritizes or "ranks" the elements for research and protection efforts. The ranking process at the state level uses criteria that include the elements rarity in the state, range, number of protected examples, ecological fragility, and possibility of destruction (Fig. 1). Since most species that are rare in one state are common in another part of their range, it is also necessary to also determine the element's global rank. This process involves obtaining information about the element's status in all areas where it occurs.

In order to assure comparability of data from diverse sources, the regional heritage task force, responsible for compiling information from the state programs, generally assists in determining global element ranks. A global element ranking form (Fig. 2) is completed for high priority elements, with the state or regional office most familiar with this element completing the first draft. Thus, each state is able to give first priority to the rarest elements. Once lists and priorities have been established, we begin collecting and processing information that allows us to map and store data on each and every known site in the state where these elements occur.

Data Management System

The data management system consists of a refined system of manual and computerized files that are augmented by computerized databases maintained at the regional and national levels. The central data unit in the Natural Diversity Inventory, and Heritage Programs around the country, is the "element occurrence." As previously discussed, this is the occurrence, at a specific locality, of a habitat that supports or otherwise contributes to the survival of a listed element. The population of the rare butterfly, the regal fritillary, *Speyeria idalia*, which inhabits an open, grassy, limestone barren in Adams County is an element occurrence. This site specific data has been gathered from sources such as herbarium sheets and specimens found in the major state and regional collections, scientific publications, personal communications, and field surveys.

Field surveys occupy much of the staff's time during the warmer months of

(6/2/83) **GLOBAL ELEMENT RANKING FORM**
State: ERO
Element Name: *Trollius laxus* ssp. *laxus* — Date: 3/14/84
Common Name: Spreading Globe Flower — Prepared by: Peggy Bliss
Class: Plant, Dicot, Ranunculaceae — Element Code: PDRAN0P022

EO SPECIFICATIONS: Individual plant or more often a contiguous population.

HABITAT OR COMMUNITY DESCRIPTION: Wetlands influenced by cold, highly alkaline groundwater seepage such as wet meadows, sloping fens, and seepage swamps.

SITE OF EXEMPLARY EO: Litchfield Co. CT, Occ. No. 004

TAXONOMIC DISTINCTNESS: see back—One North American species. Two subspecies not taxonomically distinct. ssp. *albiflorus* in Rocky Mountains ssp. *laxus* in northeast.

PERMANENCE OF EO's: Long-lived perennial, appears stable with unchanging habitat conditions.

FEDERAL STATUS: LE LT PE PT C1 **C2** C AC N
Comments: *T. laxus* ssp. *laxus* is a C2 federal candidate (11-11-83).

DEGREE OF LEGAL PROTECTION: CT: state list, no protection. NY: protected by Native Plant list which prohibits picking without landowner's permission. NJ: state list, no protection. PA: proposed plant list, no protection. OH: Div. of Nat. Areas and Preserves lists it as state endangered, no prot.

GLOBAL RANKING CONSIDERATIONS:

Estimated Total EO's: A B **C** D

Comments: About 37 populations. Populations are often clustered, and therefore, difficult to count. Searching would probably turn up others, but not enough to change rank.

Estimated Total Abundance: A B **C** D
Comments: Often population counts are estimated as individuals are too numerous.

Total Range: A1 A2 **B** C D
Comments: see back CT, NY, PA, NJ, Ohio

Estimated adequately protected EO's: U A B **C** D
Comments: 5 protected EO's; one in Ohio, one in Connecticut, three in N.Y.

Relative Threat of Destruction: A **B** C D
Comments: Wetlands subject to drainage, development; plants sensitive to change in water quality degradation or pH change. Threats from grazing, logging, and overcollecting at some sites.

Ecological Fragility: A B **C** D
Comments: Plants produce abundant, fertile seed, and seedlings reported.

Other Ranking Considerations: A conspicuous and attractive wildflower, sometimes cultivated in moist places either from seed or transplants.

GLOBAL ELEMENT PRIORITY RANK: G1 G2 G3 **G4T3Q** G5 GA GE GH GU GX
Summarize reasons: The species is secure in western U.S. About 37 populations of *T. laxus* ssp. *laxus* known, these range from 5—3000 individuals.

NUMBER OF PROTECTED EO'S NEEDED (include reasons): At least 6 additional protected EO's needed; one in CT (protected site only has 20 individuals), 2 in PA (see back)

INVENTORY/RESEARCH NEEDS: Research on the taxonomic distinctness of *T. laxus* ssp. *laxus* is needed. Documentation of population trends needed to determine effect of shading on entire population.

OTHER PROTECTION/STEWARDSHIP NEEDS: none known

FIGURE 2: Global Element Ranking Form.

ELEMENT OCCURRENCE RECORD

EO-CODE: [PDRAN0P022.501]   EL-CODE: [PDRAN0P022]
NAME:
[TROLLIUS LAXUS SSP LAXUS   ]
COMMON-NAME:
[SPREADING GLOBE FLOWER   ]
MARG-NUM: [501] IDENT: [Y] EO-RANK: [B]
EO-RANK-COMM: [500 IND IN POPULATION. QUAL-COND-VIAB-DEF ALL GOOD.]
FIELD-EVAL-DATE: [1985-04-28] LAST-OBS: (1985-04-28) FIRST-OBS: [1910]
GLOBAL-EL-RANK: [G4T2] STATE-EL-RANK: [S1] STATE: [PA]
ALL-COUNTY-CODES: [PA089   ] COUNTY-CODE: [PA089]
ALL-COUNTY-NAMES: [MONR   ]
ALL-QUAD-CODES: [4007584   ] QUAD-CODE: [4007584]
ALL-QUAD-NAMES: [BRODHEADSVILLE] [   ]
                [   ] [   ] PRECISION: [SC]
LAT: [405500] LONG: [0752730] S: [405455] N: [405510] E: [0752725]
W: [0752734] PHYS-PROV: [VA] WATERSHED: [02040104]
DIRECTIONS: [LAKE MINEOLA. 1.5 MI NE OF BRODHEADSVILLE ON PA 715. EO]
            [IS LOCATED BELOW OUTLET OF LAKE ON SOUTH FACING   ]
            [SEEPAGE SLOPE.   ]
GEN-DESC: [30% SOUTH FACING SEEPAGE SLOPE, DOMINATED BY ACER   ]
          [RUBRUM-FRAXINUS NIGRA/LINDERA BENZOIN/SYMPLOCARPUS   ]
          [FOETIDUS. SWAMP SURROUNDED BY FIELDS TO N, E, W AND   ]
          [STREAM & WOODS TO SOUTH.   ]
ELEV: [740] SIZE: [5]
EO-DATA: [500 IND SEEN ON 4/28/85 IN FLO. PLANTS OF ALL SIZES PRESENT]
         [REPRODUCING VERY WELL. PLANTS ARE GROWING IN PARTIAL   ]
         [SHADE AND SOIL IS SATURATED BUT NOT INUNDATED GRAVELLY   ]
         [LOAM.   ]
COMMENTS: [   ]
          [   ]
MA-CODE1: [------------] CONTAINED : [--] MA-CODE2: [   ]
CONTAINED2: [ ] MA-CODE3: [   ] CONTAINED3: [ ] ADDL-MAS: [   ]
MORE-LAND: [   ] MORE-PROT: [ ] MORE-MGMT: [ ] SITE-CODE: [   ]
OWNER: [JOHN BROWN   ]
OWNER-COMM: 54 EAST STREET, BRODHEADSVILLE, PA 17889
PROT-COMM: [OWNER NOTIFIED AND SEEMS INTERESTED IN PROTECTION   ]
MANAGE-COMM: [SITE STABLE & NO MANAGEMENT NEEDED AT PRESENT   ]
BEST-SOURCE: [SMITH, T.L. AND A. WILKINSON. 1985. FIELD SURVEY TO]
             [LAKE MINEOLA OF APRIL 28.   ]
ALL-SOURCE-CODES: [F85SMI34   S10LONAN   ]
                  [   ]
BEST-SOURCE-CODE: [F85SMI34] DATA-SENS: [Y] BOUNDARIES: [Y] PHOTOS: [Y]
QUAL-SURV: [Y] QUAN-SURV: [Y] OWNER-INFO: [Y] TRANSCRIBER: [85-05-15 TLS]
EA-REV: [N] CD-REV: [Y] MAPPER: [85-05-15 TLS] QC: [Y] UPDATE: [85-05-20]
UPDATE-INIT: [AMW] HAB-CODE: [PAB] FED-STATUS: [C2] STATE-STATUS: [PE]
MANUAL-FILE-LOC: [E] MA-NAME: [NONE   ]
MUNICIPAL-CODES: [45909   ]
MUNICIPAL-NAMES: [JACKSON TWP] [   ] [   ] [   ]
WATERSHED-CODES: [04778 04750 00002   ]
WATERSHED-NAMES: [MCMICHAEL CREEK   ] [BRODHEAD CREEK   ]
                 [DELAWARE RIVER   ] [   ]
ASSOC-COMMUN: [CAAFHAA----   ]
FOR-DIST: [19   ]

FIGURE 3: Element Occurence Record.

the year, as staff attempt to verify historical occurrences and locate new occurrences for elements of concern, always concentrating their efforts on the rarest elements, those most in need of conservation attention. Field investigations by Pennsylvania Natural Diversity Inventory staff and contract workers has resulted in the verification of over 600 element occurrences. In some cases, field work has turned up enough new sites that a plant previously thought to be rare is actually fairly common. The opposite has also been found, an element with numerous historic locations being found at very few sites due to habitat destruction, etc.

An Element Occurrence Record Form is filled out and computerized for every element occurrence. This form (Fig. 3) includes, in addition to the scientific and common name of the element, such key information as directions to and coordinates of the element's location as precisely as can be determined, the date(s) of observation(s) or collection(s), the identity of the source(s) supplying that record, a site description, notes on the size, health, and quality of the population, name of the landowner, and whether the site is protected and being managed for preservation of the element. General locators such as township, county, physiographic province, and watershed are also included. This system allows data to be retrieved by any one of these categories. For example, data can be retrieved on the known occurrences of the spreading globe flower (*Trollius laxus*) in the state, or on all the element occurrences found in Philadelphia County. For environmental review purposes, all element occurrences which may be affected by acid mine drainage from a proposed mining operation can be rapidly supplied. As may be obvious, any permutation and combination of information on these records is also available.

TABLE 1

Northeastern Heritage Programs

State	Month/Year Program Initiated	# Staff	Number of Mapped/Computerized Occurrences (1985 figures)				# Mapped Managed Areas
			Animals	Plants	Nat. Com.	Total	
PA	5/81	6	1255	2715	220	4190	220
MD	11/79	4	600	3800	150	4550	260
NJ	5/84	4	164	757	6	327	195
NY	10/84	5	97	598	20	715	7
OH	7/76	9	1604	7037	306	8947	ca. 400
WV	3/75	4	696	1615	983	3294	166
CT	8/83	5	602	1018	57	1677	ca. 500
ME	12/83	2	177	847	120	1144	43
MA	11/78	5	895	2087	48	3030	ca. 1500
NH	1/84	2	252	1602	140	1994	30
RI	11/78	3	351	501	31	883	176
VT	4/84	2	170	958	200	1328	360

SOURCE ABSTRACT
SA-D OF SA
SOURCE-CODE: [A79SCH51]
CITATION: [SCHUYLER, A.E. 1971. CHECK LIST OF THE AQUATIC VASCULAR]
      [PLANTS OF LAKE LACAWAC, PENNSYLVANIA. BARTONIA 46:69-70.]
      [   ]
                              [   ]
COUNTY-NAME: [   ] COUNTY-COD: [   ]
SHELF-NOTE: [LIBRARY-REPRINT FILE   ]
GEO-COVERAGE: [WAYNE CO.   ] S: [   ]
N: [   ] E: [   ]
W: [   ] SCOPE: [4   ]
ABSTRACT: [30 AQUATIC SPECIES LISTED INCLUDING ELEOCHARIS ROBBINSII]
      [AND NYMPHOIDES CORDATA.   ]
      [   ]
      [   ]
NAT-COMMUNITIES: [ ] TER-COMMUNITIES: [ ]
AQ-COMMUNITIES: [ ] FLORA: [Y]
AQ-FLORA: [Y] TER-FLORA: [ ]
NONVASC-PLANTS: [ ] VASC-PLANTS: [Y]
MICRO-ORG: [ ] FAUNA: [ ]
AQ-FAUNA [ ] TER-FAUNA: [ ]
MOLLUSCS: [ ] INSECTS: [ ]
CRUSTACEANS: [ ] OTHER-ARTHRO: [ ]
OTHER-INVERT: [ ] FISHES: [ ]
AMPHIBIANS: [ ] REPTILES: [ ]
BIRDS: [ ] MAMMALS: [ ]
OTHER: [ ] MANAGED-AREAS: [ ]
PHYSIO-TOPO: [ ] HYDRO: [ ]
GEOLOGY: [ ] SOILS: [ ]
CLIMATE: [ ] MGMT-TECHNIQUES: [ ]
ECOLOGY: [ ] ECOSYS-FUNCTION: [ ]
BIOLOGY: [ ] PHYSICAL-SCIENCE: [ ]
PROTECT-TOOLS: [ ] PROTECT-ORG: [ ]
INVENTORIES: [ ] NAT-DIVERSITY: [ ]
RESEARCH-TECH: [ ] MGMT-PLANS: [ ]
IMPACT-STUDIES: [ ]
COMMENTS: [   ]
      [   ]
U-RATING: [1]
DIGESTION-NOTES: [EO'S PROCESSED THROUGH RECENT FIELD WORK.   ]
      [   ]
INITIALS: [TLS] DATE: [84-04-30]

FIGURE 4: Source Abstract.

A summary of the number of mapped/computerized occurrence records (mid-1985 totals) for each northeastern state is provided in Table 1.

In addition to this computerized file, each state also maintains a complete set of the 7.5-minute U.S. Geological Survey topographic quadrangle maps. On these maps each element occurrence is marked as precisely as possible with a numbered, color-coded dot, and whenever possible boundaries of the suitable habitat for the element at that location are also marked. Each location is referenced in the margin with the element's name, occurrence number, and, often,

MANAGED AREA ABSTRACT

```
      MA-D OF MA
MA-CODE: [PAPNCNAWOOD1]
MA-NAME: [WOODBURNE FOREST AND WILDLIFE SANCTUARY      ]
ESTAB-DATE: [1956-4-10  ] ALL-COUNTY-CODES: [PA115          ]
COUNTY-CODE: [PA115] QUAD-CODE: [4107578] LAT: [414540] LONG: [0755330]
S: [414500] N: [414610] E: [0755235] W: [0755425] TOWN-RANGE: [           ]
SECTION: [  ] MERIDIAN: [  ] TRS-COMM: [DIAMOCK TWP—58910] CONTIG: [Y ]
DESCRIPTION: [200 AC. VIRGIN HEML. &N. HARDWD. ON PRIME SITE: SMALL BOG]
             [& AR T. POND SUPP. FLOATING MAT COMM. WHCH SUPP. EXCEL.]
             [BOG FLORA        ]
SIZE: [     60] PROT-STATUS: [1  ]
MANAGER: [STONE, TNC              ]
ADDRESS: [WOODBURNE FOREST & WILDLIFE SANCTUARY                    ]
         [BOX 307, RD #1, MONTROSE, PA 18801 (717)278-3384         ]
BOUNDARIES: [Y ]
MGMT-COMM: [SELF GUIDED NATURE TRAIL & RESIDENT NATURALIST          ]
           [                                                       ]
MAJOR-MA: [PAPNCNAWOOD1]
COMMENTS: [MONTROSE WEST QUAD                                       ]
          [                                                        ]
UPDATE: [82-11-23]
```

FIGURE 5: Managed Area Abstract.

the year of its last observation. The boundaries for all areas managed by a federal, state, or local agency, or a conservation organization are also placed on these maps and referenced in the margin. For each map there is a corresponding file folder (referred to collectively as the Geographical Manual File) in which is stored all materials pertaining to that particular map.

In addition to these core files, each state program maintains three additional files: an Element File, a Source Abstract File, and a Managed Area File. The Element File is a manual file that contains all the ecological or life history information encountered on that element. For example, the file for the Eastern Serpentine Barren Natural Community would contain articles and references describing the ecological features of this community.

The Source File is a manual and computerized data base of all sources of use to the program. It includes information on articles, books, maps, knowledgeable individuals, and various unpublished materials (field notes, reports, correspondence) that contain element or element occurrence information. A Source Abstract (Fig. 4) is completed and computerized for each source. This abstract contains the citation for the source, subjects content, geographic area covered, and where it is filed (if a document or publication). These abstracts are retrievable by any of the fields listed; thus should someone want to know all the sources on Pennsylvania insects of concern, this information could be quickly supplied.

The Managed Area File is also a computerized and manual data base consisting of one folder for each area managed by a governmental agency, or a private conservation organization. A Managed Area Abstract (Fig. 5) is also completed and computerized for each managed area. The folder for each managed area contains location maps and detailed boundary maps, regulations, species lists, correspondence, etc., for the area.

In summary each inventory program has:

1. A set of 7.5-minute topographic maps on which are plotted the locations of all known habitats supporting rare or endangered species, exemplary natural community types, and managed areas;

2. Computerized files containing back-up information on each one of these plotted locations;

3. The capability to retrieve and reorder this information in any combination the user requires;

4. A complete set of manual files containing detailed field survey information, site maps, etc.;

5. Biological information on listed species and communities;

6. A source file of articles, books, persons, theses, etc. which can supply information on the state's natural history; and

7. A full-time staff of professional biologists whose specialized knowledge continues to grow around the database, thus continuously expanding and improving it.

In addition to the state-maintained databases, the regional and national heritage staff have developed several databases to augment the power and utility of the state programs.

NATIONAL NATURAL HERITAGE DATABASES

Over the past several years the regional and national natural heritage staffs have been developing and maintaining computerized national databases designed to more efficiently manage the information necessary to establish and implement sound conservation goals. These databases rely on information supplied by state heritage programs. In turn, national and regional staff, by managing and disseminating this information, provide the state heritage programs and conservation agencies with a more comprehensive data base than they could generate on their own.

The national databases consist of files on element status, ranking, and management or stewardship. The element tracking databases include information on the global and state-by-state status of elements of conservation concern. There are separate files for vascular plants, non-vascular plants, vertebrates, invertebrates, and natural communities. The global portion of each file includes information which is element specific—a scientific name or community name, author, common name, class and family, a code to identify the element for all information management purposes, federal status, and a global priority rank. A state portion of the files is maintained for each state which lists, or tracks, the element through its Heritage program. In addition, all the state's vertebrates and selected invertebrate groups are included in this file. The state file is linked to the global file through the unique element code. The state file contains the code, state abbreviation, status of the element in the state Heritage classification, estimates of the current number of occurrences, information on whether a state rank form has been done, and the state priority rank. There is also a field to link the global record with any non-standard synonyms that are used for the element name.

These files are maintained and updated continuously by national and regional heritage staffs as new, more accurate information is obtained from heritage programs and other sources. By combining the global and state parts of these files, lists can be generated which summarize the range-wide status of any element, the status of all elements listed by a particular state, or the status of all elements in a particular region or the whole country. These lists are distributed regularly to the states by the regional and national heritage staff.

The element ranking database consists of a computerized version of the global rank form. This information is compiled with the help of state heritage staff and summarizes the reasons for assigning a specific global rank. The standard procedures used to sum up information on total range, total abundance, taxonomic distinctness, occurrence specifications, degree of protection, threats, research, inventory, and protection needs permit accurate overall priority ranks to be assigned efficiently to every element. Thus, the ranks are documented, and the forms can be revised and updated on the computer. An important aspect of this database for heritage programs is the standard definition of what constitutes an element occurrence. Without the use of standard terminology to describe an element occurrence, it would be difficult if not impossible to decide how many actual occurrences of an element exist, how many are adequately protected, and which of the unprotected occurrences are worthy of protection.

The element stewardship files consist of (1) information on the status and needs of elements occurring on Nature Conservancy preserves, as well as (2) abstracts detailing specific management needs of target species and communities that may need active management. The first is a record which tracks specific occurrences, and it includes information about population numbers and trends, monitoring or management programs underway, additional monitoring/management needs, and additional land protection needs at the site. These data help focus land management planning on those species and communities for which the preserve was established. In addition, the stewardship abstract, provides a standard, easily updated format for management needs of a particular species or community. It facilitates communication of management information among heritage programs, Conservancy staff and other land managers concerned with protecting these species and communities. By on-going communication and constant revision of the abstracts as new information comes in, the costs of duplicated efforts can be avoided. Information gaps and future research needs can be identified and all interested persons can be informed of the results as they are incorporated into the abstract.

National databases provide a quantity and scope of information not readily available or practical to maintain on a state-by-state basis. Data on range-wide and state-specific status, protection status and needs, and management needs and strategies for species and communities are available to enhance state decisions on inventory and protection priorities and actions. The ability to share and exchange information among a network of states assures that much crucial work need only be done once and not duplicated by different state agencies and others concerned with the conservation and management of these species and communities. State heritage and protection agency staff have the benefits of a national or global perspective while being able to focus their energy on their in-state work.

USES OF NATURAL DIVERSITY INVENTORY DATA

The Pennsylvania Natural Diversity Inventory (PNDI), like most state heritage programs, plays an integral role in the environmental review process. When a review is requested, it is a simple process to check the appropriate topographic quad map or search the computerized database to see if any element occurrences are located in or near the project area. In Pennsylvania, various permitting agencies within the Department of Environmental Resources (DER) have access to the database via computer terminals in their offices. If an element occurrence is near a proposed project, the PNDI staff can be contacted to obtain specific information as to what element or elements are involved, their precise location and what possible impacts the proposed project may have on the elements involved. For example, the Natural Diversity Inventory, at the request of Pennsylvania Power and Light, reviewed a number of proposed ash disposal sites in the York Haven area. DER uses the Natural Diversity Inventory to review all proposed oil and gas drilling sites for species of special concern. The Natural Diversity Inventory also assists county planning offices with local reviews, as many of these projects never reach the state level. These planning offices have a set of topo maps with element occurrences "flagged" on them so that they can then contact the Natural Diversity Inventory staff to obtain specific information on the elements in a given location.

The Natural Diversity Inventory also assists in setting preservation priorities for public and private conservation organizations throughout the state by identifying which natural communities and species are most endangered, and which areas offer the best opportunities to protect these elements of natural diversity. This identification process involves an analysis of the entire database, summarized in a "natural diversity scorecard," which prioritizes elements in order of their rank, and, for each, lists all known occurrences, the current protection status of the sites, and the level of protection necessary to secure the element occurrences. The scorecard functions as a ledger; it allows us to determine when there is an adequate number of well-protected element occurrences and those for which additional protection is necessary. Determining priority sites thus becomes a clear-cut procedure; these are the sites which contain occurrences of unprotected or underprotected high ranking elements. The various forms of protection which may be selected for these sites include acquisition and preserve status for the most critical sites; others by a verbal agreement of the landowner may be registered as natural areas.

The Pennsylvania Natural Diversity Inventory, like the other Natural Heritage Programs throughout the Northeast, has followed this pattern; the scorecard, a product of the Inventory's now extensive database, supports The Nature Conservancy's land protection efforts in eastern Pennsylvania including its acquisition program and the Eastern Pennsylvania Natural Areas Registry Program. The database and scorecard are also utilized by private and public conservation organizations throughout the state, including the Western Pennsylvania Conservancy and the Berks County Conservancy. With the aid of Natural Diversity Inventory data and staff, the Bucks County Planning Commission recently developed a comprehensive resource plan for the protection of the county's resources. The Bureau of Forestry within DER will utilize the database to help in the selection of Private Plant Sanctuaries, a recently established landowner registry program established through the Wild Resource Conservation Act.

There are now natural diversity scorecards containing information on over 2000 priority sites in 14 northeastern states. In 1984, 83 percent of 112 protection projects completed by the Conservancy in the Northeast were derived from natural diversity scorecards. Registry (voluntary protection) programs in 9 northeastern states rely exclusively on heritage scorecards for their protection agenda.

In addition to environmental review and natural area programs, the natural diversity inventories/heritage programs also aid in coordinating statewide research efforts, and in providing information to the public. For example, the Maryland Natural Heritage Program currently handles over 200 project reviews and information request per month.

Heritage programs have also published their findings in an effort to inform the public about rare species conservation needs. The Maryland Heritage Program recently published a book, *Threatened and Endangered Plants and Animals of Maryland* (Norden A.W., D.C. Forester, and G.H. Fenwick, eds. 1984. Maryland Department of Natural Resources, Maryland Natural Heritage Program, Annapolis, MD. 475p.), that provides lists of rare species and much information about their status and habitat within the state. In 1984, the Ohio Natural Heritage published 367 abstracts on state-listed plant taxa in a book

Ohio Endangered and Threatened Vascular Plants (McCance, R.M. Jr. and J.F. Burns, eds. 1984. Division of Natural Areas and Preserves, Department of Natural Resources, Columbus, Ohio. 635p.)

Federal agencies routinely use information provided by state natural heritage programs to aid in decisions on the status of species and uses of lands under their jurisdiction. The U.S. Fish and Wildlife Service has come to rely upon natural heritage databases for up-to-date information on the status of species thought to be in danger of extinction throughout all or a significant portion of their ranges. The Service has contracted with the Eastern Heritage Task Force in Boston to coordinate range-wide surveys on northeastern species based on data compiled by state natural programs. Information provided by heritage programs is providing decision-makers within the U.S. Forest Service with basis for the nomination and designation of Research Natural Areas and Special Interest Areas.

Through the establishment of the Pennsylvania Natural Diversity Inventory and sister programs throughout the nation, we have come a long way towards assuring the most cost-effective, continuous, systematic collection and management of information on our critically threatened ecological features. And thus, through the proper consideration of this information by federal and state governments, business, science, and private conservation organizations, the protection of our rich natural heritage will be ensured.

Appendix
Northeast Natural Heritage Programs

Eastern Heritage Task Force
The Nature Conservancy
294 Washington St. Room 740
Boston, MA 02108
617/542-1908
   Coordinator/Zoologist: Larry Master
   Ecologist: Tom Rawinski
   Reg. Info. Manager: Jan Cassin
   Zoologist: Dale Schweitzer
   Secretary/Data Handler: Julie Gumley

Connecticut Natural Diversity Database
Natural Resources Center
Dept. of Environmental Protection
State Office Building, Rm. 553
165 Capitol Avenue
Hartford, CT 06106
203/566-3540
   Coordinator/Botanist: Les Mehrhoff
   Biologist Data Manager: Nancy Murray
   Ecologist: Ken Metzler
   Data Handler: Megan Rollins
   Zoologist: Bob Craig

Maine Natural Heritage Program
122 Main Street
Topsham, ME 04086
207/729-5181
   Coordinator: John Albright
   Data Manager: Amy Osterbrock

Maryland Natural Heritage & Environmental Review
Dept. of Natural Resources
C-3, Tawes State Office Bldg.
Annapolis, MD 21401
301/269-3656
   Coordinator/Bot: Dan Boone
   Environmental Spec: Arnold Norden
   Man. Area Spec: Derek Richerson
   Zoologist: Ed Thompson

Massachusetts Heritage Program
Div. of Fisheries & Wildlife
100 Cambridge St.
Boston, MA 02202
617/727-9194
   Coordinator/Ecol: Henry Woolsey
   Botanist: Bruce Sorrie
   Zoologist: Scott Melvin
   Data Mgr/Env. Rev: Joanne Tribble
   Habitat Prot. Spec.: Annie Marlowe

New Hampshire Natural Heritage Program
c/o Society for the Protection of N.H. Forests
54 Portsmouth Street
Concord, NH 03301
603/224-9945
   Coordinator/Bot: Frances Brackley
   Information Manager: Edie Hentcy

New Jersey Natural Heritage Program
Office of Natural Lands Management
109 W. State Street
Trenton, N.J. 08608
609/984-1339
   Coordinator/Ecol: Thomas Breden
   Botanist: David Snyder
   Zoologist: Jim Sciascia
   Data Manager: Jane Saks

New York Natural Heritage Program
Wildlife Resources Center
Delmar, NY 12054-9767
518/439-7635 x250
   Coordinator: Pat Mehlhop
   Ecologist: Carol Reschke
   Botanist: Steve Clements
   Data Manager: Rachel Pleuthner
   L.T. Botanist: Bob Zaremba

Ohio Natural Heritage Program
OH DNR, Div. of Nat. Areas & Pres.
Fountain Square, Bldg. F
Columbus, OH 43224
614/265-6453
   Coordinator: Bob McCance
   Botanist: Allison Cuslick
   Botanist: Jim Burns
   Zoologist: Dan Rice
   Plant Ecologist: Dennis Anderson
   Data Supervisor: Pat Jones
   Data Specialist: Maryann Silagy
   Data Specialist: Lauren McEleney

Pennsylvania Natural Diversity Inventory—East
34 Airport Drive
Middletown, PA 17057
717/783-1712
   Coordinator/Ecologist: Tom Smith
   Zoologist: Anthony Wilkinson
   State Botanist: Kathy Mckenna
PA Bureau of Forestry
Box 1467
Harrisburg, PA 17120
717/783-0388

Pennsylvania Natural Diversity Inventory—West
Western PA Conservancy
316 4th Ave.
Pittsburgh, PA 19107
412/288-2777
  Ecologist: Charles Bier
  Botanist: Paul Wiegman

Rhode Island Heritage Program
Dept. of Environmental Mgmt.
Div. of Planning & Development
22 Hayes St.
Providence, R.I. 02903
401/277-2776
  Coordinator: Rick Enser
  Zoologist: Chris Raithel
  Data Manager: Lisa Hilli

Vermont Natural Heritage Program
Vermont Field Office
138 Main Street
Montpelier, VT 05602
802/229-4425
  Coordinator: Marc DesMeules
  Ecologist: Liz Thompson

West Virginia Wildlife & Natural Heritage
    Database
DNR Operations Center
P.O. Box 67
Elkins, WV 26241
304/636-1767
  Coordinator/Ecologist: Brian McDonald
  Asst. Director: Pete Zurbach
  Botanist: Garrie Rouse
  Data Handler: Sandra Mehringer

Endangered and Threatened Species Programs in Pennsylvania and other States: Causes, Issues and Management. Edited by S. K. Majumdar, F. J. Brenner and A. F. Rhoads. © 1986, The Pennsylvania Academy of Science.

Chapter Twenty-Eight

THE ECOLOGY OF THE CHESAPEAKE BAY: ITS IMPORTANCE TO RARE AND ENDANGERED SPECIES

Christopher P. White
The Mare Nostrum Foundation
93 Main Street, Suite 400
Annapolis, Maryland 21401

A survey of rare and endangered species in the Maryland and Virginia coastal plain and waters reveals certain patterns of distribution: Most rare and declining aquatic species inhabit freshwater tributaries and wetlands, rather than the Chesapeake Bay proper. The ecology of the estuarine system is briefly discussed in light of these patterns to ascertain the vulnerability of species and habitats. Fourteen endangered and threatened animal species are found within the Chesapeake Bay watershed of Maryland and Virginia. Of particular concern are the bald eagle and other rare wetlands-dependent species, many of which are not protected at this time.

INTRODUCTION

The Chesapeake Bay in Maryland and Virginia has been the subject of intensive research regarding the deterioration of water quality and the destruction of wetlands and how these environmental degradations affect commercially valuable species[1]. However, during the course of these research efforts little attention has been paid to the consequences of direct and indirect habitat impairment with regard to local endangered and threatened species. This may be due, in part, to the subdivision of the Chesapeake Bay watershed into various political regions. This volume, covering Pennsylvania and surrounding states, provides the opportunity to inventory rare and threatened species within an ecosystem, rather than within political boundaries.

TABLE 1

Federally listed endangered species in the coastal plain and waters of Maryland and Virginia (excluding marine mammals).

Common Name	Scientific Name	Habitat
INVERTEBRATES		
Hay's spring amphipod	*Stygobromus hayi*	surface spring pool[3]
FISHES		
Shortnose sturgeon	*Acipenser brevirostrum*	rivers, bay & ocean[1]
Maryland darter	*Etheostoma sellare*	clear, warm streams[2]
REPTILES		
Leatherback turtle	*Dermochelys coriacea*	coastal; rarely bay[1]
Hawksbill turtle	*Eretmochelys imbricata*	coastal; rarely bay[1]
Kemp's ridley turtle	*Lepidochelys kempii*	coastal and bay
threatened:		
Loggerhead turtle	*Caretta caretta*	coastal and bay
Green turtle	*Chelonia mydas*	coastal; rarely bay[1]
BIRDS*		
Bald eagle	*Haliaeetus leucocephalus*	bay, marshes & riparian
Peregrine falcon	*Falco peregrinus* ssp.	open country
Red-cockaded woodpecker	*Picoides borealis*	mature pine woods[4]
Bachman's warbler	*Vermivora bachmanii*	hardwood swamps[1,4]
Kirtland's warbler	*Dendroica kirtlandii*	woodlands[1]
MAMMALS		
Delmarva Peninsula fox squirrel	*Sciurus niger cinereus*	mixed forests with open understory; also wet woods and swamps

Source: Federal Register (FR) 45 (99): 33768-33781 (5/20/80) et seq.*

* The Atlantic Coast population of the eastern brown pelican, *Pelecanus occidentalis carolinensis*, was delisted from the federal endangered species list on February 4, 1985 (FR 50 (23): 4938-4945).
[1] transient species only
[2] endemic to Maryland only
[3] endemic to District of Columbia only
[4] Virginia and south only

In the Chesapeake Bay proper and the coastal plain sector of the Chesapeake watershed, 14 animal species are listed by the federal government as either endangered or threatened, excluding whales (Table 1). While the State of Virginia follows the federal list verbatim, the State of Maryland considers 5 other species to be endangered in addition to those under federal protection (Table 2). Moreover, 15 vertebrate and invertebrate species are now candidates for federal listing (Table 3). Of particular importance, with regard to protected species, the Chesapeake Bay region supports two endemic endangered species which rely on wetlands or waterways, another which inhabits wet woods, and the largest bald eagle population in the mid-Atlantic region.[2]

The Chesapeake Bay ecosystem is the nation's largest estuary and incorporates nearly 500,000 acres of surrounding tidal and non-tidal wetlands.[3] An estuary is a semi-enclosed body of water which has a free connection with the open sea and within which sea water is measurably diluted by fresh water from land drainage.[4] As a consequence of this mixture of water regimes, the Chesapeake Bay, its tributaries, wetlands and main stem, are segregated into fresh, brackish and subsaline habitats, each of which has a unique community of animals and plants.[5,6]

The majority of endangered species found in estuarine systems are confined to isolated pockets of freshwater habitat in the upper reaches of freshwater streams. Within freshwater habitats, species diversity is high, isolation is more probable, and rare endemics are more common.[7] On the other hand, in brackish estuarine environments, species diversity is low and the few tolerant species tend to have large populations.[8] Meanwhile, the highly migratory behavior of marine species tends to prevent endemism in the lower, subsaline regions of estuaries.[5]

Fishes provide a good example of these estuarine phenomena. Most of the

TABLE 2
Additional species considered "endangered" by the State in the Coastal Plain of Maryland.*

Common Name	Scientific Name	Habitat
AMPHIBIANS		
Eastern hellbender[1]	*Cryptobranchus a. alleganiensis*	rivers and streams
Eastern tiger salamander[2]	*Ambystoma t. tigrinum*	woods and fields
Eastern narrow-mouthed toad[3]	*Gastrophryne carolinensis*	swamp and stream margins; woods
REPTILES[4]		
Rainbow snake[3]	*Farancia e. erytrogramma*	streams and swamps
BIRDS		
Eskimo curlew[5]	*Numenius borealis*	beaches and tideflats

Source: Maryland Forest, Park and Wildlife Service 1984.

*NOTE: The State of Virginia only recognizes federally protected species (FR 45 (99): 33768-33781) as endangered or threatened within state boundries: see Table 1.[36]

[1]currently *under review* by the USFWS for listing as endangered or threatened (FR 47 (251): 58457; December 30, 1982); though probably extirpated from the Maryland coastal plain; i.e., lower Susquehanna Valley.[37]
[2]northern limit of range; status undetermined in Virginia.[32,38]
[3]northern limit of range; locally common in Virginia coastal plain.[5]
[4]bog turtle, *Clemmys muhlenbergi,* was delisted in 1982.[39]
[5]old records only: collected from Potomac River and Ocean city; no dates.[25]

TABLE 3

Invertebrate and vertebrate species of the Maryland and Virginia Coastal Plain Currently Under Review for Federal Listing as Endangered or Threatened Species.

Candidate Species	Scientific Name	Habitat/Reference
AMPHIPODS		
Tidewater amphipod	*Stygobromus araeus*	groundwater seeps (VA)[40]
Tidewater amphipod	*Stygobromus identatus*	seeps and wells (VA)[40]
INSECTS		
Northern coastal tiger beetle	*Cicindela d. dorsalis*	Bay sand beaches (MD)[41]
Puritan tiger beetle	*Cicindela puritana*	Bay sand beaches (MD)[41]
American burying beetle	*Nicrophorus americanus*	deciduous woods (MD & VA)[41]
Rare skipper	*Problema bulenta*	wet meadows (MD & VA)[42,43]
Regal fritillary	*Speyeria idalia*	wet meadows (MD & VA)[42]
MOLLUSCS		
Dwarf wedge mussel	*Alasmidonta heterodon*	Bay fresh tributaries (MD & VA) (Choptank, Potomac, James, and Rappahannock drainages)[34,44]
AMPHIBIANS		
Eastern hellbender	*Cryptobranchus a. alleganiensis*	rivers and streams (MD coastal plain only; probably extirpated)[32,37]
REPTILES		
Bog turtle	*Clemmys muhlenbergi*	wet meadows and streams (MD coastal plain only)[32,45]
BIRDS		
Piping plover[1]	*Charadrius melodus*	beaches and mudflats (MD & VA)[22,35]
Roseate tern	*Sterna dougallii*	tidal beaches (MD & VA) ((hist. bred: MD (1930s); VA (1927)))[22,35]
MAMMALS		
Dismal Swamp southeastern shrew	*Sorex longirostris fisheri*	swamp thickets, meadows (VA)[7,46]
Dismal Swamp short-tailed shrew	*Blarina brevicauda telmalestes*	swamp thickets, meadows (VA)[7]
Southern bog lemming	*Synaptomys cooperi helaletes*	swamp thickets, meadows (VA)[7,46]

Source: FR 49 (100): 21663-21675, (5/22/84); FR 47 (251): 58455-58460 (12/30/82).
[1] proposed for listing as *threatened*, FR 49 (218): 44712-44715 (11/8/84).

TABLE 4

Other wetland-associated vertebrate species considered "threatened" (T), rare (r), of special concern (SC), or of undetermined status (SU) in the Coastal Plain of Maryland and Virginia.*

Common Name	Scientific Name	Reference
FISHES		
Atlantic sturgeon[1]	*Acipenser oxyrhynchus*	(T);[47] (r)[7] (SC)[48,49]
American shad[1]	*Alosa sapidissima*	(SC)[49]
Striped bass[1]	*Morone saxatilis*	(SC)[49]
Marsh killifish[3,5]	*Fundulus confluentis*	(SC);[47] (r)[5]
Spotfin killifish[3,5]	*Fundulus luciae*	(SC)[48,49] (r)[5]
Mud sunfish[4,5]	*Acantharchus pomotis*	(SC)[48]
Blackbanded sunfish[4,5]	*Enneacanthus chaetodon*	(SC)[47,48] (r)[5,7]
Glassy darter[6]	*Etheostoma vitreum*	(T)[47,48]
Northern logperch[6]	*Percina caprodes semifasciata*	(X)[47] (T)[48] (r)[5,7]
AMPHIBIANS AND REPTILES		
Carpenter frog[2,3,4]	*Rana virgatipes*	(r);[50] (SU)[32]
Canebrake rattlesnake[4]	*Crotalus horridus* ssp.	(SC);[32] (r)[7] (VA only)
BIRDS		
Little blue heron[3]	*Egretta caerulea*	(SC);[22] (r)[35]
Northern harrier[3]	*Circus cyaneus*	(r)[23,35]
Wilson's plover[7]	*Charadrius wilsonia*	(T);[22] (r)[7] (r)[35]
Gull-billed tern[3,7]	*Sterna nilotica*	(T);[22] (r)[7] (r)[35]
Least tern[7]	*Sterna antillarum*	(T);[22] (r)[7] (r)[35]
Royal tern[7]	*Sterna maxima*	(SC);[22] (r)[7] (r)[35]
Sandwich tern[7]	*Sterna sandvicensis*	SC);[22] (r)[7] (r)[35]
Short-eared owl[2,3]	*Asio flammeus*	(r)[23,35]
Sedge wren[2,3]	*Cistothorus platensis*	(SC);[22] (r)[7] (r)[35]
Swamp sparrow[2,3]	*Melospiza georgiana nigrescens*	(r)[35] (r)[7]
MAMMALS		
Barrier island cottontail[3,7]	*Sylvilagus floridanus hitchensi*	(SU)[46,7] (VA only)
Marsh rabbit[3,4]	*Sylvilagus palustris*	(SC)[46] (VA only)

*NOTE: only species mentioned in both MD and VA rare lists are included here.
HABITAT KEY: [1]rivers, bay & ocean, [2]wet meadows, [4]swamps & thickets, [6]clear streams, [3]marshes, [5]weedy creeks, [7]beaches & mudflats

endangered fish in North America are freshwater species.[9] In the Chesapeake watershed, of the two endangered fishes, the Maryland darter (*Etheostoma sellare*) is a freshwater species, and the shortnose sturgeon (*Acipenser brevirostrum*) is anadromous. Nine other fish species are considered either rare, declining, or of special concern in the Chesapeake watershed of Maryland and Virginia; all are freshwater or anadromous species (Table 4). No marine species are currently threatened.

The sea turtles listed in Table 1 which occasionally enter the Bay are, of course, an exception to this generalization. Because they nest on land, these reptiles are more vulnerable to habitat destruction (i.e., loss of nesting beaches) and massive exploitation than are most other marine animals. In any case, they are not estuarine species.

Although estuarine aquatic systems, in general, do not support many endangered species, their adjacent wetlands do.[10] In view of the recent losses of wetlands in Maryland and Virginia over the past 50 years,[11,12,13] it is valuable to survey the literature to ascertain the value of wetlands nationally and within the Chesapeake Bay to federally protected species. Though the Chesapeake Bay and its associated wetlands do not harbor as many threatened species as some areas, such as the Everglades, it is important to remember that each species and its wetland inhabitat provide an extremely important sanctuary. For example, more than 400 bald eagles (*Haliaeetus leucocephalus*) utilized the Chesapeake Bay during one month (January) in 1984.[2]

VALUE OF WETLANDS TO NATIONALLY ENDANGERED SPECIES

The importance of wetlands to endangered and threatened species on a national scale was discussed by Williams and Dodd[10] and Nilsson.[14] Although wetlands comprise a small fraction of the total U.S. land area, they contain an extraordinary large percentage of unique species, and in the wake of persistent habitat destruction (e.g., marsh drainage), these systems now harbor a disproportionate number of endangered and threatened species. The whooping crane, *Grus americana*, to name just one species, is totally dependent on wetlands for nesting, migratory, and wintering sites.[5] In all, more than 50 percent of the fishes and amphibians, more than 30 percent of the reptiles and birds, and more than 15 percent of the mammals endangered or threatened in the United States are dependent on wetlands for survival.[10]

The major threat to these species is habitat destruction in the form of wetland drainage for farmland, development sites, and mosquito control, as well as habitat degradation from pollution and pesticides. Freshwater wetlands are especially vulnerable as evidenced by the fact that more than 30 species and subspecies of birds listed by the *IUCN Red Data Book* have declined as a direct result of freshwater swamp and marsh reclamation.[14]

Given the historical loss of wetlands locally and nationwide, the reason for the relatively lean inventory of endangered species within Bay-area wetlands is, perhaps, one of geography more than anything else. Chesapeake wetlands are a temperate system midway along the Atlantic flyway: there are no endemic breeding birds. By comparison, Florida has 12 endemic birds, 4 of which are endangered. Also, since many southern species reach their northern limit in the Chesapeake Bay region and similarly since various northern species reach their southern limit in the region, most of the locally rare mammalia-, herpeto-, and avifauna consist of peripheral populations.[5] Consequently, rare endemics are the exception rather than the rule.

SOUTHERN BALD EAGLE: CHESAPEAKE BAY POPULATION

The Chesapeake Bay region supports the fourth largest breeding population of bald eagles in the lower 48 states.[2] In the spring and summer of 1984, 121 nesting pairs raised 128 eaglets in the Maryland and Virginia coastal plain.[16] This is a vast improvement over past years. During the height of pesticide use in 1962, only 7 fledglings were produced in 37 known active nests (0.2 young per nest), while in 1936, before the widespread use of DDT, 39 known active nests produced 64 young, or 1.6 young per nest.[7] Between 1936 and 1970 the number of nesting pairs in the Bay region decreased from an estimated 600 pairs to less than 90.[2] DDT was banned in 1972, after its residual form, DDE, was shown to cause eggshell thinning in eagles and other birds of prey (e.g., ospreys, peregrines, and pelicans).[7]

Since 1977, the National Wildlife Federation, in cooperation with state and federal agencies, has conducted the Chesapeake Bay Bald Eagle Banding Project. During the 8 years of the project, nest productivity has increased from 0.82 to 1.11 young per active nest. At the same time the nest success (number of successful nests/number occupied nests) has increased from 48 to 65 percent.[16,17] The Chesapeake bald eagle population now exceeds a minimum maintenance level of 50 percent nest success and 0.7 rate of productivity.[18]

Today, the 121 bald eagle nests in Maryland and Virginia are found (with only two exceptions) in counties bordering the Chesapeake Bay and its tributaries (Fig. 1). Preferred nest sites are atop loblolly pines (70%) within sight of water (K. Cline, NWF, pers. comm.). In 1984 (as in other years), fish predominated the diet (39% occurrences in nests), with catfish (*Ictalurus* spp.) and carp (*Cyprinus carpio*) at the top of the list. Second in rank, after fish, were birds (35% of nests) with mallard (*Anas platyrhynchos*) as the main species. Mammals were found in 14 percent of the nests with the muskrat (*Ondatra zibethica*) as the most frequent species. Last on the list are aquatic turtles which were found in 12 percent of the nests.[16]

A computer-generated analysis of active and potential bald eagle nest sites

CHESAPEAKE BAY BALD EAGLE BREEDING TERRITORIES

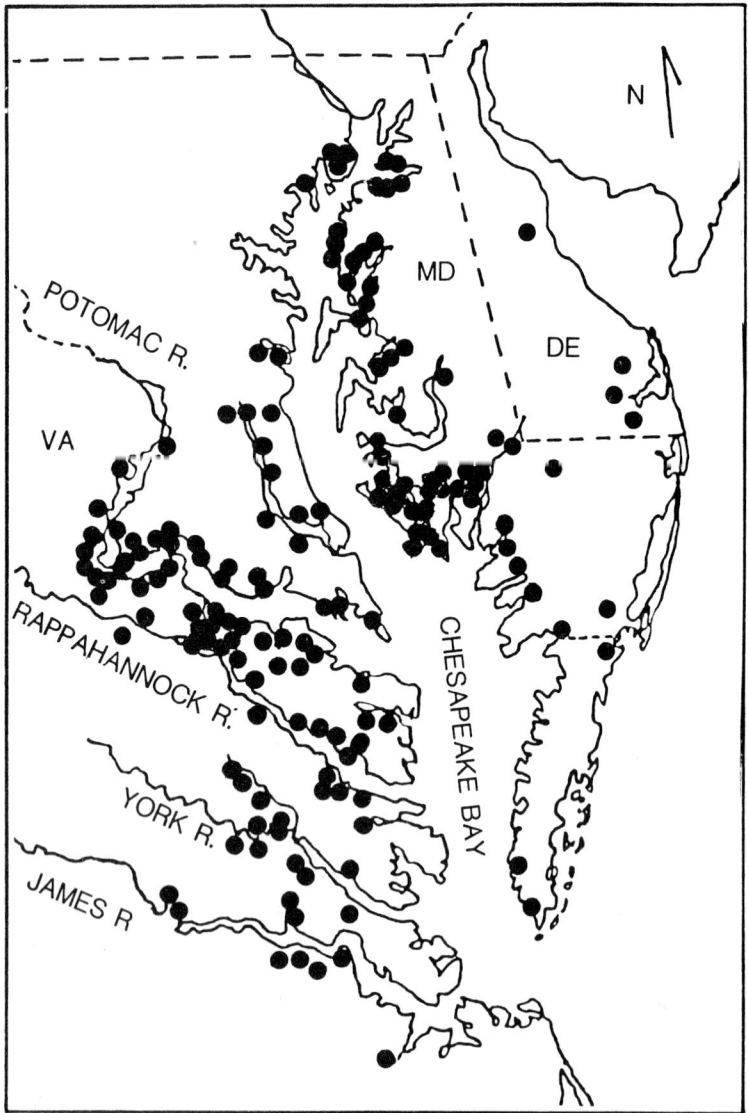

FIGURE 1. Bald Eagle Breeding Territories Occupied One or More Years, 1977-1984. Source: Cline[16]. Reprinted with permission.

showed that, in 1978, 17.5 percent of 57 active Maryland nests examined were within 1.2 km of water and 21.1 percent of the nests were within 0.6 km of wetlands.[19] Another study (70 Maryland nests) found that eagles selected nest sites in more open vegetation near water and further from human activities than random habitat plots.[20] Open forest stands were apparently chosen because of the inability of eagles to maneuver through closed canopy forests, while it has been conjectured that proximity to water may be adaptive in terms of optimizing forage success. However, Andrews and Mosher[20] concluded that, since there was no significant correlation between number of fledged young and distance to open water, the entire population in all likelihood built nests well within optimal foraging range. A similar result was found in a study of 40 nest sites in Virginia where nests ranged from 1 meter to 2.134 km from water.[21] Thus, in the Chesapeake Bay region, proximity to water seems to influence nest selection, but once the site is chosen this factor does not necessarily improve nesting success.

OTHER ENDANGERED SPECIES VISITING OR BORDERING CHESAPEAKE WETLANDS

Although the bald eagle is the only nesting endangered species directly associated with Chesapeake emergent wetlands, several other federally endangered animals either visit or border the swamp- or marshland environment. Fortunately, at least one wetland species formerly threatened by habitat degradation and pesticides, the osprey, *Pandion haliaetus*, has now recovered to a stable breeding status in the region.[22] Today, ospreys are more common within the Chesapeake watershed than anywhere else in the United States!

Another fish-eater, the eastern brown pelican, *Pelecanus occidentalis carolinensis*, was considered an endangered species by the USFWS and the Commission of Game and Inland Fisheries in the State of Virginia until February 1985, though the nearest breeding colony is located near Ocracoke Island, North Carolina.[22] Today, frequent visitors are seen along the Virginia coast and at the mouth of the Chesapeake Bay in spring, summer, and fall.[7] The peak count in Virginia was about 25 individuals at Fisherman Island on May 23, 1977.[23] This species uses marsh grasses in the construction of nests, but as there are no breeding colonies in the region, the species only benefits from Chesapeake wetlands by using them as a temporary shelter and from their contribution to fishery stocks, which are the pelican's sole source of food. Habitat loss, pollution, and pesticides were originally responsible for placing this bird on the federal list in 1970.[7] Though it has subsequently stabilized on the Atlantic Coast, it is still considered endangered in Mississippi, Louisiana, and Texas (FR 50 (23): 4938-4945).

The endangered peregrine falcon, *Falco peregrinus*, was extirpated from the eastern United States by the late 1960's because of pesticide contamination.[24] Formerly, it bred in both Maryland and Virginia.[23,25] Currently, it is being reintroduced into the Chesapeake Bay region through a captive breeding and release program coordinated by the states, USFWS, and the Cornell University Peregrine Fund. Young peregrines have been hacked on Fox Island, South Marsh, and other Bay-area sites (Mitchell Byrd, College of William and Mary, pers. comm.), and, as they return to breed permanently in the area, mallards and other wetlands-oriented waterbirds are likely to be a source of food (Andy Moser, USFWS, pers. comm.). City-dwelling peregrines, for example in Baltimore, mainly eat pigeons, which in that city comprise 93 percent of their diet (John Barber, USF&G, pers. comm.), while nesting pairs on the Chesapeake Bay Bridge and at Fishing Bay require alternate sources of prey (Gary Taylor, MD FPWS, pers. comm.). In upcoming years, the peregrine population's use of wetlands and wetlands-based prey should be monitored closely.

Bachman's warbler, *Vermivora bachmanii*, an inhabitant of hardwood swamps, is the rarest songbird in North America[26] and may be extinct.[27] Although there are no recorded nestings in Virginia, solitary males were sighted at the mouth of Pohick Creek near Fort Belvoir, Virginia, in May 1954 and May 1958[23]; the species has not been recorded in Maryland. The USFWS and the Virginia Commission of Game and Inland Fisheries consider this species to be endangered, assuming it is still transient, in Virginia.[7]

The red-cockaded woodpecker, *Picoides borealis borealis*, nests in tall, mature, longleaf and loblolly pine woods south and southeast of the James River in Brunswick, Isle of Wight, Prince George, Southampton, Suffolk, Surry, Sussex, and Virginia Beach counties, Virginia.[7] It does not currently nest in Dismal Swamp, though it is found nearby. Formerly, it nested near Blackwater National Wildlife Refuge in Dorchester County (1958) and in Worcester County (1943), Maryland.[7] Since mature loblolly pines often flank brackish marshes in the southern Chesapeake Bay,[6] thus forming tidewater forests (i.e., wooded swamps), pine woods should be surveyed for signs of red-cockaded woodpeckers before lumbering adjacent to wetlands. The last sighting in Dorchester County, Maryland, was in 1976.

The Delmarva Peninsula fox squirrel, *Sciurus niger cinereus*, is endemic to the Eastern Shore of Maryland and Virginia where it occupies mixed lowland forests, often near water, feeding on cones, acorns, and nuts.[28] In Dorchester County, some of the wet woodlands (e.g., tidewater loblolly forests) adjacent to marshes provide good habitat for the Delmarva fox squirrel (Gary Taylor, MWA, pers. comm.), and thus the same caution suggested above, regarding lumbering in tidewater loblolly forests, should be exercised within the fox squirrel's range. Currently, this species is located in Cecil, Dorchester, Kent, Queen Anne's, Somerset, Talbot, and Worcester counties, Maryland, and Accomack and Northampton counties, Virginia.[7]

Obviously, endangered fishes, like other aquatic species within the Chesapeake

Bay, are at least indirectly dependent on wetlands for food, particularly for primary production at the base of the detrital food chain, and for inherent water quality benefits.[15] The Chesapeake watershed harbors two endangered fishes: the shortnose sturgeon, *Acipenser brevirostrum*, and the Maryland darter, *Etheostoma sellare*.[7,9] The shortnose sturgeon is an anadromous species which perhaps spawned at one time in the Susquehanna River and other Chesapeake tributaries—prior to dam construction and deterioration of river and estuarine habitat.[29] The closest extant breeding population is found in the Delaware River, though individuals are rarely captured in the Chesapeake Bay. The sturgeon is dependent on benthic invertebrates for food.[7] The Maryland darter is restricted to a single, swift riffle in Deer Creek, Harford County, Maryland. This extremely rare species feeds on snails and the larvae of aquatic insects[30] which in turn feed on algae and detritus that may originate, albeit in some small part, from wetlands sources.

Last, on the list of federally endangered and threatened vertebrates within the Maryland and Virginia coastal plain, are the sea turtles. All 5 of the Atlantic species have at least been sighted in the Chesapeake Bay (Table 1). Only 2, the loggerhead turtle, *Caretta caretta*, and Kemp's ridley turtle, *Lepidochelys kempii*, regularly visit the Chesapeake Bay.[7] However, all consume invertebrates, including jellyfish, mollusks, and crustaceans that, within the Bay, may depend, in part, on wetlands and the marsh-estuarine system. Sea turtles also feed upon marine grasses; e.g., eelgrass.[31,32]

CANDIDATE SPECIES IN THE MARYLAND-VIRGINIA COASTAL PLAIN

Within the Maryland-Virginia coastal plain 8 invertebrate species and 7 vertebrate species have been placed *under review* for federal listing as endangered and threatened species (Table 3). Of these, one species, the piping plover, *Charadrius melodus*, has now been proposed for listing as a threatened species along the coast of Maryland and Virginia (FR 49 (218): 44712-44715; November 8, 1984). In addition, the Dismal Swamp shrew, *Sorex longirostris fisheri*, is expected to be proposed for listing during 1986 (Andy Moser USFWS, pers. comm.). Since it is not within the scope of this review to discuss these 15 candidate species in adequate detail, the reader is referred to the sources identified in Table 3 for detailed information on habitat, distribution, and abundance.

RARE SPECIES OF SPECIAL CONCERN

Symposia on the rare, endangered, and threatened plants and animals of Maryland and Virginia were held at Towson and Blacksburg on September 3-4,

1981, and May 12-20, 1978, respectively. The proceedings of these symposia address the endangered animals discussed above as well as a host of locally rare and threatened species.[33,34] The vertebrate species ranging the Chesapeake watershed that are associated with wetlands, either by habitat or by feeding mode, are listed in Table 4. More than half of the rare breeding birds in both Maryland and Virginia are dependent on wetlands.[22,35]

SUMMARY OF WETLAND AND ESTUARINE VALUES

Chesapeake wetlands are an important nesting, roosting, and feeding area for the bald eagle, *Haliaeetus leucocephalus*, and a potential food source for the reintroduced peregrine falcon, *Falco peregrinus* ssp. Preferred food items of the bald eagle are fish, waterfowl, muskrats, and turtles, all of which are wetlands-dependent; nests are located within a mile or two of water. The osprey and eastern brown pelican have recovered on the Atlantic Coast to a stable breeding status. The bald eagle population has improved dramatically, while the peregrine recovery is still in progress. Tidewater loblolly forests adjacent to marshes are potential nest sites for the bald eagle, red-cockaded woodpecker, and the Delmarva peninsula fox squirrel. Rare and endangered fishes and sea turtles at least occasionally feed on invertebrates that are nurtured to some degree by Chesapeake wetlands. In addition, 15 candidate species are found in the Maryland-Virginia coastal plain, while an additional 20 wetland-associated vertebrate species warrant special concern. Wherever these rare species occur, the economic and environmental value of associated wetlands is enhanced by their presence.

By comparison, the main stem of the Chesapeake Bay is not direct critical habitat for federally protected species. Nonetheless, several endangered species migrate through the Chesapeake Bay and its environs, and may rely on the Bay's aquatic resources for food during these periods.

ACKNOWLEDGMENTS

I would like to thank the following individuals for providing information used in the preparation of this paper: Andy Moser, Judy Jacobs, and John Gill, USFWS; Gary Taylor, MD Forest, Park and Wildlife Service; Richard H. Cross and John P. Randolph, VA Commission of Game and Inland Fisheries; Keith W. Cline, NWF Raptor Information Center; John Barber, USF&G Company; and Arnold W. Norden, Maryland Natural Heritage Program.

LITERATURE CITED

1. EPA. 1983. Chesapeake Bay Program; findings and recommendations. U.S. Environmental Protection Agency. Philadelphia, PA. 48p.
2. Cline, K.W. 1985. Bald eagles in the Chesapeake: a management guide for landowners. NWF Raptor Information Center. Washington, D.C. 16p.
3. White, C.P. 1985. Values of wetlands to endangered species within the Chesapeake Bay watershed: Maryland and Virginia coastal plain. *in* Groman, H.A. *et al.* (eds.) Wetlands of the Chesapeake: proceedings. Env. Law Inst. Wash, D.C. 389p.
4. Cronin, L.E., and A.J. Mansueti. 1971. The biology of the estuary. *in* A Symposium on the Biological Significance of Estuaries. Sport Fishing Inst. Wash., D.C. 26p.
5. Wass, M.L. *et al.* (compiled). 1972. A check list of the biota of lower Chesapeake Bay. VIMS. Spec. Publ. No. 65. Gloucester Point, VA. 290p.
6. White, C.P. (in press). Chesapeake Bay: the nature of the estuary—a field guide. Cornell Maritime Press. Centreville, MD. 224p.
7. White, C.P. 1982. Endangered and threatened wildlife of the Chesapeake Bay region. Tidewater Publishers. Centreville, MD. 148p.
8. McLusky, D.S. 1971. Ecology of estuaries. Heinemann Educational Books, Ltd., London. 144p.
9. Ono, R.D., J.D. Williams, and A. Wagner. 1984. Vanishing fishes of North America. Stone Wall Press. Washington, D.C. 257p.
10. Williams, J.D. and C.K. Dodd. 1978. The importance of wetlands to endangered and threatened species. *in* Greeson *et al.* (eds.) *op. cit.*
11. McCormick, J. and H.A. Somes. 1982. The coastal wetlands of Maryland. Coastal Zone Mgmt. Program. MD DNR. Annapolis, MD. 243p.
12. Settle, F.H. 1969. Survey and analysis of changes effected by man on tidal wetlands of Virginia, 1955-69. Manuscript, Virginia Polytechnic Institute, Blacksburg, Virginia, 100 + p.
13. Wass, M.L. and T.D. Wright. 1969. Coastal wetlands of Virginia. Spec. Rep. No. 10. VIMS. Gloucester Point. 154p.
14. Nilsson, G. 1983. The endangered species handbook. The Animal Welfare Institute. Washington, D.C. 245p.
15. Greeson, P.E., J.R. Clark, and J.E. Clark. (eds.) 1979. Wetland functions and values: the state of our understanding. Proceedings of the National Symposium on Wetlands. American Water Resources Assoc. Minneapolis, MN. 675p.
16. Cline, K.W. 1984. Chesapeake Bay bald eagle banding project report: 1984. NWF Raptor Information Center. Washington, D.C. 36p.
17. Cline, K.W. and W.S. Clark. 1981. Chesapeake Bay bald eagle banding project: 1981 report and five year summary. NWF Raptor Information Center. Washington, D.C. 38p.

18. D'Loughy, K.J. 1984. Status of the bald eagle in Maryland. *in* A.W. Norden *et al.* (eds.) *op. cit.*
19. Taylor, G.J. and G.D. Therres. 1981. A computer generated description of potential bald eagle nesting habitat in Maryland. MD. Power Plant Siting Program. Annapolis.
20. Andrew, J.M. and J.A. Mosher. 1982. Bald eagle nest selection and nesting habitat in Maryland. J. Wildl. Mgmt. 46:382-390.
21. Jaffee, N.B. 1980. Nest site selection and foraging behavior of the bald eagle (*Haliaeetus leucocephalus*) in Virginia. Master's thesis. Dept. Biology. College of William and Mary.
22. Byrd, M.A. 1979. Birds. *in* D.W. Linzey (ed.). Endangered and threatened plants and animals of Virginia. Virginia Polytechnic Inst. and State University. Blacksburg. 665p.
23. Larner, Y.R. 1979. Virginia's birdlife: an annotated checklist. Virginia Avifauna No. 2. VA. Soc. of Ornithology.
24. Barclay, J.H. and T.J. Cade. 1983. Restoration of the peregrine falcon in the eastern United States. Bird Conservation Vol. 1 No. 1 pp. 3-40.
25. Robbins, C.S. and D. Dystrak. 1977. Field list of the birds of Maryland. MD. Avifauna No. 2. Maryland Ornithological Society. 45p.
26. Peterson, R.T. 1980. A field guide to the birds of eastern and central North America. Houghton Mifflin Co. Boston. 384p.
27. Robbins, C.S., B. Bruun, and H.S. Zim. 1983. Birds of North America: a guide to field identification. Golden Press. New York. 340p.
28. Feldhamer, G.A., J.E. Gates, and J.A. Chapman. 1984. Rare, threatened, endangered and extirpated mammals from Maryland. *in* A.W. Norden *et al.* (eds.) *op. cit.*
29. Testaverde, S.A. *et al.* 1981. Shortnose sturgeon recovery plan. NMFS. Gloucester, MA. 122p.
30. Frisbie, C.M., L. Knapp, J. Sheridan, and R.L. Butler. 1982. The Maryland darter recovery plan. USFWS. Region 5. Boston, Mass. 27p.
31. Groves, J.D. 1984. The sea turtles of Maryland. *in* A.W. Norden *et al.* (eds.) *op. cit.*
32. Tobey, F.J. 1979. Amphibians and reptiles. *in* D.W. Linzey (ed.) *op. cit.*
33. Norden, A.W., D.C. Forester, and G.H. Fenwick. 1984. Threatened and endangered plants and animals of Maryland. MD. Nat. Heritage Program. Spec. Publ. 84-1. MD DNR. Annapolis. 475p.
34. Linzey, D.W. (ed.) 1979. Endangered and threatened plants and animals of Virginia. Virginia Polytechnic Inst. and State University. Blacksburg. 665p.
35. Robbins, C.S. and D.D. Boone. 1984. Threatened breeding birds of Maryland. *in* A.W. Norden *et al.* (eds.) *op. cit.*
36. Virginia Commission of Game and Inland Fisheries. 1983. Official Virginia endangered list: vertebrate and molluscs. *in* J.P. Randolph (ed.). Virginia's

endangered species. VA. Comm. of Game and Inland Fisheries. 13p.
37. Gates, J.E., C.H. Hocutt, and J.R. Stauffer, Jr. 1984. The status of the hellbender (*Crypto-branchus alleganiensis*) in Maryland. *in* A.W. Norden *et al.* (eds.) *op. cit.*
38. Stine, C. 1984. The life history and status of the eastern tiger salamander, *Ambystoma tigrinum tigrinum* (Green) in Maryland. Bull. MD. Herp. Soc. 20(3): 65-108.
39. Taylor, G.J. 1984. The Maryland endangered species program: a history. *in* A.W. Norden *et al.* (eds.) *op. cit.*
40. Holsinger, J.R. 1979. Freshwater amphipod crustaceans. *in* D.W. Linzey (ed.) *op. cit.*
41. Opler, P.A. 1984. Endangered and threatened insects of Maryland *in* A.W. Norden *et al.* (eds.) *op. cit.*
42. Fales, J.H. 1984. Status of Maryland's less-common butterflies. *in* A.W. Norden *et al.* (eds.) *op. cit.*
43. Opler, P.A. 1979. Freshwater and terrestrial arthropods *in* D.W. Linzey (ed.) *op. cit.*
44. Gerberich, A. 1984. The endangered and threatened freshwater molluscs of Maryland. *in* A.W. Norden *et al.* (eds.) *op. cit.*
45. Dawson, S.A. 1984. The status of the bog turtle (*Clemmys muhlenbergi*) in Maryland. *in* A.W. Norden, *et al. op. cit.*
46. Handley, C.O., Jr. 1979. Mammals. *in* D.W. Linzey (ed.) *op. cit.*
47. Jenkins, R.E. 1979. Freshwater and marine fishes. *in* D.W. Linzey (ed.) *op. cit.*
48. Lee, D.S., S.P. Platania, A.W. Norden, and C.R. Gilbert. 1984. Endangered, threatened, and extirpated freshwater fishes of Maryland. *in* A.W. Norden *et al.* (eds.) *op. cit.*
49. Wiley, M.L. 1984. Endangered and threatened marine and estuarine fishes in Maryland. *in* A.W. Norden *et al.* (eds.) *op. cit.*
50. Brosnan, M.C. 1984. The rare and endangered animals of Maryland. *in* A.W. Norden *et al* (eds.) Threatened and endangered plants and animals of Maryland. Maryland Nat. Heritage Program. MD DNR. Annapolis. 475p.

Endangered and Threatened Species Programs in Pennsylvania and other States: Causes, Issues and Management. Edited by S. K. Majumdar, F. J. Brenner and A. F. Rhoads. © 1986, The Pennsylvania Academy of Science.

Chapter Twenty-Nine

ENDANGERED WILDLIFE MANAGEMENT IN OHIO

Denis S. Case
Ohio Department of Natural Resources
Division of Wildlife
Fountain Square
Columbus, OH 43224

Endangered wildlife has been a part of Ohio's history from the first white settlements in the mid-eighteenth century. Bison (*Bison bison*) and elk (*Cervus canadensis*) were nearly eliminated from the state by the year 1800[1]. Many other terrestrial species became endangered or extirpated in the first half of the nineteenth century, mostly as a result of deforestation and wetland drainage.[2,3] These included black bears (*Ursa americanus*), gray wolves (*Canis lupus*), martens (*Martes americanus*), fishers (*M. pennanti*), and mountain lions (*Felis concolor*). Beavers (*Castor canadensis*) were extirpated through over-exploitation.

Many species of fish also began to show dramatic population declines during this period, especially the larger, migratory fishes.[4] These included the muskellunge (*Esox masquinongy*), northern pike (*E. lucius*), and lake sturgeon (*Acipenser fulvescens*). Principal causes for the declines were: (1) the construction of mill dams, (2) water pollution from lumber mills, slaughter houses, and breweries, (3) wetland drainage, (4) stream ditching, (5) lowered water table and reduced water flows, and (6) an increase in commercial seining.[4]

These events also resulted in the earliest efforts to attempt to deal with threatened and endangered wildlife. In 1829, a law was passed establishing a closed season on muskrats (*Ondatra zibethicus*), for the stated purpose of protecting the fur trade.[5] This was the first action taken in which the idea existed of a threat to wildlife, and for which some positive conservation action was required. In following years, similar actions were taken for many species of wildlife, including a law prohibiting the taking of nesting or roosting passenger pigeons (*Ectopistes migratorius*) in 1876.[5] Protection of the passenger pigeon is the first instance in Ohio involving a species that was recognized as actually endangered throughout its range, and which subsequently became extinct.

Enactment of legislation to restrict or prohibit the taking of threatened or endangered wildlife continued to be the principal response of state government up to the middle of the twentieth century. However, also during this period many Ohioans began to consider the broader relationships between wildlife populations and changes in land and water use patterns. [6,7,8,9,10] The thoughts and efforts of these individuals, among others, began to form the basis for a more comprehensive approach to the problem of endangered wildlife.

One of the first concrete responses by state governments was passage of the state endangered wildlife law in 1973.[11] It allowed the Chief of the Division of Wildlife to classify animals as endangered, if they were threatened with extirpation from the state. This legislation was deficient, and still is, in that it had no provision for habitat protection. It only prohibited the taking of the animal itself. More significantly, however, this legislation broadened the authority of the Division to include many additional species of wildlife (especially invertebrates), and was of material value in helping to shift the focus of state government toward total wildlife management.

In 1974, a Division of Wildlife committee recommended the first list of endangered animals, with force of law behind it. This committee benefitted from a previous list compiled by the Ohio Chapter of The Wildlife Society, published in 1973.[12] In 1975, a formal nongame wildlife program was established, and a full-time wildlife biologist was hired to plan and coordinate its development. Responsibilities for endangered wildlife became a part of this overall nongame wildlife program. Animals presently classified as endangered in Ohio are listed in Table 1.

PRESENT ENDANGERED WILDLIFE PROGRAM

In the decade since establishment of the nongame wildlife program, endangered wildlife management has increased substantially. An important aspect of program development has been to integrate endangered wildlife activities throughout the Division of Wildlife, rather than to create a separate nongame or endangered wildlife unit. The result has been broad involvement of the Division in these newer programs and has maximized the amount of manpower, facilities and experience that have been brought to bear on endangered wildlife problems.

Legislation for a state income tax return checkoff system, allowing for tax-

TABLE 1

Wildlife Classified as Endangered in Ohio

Mammals
    River Otter - *Lutra canadensis*
    Bobcat - *Felis rufus*
    *Indiana Myotis - *Myotis sodalis*
    Eastern Woodrat - *Neotoma floridana*

Birds
    *Peregrine Falcon - *Falco peregrinus*
    Sharp-shinned Hawk - *Accipiter striatus*
    *Bald Eagle—*Haliaeetus leucocephalus*
    King Rail - *Rallus elegans*
    *Kirtland's Warbler - *Dendroica kirtlandii*
    Upland Sandpiper - *Bartramia longicauda*
    Common Tern - *Sterna hirundo*

Reptiles
    Spotted Turtle - *Clemmys guttata*
    Copperbelly Water Snake - *Nerodia erythrogaster neglecta*
    Eastern Plains Garter Snake - *Thamnophis radix radix*

Amphibians
    Blue Spotted Salamander - *Ambystoma laterale*
    Green Salamander - *Aneides aeneus*
    Cave Salamander - *Eurycea lucifuga*
    Four-toed Salamander - *Hemidactylium scutatum*
    Wehrle's Salamander - *Plethodon wehrlei*

Fish
    Ohio Lamprey - *Ichthyomyzon bdellium*
    Northern Brook Lamprey - *Ichthyomyzon fossor*
    Mountain Brook Lamprey - *Ichthyomyzon greeleyi*
    Silver Lamprey - *Ichthyomyzon unicuspis*
    American Brook Lamprey - *Lampetra appendix*
    Lake Sturgeon - *Acipenser fulvescens*
    Paddlefish - *Polyodon spathula*
    Spotted Gar - *Lepisosteus oculatus*
    Shortnose Gar - *Lepisosteus platostomus*
    Mooneye - *Hiodon tergisus*
    Cisco - *Coregonus artedii*
    Great Lakes Muskellunge - *Esox masquinongy masquinongy*
    Rosyside Dace - *Clinostomus funduloides*
    Tonguetied Minnow - *Exoglossum laurae*
    Bigmouth Shiner - *Notropis boops*
    Ghost Shiner - *Notropis buchanani*
    Blacknose Shiner - *Notropis heterolepis*
    Silver Chub - *Hybopsis storeriana*
    Longnose Sucker - *Catostomus catostomus*
    Greater Redhorse - *Moxostoma valenciennesi*
    Blue Sucker - *Cycleptus elongatus*
    River Redhorse - *Moxostoma carinatum*
    Lake Chubsucker - *Erimyzon sucetta*
    *Scioto Madtom - *Noturus trautmani*
    Northern Madtom - *Noturus stigmosus*
    Mountain Madtom - *Noturus eleutherus*
    Pirateperch - *Aphredoderus sayanus*
    Burbot - *Lota lota*

TABLE 1

Banded Killifish - *Fundulus diaphanus*
Iowa Darter - *Etheostoma exile*
Longhead Darter - *Percina shumardi*
River Darter - *Percina macrocephala*
Eastern Sand Darter - *Ammocrypta pellucida*
Channel Darter - *Percina copelandi*
Tippecanoe Darter - *Etheostoma tippecanoe*
Slenderhead Darter - *Percina phoxocephala*
Spotted Darter - *Etheostoma maculatum*

Crustaceans
Allegheny Crayfish - *Orconectes obscurus*

Mollusks
Smooth Cob Shell - *Quadrula cylindrica*
Northern Club Shell - *Pleurobema clava*
Ohio Fan Shell—*Cyprogenia stegaria*
*Ohio Mucket—*Lampsilis abrupta* (=orbiculata)
*White Cat's Paw - *Epioblasma obliquata perobliqua* (=*sulcata delicata*)
Northern Riffle Shell - *Epioblasma rangiana*
Simpson's Shell - *Simpsonaias ambiqua*
Sharp Ridged Pocketbook - *Lampsilis ovata*
Yellow Sand Shell - *Lampsilis teres*
Fragile Heelsplitter - *Potamilus ohiensis*
Winged Pimpleback - *Quadrula nodulata*
Knobbed Rock Shell - *Quadrula metanevra*
Common Bullhead - *Plethobasus cyphyus*
Butterfly Shell - *Plagiola lineolata*
Longsolid - *Fusconaia maculata*
Ohio Pigtoe - *Pleurobema cordatum*

*Listed as endangered by both the State of Ohio and the United States.

payers to contribute to a special account for nongame and endangered wildlife management, was passed in 1983.[11] This system has been very successful. During the first two years in which the option appeared on the tax form, nearly $1,000,000 were contributed (Table 2).

Concerned citizens have been actively involved in developing guidelines for expenditure of these funds. Citizen involvement is thought to be especially important, because of the voluntary nature of the funding base. Major input was provided through a public workshop in October, 1984. Nearly 200 persons representing conservation organizations, academic institutions, and governmental agencies participated in the workshop. Significant problems and their solutions were identified for mammals, birds, reptiles and amphibians, terrestrial invertebrates, fish, aquatic invertebrates, and the following habitats: (1) forests, (2) wetlands, (3) agricultural lands and prairies, (4) urban and suburban areas, (5) inland lakes and streams, and (6) Lake Erie. These recommendations were formulated into a project-oriented plan, with funds allocated for priority projects.[13] Projects dealing with endangered species under this plan, and since the start of the program in 1975, are listed in Table 3.

TABLE 2

State Income Tax Return Checkoff Contributions to the Ohio Nongame and Endangered Wildlife Program, in 1984 and 1985

Item	1984	1985	Total
# Eligible Taxpayers	2,701,676	2,852,086	5,553,762
# Contributors	135,758	118,609	254,367
Average Contribution	$3.60	$4.28	$3.92
% Contributing	5.0%	4.3%	4.6%
$ Contributed	$489,234	$507,962	$997,196

TABLE 3

Annotated List of Ohio Division of Wildlife Endangered Wildlife Projects from 1975 through 1985

Mammals
 1. Reintroduction of the Eastern Woodrat (*Neotoma floridana*). The objectives of the project were to develop reintroduction techniques, and to restore a population of woodrats in a portion of its former range.
 2. Survey of Southeastern Ohio for the Indiana Myotis (*Myotis sodalis*). The objective of the project was to determine if the Indiana bat was distributed in southeastern Ohio, especially on the Wayne National Forest.
 3. Reintroduction of the River Otter (*Lutra canadensis*). The initial objective is to determine the feasibility of reintroducing otters to Ohio.

Birds
 1. Evaluation of a Census Technique for Woodland Hawks. The objective is to evaluate the feasibility of using raptor sound recordings to estimate the density of nesting woodland hawks.
 2. Management of Bald Eagles (*Haliaeetus leucocephalus*). The objective is to restore the nesting population of eagles to a minimum of 10 productive pairs.
 3. Management for Grassland Dependent Birds. The objective is to restore sufficient, undisturbed grassland acreage in Ohio, to allow for increased populations of grassland dependent birds (including upland sandpipers, *Bartramia longicauda,* and common barn owls, *Tyto alba*).
 4. Management of Common Terns (*Sterna hirundo*). The objective is to develop and maintain habitat, set aside specifically for common tern nesting colonies.

Reptiles and Amphibians
 1. Management of the Eastern Plains Garter Snake (*Thamnophis r. radix*). The objectives were to determine the distribution of the snake in Ohio, to determine if it was in competition with the eastern garter snake (*T. s. sirtalis*), and to develop habitat management guidelines.
 2. Development of a Herpetological Data Base. The objective is to compile all existing information on the distribution and status of reptiles and amphibians in Ohio.
 3. Survey for the Hellbender (*Cryptobranchus alleganiensis*). The objective is to determine the distribution of hellbenders in Ohio.

Fish
 1. Survey for the Scioto Madtom (*Noturus trautmani*). The objective is to determine if this endemic madtom is still extant in Ohio.
 2. Survey of Lampreys in Northeastern Ohio. The objective is to determine the distribution of both sea lampreys (*Petromyzon marinus*) and native lampreys in streams tributary to Lake Erie.

OTHER AGENCIES AND ORGANIZATIONS

There are other entities in Ohio which contribute significantly to the protection of endangered wildlife. The Division of Natural Areas and Preserves (also in the Department of Natural Resources) is responsible for endangered plants, maintains a Natural Heritage Data Base, and is responsible for designation of scenic rivers and natural areas. The state Environmental Protection Agency has an important role in the protection of water quality. This is critical since the majority of the endangered wildlife in Ohio are aquatic species. The Ohio Biological Survey is a consortium of colleges, universities and government agencies, which has been instrumental in the identification of endangered species and their habitats. It also has served an invaluable function in publishing the results of these surveys. The U.S. Fish and Wildlife Service has interacted with the state in several ways, the most important of which have been through the Federal Endangered Species Act and through protection of bald eagles on the Ottawa National Wildlife Refuge. The U.S. Forest Service has incorporated endangered species protection into management plans for the Wayne National Forest.

Private organizations have become increasingly valuable for endangered species protection. They not only engage in their own programs, but fulfill a helpful "oversight" role for governmental agencies. Organizations of special significance have been Audubon Chapters, The Ohio Chapter of the American Fisheries Society, The Ohio Chapter of The Wildlife Society, the Ohio Environmental Council, the Ohio Wildlife Management Association, the Sierra Club, and The Nature Conservancy. Many other groups have contributed, especially for issues of a more local nature.

SUMMARY

Endangered wildlife management and protection have evolved in Ohio over the last 150 years, and have received special emphasis over the last 15 years. Programs and a significant funding base are firmly in place, and endangered wildlife will continue to be an important responsibility of the Division of Wildlife in the future. This responsibility is met through a program of management for nongame wildlife, and reflects an important, fundamental broadening of interest to the protection of all forms of wildlife.

LITERATURE CITED

1. Brayton, A. M. 1882. Report on the Mammalia of Ohio. pp. 3-185. *In:* Report of the Geological Survey of Ohio. Volume IV. Zoology and Botany. Part I. Zoology. Nevins and Myers, State Printers, Columbus, Ohio.

2. Laub, K. W. 1979. Changing Land Use: Forests, Farm Lands, and Wildlife. In: pp. 244-281. M. B. Lafferty (ed.). Ohio's Natural Heritage. Ohio Academy of Science, Columbus, Ohio.
3. Trautman, M. B. 1978. The Ohio Country from 1750 to 1977 - A Naturalist's View. Ohio Biological Survey Biological Notes Number 10. 25 pp.
4. _____. 1981. The Fishes of Ohio. Ohio State University Press, Columbus, Ohio. 782 pp.
5. Finfrock, C.M. 1939. History of Conservation Legislation in Ohio. Master's Thesis. Oberlin College, Oberlin, Ohio. 69 pp.
6. Osborn, H., J. E. Carman, F. H. Herrick, C. G. Shatzer, E. N. Transeau, and M. M. Metcalf. 1921. Report of Committee on Preservation of Wildlife of State. Annual Report Ohio Academy of Science 7(6):184.
7. Sears, P. B. 1942. History of Conservation in Ohio. pp. 219-240. *In:* The History of the State of Ohio. VI. Ohio in the Twentieth Century. State Archeological and Historical Society, Columbus, Ohio.
8. Hicks, L. E. 1943. Rare and Endangered Species in the Ohio Valley and the Lower Great Lakes Region. Ohio Wildlife Research Station Release 181. Ohio State University, Columbus, Ohio. 9 pp.
9. Trautman, M. B. 1940. The Birds of Buckeye Lake. University of Michigan Press, Ann Arbor, Michigan. 469 pp.
10. Dambach, C.A. 1948. The Relative Importance of Hunting Restrictions and Land Use in Maintaining Wildlife Populations in Ohio. Ohio Journal of Science 48(6):209-279.
11. Ohio Revised Code Annotated. Sections 1531.25-26 (Baldwin, 1984).
12. Smith, H.G., R.K. Burnard, E.E. Good, and J.M. Keener. 1973. Rare and Endangered Vertebrates of Ohio. Ohio Journal of Science 73(5):257-271.
13. Case, D. S. and K. R. Fritz. 1985. Ohio Nongame Wildlife Plan. Ohio Department of Natural Resources, Division of Wildlife, Columbus, Ohio. 32 pp.

Endangered and Threatened Species Programs in Pennsylvania and other States: Causes, Issues and Management. Edited by S. K. Majumdar, F. J. Brenner and A. F. Rhoads. © 1986, The Pennsylvania Academy of Science.

Chapter Thirty

VIRGINIA'S ENDANGERED SPECIES PROGRAM

John P. Randolph
Assistant Executive Director
Virginia Commission of Game and Fisheries
Richmond, Virginia 23230-1189

Virginia's Endangered Species Program began in 1976 when, using funds available under the Endangered Species Act, the Virginia Game Commission initiated a recovery program for the bald eagle. Endangered species programs, however, were enhanced with the enactment of the Endangered Species and Non-Game Income Tax Check-Off system in 1981.

The Virginia Commission of Game and Inland Fisheries is charged with the administration of the endangered species program for all fauna of the Commonwealth. While the commission has been authorized to designate state endangered species, it has, to date, elected not to do so. Only those species designated on the federal list of endangered species are recognized as endangered in Virginia.

Research and recovery programs for endangered species are afforded the highest priority in Virginia; but with the commencement of the endangered species and non-game program supported by contributed funds, in fiscal year 1983, the Commission broadened its goals, not only working with endangered species, but taking action to ensure that species currently viable in the Commonwealth are monitored to identify problems before the species becomes threatened or endangered.

It is also important to note that endangered species recovery programs, while in themselves are vital, the problem of threatened and endangered species must be approached on a broader front, not isolated or confined to the endangered species themselves. For this reason the endangered species program in Virginia, while directed primarily at the species of concern, is also broadened to involve the public and to protect habitats critical to their existence. While the specific species programs are of primary concern, our computerized wildlife and habitat inventory system, called BOVA (Biota of Virginia), is used to enhance our data base as well as outreach programs.

Our BOVA data base currently maintains life history, distribution, habitat, and other data, including a bibliography of known literature for 960 species of fish, amphibians, reptiles, birds, and mammals. Additional species will be added on an as required basis. The system, which resides on computers at Virginia Polytechnic Institute and State University (VPI & SU) at Blacksburg, is the property of the Commission.

BOVA is currently being enhanced with the addition of the Geographic Information System (GIS) and the River Reach System. This will give BOVA the capability of producing information graphically as plotted data on map overlays, as well as through conventional printouts. Endangered species, of course, reside within the BOVA data base.

The Commission serves as a clearinghouse for permitting actions involving construction, water use, or impacts upon riparian or other habitats. While we do not have permitting authority, we provide input to the permitting agencies. By checking all such applications against the BOVA system, we quickly identify those actions that may impact upon an endangered or threatened species. This enables us to make a more intelligent evaluation of the impact of the project and to make appropriate comments. The BOVA output, of course, is balanced with observations of the field biologist responsible for the project area.

The public outreach program brings to the public the findings of the scientific staff. In addition to the important function of involving the public in the total program, thereby maintaining the level of contributions, the program keeps the public aware of the existence of endangered species and actions that can be taken by them to protect the habitat and to conserve the species. For example, not disturbing eagles during nesting, not throwing clear plastic bags overboard that may be mistaken by sea turtles for jellyfish, or simply not shooting raptors, involved the public in these important aspects of recovering our endangered species. We are acutely aware that scientific research, while necessary, is useless unless applied and, where possible, the public is involved in the programs. We consider the public outreach phase of the program to be equally important as the species management phase.

To enhance the public awareness of the needs of endangered and threatened species, we have used our weekly television show: *Virginia Wildlife* magazine; a free booklet, "Virginia's Endangered Species"; and a full color comprehensive wildlife guide, "Virginia's Wildlife." We have produced a movie covering Virginia's birdlife, "Virginia's Flying Colors."

It is against this background that our endangered species programs exist. Being a total wildlife agency, we have not subscribed to the practice of establishing special game and non-game or endangered species groups or units. Each district biologist is responsible for all species within his geographic area of responsibility.

The endangered species program in Virginia relies heavily upon the expertise available in colleges and universities of the Commonwealth. Most of our species-specific programs are contracted with the best people in the field throughout schools in the state. This policy has proven to be effective and rewarding. However, each project is administered by a biologist on our staff. As a feature of each contract, the contractor is required to meet certain parameters and, as part of the deliverables from the project, he is required to produce stylized input for BOVA.

SPECIFIC PROGRAMS

Bald Eagle (Cooperator—Dr. Mitchell A. Byrd, College of William and Mary)

The history of the bald eagle (*Haliaeetus leucocephalus*) and its decline, primarily due to the ingestion of chlorinated hydrocarbons, is well-known and well-documented. Eagles in Virginia were not spared from this decline.

The Commission initiated its bald eagle research program in 1976 with the following objectives:

1. To determine the size of the breeding population and its productivity in Virginia.
2. To obtain a winter inventory of bald eagle numbers and determine the range of these birds in Virginia.
3. To monitor activities of two active eagle nest sites from egg laying through fledging of the young through the use of video equipment. In addition, all aspects of incubation and post-incubation behavior will be observed from two blinds at two additional sites.
4. To determine post nesting dispersal and other movements of young eagles through the use of radio telemetry.
5. To develop and utilize techniques to introduce bald eagles into formerly occupied habitat through hacking techniques and to introduce captivity-reared bald eagle young into foster parent nests.

The fate of the bald eagle is closely associated with the condition of Chesapeake Bay. Primarily a fish eater, the bald eagle lives along the bay and the tidal rivers. Most of our eagles are found along the Potomac, Rappahannock, James, and Chickahominy rivers.

At the time the project was initiated in 1976 there were thirty-three active nests in Virginia, of which only 13 were productive. Surveys conducted during the late winter and spring of 1984 located 60 active nests, 8 more than the previous year. The nests produced 65 young, of which 58 survived. Some of the young perished in a May storm that occurred in the eastern part of the state, and a few simply fell out of the nest. One young eagle was shipped to North Carolina where it contributed to that state's eagle recovery program. Forty-five of the eaglets were banded and marked for future identification.

A large summer population of bald eagles resides on the Potomac and James rivers. Surveys were conducted on both rivers during the summer of 1983 revealing that between 60 and 100 eagles residing on each river. We are planning to use radio telemetry to further our studies of these summer visitors.

The mid-winter survey revealed a significant increase in the number found. A total of 217 were counted in 1984, as opposed to 171 the previous year. The James river hosted the largest number of wintering eagles.

One of the more interesting studies of eagles was conducted at Caledon State Park. This park and the adjoining Cedar Grove Farm on the Potomac River harbor one of the most largest concentrations of bald eagles on the Atlantic Coast. The problem is to determine how the public may use the yet-to-be-opened park without disturbing the eagles. The study was designed to determine the areas used most by eagles during each season of the year.

The park and farm border on the Potomac River where the eagles feed. They were counted by setting up a census route along the shore which was traversed by boat several times each week from March through November. The greatest number of eagles was present in August when 39 were counted per census. The highest count for any one day was 55. More adults were noted in July, while immature birds were most prevalent in late August. Because there were undoubtedly more eagles present in the forest beyond the shoreline, the numbers counted represent a conservative count of the numbers of eagles actually present.

Foot surveys were also conducted inland to find concentrations of eagles and areas they used extensively as a basis for recommendations of areas that must be protected from traffic.

While eagles appear to be on the increase and breeding success appears to be sufficient to maintain populations, efforts will continue to safeguard the future of this species. In addition to continued monitoring of the breeding population, continued effort will be made to monitor known summer and winter concentration areas for eagles and to locate new areas which are significant.

A new initiative has been launched, using commission personnel, to contact landowners of areas where eagles nest or concentrate to develop cooperative agreements or negotiate conservation easements to afford a degree of protection to these critical areas. We believe that, while a great deal of effort has been devoted to monitoring populations and migrations, this is the first concrete action we have taken to actually benefit the birds and ensure their future viability.

More work needs to be done to determine the types of human activity that have an adverse effect upon nesting success and to develop parameters to evaluate such activity, as well as means to protect the eagles from such activity during the nesting period.

Peregrine Falcon (Cooperator—Dr. Mitchell A. Byrd, College of William and Mary)

When the Commission of Game and Inland Fisheries began its program to work with peregrine falcons (*Falco peregrinus*), the species was extirpated as a breeding bird in the Commonwealth. Known nesting sites in the western mountains had been abandoned for many years, a fact substantiated as the Commission's program progressed.

The program was initiated in 1976 with the following objectives:

1. Locate and monitor all known historical eyries and evaluate their present suitability for occupancy by peregrines.
2. Re-introduce peregrines into Virginia through the technique of hacking.
3. Monitor transient populations of peregrines in Virginia.

A total of 15 known valid sites for eyries were identified within the western region of the state. Of these, 13 historical nesting sites were thoroughly evaluated and 7 were rated as suitable for re-occupancy or the release of captive-produced birds. Human activity in the vicinity of nesting sites is recognized as a limiting factor in selecting viable nesting sites.

Nineteen releases of captive-produced peregrines were conducted from 8 release sites in eastern Virginia between 1978 and 1984. The release sites were mainly hack towers, except one was released from a roof and another from a cupola. The success rate of peregrine releases in Virginia has been 90 percent. The greatest known cause of mortality in Virginia is due to returning subadult and adult peregrines. In one instance, a released female is believed to have followed a subadult tiercel away from the site and was listed as lost because the subadult was never observed to feed and she was considered too young to hunt proficiently. An adult male or a pair that returned to a hack site forced three young males away from the site before they were competent hunters. This incident was repeated at another site and it is anticipated that this problem may occur more frequently in the future as more adults return to towers where young are present. However, in eastern Virginia the peregrines are largely spared predation by great horned owls which are rare in the salt marsh habitat. Great horned owl predation may be a factor as hacking activities commence in the western part of the state.

The first nesting of released peregrine falcons occurred at Assateague Island in 1982 where a pair successfully reared three young. A pair at this same release site subsequently produced four young in 1983 and four (including two foster young) in 1984. Four more young, including 3 foster young, were successfully reared at Great Fox Island in 1984. Although successful nesting occurred at only two sites in 1984, single or paired adults occurred at 8 of 10 sites. The chances for future nesting success appear to be quite good.

Three stations for monitoring raptor movements during the fall migration have been operating for several years at locations on the Eastern Shore. These stations were manned a total of 69 station days in 1983 and 62 station days in 1984. In 1983, a total of 87 peregrines were observed, as opposed to 191 in 1984. These observations, of course, are heavily influenced by the weather; but over the years the trend has been upwards, probably reflecting a recovery of tundra populations in the north. Monitoring activities throughout the winter on the Eastern Shore and Tidewater Virginia indicates an increase of wintering populations, probably as a result of the hacking program as well as a larger number of wintering tundra birds.

Current plans call for continued monitoring of the status of nesting pairs that have resulted from the reintroduction efforts. Brood supplementation with captive-reared young will continue as appropriate.

The program will undertake a major new initiative as it moves westward to the Appalachians. Birds will be released at cliff sites in an attempt to reintroduce peregrines in the historic range of the species.

Red-cockaded Woodpecker (Cooperator—Dr. Mitchell A. Byrd, College of William and Mary)

This program involves locating colonies of red-cockaded woodpeckers (*Picoides borealis*) and negotiating with landowners to protect the fragile mature pine habitat required to sustain the species. The objectives of the Game Commission's program are:

1. To initiate a comprehensive survey of suitable habitat areas in southeastern Virginia in an effort to determine the present population levels and to estimate past population levels.

2. To describe the habitat comprising the support stand of known active or recently active clan sites, to describe characteristics of the cavity trees, and to explore relationships between the cavity tree and the support stand.

3. To estimate nesting success in areas with known red-cockaded woodpecker activity.

4. To develop plans for effective management of the species in Virginia.

In 1982, seven active nests were found, of which six successfully produced young. Nine young were produced averaging 1.28 per active nest. These young birds, plus 22 known adults, constituted the total known population found in Virginia.

This endangered species has reached this precarious state largely because it demands larger, mature pines into which it drills the holes for its nest. It appears that mature pines and the woodpecker are sharing the same fate.

Through the cooperation of the Union Camp Corporation and the Gray Lumber Company, a few known nesting sites of this rare woodpecker have been spared; but this may not be sufficient. Because of the small numbers, there may not be genetic diversity required to ensure the viability of the species in Virginia, which is at the extreme northern edge of its range.

In 1984, isolated birds were found at one site in each of two counties. Active breeding was determined at 4 sites, 3 of which were successful in producing 3 young each. Including these chicks, the Virginia population was estimated at 25 in 1984.

A graduate student is now studying the winter foraging requirements of the species. However, the population is quite tenuous at this time. The species has no chance for survival in Virginia unless present and adjacent habitats are placed in a protected management status.

Steps are presently being taken with major conservation groups to acquire all or portions of significant habitats in the state which are occupied by red-cockaded woodpeckers. Should these endeavors be successful, attempts might then be made to introduce birds from populations where density is higher.

Delmarva Fox Squirrel (Project Officer—Karen Terwilliger, Virginia Commission of Game and Inland Fisheries)

The Commission program for the recovery of the Delmarva fox squirrel (*Sciurus niger cinereus*) includes the following actions:
1. Habitat protection.
2. Nest box and/or den tree provisions.
3. Reduction of competition from gray squirrels (*sciurus cerolinus*).
4. Protection from hunting or other controllable mortality factors.
5. Habitat management for adequate food supply and understory reduction through planned forestry practices.
6. Translocation of squirrels to suitable habitat within former range.

The Delmarva fox squirrel has suffered from lack of suitable habitat due to land use practices. In order to restore it to viable numbers, suitable habitat must be identified and re-populated.

In June of 1982, a total of 24 squirrels were live-trapped on the Chincoteague National Wildlife Refuge and translocated to Brownsville, an antebellum plantation owned by The Nature Conservancy. The actual relocation covered about a year, being completed in July of 1983. Nest boxes were erected and feeders installed in Brownsville's mature pine forests in an attempt to meet all of the species needs.

To prevent dispersion from the release site, the "soft release" technique was employed. The animals were transported to the release sites in their nest boxes and the boxes were placed in a large holding pen (soft release cage) where they were free to roam. They were monitored as they were fed and watered for 3 to 5 days before they were permitted to exit the cage.

Subsequent to the release, feeder watches and nest box checks have been conducted to monitor the status of the population. Extra feeders and nest boxes were installed to be sure all needs were satisfied.

Feeders filled with corn were effective in attracting squirrels for observation, particularly during the winter months. However, additional measures were required to assess the population and reproductive success.

Thirty-five nest boxes had been placed, hoping that the squirrels would use them for reproduction as well as winter denning. To date, however, observations have found only one Delmarva and several gray squirrels using the boxes.

This behavior is typical in suitable habitat. Seasonal box checks, consequently, documented very little use. Birds, however, used the boxes as winter roosts.

A mark and recapture program was initiated in January of 1984. Forty live traps baited with corn were set and checked daily. After 2 weeks, only 4 Delmarva fox squirrels were captured. Two were adult females which were brought from Chincoteague. The other two were unmarked young males. This means that either reproduction had occurred or, more likely, that one of the females was pregnant when transplanted. During this trapping period, 16 gray squirrels were removed from the area.

The low number of Delmarvas caught could indicate they have dispersed from the area, that they suffered high mortality, or that their activity level was low during the winter month in which trapping was conducted.

The following fall 40 traps were pre-baited in October and set in November, resulting in the capture of 5 Delmarvas, 5 grays, and 3 opossums. Two of the Delmarvas were adult males and one, an adult female which showed evidence of having reproduced since the previous January when it had been trapped (££) across a salt marsh from the previous capture locations. The remaining 2 were young of the year females

Monitoring of this small transplanted population will continue as we continue to search for other suitable release sites.

Marine Turtles (Cooperators—Dr. Jack Musick and Richard Byles, Virginia Institute of Marine Science)

Recognizing that marine turtles qualified as endangered species in Virginia, the Commission of Game and Inland Fisheries has been partially funding marine turtle research being conducted by the Virginia Institute of Marine Science, a division of the College of William and Mary.

Studies so far have indicated that juvenile loggerhead (*Caretta caretta*) and Atlantic ridley (*Lepidochelys kempii*) turtles migrate into Chesapeake Bay each summer to feed in this productive estuary. No one knows where they come from, what routes they follow, where they go when they leave, or where they winter. Prior research has shown that a significant number of turtles die in the bay each year, many due to accidental drownings in fixed fishing gear. Virginia Institute of Marine Science (VIMS) studies under Dr. Jack Musick and doctoral candidate Richard Byles are designed to answer the above questions and to help reduce mortality in the bay.

Research includes biotelemetry studies to determine the behavior and migratory routes of individual turtles, including aerial surveys to determine to what extent the turtles use the bay and how many are present. Every carcass found is examined to determine cause of death. These studies are aimed at improving the protection of sea turtles in Virginia waters.

In 1983, six loggerheads and one Atlantic ridley (the rarest of all sea turtles)

were equipped with two types of telemetric devices and tracked by aircraft and small boats.

One transmitter sent signals over long distances but would not transmit underwater. The second was an underwater sonic transmitter which had smaller range. Since turtles spend most of their time underwater, the sonic transmitter was advantageous. Both types were attached to each turtle. By the end of fiscal year 1984 the studies had resulted in the following determinations:

1. Of the time monitored, the loggerheads spent only 5 percent of their time on the surface. This indicated a ratio of 20 to 1 underwater to surface time.

2. The above ratio of underwater to surface time was used to strengthen population estimates derived from aerial surveys. The ratio was used as a multiplier to account for unseen underwater turtles along the flight path. In 1983, an estimated 3600 loggerhead turtle were present at the mouth of the bay in the 750 Km^2 study.

3. Turtles are apparently more abundant in the lower bay. Very few reports of sea turtles have been collected north of the Potomac River. Flights being conducted in fiscal year 1985 compare the mid and upper reaches of the Chesapeake Bay to the lower bay study area.

4. Both species of turtles appear to select preferred feeding ranges after entering the bay. Evidence indicates that loggerheads return to the same sites year after year. Two loggerheads were intentionally removed from their capture sites to test their preference for a particular range. Monitored telemetrically, both turtles swam nearly directly back to their capture sites, covering distances of about 48 Km (30 miles) and 74 Km (46 miles).

5. The loggerhead and ridley have different food preferences and feeding ranges. The predominate prey found in loggerhead stomachs was horsehoe crabs while Ridleys fed almost exclusively on blue crabs. Differences were also noted in feeding areas. Both species displayed a tendency to orient on freshwater outflows at river mouths, but the ridley favored shallower water, ranging from 0.3 (12 ft) to 18 m (66 ft) in depth or in waters near channels.

6. There is no evidence of turtles wintering in the bay. Turtles are physiologically capable of hibernation, but the bottom water temperatures in all probability during the winter are too cold for sea turtles to overwinter in Virginia. Turtles have been found to be present in Virginia when water temperatures are above 68°F. These temperatures are normally found in Virginia from May into October. Although turtles tagged on both coasts of Florida have been recovered in the Chesapeake, none from the bay have been tracked to their wintering grounds. They have been observed on their northward spring migration along the coast and into the bay, and southward to Cape Hatteras, North Carolina in the fall. Contact with radio-tracked turtles has not been maintained beyond Cape Hatteras.

7. A new sonic device developed in 1983-84 is currently being tested. In addition to simply locating turtles, this device will furnish information concerning

feeding and swimming activity, depth of the turtle, as well as internal and external temperatures.

8. A new state-of-the-art satellite transmitter is being developed specifically for work with sea turtles. This new unit is smaller, more powerful than older models and will be able to transmit locations, depth of dives, and temperatures from migrating turtles. The first unit should be available shortly, but failure of a NASA satellite has delayed placing a transmitter on a turtle. When deployed this system will enable VIMS to track a turtle for a year regardless of weather conditions. This new equipment should enable VIMS scientists to find the wintering sites of the Chesapeake Bay turtles and provide data concerning behavioral changes that take place during migration.

Programmed activities for fiscal year 1986 include continued aerial surveys and population estimates, pound net monitoring, rescue and salvage of carcasses, determination of preferred turtle habitats in the bay, construction of a turtle holding pen, enhancement and continuation of the satellite tracking program, and aid with carcass salvage and mortality investigations to include blood collection and examination, maintenance of a stranding network, and continuing studies of turtle aging techniques.

Endangered Bats (Cooperator—Dr. Virginia Tipton, Radford University)

This project commenced in 1983 with a survey of known caves. A total of 17 caves in southwest Virginia were explored the first year, with the search centering on endangered Virginia long-eared bats (plecotus townsendii virginianus *M. sodais* and Indiana bats. No big-eared bats were found in 1983, but Indiana bats were found in 2 caves.

In 1984, 28 caves previously unexplored caves were checked and 2 of the caves had significant numbers of little brown bats (*Myotis iucifugus*) and pipistrelle bats (*Pifistrellus subflavus*). A major discovery was a cave serving as a hibernaculum for 2 endangered species of bats, the Virginia big-eared bat and the Indiana bat. Negotiations have been completed with the landowner to protect this important habitat.

The other known cave used by hibernating Indiana bats was survived and the results indicated that the population had declined from the previous years. This decline was attributed to a major disturbance caused by efforts to rescue a lost person from the cave about a month before the survey.

A list of caves to be censused was obtained from the Commission's wildlife data base, BOVA. The caves were visited once or twice a year as dictated by their complexity. All bats, including endangered and non-endangered species, observed during the visits were counted and ambient temperatures and humidities recorded. Records were kept on other life forms found in caves. All of this information will contribute to a comprehensive report as the study continues.

An ultrasonic bat detector purchased by the Commission was used to help detect bat activity within the caves. The detector picks up the ultrasonic calls of bats which are converted into sound audible to humans. These sounds are also converted to electrical pulses which are displayed on a portable oscilloscope, which enables the investigators to locate and identify the bats.

Further studies include determining when Virginia big-eared bats leave the maternity roost cave in the fall and when they return in the spring. This hibernation cave was also monitored to determine when they departed for the season. Since this cave was only recently discovered, arrival time of the bats could not be determined; but this will be solved this year.

Two additional caves were found to be important hibernation areas for large numbers of non-endangered bats. Both caves have adequate protection provided by the landowners to ensure their viability.

The most significant discovery so far was the finding of the cave that supported the two endangered species during hibernation. This find located about 250 big-eared bats and 4,000 Indiana bats but the summer range of the Indiana bats has not been determined at this time.

Endangered Mussels (Cooperator—Dr. Richard Neves, Virginia Polytechnic Institute and State University)

Remnant populations of 9 endangered species of mussels currently survive in portions of the Holston, Powell, and Clinch rivers in southwest Virginia. These include the shiny pigtoe pearly mussel (*Fusconaia edgariana*), fine-rayed pigtoe pearly mussel (*Fusconaia cuneolus*), birdwing pearly mussel (*Conradilla caelata*), dromedary pearly mussel (*Dromus dromas*), tan riffle shell mussel (*Epioblasma walkeri*), green-blossom pearly mussel (*Epioblasma torulosa gubernaculum*), Appalachian monkeyface pearly mussel (*Quadrula sparsa*), and the Cumberland monkeyface pearly mussel (*Quadrula intermedia*). The ninth species, the rough pigtoe pearly mussel (*Pleurobema plenum*) has been extirpated from Virginia waters.

In fiscal year 1983, the Commission supported two mussel projects which were directed by Dr. Richard Neves of Virginia Polytechnic Institute and State University (VPI & SU).

It is known that certain fish act as intermediary hosts during the reproductive cycle of mussels. In one of the two studies Dr. Neves infected certain known host fish with the larvae (glochidia) of three non-endangered mussels and transplanted them to specific test sites in the Clinch and Holston rivers. These larvae, residing in the gills of the host fish, will eventually drop off and, hopefully, start a new mussel population. This procedure could be a useful tool in expanding the range of endangered mussels. A previous transplant of mussels not using host fish, but simply transplanting adult mussels, has proven to be successful. Previous transplants are being evaluated to determine the number of mussels, males and females, that can be relocated after 2 years. Initial sampling efforts on the North Fork of the Holston River found 30 to 50 percent of transplants placed in 1981. Those not found are believed to be nearby but washed downstream by high water conditions.

The second study was designed to evaluate the habitats favored by juvenile mussels. No one knows where juveniles reside in the stream bed. Field sampling for juvenile mussels began in 1983. Substrates in major habitat types were collected with a bucket sampler in March, May, and June. These samples of stream bottoms were preserved, stained, and sorted under a binocular microscope in the laboratory. From 26 samples, 14 juvenile mussels have been collected from pool, run, and riffle habitats. Preliminary results indicate that preferred habitat may be near stream banks and behind boulders in streams. Core sampling will determine depth and bottom type (substrate) preferences. There appears to be an extremely high mortality between newly transformed juvenile mussels and those that reach one year of age. There is presently no way of determining the species of juvenile mussels, but these studies include efforts to develop an accurate identification technique. Further sampling is planned to determine whether the habitat requirements of adults and juveniles are the same or if they differ significantly.

In 1984, work on habitat requirements for juvenile mussels continued on Big Moccasin Creek which flows more than 80 Km (50 miles) through Scott and Russell counties, joining the North Fork of the Holston near Weber City. Seven species of mussels occur in this area.

To understand this work one must appreciate that a juvenile mussel is not much larger than a grain of sand. It is about a millimeter long, transparent, and very difficult to sort out of the substrate which is sand, mud, and litter gathered from the creek bottom. In addition, all living material in the sample must be identified, cataloged, and counted. The process involves taking a sample, baking it in an oven, and then painstakingly sorting through it with the aid of a microscope.

This 1984 study produced 36 samples from which 46 juveniles were isolated.

Early information indicates that juveniles are present in all substrates where adults are found. Work in progress this year includes corroboration of the juvenile/adult relationship, confirmation of the Big Moccasin data in another stream, and obtaining better ecological data on the early life stages of mussels.

Another study, this one dealing with predation of mussels, suggests that predation by muskrats can be a limiting factor on mussel populations.

Fringed Mountain Snail (Cooperator—Dr. Robert E. Batie, Radford University)

The Virginia Fringed Mountain Snail (*Polygyriscus virginianus*) is considered to be one of the rarest snails in North America. Its known range is restricted to a single collection site on the banks of the New River near Radford, Virginia.

Virtually nothing is known about the basic population structure, population size, distribution, or basic biological requirements of this species. In order to implement a recovery plan, initial studies are necessary to describe its basic distribution and abundance.

This project, commencing in July 1985, involves the survey of potential habitats within a 16 Km (10 mile) radius of the single known habitat. Further, the known habitat will be carefully surveyed to determine the status of the population of this rare snail.

Threatened Species

Osprey (Cooperator—Dr. Mitchell A. Byrd, College of William and Mary)

The osprey (*Pandion haliaetus-carolinensis*) population in Virginia was in decline through the 1960s' and 1970s' due to egg failure and other causes. In the late 1960s', the Redbook of "Rare and Endangered Fish and Wildlife of the United States" classified the osprey as "status undetermined."

Using endangered and non-game species check-off funds, the Virginia Commission of Game and Inland Fisheries initiated its osprey program in 1983. The objectives were:

1. Make a complete aerial and ground survey of active osprey nests to determine the total breeding population size.

2. Measure hatching and fledging success of a sample of osprey nests representative of Virginia.

3. Coordinate all transfer of young ospreys from Virginia to other states involved in re-introduction programs for this species.

4. Study the population dynamics of the species based upon a large banded sample of adults.

Dr. Byrd has been involved with osprey research since 1970 and the Commission's program has benefited from his long experience with this species. Statewide surveys of ospreys were conducted from 1982 to 1985. During fiscal year 1983 a total of 700 breeding pairs were located. In fiscal year 1984, the number of ospreys increased significantly to 800 breeding pairs.

Four hundred to 525 nests are being monitored 3 times during the breeding season to determine nesting success. Productivity is exceeding one fledgling per active nest.

For the past 5 years, Virginia has provided 10 to 25 young per year to Tennessee and Pennsylvania for hacking purposes. Young have been provided based upon nesting productivity in Virginia.

Dr. Byrd has banded over 3000 nesting ospreys in Virginia since 1976. In 1983, a program to trap and identify banded birds was started and a total of 66 adults were captured, of which 51 were banded. The banded birds ranged from 4 to 14 years of age. The average age of trapped males was 5.9 years and the average age of females was 8.8 years. The average age of all banded birds captured was 6.9 years. Further study will be required to determine why the paucity of 3 to 5 year old birds occurred. It is possible there are many non-breeders in this age group. Trapping samples also enabled researchers to determine dispersal distances between natal and breeding areas. Two birds dispersed over 100 Km, but most appeared to nest within 30 Km of where they were hatched.

In 1984, severe May storms resulted in the loss of many osprey nests. Over 100 were lost on the Eastern Shore alone. The losses were not as severe on the western shore of Chesapeake Bay, but some areas experienced a 30 to 50 percent of the nests. Because the storms came so late, the adults did not attempt to re-nest, resulting in osprey productivity that was substantially below that of 1983. It was so low that production at that level would be insufficient to support the population.

Future efforts with this species will be concerned with population studies, monitoring continued availability of nest sites, and providing young to other states for hacking purposes.

An interesting aspect study arose when it was noted that the Coast Guard was placing channel marker to the poles at a point so low that the pointed top of the sign did not project above the top of the pole. This practice prevented ospreys from anchoring nests on these markers. Coordination with the Coast Guard should prevent this from happening in the future.

Roanoke Log Perch and Orangefin Madtom (Cooperator—Dr. Richard Neves, Virginia Polytechnic Institute and State University)

The Roanoke Log Perch (*Percina rex*) and the Orangefin Madtom (*Notorus gilberti*) are considered to be candidate species for threatened status in Virginia by the U.S. Fish and Wildlife Service. Little information is available on their current distribution, life histories, or habitat requirements within the state. In 1984, a study was initiated to collect sufficient distributional and population data on these two species to assess their status and provide recommendations for their protection.

Using electrofishing equipment, seines, and snorkels with slurp guns, sampling was initiated in 1984 with initial emphasis on the orangefin madtom. Efforts were concentrated in areas where the orangefin madtom was known to occur. Starting at this point, the collection team found this species in areas where it was not reported before, extending the range of the species from 17.6 Km (11 miles) on one stream to 106.7 Km (66.8 miles) and extending it on another stream from 1.6 Km (1 mile) to 16.5 (10.3 miles).

Additional sampling for both species will continue this year.

Related Projects

In addition to the projects noted above, the Commission is conducting continuing studies of various species of colonial nesting birds, shore birds, the loggerhead shrike (*Lanius ludovicianus*), barn owl (*Tyto alba pratincoa*), small mammals, reptiles, and amphibians. We are cooperating with the Virginia Society of Ornithology in their breeding bird survey and support a bird banding station on the Eastern Shore. A comprehensive book of the fishes of Virginia is being assembled by Dr. Robert Jenkins of Roanoke College, and the Virginia Institute of Marine Science is assembling marine vertebrate data for BOVA. Last year Dr. James Fraser, VPI & SU, completed a non-game attitude study which assessed the public concept of the program and provided guidance for the future.

Author's Note: Material for this chapter was, in part, furnished by the cooperators mentioned above for each of the species addressed. Their comments were incorporated into the text without credit. I wish to acknowledge the contribution of each one.

Endangered and Threatened Species Programs in Pennsylvania and other States: Causes, Issues and Management. Edited by S. K. Majumdar, F. J. Brenner and A. F. Rhoads. © 1986, The Pennsylvania Academy of Science.

Chapter Thirty-One

THREATENED AND ENDANGERED SPECIES IN WEST VIRGINIA

Kenneth B. Knight
Wildlife Biologist
West Virginia Department of Natural Resources
P.O. Box 67, Elkins, WV 26241

INTRODUCTION

Eight animals currently or formerly found in West Virginia are listed by the federal government as endangered and one is listed as threatened. There are no plant species listed as threatened or endangered, although several are currently under review.

West Virginia has no endangered species legislation at the state level. The West Virginia Department of Natural Resources (WVDNR) maintains lists of plants and animals deemed to be rare in the state. Information on each of these species is stored in manual and computer files and each occurrence is recorded on USGS topographic maps. This information is used in the review of mining and construction permit applications, to fulfill requests for environmental information, and in the identification of significant biological areas.

In September 1982 WVDNR entered into an Endangered Species Cooperative Agreement with the U.S. Fish and Wildlife Service. The cooperative agreement opened the door for federal assistance matching monies under Section 6 of the Endangered Species Act and a major, coordinated effort to conserve threatened and endangered fish and wildlife within the state. These funds are matched by state nongame wildlife tax check-off receipts. To date, Section 6 projects have included studies of the Virginia big-eared bat, Indiana bat, flatspired three-toothed land snail, bald eagle, and peregrine falcon.

BALD EAGLE
Haliaeetus leucocephalus

Historical Status

The bald eagle was not known to nest in West Virginia before 1981, but this is not to say that the bald eagles have never nested in the state. The rugged landscape and extensive remote areas may have harbored an occasional nest, but it is probably safe to say that no self-sustaining population has existed in the past 100 years.

Current Status

In June 1981, a bald eagle nest was discovered along the South Branch of the Potomac River in Hardy County (Fig. 1). The size of the nest indicated that it was relatively new, probably a first year nest. Two nestlings were fledged in 1981 and every subsequent year through the present (1985). The origin of the adults is not known; the closest known nest is 160 km (100 miles) to the east, on the western shore of the Chesapeake Bay.

FIGURE 1. Current known nesting site of the bald eagle in West Virginia.

The nest is unfortunately along a remote, but very popular section of river for fishing, camping, canoeing, and hunting. The location of the nest is widely known, and consequently is frequently visited by photographers and others hoping to get a glimpse of an eagle. Since the nest tree is on a steep slope, the nest and its contents may be peered into simply by climbing up the mountain a few 100 feet above the river. This, of course, is disruptive, particularly to nesting birds, but, to date, has not resulted in reproductive failure or mortality of nestlings.

Bald eagles are frequently observed in all parts of the state during fall migration and winter. Single adult birds, apparently nonbreeders, are also occasionally seen during the nesting season, but no additional nests have been located.

The bald eagle was listed as endangered in 1967.

Reasons for Status

The lack of natural lakes in West Virginia and relative isolation from other breeding populations probably accounts for the historical absence of bald eagles in the state.

Current Research

Since 1984 the WVDNR has contracted with the National Wildlife Federation Raptor Information Center to band the eagle nestlings. Each bird receives a standard federal aluminum band and a white plastic band with a black engraved alpha-numeric code. Otherwise, we have a policy of minimal disturbance with only occasional monitoring to determine nesting chronology and success.

Current Management

Through contact with the landowner, we expect no alteration of habitat near the nest as long as the birds are nesting at that location. Public education efforts via the news media, the state natural resources magazine, and DNR brochures should help assure that this species will continue to nest and flourish in West Virginia.

The Future

Planning has recently been initiated for a small-scale (1-2 pairs) bald eagle captive breeding program at the French Creek Game Farm in central West Virginia. Progeny would be used for hacking and/or fostering.

As eagle populations in nearby states continue to expand and with each year of successful reproduction at the West Virginia nest, it is expected that this species will eventually establish a breeding population in the state providing a link between populations in the Chesapeake Bay area and the Great Lakes region.

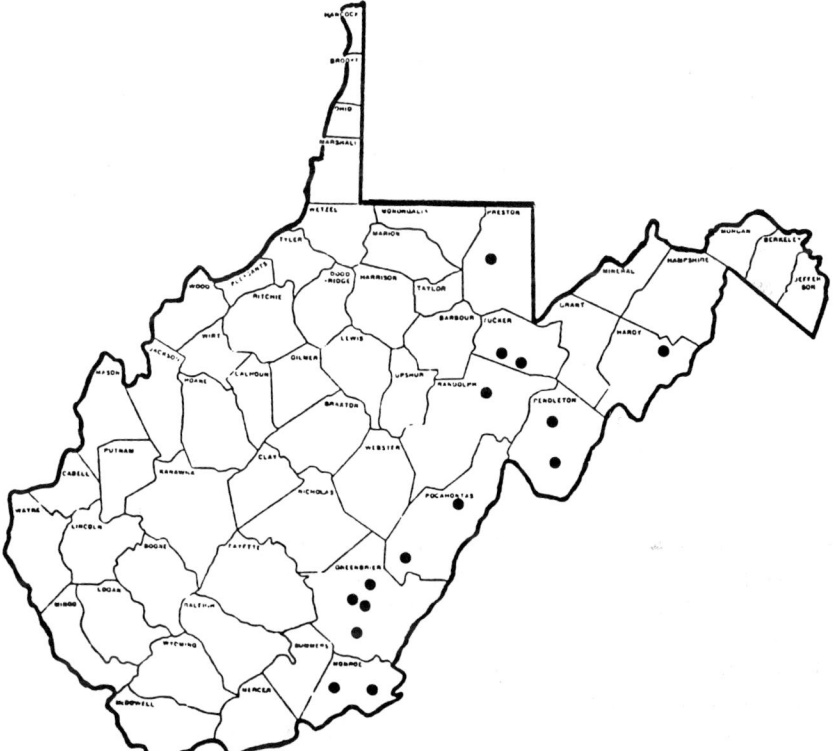

FIGURE 2. Recorded occurrences of the Indiana bat in West Virginia.

INDIANA BAT
Myotis sodalis

Historical Status

West Virginia is at the eastern periphery of the distributional range for the Indiana bat. It is found here in relatively small and widely scattered populations throughout the cavernous limestone region in the eastern mountains (Fig. 2). Some population estimates are available from the early 1940's, about the time when sport caving began to gain rapidly in popularity. From available sources, it appears that during the 1940's the known Indiana bat population in the state numbered about 5,000 individuals. Many old publications and museum specimens list the cave name, but yield no information on colony size. Also, given the large number of caves in the state and the fact that caves are still being found, there have no doubt been and may still be, undiscovered bat colonies. Thus, the figure of 5,000 individuals is probably a minimum value.

Current Status

Despite the increased level of cave exploration in recent years, no major hibernating colonies of *Myotis sodalis* have been discovered since the 1950's. The total known population in the state is currently about 3626 bats, and only 4 caves currently contain more than 25 individuals. One colony which numbered 1,600 to 2,400 *M. sodalis* in the early 1940's has been reduced to only 2 individuals in 1985. Another which contained 1,500 Indiana bats in 1974 had over 3,300 in the winter of 1986. This is currently the largest known population in the state, and it has been closed to human entry in winter since 1981.

The Indiana bat was listed as endangered in 1967.

Reasons for Status

The use of chlorinated hydrocarbon pesticides and disturbance by vandals, bat researchers, and recreational cavers are perhaps the primary decimating factors. Pesticides not only reduced the available food supply, but they also contributed directly to bat mortality.[1,2] Indiana bats are extremely sensitive to disturbance during hibernation, awaking quickly and flying about. If harassed too frequently or for prolonged periods, their remaining energy reserves may not be sufficient for them to survive the winter.

Current Research

In the mid-1970's the WVDNR funded a Master's degree project to determine the historic and current status of bats in West Virginia.[3] At about the same time various levels of research were also conducted or funded by the U.S. Fish and Wildlife Service and the U.S. Forest Service. In 1983, WVDNR initiated a bat research project with Section 6 endangered species federal assistance matching monies. The primary purpose of the project was to locate, protect, and monitor existing hibernating colonies of *M. sodalis* in West Virginia. In 3 winters of fieldwork, 60 caves have been surveyed, and one new major colony has been located.[4,5]

Management

One of the few management tools for protecting *M. sodalis* hibernacula is the closure of the occupied caves, via a gate or chain-link fence, from 1 September through 30 April. These structures must be faithfully maintained, however, as they gain the particular attention of often-ingenious vandals. Resurveys of these populations are resurveyed every 2 years, thus minimizing disturbance.

The Future

Although many of the most detrimental pesticides have been banned or restricted in use and the major hibernacula have been protected, the future of the Indiana bat in West Virginia is questionable. The species may be so reduced in number as to preclude an increase. Our best hope lies in the discovery of a new colony in a cave little known to sport cavers or the recolonization of a cave or caves currently closed in winter.

VIRGINIA BIG-EARED BAT
Plecotus townsendii virginianus

Historical Status

A subspecies of the Western or Townsend's big-eared bat, the Virginia big-eared bat is found in only 3 small disjunct populations, with one each in Kentucky, Virginia, and West Virginia. Historical population figures from West Virginia are even less available than for the Indiana bat. For this reason, we cannot document a population decline per se, but the existing population is so small and vulnerable, that the subspecies merits special consideration.

Current Status

Virginia big-eared bats are unique in West Virginia in that they require caves for reproduction in summer as well as hibernation in winter. In summer, the females form maternity or nursery colonies where the young are born and reared. The location of the males in summer in unknown. Currently, 9 maternity colonies, totalling over 3,700 adult females have been located. These colonies range in size from about 150 to over 800 bats.[6] In winter they may or may not inhabit the same caves. Only about 3,640 big-eared bats have been located in hibernacula, the largest of which numbers about 2,914 bats. The distributional range in West Virginia appears to be restricted to only 5 counties in the northern mountains (Fig. 3).

The Virginia big-eared bat was listed as endangered in 1979.

Reasons for Status

The 3 disjunct populations of the Virginia big-eared bat are thought to be natural relicts of a once-widespread population.[7,8] In recent times, they probably also have been affected by pesticides and disturbance by sport cavers and vandals. Many of the caves currently used by this species were the sites of saltpeter extraction operations, particularly during the Civil War. This activity would certainly have been detrimental to all bats, but its effects have not been documented.

Current Research

Building on bat surveys done in West Virginia in the 1970's[3,9,10,11] WVDNR initiated an endangered species federal assistance project in 1983. The purpose of the project is to locate, monitor, and protect all colonies of Virginia big-eared bats in West Virginia. Fieldwork has been aimed primarily at locating the hibernacula. Monitoring of the maternity colonies is accomplished via the nightscope technique.[12] Briefly, the technique involves lighting the entrance or a con-

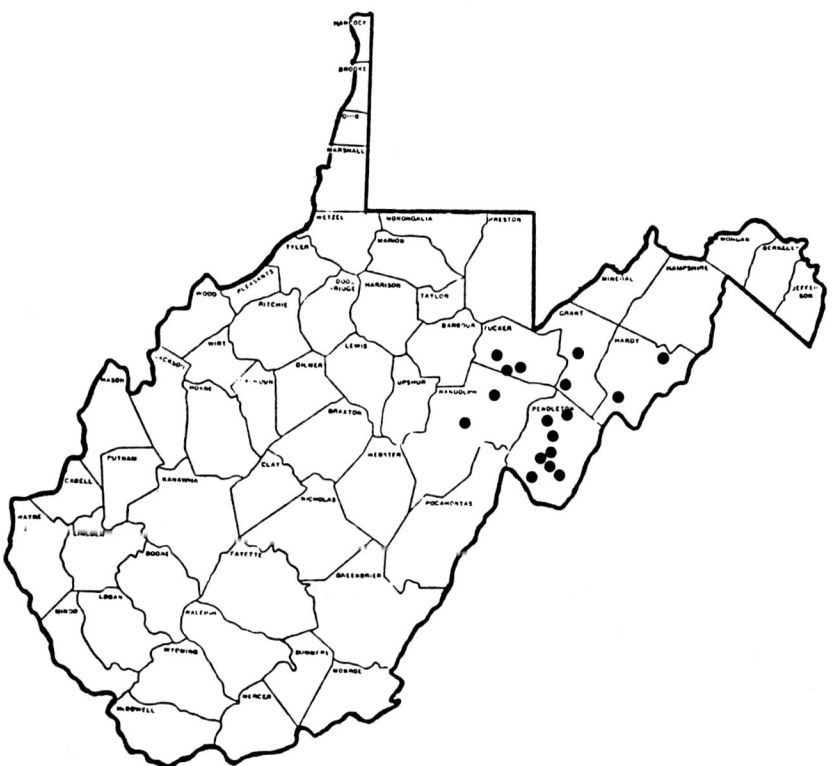

FIGURE 3. Recorded occurrences of the Virginia big-eared bat in West Virginia.

striction in the cave passage with infrared lights. Then, by using a night scope or starlight scope, which gathers and greatly intensifies available light including infrared, the bats are counted as they emerge in the evening to feed. All maternity colonies are monitored annually, while hibernating colonies are monitored every other year.

Management

As with Indiana bats, gating or fencing of the cave entrance is the most effective means of protecting bat colonies. The closure period is 1 April through 15 September for maternity colonies and 1 September through 15 May for hibernacula. Caves which harbor big-ears in summer and winter are generally closed year-round. Six of the 9 summer colonies have been fenced or gated and all 4 of the major winter colonies (over 25 individuals) have been gated or fenced.

The Future

The West Virginia population of the Virginia big-eared bat appears to be relatively stable, and barring unforeseen circumstances, should continue to remain stable or slowly increase.

One major unknown is the location of the more than 3,000 hibernating big-ears. Thus, the population must be considered to be somewhat in jeopardy until these bats are located and protected.

PEREGRINE FALCON
Falco peregrinus

Historical Status

The peregrine falcon nested in West Virginia as late as 1949.[13] By 1964 it had been extirpated as a breeding species throughout the eastern United States.[14] In West Virginia, preferred nesting sites were high cliffs, primarily in the eastern panhandle (Fig. 4). It is not known what the maximum population might have been, but it probably was in the range of 4 to 8 pairs. The total eastern United States population before the decline has been estimated at 3506 pairs.[15]

FIGURE 4. Recorded historic nesting sites of the peregrine falcon in West Virginia.

Current Status
There are currently no known active peregrine eyries in West Virginia. Peregrines are occasionally observed during migration.
The peregrine falcon was listed as endangered in 1970.

Reasons for Status
The rapid decline of the peregrine falcon has been primarily ascribed to the effects of DDT and related pesticides. Wanton shooting and egg collecting probably also contributed to the decline. No additional factors are known to have affected peregrines in West Virginia.

Current Research
Since 1983, WVDNR has been pursuing the goal of reintroducing peregrine falcons into West Virginia. Nine historic eyrie cliffs have been identified and evaluated for current nesting or hacking suitability. Several other cliffs, not known to be historic nesting sites, have also been evaluated. Most of the best cliffs for hacking are located in the eastern panhandle, specifically Pendleton, Grant, Mineral, Hampshire, and Morgan counties. These cliffs are monitored annually for the presence of single peregrines, pairs, and/or nests.

Management
No management for peregrines is underway in West Virginia.

The Future
The Peregrine Falcon Recovery Team intends to start a major release effort in the Southern Appalachian Region, which includes West Virginia, in 1986. Limited releases were made in this region at 2 sites in 1984 and 6 sites in 1985. As a result of 10 years of hacking in the east, the number of natural nests is growing annually. It is reasonable to expect that peregrines will again nest in West Virginia within the next decade.

NORTHERN FLYING SQUIRREL
Glaucomys sabrinus fuscus

Historical Status
Nothing is known of the historical status of West Virginia populations of the northern flying squirrel. Discovered and described in 1936,[16] the type locality of the subspecies *G.s. fuscus* is Cranberry Glades in Pocahontas County. Only 10 occurrences of the species were recorded between 1936 and 1984; these were from 3 general areas in two counties, and all were above 990 m (3,300 ft.) in elevation (Fig. 5).

FIGURE 5. Recorded occurrences of the northern flying squirrel in West Virginia.

Current Status

Little is still known of the status of West Virginia populations. Concern over the relative lack of records for the species and evidence of general population rarity,[17] led to the federal listing in 1985 of two subspecies found in the southern Appalachians: *G. s. fuscus* (found in West Virginia and Virginia) and *G. s. coloratus* (found in North Carolina and Tennessee).

Reasons for Status

Whether currently declining in numbers or not, *G. sabrinus* appears to be severely restricted in distributional range in the southern Appalachians. The gradual reduction of the species' preferred habitat, spruce-fir-mature northern hardwoods, in this region is presumed to have further restricted its distribution. Weigl[18] postulated that the more aggressive southern flying squirrel (*Glaucomys volans*) may out-compete the northern flying squirrel for nest cavities where the ranges of the two species overlap. In addition, *G. volans* harbors a parasite (*Strongyloides*) without apparent harm, which when transferred to *G. sabrinus*, may have fatal results.[19]

Current Research

Research efforts in West Virginia are focused on determining the distribution of *G. sabrinus* in the state and specific habitat preferences. Thus far in 1985, northern flying squirrels have been caught at two locations; most of these captures were in nesting boxes, some erected specifically for flying squirrels and others for bluebirds. At one of these locations, southern flying squirrels were also captured at a slightly higher elevation and in what appeared to be typical northern flying squirrel habitat. Clearly, much more information regarding habitat requirements and preferences is needed.

Management

Most of the suitable range for *G. sabrinus* in West Virginia is within the Monongahela National Forest. Thus, standards and guidelines for management of this species on the national forest have been developed. As our knowledge of habitat requirements improves, management procedures will be refined, particularly in regard to timber management.

The Future

The federal listing of the northern flying squirrel as endangered and the concurrent increase in research regarding the species have probably taken place at an early stage in its decline, if such a decline is occurring at all. Suitable habitat, based on our current knowledge, seems to be relatively abundant in West Virginia. Management and protection under the Endangered Species Act should ensure the continued existence of this species in the state.

EASTERN COUGAR
Felis concolor couguar

Historical Status

The mountain lion was once found throughout West Virginia. This is confirmed by numerous accounts of the early settlers and naturalists as well as local bounty records. One of 8 existing specimens of this subspecies was taken in West Virginia.[20] By about 1900 the cougar was presumed extinct in the state, with the last recorded specimen taken in 1887.[21] There have been numerous reports of sightings of these animals and their tracks in this century but no confirmed occurrences.

Current Status

Whether or not the cougar currently exists in West Virginia is not known.

Despite dozens of reports annually to the contrary, indisputable proof of a population or an individual is not available. At this time, the origin of any cougars found would be questionable.

The eastern cougar was listed as endangered in 1973.

Reasons for Status

Relentless shooting (often encouraged by bounty payments), the destruction and fragmentation of habitat through clearcutting and settlement, and the decline of its primary prey species, the white-tail deer, in the late 1800's are the major reasons for the extirpation of the eastern cougar.

Current Research

The West Virginia Department of Natural Resources records all reported sightings of cougars in the state. Occasionally, field investigations follow-up these reports, particularly when good footprints are found or when several reports are received from the same general area. Many reports seem to be reliable; some, in fact, have been made by WVDNR or U.S. Fish and Wildlife Service biologists.

Management

No active management is done specifically for cougars. Two primary requirements, an adequate food supply and sufficient remote, undeveloped areas, are probably met in West Virginia. The West Virginia deer herd is estimated at over 500,000 and continues to expand. Extensive roadless tracts on national forest and private lands would provide the seclusion the cougar seems to require.

The Future

The future of the cougar in West Virginia seems to depend on its ability to adapt to changing habitat conditions and whether there exists a population from which to expand.

TUBERCULED BLOSSOM PEARLY MUSSEL
Epioblasma (=Dysnomia) torulosa torulosa

Historical Status

This freshwater mussel was once common and relatively widespread in the state. It has been reported from four major river drainages: Tennessee, Cumberland, Ohio, and St. Lawrence.[22] In West Virginia, it has been found only in the Kanawha River,[23] but no live specimens have been found in this century (Fig. 6).

Current Status
The subspecies *Epioblasma t. torulosa* is thought to be extinct.[24] It was listed as endangered in 1976.

Reasons for Status
Like most freshwater mussels, this species requires highly oxygenated, clean waters with a substrate of sand and gravel. Impoundments and pollution have been the major factors in its decline.

Current Research
Recent efforts have primarily involved mussel surveys by various individuals and agencies.[23,25,26,27]

Management
The only chance for survival of *E. torulosa* is the improvement of water quality in the few remaining unimpounded portions of its range.

The Future
All forms of *Epioblasma torulosa* are endangered and may be extinct. There is little chance of recovery for this species.

PINK MUCKET PEARLY MUSSEL
Lampsilis orbiculata (=abrupta) orbiculata

Historical Status
Though generally considered uncommon throughout its range, this freshwater mussel was once relatively widespread, having been reported from 24 river systems, from the Niagara River in New York to the Ouachita River in Arkansas.[22] In West Virginia, it has been recorded from the Elk River[25] and the Kanawha River (Fig. 6).[27,28]

Current Status
Clarke[27] estimated 1,000 individuals of this species in the Kanawha River. However, the population is in a relatively short portion of the river and is, therefore, highly vulnerable to destruction by a single pollution or sediment event.
Lampsilis o. orbiculata was listed as endangered in 1976.

Reasons for Status
Habitat degradation in the form of river impoundment, pollution, and sedimentation is the major factor in this species' decline.

FIGURE 6. Current known range of the tuberculed blossom pearly mussel and the pink mucket pearly mussel in West Virginia.

Current Research
   Mussel surveys are ongoing by various individuals and agencies.[23,25,26,27]

Management
   Little can be done to manage this species other than safeguarding water quality at and above its beds. Clarke[27] also suggested a program of artificial culture and release of young mussels.

The Future
   Barring further degradation of the Kanawha River within range of the species and it will probably remain rare but relatively stable in numbers.

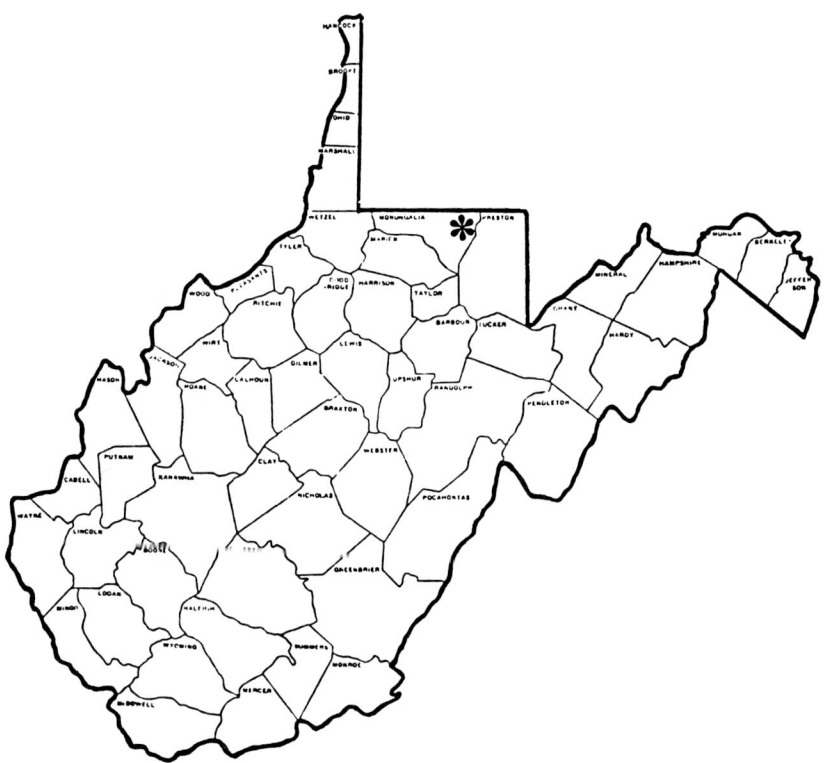

FIGURE 7. Current known range of the flatspired three-toothed land snail.

FLATSPIRED THREE-TOOTHED LAND SNAIL
Triodopsis platysayoides

Historical Status

This land snail was discovered and described by S.T. Brooks in 1933. From its discovery until 1981, it was thought to occur at only one localized site within Coopers Rock State Forest along the rim of the Cheat River canyon. The total population was estimated at 300-500 individuals.[29] It is not known whether the species was once more widespread in recent times or is a natural relict.

Current Status

In 1978, *Triodopsis platysayoides* was listed by the federal government as threatened. At that time, only one small population was known to exist. Since then, field surveys by the WVDNR and the U.S. Fish and Wildlife Service have located 6 additional populations. All 7 sites are within an area of about 2.6 km² (1 mile²) (Fig. 7). A population estimate is difficult to produce given the species' small size, its secretive nature, and the inaccessibility of the numerous sandstone fissures in which it resides.

Reasons for Status

It is not known why *T. platysayoides* is so restricted in distribution. If it was more widespread in recent times, it may have been affected by logging and the fires that generally occurred after logging.

Current Research

The major objective of current research is to determine the distributional range of the species. Other objectives include determining habitat characteristics and preferences, seasonal activity periods, growth rates, longevity, and general life history information.

Management

Management for *T. platysayoides* consists of habitat protection.

The Future

The field investigations currently underway should enable biologists to refine techniques for locating additional populations, if they exist. Since much of the known range is on state-owned lands, protection should be adequate in the future.

REFERENCES CITED

1. Geluso, K.N., J.S. Altenbach, and D.E. Wilson. 1976. Bat mortality: pesticide poisoning and migratory stress. Science 194:184-186.
2. Clark, D.R., Jr. 1981. Bats and environmental contaminants: a review. U.S. Dept. of the Interior, Fish and Wildl. Serv. Spec. Sci. Rep.—Wildl. No. 235, 27pp.
3. Dotson, T.L. 1977. The status of bats in West Virginia. M.S. Thesis Marshall Univ., Huntington, WV. 63pp.
4. Knight, K.B. and J.M. Crum. 1984. Virginia big-eared bat/Indiana bat recovery. Federal Assistance Endangered Species Performance Report. Proj. No. E-1-1. W. Va. Dept. Nat. Resour., Elkins. 15pp.
5. _____. 1985a. Virginia big-eared bat/Indiana bat recovery. Federal Assistance Endangered Species Performance Report. Proj. E-1-2. W. Va. Dept. Nat. Resour., Elkins. 13pp.
6. _____. 1985b. Censuses of *Plecotus townsendii virginianus* maternity colonies in West Virginia, 1985. Unpub. rept. to U.S. Fish and Wildl. Serv., W. Va. Dept. Nat. Resour., Elkins. 4pp.

7. Handley, C.O., Jr. 1959. A revision of American bats of the genera *Euderma* and *Plecotus*. Proc. U.S. Nat. Mus. 110:95-246.
8. Humphrey, S.R. and T.H. Kunz. 1967. Ecology of a Pleistocene relict, the western big-eared bat (*Plecotus townsendii*) in the southern Great Plains. J. Mammal 57:470-494.
9. Hall, J.S. 1972. The status of *Myotis sodalis*, the Indiana bat, in West Virginia. Unpub. Rept. to WVDNR. 9/24/72. 9pp.
10. _____. 1975. The status of the Indiana bat, *Myotis sodalis*, in the Monongahela National Forest. Unpub. Rept. to the U.S. For. Serv. 9pp.
11. _____. 1977. The continuation of the survey of the Indiana bat (*Myotis sodalis*) and the big-eared bat (*Plecotus townsendii*) in Monongahela National Forest, West Virginia. Unpub. Rept. to U.S. For. Serv., Aug. 1977. 6pp.
12. Bagley, F. and J. Jacobs. 1983. Development of a non-intrusive population survey technique for Ozark and Virginia big-eared bat maternity colonies. U.S. Fish and Wildl. Serv., Jackson, Mississippi. 94pp + Append.
13. DeGarmo, W.R. 1950. Ornithological results of 1949 foray in the eastern panhandle of West Virginia. The Redstart 17(3):29-38.
14. Berger, D.D., C.E. Sindelar, Jr., and K.E. Gamble. 1969. The status of breeding peregrines in the eastern United States. pp. 165-173 In: *Peregrine Falcon Populations: Their Biology and Decline.* Edited by J.J. Hickey. Univ. of Wisc. Press, Madison.
15. Hickey, J.J. 1942. Eastern population of the duck hawk. Auk 59:176-204.
16. Miller, G.S., Jr. 1936. A new flying squirrel from West Virginia. Proc. Biol. Soc. Wash. 49:143-144.
17. Linzey, D.W. 1983. Status and distribution of the northern water shrew (*Sorex palustris*) and two subspecies of northern flying squirrel (*Glaucomys sabrinus coloratus* and *Glaucomys sabrinus fuscus*). Final Rept. to U.S. Fish and Wildl. Serv. 42pp.
18. Weigl, P.D. 1978. Resource overlap, interspecific interactions and the distribution of the flying squirrels *Glaucomys volans* and *G. sabrinus.* Amer. Midl. Nat. 100:83-96.
19. _____. 1975. Parasitism as a possible biological weapon affecting the ranges and interactions of the flying squirrels *Glaucomys volans* and *Glaucomys sabrinus*. Paper presented at 55th Annual Meeting Amer. Soc. Mammalogists, Univ. Montana. 6pp.
20. Downing, R.L. 1981. Eastern cougar recovery plan. U.S. Fish and Wildlife Service, Atlanta, GA. 17pp.
21. Brooks, A.B. 1924. West Virginia's vanished and vanishing wild life. West Virginia Wildlife, May.
22. Ahlsted, S.A. 1983. Molluscan fauna of the Elk River in Tennessee and Alabama. Bull. Amer. Malacol. Union. 1:43-50.
23. Stansbery, D.H. 1980. The naiad mollusks of the Kanawha River below Kanawha Falls with special attention to endangered species (Bivalva:

Unionida: Unioidae). Rept. to the Enviro. Prot. Agency, Philadelphia. EPA Contract No. C-540383. 16pp.
24. _____. 1976. Naiad mollusks. pp.42-52 In: *Endangered and Threatened Plants and Animals of Alabama.* Bull. Alabama Mus. Nat. Hist., No. 2.
25. Taylor, R.W. 1980. A survey of freshwater mussels of the Ohio River from Greenup locks and dam to Pittsburgh, Pa. Huntington/Pittsburgh Districts, U.S. Army Corps of Engineers. 71pp.
26. _____ and R. Hughart. 1981. The freshwater naiads of Elk River, West Virginia with a comparison of earlier collections. Nautilus 95(1):21-25.
27. Clarke, A.H. 1982. Survey of the freshwater mussels of the upper Kanawha River (RM 91-95), Fayette County, West Virginia, with special reference to *Epioblasma torulosa torulosa* (Rafinesque) and *Lampsilis abrupta* (Say) (= *Lampsilis orbiculata*) (Hildreath) (of authors). Final Rept. to U.S. Fish and Wildl. Serv., Order No. 50181-0546-2, Newton Corner, MA. 104pp.
28. Stansbery, D.H. 1972. A preliminary list of the naiad shells recovered from the Buffalo site. Appendix A. pp. 105-106 In: *A Late 17th Century Indian Village Site (46 Pu 31) in Putnam County, West Virginia* by B.H. Broyles. Rept. of Archeological Investigations No. 5, W. Va. Geol. and Econ. Surv., Morgantown.
29. Grimm, F.W. 1972. Office of Endangered Species Information form. U.S. Fish and Wildl. Serv., Washington.

Endangered and Threatened Species Programs in Pennsylvania and other States: Causes, Issues and Management. Edited by S. K. Majumdar, F. J. Brenner and A. F. Rhoads. © 1986, The Pennsylvania Academy of Science.

Chapter Thirty-Two

MARYLAND ENDANGERED SPECIES PROJECTS

Gary J. Taylor

Nongame and Endangered Species Program Manager
Maryland Department of Natural Resources,
Wye Mills, Maryland 21679

A program to address the research and management needs of Nongame and Endangered Species in Maryland was established within the Wildlife Administration (now the Forest, Park and Wildlife Service) of the Department of Natural Resources in 1973. The Maryland General Assembly authorized the addition of a full time biologist with logistical support to be created in the agency to administer this program. Significantly, it also authorized the appropriation of General Funds (derived from tax revenue) to support this work. The remainder of the agency continued to be supported by sportsmen's dollars derived through the sale of sport hunting licenses. This, along with Federal matching dollars derived from taxes on sport hunting equipment, traditionally was the primary source of budget support for State fish and wildlife conservation agencies.

From modest beginnings in 1973, the Nongame and Endangered Species program grew to a full time staff of 3 biologists in 1981, supported by General Funds and Federal Grant-in-Aid matching dollars under the Federal Endangered Species Act of 1973. However, fiscal austerity at both the State and Federal levels subsequently reduced the program to the original one biologist staff. State General Funds were lost in 1981, and the program is now supported by hunting license dollars and Federal Grant-in-Aid matching dollars for endangered species and wildlife restoration. Numerous attempts to pass check-off legislation in Maryland have failed in the General Assembly.

The history of this program is further detailed in Taylor[1]. The remainder of this chapter will be used to describe the research, management and recovery programs for four select endangered species in Maryland. Research, management and recovery programs for other species are described further in the published literature (Literature Cited 2nd Program Bibliography).

Delmarva fox squirrel (Sciurus niger cinereus)

Historically known from southeastern Pennsylvania, south-central New Jersey and the Delmarva peninsula of Maryland, Delaware and Virginia, this subspecies by 1970 was restricted to portions of 4 counties on the Eastern Shore of Maryland. The life history, habitat needs, reasons for decline, etc. are well documented in Taylor;[2,3] Taylor and Flyger;[4] and The U.S. Fish and Wildlife Service approved Delmarva Fox Squirrel Recovery Plan.[5] Loss of preferred habitat (small stands of large, mature mixed hardwoods—pine interspersed with agriculture, river borders, and wooded hedgerows) and increased competition with the gray squirrel are believed to have caused the decline of this subspecies.

Our initial investigations were designed to further detail the life history, needs, and habitat use by this subspecies within its remaining extant range. Over a period of 4 field seasons (1977-1980) we collected data on squirrels using several hundred wood nesting boxes placed throughout the range of the Delmarva fox squirrel in Maryland. In summary, we found the following.

The Delmarva fox squirrel co-exists with the gray squirrel throughout its range. The two species compete for food and nesting cavities. However, in areas of preferred habitat, the Delmarva fox squirrel can successfully compete with the gray squirrel, and thus has persisted in certain areas. Throughout its range, on the basis of over 10,500 individual nest box examinations, we found a ratio of approximately 1 Delmarva fox squirrel for every 8 gray squirrels. While finite numbers on a total population size are unavailable for the Delmarva fox squirrel, this will give the reader a relative concept for the abundance of this subspecies.

We further substantiated a much larger home range in the Delmarva fox squirrel than the gray squirrel. There was seasonal use of different habitat types (hedgerows, forest edges, etc.). The Delmarva fox squirrel makes significantly greater use of agricultural products (corn and soybeans, primarily), than the gray squirrel. There are two breeding peaks (late winter and mid-summer), but the winter parturition of the Delmarva fox squirrel preceeded that of the gray squirrel in the same area. Average litter size was three.

Based on this information, we proposed a restoration effort centered around the translocation of a small number of individuals to select areas of historic range determined (by the recovery team) to have potential to support this subspecies. Beginning in 1979, we have released over 100 individuals at 7 different sites in the following Maryland counties: Cecil (1 release site); Kent (2); Somerset (2); Worcester (2). With the exception of one of the Somerset county release sites, survival of released individuals has been good and reproduction in the released populations has been widely documented. Details of the translocation project can be found in the recovery plan[5] and Federal Aid documents (Maryland Forest, Park and Wildlife Service 1977-84). We expect to continue Maryland translocations, and have also provided Delaware with squirrels for the restoration project in that state.

The recovery objective for this subspecies is the maintenance of the extant population and the establishment of 30 self-sustaining translocated populations within the historic range. The success of our initial efforts demonstrates the feasibility of restoration through translocation. With continued support from all involved agencies, we feel that recovery is an achievable goal within the next decade.

Bald eagle (Haliaeetus leucocephalus)

Historically (circa 1930), there may have been as many as 600 nesting pairs of this endangered species in the Chesapeake Bay region (MD-DE-VA).[6] By the early 1960's, observers were able to document only an estimated 150 nesting pair with a reproductive rate far below that required for population maintenance.[7] By 1970, nesting pairs were reduced to an estimated 90 pair, while productivity had improved slightly from a decade earlier.[7,8]

The reasons for the precipitous decline in the bald eagle population in the Chesapeake region and elsewhere are well documented. The U.S. Fish and Wildlife Service approved recovery plan for the Chesapeake region[9] details limiting factors and provides an extensive literature citation. A recent keyworded, computer-based bibliography[10] contains thousands of entries on the species. This species has received considerable attention in the last 10-15 years as a symbol of endangered species, and much has been published on its status.

We started intensive monitoring of the bald eagle in Maryland in 1976. Using a single-engine high wing aircraft, we survey the Coastal Plain physiographic province of Maryland several times each year from early January through May. These flights are timed to search out nest territories, document occupied territories, track incubation, and determine final productivity in the nesting population for that season. Both the number of nest territories and population productivity have improved significantly since 1976 (Table 1). Productivity in Maryland (and the entire Chesapeake region) is now at a level capable of continuing a population increase.

Since 1977, we have been banding and color-making eaglets in Maryland (and Virginia and Delaware). Our purpose of banding is multiple: to provide a data base of known aged marked individuals for survival/mortality determinations through band recoveries; to document movements in all aged birds through recoveries; to substantiate natal territory fidelity; to collect diet information through the collection of prey items during nest visitations; and to characterize the physical components of the nest site and territory. We expect to continue banding for one additional nesting season (through 1986) and then evaluate

TABLE 1

Bald Eagle Nesting Productivity in Maryland, 1976-1985.

	1976	1977	1978	1979	1980	1981	1982	1983	1984	1985
Occupied Nests	—	—	—	—	—	—	—	59[1]	60	62
Active Nests	43	44	45	48	47	49	56	55	55	59
Nests of Known Outcome	—	43	44	48	47	49	56	59	60	62
Nests with Young	24	27	27	24	25	30	35	—[2]	—	—
Successful Nests	—	—	—	—	—	—	—	40[1]	40	41
Number of Young Fledged	36	45	38	38	35	51	55	59	70	77
nests with 3 young	—	2	2	1	0	3	6	4	6	7
nests with 2 young	—	16	8	12	10	15	8	10	18	22
nests with 1 young	—	9	17	11	15	12	21	27	16	12
Number Young Fledged per Nest With Known Outcome	—	1.0	.85	.79	.74	1.0	.98	1.0	1.17	1.24
Number of Young Per Successful Nest	1.5	1.7	1.41	1.58	1.40	1.7	1.57	1.47	1.75	1.88

[1] Reporting terms added to further refine productivity data and provide for uniform terminology among cooperating agencies in the bald eagle recovery effort.
[2] Reporting terms deleted to further refine productivity data.

our data. Much has already been learned and reported.[11,12]

We are continuing to work with private landowners, land-use agencies and planning and zoning agencies to protect and secure both occupied habitat and potential nesting habitat for population recovery. The Chesapeake Bay Region now supports the fourth largest breeding concentration of bald eagles in the United States, excluding Alaska. Recovery of our resident population in this area now equals that of anywhere else in the United States. If we, through the various government agencies and private conservation organizations, with the cooperation of the private landowners, can secure the habitat necessary to support a recovering population, then we feel there is a promise of a more secure future for the bald eagle in Maryland.

Muhlenberg (bog) turtle (Clemmys muhlenbergi)

This species was believed at one time by herpetologists to be one of the rarest reptiles in the Eastern United States, and was originally listed as state "endangered" in Maryland. We determined the distribution and population status of the Muhlenberg turtle in Maryland by intensive field investigations of potential habitat characterized by certain soil type associations. Prior to our investigation, this species was known from only 17 active sites (in 1975) in Maryland. We identified 173 previously unknown sites for this species in Maryland and described occupied habitat. The Muhlenberg turtle in Maryland is restricted to portions of the Piedmont physiographic province. Habitats for this species here are permanently wet, small (2 acres or less) sedge meadows exhibiting moderate to dense herbaceous vegetation. The majority of known sites exist on private property, and we received excellent cooperation in our study from the private landowners. Surveys conducted subsequent to our initial investigations have documented minimal loss or degradation of habitat. We believe the Muhlenberg turtle is secure in Maryland and this species has consequently been delisted as state endangered. Further details on this study can be found in Taylor et al.[13]

Jefferson salamander (Ambystoma jeffersonianum)

Originally classified as state "endangered" in 1973, this species was known from only seven (7) historic sites in the Piedmont physiographic province of Western Maryland at the time it was listed. Extensive surveys conducted from 1977-78 identified 54 additional vernal pools where this species was documented to be using as breeding sites. The range of this species in Maryland was extended into the Allegany Plateau (Garrett county) and breeding sites were distributed in several parallel belts running in a northeast-southeast direction, generally coinciding with mountain ridges. Breeding sites were found to be isolated upland pools usually surrounded by forest land and a dense border of shrubs and/or trees. Several additional breeding sites have been located since the completion of the original survey, and the status of this species in Maryland appears secure. It has thus been delisted as endangered in Maryland. Additional information on this species can be found in Thompson;[15] Thompson et al;[15] and Thompson and Gates.[16]

SUMMARY

These short synopses on these four species will give the reader an insight into the types of programs being undertaken in Maryland on threatened and endangered species. Projects exist on several other species; time precludes addressing all of these here, however. The interested reader is referred to the Program Bibliography for more detailed information on these four species, and/or project information on additional species.

LITERATURE CITED

1. Taylor, G.J. 1984a. The Maryland endangered species program: a history. Proc. 1981 Symposium on Threatened and Endangered Plants and Animals of Maryland. MD Dept. Natural Resources,'Natural Heritage Program, Special Publication 84-1, Annapolis. 43-49.

2. Taylor, G.J. 1974. Present status and habitat survey of the Delmarva fox squirrel (*Sciurus niger cinereus*) with a discussion of reasons for its decline. Proc. Southeastern Assoc. Game and Fish Comm. 27:278-289.
3. Taylor, G.J. 1976. Range determination and habitat description of the Delmarva fox squirrel in Maryland. MS thesis, Univ. of MD, College Park.
4. Taylor, G.J. and V. Flyger. 1973. Distribution of the Delmarva fox squirrel (*Sciurus niger cinereus*) in Maryland. Chesapeake Science 14:59-60.
5. U.S. Dept. of Interior, Fish and Wildlife Service. 1983. Recovery Plan for the Delmarva Fox Squirrel, First Revision. Washington, D.C. 49 pp.
6. Tyrell, W.B. 1936. Unpublished report of bald eagle nest survey of the Chesapeake Bay region. National Audubon Society library files.
7. Abbott, J.M. 1978. Chesapeake Bay bald eagles. Del. Cons. 22:3-9.
8. Abbott, J.M. 1970. 1970 Bald eagle nest survey. Atlantic Nat. 25:169-171.
9. U.S. Dept. of Interior, Fish and Wildlife Service. 1982. Chesapeake Bay Bald Eagle Recovery Plan. Washington, D.C. 81 pp.
10. Lincer, J.L., W.S. Clark and M. LeFranc. 1979. Working bibliography of the bald eagle. Pub. 2, National Wildlife Federation Scientific/Technical Series, Washington, D.C.
11. Cline, K.W. 1985b. Chesapeake Bay bald eagle banding project: report. Raptor Information Center, National Wildlife Federation, Washington, D.C. 42 pp.
12. Lefranc, M.N., Jr. and K.W. Cline. 1983. The occurrence of birds as prey at active bald eagle nests in the Chesapeake Bay region. *in* Bird, D.M., N.R. Seymour, and J.M. Gerrard, eds. Biology and Management of Bald Eagles and Osprey. Raptor Research Foundation, Inc. 325 pp.
13. Taylor, G.J., S.A. Dawson, S.A. Beall and J.E. Schaeffer. 1984. Distribution and habitat description of the Muhlenberg (bog) turtle (*Clemmys muhlenbergi*) in Maryland. Trans. 41st Northeast Fish Wildl. Conf., Ocean City, MD. 45-58.
14. Thompson, E.L. 1980. Breeding site ecology of Ambystomatid salamanders in Maryland; Part 1: Distribution and breeding habitat selection of the Jefferson salamander, *Ambystoma jeffersonianum*, in Maryland; Part 2: Breeding pool segregation by *Ambystoma jeffersonianum* and *A. maculatum* in a region of sympatry. MS thesis, Frostburg State College, 55 pp.
15. Thompson, E.L., J.E. Gates and G.J. Taylor. 1980. Distribution and breeding habitat selection of the Jefferson salamander, *Ambystoma jeffersonianum*, in Maryland. J. Herp. 14:113-120.
16. Thompson, E.L. and J.E. Gates. 1982. Breeding pool segregation by the mole salamanders, *Ambystoma jeffersonianum* and *A. maculatum*, in a region of sympatry. Oikos. 38:273-279.

ADDITIONAL PROGRAM BIBLIOGRAPHY

Chase, J.D. 1983. Habitat characteristics, population size, and home range of the bog turtle, *Clemmys muhlenbergii*, in Maryland. MS thesis, Frostburg State College. 48 pp.

Chase, J.D., K.R. Dixon, J.E. Gates, D. Jacobs, and G.J. Taylor. 1986. Habitat characteristics, population size, and home range of the bog turtle, *Clemmys muhlenbergii*, in Maryland. (in prep.).

Clark, W.S. and J.L. Lincer. 1977. Chesapeake Bay bald eagle banding project: progress report. Raptor Information Center, National Wildlife Federation, Washington, D.C. 21 pp.

Cline, K.W. 1983. Chesapeake Bay bald eagle banding project: report. Raptor Information Center, National Wildlife Federation, Washington, D.C. 46 pp.

Cline, K.W. 1984. Chesapeake Bay bald eagle banding project: report. Raptor Information Center, National Wildlife Federation, Washington, D.C. 36 pp.

Cline, K.W. 1985a. Bald eagles in the Chesapeake: a management guide for landowners. Raptor Information Center, National Wildlife Federation, Washington, D.C. 16 pp.

Cline, K.W. and W.S. Clark. 1981. Chesapeake Bay bald eagle banding project: 1981 report and five year summary. Raptor Information Center, National Wildlife Federation, Washington, D.C. 38 pp.

Cline, K.W. and W.S. Clark. 1982. Chesapeake Bay bald eagle banding project: report. Raptor Information Center, National Wildlife Federation, Washington, D.C. 44 pp.

Dawson, S.A. 1984. The status of the bog turtle (*Clemmys muhlenbergi*) in Maryland. Proc. 1981 Symposium on Threatened and Endangered Plants and Animals of Maryland. MD Dept. Natural Resources, Natural Heritage Program, Special Publication 84-1, Annapolis. 360-362.

D'Loughy, K.J. 1984. Status of the bald eagle in Maryland. Proc. 1981 Symposium on Threatened and Endangered Plants and Animals of Maryland. MD Dept. Natural Resources, Natural Heritage Program, Special Publication 84-1, Annapolis. 390-394.

Devlin, W.J. 1979. Woodpeckers nesting in red-cockaded woodpecker habitat. MS thesis, Frostburg State College. 45 pp.

Devlin, W.J., J.A. Mosher and G.J. Taylor. 1980a. History and present status of the red-cockaded woodpecker in Maryland. Am. Birds 34:314-316.

Devlin, W.J., J.A. Mosher and G.J. Taylor. 1980b. Potential red-cockaded woodpecker habitat in Maryland. Natural History Miscellanea of the Chicago Academy of Sciences, no. 212. 7 pp.

Dittrick, R. and W.S. Clark. 1978. Chesapeake Bay bald eagle banding project: progress report. Raptor Information Center, National Wildlife Federation, Washington, D.C. 54 pp.

Gates, J.E., G.A. Feldhamer, L.A. Griffith, and R.L. Raesly. 1984. Status of cave-dwelling bats in Maryland: importance of marginal habitats. Wildl. Soc. Bull. 12:162-169.

Gates, J.E., C.H. Hocutt, and J.R. Stauffer, Jr. 1984. The status of the hellbender (*Cryptobranchus alleganiensis*) in Maryland. Proc. 1981 Symposium on Threatened and Endangered Plants and Animals of Maryland. MD Dept. Natural Resources, Natural Heritage Program, Special Publication 84-1, Annapolis. 329-335.

Gates, J.E., C.H. Hocutt, J.R. Stauffer, Jr., and G.J. Taylor. 1985. The distribution and status of *Cryptobranchus alleganiensis* in Maryland. Herp. Review 16:17-18.

Maryland Dept. Natural Resources, Forest, Park and Wildlife Service. 1977-1984. Resident Endangered Species Investigations. Federal Aid to Endangered Species Project E-1 Annual Reports: 1977-1984. Annapolis.

McKee, R.M. and G.J. Taylor. 1983. Preliminary report on the effectiveness of translocating Delmarva fox squirrels (*Sciurus niger cinereus*) to re-establish populations in former range. Poster with abstract. Proc. 40th Northeast Fish Wildl. Conf., Mt. Snow, VT (in press).

Pramstaller, M.E. and W.S. Clark. 1979. Chesapeake Bay bald eagle banding project: progress report. Raptor Information Center, National Wildlife Federation, Washington, D.C. 20 pp.

Pramstaller, M.E. and W.S. Clark. 1980. Chesapeake Bay bald eagle banding project: progress report. Raptor Information Center, National Wildlife Federation, Washington, D.C. 24 pp.

Stine, C.J. 1984. The life history and status of the Eastern tiger salamander, *Ambystoma tigrinum tigrinum* (Green) in Maryland. Bull. MD. Herpetol. Soc. 20:65-108.

Stouffer, R.J., Jr., J.E. Gates, C.H. Hocutt, and J.R. Stauffer, Jr. 1983. Surgical implantation of a transmitter package for radio-tracking endangered hellbenders. Wildl. Soc. Bull. 11(4):384-386.

Taylor, G.J. 1977. Maryland's Delmarva fox squirrel. Fact sheet, MD Dept. of Natural Resources, Wildlife Administration, Annapolis. 2 pp.

Taylor, G.J. 1982. Investigations of Maryland Endangered Herptiles. Unpubl. MS presented at the 10th Annual meeting of the Eastern Seaboard Herpetological League: March 20; Baltimore, MD Abstract only publ. in Bull. MD Herpetol. Soc. 18:18-19.

Taylor, G.J. 1983. The status of the bald eagle in the Chesapeake Bay. Proc. 1982 Bald Eagle Days (EVE) Conference. Rochester, NY pp143-147.

Taylor, G.J. 1984b. The black bear in Maryland. Proc. Seventh Eastern Workshop on Black Bear Research and Management. Homosassa, Fla. Fla. Game and Freshwater Fish Commission. pp10-11.

Taylor, G.J. and M.A. Byrd. 1978. Chesapeake Bay bald eagle nesting success: a summary. Unpubl. MS presented at the Raptor Research Foundation

Meetings, Allentown, Pennsylvania.

Taylor, G.J. and T. Cofield. 1980. Return of the peregrines. MD Conservationist. 56(3):28-30.

Taylor, G.J. and S.A. Dawson. 1981. Brown pelican in Maryland in winter. Bull. Md. Ornith. Soc. 37(1):4.

Taylor, G.J. and G.D. Therres. 1981. A computer generated description of potential bald eagle nesting habitat in Maryland. MD Dept. Natural Resources, Power Plant Siting Program, Report No. PPRP-55, Annapolis. 12 pp.

Therres, G.D. and G.J. Taylor. 1984. Maryland and District of Columbia breeding bird atlas project: a preliminary report. Trans. 41st Northeast Fish Wildl. Conf., Ocean City, MD. 182-191.

Thompson, E.L. 1984. A report on the status and distribution of the Jefferson salamander, green salamander, mountain earth snake, and Northern coal skink in Maryland. Proc. 1981 Symposium on Threatened and Endangered Plants and Animals of Maryland. MD Dept. Natural Resources, Natural Heritage Program, Special Publication 84-1, Annapolis. 338-351.

Thompson, E.L. and G.J. Taylor. 1985. Notes on the green salamander, *Aneides aeneus*, in Maryland. Bull. MD Herpetol. Soc. 21:107-114.

Williams, R.D., J.E. Gates, and C.H. Hocutt. 1981. An evaluation of known and potential sampling techniques for hellbender, *Cryptobranchus alleganiensus*. J. Herp. 15(1):23-27.

Williams, R.D., J.E. Gates, C.H. Hocutt and G.J. Taylor. 1981. The hellbender: a nongame species in need of management. Wildl. Soc. Bull. 9(2):94-100.

Chapter Thirty-Three

RECOVERY OF THE PEREGRINE FALCON IN THE EASTERN UNITED STATES

Martin J. Gilroy and John H. Barclay

The Peregrine Fund, Inc.
Cornell Laboratory of Ornithology
159 Sapsucker Woods Road
Ithaca, New York 14850

More than 750 peregrine falcons (*Falco peregrinus*) have been released by hacking or fostering in the eastern United States since 1975. Releases have been concentrated in three geographical regions: the mid-Atlantic coast between New York City and Norfolk, Virginia where falcons have been released from specially constructed towers and other man-made structures, and the mountains of New England and the southern Appalachians. Successful nesting by released peregrines first occurred in 1980; the founding population has increased steadily since then, with an intrinsic rate of growth of approximately 0.44. Through 1985 there have been 63 confirmed nesting attempts, 47 (75%) of which were successful, producing 128 young. Productivity has been 2.03 young per attempt and 2.72 young per successful attempt. In 1985 40 pairs were recorded, 25 attempted to nest and 16 produced 47 young. A simulation study shows that the rate with which recovery is achieved will be dependent on the level and duration of future recovery efforts.

INTRODUCTION

The decline of the peregrine falcon (*Falco peregrinus*) population in eastern North America began in the years following World War II. This population, estimated at approximately 350 breeding pairs,[1] had been characterized by remarkable stability; more than 80% of the 408 eyries known to have been used historically were still active when Hickey[1] conducted his study in the late 1930's and early 1940's. By 1965 when Hickey convened the International Peregrine Conference[2] to investigate the factors responsible for the decline, there were no known breeding Peregrines east of the Mississippi River.[3] The conferees presented evidence linking the decline to the use of DDT and other pesticides, but it was not until several years later that the mechanisms were fully understood and had been demonstrated experimentally. The extirpation has been attributed to the biological concentration of persistent, organochlorine residues in the food chain of the falcon, and to the effects of these chemicals on eggshell formation and consequent reproductive failure.[4,5]

The peregrine was officially listed as an endangered species in the United States in 1969. It became a conservation symbol, focusing public attention on wildlife threatened by man's environmental degradation. This awareness facilitated the restriction of DDT and related chemicals in 1972,[6] and resulted in a cadre of devotees eager to save the peregrine.

In 1970, The Peregrine Fund, a private, non-profit organization affiliated with Cornell University, established a program to develop methods for propagating peregrines in captivity as a source of falcons for introduction into the vacant eastern breeding range.[7] The first twenty young peregrines were produced at the Behavioral Ecology Building, Cornell University, in 1973 by four laying females. The methods were sufficiently refined and production high enough by 1975 that restocking appeared feasible. The first experimental release of two captive-bred falcons took place in 1974 with the cooperation of Dr. Heinz Meng at the State University of New York at New Paltz, and large-scale releases began the following year.

The U.S. Fish and Wildlife Service appointed an Eastern Peregrine Falcon Recovery Team[8] in 1975 which has developed a Recovery Plan[9] detailing the management activities required to restore the peregrine in the east. The Plan is based on the establishment of a new Eastern Peregrine population by introducing captive-produced falcons into the wild, with the goal of restoring a self-maintaining population at a level of 50 percent of the number of breeding pairs estimated to have occurred in the 1940's, or to a level the present environment will support.

Releases have continued since 1975 and these efforts have proven to be effective.[10] A rapidly growing breeding population of peregrines once again exists in this region devoid of the species for some 30 years.

MATERIALS AND METHODS

The peregrines in the breeding colony at Cornell come from seven main sources: The North American tundra (Alaska and Canada); the North American taiga (Alaska and Canada); the Pacific Northwest (Aleutians and Queen

Charlotte Islands); western United States; Scotland; Spain, and Chile.

The origin of the captive breeding stock from which the reintroduced young derive remains, for some, a controversial issue of this program and warrants a brief review. This issue was first fully discussed at a conference sponsored by the National Audubon Society in 1974.[11]

The extirpation of the eastern "Appalachian" or "Rock" peregrine was complete, thus none of these birds, representing an ecotype adapted to the eastern environment,[12] were available for captive propagation. Consequently all of the captive-bred peregrines released in the East are the progeny of falcons drawn from non-indigenous populations. Falcons from neighboring populations might be expected to be most similar to the extirpated eastern peregrine and thus be good candidates for reintroduction; however, at the time the captive colony was being founded, the neighboring populations to the West and North were themselves endangered and unable to withstand intensive harvesting. Furthermore, birds from neighboring populations may not be as well adapted to the current environment as falcons from other, more distant populations. The Spanish peregrines discussed by Cade[13] that have adapted to breeding in close proximity to human activity serve as an example. These falcons may be better pre-adapted to survival in the man-dominated eastern United States than birds of remote Arctic populations, for example.

Another view, put forth at the Audubon conference by William Drury[14] and Ian Nisbet and agreed upon by the conferees, suggested that the captive population be drawn from several sources and then these stocks deliberately mixed to achieve greater genetic variability. Natural selection would then act on these "hybridized" individuals and pick out those able to survive and reproduce in the current environment. The Audubon conferees recognized that the resulting peregrine "will not be a Rock peregrine, but still a proper peregrine adapted to today's environment". However, if the same selective forces that produced the original duck hawks are still operative, then it is reasonable to predict that the new population will converge genetically and phenotypically on the old; if, as seems more likely, new and different selective forces are now associated with the much altered eastern environment, then a somewhat different peregrine will result.[10]

Such an approach recognizes both our inability to determine *a priori* which kind of peregrines are adapted for survival in the current eastern environment, and the inherent genetic problems of small populations, a subject which has received a great deal of thought in recent years.[15,16,17,18] Founding a captive population represents a severe genetic bottleneck which, along with genetic drift occurring in the ensuing generations while the population is small, results in loss of alleles and genetic variability.[19,20] Maintaining separate lines in the captive population exacerbates this problem since each line represents a separate founding event and becomes subject to these forces, whereas managing the captive population as a single unit results in a larger effective population size and lessens their effect. Cooperation among the increasing number of private and institutional breeders, though not yet developed to its potential, offers the ability to control such factors as allele loss and inbreeding through the incorporation of new founders into captive colonies. The work of Templeton et al.[21] suggests that disruption of locally adapted or genetically coadapted gene complexes (outbreeding depression) is unlikely in a species such as the peregrine.

This approach has been corroborated by Corbin,[22] Templeton,[23] and the Species Survival Plan Subcommittee, of the Management and Conservation Committee of the American Association of Zoological Parks and Aquariums.[24] It is consistent with the Endangered Species Act in focussing on the species as the taxon of importance for preservation rather than the local population. Its goal is to maintain the species as a population of ecologically adapted individuals and to increase their numbers in geographic regions where they have declined or disappeared.[10]

This philosophy has been endorsed by the Fish and Wildlife Service in the Recovery Plan and has since become a working assumption of the eastern peregrine reintroduction program.

The captive propagation techniques have been covered in great detail elsewhere.[25,26,27,28,29,30] Innovative manipulative techniques are used to maximize productivity. In 1985, hatchability of fertile eggs was up to 88 percent and chick survival was up to 96 percent. Productivity of captive-bred F_1 falcons does not appear to differ significantly from that of founders.[30]

The selection of release sites was also thoroughly discussed at the Audubon conference.[11] It was determined that selection criteria should include: the presence of suitable, open terrain over which the falcons could hunt; a sufficient quantity of prey; a minimum of human disturbance; and security from potential predators. Release sites used in the eastern recovery efforts have included natural cliff sites and artificial sites consisting of city buildings and man-made towers located in regions lacking suitable natural nesting structures. Sites were widely distributed among the eastern states at first but were subsequently clustered in areas of high initial success, resulting in a concentration of artificial sites along the mid-Atlantic coast and more widely scattered natural sites inland.

The use of artificial release sites has also been a controversial aspect of the program, though the controversy seems to be based more on aesthetic considerations than biological principles. While peregrines most commonly nest on cliff ledges, they have been reported nesting in a wide variety of situations throughout their cosmopolitan range, including cut-banks, dunes, tree cavities, tree nests appropriated from other species, a variety of man-made buildings and structures, and even on the ground in arctic bogs,[31] (see review in Hickey and Anderson, 1969). In the eastern United States tree-nesting was localized but apparently not uncommon where suitable trees were available.[32,33,34] Groskin[35] and Herbert and Herbert[36] describe urban-nesting peregrines in the Northeast, and there are at least two records of peregrines nesting on the mid-Atlantic coast.[37,38]

The artificial sites were used in the hope that the peregrine's usual preference for nest habitat and nest site might be modified.[39] It was hypothesized that if the falcons were raised and released on such structures they would become "imprinted" to them and to the local area and that they would return to a similar structure and habitat for breeding.[27] In addition to these criteria, tower sites could be located at will and thus clustered so as to increase the probability that the released falcons would encounter one another and form breeding pairs. They are often simpler to operate than cliff sites and facilitate behavioral studies.[40] Urban sites permit releases near potential cliff nest sites that are unusable because of predators, and prey at urban sites may harbor lower levels of contaminants than prey at other types of sites.[4]

Two techniques have been used to release peregrines in the East: "hacking" and "fostering". The details of hacking, a modification of a traditional falconer's method,[41] have been presented elsewhere.[42,43,44] Briefly, it involves placing broods of young peregrines in a protective enclosure (a "hack box") at the release site about one week before they can fly. They are fed and cared for in the box by on-site attendants until they are capable of sustained flight (approximately 40-45 days of age). The hack box is then opened allowing the falcons to fly at will. The site attendants continue to provide food for 5-6 weeks until the young falcons become self-sufficient and disperse from the hack site.

The establishment of breeding pairs and lone resident adult falcons resulting from previous releases has permitted a small proportion of the captive-bred young to be released by "fostering" to wild falcons. Fostering involves supplementing the existing clutch or brood of a nesting pair or lone peregrine with captive-bred young. It has been employed extensively in the peregrine recovery efforts in the western United States and is discussed in detail by Burnham et al.[45] and Cade.[27]

RESULTS

Since 1975 more than 750 peregrines have been released at more than 50 locations in 15 eastern states. Approximately 45 percent have been released from tower and urban sites along the mid-Atlantic coast between New York City and Norfolk, Virginia; the remaining 55 percent have been released at inland cliff and urban sites (Fig. 1). Greater survival during hacking and more rapid colonization by adult falcons at coastal sites during the first few years led to an emphasis in the coastal region and fewer releases at inland sites from about 1978-1981. As the coastal sites became occupied, efforts in that region have been reduced to mainly fostering captive-bred young to wild pairs, and the emphasis has shifted to hacking in the inland region.

The results according to release method (hack vs. foster) and type of site summarized in Table 1 are used (tower, urban, or cliff). The percentage of birds

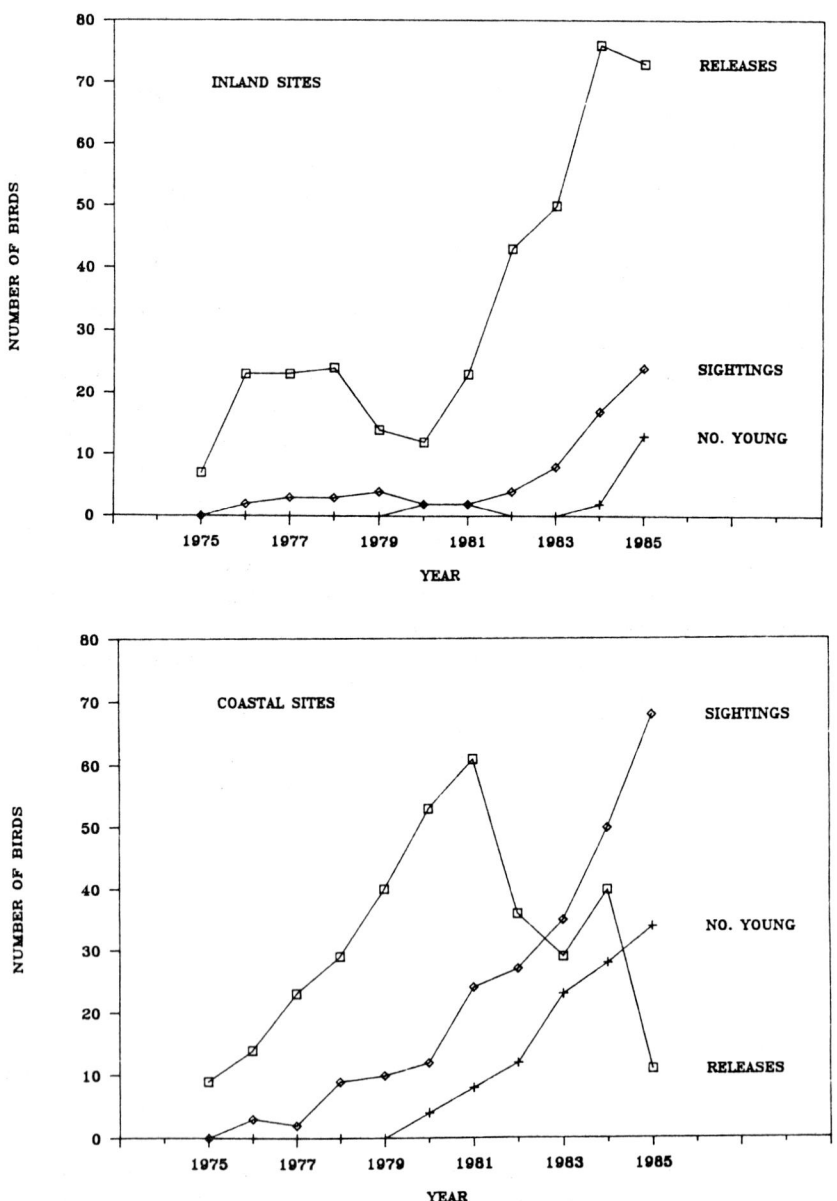

FIGURE 1. Distribution of eastern peregrine falcon releases, sightings, and production of young. Redrawn with permission from Barclay, in Cade et al. (in press).

TABLE 1

Peregrine reintroduction success by type of release site and method of release. Percent dispersed normally (number released). Fostering has not yet been employed at cliff sites.

Year	Tower Hack	Tower Foster	Urban Hack	Urban Foster	Cliff Hack	Total
1975	90(10)	—	—	—	50(6)	75(16)
1976	71(14)	—	—	—	65(23)	68(37)
1977	89(18)	100(5)	—	—	61(23)	76(46)
1978	71(24)	100(5)	—	—	50(24)	64(53)
1979	74(27)	80(5)	100(4)	100(4)	67(12)	77(52)*
1980	87(31)	100(2)	93(14)	100(4)	58(12)	84(63)*
1981	63(35)	50(2)	68(19)	100(5)	83(23)	71(84)
1982	97(31)	0(2)	—	100(3)	91(43)	91(79)
1983	83(24)	100(3)	—	0(2)	92(50)	87(79)
1984	100(24)	100(16)	50(6)	—	97(78)	96(124)
1985	29(7)	75(4)	78(18)	—	90(88)	84(117)
Total	80(245)	89(44)	77(61)	89(18)	83(382)	82(750)

* Does not include 5 (1979) and 4 (1980) birds hacked for recapture and subsequent training for release as adults.

that successfully dispersed from the coastal hack towers was higher than for the inland cliff sites from 1975 to 1981. Hacking success at sites subsequently improved when sites were more carefully selected to avoid predation by great horned owls (*Bubo virginianus*), a major cause of mortality. Urban hack sites have been generally successful, but they expose the young falcons to a variety of hazards. Fostering young falcons to wild adults has been a successful technique, as expected, but still results in some losses. Comparing the 11 year cumulative results yields no significant differences in reintroduction success among site types for hacking ($X^2 = 1.76$, df = 2, $p > 0.05$) or for fostering ($X^2 = 2.32$, df = 1, $p > 0.05$). Then pooling the results from the three site types shows no significant difference between the two methods, hacking and fostering ($X^2 = 1.92$, DF = 1, $P > 0.05$). The overall reintroduction success from 1975 to 1985 has been 82 percent or a mortality rate of 18 percent; this compares favorably with estimates of mortality in wild raptor populations during the post-fledging dependency period.[10]

Figure 2 presents the results of loss and mortality of peregrines until four weeks after release—the point at which the falcons generally begin to disperse from the release site. The table includes birds released by both hacking and fostering and losses that occurred prior to release, and those resulting in the return of falcons to captivity. The 3 major mortality factors have been premature dispersal, predation by Great horned owls, and harassment by adult peregrines.

Premature dispersal represents cases in which birds disappeared at a point in the hacking process when it was unlikely that they could have been self-sufficient. This includes some for which other factors, such as owl predation were suspected but for which evidence was lacking. However, some of the these

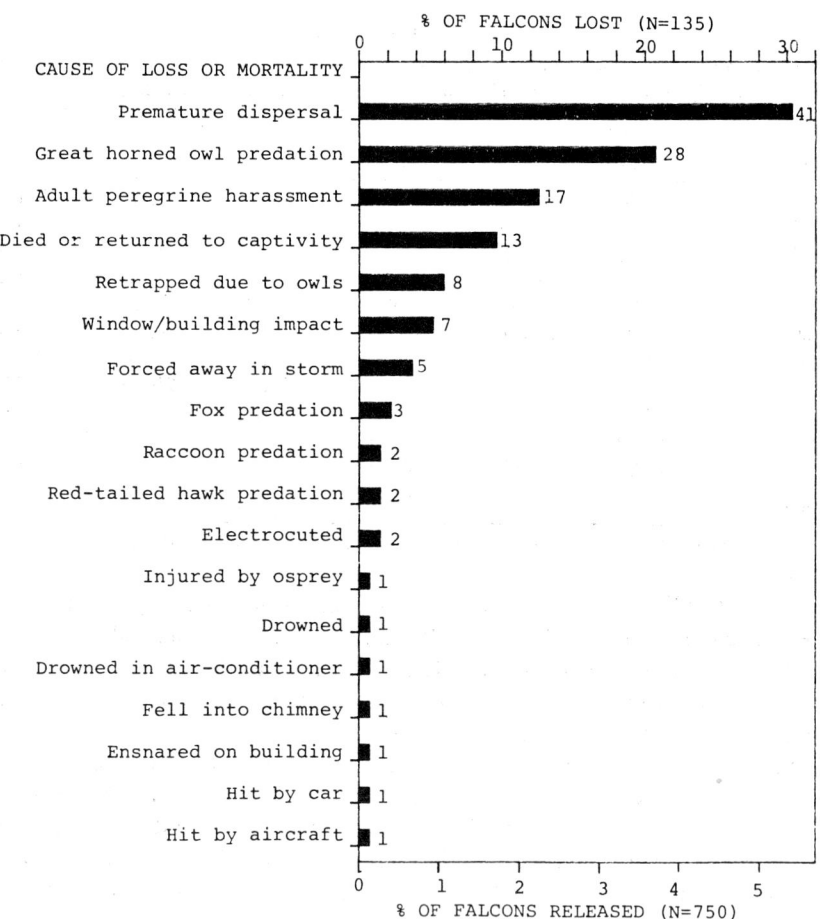

FIGURE 2. Losses of peregrine prior to dispersal from release sites.

falcons have later been identified as breeders, so not all perish.

Predation by great horned owls has been the second highest loss factor. In addition to the 28 falcons killed by owls, 8 more were retrapped from release sites and returned to captivity because owl predation was imminent. Thus, owl predation accounts for the effective loss of 36 birds (26.67% of the total lost; 4.80% of the total released) from the population. It has occurred at both coastal and cliff sites and is known to have been responsible for the death of at least one fostered falcon at a site with wild parents present. Owl trapping proved to be very labor intensive, and largerly ineffective owing to reoccupation by owls from adjacent territories. The only way found to reduce owl predation to date has been to avoid the owls themselves. The many historical eyries at low-elevation cliffs in mixed agricultural and forested regions throughout Pennsylvania, New York, Connecticut, and Massachusetts where owls are common, have been abandoned as hack sites in favor of the higher-elevation cliffs in the mountains of upstate New York, northern New England, the southern Appalachians, and the expansive coastal marshes away from owl habitat. Urban sites near such historical eyries which are unusable because of owls offer safe, owl-free zones from which falcons can be released into otherwise suitable regions. It is presumed that nesting adults could coexist with the owls and that predation of their young would be minimal.

Harassment of falcons at release sites by previously released subadult or adult falcons was an unexpected mortality factor. Young have been lost to injuries sustained from overtly aggressive returning falcons, to starvation after having been driven from the release site by territorial adults before the young falcons were capable of fending for themselves, and to starvation resulting from the mis-directed food-seeking behavior of young falcons toward non-parentally motivated subadults or adults. These encounters have become more frequent over the years as the free-living peregrine population has increased and have occurred at cliff, coastal and urban release sites. The outcome of such encounters seems to have been largely dependent upon their timing during the hacking period. If the encounter occurred right after release, while the young were still unfamiliar with their surroundings, they seem to have become lost while fleeing from the territorial adult. If the subadult or adult arrived later, when the young were more skilled flyers and knew their surroundings, the young were able to lie low and wait out the aggression. In several cases, the aggressive behavior of the returning bird has been short-lived, giving way to ambivalent, or even parental behavior in a matter of just a few days. Once past the aggressive period, the young birds being hacked probably benefitted from the presence of the adult, in much the same ways as young wild peregrines benefit from their parents. Harassment by adults has made proximity to territorial adult falcons an important factor in the selection of release sites and increased the need for surveys of sites prior to releases. This problem is made more difficult by the low degree of site tenacity exhibited by these floating subadult or unpaired adult falcons that may wander great distances and then appear at a hack site.

Barclay and Cade[10] have analyzed the mortality and movements of peregrines after departure from release sites. Their estimates of mortality compare favorably with those of Young[46] for wild peregrine populations.

Their analysis of recoveries and sightings of hacked peregrines reveals a pattern of "unoriented wandering" characteristic of first-year peregrines in sedentary populations.[47] There seems to be general movement in a southerly direction toward the coast in fall and winter in response to prey availability, but no strong migratory movement *per se*. A recent recovery of a falcon hacked in the Appalachian mountains of North Carolina, trapped on the Virginia coast in late fall, and then sighted back at its hack site the following spring is typical of the upland-to-coastal movements of the historic eastern peregrine popula-

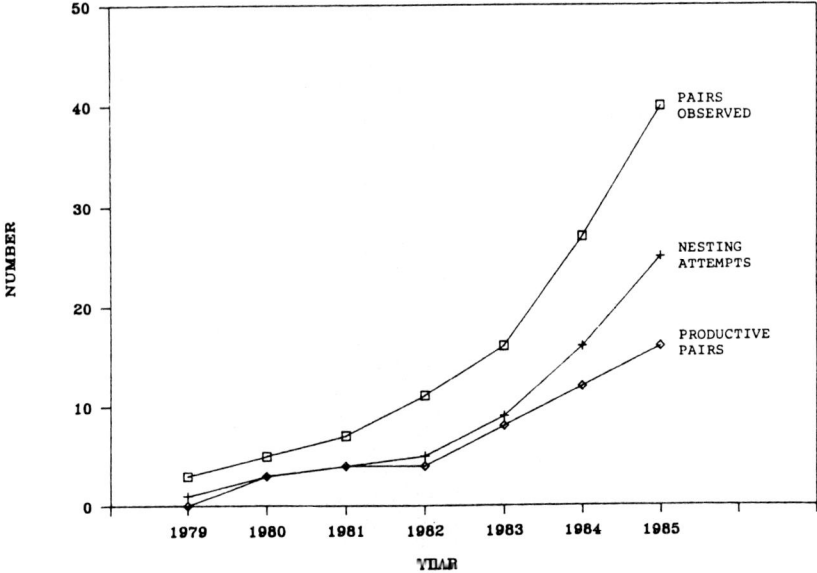

FIGURE 3. Growth of the eastern peregrine population. Redrawn with permission from Barclay, in Cade et al. (in press).

tion.[2] There is no evidence to bear out concerns expressed in the early years of the program that migration might be under genetic control and that birds from non-indigenous populations, hacked in the East, would show migratory tendancies of the populations from which they were derived[27]—e.g. falcons from Arctic populations hacked on the mid-Atlantic coast migrating to South America for the winter and then to Arctic breeding grounds the following spring.

Promising results were realized as early as 1976 when a male falcon returned to the site in New Jersey where he had been hacked the year before. Again in 1977 and 1978 he (or perhaps another bird) returned, each time adopting the young that were being hacked at the site and providing them with prey he had killed. He paired with a subadult female that returned to the site later in the 1978 season, forming the first known pair of reintroduced peregrines.

Also in 1978, a female peregrine named Scarlett, released at a tower site some 15 to 20 km. from Baltimore, MD, took up residence on that city's tallest building. She was provided nest boxes and in 1979 laid three infertile eggs. These were later replaced with captive-bred peregrine chicks, hatched at the Cornell breeding facility, which she successfully raised to independence. Another coastal tower in New Jersey was occupied by a pair in 1979, and though the female was a subadult, she laid fertile eggs. This attempt later failed however because of interference by crows (*Corvus ossifragus* and *Corvus brachyrhynchos*). Pairs of first-year peregrines occupied two other towers in New Jersey that year but did not attempt to breed.

Three pairs occupied coastal towers in New Jersey in 1980. Two of the pairs succeeded in producing a total of four young, while the third was preempted by barn owls (*Tyto alba*) that attempted to nest at the tower. A fourth pair at a cliff in southern Quebec, one member of which is known to have been released in the United States, successfully produced two young. These represented the first successful nestings of peregrines east of the Mississippi River in more than 20 years and proved the effectiveness of the methods developed in this program for restoring the extirpated eastern peregrine population.

Since 1979 a total of 128 young have been produced; 47 of 63 documented nesting attempts (75%) have been successful, for an average of 2.03 young per attempt and 2.72 young per successful attempt (Fig. 3). Since 1982, the number of nesting attempts has increased at an average annual rate of 71 percent and successful nestings have increased at an average annual rate of 61 percent. The intrinsic rate of natural increase (r),[48] during this period has been approximately 0.44. Altogether in 1985, 40 pairs were recorded, 25 attempted to nest and 16 produced 47 young (1.88 young per attempt; 2.94 young per successful attempt).

The progress of the reintroduction broken by region is summarized in Fig. 1. Natural production has offset the reduction in releases at the coastal sites and this population continues to grow at a rapid rate. The critical density of falcons of reproductive age in the inland region has apparently just been reached in the past year or so, with 5 of 7 nesting attempts successful in 1985. It is interesting to note that several of the inland pairs have occupied historic eyries that have never been used as hack sites. This parallels the reoccupation of long-vacant eyries seen in the British peregrine recovery,[5] and may support Hickey's[1] theory of "ecological magnetism".

The number of sightings of falcons in the inland region has not closely followed the number of releases as was seen in the coastal region, owing in part to the increased difficulty of finding peregrines in mountainous terrain. These figures therefore represent minimum estimates of population size since only documented sightings are recorded and surely some falcons go undetected.

DISCUSSION

The Eastern Peregrine Recovery Team recently defined more specific goals of at least 20 successfully nesting pairs in each of 5 regions for 3 consecutive years before downlisting to threatened status would be recommended, and a total of 175 pairs for complete recovery and de-listing (Nickerson, et al., in prep.). Region 1 contains the population of falcons nesting on artificial towers along the mid-Atlantic coast. Region 2 includes the mountains of New York and New England where releases have been emphasized since 1981. Region 3 is the

FIGURE 4. Recovery regions defined in revised Eastern Peregrine Recovery Plan (Nickerson et al., in prep.). Reprinted with permission from Barclay, in Cade et al. (in press).

southern Appalachians where releases began in 1984. The fourth region comprises the upper Great Lakes area where releases were tried in 1976 and 1977, but discontinued due to owl predation (Fig. 4). A release program under the direction of Dr. P.T. Redig and Dr. H.B. Tordoff of the University of Minnesota and the Bell Museum of Natural History (respectively) was begun in 1982 and has released 56 birds to date. Region 5 lacks clear boundaries and is comprised of sites scattered throughout several eastern states. Many of these were abandoned as hack sites in the past because of owl predation. Recovery in this region will require alternative release strategies such as the use of urban sites to avoid owl predation, though the best prospect here may be to await dispersal and colonization by falcons from adjacent regions.[49]

Only a small number of the breeding peregrines in the East have been individually identified to date, but there is evidence of movement of falcons between the coastal and northeastern inland sites (regions 1 and 2). Since 1983, peregrines have bred on tall bridges in New York City;[50] some of these birds have come from the coastal towers to the south and others have come from the northern cliff sites, demonstrating their flexibility with respect to nest site selection. One male falcon that bred in New York, in 1983 was the offspring of one of the first cliff-nesting pairs resulting from the reintroduction program, and sired young in his second year. Although breeding by subadults is generally considered unusual[5], it is more of a reflection of the structure of this founding population than a physiological feat. In a stable population the presence of territorially dominant older birds would no doubt restrict the opportunities of subadults to acquire nesting territories.[10] More recently, peregrines have colonized bridges near Annapolis, Marlyland, Wilmington, Delaware, and Philadelphia, Pennsylvania, and have been sighted near cliffs in the Delaware Water Gap (L.M. Rymon, pers. comm.). The mean dispersal distance of 9 known eastern breeders is 172.6 km. (SE = 41.2 km.) or 107.2 mi. (SE = 25.6 mi.); although this is too small a sample to permit broad conclusions to be drawn, it suggests that dispersal and colonization of vacant adjacent regions is a reasonable expectation. Conversely, many falcons do not seem to be dispersing far from their site of origin, instead joining the floating population of non-breeding falcons awaiting recruitment when an opportunity becomes available. This pattern of regional philopatry, accompanied by more widespread dispersal of a small component of the population, is like that described by White[51] as typical of most peregrine populations, and indeed, most other organisms.[52] Ratcliffe[5] has discussed the importance of this non-breeding element in the maintenance of a stable population structure, and that rapid mate replacement in instances in which one member of a pair dies is the chief evidence for its existence. The rapid replacement of "Scarlett", the Baltimore female, is a favorable indication of the status of the mid-Atlantic coastal peregrine population. This falcon, which raised 18 fostered young before finally attracting a mate and raising four young of her own, died in 1984 from a *Pseudomonas* infection in ther pharynx,[56] but it was replaced in just 4 days by a 2-year old female released at a tower 164 km. (102 mi.) away in New Jersey. However, these floating birds may present some problems in the recovery of the peregrine population; in addition to the problem of harassment at hack sites already described, the nesting attempt of at least one pair at a New Jersey tower in 1985 was thwarted because of interference by some of these surplus birds.

Cade[27] has addressed the basic biological requirements necessary to achieve recovery of the eastern peregrine population. Released birds must possess: 1) behavioral patterns allowing social interaction and reproduction to occur in the wild; 2) strong site-specific attachment to areas where they are released; 3) migratory habits allowing them to breed successfully in release areas; and 4) a survival potential comparable to a wild falcon. Finally, 5) the environment must be sufficiently free of pollutants and harmful chemicals to allow released peregrines to live and breed successfully. Based upon the results of this program to date, it is reasonable to assume that the first four requirements have been attained. There is still concern, however, that chemical residues in the environment may continue to interfere with reproduction. In a preliminary investigation of this problem, Gilroy and Barclay[53] analyzed 39 infertile or addled eggs and shell fragments collected from peregrines at 9 coastal tower and urban breeding sites in the East. The sample had the following means: shell thickness = 0.340 mm; Ratcliffe Index = 1.75; and DDE residues = 6.203 ppm lipid wet weight, but varied significantly among sites. Residue levels in eggs from urban sites were significantly lower than those in eggs from coastal towers, a finding predicted by Peakall.[4] Comparison of eggs from successful and unsuccessful clutches showed that residue levels and shell thinning have not been severe enough to have affected reproduction. Any problems that may develop then are likely to be specific to certain localities, thus posing at most a local, rather than widespread threat. This study, however, indicates the need for continued monitoring of chemical residues as population restoration proceeds.

Grier and Barclay[54] performed a simulation study, based on the observed growth rate of the eastern peregrine population to date, in order to assess the time frame required for recovery. Under the assumptions of their model, the current population is theoretically capable of reaching the recovery goals entirely by natural reproduction, with no further augmentation, but would do so at a very slow rate. They show that the rate with which restoration is achieved will be dependent on the level and duration of future recovery efforts.[55] Since reintroduced peregrines first bred in 1980, peregrine recovery has shifted from the experimental to an operational phase, marked by increasing involvement by state wildlife management agencies. As the recovery and management of this species becomes more routine, it is important to guard against an attitude of complacency. It must be remembered that in 1985 the entire breeding population of eastern peregrines comprised just 25 pairs, only 16 of which produced young, and is therefore still very much endangered. Recovery of the eastern peregrine population now appears to be within reach and can be achieved if man is willing to continue his stewardship on behalf of this species.

ACKNOWLEDGEMENTS

The eastern peregrine recovery program is a large cooperative effort which owes much of its success to the varied contributions, both financial and logistical, of numerous federal and state agencies and private organizations and individuals; a complete listing can be found in The Peregrine Fund Newsletter vols. 1-13 (1973-1985). We extend our special thanks to those individuals, too numerous to list, who have worked as release site attendants, and to our dedicated co-workers, past and present, at The Peregrine Fund. The assistance of Jonathan D. Ballou in preparation of the graphs is gratefully acknowledged.

REFERENCES CITED

1. Hickey, J.J., 1942. Eastern population of the duck hawk. Auk 59:176-204.
2. Hickey, J.J. (Ed.), 1969. Peregrine falcon populations: their biology and decline. University of Wisconsin press, Madison.

3. Berger, D.D., C.E. Sindelar, Jr., and K.E. Gamble, 1969. The status of breeding peregrines in the eastern United States. *In*: J.J. Hickey (Ed.) Peregrine falcon populations: their biology and decline. University of Wisconsin Press, Madison, pp.165-173.
4. Peakall, D.B., 1976. The peregrine falcon (*Falco peregrinus*) and pesticides. Can. Field-Naturalist 90:301-307.
5. Ratcliffe, D.A., 1980. The peregrine falcon. Buteo books, Vermillion, SD.
6. Wurster, C.F., 1973. DDT proved neither essential nor safe. Bioscience 23:105-106.
7. Cade, T.J., 1974. Current status of the peregrine in North America. *In*: Proceedings of the Conference on Raptor Conservation Techniques, Fort Collins, Colorado, 22-24 March 1973 (Part 6). Raptor Research Report No. 3. pp3-12.
8. Porter, R.D. and D.B. Marshall, 1977. The recovery team approach to restoration of endangered species. *In*: R.d. Chancellor (Ed.) World conference on birds of prey, report of proceedings, Vienna 1975, Int. Council for Bird Preservation. pp.314-319.
9. Bollengier, R.M., Jr., J. Baird, L.P. Brown, T.J. Cade, M.G. Edwards, D.C. Hagar, B. Halla, and E. McCaffrey, 1979. Eastern peregrine falcon recovery plan. U.S. Fish and Wildlife Service. Mimeographed. 147pp.
10. Barclay, J.H. and T.J. Cade, 1983. Restoration of the Peregrine falcon in the Eastern United States. Bird Conservation 1:3-40.
11. Clement, R.D., (Ed), 1974. Peregrine falcon recovery, proceedings of a conference on peregrine falcon recovery, 13-15 February, 1974. Audubon conservation report No. 4. National Audubon Society, New York.
12. White, C.M., 1968. Diagnosis and relationships of the North American tundra-inhabiting peregrine falcons. Auk 85:179-191.
13. Cade, T.J., 1974b. Plans for managing the survival of the peregrine falcon. *In*: Proceedings of the Conference on Raptor Conservation Techniques, Fort Collins, Colorado, 22-24 March 1973 (Part 6). Raptor Research Report No. 3. pp.89-104.
14. Drury, W.H., 1974. Rare species. Biological Conservation 6(3):162-169.
15. Schonewald-Cox, C.M., S.M. Chambers, B. MacBryde, and L. Thomas, (Eds.) Genetics and conservation: a reference for managing wild animal and plant populations. Benjamin Cimmings, Menlo Park, CA 722pp.
16. Soule, M.E. and D. Hales, in press. Conservation biology: science of diversity. Sinauer Associates, Sunderland, MA.
17. Frankel, O.H. and M.E. Soule, 1981. Conservation and evolution. Cambridge University Press, Cambridge, England.
18. Soule, M.E. and B.A. Wilcox, (Eds.), 1980. Conservation biology: an evolutionary-ecological perspective. Sinauer Associates, Sunderland, MA.
19. Franklin, I.R., 1980. Evolutionary change in small populations. *In*: M. Soule and b. Wilcox (Eds.) Conservation Biology: an evolutionary-

ecological perspective. Sinauer Associates, Sunderland, MA.
20. Carson, H.L., 1983. The genetics of the founder effect. *In*: C. Schonewald-Cox, S.M. Chambers, B. MacBryde, W. Thomas (Eds.) Genetics and conservation: a reference for managing wild animal and plant populations. Benjamin Cummings, Menlo Park, CA pp.189-200.
21. Templeton, A.R., H. Hemmer, G. Mace, U.S. Seal, W.M. Shields, and D.S. Woodruff, 1986. Local adaptation, coadaptation, and population boundaries. *In*: K. Ralls and J.d. Ballou (Eds.) Genetic management of captive populations. Zoo Biology 5(2).
22. Corbin, K.W., 1978. Genetic diversity in avian populations. *In*: Temple, S.A. (Ed.) Endangered birds: management techniques for preserving threatened species. University of Wisconsin Press, Madison, pp. 291-302.
23. Templeton, A.R., in press. Coadaptation and outbreeding depression. *In* M.E. Soule and D. Hales (Eds.) Conservation biology: science of diversity. Sinauer Associates, Sunderland, MA.
24. Wharton, D., 1985. The SSP subspecies dilemma: a report of an exploratory meeting of the AAZPA Species Survival Plan Subcommittee (SSPC) of the Wildlife Management and Conservation Committee. *In*: AAZPA 1985 Annual conference proceedings, pp. 47-54.
25. Cade, T.J., J.D. Weaver, J.B. Platt, and W.A. Burnham, 1977. The propagation of large falcons in captivity. Raptor Research 11:28-48.
26. Cade, T.J. and R.W. Fyfe, 1978. What makes peregrine falcons breed in captivity? *In*: Temple, S.A. (Ed.) Endangered birds: management techniques for preserving threatened species. University of Wisconsin Press, Madison, pp. 251-262.
27. Cade, T.J., 1980. The husbandry of falcons for return to the wild. Int. Zoo Yearbook. 20:23-35.
28. Burnham, W.A., 1983. Artificial incubation of falcon eggs. J. Wildl. Manage. 47(1):158-168.
29. Weaver, J.D. and T.J. Cade (Eds.), 1983. Falcon propagation. The Peregrine Fund, Inc., Ithaca, N.Y.
30. Cade, T.J. and V.J. Hardaswick, 1985. Summary of peregrine falcon production and reintroduction by The Peregrine Fund in the United States 1973-1984. Aviculture 91 (1-2):79-92.
31. Kumari, E., 1974. Past and present of the peregrine falcon in Estonia. *In*: E. Kumari (Ed.) Estonian wetlands and their life. Estonian contribution to IBP, No. 7 Acad. Sci. Estonian S.S.R., pp.230-252.
32. Goss, N.S., 1878. Breeding of the duck hawk in trees. Bull Nuttal Ornithol. Club 3:32-34.
33. Ridgway, R., 1895. Nesting of the duck hawk in trees. Nidologist 3(4-5):42-44.
34. Ganier, A.F., 1932. Duck hawks at the Reelfoot heronry. Migrant 3(2):28-32.
35. Groskin, H., 1952. Observations of duck hawks nesting on man-made struc-

tures. Auk 69:246-253.
36. Herbert, R.A. and K.G.S. Herbert, 1965. Behavior of peregrine falcons in the New York City region. Auk 82:62-94.
37. New Jersey State Geologist Report, 1890. Final report of the state geologist: mineralogy, botony, zoology. Vol. 2, J.L. Murphy Co., Trenton.
38. Jones, F.M., 1946. Duck hawks of eastern Virginia. Auk 63:592.
39. Cade, T.J., 1978. Manipulating the nesting biology of endangered birds. *In*: Temple, S.A. (Ed.). Endangered birds: management techniques for preserving threatened species. University of Wisconsin Press, Madison, pp. 167-170.
40. Sherrod, S.K., 1983. Behavior of fledgling peregrines. The peregrine Fund, Inc., Ithaca, NY.
41. Michell, E.B., 1900. The art and practice of hawking. D.R. Hillman and Son's, Ltd., Great Britain.
42. Cade, T.J. and S.A. Temple, 1977. The Cornell University falcon programme. *In*: R.D. Chancellor (Ed.) World conference on birds of prey, report of proceedings, Vienna. 1975. Int. Council for Bird Preservation. pp. 353-368.
43. Sherrod, S.K. and T.J. Cade, 1978. Release of peregrine falcons by hacking. *In*: T.A. Geer (Ed.) Birds of prey management techniques. British Falconer's Club.
44. Sherrod, S.K., W.R. Heinrich, W.A. Burnham, J.R. Barclay, and T.J. Cade, 1982. Hacking: a method for releasing peregrine falcons and other birds of prey. The Peregrine Fund, Inc., Ithaca, NY.
45. Burnham, W.A., J. Craig, J.H. Enderson, and W.R. Heinrich, 1978. Artificial increase in reproduction of wild peregrine falcons. J. Wildl. Manage. 42:626-628.
46. Young, H.F., 1969. Hypotheses on peregrine population dynamics. *In*: J.J. Hickey (Ed.) Peregrine falcon populations: their biology and decline. University of Wisconsin Press, Madison, pp. 513-519.
47. Hickey, J.J. and D.W. Anderson, 1969. The peregrine falcon: life history and population literature. *In*: J.J. Hickey (Ed.) Peregrine falcon populations: their biology and decline. University of Wisconsin Press, Madison, pp.3-42.
48. Pianka, E.R., 1978. Evolutionary ecology. Second edition. Harper and Row, New York, NY.
49. Barclay, J.H., in press. Restoration of the peregrine falcon in the eastern United States. *In*: T.J. Cade, C.M. White, J. H. Enderson, and C.G. Thelander (Eds.) Peregrine falcon populations: their management and recovery. The Peregrine Fund, Inc., Ithaca, NY.
50. Cade, T.J. and P.R. Dague, 1983. The Peregrine Fund Newsletter. No. 11.
51. White, C.M., 1969. Is there a genetic continuity concerned in eyrie maintenance? *In*: J.J. Hickey (Ed.) Peregrine falcon populations: their

biology and decline. University of Wisconsin Press. Madison, pp. 391-397.
52. Shields, W.M., 1982. Philopatry, inbreeding, and the evolution of sex. State University of New York Press, Albany, NY.
53. Gilroy, M.J. and J.H. Barclay, in press. DDE residues and shell characteristics of eggs of re-established peregrines in eastern United States. *In*: T.J. Cade, C.M. White, J.H. Enderson, and C.G. Thelander (Eds.) Peregrine falcon populations: their management and recovery. The Peregrine Fund, Inc., Ithaca, NY.
54. Grier, J.W. and J.H. Barclay, in press. Dynamics of founder populations established by reintroduction. *In*: T.J. Cade, C.M. White, J.H. Enderson, and C.G. Thelander (Eds.) Peregrine falcon populations: their management and recovery. The Peregrine Fund, Inc., Ithaca, NY.
55. Cade, T.J., C.M. White, J.H. Enderson, and C.G. Thelander (Eds.). Peregrine falcon populations: their management and recovery. The Peregrine Fund, Inc., Ithaca, NY, in press.
56. DeMent, S.H., J.J. Chisolm, Jr., J.C. Barber, and J.D. Strandberg, 1986. Land exposure in an "urban" peregrine falcon and its avian prey. J. Wildlife Diseases 22(2).238 244

Endangered and Threatened Species Programs in Pennsylvania and other States: Causes, Issues and Management. Edited by S. K. Majumdar, F. J. Brenner and A. F. Rhoads. © 1986, The Pennsylvania Academy of Science.

Chapter Thirty-Four

AIR POLLUTION STRESSORS AND FOREST DECLINE—A REVIEW

J. Robert Halma[1], Denise Rieker[1] and Shyamal K. Majumdar[2]

[1]Cedar Crest College
Allentown, PA 18104
and
[2]Lafayette College
Easton, PA 18042

Certain tree species in sensitive areas of the eastern forests of North America are in different stages of decline. Some of the evidence suggests that the decline parallels the upstart and continuation of acid deposition. Other research points to ozone as a causal agent. The effects vary from severe dieback of red spruce at high elevations to somewhat subtle decreases in growth rates of several other species in various forest settings.

INTRODUCTION

The effect of changing acidity in aquatic ecosystems has been repeatedly observed in the Adirondacks,[1] Canadian lakes,[2] the Poconos[3,4,5] and elsewhere. The detrimental effects, in later stages, become obvious in severely depressed pH values, gradual loss of the normal biota, and, most overtly, in the disappearance of game fish. These aquatic changes are most closely associated with those areas lacking bedrock and soil systems necessary to effectively neutralize the acid inputs.

Carbonate-rich limestone and dolomite, which have high buffering capacities, can neutralize virtually all acid inputs.[6] In contrast, granitic gneisses and quartz sandstones, as in much of New England and eastern Canada, have low to no buffering capacity. Some sandstones, shales, and conglomerates have medium to low buffering capacity.[7] Various maps have been generated for North America in which bedrock geology is used as an indicator for regions sensitive to acid precipitation.

Unlike aquatic ecosystems, changes in tree growth and vigor are less obvious. Unless an acute stage is reached, as when high rates of tree dieback occur, a forest may show little or no external signs of changes. For this reason, it is necessary to measure the annual growth increments over the life of the trees.

METHODS AND MATERIALS

In studying tree growth, most researchers follow the protocol outlined in Fritts.[8] A special hollow drill, called an increment corer (borer), is inserted along a radius of the tree (Figure 1). The resultant core is then removed with an extracter, mounted on a suitable wooden block, sanded, and examined with a stereoscope so that each annual increment can be accurately measured. The data are then subjected to computer analysis using several approaches. For single species-single area studies, indexing is most commonly used, followed by the removal of the weather factor, and thus leaving a "straight line" growth curve—unless other external factors act upon that line. In other cases, where the mean growth increments of a species drop sharply at some point and maintain that below-normal condition, the shift is compared with environmental perturbations. In comparative studies (same species, but in proximal sensitive and nonsensitive areas) the growth rates are plotted simultaneously for examination of trends. The approach has been to examine the long term trend of a given species' growth, minimize the variables, and then look for recent growth changes. In the laboratory, simulated acid rain, ozone and combinations of these, have been used primarily with young plants.

Another approach has been to examine the wood increments chemically for the presence and/or absence of certain metals that may be air pollution related.[9]

RESULTS AND DISCUSSION

The forest soil is composed of parent rock particles, gases, dissolved and suspended materials, organic matter, and a micro flora and fauna. A pH range of 6-7 is optimum for the biological regime.[10] Acid precipitation causes leaching of basic materials and results in a pH depression. The availability of phosphorus below a pH of 5.0 becomes limiting, and others elements, such as aluminum and lead, can become toxic. Nitrification becomes limiting below a pH of 5.0. Fungi and bacteria also show diminishing activity as the pH drops. In short, as the soil acidity drops, so do the normal biological processes and, hence, the effect if passed on to the trees. In agricultural settings, the effect is offset with liming—an impossible task for forests.

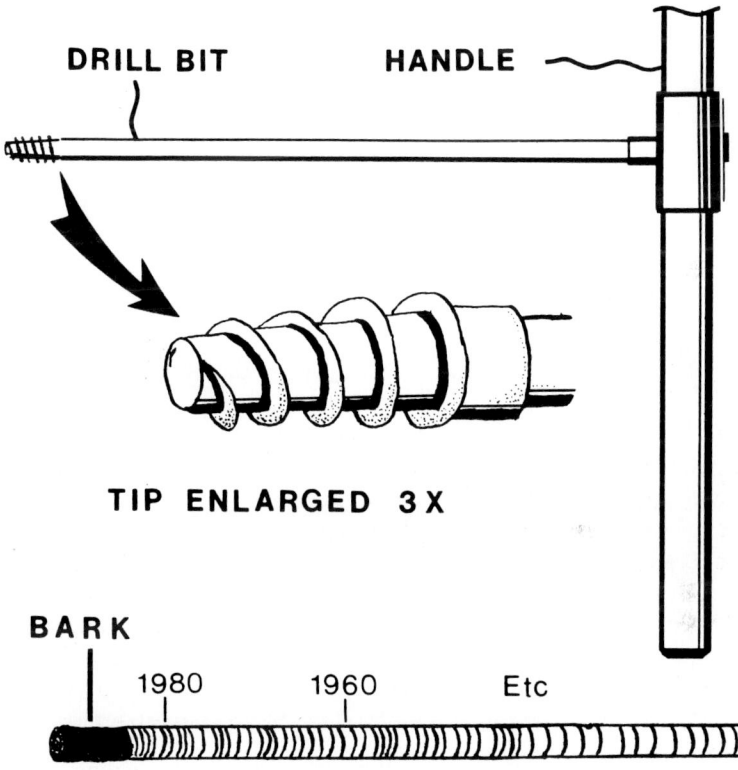

FIGURE 1. Corer and Core Sample.

Forest decline and tree dieback were first noted in Europe. Observations of many older silver fir trees (*Abies albo*) in West Germany showed progressive deterioration from foliage yellowing to defoliation and, finally, death. Norway spruce (*Picea abies*), pine (*Pinus*), and several deciduous species were added to the list of affected trees. The 1984 forest survey of West Germany put the damaged area of the forests at 50 percent. Other countries in Europe have also reported damaged areas ranging from ± 3 to 35 percent. The European experience is summarized by the Interagency Task Force on Acid Precipitation.[11]

In 1975, the U.S. Forest Service sponsored the first acid precipitation symposium in this country. In the following we summarize some representative studies of the possible effects of air quality on the forests in the eastern United States.

Siccama, Bliss and Vogelmann[12] studied red spruce (*Picea rubens*) in the Green Mountains of Vermont and found that it had declined by about half in basal

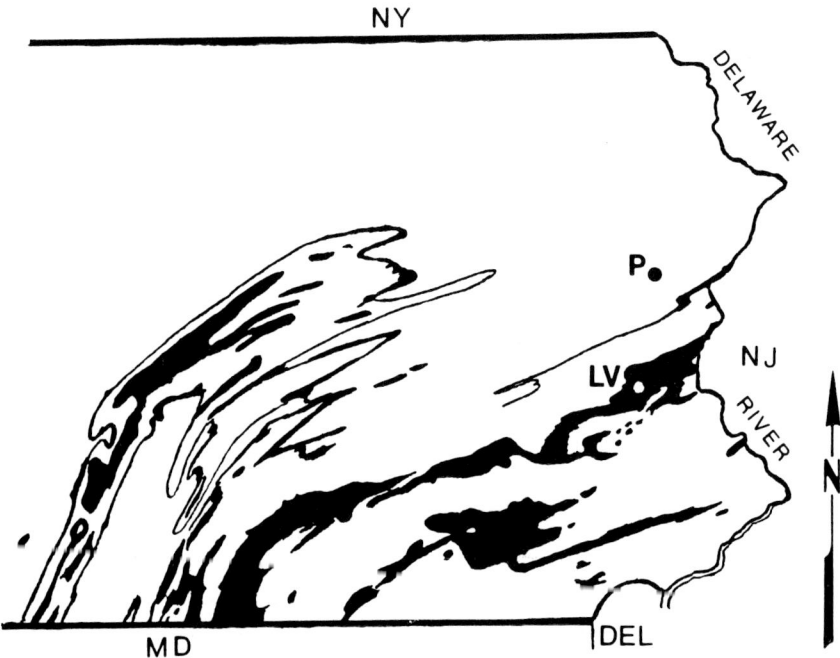

FIGURE 2. Occurrence of Limestone in Eastern Pennsylvania Sampling Sites: P = Poconos, LV = Lehigh Valley. Map after *Pennsylvania Geology* 10(2), 1979. Topographic and Geologic Survey.

area and density in virgin mid to high elevations between 1964 and 1979. Cloud moisture, common as a source of water above 800 m., is about 0.5 to 1.0 pH units lower than rain. In air reconnaissance observations of the Adirondack Mountains, they also noted similar spruce mortality and yellowing of the younger spruce trees.

Puckett[13] studied the growth patterns of white pine (*Pinus strobus*), eastern hemlock (*Tsuga canadensis*), pitch pine (*P. rigida*), and chestnut oak (*Quercus prinus*) in the Shawangunk Mountain area of southeastern New York. After removing the climatic variables, he found that hemlock showed no consistent trends, but that the remaining three species showed dramatic downward changes in their growth rates since the 1950's.

In studies of red spruce (*P. rubens*) from North Carolina to New Hampshire, Johnson and Siccama[14] found that, in the last 15-20 years, mortality has occurred rather evenly across all class sizes from the Catskills northward. On some plots, balsam fir (*Abies balsamea*) and white birch (*Betula papyrifera*) showed reductions in both basal area and density.

Studies of several pine species (pitch pine, *P. rigida;* shortleaf pine, *P. echinata;* and loblolly pine, *P. taeda)* in the Pine Barrens region of southern New Jersey, indicate an abnormal decrease in growth rates over the last 25 years.[15] Their studies

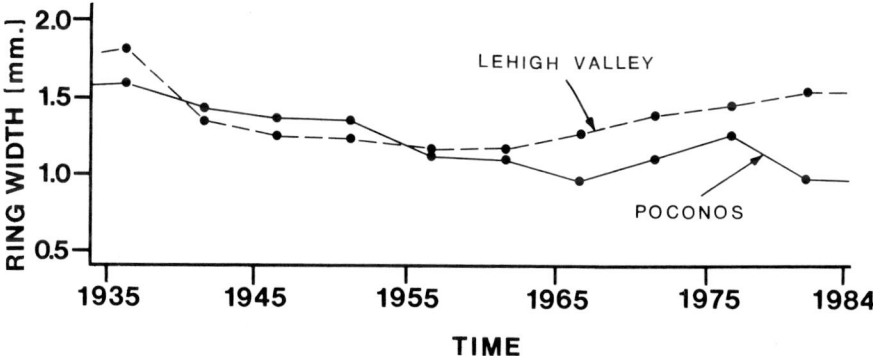

FIGURE 3. Ring Width vs. time for White Oak in the Poconos and Lehigh Valley. Points are five year means.

show a strong statistical relationship between lowered stream pH and declining growth rates of the trees.

Mineo et. al.[16] studied ectomycorrhizal distribution in the Lehigh Valley and Pocono forests. Soil pH was markedly depressed in the Pocono sites compared with those of the Lehigh Valley. Mycorrhizal activity was found to be less prominent in the Pocono forests than in the less acidic soils of the Lehigh Valley woodland. In eastern Pennsylvania Majumdar et. al[17] compared the growth of white oak (*Quercus alba*) in the sensitive sandstone bedrock area of the Poconos and the non-sensitive limestone of the nearby Lehigh Valley (Figure 2). Both sites showed similar growth patterns from the 1930's to about 1965. From 1965 to the present the Pocono forest had gradually diminished growth rates (Figure 3). Paired t-tests statistically confirmed the intuitive relationship between the two population means.

The assumption, in part triggered by the European experience and a widely publicized account of acid rain[18] in North America, has been that acid rain is a causal agent. Recent laboratory studies by Reich and Amundson[19], however, have shown that increasing ozone concentrations cause decreased photosynthetic rates, which in turn are related to growth. Their studies further show that, in the laboratory, acid rain has no effect on the seedlings of several tree species.

While widespread evidence of declining tree growth continues to accumulate, conclusive cause-and-effect relationships remain to be demonstrated. Some trees seem unaffected by the increased acidity, others respond less punctually to environmental perturbations, and some have shown a positive response to acid precipitation in the seedling stage.[20]

Bormann[21] has suggested a continuum of progressive decline leading to ecosystem collapse (here summarized):

Stage O. Pristine systems.
Stage I. Low levels of anthropogenic pollutants. No effect.
Stage IIA. Sensitive species subtly and adversely affected.
Stage IIB. Sensitive species decline, but others remain as insignificant components.
Stage IIIA. Large species die. Basic structure of the ecosystem changes.
Stage IIIB. Ecosystem collapse.

One may debate where the forests of eastern North America fall on the suggested continuum, but evidence points to Stage II for a number of species, and Stage IIIA for a few species. In extreme local conditions, Stage IIIB has been reached.[22] In the long run, we might look to the loss of American chestnut to chestnut blight disease and the resulting changes in forest composition as an indication of things to come. Unfortunately, trees are slow to mature, genetic turnover is slow, and therefore the development of resistant or tolerant populations within affected species is a very long term process.[10] Alternatively, should regulatory changes occur so as to markedly reduce acid deposition and other pollutants at their sources, existing forest species could rebound to their prior growth levels.

Although the studies in North America have focused primarily on the northeastern states because of their meteorological juxtaposition to the high emission Ohio Valley, recent concern has been raised about the western states.[23] And while the concern shifts westward, debate continues about pollutant sources in the northeast vs. those from the midwest.[24] *Debate* itself, it seems, has been the pivotal word surrounding the whole air pollution—environmental stress issue. SO_2, NO_x, and O_3 all can have toxic effects on plants and they are unevenly generated and distributed. Abelson[25] recently pointed out that any initiations to reduce acid precipitation, should include all source types.

In the context of the theme of this book, however, the question remains of threatened and endangered species. Research on tree growth has focused on common species and acid deposition, and air pollution is viewed as a stressor. Stressors generate a host of ecosystem changes,[26] and among these will surely be the loss of sensitive species unable to cope with the changing environment.

ACKNOWLEDGEMENTS

This research was funded by Pennsylvania Power and Light Company. Study site permissions were granted by the Allentown Parks, Don Frederick, Inc., and Nature Conservancy.

REFERENCES CITED

1. Schofield, C.L. 1977. Acid precipitation's destructive effects on fish in the Adirondacks. *New York Food Life Sci. Q.* 10(3): 12-15.
2. Beamish, R.J. 1976. Acidification of lakes in Canada by acid precipitation and the resulting effects on fish. *Water, Air, and Soil Poll.* 6:501-514.
3. Bradt, P.T. and M.B. Berg. 1983. Preliminary survey of Pocono Mountain lakes to determine sensitivity to acid deposition. *Proc. PA. Acad. Science.* 57: 190-194.
4. Bradt, P.T. and J.L. Dudley. 1984. The ecological effects of acid deposition in eastern North America, pp. 221-236. In S.K. Majumdar and E.W. Miller (Eds.) *Solid and Liquid Wastes: Management and Socioeconomic Considerations.* The Pennsylvania Academy of Science Publication, pp. 412.
5. Majumdar, S.K., G. Rall, A. Mrowca, P. Steed, J. Tabak, and L. Mineo. 1984. Bacteriological survey of two acid-stressed lakes in the Poconos before limestone application. *Proc. PA. Acad. Sci.* 58: 181-186.
6. Johnson, N.M. 1984. Acid rain neutralization by geologic materials, in Bricker, O.P. (ed.), *Geological Aspects of Acid Deposition.* Butterworth Publishers, Boston, MA.
7. Glass, N.R., D.E. Arnold, J.N. Galloway, G.R. Hendrey, J.J. Lee, W.W. McFee, S.A. Norton, C.F. Powers, D.L. Rambo, and C.L. Schofield. 1982. Effects of acid precipitation. *Env. Sci. and Tech.* 16(3): 162-169A.
8. Fritts, H.C. 1976. *Tree Rings and Climate.* Academic Press, N.Y.
9. Baes, C.F. III, and S.B. McLaughlin, 1984. Trace elements in tree rings evidence of recent and historical air pollution. *Science* 224: 494-497.
10. Department of Environmental Resources. *Pennsylvania Perspective on Acid Rain.* The Pennsylvania Department of Environmental Resources, May, 1984.
11. Interagency Task Force on Acid Precipitation. 1984. Annual Report, 1984 to the President and Congress. National Acid Precipitation Assessment Program, Washington, D.C.
12. Siccama, T.G., M. Bliss, and H.W. Vogelmann. 1982. Decline of the red spruce in the Green Mountains of Vermont. *Bull. Torrey Bot. Club.* 109(2): 162-168.
13. Puckett, L.J. 1982. Acid rain, air pollution, and tree growth in southeastern New York. *J. Envir. Qual.* 11(3): 1982.
14. Johnson, A.H., and T.G. Siccama. 1983. Acid deposition and forest decline. *Environ. Sci. Technol.* 17(7): 294t-305t.
15. Johnson, A.H., T.G. Siccama, D. Wang, R.S. Turner, and T.H. Barringer. 1981. Recent changes in patterns of tree growth rate in the New Jersey pinelands: a possible effect of acid rain. *J. Environ. Qual.* 10(4): 427-430.

16. Mineo, L., S.K. Majumdar, G. Rall, J. Francis A. Segal and A. Mrowca. 1984. Preliminary study of the ectomycorrhizal distribution of white oaks in eastern Pennsylvania forests. *Proc. PA. Acad. of Sci.* 58: 92-98.
17. Majumdar, S.K., L. Mineo and J.R. Halma. 1985. Progress Report on the Acid Precipitation Studies in the Poconos, Pennsylvania Power and Light Company, Allentown, PA.
18. Likens, G.E., R.F. Wright, J.N. Galloway, and T.J. Butler. 1979. Acid rain. *Scientific American* 241: 43-51.
19. Reich, D.B. and R.G. Amundson. 1985. Ambient levels of ozone reduce net photosynthesis in tree and crop species. *Science.* 230: 566-570.
20. Wood, T., and F.H. Bormann. 1977. Short-term effects of a simulated acid rain upon the growth and nutrient relations of *Pinus strobus L. Water, Air and Soil Pollut.* 7: 479-488.
21. Bormann, F.H. 1985. Air pollution and forests: an ecosystem perspective. *BioScience* 35(7):434-441.
22. Jordan, M.J. 1975. Effects of zinc smelter emissions and fire on a chestnut-oak woodland. *Ecology* 56: 78-91.
23. Sun, M. 1985. Possible acid rain woes in the West. *Science* 228(4695): 34-35.
24. Rahn, K.A., and D.H. Lowenthal. 1985. Pollution aerosol in the northeast: northeastern-midwestern contributions. *Science.* 228(4697): 275-284.
25. Abelson, P.H. 1985. Air pollution and acid rain. *Science.* 230(4726): 617.
26. Odum, E.P. 1985. Trends expected in stressed ecosystems. *BioScience.* 35(7): 419-422.

Endangered and Threatened Species Programs in Pennsylvania and other States: Causes, Issues and Management. Edited by S. K. Majumdar, F. J. Brenner and A. F. Rhoads. © 1986, The Pennsylvania Academy of Science.

Chapter Thirty-Five

IMPACTS OF ACIDIFICATION ON TROUT AND BENTHIC INSECTS OF HEADWATER STREAMS: AN OVERVIEW

William G. Kimmel
Department of Biological and Environmental Sciences
California University of Pennsylvania
California, PA 15419

INTRODUCTION

Acidification of stream ecosystems in Pennsylvania is a phenomenon as old as the state's coal-mining industry. Both the well-documented pollution from acid mine drainage (AMD) and the current threat from atmospheric deposition of acids involve the element sulfur and its conversion to sulfuric acid. Acid mine drainage stems from the exposure of pyritic materials to the action of air, water, and microbes during and after mining operations. The resultant drainage, a mixture of sulfuric acid, heavy metals, and silt, has degraded approximately 4,800 km of surface streams in the Commonwealth.[1,2] By contrast, acid deposition is the end result of a complex series of atmospheric reactions. Combustion of fossil fuels, metal smelting, and various industrial processes release oxides of sulfur and nitrogen into the atmosphere where they are converted into aerosols of sulfuric and nitric acids. The introduction of these substances into aquatic ecosystems may be accomplished by either wet fallout as rain, snow, sleet, and hail (wet deposition) or by gravitational settling of coarse particulates and fine aerosols (dry deposition).[3,4] Increasing acidity of precipitation over the northeastern United States and Canada has been implicated in the loss of fish populations from sensitive lakes and streams.[5]

The Commonwealth of Pennsylvania ranks as both a major emitter and recipient of airborne mixtures of acidic pollutants. Indeed, a "double-dose" acidification effect from both the extraction and combustion of high-sulfur coal may be experienced. Prevailing winds carry sulfur emissions from the large concentration of electric power generating stations in the Ohio Valley into Pennsylvania where they combine with local pollutants to acidify ambient precipitation. The mean annual pH of precipitation falling in Pennsylvania is about 4.0 and is as acidic as anywhere in the nation.[6]

SENSITIVITY TO ACIDIFICATION

Three major factors governing the sensitivity of a watershed to acidification are size of drainage basin, buffering capacity, and topography.[7,8] Dilution capacity is largely dependent upon the quantity of surface runoff and groundwater inflow; therefore, large watersheds are less susceptible to acidification than are small watersheds. Buffering capacity is the ability of water to neutralize the addition of an acid or base without attendant changes in pH. In natural waters, bicarbonate (HCO_3^-) and carbonate (CO_3^{-2}) ions are the principal buffering agents. Streams draining watersheds underlain by limestone or other calcareous bedrock may have high concentrations of these substances in solution and exhibit pH levels at or above neutrality (pH 7.0). Addition of acids to such streams will result in neutralization (and no pH decline) until the supply of bicarbonate and carbonate ions is exhausted. At this point, pH will begin to decline. The higher the concentrations of these ions (alkalinity), the greater the buffering capacity. This important chemical system protects aquatic organisms from rapid changes in pH and renders most toxic heavy metals insoluble. By contrast, streams draining watersheds lacking carbonate minerals typically exhibit baseflow pH values of 6.0—6.5 and little buffering capacity. An accepted criterion of sensitivity to acidification is base-flow surface water alkalinity of ≤ 10 mg/l as $CaCO_3$.[9] For Pennsylvania, these regions are shown in Figure 1. While this map provides a useful geographic overview, it must be emphasized that local variations in sensitivity are likely to occur even in adjacent watersheds. The topography of a region also has a significant influence on the susceptibility of its lakes and streams to acidification. Mountainous areas are likely to have shallower soils and more exposed insoluble bedrock than lowlands, and are hence more vulnerable to the impacts of acid deposition. Pristine headwater streams located on mountain ranges from the Laurel Highlands in the southwest to the Poconos in the northeast frequently exhibit all three sensitivity factors.

Mountain streams draining undeveloped forested watersheds are an important economic resource in Pennsylvania. They represent the prime habitat for wild naturally-reproducing populations of the brook trout (*Salvelinus fontinalis*) and other wild and hatchery-reared salmonids. The value of coldwater angling

Adapted from: Omernik, J. 1980. Total alkalinity of surface water in the Appalachian region. U.S. Environmental Protection Agency, EPA-600/D-8L-333.

FIGURE 1. Areas with total average surface water alkalinity of ≤ 10 mg/l in Pennsylvania.

per day in Pennsylvania was estimated at $43.00 in 1981[10] and the resource is the most heavily utilized in the nation.[11] In addition, many communities are served by water supply reservoirs on such streams since disinfection is frequently the only treatment required for potability. These low-order streams (orders 1—3) constitute the majority of flowing waters in the Commonwealth and are frequently cited by conservation agencies as "high quality" environments demanding protection from development.

THE STREAM ECOSYSTEM

Dynamic stream ecosystems support a wide variety of aquatic organisms which function as producers, consumers, and decomposers. The aquatic food chain, often based on terrestrial detritus (fall inputs of leaves), culminates in the brook trout, the state fish of Pennsylvania. Aquatic insects are an important component of the food chain in headwater streams and populate benthic stream communities. Certain insects of the Orders Ephemeroptera (mayflies), Plecoptera (stoneflies), Trichoptera (caddisflies), Odonata (dragonflies and damselflies), Coleoptera (beetles), Megaloptera (alderflies and fishflies), and Diptera (true flies) have partially or wholly aquatic life cycles. These organisms, along with other microscopic and macroscopic invertebrates function in detritus processing as shredders and collectors and as grazers on attached algae and

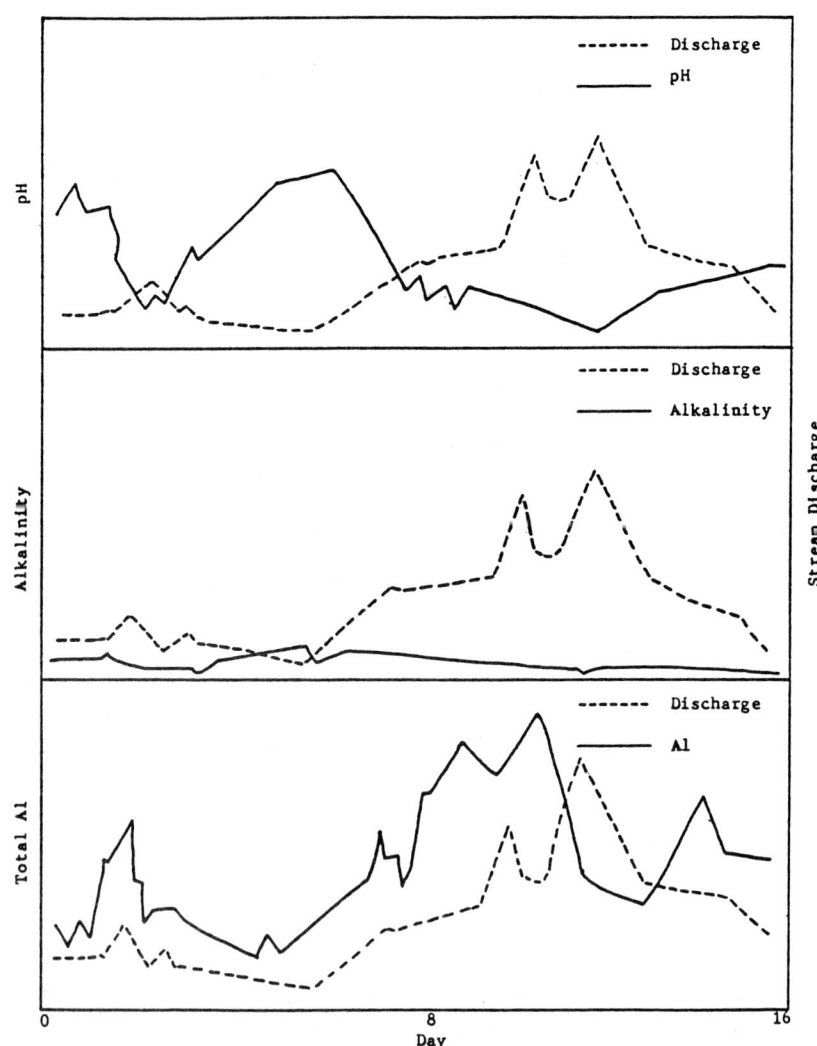

Adapted from: Sharpe, et. al. 1984. Causes of acidification of four streams on Laurel Hill in southwestern Pennsylvania. *J. Environ. Qual.* 13(4): 627,628.

FIGURE 2. Temporal behavior of pH, alkalinity, and total aluminum (Al) during a major dormant season runoff event on McGinnis Run.

predators. Aquatic macroinvertebrate taxa vary considerably in their respective abilities to tolerate various types of pollutants, and this phenomenon has prompted the use of benthic community structure as a tool of water pollution biologists. The entire community is an important link in the transfer of energy to the apex of the food chain—the trout.

The headwater stream fish community in Pennsylvania often consists of only two species—the brook trout and either the slimy (*Cottus cognatus*) or mottled sculpin (*Cottus bairdi*). Both rely on aquatic invertebrates as their primary food source although brook trout will feed on terrestrial insects that fall into streams. In response to the rigors of life in a fluctuating environment, brook trout spawn at an early age and small size and their populations fluctuate widely from year to year. This, most acid-tolerant species of the salmonid family, is often the final victim of progressive acidification.

MECHANISMS OF TOXICITY

Much of the atmospheric acidification currently experienced by Pennsylvania brook trout streams can best be described as intermittent. That is, water quality fluctuates with stream discharge. Increased discharge, as a result of precipitation or snow-melt runoff results in a decline in pH and total alkalinity and an elevation in toxic heavy metal concentrations, particularly aluminum. While peak flows can occur at any time of the year, rapid melting of accumulated snow packs in late winter or early spring can be particularly damaging. Depression in pH of nearly 2 units during dormant season peak discharges have been reported from streams on the Laurel Hill in southwestern Pennsylvania.[12] Figure 2 depicts the behavior of selected water quality parameters during a February 1981 snow-melt runoff event on McGinnis Run.[12] Solar radiation and elevated temperatures cause the snowpack to melt from top to bottom releasing into solution accumulated pollutants. As the resultant acidic meltwater passes through the soil, it leaches aluminum, a common component of forest mineral soils in Pennsylvania. Bound to clay materials in the soil, aluminum may be mobilized by sulfate (SO_4^{-2}) and hydrogen ion (H^+) activity once soil buffering capacity has been exhausted. The rapid influx of surface runoff and soil leachate into a stream can severely degrade water quality for the duration of the "acid shock" episode. Loss of soil buffering capacity is a progressive phenomenon and may be irreversible.

Impacts of acidification on benthic insects depend upon species tolerance, stage in the life cycle, and severity and duration of the episode. Within any taxonomic group, species of varying sensitivity to pH depressions may be found. In general, pH sensitivity declines at the order level as follows: Odonata, Trichoptera, Ephmeroptera, Hemiptera, Diptera, Coleoptera, Plecoptera.[13] Extreme conditions of acid/aluminum stress may result in mortality and/or mor-

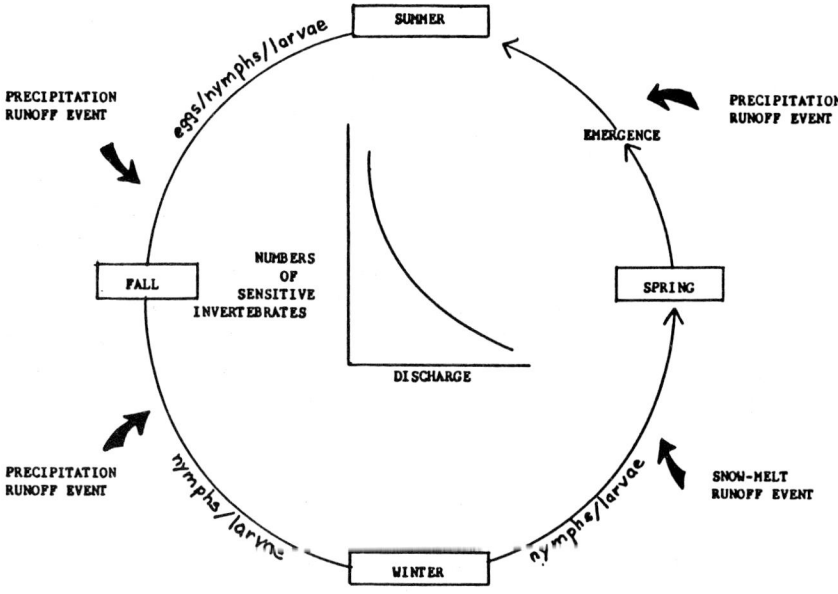

FIGURE 3. Seasonal impacts of intermittent acidification on benthic stream insects.

bidity of sensitive organisms. Catastrophic drift may depopulate areas of stream bottom for the duration of the episode. Upon return to the favorable chemical environment provided by base-flow conditions, recolonization from various sources may commence. Alkaline spring seeps or tributaries may yield immigrants in the form of behavioral drift while upstream flight of egg-laying adults may also serve to repopulate headwater reaches. This cyclic effect is summarized in Figure 3. Benthic macroinvertebrate community structure may thus fluctuate considerably during the year depending upon the frequency and severity of runoff episodes.[14]

Susceptibility of trout populations to acidification also depends upon species, life cycle stage, and severity and duration of the episode. Brook trout are the most tolerant followed by brown trout (*Salmo trutta*) with rainbow trout *(Salmo gairdneri)* the most sensitive. In recognition of this variability in species tolerance and the seasonal nature of acidification, the Pennsylvania Fish Commission has adopted the following stocking criteria for impacted streams:

    A. Pre-season stocking eliminated or curtailed to appropriate species due to acidity.
    B. Rainbow trout no longer stocked at any time due to acidity.
    C. Brown trout no longer stocked at any time due to acidity.
    D. Only brook trout stocked due to acidity.
    E. Brook trout no longer stocked at any time due to acidity.

F. Stocking terminated due to acidity.

Acidification toxicity to trout is due primarily to synergistic acid/aluminum stress acting on the gills.[15,16] The gills, one of the few areas of the body permeable to salts and water, function in salt and water balance (osmoregulation) as well as respiration. The dilute medium of headwater streams requires compensation for diffusional losses of ions such as sodium (Na^+) and chloride (Cl^-) and gains of water. Excess water is voided as a dilute and copious urine while drinking is avoided. Salt loss is replaced by specialized cells in the gills which actively transport ions across the gill membrane. This osmoregulatory mechanism is inhibited by acid/aluminum stress with lethal toxicity dependant upon pH level and the form and concentration of aluminum.[5] Fish under acid/aluminum stress frequently exhibit loss of equilibrium and hyperventilation. Post-mortem examination of such fish frequently reveals accumulations of yellowish mucus on the gills.[17,18] Respiratory distress is likely a secondary consequence of acid/aluminum stress. At the population level, acidification may block upstream migration of spawners, eliminate fish from certain streams or reaches of streams periodically, and kill eggs and/or fry resulting in loss of year classes. Mortality of adult fish appears to be uncommon presumably due to their mobility.

SUMMARY

The Pennsylvania Fish Commission recognizes a large number of Pennsylvania headwater trout streams as either intermittently acidified or vulnerable to acidification. Frederick Johnson of the Pennsylvania Fish Commission forecasts a dismal future for these resources if present levels of emissions of sulfur and nitrogen oxides are not reduced.[10,18] In a comprehensive review of stream water quality data from Fish Commission files, he found historical declines in alkalinity and concomitant losses of fish populations. Johnson estimates that fully 30 percent of the nearly 8,045 km of stocked streams and 40 percent of 14,481 km of unstocked streams in Pennsylvania are vulnerable to acidification. Unless emissions are reduced, at least half of these sensitive streams may lose their fisheries by 1999. The concomitant loss of 1.15 million angler days could result in a recreational loss of $50 million annually. Acidification of headwater trout streams appears to be a real and progressive phenomenon. Since loss of buffering capacity may be irreversible, the biological and social amenities provided by these endangered ecosystems should not be sacrificed for short-term energy objectives.

REFERENCES

1. Sopper, W. and S. Kerr. 1981. Revegetating strip-mined land with municipal

sewage sludge. Environmental Protection Agency report number, EPA-600/s2-81-182.
2. Barnes, H. and S. Romberger. 1968. Chemical aspects of acid mine drainage. *JWPCF* 40:371-384.
3. Likens, G., R. Wright, J. Galloway, and T. Butler. 1979. Acid rain. *Sci. Amer.* 241:43-51.
4. Cowling, E. 1982. Acid precipitation in historical perspective. *ES&T* 16:110A-123A.
5. Haines, T. 1981. Acid precipitation and its consequences for aquatic ecosystems: a review. *Trans. Am. Fish. Soc.* 110:669-707.
6. Barrie, L. 1982. Environment Canada's long range transport of atmospheric pollutants program: atmospheric studies. pp. 141-161. *In: Acid precipitation effects on ecological systems,* F. D'Itri, Ed., Ann Arbor Science, Michigan, 506 pp.
7. Hendrey, G., J. Galloway, S. Norton, C. Schofield, P. Shaffer, and D. Burns. 1980. Geological and hydrochemical sensitivity of the eastern United States to acid precipitation. Brookhaven National Laboratory, Upton, NY, EPA-600/3-80-024.
8. Kaplan, E., H. Thode, Jr., and A. Protas. 1981. Rocks, soils, and water quality. Relationships and implications for effects of acid precipitation on surface water in the NE United States. *ES&T* 15:539-544.
9. Altshuller, A. and G. McBean. 1979, 1980. The LRTAP problem in North America: A preliminary overview prepared by the United States-Canada bilateral research consultation group on the long-range transport of air pollutants. Atmosp. Envir. Serv. Downsview, Ontario, 48 pp. Part 1 (1979), 48 pp. Part 2 (1980), 39 pp.
10. Johnson, F. 1983. Trends of alkalinity and pH in Pennsylvania's low order stocked mountain trout streams and potential economic implications. Unpub. report NE Fish and Wildlife Conference, Mount Snow, Dover, Vermont.
11. Martin, R. 1977. Trends in angling pressure and license sales. *Fisheries* 2(4) pp. 11-16.
12. Sharpe, W., D. DeWalle, R. Leibfried, R. Dinicola, W. Kimmel, and L. Sherwin. 1984. Causes of acidification on four streams on Laurel Hill in southwestern Pennsylvania. *J. Environ. Qual.* 13:619-631.
13. Eilers, J. and R. Berg. 1981. Sensitivity of aquatic organisms to acidic environments. U.S. Environmental Protection Agency, Environmental Research Laboratory, Draft, Duluth, MN.
14. Kimmel, W., D. Murphey, W. Sharpe, and D. DeWalle. 1985. Macroinvertebrate community structure and detritus processing in two southwestern Pennsylvania streams acidified by atmospheric deposition. *Hydrobiologia* 124:97-102.

15. Baker, J. and C. Schofield. 1980. Aluminum toxicity to fish as related to acid precipitation and Adirondack surface water quality. pp. 292-293 *In: Ecological impact of acid precipitation*, Proceedings of an international conference, Drablos, D. and A. Tollan, Eds., Sandefjord, Norway. Oslo-As, Norway, SNSF Project. 383 pp.
16. Schofield, C. and J. Trojnar. 1980. Aluminum toxicity to fish in acidified waters. pp. 341-346 *In: Polluted rain,* Toribara, T., M. Miller, and P. Morrow, Eds., Plenum Press, New York, NY, 502 pp.
17. Muniz, I. and H. Leivestad. 1980. Acidification—effects on freshwater fish. pp.84-92 *In: Ecological impact of acid precipitation,* Proceedings of an international conference, Drablos, D. and A. Tollan, Eds., Sandefjord, Norway. Oslo-As, Norway, SNSF Project, 383 pp.
18. Johnson, F. 1983. Acid precipitation. Supplement to *Pennsylvania Angler* 52 p. 4.

Chapter Thirty-Six

IMPACT OF ACID PRECIPITATION AND LIMESTONE NEUTRALIZATION ON BACTERIAL AND DIATOM POPULATIONS IN TWO LAKES IN THE POCONOS, PENNSYLVANIA

S.K. Majumdar, P.M. Steed, G.F. Rall,
O. DeLucia, R.W. Snyder, L. Mineo, R.L. Morris,
C.A. Barthelmes, K.R. Berger and T.A. Baker

Department of Biology
Lafayette College, Easton, Pennsylvania 18042

This study examined water and sediment samples from the acid-stressed Bruce Lake (pH 5.5-6.1) and the limestone neutralized White Deer Lake (pH 6.6-7.5) for several seasons to assess the impacts of acidification and neutralization on bacterial and diatom populations. Live and dead bacterial densities were determined by direct count through epifluorescence microscopy. Spot plating and most probable number methods were utilized to enumerate aerobic heterotrophic, proteolytic, nitrogen cycle and sulfur cycle bacteria. Diatom densities in water and sediment samples of the two lakes were analyzed by acridine orange direct counts using epifluorescence microscopy. Bacterial densities in the two lakes prior to limestone neutralization of White Deer Lake were similar. With a few exceptions, total bacterial counts in Bruce Lake in 1985 were similar to those observed in 1984. Bacterial densities enumerated by epifluorescence microscopy in water and sediment samples taken from White Deer Lake after liming were consistently higher than those observed for acid-stressed Bruce Lake. Higher values were also observed for heterotrophic and proteolytic bacteria in the neutralized White Deer Lake. Sulfur cycle and nitrogen cycle bacteria, however, showed only a marginal increase without any definite trend in the neutralized lake. Diatom densities were dramatically higher throughout the study period in White Deer Lake than in the acid-stressed Bruce Lake. Analysis of

---

This study was made possible through a research contract grant provided by the Pennsylvania Power and Light Company, Allentown, Pennsylvania

variance and Tukey's test revealed that bacterial and diatom densities in White Deer Lake sediment after liming were significantly higher than in Bruce Lake. It thus appears that neutralization by limestone reintroduced a favorable environment for certain bacterial and diatom species in the aquatic environment which had been previously stressed by acid precipitation.

INTRODUCTION

Recent attention has brought the phenomenon of acid precipitation into public light even though the problem has existed for many years. This increased interest stems from the fact that although the precipitation falling on the northeastern United States has been acidic for some time, the effects of such conditions have become more acute in the past few decades.[2,3] In fact, the rainfall around world has become five to thirty times more acidic than the lowest expected value (pH 5.6) for an unpolluted atmosphere.[1] This phenomenon is caused by natural as well as man-made stressors, many of which are atmospheric pollutants such as sulfur and nitrogen oxides produced by the burning of fossil fuels.[1,2,3,4] The resulting acid precipitation produces devastating effects on the ecosystem,[5,6] causing the breakdown of the biota's structure and function[7] and thereby posing a great threat to individual species of a balanced ecosystem.

The decrease in pH causes the population densities of many indigenous organisms to dwindle. A secondary effect of this pH stress is the influx of heavy metals, particularly aluminum, into aquatic and terrestrial systems. These metals come from both the soil and the atmosphere.[8] The lakes of the Poconos are particularly susceptible to acid stress due to their geological characteristics. Bedrock of the lakes is composed of siliceous rocks such as sandstone and conglomerate which have poor buffering capacity and are unable to compensate for increasing hydrogen ion concentration.

Most investigations of the impacts of acidification in aquatic systems included studies of fish, phytoplankton and zooplankton populations.[9,10,11] The adverse effects of increased acidity on aquatic microorganisms have been demonstrated only recently. Studies of acid-stressed lakes (pH 4.5 to 5.5) revealed bacterial population counts as much as an order of magnitude lower than those of non-acid-stressed lakes.[12] Survey of bacterial populations in two acid-stressed lakes in the Poconos exhibited a similar lower trend in bacterial densities.[13,14] In another study, composition of heterotrophic bacteria in acid-stressed lakes was found to be different from those of nonstressed lakes.[15]

Bacteria and diatoms are the beginnings of the food chain, and biodegradation in aquatic systems is mainly accomplished by bacteria. It has been shown that acidic conditions are unfavorable to microorganisms,[16] and the rate of decomposition has decreased creating a build up of organic material.[17] This is particularly due to a shift in decomposing organisms from rapidly decomposing bacteria to slower acting fungi.[18]

Neutralization by limestone has been shown to be an effective method in the rejuvenation of lakes. This technique has been successful in reestablishing game fish populations in Sweden[19] and in New York State.[20] These studies also reported an upward succession in phytoplankton and zooplankton after neutralization. Studies have indicated that the monitoring of large game fish is a poor method for detecting early effects of environmental stressors.[6] A more effective approach is to monitor microorganisms that reproduce rapidly and respond quickly to changes in the ecological balance.[21]

In this study, water and surface sediment samples from two acid-stressed lakes in the Poconos were monitored for several seasons before and after limestone treatment to assess the impacts of acidification and neutralization on bacterial and diatom populations. White Deer Lake was neutralized with limestone in February, 1985 while Bruce Lake was kept undisturbed in its natural state throughout the study.

MATERIALS AND METHODS

Samples were taken from each of the lakes at four sites situated upon the long axis of the lakes at three depths per site: subsurface (15 centimeters below the water surface), middle (one-half depth at that site), and sediment pH was determined in the field with a Fisher Acumet field pH meter. The lakes were similar before liming in that both pH and temperature parameters exhibited similar changes.[13,14]

Direct count (spot plate method) and most probable number (MPN) dilution exclusion series tests were performed on the water and sediment samples using several types of media that are highly selective for the following types of bacteria: heterotrophic, proteolytic, nitrogen cycle and sulfur cycle. The Young Spot Plate Method was used to detect the heterotrophic, proteolytic, and nitrogen cycle bacteria.[22] The five tube most probable number dilution exclusion test was performed to detect nitrogen cycle and sulfur cycle bacteria.[23] Heterotrophic bacteria were enumerated on Foot and Taylor agar,[22] proteolytic bacteria on Glycerol Beef-Peptone agar,[23] ammonifying bacteria on Peptone-Salt Medium, nitrifying bacteria on Winogradsky Medium, and denitrifying bacteria on Giltay Medium.[23] Starkey Medium[24] was used to detect sulfate reducing bacteria while Postgate Medium[25] was used to count sulfur oxidizing bacteria. Agar counts were made on days 2, 6 and 9 while MPN counts were obtained after 9 and 16 days of incubation; plates and tubes were incubated at 22-24 degrees Celsius.

Live and dead counts for both bacteria and diatoms were obtained by the use of acridine orange epifluorescence microscopy. Water and surface sediment samples were fixed in 4% buffered formalin at the collection site. One milliliter of each sample was stained in acridine orange solution for eight to ten minutes and filtered through a nuclepore filter.[26,27] A Bausch and Lomb microscope

TABLE 1
Seasonal Variations of pH and Temperature in the Pocono Lakes

Month		Bruce Lake 1984 Water	Bruce Lake 1984 Sediment	Bruce Lake 1985 Water	Bruce Lake 1985 Sediment	White Deer Lake 1984 Water	White Deer Lake 1984 Sediment	White Deer Lake 1985** Water	White Deer Lake 1985** Sediment
May	pH	—	—	5.68	5.81	4.40	4.70	7.47	6.15
	Temp*	—	—	16.7	16.1	13.8	13.7	18.6	15.6
June	pH	6.30	5.60	6.18	6.05	4.60	4.80	7.17	6.33
	Temp*	27.6	26.2	18.7	17.1	16.0	16.0	19.3	17.7
July	pH	6.40	6.20	6.21	6.04	6.60	6.60	7.45	6.00
	Temp*	26.1	26.0	22.8	19.2	23.9	23.9	23.6	20.2
August	pH	6.40	6.40	5.87	5.85	6.40	6.40	6.64	6.55
	Temp*	24.7	24.4	25.8	25.5	26.6	23.9	24.8	24.5
September	pH	6.60	6.60	6.00	5.72	6.40	6.30	6.88	6.83
	Temp*	18.5	18.5	17.0	17.0	16.4	16.7	19.3	19.2
October	pH	5.90	5.80	6.20	6.10	6.30	6.10	7.04	6.84
	Temp*	15.7	15.2	14.2	14.3	14.4	14.5	14.4	15.2
November	pH	6.30	6.10	6.30	6.05	6.40	6.00	6.96	6.87
	Temp*	9.5	9.5	6.7	7.4	9.6	9.2	7.0	7.9

*Temperature in degrees centigrade
**Limestone applied February, 1985
—Not measured

equipped with an incident-fluorescence system was used for the counts. Live and dead bacteria and diatoms were counted in 25 microscopic fields under an oil immersion objective. The areas of the filter and of each objective field were measured to obtain the number of bacteria and diatoms per milliliter of water or sediment slurry. Since subsurface and middle layer water counts were very similar, they were averaged and presented in one category. The data were analyzed using analysis of variance (ANOVA). When significant differences ($P < 0.05$) were found with ANOVA tests, the Tukey's test was used to determine which bacterial and diatom densities resulted in significant differences in numbers.[28] Linear regression analysis was performed to test the relationship between population densities and pH ranges.

RESULTS

Temperature and pH parameters:

The temperature and pH data obtained on water and sediment samples from the lakes are summarized in Table 1. Temperatures did not vary greatly between 1984 and 1985 study periods. For both years, temperature readings of Bruce Lake ranged from 6.7°C to 27°C, while the values for White Deer Lake varied from 7°C to 26°C. On the average, sediment temperatures were 1.0 to 1.5 degrees less than the water samples. Temperature readings for both lakes followed a seasonal pattern, appearing relatively low in May, peaking during the summer months and then dropping sharply in November.

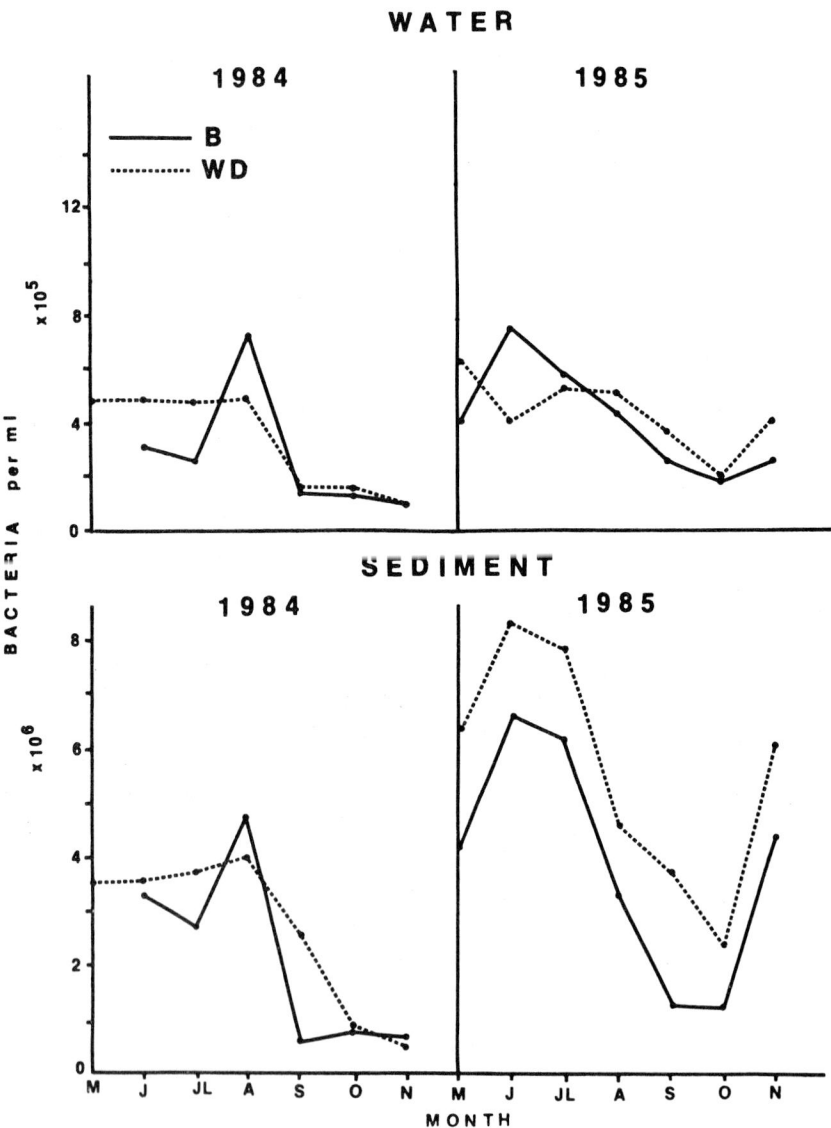

FIGURE 1. Epifluorescence Counts of Bacterial Densities.

The pH regimes of the two lakes in 1984 (before limestone addition) were somewhat similar, although White Deer Lake was slightly more acidic than Bruce Lake. The pH readings obtained from White Deer Lake after limestone treatment, however, were higher throughout the 1985 study period (Table 1). The pH values obtained for Bruce Lake were analogous for both years of study. For White Deer, the pH values for 1984 (May to November) ranged from 4.40 to

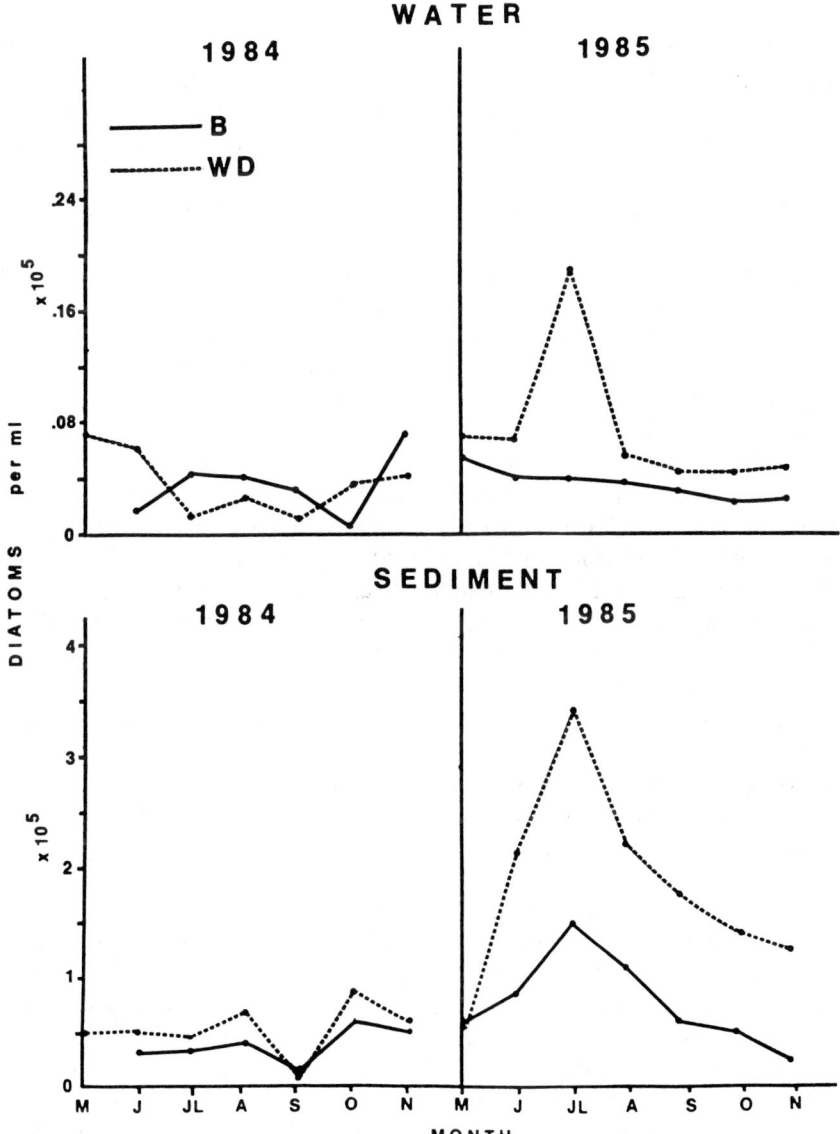

FIGURE 2. Epifluorescence Counts of Diatom Densities.

6.60, while the 1985 pH for the same period ranged from 6.00 to 7.47. It may be noted that the pH readings of the sediment in White Deer Lake were slightly lower (6.00-6.87) than those of the water sample values (6.64-7.47).

Epifluorescence Microscopy—*Total bacterial density*

Bacterial densities in water and surface sediment samples of the two lakes before and after limestone addition were determined by acridine orange direct counts using epifluorescence microscopy and are presented in Figure 1. The distribution of bacterial populations in the two lakes exhibited seasonal fluctuations. Bacterial counts obtained from Bruce Lake during 1984 and 1985 varied somewhat but the difference was not significant in analysis of variance test (ANOVA). Comparisons of bacterial populations obtained in 1985 from water samples of the two lakes revealed the presence of more bacteria in the White Deer Lake water except for the month of June. Although the increase in White Deer Lake in some instances was as much as two times higher than in Bruce Lake, the difference was not significant in the ANOVA statistics. Bacterial densities in the White Deer Lake sediment after neutralizaton were consistently higher than those found in Bruce Lake and in White Deer Lake prior to neutralization (Fig. 1).

Analysis of variance and Tukey's test[28] revealed that while the two lakes were similar before limestone neutralization, sediment values for White Deer Lake after neutralization were significantly higher ($P < 0.01$) than those of acid-stressed Bruce Lake. One notable observation revealed by epifluorescence microscopy was that the increase in bacterial density after limestone addition was due primarily to live bacteria which existed in the range of 1.35×10^6 to 6.73×10^6 per ml compared to the range of 6.7×10^5 to 5.3×10^6 per ml in the sediment of Bruce Lake.

It appears from the above that bacterial populations are adversely affected by low pH stress and favored by neutral pH environment. Linear regression analysis of total bacterial densities in water and sediment samples and corresponding pH values showed significant correlation ($P < 0.05$) between pH and bacterial density.

Epifluorescence Microscopy—*Total diatom density*

Diatom counts from water and surface sediment samples of both lakes recorded during May-November, 1984 and in 1985 are given in Figure 2. An examination of the data reveals a sharp increase in diatom density in White Deer Lake after limestone treatment, particularly in the sediment samples.

The 1984 water data from both lakes demonstrated fluctuations between 7.9×10^2 and 6.7×10^3 diatoms per ml. This range remained more or less similar for Bruce Lake in 1985, but rose substantially for White Deer to a summit of 1.8×10^4 while consistently maintaining a margin of 2×10^3 diatoms per ml over 1985 Bruce Lake values. The sediment readings showed an even more noticeable increase in diatom density in the treated lake. The 1984 sediment values for both lakes were found in the area of 1.5×10^4 to 8.7×10^4 diatoms per ml of sediment slurry, and this range increased to 1.5×10^5 for Bruce Lake in July, 1985. However, readings obtained from sediment samples of White Deer Lake in 1985 after liming were consistently found to be about twice those of Bruce Lake, peaking as high as 3.4×10^5 in July.

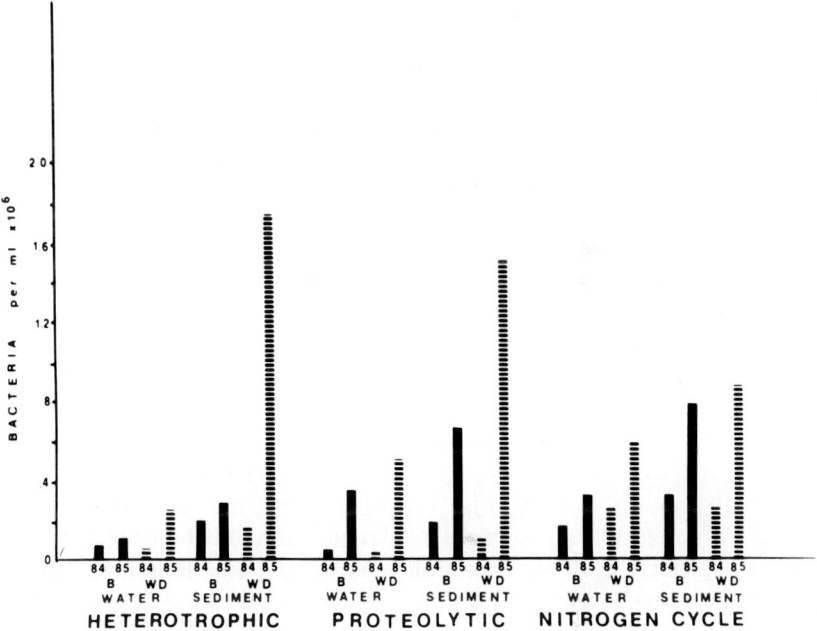

FIGURE 3. Seasonal Totals of Bacterial Densities in Spot Plate Method.

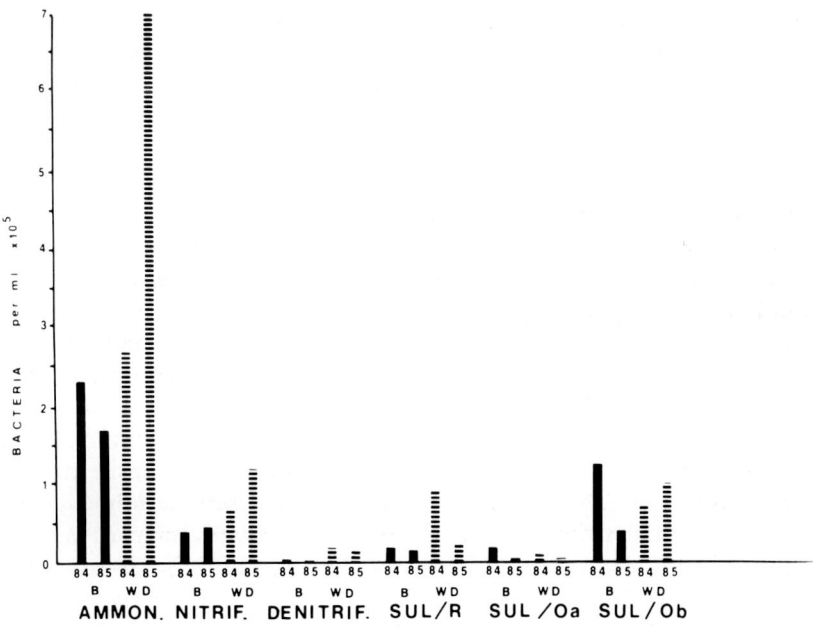

FIGURE 4. Seasonal Totals of Bacterial Densities in Most Probable Number Method.

In general, the densities of diatom populations in 1985 increased from May to July and then decreased from August to November. The consistent increase of diatom densities after liming of White Deer Lake observed in this study gives an indication that certain diatom populations prefer a less acidic environment, and diatom communities in general are affected by increased acidity. Previous studies[29,30] found that certain diatoms were sensitive to pH changes.

Spot Plating Method (SP)—*Live bacterial density*

The SP method was used to detect the presence of live aerobic heterotrophic, proteolytic, ammonifying, nitrifying and denitrifying bacteria in water and sediment samples. Seasonal totals of bacterial densities are illustrated in Figure 3. Ammonifying, nitrifying and denitrifying data are combined under the nitrogen cycle category.

Total heterotrophic and proteolytic counts of water and surface sediment bacteria in 1984 did not vary widely. In general, bacterial types increased proportionally from May to August and then decreased from September to November, corresponding to peaks in temperature and pH as noted in Table 1. Bacterial counts for Bruce Lake in 1985 were somewhat consistent with the 1984 data. White Deer readings after liming on the other hand, showed significant increases in two types of bacteria. The ranges of heterotrophic and proteolytic bacteria in White Deer Lake after liming (1985) varied from 1.0×10^3 to 9.0×10^5 and 5.0×10^2 to 1.0×10^6, per ml of sample, respectively. In contrast, heterotrophic bacteria in Bruce Lake varied from 1.3×10^3 to 1.3×10^5 per ml and proteolytic bacteria did not exceed 3.0×10^5 per ml. This difference is clearly visible in the bar graph of Figure 3.

Nitrogen cycle bacteria increased marginally in White Deer Lake; however, no apparent trend could be established.

Most Probable Number (MPN)—*Live Nitrogen cycle and Sulfur cycle bacteria in surface sediment.*

The results are depicted in Figure 4. Nitrogen cycle bacterial densities recovered in MPN method from Bruce Lake were found to be more or less similar during the survey periods in 1984 and 1985. Yearly ammonifying bacterial counts for Bruce Lake decreased slightly from 2.4×10^5 per ml of sediment slurry in 1984 to 1.7×10^5 per ml in 1985, while readings from White Deer escalated from 2.7×10^5 per ml in 1984 to 7.0×10^5 in 1985 after liming ($P < 0.05$). Nitrifying bacterial density in Bruce Lake remained almost unchanged over the two year period, while White Deer counts after neutralization elevated from 7.1×10^4 to 1.2×10^5 per ml of slurry. On the other hand, yearly denitrifying bacterial counts showed slight decreases (4.4×10^3 to 3.6×10^3) for Bruce Lake and for White Deer Lake as well (2.1×10^4 to 1.7×10^4).

Three kinds of sulfur bacteria were enumerated in the MPN method: sulfur reducing (S/R), sulfur oxidizing acidophilus (S/Oa) and sulfur oxidizing alkaliphilus (S/Ob). Sulfur oxidizing acidophilus bacteria grow best at pH 5.0 and alkaliphilus grow at pH around 7.5. Results obtained for S/R and S/Oa from the two lakes revealed no definite trend. However, values for sulfur oxidizing bacteria that favor neutral to slightly alkaline environment increased from 7.3×10^4 to 9.8×10^4 per ml of slurry in White Deer after liming. The values for Bruce Lake however, did not increase in 1985.

DISCUSSION AND CONCLUSIONS

Acid precipitation has been shown to be a serious environmental stressor, causing detrimental effects on individual species of freshwater organisms at all trophic levels.[1,5] Acidic deposition into the lakes reduces the pH ranges of water and sediment, thereby producing inhibitory effects on the indigenous organisms such as phytoplankton, zooplankton, and on several species of fish.[10,11,31,32] A number of investigators[5,6,21] suggested that monitoring of aquatic microorganisms is a more sensitive indicator in determining early changes produced by acid precipitation. This is due to microorganisms' short life cycles which allow them to respond quickly to changes in the ecosystem.

In a previous study, two acid-stressed lakes (Bruce and White Deer) in the Pocono Mountains of northeastern Pennsylvania were surveyed to assess the impact of acid precipitation on bacterial populations.[13,14] Bacterial densities recovered from these two acid-stressed lakes compared to other non-acid stressed lakes were very low. However, these values were comparable to those reported for other lakes receiving acid precipitation.[12,33]

Both the depression in bacterial density and the reduction of microbial activity are the results of stresses on biochemical processes. Several studies demonstrated the accumulation of organic matter in the sediment of acid stressed lakes.[17,34,35,36] Acidification in general inhibits bacterial activity, especially of certain bacteria which are efficient decomposers.[1] This, presumably, brings about a change in the population structures from predominantly fast acting bacteria to slow acting fungi resulting in the buildup of organic material.[18]

The addition of lime and other neutralizing agents has been used to counteract the acidification of lakes in Europe and North America. The present study examined water and sediment samples from the acid-stressed Bruce Lake and the limestone neutralized White Deer Lake to determine the influence of acidification and neutralization on bacterial and diatom populations. After treatment, the pH of White Deer Lake water and sediment samples rose considerably and maintained neutrality throughout the study. This rise in pH coincided with increases in bacterial and diatom densities in the lake. Epifluorescence microscopy enumeration revealed that this increase was found mainly in sediment samples. Heterotrophic and proteolytic bacteria counts obtained from the Spot Plate enumeration method indicated a large elevation in the densities of these bacteria after neutralization. The Most Probable Number study showed only a slight increase in ammonifying and sulfur oxidizing alkaliphilus bacteria.

Liming in acid lakes has shown increased bacterial densities, microbial activity, and an acceleration of organic decomposition.[37,38,39] Scheider et al.[38] noticed this increase to be most pronounced in heterotrophic bacteria. Diatom densities have also been found to rise as a result of liming.[39] In contrast, acidification of freshwater ecosystems is known to decrease decomposition rates and exert inhibitory effects on aquatic macro and microorganisms.[40]

In general, acidity has been shown to have adverse effects on freshwater ecosystems. Results of this study clearly indicate that the treatment of acid-stressed White Deer Lake with limestone successfully raised the pH range which in turn increased the densities of certain bacterial and diatom populations. From these results it follows that acidity in the untreated lakes acted as an environmental stressor to the existence of various bacterial and diatom communities. It is apparent from the literature review presented and this investigation that limestone neutralization of lakes produces a favorable environment for normal growth and reestablishment of several bacterial and diatom communities presumably threatened by the acid stressed environment. The effects of lake neutralization on microbial populations are poorly understood. However, only limited studies have been carried out to determine the effects of liming on aquatic microbial numbers, population structures, and activities. This study is being continued with an emphasis on the analysis of sediment chemistry. It is our hope that this would provide greater insight into microbial processes important in biochemical cycles in lake sediment affected by acid precipitation and limestone neutralization.

LITERATURE CITED

1. Likens, G.E., R.F. Wright, J.N. Galloway and T.J. Butler. 1979. Acid Rain. Sci. Amer. 241:43-51.
2. DePena, R.G. 1983. Coal and Air Pollution, pp. 371-387. In S.K. Majumdar and E.W. Miller (Eds.), *Pennsylvania Coal: Resources, Technology and Utilization.* The Pennsylvania Academy of Science Publication, pp. 594.
3. Halma, J.R., D. Rieker and S.K. Majumdar. 1986. Air Pollution Stressors and Forest Decline—A Review. In S.K. Majumdar, F.J. Brenner and A.F. Rhoads (Eds.), *Endangered and Threatened Species Programs in Pennsylvania and Other States: Causes, Issues and Management.* The Pennsylvania Academy of Science, In Press.
4. Abelson, P.H. 1985. Air Pollution and Acid Rain. Science. 230:617.
5. Odum, E.P. 1985. Trends Expected in Stressed Ecosystems. Bioscience. 35:419-422.
6. Schindler, D.W., K.H. Mills, D.F. Malley, D.L. Findlay, J.A. Shearer, I.J. Davies, M.A. Turner, G.A. Linsey, and D.R. Cruikshank. 1985. Long-Term

Ecosystem Stress: The Effects of Years of Experimental Acidification on a Small Lake. Science. 228:1396-1401.
7. Van Voris, P., R.V. O'Neill, W.R. Emanual and H.H. Shugart, Jr. 1980. Ecology 61:1352.
8. Bengtsson, B., W. Dickson and P. Nyberg. 1980. Liming Acid Lakes in Sweden. Ambio 9:34-36.
9. Bradt, P.T. and M.B. Berg. 1983. Preliminary Survey of Pocono Mountain Lakes to Determine Sensitivity to Acid Deposition. Proc. Pa. Acad. Science. 57:190-194.
10. Bradt, P.T. and J.L. Dudley. 1984. The Ecological Effects of Acid Deposition in Eastern North America, pp. 221-236. In S.K. Majumdar and E.W. Miller (Eds.) *Solid and Liquid Wastes: Management and Socioeconomic Considerations*. The Pennsylvania Academy of Science Publication, pp. 412.
11. Luoma, J.L. 1980. Troubled Skies, Troubled Waters. Audubon. 82:88.
12. Rao, S.S. and B.J. Dutka. 1983. Influence of Acid Precipitation on Bacterial Populations in Lakes. Hydrobiologia 98: 153-157.
13. Majumdar, S.K., G. F. Rall, A. M. Mrowca, P. M. Steed, J. Tabak and L. C. Mineo. 1984. Bacteriological Survey of two Acid-Stressed Lakes in the Poconos before Limestone Application. Proc. Pa. Acad. Sci. 58:181-186.
14. Majumdar, S.K., A.M. Mrowca, G.F. Rall and L.C. Mineo. 1985. Bacteriological Survey of two Acid-Stressed Lakes in the Pocono Mountains of Northeastern Pennsylvania. Abstract presented at the Annual Meeting of the American Society for Microbiology, pp. 233.
15. Boylen, C.W., M.O. Shick, D.A. Roberts and R. Singer. 1983. Microbiological Survey of Adirondack Lakes in USA with various pH values. Appl. Environ. Microbiol. 45:1538-1544.
16. Hasler, A., O.M. Brynildson and W.T. Helm. 1951. Improving Conditions for Fish in Brown-Water Bog Lakes by Alkalization. J. Wildlife Management, 15:43-51.
17. Gahnstrom, G., G. Anderson, and S. Fleischer. 1980. Decomposition and Exchange Process in Acidified Lake Sediment, pp. 306-307. In D. Drablos and A. Tollan (Eds.),*Ecological Impact of Acid Precipitation*. SNSF Project, Norway.
18. Tollan, A. 1981. Effects of Acid Precipitation on Aquatic and Terrestrial Ecosystems, pp. 438-445. In *Acid Precipitation: Effects on Forest and Fish*. SNSF Project, Norway.
19. Hultberg, H. and I.B. Anderson. 1982. Liming of Acidified Lakes: Induced Long Term Changes. Water and Soil Pollution. 18:311-331.
20. Blake, L.M. 1982. Liming Acid Ponds in New York. In F.M. D'Itri (Ed), Acid Precipitation, Effects on Ecological Systems. Ann Arbor Science, Ann Arbor, MI, pp.251-260.
21. Ivanovici, A.M., and W.J. Wiebe. 1981. Towards a Working Definition of

Stress: A Review and Critique. pp. 13-27. In G.W. Barrett and R. Rosenberg, (Eds.), *Stress Effects on Natural Ecosystems*: John Wiley & Sons, New York.
22. Young, M. 1979. A Modified Spread Plate Technique for the Determinations of Concentrations of Viable Heterotrophic Bacteria, pp. 41-51. In C.D. Litchfield and P.L. Seyfried (Eds), *Methodology for Biomass Determinations and Microbial Activities in Sediments*. ASTM Special Technical Publication, pp. 673.
23. Rodina, A.G. 1972. *Methods in Aquatic Microbiology*. University Park Press, Baltimore, pp. 504.
24. Starkey, R.L. 1948. Characteristics and Cultivation of Sulfate Reducing Bacteria. J. Amer. Water Works Assoc. 40:1291-1298.
25. Postgate, A. 1966. Media for Sulfur Bacteria. Lab. Pract. 15:1239-1244.
26. Hobbie, J.E., R.J. Daley and S. Jasper. 1977. Use of Nucleopore Filters for Counting Bacteria by Fluorescence Microscopy. Appl. Environ. Microbiol. 33:1225-1228.
27. Zimmerman, R. and L.A. Meyer-Reil. 1974. A New Method for Fluorescence Staining of Bacterial Populations on Membrane Filters. Ausdem Institut for Meereskunde an der Universitat Kiel. 30:24-27.
28. Snedecor, G.W. 1956. *Statistical Methods*. The Iowa State University Press, Ames, Iowa, pp. 534.
29. Van Dam, H., G. Surrmond, and C.T. Braak. 1980. Impact of Acid Precipitation on Diatoms and Chemistry of Dutch Moorland Pools, pp. 298-299. In D. Drablos and A. Tollan (Eds.), *Ecological Impact of Acid Precipitation*. SNSF Project, Norway.
30. Davis, R.B. and F. Berge. 1980. Atmospheric Deposition in Norway During the Last 300 Years as Recorded in SNSF Lake Sediments II. Diatom Stratigraphy and Inferred pH, pp. 270-271. In D. Drablos and A. Tollan (Eds.), *Ecological Impact of Acid Precipitation*. SNSF Project, Norway.
31. Rheinheimer, G. 1971. *Aquatic Microbiology*, John Wiley and Sons, New York, pp. 184.
32. McKinley, V.L., and J.R. Vestal. 1982. The Effects on Litter Decomposition in an Arctic Lake. Abst. Ann. Am. Soc. Microbiol. N-70.
33. Scheider, W. and P.J. Dillon. 1976. Neutralization and Fertilization of Acidified Lakes Near Sudbury, Ontario, Water Pollut. Res. Can. 11: 93-100.
34. Traaen, T.S. 1980. Effects of Acidity on Decomposition of Organic Matter in Aquatic Environments. pp. 340-341 in,*Ecological Impact of Acid Precipitation,* D. Drablos and a. Tollen, Eds. (Oslo-As, 1980).
35. Laake, M. 1976. Effects of Low pH on Some Biological Processes in Natural and Artificial Lake Sediments.
36. Grahn, O.J., H. Hultberg and L. Landner, 1974. Oligotrophication—A Self Accelerating Process in Lakes Subjected to Excessive Supply of Acid Substances, Ambio, 3:93-94.

37. *Acidification Today and Tomorrow.* 1982. Swedish Ministry of Agriculture Environment 1982 Committee, pp. 200-227.
38. Scheider, W., J. Adamski and M. Payler. 1975. Reclamation of Acidified Lakes Near Sudbury, Ontario. Ontario Ministry of the Environment, Ontario.
39. Overrein L.N., H.M. Seip and A. Tollan. 1980. *Acid Precipitation-Effects on Forests and Fish,* SNSF Project, Norway.
40. Cowling, E.B. 1980. Acid Precipitation and its Effects on Terrestrial and Aquatic Ecosystems. Ann. New York Acad. Sci, 338:540-555.

Endangered and Threatened Species Programs in Pennsylvania and other States: Causes, Issues and Management. Edited by S. K. Majumdar, F. J. Brenner and A. F. Rhoads. © 1986, The Pennsylvania Academy of Science.

Chapter Thirty-Seven

Acid Precipitation: A Review of the Potential and Observed Effects on Vegetation, with Particular Reference to Forest Communities

David R. Vann[1] and Arthur H. Johnson[2]

[1]Research Associate and [2]Professor of Geology
Department of Geology
University of Pennsylvania
Philadelphia, PA 19104

Acid precipitation, although recognized over a century ago as a potential problem by Angus Smith, has only been seriously addressed in the past decade and a half.[1] Although pollution is generally regarded as a public health problem, acid precipitation has become a political issue of international concern.[2] This concern has led to a number of studies, and several books and reviews have been published discussing the known and hypothetical problems associated with this phenomenon.[3,4,5,6]

Most of the literature concerning airborn pollution has dealt with gaseous pollutants, principally SO_2, NO_x and ozone. Historically, precipitation has been considered as a "scavenging" process,[7] reducing the quantity of airborn chemicals. The precise nature of this process has been extensively studied and reviewed.[8,9] One of the important observations from this research is that the scavenging process becomes less efficient as the pH of the atmospheric water decreases,[10] particularly for SO_2. As air pollutants accumulate in atmospheric water, pH decreases. Whereas gaseous pollutants tend to decrease with increasing distance from the source, pollutants dissolved in atmospheric moisture can be dispersed to great distances.[10]

This review will be principally concerned with effects related to acid deposition, as opposed to injuries due to gaseous pollutants, however, it should be noted that many regions experiencing high levels of acid deposition are also subject to the presence of photochemical oxidants. In some instances, the effects of each category may not be clearly separable, so data from gaseous exposure experiments will be presented where relevant. The principal concerns about acidic deposition relate to the effects of the hydrogen ion concentration and the accompanying anions.

This paper addresses the effects of acidic precipitation on woody plants in forest communities. Much of the available data is on herbaceous plants. This is particularly true for biochemical and physiological data, mainly due to the ease of experimental manipulation. We have focussed on woody species where information is available, citing supplementary data from studies with herbaceous plants where relevant. Broader aspects of herbaceous plant production, such as yield data, are not included as these have been reviewed elsewhere.[4,11] Some discussion of alterations in forest biomass production and community structure is provided. These effects are difficult to quantify, and most of published material is of a theoretical nature. Although these and other hypothetical effects are discussed, it is the intent of this review to focus on documented injuries and physiological disturbances.

The modes of action of any given stress may be summarized as follows: effects may be direct, acting on the anatomy or physiology of the plant; they may be indirect, operating via an alteration of the plant's environment; or they may be consequential, occurring as a result of disturbances arising from the processes described above, and causing a reduction in overall fitness or competitive ability. Mechanical breakage and toxic disruption of metabolism are examples of direct effects. These injuries could lead to consequential effects such as increased pathogen damage or reduced tolerance to other stresses. Alteration of the environment may act in a similar manner, particularly as a result of changes in nutritional status.

INDIRECT EFFECTS

Soil Chemistry

Most of the indirect effects which have been identified and studied relate to alterations in soil chemistry. A number of effects of acid rain on soils have been postulated; they have been reviewed by a number of authors.[12,13,14] Acidification of the soil may result in displacement of base cations, reducing cation-exchange capacity and lowering the nutritional status of the forest floor;[15] or it may cause release of toxic metals, especially aluminum.[16] The severity of these effects is dependent on the soil composition, and may, in fact, be of little concern in many soils, particularly the naturally acid spodosols of the coniferous forests[14] and well-buffered mineral soils, such as mollisols and alfisols.[17] As soil pH decreases, sulfate mobility also declines, reducing its ability to leach cations. Soils having sufficient reserves of iron and aluminum oxides have a large capacity to bind sulfates, also reducing their leaching ability.[18] In fact, McFee, et al,[4] using the data of Likens, et al[18] calculated half-lives of upwards of a century for the displacement of base cations as a result of acid input in most soils.

Another hypothesis involves aluminum toxicity, which results in membrane damages associated with Ca^{2+} uptake.[9] Damage may occur before visible symptoms are apparent on shoots of red spruce (*Picea rubens*);[20] however, the concentrations of aluminum reported to be detrimental to seedlings were higher than those found at most forest sites.[21,22,23] In contrast, Rorison[118] found that concentrations of 20 ppm (at the low end of site values) reduced phosphorus incorporation into nucleotides by as much as one-third. Similarly, Hutchison[24] found significant effects at 20-40 ppm; however, he also examined natural soils presumably unexposed to pollution and found values within this range. He concluded that aluminum may form organic complexes of low mobility. In addition, mineral soils are buffered with complex aluminum hydroxides,[25] thus it is not clear to what extent acid precipitation may actually mobilize this metal, particularly in naturally acidic soils.

In summary, the effects of acid deposition on edaphic factors may not be as important as once assumed; in fact, forest inputs of xenogenic materials may equal outputs (e.g.[26]), with effects more important in aquatic systems.[27,28] A recent paper by Cronan, et al,[21] provides an extensive study of the effects of localized differences in vegetative and edaphic factors on watershed throughput, as well as summarizing the major concerns in this regard.

Soil Microflora

Besides such abiotic influences, a potential for disturbances of soil microflora has been identified.[29] The systemic result of such disturbances is little understood. Parameters which have been demonstrably altered include microbial degradation of litter (decreases),[29,30,116] nitrification (decrease),[32] denitrification (increase), and mycorrhizal infection (decreases).[34] Kelly and Strickland[35] measured CO_2 evolution in the field and found no measurable effect; however, when horizons were separated and measured in the laboratory, significant decreases were seen in the activity in the O_2 layer, from which plants receive a large portion of their nutrients. In a longer term experiment, Novick, et al.[36] found that simulated acid precipitation initially reduced mineralization rates of nitrogen, but inhibition decreased with time, depending on soil origin. This implies a recovery mechanism, due either to organismal adaptation or to a change in the microbial community. This group also found that nitrification rates were reduced, independent of soil type, although ammonia levels did not change. The net result of these changes is principally an alteration of nutrient cycling rates, typically resulting in lower residence times of critical ions, potentially reducing fertility. Such decreases could subsequently reduce productivity and stability of ecosystems.[37] Altered nutrition may also affect resistance to additional injury from air pollution. Noland and Kozlowski[38] found that increased potassium nutrition increased stomatal opening, aggravating ozone injury. On the other hand, Baba and Sakai[39] reported that deficiencies of nitrogen, phosphorus or potassium, or excesses of nitrogen resulted in increased injury in rice due to SO_2. They found that injury was correlated with decreases in the electrical conductivity (total dissolved ions) of the tissue.

DIRECT EFFECTS

With reference to direct effects upon plants, two main types of injury are generally identified; either mechanical damage of the cuticle or physiological disturbances within the cell. Both types of injuries have the potential to result in a variety of effects. The following sections will concentrate on presenting the observed direct effects in greater detail, as well as discussing indirect consequences related to biotic factors.

Uptake

Deposition, whether occurring through wet or dry processes, impacts the above-ground portions of the plant, i.e. the leaf or stem. Due to the relative area and surface characteristics, the stem is probably not the principal point of entry. Within the leaf, two tissues may be identified as sites for uptake—the cuticle and the stomata.

Although the stomata are considered the principal point of absorption for gaseous pollutants,[40,41] uptake of liquids is considered to be insignificant, as a result of the small aperture and steep angle of entry required.[42] However, as guard cells are epidermal, it has been argued that acid precipitation may affect their functioning, thereby altering the gas exchange characteristics of the plant.[43] This might occur either as a result of mechanical damage to the cells, related to membrane damage or cuticle loss, leading to dehydration, or it may have a physiological basis, related to ionic effects on the potassium pump which serves to maintain cell turgor. Evans, et al[28] did find a reduced diffusion resistance in *Phaseolus* leaves exposed to simulated acid rain at pH 3.4 or less. This is similar to the effects of SO_2 on stomatal resistance.[40,45,46] Other ions (nitrite, ammonia) generally result in increases in resistance,[47] as does ozone.[25] As these various compounds occur as admixtures in polluted atmospheres, it is not clear how they will affect stomatal control in the field. Several references include discussions of effects of mixtures.[49,50,125]

The net effect of pollutants on stomatal operation is important to a variety of physiological processes. An increase in aperture could result in lowering of the water potential, causing stress effects related to dehydration. Increasing resistance could reduce photosynthesis, and therefore, productivity. Evans[4] also comments that reducing resistance could increase CO_2 uptake; however, it should be noted that uptake tends to be limited by mesophyll resistance to diffusion.[51] Therefore, unless both stomatal and mesophyll resistances are affected, no net change in CO_2 flux would occur. It is difficult to demonstrate deleterious effects on stomatal relations, as a large number of environmental factors influence operation. In fact, the plant may be able to compensate within the range of most acid precipitation. Probably the greatest concern expressed deals with possible alterations of stomatal functioning during the winter, as this may result in excessive dehydration of the plant, causing winter injuries.[52]

Aside from these consequential effects, then, stomatal uptake of acidic precipitation is most likely unimportant; rather, the cuticle constitutes the principal site of entry for deposited substances.[4] Cuticular uptake is dependent on a variety of processes related to wettability, from angle of impact to composition of epicuticular waxes.[53] In addition, rate of uptake may be influenced by solution acidity;[54] the presence of pores;[55] and epidermal structures such as trichomes.[56] Thus, penetration occurs differentially among regions of the leaf, with the fastest rates near guard and subsidiary cells, cuticular appendages and vascular structures.[4]

Furthermore, uptake may be influenced by alterations in the cuticle itself. Changes in both the biochemistry and structure of epicuticular waxes in the presence of acid fog and mist have been postulated.[57,58] Erosion of epicuticular waxes has been attributed to acid precipitation, although evidence is contradictory,[4] with species demonstrating a range of tolerance.[59,60] Fowler, et al,[61] studying damage to conifers subjected to combinations of wet and dry deposition, observed cuticular degradation apparently more related to alterations in form than to loss of material. This is similar to observations reported by Percy and Riding.[62] Rehfeuss[63] reported no significant injuries beyond a possible premature loss of stomatal plugs in spruce studied in high-altitude forests in Germany. Another recent paper[64] described erosion, principally around stomata, in concurrence with the observations of Finnish workers, who have more clearly shown erosion as a result of gaseous SO_2.[65] This may indicate a role for dry deposition of SO_2. Some of the discrepancies in the reported observations can no doubt be attributed to the variations in cuticle morphology. The most recent work, a synthesis of contact angle, surface morphology, etc. indicates that the greatest concern may not be erosion so much as wettability and retention characteristics.[66]

The chemical nature of cuticular waxes is such as to make them resistant to degradation by any but the strongest acids; however, the underlying cells may be affected.[45,67] This would likely alter the plant's ability to repair damage or result in stress-induced changes in the biochemical composition of the waxes. Such alterations may cause a variety of consequential effects, including increased water loss. Also likely to be affected is accessibility of the leaf to surface pathogens.[65,68]

The aspect of the leaf-environment relationship that has been most clearly demonstrated as being affected by acid precipitation is its ion-exchange characteristics. Alterations in rain fall through chemistry as a result of foliar contact are well documented.[69] Acidic precipitation alters the rate of leaching by increasing the exchange of hydrogen ions for base cations.[70,71] The rate of such exchanges increases with a decrease in pH for most cations.[72,73] Evans, et al,[28] however, found the potassium leaching to be higher at pH 5.7 than at lower values. Several of these groups have also found that anion leaching (in particular, sulfate and nitrate) increased with acidity.[28,73] Lovett, et al[70] attributed 40-60 percent of the base cation leaching to hydrogen ion exchange on the basis of electrical equivalence, with the remainder of the balance coming from plant-derived anions, most likely organic acids derived from metabolic cycles (e.g. malate) or from cuticular oxidation.

The other side of the question deals with the input of materials into the foliage. In addition to H, S, and N, a variety of other materials may be present in precipitation, including heavy metal ions.[74,75] Such inputs may lead to toxic effects on enzymes; in particular, polyvalent cations are known to interfere with membrane regulatory aspects, as demonstrated for lead by Lane et al.[76] However, foliar uptake of heavy metals has not been extensively studied.[77,78] The remainder of this discussion will be confined to effects of the dominant ions, H^+, NO_x^-, NH_4^+, and SO_x^{2-}.

One result of foliar uptake could be enhanced nutritional status, particularly on deficient soils. Relatively few experiments have been conducted to assess this possibility. Evans, et al[28] did find uptake of sulfate, although it was at a rate three orders of magnitude slower than that of water. Whether or not there is sufficient N or S to enhance nutrition is not clear; Evans, et al[79] found no response in soybeans treated with amounts ten times higher than normally measured in rainfall. Conversely, Jacobson,[80] found changes in the reproductive: vegetative allocation ratio, concluding that an increase in nutrition had occurred. In light of the leaching rates discussed above, the greater concern is more likely a lowering of nutritional status.

Loss of materials from the foliage must be compensated for, or the plant will become nutrient-deficient. Plants may respond by increasing the uptake of these nutrients; the process of uptake and translocation is, however, energy-dependent. In addition, the nutrients must be available for uptake, a condition related to soil characters and the mobility of anions associated with precipitation. Replacement of nutrients is also dependent on the health of the roots, which may in turn be affected by acid precipitation. Of course, rainfall seldom comes in direct contact with roots, but alterations in soil solution chemistry may effect changes in root status. In particular, as the principal uptake process for cations involves exchanging hydrogen ions, root uptake and growth may be hampered in acidic solutions.[81] Events altering the energy status of the plant will also change the physiological status of the roots, in turn affecting uptake. Also, acid precipitation may increase the ion concentration in the soil solution, thereby increasing its osmotic potential; this may affect the plant-water status.

Metals in the solution may also have toxic effects; this has been postulated as an effect of the atmospheric deposition of heavy metals. A summary of recent research indicates that mobility is sufficiently low for these metals that this is not likely to be a major concern.[82] As discussed above, aluminum has been postulated to become more mobile in acidified soils, causing toxic effects. Again, data does not support this conclusion. Many soils are buffered by aluminum-Al hydroxide complexes,[25] and plants native to these and to acidic soils are likely to have high natural tolerances to aluminum.[83] Hutchison[24] examined soil not known to be near pollution sources and found values as high as 40 ppm in the organic layer; however, these were considered to be tightly bound and similar conclusions were obtained by other investigators.[84,85]

In summary, the most important point of contact is the foliage; leaching of base cations from foliage probably exceeds input, leading to potential nutritional deficiencies. Cuticular degradation has not been clearly demonstrated, although it is likely that underlying cells may be injured, thus altering repair mechanisms. Root uptake may or may not be affected, depending on soil type and nutritional status of the plant.

Biochemical and Physiological

To date, little data has been accumulated on the potential alterations in secondary metabolic processes; some studies are available, however, on influences upon the primary pathways of photosynthesis and respiration. As noted above, references cited which deal with biochemical effects are largely derived from studies of gaseous pollutants; they are considered applicable since the principal agents of toxicity are the sulfite, nitrite and ammonium ions. In fact, some researchers have concluded that toxicity associated with low levels of sulfur dioxide and pH effects are indistinguishable.[86] Some injuries may also be related to gaseous SO_2 arising from changes in solution equilibrium.[87]

In studies which evaluate photosynthesis and respiration via CO_2 exchange, no clear detrimental effects have been demonstrated as a result of acid precipitation. Ferenbaugh[88] found increased rates of both processes accompanied by reduced growth rates. This was considered evidence for the uncoupling of photophosphorylation. Similar increases were reported in Irving and Miller.[89] Reich, et al[90] found no effect on red oak (*Quercus rubra*) or sugar maple (*Acer saccharum*) photosynthesis during the course of a single growing season. Emmons, et al[91] found decreases in photosynthesis and increases in respiration for *Liriodendron* exposed to acidic mist at pH 3. Although Sigal and Johnston[92] found no effect on photosynthesis in three lichen species upon initial exposure, rates declined during the course of a week, accompanied by necrosis and bleaching of the thallus at pH 4 and below. They observed more rapid and intense declines in a species of *Lobaria*.[31] These variations may be related to the phycobiont; the latter species contains a blue-green alga, which lacks chloroplasts. The differences in response within lichen types and between lichens and higher plants implies that sensitivity to acidity may be reduced in plants having increasingly complex structural organization. This protection would occur as a result of additional membranes, the cuticle, surface characters, etc., as well as more advanced physiological detoxification mechanisms.

Relatively few experiments relating acid precipitation to the biochemistry of photosynthesis have been performed. Somewhat more is known from SO_2 fumigation. Malhotra and Khan[41] provide a complete discussion of the biochemical action of the various ions. The reported effects on photosynthetic pigments are inconsistent. No changes in chlorophyll contents were found in either sugar maple[90] or pines (*Pinus spp*).[93] Contrary to this, Malhotra[94] found decreases in chlorophyll content of pine needles when aqueous solutions of SO_2 were applied. In acidic environments, Mg^{2+} may be displaced from the phaeophytin molecule, altering its spectrum. This may be the explanation for the bleaching and lesions described by Evans et al.[79] On the other hand, intracellular concentrations may never achieve levels high enough to cause this displacement. Sugahara, *et al*[48] reported that *in vitro* chlorophyll and chlorophyll-protein complexes were unaffected by concentrations of sulfite as high as 40 mM. However, they did note that the ion inhibited photo-conversion of the 'dark' form of the chlorophyllide complex to the active form. For ribulose bisphosphate carboxylase, the principal CO_2 fixing enzyme, Emmons, *et al*[91] found reductions in activity without changes in chlorophyll or protein content or chlorophyll a:b ratio. Gezelius and Hallgren[96] found that the sulfite ion causes noncompetitive inhibition of this enzyme, but this was not the cause of reductions in photosynthesis, based on measurements of quantum yield (grams carbon fixed per mole of photons intercepted) in pine seedlings.[93] *In vitro* measurements have demonstrated that the sulfite ion does not actually decouple photophosphorylation,[41] as proposed by Ferenbaugh,[88] (discussed above); however, the acidic nature of the ion may reduce intermediates in electron chains, such as NADP or ATP. The net result, in terms of growth processes, would be similar.

Nitrogen in its various forms generally has relatively little effect on either photosynthesis or respiration,[93] as it can be rapidly incorporated into amino acids via photorespiration in the case of ammonia, and reduced for incorporation into amino acids by the nitrate-nitrite reductase complex.[91] Sufficient accumulations of ammonia are toxic to photosynthesis.[97] Takeuchi, *et al*[98] found inhibitions of nitrate reductase activity in the presence of NO_2 in *Cucurbita*, and Sigal and Johnston[31] found a reduction in nitrogen fixation in lichen as a result of acid precipitation. Neither of these observations is particularly surprising, as nitrate is known to inhibit nitrogen fixation, and nitrite similarly inhibits nitrate reductase *in vitro*.[99] As noted for sulfur above, the reductive power of the ion may reduce electron chain intermediates, but it is doubtful that sufficient quantities are present in acid precipitation.

If intracellular levels are low, the sulfite ion is oxidized to sulfate, which is less toxic.[93] Sulfate and sulfite may be subsequently reduced to sulfhydryl, and either incorporated into amino acids and glutathione,[100,101] or be re-emitted as H_2S.[102] The latter process varies with species and may be an indication of adaptive resistance. The accumulation of both sulfate and nitrate can reach levels which are toxic to membranes, requiring the cells to reduce these compounds to less harmful forms. The reduction of sulfur and nitrogen both require carbon skeletons and reductive energy derived from photosynthesis. Depending on the energy status of the plant, the requirements for reductant may induce greater carboxylase activity. If the plant is photosynthesizing at capacity (often the case in agriculture), diversion of photosynthate may result in growth declines. Thus, the variations in response to acid precipitation at levels which do not induce acute effects may be explained, at least in part, by amplification of normal metabolic processes.

A number of other metabolic process may be affected by sulfur and nitrogen ions. Malhotra and Sarkar,[42] studying pine seedlings, reported an increase in amino acids, as well as an apparent conversion of non-reducing to reducing sugars, probably as a result of increasing acidity. They attributed this to an increased proteolytic rate, possibly as a result of damage to membrane proteins. Evidence also implicates the sulfite ion in alterations in lipid chemistry, probably as a result of changes in the elongation and desaturating processes.[103] This may have an effect on a variety of cellular activities dependent on membrane characters. It may also affect cold hardening.[104] No experiments have measured these effects with specific respect to acid precipitation, so no evaluation can be made of the severity of injuries to these systems. A review of what is known about the effects of gaseous pollutants (and to some extent aqueous solutions) is presented by Malhotra and Khan.[93]

In addition to disruption of normal metabolic events, some plants show evidence of induction of known stress responses. Karolewski[105] found increased levels of proline in *Populus* in response to SO_2. Increases in peroxidases (enzymes which scavenge free radicals, thereby protecting membranes) have been reported for various conifers,[106,107] and several crop plants.[108]

Although little literature is available on the subject, alterations may also occur in the secondary metabolic pathways, either as a direct result of exposure, or as a consequence of lowered carbon status of the plant. Such alterations may affect the plant internally or may affect the competitive ability of the plant. Hoque[109] found autotoxic levels of picein and its derivatives in Norway spruce subjected to pollution. Many secondary compounds have allelopathic properties, and changes in production may alter the plant's resistance to predation and pathogenic infection. On the other hand, there is evidence to indicate that acid precipitation reduces soil pathogen infection[110] as well as the incidence of surface pathogens[111] In either event, injured plants definitely show increased numbers of secondary pathogens[112] The various pathogenic interactions and available literature have been discussed and reviewed.[65,112]

Effects on the Whole Plant

Anatomical effects of acid precipitation reported include necrosis and lesions on foliage (*Populus*;[91] *Glycine*[4]). Such responses only occur under very acid conditions, generally below pH 3. These symptoms are most pronounced on expanding leaves and reproductive tissues[4,67] and at leaf veins, trichomes and other cuticular features which retain more precipitation.[66] Complete abcission of leaves without visible effects on leaflets was reported for *Robinia* by Haines, et al.[66] Reich, et al[90] did not describe any visible injuries on either red oak or sugar maple. The only documented injuries in field plants that could be clearly correlated with acid precipitation were those reported by Evans, et al.[13] This is in contrast to the extensive injuries reported at both visible and cellular levels after SO_2 exposure in both the field and laboratory.[64,114,115] These injuries involve cell death; other workers have reported gall formation on the leaves of herbaceous plants.[116,117] Areas so affected did not subsequently retain water. Evans[3] postulates that such hyperplastic responses reduce further injury and represent a stress response accounting for differential sensitivities of species.

The appearance of visible symptoms is generally taken to indicate a potential effect on growth rates, however, Wood and Bormann[118] found that reduction was significant only in very young birch seedlings, in spite of visible damage. In addition, the forest growth model of Botkin and Aber[119] was insensitive to as much as a 5.5 percent loss of foliage. Hindawi and Ratsch[120] reported inhibition of pine needle elongation by acid solutions applied to immature fascicles. Reich, et al,[90] reported no effect on growth of red oak or sugar maple as a result of simulated acid rain as low as pH 3. In field studies in areas known to be exposed to acid deposition and photochemical pollutants, a number of reports of decrease in radial growth of trees exist.[121,122,123,124,125]

This lack of consensus in the data on growth effects is prevalent throughout the literature for both woody and herbaceous[4] plants, and may arise as a result of various indirect effects or variability in field conditions. To date, it does not appear that acid precipitation has significant short-term effects on vegetative growth. More attention should, however, be paid to the photochemical pollutants generally present in regions receiving quantities of acid deposition. Significant growth reductions can occur with chronic doses below 50 ppb O_3,[126] well within the values commonly reported.

Another explanation of the variability in the growth response may be related to differential resistance of species. Umbach and Davis studied the effects of short-term exposure to SO_2 (900 ppb) on 57 tree species and found a positive correlation between resistance to injury and shade tolerance.[12] Similar variability within provenances of pine, correlated with sugar content, were reported by Mejnartowicz and Lukasiak.[95]

If relatively little work has been done on vegetative growth, even less attention has been devoted to phenology, reproductive growth and seed germination. Lee and Weber[127] and Raynal, et al[128] tested emergence of a variety of woody species and found effects on germination were minimal; species native to acidic soils germinated better at low pH than at neutrality. This is in accord with early experiments by Baldwin[129] on red spruce. Other species were unaffected, with the exception of birch, maple and sumac, which were inhibited slightly. It seems unlikely that seed germination will be affected significantly in the field, unless extreme acidity occurs. Studies on reproduction have indicated a potential for alterations in resource allocation.[80] Cox[130,131] has determined that pollen germination is sensitive to acidity and he has discussed the implications for reproduction.

Phenological alterations in flowering, seed set, and so forth may arise as a result of alterations in resource allocation or interference with hormone metabolism; however, these are only hypothetical consequences. For woody plants, an important aspect of seasonal timing is related to overwintering ability. Huttunen,[65] and Havas and Huttunen[52] have presented a case for injuries during the winter as a result of SO_2 exposure. These are principally related to cuticular damages and stomatal regulation, resulting in an increase in water loss.[132] Keller[106] and Michael[133] have also reported a variety of physiological consequences as a result of winter fumigation. Whether or not similar effects may arise as a result of winter acid precipitation is questionable; nevertheless, acid snow may remain in contact with twigs and needles for several months, possibly allowing deterioration to occur. More recently, Friedland, et al[33] have postulated that extensive winter injuries reported for red spruce may arise as a result of pollutant exposure, possibly caused by a delaying of the cessation of growth required for hardening events.[134] Winter damage is particularly severe in conifers, as the needles and twigs, which store carbohydrate reserves, are exposed to injury.

Community and Ecosystem Effects

The various factors discussed above—growth alterations, foliar leaching, increased pathogen/predation susceptibility, etc.—all alter the competitive ability of the plant. Countering this is the fact that individuals have varying resistance to pollution.[95,135] Resistance requires diversion of resources, again potentially altering the status of the plant within the community.

In general, environmental stress at the population level may lead to species extinction. In less severe cases, plants may adapt; however, this is likely to result in genetic drift and a loss of gene polymorphism. Drift does appear to be occuring in response to pollution.[135] At the community level, stress will alter the structure and species distribution, shifting to the more tolerant individuals, which are, in many cases, invasive species. Such a loss of community diversity results in a loss of gene heterogeneity and therefore a loss in ecosystem resilience to further or alternate perturbations.[136] Due to the widespread nature of atmospheric pollution, there are implications for alterations of landscapes. Although acute effects on the physiology of plants have not been clearly demonstrated, more subtle and long-term effects are very likely to occur, due to the various processes mentioned above. Discussions of these concerns are provided by Materna[137] and McLaughlin, et al.[138] Several attempts have been made to estimate the potential long-term impact on ecosystems due to acid deposition and other atmospheric pollutants.[139,140,141] The modelling approaches of the Finnish groups agree that a net decline in productivity as a result of pollutants will occur, probably reaching important levels by the year 2040. Aber's group found the predictions to be dependent on the effect on forest floor nutrient cycles. However, using various constraints in the model, they concluded that 'significant' reductions were not likely to occur unless a 50 percent reduction in soil biological activity occurred. None of these groups have addressed the question of changes in community composition.[139]

In summary, it can be stated that certain processes within the plant are affected by atmospheric input, particularly by the sulfite ion. These processes include certain aspects of photosynthesis and electron transport. Other metabolic consequences have not been fully explored, although damage to membranes is a distinct possibility. Acid precipitation definitely increases foliar leaching of ions, leading to a potential for nutritional deficiencies. The overall effect on plant growth is not clear, due to tolerance mechanisms within plants. The variation in responses between species could result in alterations in species distributions within communities. This may not result in total biomass reductions within ecosystems, unless soil fertility is altered.

LITERATURE CITED

1. Cowling, E.B. 1982. Acid Precipitation in Historical Perspective. *Environ. Sci. Technol.* 16A:110-123.
2. Brady, G.L., and J.C. Selle. 1985. Acid Rain: The International Response. *Int. J. Env. Stud.* 24:217-230.
3. Evans, L.S. 1984. Acidic precipitation effects on terrestrial vegetation. *Ann. Rev. Phytopathol.* 22:397-420.
4. Evans, L.S. 1985. Botanical aspects of acidic precipitation. *Bot. Rev.* 50:449-490.
5. Hutchison, T.C. and M. Havas. 1980. *Effects of Acid Precipitation on Terrestrial Ecosystems.* Plenum Press. New York. xxi + 456p.

6. Treshow, M. ed. 1984. *Air Pollution and Plant Life.* John Wiley & Sons. Chichester. xii + 486p.
7. Junge, C.E. 1963. *Air Chemistry and Radioactivity.* Academic Press. New York. xii + 382p.
8. Hales, J. 1984. Precipitation Scavenging Processes, A6. in: *The Acidic Deposition Phenomenon and its Effects. Vol. I. Atmospheric Sciences.* EPA-600/8-83-016BF. J.S. Nader, L.E. Niemeyer, N.V. Gillani, D.F. Miller, eds. Environmental Protection Agency. Washington, D.C.
9. Robinson, E. 1984. Dispersion and Fate of Atmospheric Pollutants, pp. 15-38. in: ref. 141.
10. Ottar, B., H. Dovland, and A. Semb. 1984. Long Range Transport of Air Pollutants and Acid Precipitation, pp. 39-72. in: ref. 6.
11. Heggestadt, H.E., and J.H. Bennett. 1984. Impact of Atmospheric Pollution on Agriculture, pp. 356-396. in: ref. 141.
12. Bache, B.W. 1980. The Acidification of Soils, pp. 183-202. in: ref. 5.
13. McFee, W.W. 1983. Sensitivity ratings of soils to acid deposition: A review. *Env. Exp. Bot.* 23:203-210.
14. McFee, W.W., F. Adams, C.S. Cronan, M.K. Firestone, C.D. Roy, R.D. Harter, and D.W. Johnson. 1984. Effects on Soil Systems, pp. 2:1-2:71. in: *The Acid Deposition Phenomenon and its Effects. Vol. II. Effects Sciences.* EPA-600/8-83-016BF. A.P. Altshuller and R.A. Linthurst, eds. Environmental Protection Agency. Washington, D.C.
15. Cronan, C.S., W.A. Reiners, R.L. Reynolds, and G.E. Lang. 1978. Forest floor leaching: Contributions from mineral, organic and carbonic acids in New Hampshire subalpine forests. *Science.* 200:309-311.
16. Bache, B.W. 1974. Soluble aluminum and calcium-aluminum exchange in relation to the pH of dilute calcium chloride suspensions of acid soils. *J. Soil Sci.* 25:320-332.
17. Richter, D.D., and D.W. Johnson. 1982. Effects of Acid Rain on Forest Soil Change, pp.379-403. in: *A Specialty Conference on: Atmospheric Deposition,* Nov. 7-10, Detroit, MI. Air Pollution Control Ass'n, ed.
18. Likens, G.E., F.H. Borman, R.S. Pierce, J.S. Eaton, and N.M. Johnson. 1977. *Biogeochemistry of a Forested Ecosystem.* Springer-Verlag. New York. xi + 179p.
19. Edwards, J.H., B.H. Horton, and H.C. Kirkpatrick. 1976. Aluminum toxicity symptoms in peach seedlings. *J. Am. Soc. Hort. Sci.* 101:139-142.
20. Schier, G.A. 1984. Response of red spruce and balsam fir seedlings to aluminum toxicity in nutrient solutions.*Can. J. For. Res.* 15:29-33.
21. Cronan, C.S. 1985. Biogeochemical influence of vegetation and soils in the ILWAS watersheds. *Water Air Soil Pollu.* 26:355-371.
22. Matzner, E. 1983. Balances of Element Fluxes within Different Areas Impacted by Acid Rain, pp. 147-155. in:*Effects of Accumulation of Air Pollutants in Forest Ecosystems.* B. Ulrich and J. Pankrath, eds. D. Reidel

Pub. Co.Dordrecht, F.R.G.
23. Ulrich, B. 1983. Interaction of Forest Canopies with Atmospheric Constituents, pp. 33-45. in: *Effects of Accumulation of Air Pollutants in Forest Ecosystems.* B. Ulrich and J. Pankrath, eds. D. Reidel Publ. Co. Dordrecht, F.R.G.
24. Hutchison, T.C. 1985. Responses of conifer seedlings to aluminum stress in boreal forest soils, p. 163-164. *Proc. Int. Symp. on Acidic Precipitation,* Sept. 15-20, Muskoka, Canada.
25. Brady, N.L. 1974. *The Nature and Properties of Soils.* 8th Ed. MacMillan. New York. xvi + 639p.
26. Ulrich, B. 1984. Effects of air pollution on forest ecosystems and waters: the principles demonstrated at a case study in Central Europe. *Atmos. Environ.* 18:621-628.
27. Magnuson, J.J., and F.J. Rahel. 1984. Effects on Aquatic Biology, pp. 5:1-5:196. in: *The Acid Deposition Phenomenon and Its Effects. Vol. II. Effects Sciences.* A.P. Altshuller and R.A. Linthurst, eds. Environmental Protection Agency. Washington, D.C.
28. Evans, L.S., T.M. Curry, and K.F. Lewin. 1981. Responses of leaves of *Phaseolus vulgaris* to simulated acid rain. *New Phytol.* 88:403-420.
29. Alexander, M. 1980. Effects of Acidity on Microorganism and Microbial Processes in Soil, pp. 363-374. in: ref. 5.
30. Boath, E.B., B. Berg. U. Lohn, B. Lundgren, H. Lundqvist, T. Rosswall, B. Soderstrom, and A. Wiren. 1980. Soil Organisms and Litter Decomposition in a Scots Pine Forest—Effects of Experimental Acidification, pp. 375-380. in: ref. 5.
31. Sigal, L.L., and J.W. Johnston. 1986. Effects of acid rain and ozone on nitrogen fixation and photosynthesis in the lichen *Lobaria pulmonaria* (L.) Hoffm. *Env. Exp. Bot.* 26:59-64.
32. Strayer, R.F., C.J. Liu, and M. Alexander. 1981. The effect of simulated acid rain on nitrification and nitrogen mineralization in forest soils. *J. Environ. Qual.* 10:547-552.
33. Friedland, A.J., R.A. Gregory, L. Karenlampi, and A.H. Johnson. 1984. Winter damage to foliage as a factor in red spruce decline. *Can. J. For. Res.* 14:963-965.
34. Reich, P.B., A.W. Schoettle, H.F. Stroo, J. Troiano, and R.G. Amundson. 1985. Effects of O_3, SO_2, and acidic rain on mycorrhizal infection in northern red oak seedlings. *Can. J. Bot.* 63:2049-2055.
35. Kelly, K.M., and R.C. Strickland. 1984. CO2 Efflux from Deciduous Forest Litter and Soil in Response to Simulated Acid Rain Treatment. *Water Air Soil Pollu.* 23:431-440.
36. Novick, N.J., T.M. Klein, and M. Alexander. 1984. Effect of simulated acid precipitation on nitrogen mineralization and nitrification in forest soils. *Water Air Soil Pollu.* 23:317-330.

37. DeAngelis, D.L. 1980. Energy Flow, Nutrient Cycling, and Ecosystem Resilience. *Ecology.* 61:764-771.
38. Noland, T.L., and T.T. Koslowski. 1979. Influence of potassium nutrition on susceptibility of silver maple to ozone. *Can. J. For. Res.* 9:501-503.
39. Baba, I., and s. Sakai. 1976. Physiological studies on the mechanism of the occurence of air pollution damage in crop plants. *Rep. Inst. Agric. Biol. Sci. Okayana Univ.* 55:189-198.
40. Freer-Smith, P.H. 1985. The Influence of SO2 and NO2 on the Growth, Development and Gas Exchange of *Betula pendula* Roth. *New Phytol.* 99:417-430.
41. Malhotra, S.S., and A.A. Khan. 1984. Biochemical and Physiological Impact of Major Pollutants, pp. 113-158. in: ref. 6.
42. Schoenherr, J., and M.J. Bukovac. 1972. Penetration of stomata by liquids: Dependence on surface tension, wettability, and stomatal morphology. *Plant Physiol.* 49:813-819.
43. Tamm, C.O., and E.B. Cowling. 1977. Acidic precipitation and forest vegetation. *Water Air Soil Pollu.* 7:503-511.
44. Francis, A.J., D. Olson, and R. Bernatsky. 1980. Effects of acidity in microbial processes in a forest soil, pp. 166-167. in: *Proc. Int'l. Conf. Ecological Impact of Acid Precipitation,* Sandefjord, Norway (3/11-14/80). D. Drablos and A. Tollan, eds. SNSF Project. Oslo, Norway.
45. Black, C.R., and V.J. Black. 1979. Light and scanning electron microscopy of SO2-induced injury to leaf surfaces of field bean (*Vicia faba*). *Plant Cell Env.* 2:329-333.
46. Noland, T.L., and T.T. Kozlowski. 1979. Effect of SO2 on stomatal aperture and sulfur uptake of woody angiosperm seedlings. *Can. J. For. Res.* 9:57-62.
47. Srivasta, H.S., P.A. Joliffe, and V.C. Runeckles. 1975. Inhibition of gas exchange in bean leaves by NO2. *Can. J. Bot.* 53:466-474.
48. Sugahara, K., S. Uchida, and M. Takimoto. 1980. Effect of sulfite ions on water soluble chorophyll proteins. *Res. Rep. Nat. Inst. Env. Stud. Japan* 11:103-112.
49. Reinert, R.A. 1984. Plant responses to air pollutant mixtures. *Ann. Rev. Phytopathol.* 22:2049-2055.
50. Runeckles, V.C. 1984. Impact of Air Pollutant Combinations on Plants, pp. 239-258. in: ref. 6.
51. Bazzaz, F.A., and J.S. Boyer. 1972. A compensating method for measuring carbon dioxide exchange, transpiration, and diffusive resistances of plants under controlled environmental conditions. *Ecology* 53:343-349.
52. Havas, P., and S. Huttunen. 1980. Some special Features of the Ecophysical Effects of Air Pollution on Coniferous Forests during the Winter, pp. 123-150. in: ref. 5.

53. Juniper, B.E., and C.E. Jeffree. 1983. *Plant Surfaces*. Arnold Press. London. 229p.
54. Schoenherr, J., and H.W. Schmidt. 1979. Water permeability of plant cuticles: Dependence of permeability coefficients of cuticular transpiration on vapor pressure saturation deficit. *Planta* 144:391-400.
55. Crafts, A.S. 1961. *The Chemistry and Mode of Action of Herbicides*. Wiley Interscience. New York.
56. Evans, L.S., and T.M. Curry. 1979. Differential responses of plant foliage to simulated acid rain. *Am. J. Bot.* 66:953-962.
57. Hoffman, W.A., S.E. Lindberg, and R.R. Turner. 1980. Some observations of organic constituents in rain above and below the forest canopy. *Environ. Sci. Technol.* 14:95-100.
58. Tukey, H.B. 1980. Some Effects of Rain and Mist on Plants with Implications for Acid Precipitation, pp. 141-150. in: ref. 5.
59. Haines, B., M. Stephani, and F. Hendrix. 1980. Acid rain: threshold of leaf damage in eight plant species from a southern Appalachian forest succession. *Water Air Soil Pollu.* 14:403-407.
60. Neufeld, H.S., J.A. Jernstedt, and B.L. Haines. 1985. Direct foliar effects of simulated acid rain. I. Damage, growth and gas exchange. New Phytol. 99:389-405.
61. Fowler, D., J.N. Cape, I.A. Nicholson, J.W. Kinnaird, and I.S. Paterson. 1980. The Influence of a Polluted Atmosphere on Cuticle Degradation in Scots Pine (*Pinus sylvestris*). in: *Ecological Impact of Acid Precipitation: Proc. Int'l. Conf.,* Sandefjord, Norway. D. Drablos and A. Tollan, eds. SNSF Project. Oslo, Norway.
62. Percy, K.E., and R.T. Riding. 1978. The epicuticular waxes of *Pinus strobus* subjected to air pollutants. *Can. J. For. Res.* 8:474-477.
63. Rehfuess, K.E., C. Bosch, and E. Pfannkuch. 1983. On the Norway spruce decline at higher altitudes of the Bavarian forest. in: *Acid Precipitation — Origin and Effects*. Proc. Conf. Lindau, F.R.G., June. VDI-Berichte #500, Dusseldorf, Verlag, GmbH.
64. Parameswaran, N., S. Fink, and W. Liese. 1985. Feinstukturelle Untersuchungen an Nadeln geschaedigter Tannen and Fichten aus Waldschadensgebieten im Schwartzwald. *Eur. J. For. Pathol.* 15:168-182.
65. Huttunen, S. 1984. Interactions of Disease and Other Stress Factors with Atmospheric Pollution, pp. 332-356. in: ref: 6.
66. Haines, B.L., J.A. Jernstedt, and H.S. Neufeld. 1985. Direct foliar effects of simulated acid rain II. Leaf surface characteristics. *New Phytol.* 99:407-416.
67. Papparozzi, E.T. 1981. The effects of simulated acid precipitation on leaves of *Betula alleghaniensis* Britt. and *Phaseolus vulgaris* cv. Red Kidney. Ph. d. Diss., Cornell Univ., Ithaca, New York.

68. Laurence, J.A. 1981. Effects of air pollutants on plant-pathogen interactions. *Z. Pflanzenkr. Pflanzenschutz.* 88:156-172.
69. Eaton, J.S., G.E. Likens, and F.H. Bormann. 1973. Throughfall and stemflow chemistry. *J. Ecol.* 61:495-508.
70. Lovett, G.M., S.E. Lindberg, D.D. Richter, and D.W. Johnson. 1985. The effects of acidic deposition on cation leaching from three deciduous forest canopies. *Can. J. For. Res.* 15:1055-1060.
71. Van Breemen, N., P.A. Burrough, E.J. Velhorst, H.F. van Dobben, T. de Wit, T.B. Ridder, and H.F. Reijinders. 1982. Soil acidification from atmospheric ammonium sulfate ir forest canopy through-fall. *Nature* 299:548-550.
72. Fairfax, J.A.W., and N.W. Lepp. 1975. Effect of simulated"acid rain' on cation loss from leaves. *Nature* 255:324-325.
73. Wood, T., and F.G. Bormann. 1977. Short-term effects of simulated acid rain upon the growth and nutrient relations of *Pinus strobus* L. *Water Air Soil Pollu.* 7:479-488.
74. Galloway, J.N., J.D. Thornton, S.A. Norton, H.L. Volchok, and R.A. McLean. 1982. Trace metals in atmospheric deposition: A review and assessment. *Atmos. Environ.* 16:1677-1700.
75. Scherbatskoy, T., and M. Bliss. Occurence of acidic rain and cloud water in high elevation ecosystems in the green mountains of Vermont. in: *The Meteorology of Acidic Deposition.* Proc. of the APCA Specialty Conf., Hartford, CT, Oct. 16-19, 1983. P.J. Samson, ed. Air Pollution Control Assoc. Pittsburgh, PA.
76. Lane, S.D., E.S. Martin, and J.F. Garrod. 1978. Lead toxicity effects on indole-3-acetic acid induced cell elongation. *Planta.* 144:79-84.
77. Kothny, E.L. 1973. *Trace Elements in the Environment.* American Chemical Society. Washington, D.C. ix + 149p.
78. Ormrod, D.P. 1984. Impact of Trace Element Pollution on Plants, pp. 291-319. in: ref. 6.
79. Evans, L.S., K.F. Lewin, M.J. Patti, and E.A. Cunnigham. 1983. Productivity of field-grown soybeans exposed to simulated acid rain. *New Phytol.* 93:377-388.
80. Jacobson, J. 1980. The Influence of Rainfall Composition on the Yield and Quality of Agricultural Crops, pp. 41-46. in: *Ecological Impact of Acid Precipitation:* Proc. Int. Conf., Sandefjord, Norway. D. Drablos and A. Tollan, eds. SNF Project. Oslo, Norway.
81. Fitter, A.H., and R.K.M. Hay. 1981. *Environmental Physiology of Plants.* Academic Press. New York. xii + 354p.
82. Friedland, A.J., and A.H. Johnson. 1985. Lead Distribution and Fluxes in a High-Elevation Forest in Northern Vermont. *J. Environ. Qual.* 14:332-336.
83. Foy, C.D., K.L. Chaney, and M.C. White. 1978. The physiology of metal

toxicity in plants. *Ann. Rev. Plant Physiol.* 29:511-566.
84. Johnson, A.H., and T.G. Siccama. 1983. Acid deposition and forest decline. *Environ. Sci. Technol.* 17A:294-305.
85. Turner, R.S., A.H. Johnson, and D. Wang. 1985. Biogeochemistry of aluminum in McDonalds Branch Watershed, New Jersey Pine Barrens. *J. Environ. Qual.* 14:314-323.
86. Grennfelt, P., C. Bengtsong, and L. Sharby. 1980. An Estimation of the Atmosphere Input of Acidifying Substances to a Forest Ecosystem, pp. 29-40. in: ref. 66.
87. Cape, J.N. 1984. The importance of solution equilibria in studying the effects of sulfite on plants. *Environ. Pollu.* 34A:265-274.
88. Ferenbaugh, R.W. 1976. Effects of simulated acid rain on *Phaseolus vulgaris* L. (Fabaceae). *Am. J. Bot.* 63:183-188.
89. Irving, P.M., and J.E. Miller. 1980. Response of Field-Grown Soybeans to Acid Precipitation Alone and in Combination with Sulfur Dioxide, pp. 170-171. in: *Ecological Impact of Acid Precipitation:* Proc. Int. Conf., Sandefjord, Norway. D. Drablos and A. Tollan, eds. SNF Project. Oslo, Norway.
90. Reich, P.B., A.W. Schoettle, and R.G. Amaundson. 1986. Effects of 03 and acidic rain on photo-synthesis and growth in sugar maple and Northern red oak seedlings. *Environ. Pollu.* 40A:1-15.
91. Emmons, C.L., R.D. Noble, and K.F. jensen. 1985. Effects of simulated acid mist on *Liriodendron tulipifera*. *Plant Physiol.* 75 supp:67.
92. Sigal, L.L., and J.W. Johnston. 1986. Effects of simulated acidic rain on one species each of *Pseudoparmelia, Usnea,* and *Umbilicaria*. *Water Air Soil Pollu.* 27:315-322.
93. Hallgren, J.E., and K. Gezelius. 1982. Effects of SO2 on photosynthesis and ribulose bisphophate carboxylase in pine tree seedlings. *Physiol. Plant.* 54:153-161.
94. Malhotra, S.S. 1977. Effects of aqueous sulfur dioxide on chlorophyll destruction in *Pinus contorta*. *New Phytol.* 78:101-109.
95. Mejnartowicz, L.E., and H. Lukasiak. 1985. Level of sugars in Scots pine trees of different sensitivity to fluoride and sulphur dioxide. *Eur. J. For. Pathol.* 15:193-198.
96. Gezelius, K., and J. Hallgren. 1980. Effects of SO_3 on the activity of ribulose bisphosphate carboxylase from seedlings of *Pinus sylvestris*. *Physiol. Plant.* 49:354-358.
97. Avron, M. 1960. Photophosphorylation by Swiss chard Chloroplasts. *Bioc. biop. Acta* 40:257-272.
98. Takeuchi, Y., J. Nihira, N. Kondo, and T. Tezuka. 1985. Change in Nitrate-Reducing Activity in Squash Seedlings with NO2 Fumigation. *Plant Cell Physiol.* 26:1027-1035.
99. Beevers, L., and R. Hageman. 1980. Nitrate and Nitrite Reduction, pp.

115-168. in: *The Biochemistry of Plants*. B.J. Mifflin, ed. Academic Press. New York.
100. Hewitt, E.J. 1975. Assimilatory nitrate-nitrite reduction. *Ann. Rev. Plant Physiol.* 26:73-100.
101. Schiff, J., and R.C. Hodson. 1973. The metabolism of sulfate. *Ann. Rev. Plant Physiol.* 24:381-414.
102. Hallgren, J.E., S. Linder, A. Richter, E. Troeng, and L. Granat. 1982. Uptake of SO2 in shoots of Scots pine: field measurements of net flux of sulphur in relation to stomatal conductance. *Plant. Cell Env.* 5:75-83.
103. Khan, A.A., and S.S. Malhotra. 1977. Effects of aqueous sulphur dioxide on pine needle glycolipids. *Phytochem.* 16:539-543.
104. Steponkus, P.L. 1984. Role of the Plasma Membrane in Freezing Injury and Cold Acclimation. *Ann. Rev. Plant. Physiol.* 35:466-474.
105. Karolewski, P. 1985. The role of free proline in the sensitivity of poplar (Populus 'Robusta') plants to the action of SO_2. *Eur. J. For. Pathol.* 15:199-206.
106. Keller, T. 1981. Folgen einer winterlichen SO2—Belastung fuer die Fichte. *Gartenbauwi.* 46:170-178.
107. Keller, T. 1984. The influence of SO2 on CO2 uptake and peroxidase activity. *Eur. J. For. Pathol.* 14:354-359.
108. Varshney, S.R.K., and C.K. Varshney. 1985. Response of peroxidase to low levels of SO2. *Exp. Env. Bot.* 25:107-114.
109. Hoque, E. 1984. Norway spruce die-back: isolation, biological activity, measurement of concentration of p-hydroxy acetophenone and its O-glucoside (picein) by gas chromatography. *Eur. J. For. Pathol.* 14:377-382.
110. Shafer, S.R., R.I. Bruck, and A.S. Heagle. 1985. Influence of Acidic Rain on *Phythophora cinnamoni* and Phythophora Root Rot of Blue Lupine. *Phytopathol.* 75:996-1003.
111. Shriner, D.S. 1977. Effects of simulated rain acidified with sulfuric acid on host-parasite interactions. *Water Air Soil Pollu.* 8:9-14.
112. Schmidt, O. 1985. Occurence of microorganisms in the polluted wood of Norway spruce trees from polluted sites. *Eur. J. For. Pathol.* 15:1-10.
113. Evans, L.S., K.F. Lewin, E.A. Cunnigham, and M.J. Patti. 1982. Effects of simulated acid rain on yields of field-grown crops. *New Phytol.* 91:429-441.
114. Umbach, D.M., and D.D. Davis. 1984. Severity and frequency of SO2-induced leaf necrosis on seedlings of 57 tree species. *Forest Sci.* 30:587-596.
115. Soikkeli, s., and L. Karenlampi. 1984. Cellular and Ultrastructural Effects, pp. 159-174. in: ref. 141.
116. Adams, C.M. 1980. The response of *Artemisia tilesii* to simulated acid precipitation. M.S. Thesis. Univ. Toronto, Ont. Canada. in Evans, L.S. (1985).

117. Evans, L.S., N.F. Gmur, and F. Da Costa. 1978. Foliar response of six clones of hybrid poplar to simulated acid rain. *Phytopathol.* 68:847-856.
118. Wood, T., and F.H. Bormann. 1974. The effects of an artificial acid mist upon the growth of *Betula alleghaniensis* Britt. *Environ. Pollu.* 7:259-268.
119. Botkin, D.B., and J.D. Aber. 1981. Some Potential Impacts of Acid Rain on Forest Systems: Implications of a Computer Simulation. *Brookhaven Natl. Lab. Rep.* BNL-50889.
120. Hindawi, I.J., and H.C. Ratsch. 1974. Growth abnormalities of Christmas trees attributed to sulfur dioxide and particulate acid aerosol. p. 252. *Proc. 67th Ann. Meet. Air Pollu. Control Assoc.*
121. Adams, H.S., S.L. Stephenson, T.J. Blasing, and D.N. Duvick. 1985. Growth trend declines of spruce and fir in Mid-Appalachian subalpine forests. *Env. Exp. Botany* 25:315-325.
122. Johnson, A.H., T.G. Siccama, D. Wang, R.S. Turner, and T.H. Barringer. 1981. Recent changes in patterns of tree growth rate in the New Jersey pinelands: a possible effect of acid rain. *J. Environ. Qual.* 10:427-430.
123. Scott, J.T., T.G. Siccama, A.H. Johnson, and A.R. Breisch. 1984. Decline of red spruce in the Adirondacks, New York. *Bull. Torr. Bot.* 111:438-444.
124. Siccama, T.G., M. Bliss, and H.W. Vogelmann. 1982. Decline of Red Spruce in the Green Mountains of Vermont. *Bull. Torr. Bot.* 109:162-168.
125. Guderian, R., D.T. Tingey, and R. Rabe. 1985. Effects of Photochemical Oxidants on Plants, pp. 129-295. in: *Air Pollution by Photochemical Oxidants.* R. Guderian, ed. Springer-Verlag. Berlin.
126. Heagle, A.S., V.M. Lesser, J.O. Rawlings, W.W. Heck, and R.B. Philbeck. 1986. Response of soybeans to chronic doses of ozone applied as constant or proportional additions to ambient air. *Phytophatol.* 76:51-56.
127. Lee, J.J., and D.E. Weber. 1979. The effect of simulated acid rain on seedling emergence and growth of eleven woody species. *Forest Sci.* 25:393-398.
128. Raynal, D.J., A.L. Leaf, P.D. Manion, and C.J.K. Wang. 1982. Response of tree seedlings to acid precipitation. I. Effect of substrate acidity on seed germination. *Env. Exp. Bot.* 22:337-384.
129. Baldwin, H.I. 1934. Germination of the Red Spruce. *Plant Physiol.* 9:491-532.
130. Cox, R.M. 1985. Acid Rain Effects on Plant Reproduction. p. 251. *Proc. Int. Symp. on Acid Precipitation*, Sept. 15-20, Moskoka, Canada.
131. Cox, R.M. 1983. Sensitivity of forest plant reproduction to long range transported air pollutants: *in vitro* sensitivity of pollen to simulated acid rain. *New Phytol.* 95:269-276.
132. Huttunen, S., P. Havas, and K. Laine. 1981. Effects of air pollutants on the wintertime water economy of the Scots pine, *Pinus sylvestris. Holarctic Ecol.* 4:94-101.
133. Michael, G., S. Feiler, H. Ranft, and M. Tesche. 1982. Der Einfluss von Schwefeldioxid und Frost auf Fichten (*Picea abies* (L.) Karst.). *Flora*

172:317-326.
134. Christersson, L. 1977. Vaextnaeringens inverkan pa plantors tolerans mot frost och torka. *Exp. Genecology* 1977:83-9.
135. Scholz, F., and F. Bergmann. 1984. Selection pressure by air pollution as studied by isozyme-gene-systems in Norway spruce exposed to sulphur dioxide. *Silvae Genet.* 33:238-240.
136. Ricklefs, R.E. 1973. *Ecology.* Chiron Press. New York. xii + 966p.
137. Materna, J. 1984. Impact of Atmospheric Pollution on Natural Ecosystems, pp. 397-416. in: ref. 6.
138. McLaughlin, S.B., D.J. Raynal, A.H. Johnson, and S.E. Lindberg. 1984. Effects on Vegetation: Biomass Production; Forests, pp. 3:26-3:41. in: *The Acid Deposition Phenomenon and Its Effects. Vol. II. Effects Sciences.* A.P. and R.A. Linthurst, eds. Environmental Protection Agency. Washington, D.C.
139. Aber, J.D., G.R. Hendrey, A.J. Francis, D.B. Botkin, and J.M. Melillo. 1983. Potential Effects of Acid Precipitation on Soil Nitrogen and Productivity of Forest Ecosystems, pp. 411-433. in: *Acid Precipitation: Effects on Ecological Systems.* F.M. D'Itri, ed. Ann Arbor Science. Ann Arbor, MI.
140. Hari, P., T. Raunemaa, and A. Hautojaervi. 1986. The effects of forest growth of air pollution from energy production. *Atmos. Environ.* 20:129-137.
141. Kauppi, P. 1985. Sensitivity of boreal forests to possible climatic warming. *Gartenbauwi.* 46:170-178.
142. Malhotra, S.S., and S.K. Sarkar. 1979. Effects of sulphur dioxide on sugar and free amino acid content of pine seedlings. *Physiol. Plant.* 47:223-228.

Subject Index

Abiotic factors, 54-58
Abortions, 315
Acid deposition, 456, 463
Acid mine drainage, 363
Acid mine drainage (AMD), 463
Acid precipitation, 91, 473, 486, 495, 497
Acid rain, 456, 459, 460
Acid-stress, 472, 482
Acid/aluminum stress, 467, 469
Acidification
  atmospheric, 467, 487
  sensitivity to, 464
Acidiphiles, 138
Acquisition program, 369
Adirondack mountains, 238, 242
Aerosols, 463
Agricultural and Consumer Protection Act, 352
Agricultural Conservation Program, 350
Agricultural production zone, 285
Air Pollution, 58, 59, 63
Alala or Hawaiian crow, 3
Alder (*Alnus*), 60
Allegheny chinkapin (*Castanea pumila*), 106
Allegheny mountain section, 129, 140
Allegheny River, 204
Allele diversity, 12
Allele loss, 3,5
Allelopathy, 57
Allogenic forces, 54, 58
Allogenic plant succession, 55
Aluminum, 456
Aluminum toxicity, 487
Ambystroma tigrinum, 204
American beech (*Fagus grandifolia*), 148
American bison (*Bison bison*), 75
American chestnut *(Castanea dentata*), 59, 60, 145, 148, 150, 460
American eel, 187
American Revolution, 204
American shad, 187, 188, 189
American vestrels, 214
Analysis of variance (ANOVA), 475
Aneides aeneus, 206, 207
Annual fimbry (*Fibristylis annua*), 108
Antelope, 22
Appalachian monkeyface pearly mussel (*Quadrula sparsa*), 405
Appalachian oak forest, 103
Appalachian plateaus province, 113, 129, 140
Appalachians, 207

Aquatic ecosystems, 463
Aquatic habitat aquisition, 18
Aquatic habitats, 37, 38, 61, 259
Aquatics, 138
Arrow-head (*S. subulata*), 106
Arrow-head (*Sagittaria calycina* var *spongiosa*), 106
Artificial replenishment, 67
Artificial regeneration, 147
Ashtabula County, Ohio, 238
Aspen, (*Populus*), 60
Assateague island, 399
Assembly bill A-2151, 295
Aster-like boltonia (*Boltonia asteroides*), 106
Atlantic ridley, (*Lepidochelys kempii*), 402, 403
Atlantic sturgeon, 187, 190, 191
Atlantic white cedar (*Chamaecyparis thyoides*), 280
Audubon Chapters, 393
Autogenic forces, 54

Bachman's sparrow, 225
Bachman's warbler (*Vermivora bachmanii*), 382
Bacteria, 456, 473, 481
Badger (*Taxidea taxus*), 238, 246
Bald eagle (*Haliaeetus leucocephalus*), 225, 226, 227, 298, 301, 302, 375, 379, 381, 384, 395, 397, 410, 411, 430, 431
Bald Eagle Act of 1940, 76, 212
Bald Eagle Creek, 337
Bald eagle research program, 397
Bald eagles, 20, 393
Balsam fir (*Abies balsamea*), 458
Banded sunfish, 193
Barn owl (*Tytoalba pratincola*), 409
Barn owls, (*Tyto alba*), 446
Barrens, 108
Basswood (*Tilia americana*), 60, 148
Bayonet rush (*Juncus militaris*), 104
Beachnester species, 298
Beaver (*Castor conadensis*), 234, 245, 246, 388
Beaver and Lake Erie Canal, 204
Beech (*Fagus grandifolia*), 60
Benthic fauna, 182
Berks County Conservancy, 369
Bicarbonate, 464
Bicknell's sedge (*Carex bicknelli*), 108
Big Horn sheep, 22
Big Moccasin Creek, 406
Bindweed (*Convolvulus spithamacus*), 42

508 Endangered and Threatened Species Programs in Pennsylvania and other States

Biodegradation, 473
Biological factors, 246
Biotelemetry studies, 402
Biotic factors, 54, 56, 57
Birch, 495, 496
Birdwing pearly mussel (*Conradilla caelata*), 405
Bison (*Bison bison*), 242, 245, 246, 247, 388
Black bass, 22
Black bear (*Ursus americanus*), 22, 237, 243, 245, 246
Black bears (*Visa americanus*), 388
Black cherry (*Prunus serotina*), 149
Black gum (*Nyssa sylvatica*), 149
Black locust (*Robinia pseudoacacia*), 148
Black oak (*Q. velutina*), 148, 149
Black spruce (*Picea mariana*), 60
Black-footed ferret, 19
Black-stemmed spleenwort (*A. resiliens*), 106
Blackbanded sunfish, 193, 195
Blackjack oak (*Quercus marilandica*), 280
Blazing star (*Liatris spicata*), 42
Blood composition, 316
Blue pike (*Stizostedion vitreum glaucum*), 163, 172, 173
Blue-gill, 22
Blue-spotted sunfish, 193, 194, 195
Blunt-leaved pondweed (*Potamogeton obtusifolius*), 104
Bobcat, 22, 23
Bobcat (*Lynx rufus*), 240, 243, 245, 248
Bobolink (*Dolichinyx orgyzivorus*), 47, 49
Bobwhite quail (*Colinus virginianus*), 49, 258, 269, 270, 271, 272, 273, 274
Bog sedge (*Carex paupercula*), 104
Bog turtle (*Clemmus insculpta*), 298
Boggy areas, 183
Bogs, 139, 142
Bosque del Apache National Wildlife Refuge, 68
Bounty system, 243
BOVA (Biota of Virginia), 396, 404, 409
Bradley's spleenwort (*Asplenium bradleyi*), 106
Brain worm parasite (*Parelaphostrongylus tenuis*), 248
Breeding Bird Atlas Programs, 220, 225, 226, 227
Breeding management, 316
Breeding pairs, 440
Breeding records, 2
Bridle shiner, 193, 195
Brook lobelia (*Lobelia Kalmii*), 108
Brook trout (*Salvelinus fontinalis*), 332, 464, 465, 467, 468
Brown bats (*Myotis lucifugus*), 404
Brown pelican (*Pelecanus occidentalis*), 216
Brown trout (*Salmo trutta*), 22, 332, 468
Bruce Lake, 472, 474, 476
Brucellosis, 10
Bucks County, 105, 106

Bucks County Planning Commission, 369
Buffalo, 344
Bull sedge (*Carex bullata*), 106
Bureau of Environmental Planning, 90
Bureau of Land Management (BLM), 218
Bureau of State Forests, 90

Calcareous marshes, 139, 142
Calciphiles, 138, 139
Caledon state park, 398
California condor (*Gymnogyps californianus*), 20, 68
California Natural Diversity Data Base (CNDDB), 71
Canada, 35, 463
Canal resources, 60
Capillary beak-rush (*Rhyncospora capillacea*), 108
Captive breeding, 311, 314, 315
Captive breeding specialists group, 317
Carbon County, 104
Carbonate, 464
Caribou (*Langifer tarandus*), 242, 245, 247
Carnegie Museum of Natural History in Pittsburgh, 35
Carnivora, 253
Carp (*Cyprinus carpio*), 379
Carrying capacity, 47
Cash grain, 270
Casual escapes, 111
Catfish (*Ictalurus* spp.), 379
Catskill Game Farm, 314
Catskill mountains, 238
Cave-dwelling bats, 257
Caves, 257
Cedar grove farm, 398
Ceratocystis ulmi, 59
Chain pickerel, 184, 192
Chamisso's miner's lettuce (*Montia chamissoi*), 105
Channel catfish, 195
Channelization, 47
Chesapeake bay, 397, 402, 403, 408
Chesapeake Bay Bald Eagle Banding Project, 379
Chester County, 104, 108
Chestnut blight, 59, 60
Chestnut blight fungus (*Endothia parasitica*), 146, 149, 150, 151, 152
Chestnut borer (*Agrilus bilineatus*), 60
Chestnut oak (*Quercus prinus*), 60, 147, 148, 149, 458
Chickahominy river, 397
Chincoteague national wildlife refuge, 401, 402
Chinese Chestnut (*Castanea mollisima*), 59
Chiropterm, 253
Chloride (Cl⁻), 469

Chlorinated hydrocarbons, 397
Chromosomal studies, 310
Citizen Nongame Species Advisory Committee, 298
Clemmys muhlenbergii, 207
Cliff swallows (*Petrochelidon pyrrhonota*), 298
Clinch river, 405
Clinton County, 104
Clomophis kirtlandii, 208
Cloud moisture, 458
$CO(2)$ exchange, 490
Coast guard, 408
Coastal plain, 103, 105, 113, 141, 142,
Coastal plain habitat, 206
Coastal plain leopard frog (*Rana atricularia*), 45
Coastal plain province, 132, 140
Coggerhead shrike (*Canius ludovicianus*), 409
Coleoptera (beetle), 465, 467
Collin's sedge (*Carex collinsii*), 104
Colonial nesting birds, 409
Colonial waterbirds, 298, 300
Colorado Game and Fish Department, 345
Commission on Fisheries and Game, 344
Common loon, 226
Computer-assigned mapping (MAPIT), 70
Computer-generated maps, 69
Conglomerates, 455
Conifers, 490, 494
Conservation easement, 273
Conservation groups, 295
Conservation reserve, 273, 351
Consultation, 80
Control of species, 243
Convention on International Trade in Endangered Species of Wild Fauna and Flora, 217
Copperhill, Tennessee, 59
Corn snake (*Elaphe guttata guttata*), 278, 280, 281
Cornell University Peregrine Fund, 382
County, 104, 105, 108
Coyote (*Canis latrans*), 236, 246
Crappie, 22
Crawford County, 204
Creeping snowberry (*Gautheria hispidula*), 104
Crestwood Interceptor, 286, 290
Critical habitat, 290
Crop Adjustment Act, 350
Crop rotation, 270
Cross-fertilization, 5
Crotalys horridus, 207, 208
Crows (*Corvus ossifragus*), 446
Cryptobranchus alleganiensis, 205
Cucumber tree (*Magnolia acuminata*), 149
Cumberland monkeyface pearly mussel (*Quadrula intermedia*), 405

Data analysis, 69, 70, 71
Data collection, 70, 71
Data management, 69, 70, 72
Data management system, 360
Davenport Cluster, 283, 287
DDT, 308, 418, 437
Declining species, 202, 207, 208
Deer-poaching, 25, 27
Degradation, 47
Delaware County, 104, 105, 108, 258
Delaware River, 105, 106
Delaware River Basin Commission, 188
Delmarva fox squirrel (*Sciurus niger cinereus*), 260, 401, 402, 429
Delmarva Fox Squirrel Recovery Plan, 429
Delmarva peninsula, 206
Delmarva Peninsula fox squirrel (*Sciurus niger cinereus*), 20, 382, 384
Demographic management, 317
Demographic structure, 7, 48
Demographic structure optimum complexity, 12, 13
Denitrification, 488
Department of Agriculture, 75
Department of Environmental Protection, 298
Department of Environmental Resources (DER), 89, 90, 368
Department of Environmental Resources Bureau of Forestry, 356, 369
Department of the Interior, 18
Desert bighorn sheep, 3
Development plans, 272
Diatoms, 472, 477
Dickcissel (*Spiza americana*), 49
Diploid animals, 2
Diptera (true flies), 465, 467
Direct count (Spot Plate Method) (SP), 474
Dirrgell-Johnson program (DJ), 19
Disease, 57
Dismal swamp shrew (*Sorex longirostris fisheri*), 38
Display, 69, 70, 72
District Game Protectors, 36
Division of Coastal Resources, 281, 282, 288
Division of Fish, Game and Wildlife, 294, 295
Division of Natural Areas and Preserves, 393
Division of Wildlife, 389
Dolomite, 138, 139, 141, 455
Domestic horse (*Equus caballus*), 310, 314
Drainage basins, 183
Dredging, 190
Dromedary pearly mussel (*Dramus dramas*), 405
Duck Stamp, 348
Dusky seaside sparrow (*Ammospiza maritima nigrescens*), 216
Dutch Elm Disease, 59

Eagle Protection and Migratory Bird Treaty Acts, 22
Eagles, 396
East weasel (*Mustela nivalia*), 256
Eastern brown pelican (*Pelecanus occidentalis carolinensis*), 381, 384
Eastern cottontail (*s. floridanus*), 256, 259, 260
Eastern cougar (*Felis concolor couguar*), 420
Eastern Deciduous Forest Biome, 43, 212
Eastern elk, 241
Eastern hemlock (*Tsuga canadensis*), 60, 458
Eastern Heritage Task Force, 370
Eastern oysters (*Crassostrea virginica*), 40
Eastern PA Chapter of the Nature Conservancy (TNC), 90
Eastern Pennsylvania Natural Areas Registry Program, 369
Eastern Pennsylvania Plants, 36
Eastern Peregrine, 438
Eastern Peregrine Falcon Recovery Team, 438, 447
Eastern sand darter, (*Ammoncrypta pellucida*), 163, 171, 172
Eastern state, 103, 104, 108
Eastern white pine (*Pinus strobus*), 146, 148
Eastern woodrat (*Neotoma floridana*), 36, 46, 260, 261
Ebony sedge (*Carex eburnea*), 104
Ecological Inventory Maps, 73
Ecological magnetism, 447
Ecosystem, 53, 55, 56
Ecosystem collapse, 459
Effective population size (Ne), 4, 10, 11
Element, 358, 364
Element File, 365
Element occurrence (EO), 358
Element Occurrence Record Form, 363
Elk (*Cervus canadensis*), 388
Elk (Cervus elaphus), 10, 11, 12, 22
Emmigration, 6
Emydoidea blandingii, 204
Endangered and Nongame Species Program (ENSP), 295, 296, 298
Endangered and Threatened Amphibians and Reptiles, 36
Endangered habitats, 61
Endangered species & non-game income tax check-off system, 395
Endangered Species Act, 67, 295, 296, 395, 440
Endangered Species Act (Act), 17, 18, 19
Endangered Species Act of 1973, 76, 79, 86-89, 217
Endangered Species Conservation Act of 1969, 76
Endangered Species Cooperative Agreement, 410
Endangered Species Information System (ESIS), 71
Endangered species management, 67
Endangered Species Preservation Act of 1966, 76
Endangered Species Prog. of the Fish & Wildlife Service, 76, 78, 79
Endangered Wildlife Program, 389
Endemic species, 262, 263
Endothia parasitica, 59
Entrapment defense, 27, 28, 31
Environmental controls, 67
Environmental Impact Statements, 87, 91
Environmental performance, 290
Environmental pollution, 252
Environmental Protection Agency, 393
Environmental revolution, 202
EPA, 105
Epifluorescence microscopy, 474, 478
Epilemcroptera (may flies), 465, 467
Ermine (*M. erminea*), 256
Erosion, 490
Estuarine wetland system, 39
Estuary, 375
Eumeces anthracinus, 208
Eumeces latceps, 206
European chestnut (*Castanea sativa*), 151
European colonization, 202
European starling (*Sturnus vulgaris*), 217
Evening primrose (*Oenothera argillicola*), 42
Exotics, 252
Exploitation of mammals, 244
Extirpated species, 202, 203, 205

Falcon (*Falco peregrinus*), 381, 382, 384
Falconry, 295
Fall line, 177, 193
Fallfish (*Semotilus corporalis*), 332
Fed. Interagency Coordinating Comm. on Digital Cartography, 70
Federal Aid in Wildlife Restoration Act (P-R), 348
Federal Endangered Species Act, 393
Federal Endangered Species Act of 1973, 428
Federal Endangered Species List, 191
Federal Register, 77, 78, 87
Feed grain program, 351
Felis concolor cougar, 240
Fertility, 315, 316
Few-seeded sedge (*Carex oligosperma*), 104
Field sparrows, 214
Fine-rayed pigtoe pearly mussel (*Fusconaia cuneolus*), 405
Fish, 473
Fish and Wildlife Service (FWS), 76, 77, 217, 218, 219, 220
Fish and Wildlife Services Ecological Inventory Series, 68

Fish hatcheries, 35
Fisher (*Martes pennanti*), 23, 238, 243, 246, 388
Flatspired three-toothed land snail (*T. platysayoides*), 410, 424
Floating heart (*Nymphoides cordata*), 104
Flood plain development, 38
Floristic survey, 112
Flowering dogwood (*Cornus florida*), 148
Food chain, 473
Forest floor nutrient cycles, 497
Forest Management, 274
Fostering, 441, 443
Found. for Preservation & Protection of Przewalski Horse, 315, 318, 319
Founder genotypes, 8
Fox squirrel (*Sciurus niger vulpinus*), 259
Franklin's demonstration, 11
Fraser magnolia (*Magnolia fraseri*), 148
Fresh water intertidal zone, 106
Freshwater drum (*Aplodinotus grunniens*), 45
Fund DER's Wild Plant Management Program, 35
Fungi, 456, 481
Furbish lousewort (*Pedicularis furbishae*), 88

Game animals, 259
Game fish populations, 473
Garden Club Federation of Pennsylvania, 35
Gene pools, 214, 215, 269
General funds, 428
Genetic Deterioration, 48, 270
Genetic diversity, 47, 48
Genetic drift, 11, 317, 439
Genetic variability, 439
Genetics and Hereditory Diseases of Prezewalski Horse, 315
Geographic Information System (GIS), 70, 71, 73, 396
Geographic range, 45
Geological features, 103, 104
Geophileus, 257
Ginseng (*Panax quinquefolia*), 109
Glacial bogs, 103, 104, 105
Glacial deposits, 140
Glacial lakes, 103, 104, 105
Glaciated sections, 123, 136, 140, 141
Glaciation, 103, 183
Glaucomys Sabrinus coloratus, 419
Gleasonian model, 55
Globe flower (*Trollius laxus*), 363
Golden eagle, 219, 301
Golden seal, (*Hydrastis canadensis*), 109
Gradient, 38
Granitic gneisses, 455
Grass pickerel, 193
Gray bat, 20
Gray lumber company, 400

Gray squirrel, 429
Gray squirrel (*S. carolinensia*), 260
Gray squirrel (*Sciurus cerolinus*), 401, 402
Gray wolf (Canis lupus), 237, 243, 248
Great fox island, 399
Great Smokey Mountains National Park, 59, 63
Green & gold (*Chrysogonum virginianum*), 106
Green salamander (*Aneides aeneus*), 45, 358
Green-blossom peraly mussel (*E. torulosa gubernaculum*(, 405
Greenbelts, 274
Grey birch (*Betula populifolia*), 60
Grizzly Bear, 19
Groundwater chemistry, 91
Groundwater inflow, 464
Gypsy moth, 151

Habitat alterations, 245
Habitat development, 49
Habitat disturbance, 252
Habitat diversity, 47
Habitat dynamics, 53
Habitat elimination, 5
Habitat enhancement, 290
Habitat generalists, 257
Habitat specialists, 257, 258, 263
Hacking, 20, 441, 443, 445
Hacking program (bald eagle), 301, 302, 303
Hawaiian goose, 20
Heavy metals, 59, 463, 464, 467, 473
Helianthus annuus, 57
Hemlock (*Tsuga canadensis*), 148, 149, 332,
Herbaceous plants, 487, 495
Herbicides, 61
Herborium sheets, 360
Herd composition, 316
Heron species, 300
Herpeto fauna, 204, 205
Heterodon platyrhinos, 208
Heterotrophic bacteria, 474
High-Sulfur coal, 464
Holston river, 405, 406
Horned owls, (*Buba virginianus*), 399, 441, 443
House Committee on Environment and Public Works, 217
House sparrow (*Passer domesticus*), 217
Husbandry, 316
Hybrid corn, 347
Hybridization, 252, 258
Hydric soil, 39
Hydrocarbons, 183
Hydrogen Ion, 467, 491
Hydrophytes, 38, 39
Hypovirulent hyphae, 152, 153

ICBP Red Data Book, 214
Ideal population, 4

Illinois prairie chicken (*Tympanuchus cupido*), 271
Immigration, 6
Impoundments, 422
Imprinted, 440
Inbreeding, 48
Inbreeding coefficient, 314, 315, 316, 319, 320
Inbreeding depression, 12
Increment corer, 456
Indexing, 456
Indiana bat (*Myotis sodalis*), 20, 404, 405, 410, 413, 414
Insectivorm, 253
Interagency Tasks Force on Acid Precipitation, 457
Interbreeding, coefficient (f), 2, 11, 13
International Peregrine Conference, 437
International zoo community, 2
Intertidal endemics, 156, 157
Intn'l. Union for Cons. of Nature & Natural Res. (IUCN), 316, 318, 319, 320
Introduced species, 258
Inventory of Wild Plants on Presque Isle, 35
Invertebrates, 77
Iowa Conservation Commission, 345
Ironcolor shiner, 193, 195
IUCN Red Data Book, 378
IV (Importance value), 149

James River, 397, 398
Japanese Chestnut (*Castanea crenata*), 59
Jefferson salamander (*Ambrystoma jeffersonianum*), 432
Juvenile loggerhead (*Caretta caretta*), 402, 403
Juvenile mortality, 315

Kemp's ridley turtle (*Lepidochelys kempii*), 383
Keystone state borders, 34
Kinosternon subrubrum, 206

L. a. virginianus, 259
Labrador tea (*Ledum groenlandicum*), 104
Lacey Act, 75, 216
Lackawanna County, 104
Lagomorphs, 253, 256
Lake sturgeon (*Acipenser fulvescens*), 166, 167, 168, 388
Lake trout (*Salvelinus namaycush*), 22, 164
Lampropeltis getulis, 206
Lancaster County, Pennsylvania, 106, 108, 238
Land habitat acquisition, 18, 19
Lasiorycteris noctivagans, 257
Lasiurus seminolis, 464, 467
Leaching, 456, 488, 491, 492, 496
Lead, 456
Lead deposition, 59
Lepus americanus struthopus, 259, 263

Lichens, 492, 493
Life spans, 315
Limestone, 138, 139, 455, 459
Limestone barren, 360
Limestone beds, 103, 104, 108
Limestone neutralization, 472, 473, 482
Limnetic zone, 38
Linear regression analysis, 475
List of Endangered & Threatened Wildlife & Plants, 76, 80, 81
Listing, 77
Litter, 488
Littoral zone, 38
Livestock, 270
Locality, 7
Locustrine wetland system, 39
Loggerhead turtle (*Caretta caretta*), 383
Londongrove, Chester County, 204
Long Pond, 325
Longnose gar, 192, 195
Lotic habitats, 171
Low-growing plants, 158, 160
Luzerne county, 104
Lymantria dispar (Gypsy moth), 59, 60
Lynx, 22, 23
Lynx (*Lynx canadensis*), 238, 243, 245, 246, 248

M. liebii, 257
M. sodalis, 257
Mallard (*Anas platyrhynchos*), 379, 382
Man-made stressors-sulfur & nitrogen oxides, fossil fuels, 473
Managed Area File, 365
Management decisions, 72
Manually drafted maps, 68
Marine turtle, 402
Martens (*Martes americanus*), 388
Maryland darter (*Etheastoma sellare*), 378, 383
Maryland Natural Heritage Program, 369
Massassauga rattlesnake (*Sistrurus catenatus*), 42
McGinnis Run, 467
Meadowcroft Rockshelter, Washington County, 204, 205
Megaloptera (alder flies, fish flies), 465
Mesophyte, 39
Microbial populations, 482
Migration, 4, 10
Migratory Bird Act, 216
Migratory Bird Treaty Act, 216
Migratory Bird Treaty Act of 1918, 76
Mineral extraction, 274
Minimum effective population, 8, 10
Minnesota Department of Conservation, 345
Minnesota Division of Game and Fish, 350
Mississippi Valley, 206
Mixed mesophytic, 212

Monongahela National Forest, 420
Monroe County, 104, 108
Montgomery County, 106
Montia chemissoi, 109
Moose (*Alces alces*), 241, 245, 247
Morro Bay kangaroo rats, 20
Mosses, 36
Most Probable Number (MPN) dilution exclusion series test, 474
Mottled sculpin (*Cotrus bardi*), 467
Mountain clove *(Trifolium virginicum)*, 42
Mountain goats, 22
Mountain lion (*Felis concolor*), 22, 240, 241, 243, 244, 247, 388
Mountain pine (*Pinus pungens*), 148
Mouse-ear chickweed (*Cerastium arvense* var *villosissimum*), 108
Mud sunfish, 193, 195
Muhlenberg (bog) turtle (*Clemmys muhlenbergi*), 431, 432
Mule deer, 22
Multi-prime, 330
Muskellunge (*Esox masquinongy*), 388
Muskrat (*Ondatra zibethica*), 379, 388
Mutation, 4, 9
Mycorrhizal association, 58
Mycorrhizal infection, 488
Myotis keeni, 257

National Audubon Society, 438, 440
National databases, 366, 368
National Marine Fisheries Service, 76
National natural heritage, 366
National Park Service (NPS), 218
National Parks and Recreation Act, 281
National Species of Special Emphasis (NSSES), 218
National Wildlife Federation, 379
National Wildlife Federation Raptor Information Center, 412
National Wildlife Refuge System, 76
Native amphibian and reptile fauna of Pennsylvania, 203
Natural Areas Preservation System, 226
Natural diversity, 357, 358
Natural Diversity Inventory, 368
Natural diversity scorecard, 368
Natural Heritage Data Base, 393
Natural Heritage Programs, 356, 357, 367, 369
Nature Conservancy, 62, 63, 219, 220, 356, 357, 367, 369, 393, 401
Nature preserves, 273
Nene, 3
New England cottontail (*Sylvilagus transitionalis*), 256, 260
New England province, 132

New Jersey chorus frog (*Pseudacris triseriata Kalmi*), 45
New Jersey Coastal Area Facility Review Act (CAFRA), 281
New Jersey Division of Fish, Game, and Wildlife, 281, 285, 288
New Jersey Natural Lands Trust, 289
New Jersey Pinelands Comprehensive Management Plan, 282, 283
New River, 406
New York Department of Conservation, 301
Night-scope technique, 415
Nitric acid, 463
Nitrification, 488
Nitrogen, 463
Nitrogen cycle bacteria, 474
Nitrogen oxide, 469
NO(4), 460
NO(x), 486, 491, 493
Non-game wildlife and native wild plants, 33, 34
Non-game Wildlife Biologist, 35
Non-hydric soil, 39
Non-tidal localities, 158, 159
Nongame and endangered species, 428
Nongame unstable birds, 219
Nongame Wildlife Program, 389
North American Breeding Bird Survey, 218
Northeastern United States, 463
Northern Cardinals, 214
Northern Deciduous Forest Biome, 212
Northern Flying Squirrel (*Glausomys Sabrinus coloratus*), 419
Northern Hardwood Climax, 212
Northern hardwood forest, 103
Northern pike (*E. lucius*), 388
Northern pine snake (*Pituphis melanoleucus melanoleucus*), 278, 281, 282, 283, 284, 286, 287, 289, 291
Northern red oak (*Q. rubra*), 147, 148
Northern species, 103, 104, 105
Norway rat (*Rattus norvegicus*), 258
Norway spruce (*Picea abies*), 457
Nutrical, 329
Nutrient cycling, 56
Nycticeius humeralis, 257

Oak-chestnut, 212
Ocean County Utilities Authority, 286
Odonata (dragon flies, damsel flies), 465, 467
Office of Endangered Species, 77, 78
Ohio Biological Survey, 393
Ohio Chapter of the American Fisheries Society, 393
Ohio Chapter of the Wildlife Society, 393
Ohio Cooperative Wildlife Research Unit, 349
Ohio Environmental Council, 393

Ohio Natural Heritage, 369
Ohio River, 35
Ohio River system, 204
Ohio Wildlife Management Association, 393
Operation Abscam, 23
Operation Falcon, 22, 23
Operation Gillnet, 22, 25
Operation Torphy Kill, 22, 25
Operation Wildflower, 35
Opheodrys aestivus, 206
Opossums, 402
Orangefin madtom (*Notorus gilberti*), 408
Organic contaminents, 183
Organic industrial waste, 182
Organochlorine, 438
Osmoregulatory mechanism, 469
Osprey (*Pandion haliaetus carolinensis*), 36, 219, 225, 227, 301, 407
Osprey (*Pandion haliaetus*), 381, 384
Ottawa National wildlife Refuge, 393
Otter, 23
Outbreeding, 5, 8, 10, 13, 48
Outbreeding depression, 139
Outer continental shelf oil and gas, 68
Overharvesting, 252
Oxygen depletion, 190
Ozone, 58, 486, 488, 489
Ozone, [O(3)], 456, 457

PA Dept. of Natural Resources—Bureau of Forestry, 62, 63
PA Fish Commission and PA Game Commission, 34
PA Game Commissions Working Together for Wildlife Prog., 323, 327
Pacific Coast Ecological Inventory, 68
Pale laurel (*Kalmia polifolia*), 104
Paleo-indian sites, 204
Paleozoic chaly outcrops, 138
Palustrine wetland system, 39
Parasitism, 57
Passenger pigeon (*Ectopistes migratorius*), 75, 389
Pathogens, 491, 495, 496
Pelican Island Bird Sanctuary, 75
Pennsylvania, 472
Pennsylvania Bald Eagle Recovery Project, 301, 308
Pennsylvania Biological Survey, 238
Pennsylvania Breeding Bird Atlas Project, 225
Pennsylvania Breeding Birds Atlas Survey, 35
Pennsylvania Department of Environmental Resources, 90, 105
Pennsylvania elk (*Cercus canadensis*), 49
Pennsylvania Fish and Wildlife database, 35
Pennsylvania Fish Commission, 206, 331, 468, 469

Pennsylvania Fish Commission's Threatened and Endangered Species Committee, 163, 166, 168, 174
Pennsylvania Game Commission, 35, 248, 301, 303, 305, 307, 308, 309
Pennsylvania Natural Diversity Inventory (PNDI), 35, 36, 39, 62, 90, 91, 356, 357, 363, 368, 370,
Pennsylvania Power and Light, 368
Pennsylvania Reptiles and Amphibians, 35
Pennsylvania River Otter Reintroduction Program, 35
Pennsylvania Trappers Association, 323
Pere David's deer, 3
Peregrine falcon (*Falco peregrinus*), 226, 227, 298, 399, 410, 417, 418, 437, 438, 439, 440, 441
Peregrine Falcon Recovery Team, 418
Peregrine Falcons, 301
Peregrine Fund, 438
Peripheral species, 202, 206, 207, 208, 262, 263
Pesticides, 379, 381, 414, 415, 418, 437
Pheasant-quail management research project, 349
Phenodynamic distortions, 141
Photochemical oxidants, 487
Phyto- and zooplankton, 473, 481
Piedmont province, 131, 141, 142
Piedmont regions, 237
Pignut hickory (*Carya glabra*), 148, 149
Pike County, 104
Pine (*Pinus*), 457, 493
Pine barrens, 183, 194
Pine Barrens treefrog (*Hyla andersoni*), 280, 282, 283, 298
Pine Creek, 326, 331, 332, 333, 334, 335, 337, 338, 339, 340, 341
Pinelands Commission, 281, 283, 284, 285, 286, 287
Pinelands National Reserve, 47
Pink mucket pearly mussel (*Campsilis orbiculata orbiculata*), 422
Piping plover (*Charadrius melodus*), 383
Pipistrelle bats (*Pipistrellus subflavus*), 404
Pirate perch, 193, 194, 195
Pitch pine (*P. rigida*), 148, 280, 458
Pitch pine/scrub oak barren, 358
Pittman-Robertson program (PR), 358
Plant pests, 59, 63
Plants, 77
Plants of Special Concern in Pennsylvania, 62
Plecoptera (stone flies), 465, 467
Plymouth red-bellied turtle, 19
Poconos, 464, 472
Pod-grass (*Scheuchzeria palustris*), 104
Poletimber, 43
Pollination, 9
Pollinators, 91

Pollution, 45, 422, 486, 489, 492, 497
Polyploidy, 6
Population density, 214
Porcupine (*Erethizon dorsatum*), 236, 246
Potomac drainage, 206
Potomac river, 397, 398, 403
Prairie dropseed (*Sporobolis heterolepis*), 108
Predator control, 67
Presque Isle, 204
Privant Plant Sanctuaries, 369
Proghorn, 344
Prostate sand cherry (*Prunus pumila* var *depressa*), 105
Proteolytic bacteria, 474
Przewalski horse (*Equus przewalskii*), 310, 311, 314, 315, 316, 317, 319, 320, 321
Przewalski Horse Committee, 317, 318, 319, 320
Pseudacris triseriata Kalmi, 206
Pseudemys rubriventris, 206
Pseudotriton montanus, 204
Public education projects, 35
Public outreach program, 396
Purple bladderwort (*Utricularia purpurea*), 104
Pymatuning Region, 36
Pymatuning Wildlife Management Area, 302
Pyritic Materials, 463

Quail management programs, 268, 269
Quartz sandstones, 455

Radio telemetry, 397, 398
Radio tracking, 322, 333, 338
Ragwort (*Senecio antennariifolius*), 42
Rainbow trout (*Salmo gairdneri*), 22, 332, 468
Raised water levels, 104
Rana utricularia, 206
Range reductions, 157
Rappahannock River, 397
Raptors, 396, 399
Rare and endangered fish and wildlife of United States, 407
Rattlesnake, 35
Reclamation of surface mined lands, 35
Recombination, 6
Recovery, 81
Recovery Plan, 438, 440
Recovery Team, 218
Red fox, 243
Red mangrove (*Rhizophore mangle*), 40
Red maple (*Acer rubrum*), 148, 149
Red oak (*Quercus rubra*), 148, 492, 495
Red pine (*Pinus resinosa*), 146
Red spruce (*Picea rubens*), 457, 458, 488, 496
Red-cockaded woodpecker (*Picoides borealis borealis*), 382, 384
Red-cockaded woodpecker (*Picoides borealis*), 400

Reed grass (*Phragmites australis*), 106
Regal fritillary, *Speyeria idalia*, 360
Regional heritage task force, 360
Regression, 10, 12
Reintroduction, 318, 319, 320
Relational Database Management System (DBMS), 71
Reproductive potential, 9
Reptiles, amphibians, non-game fish, 35
Research Natural Areas, 370
Reservation of game lands, 67
Resource mapping systems, 67
Restriction of hunting, 67
Rhizobium, 57
Rice rat (*Oryzomys palustris*), 258, 263
Ring-necked pheasant *(Phasianus colchicus)*, 343, 344, 345
Riparian forests, 274
River birch (*B. nigra*), 60
River bullrush (*S. fluviatilis*), 106
River herrings, 187
River otter, *(Cutra canadensis)*, 238, 248, 322, 326, 327, 334, 338
River reach system, 396
Riverine intertidal zones, 157
Riverine systems, 38, 44
Roanoke cog perch (*Percina rex*), 408
Robbins' spike-ruch (*Eleocharis robbinsii*), 104
Rock bass (*Ambloplites rupestris*), 332
Rock dove (*Columba livia*), 217
Rock shrew (*Sorex dispar*), 257
Rock vole (*Micotus chrotorrhinus*), 257
Rodentia, 253
Roseroot sedum (*Sedum rosea*), 105
Rotation breeders, 318
Rough cotton grass (*Eriophorum tenellum*), 104
Rough pigtow pearly mussel (*Pleurobema plenum*), 405
Round-leaved fame flower (*Talinum teretifolium*), 108
Rowcrop lands, 273
Runoff, 168

S. multistriatus, 59
Salinity, 177, 192
Salmon, 22
Salt line, 177, 182
Salt marsh harvest mouse, 68
San Francisco Bay National Wildlife Refuge, 68
Sandhill cranes, 3
Sandstone and conglomerate bedrock, 473
Saskatchewan Department of Parks and Natural Resources, 305, 306, 307, 308
Sassafras (*Sassafras albidum*), 57, 149, 403
Satellite transmitter, 403
Sauger (*Stizoztedion canadense*), 45
Saw Creek Lake, 325, 326

Sawtimber, 43
Scarlet oak (*Quercus coccinea*), 148
Sciurids, 256
Scolytus scolytus, 59
Scotch pine (*Pinus resinosa*), 146
Sea turtles, 378, 379, 383, 396
Seaside sparrow (*A. m. nicgrescens*), 228
Second World Conf. on Breeding Endg. Species in Captivity, 315
Section 6 (Act), 18, 19, 20
Selection, 4, 11
Self-fertilization, 5, 6
Senate Committee on Environment and Public Works, 217
Serpentine aster (*Aster depauperatus*), 108
Serpentine barrens, 137, 139, 142, 358
Serpentine rock, 103, 108
Serviceberry (*Amelanchier arborea*), 150
Sewage, 182
Shade-intolerant plants, 57
Shade-tolerant plants, 56
Shale barrens, 42, 103, 113, 138, 139, 142
Shales, 455
Shiny pigtoe pearly mussel (*Fusconaia edgariana*), 405
Shoestring root rot (*Armillaria mella*), 60
Shore birds, 409
Short-eared owl (*Asio flammeus flammeus*), 214
Shortnose sturgeon (*Acipenser brevirostrum*), 163, 164, 165, 166, 189, 378, 383
Shrubby cinquefoil (*Potentilla fruticosa*), 108
Sida (*Sida hemaphrodita*), 106
Sierra Club, 393
Silt, 463
Siltation, 168, 190
Silver fir trees (*Abies alba*), 457
Silverbell (*Halesia carolina* var *monticola*), 148
Silvicultural, 146
Sistrurus catenatus, 207
Slender rockbrake (*Cryptogramma stelleri*), 104
Slender water-milfoil (*Myriophyllum tenellum*), 104
Slimy sculpin (*Cotrus cognatus*), 467
Small Mammal, 253
Small-Whorled Pogonia (*Isotria medeoloides*), 58, 59, 63
Smallmouth bass (*Micropterus dolomieui*), 332
Smith's bullrush (*Scirpus smithii*), 106
Snake hunts, 35
Snakes and snake hunting, 278
Snow-melt runoffs, 467
Snowshoe hare, 259, 260
$SO(2)$, 259, 260, 460, 486, 489-497
Social dysfunction, 48
Sodbuster, 273
Sodium (Na^+), 469
Soil bank, 351

Soil bank program, 350
Soil chemistry, 487
Soil Conservation and Domestic Allotment Act, 350
Soil Conservation Service, 349
Soil erosion, 61, 63, 273
Soil leachate, 467
Soil microflora, 498
Source File, 365
Sourwood (*Oxydendrum arboreum*), 149
South Dakota Department of Game, Fish and Parks, 345
South Mountain, Cumberland County, 204
Southern flying squirrel (*Glaucomys volans*), 419
Southern species, 103, 106
Soybeans, 491
Spanish peregrines, 439
Spawning movements, 168
Special Interest Areas, 370
Specialty cropping, 270
Species of special concern, 203
Species of special concern in Pennsylvania, 35
Species Survival Plan Subcommittee, 440
Spekes gazelle, 3
Spoil deposition, 47
Spotted skunk (*Spilogale putorius*), 256
Spreading globeflower (*Trolliums laxus*), 108
Spruce, 490, 494
Stallion depots, 317, 318
Stallion exchange, 316
State Endangered Wildlife Law, 389
State Federation of Sportsmen's Clubs, 296
State Natural Heritage Program, 63
Stenothermic species, 257
Steppe tarpan, 311
Stewardship files, 367
Stillborn or premature foals, 315
Stomata, 489, 490
Stream ecosystem, 465
Stream ecosystem, acidification of, 463, 469
Stream turbidity, 91
Streams: Benthic, 467
Streams: Headwater, 467, 468, 469
Streams: Low-order, 465
Streams: Stocked & Unstocked, 469
Striped bass, 22, 184, 189
Srongyloides, 420
Substrate, 38
Succession, 37, 42, 47, 54-59, 146, 147, 149, 212, 214, 280
Succession primary, 54
Succession secondary, 54
Sugar maple (*Acer saccharum*), 148, 149, 492, 493, 495, 496
Sulfate, 467
Sulfur, 463

Sulfur cycle bacteria, 474
Sulfur dioxide, 58
Sulfur oxide, 469
Sulfuric acid, 463
Sullivan County, 104
Sumac (*Rhus typhiona*), 60, 496
Surface runoff, 464, 467
Susquehanna County, 104
Swamp beggar-ticks (*Bidens bidentoides*), 106
Swamp darter, 193, 194, 195
Swamp-Pink (*Arethusa bulbosac*), 58
Swampbuster, 273
Swampland acts, 344
Sweet bayberry (*Myrica gale*), 104
Sweet birch (*Betula lenta*), 148, 149
Sweet clover, 347
Sweetbay magnolia (*Magnolia virginiana*), 105
Sycamore (*Platanus occidentalis*), 332
Symbiotic interactions, 57

Tadpole madtom, 193, 195
Tall gramma (*Bouteloua curtipendula*), 108
Tan riffle shell mussel (*Epioblasma walkeri*), 405
Tax check-off, 295, 296
Tax check-off funding, 33, 36
Tern (*Sterna albifrons*), 68
Tern (*Sterna hirundo*), 49
The Nature Conservancy, 35
The Pennsylvania Department of Environmental Resources, 58
Third Intn'l. Symp. on Preservation of Przewalski Horse, 315
Thread-ruch (*Juncus filiformis*), 104
Three-spine stickleback, 191
Three-toothed cinquefoil (*Potentilla tridentata*), 104
Threespine stickleback (*Gasterosteus aculeatus*), 168, 169, 170
Tidal localities, 158, 159
Tidal marshes, 159
Tidal system, 38
Tillage, 273
Tinicum marsh, 106
Tinicum marshes, 258
Torrey's bullrush (*Seirpus torreyi*), 104
Toxicity, mechanisms of, 467
Trailways, 274
Tree bats, 257
Tree-nesting, 440
Treenesting bats, 300
Trichoptera (caddis flies), 465, 467
Trionyx muticus, 204
Tuberculed blossom pearly mussel (*E. torulosa torulosa*), 421
Tuckerman's pond weed (*Potamogeton confervoides*), 104
Tukey's test, 475
Tule elk, 3

U.S. Department of Agriculture (USDA), 349, 352, 353
U.S. Department of the Interior, 285
U.S. Endangered Species Act, 61
U.S. Endangered Species Act of 1966, 212, 214, 217, 218, 220
U.S. Fish and Wildlife Service, 18, 21, 22, 23, 25, 26, 30, 31, 188, 189, 295, 303, 370, 393, 408, 410, 414, 421, 424, 429, 430, 438, 440
U.S. Fish and Wildlife Service (USF&WS), 86, 87, 89
U.S. Forest Service, 43, 370, 393, 414, 457
U.S. Forest Service (USFS), 218, 220
U.S. Geological Survey, 73, 364
Ultrasonic bat detector, 405
Umbrella magnolia (*Magnolia tripetala*), 106
Union camp corporation, 400
United States Department of Agriculture, 273
United States Fish and Wildlife Service, 105
United States Fishery Commission, 344
Upland Sandpiper (*Bartramia longicauda*), 49
Upper Allegheny river basin, 245
Upper Tunkhannock Creek, 325, 326
Urban development, 47
Urban management plans, 272
USFWS, 381, 382

Valley and ridge province, 130
Variable sedge (*Carex polymorpha*), 104
Vertebrates, 77
Virginia big-eared bat (*Plecotus townsendii virginianus*), 410, 415
Virginia Commission of Game and Inland Fisheries, 381, 395, 398, 400, 402, 404, 405, 407, 409
Virginia fringed mountain snail-*Polygyriscus virginianus*, 406
Virginia Institute of Marine Science (VIMS), 402, 404, 409
Virginia long-eared bats-*Plecotus townsendii virginianus*, 402, 404, 409
Virginia pine (*Pinus virginiana*), 148
Virginia Polytechnic Institute & State Univ. (VPI&SU), 396, 405, 409
Virginia society of Orinthology, 409
Virginia Wildlife magazine, 396
Virginia's endangered species, 396
Virginia's flying colors, 396
Virginia's wildlife, 396

Walleye, 173
Walter's barnyard grass (*Eichinochloa walteri*) 106
Wapiti (*Cervus elaphus*), 241, 244, 245, 246
Water fowl, 348
Water lobelia (*Lobelia dortmanna*), 104
Water permanence, 38

Water shrew (*Sorex palustris*), 259, 263
Water velocity, 38
Watershed: Buffering capacity, 464, 467, 469
Watershed: Dilution capacity, 464
Wayne County, 104
West Virginia Department of Natural Resources (WVDNR), 410, 412, 414, 415, 418, 424
Western Pennsylvania Conservancy (WPC), 35, 62, 63, 89, 90, 356
Western sand darter (*Ammocrypta clara*), 172
Wetland habitats, 289
Wetlands, 37, 44, 46, 47, 49, 271, 373, 375, 378, 381, 382, 384
Wheat program, 351
White ash (*Fraxinus americana*), 148, 149
White birch (*Betula papyrifera*), 60, 458
White Deer Lake, 472, 474, 475, 476
White oak (*Quercus alba*), 59, 147, 148, 459
White pine (*Pinus strobus*), 58, 458
White sucker (*Catostomous commersoni*), 332
White-tailed deer (*Odocoileus virginianus*), 235, 247, 260, 421
Whooping crane (*Grus americana*), 68, 378
Whorled nutrush (*Seleria verticillata*), 108
Wild Resource Conservation Act, 62, 89, 108, 323, 369
Wild Resource Conservation Fund, 34, 35
Wild Resource Conservation Fund Activity Storybook, 36
Wildflowers, 91
Wildlife Administration of Dept. of Natural Resources, 428
Wildlife Management Institute, 349
Wildlife Society, 389
Wildrice (*Zizania quatica*), 106
Willows (*Salix*), 60
Wolverine (*Gulo gulo*), 238, 246
Wood rat (*Neotoma floridana*), 298
Woodlots, 270, 274
Woodstream Trap Corporation, 327
Woody plants, 487, 495
Working Together for Wildlife, 308
Wright's formula, 11

Xerophyte, 39

Yellow birch (*Betula alleghaniensis*), 149, 332
Yellow bullhead, 193
Yellow-poplar (*Liriodendron tulipifera*), 148, 149
Young Spot Plate Method, 474

Zoning, 289

OFFICERS OF THE PENNSYLVANIA ACADEMY OF SCIENCE

SHYAMAL K. MAJUMDAR, President, Professor of Biology, Lafayette College, Easton, Pennsylvania 18042

KURT C. SCHREIBER, President Elect & Director, Science Talent Search, 1812 Wightman Street, Pittsburgh, Pennsylvania 15217

GEORGE C. SHOFFSTALL, Immediate Past- President/Executive Secretary, 502 Misty Drive, Suite 1, Lancaster, Pennsylvania 17603

SHERMAN S. HENDRIX, Treasurer, Department of Biology, Gettysburg College, Gettysburg, Pennsylvania 17325

RALPH CAVALIERE, Assistant Treasurer, Department of Biology, Gettysburg College, Gettysburg, Pennsylvania 17325

HOWARD S. PITKOW, Corresponding Secretary, Professor of Physiology, Pennsylvania College of Podiatric Medicine, Eighth at Race Street, Philadelphia, Pennsylvania 19107

DANIEL KLEM, JR., Editor of the Proceedings, Department of Biology, Muhlenberg College, Allentown, Pennsylvania 18104

FRED J. BRENNER, Newsletter Editor, Biology Department, Grove City College, Grove City, Pennsylvania 16127

J. ROBERT HALMA, Historian, Department of Biology, Cedar Crest College, Allentown, Pennsylvania 18104

VIOLA YAKSTIS, Recording Secretary

EDWARD TESTA, Director of Junior Academy, Valley View High School, Archbald, Pennsylvania 18403

JUSTICE JOHN P. FLAHERTY, Advisory Council Chairman

SISTER M. GABRIELLE MAZE, Fund Raising, Past-President, Grove and McRobert Road, Pittsburgh, Pennsylvania 15234